Architectural Theory

ARCHITECTURAL THEORY

Volume I
An Anthology from Vitruvius to 1870

Edited by Harry Francis Mallgrave

Blackwell Publishing

Editorial material and organization © 2006 by Harry Francis Mallgrave

BLACKWELL PUBLISHING
350 Main Street, Malden, MA 02148-5020, USA
9600 Garsington Road, Oxford OX4 2DQ, UK
550 Swanston Street, Carlton, Victoria 3053, Australia

First published 2006 by Blackwell Publishing Ltd

5   2010

Library of Congress Cataloging-in-Publication Data

Architectural theory, volume I: an anthology from Vitruvius to 1870 /
edited by Harry Francis Mallgrave.
p. cm.
Includes bibliographical references and index.
ISBN: 978-1-4051-0257-5 (hard cover : alk. paper)
ISBN: 978-1-4051-0258-2 (pbk. : alk. paper)
1. Architecture–Philosophy. I. Mallgrave, Harry Francis.

NA2500.A7115 2005
720′.1–dc22
2004030886

A catalogue record for this title is available from the British Library.

Set in 10/13pt Dante
by SPI Publisher Services, Pondicherry, India
Printed and bound in Singapore
by C.O.S. Printers Pte Ltd

The publisher's policy is to use permanent paper from mills that operate a sustainable forestry policy, and
which has been manufactured from pulp processed using acid-free and elementary chlorine-free practices.
Furthermore, the publisher ensures that the text paper and cover board used have met acceptable
environmental accreditation standards.

For further information on
Blackwell Publishing, visit our website:
www.blackwellpublishing.com

CONTENTS

Part III: Neoclassicism and the Enlightenment   119

A. Early Neoclassicism   121

Part IV: Theories of the Picturesque and the Sublime   221

A. Sources of the Picturesque   223

C. Consolidation of Picturesque Theory   **290**

Part V: The Rise of Historicism in the Nineteenth Century   331

A. Challenges to Classicism in France, 1802–34   333

B. The Gothic Revival in Britain, Germany, and France   362

C. The German Style Debate   395

D. The Rise of American Theory 425

C. Tectonics and Style in Germany   529

PREFACE

T he idea of sketching an architectural cross-section through the lines of Western cultural development is a compelling one, if only because the profile of the ideological continuum is on occasions tenuous at best. Theory possesses no tangible form. It exists in large and heavy tomes as well as in short and spirited manifestoes. It is found in the angle of a molding, the silhouette of a roofline, as well as in the impassioned assertions of the confident practitioner. Theory is at times imbued with revolutionary fervor, and it admittedly emanates or takes its lead from larger cultural sensibilities. Architectural theory, for all its occasional abstraction, is nothing less than the history of our ideas regarding our constructed physical surroundings.

If we accept this broad definition of theory, we must also accept a wide-ranging approach to the problem of an anthology, one that responds from many sides. Theory needs its context, just as any history of ideas needs its intellectual framework, and the expense and materiality of architecture perhaps make it even more a closely guarded pawn of political ambition, wars, and economic downturns. But ideas also move with a certain volition and tempo of their own, fascinating in their own right. The famous seventeenth-century "quarrel" between the Ancients and the Moderns, for instance, was not only a learned academic dispute concerning past and present accomplishments, but one whose momentous implications for the sciences and arts required more than a century to unfold. Similarly, the seemingly innocent notion of the "picturesque" in late eighteenth-century Britain demanded the same 100 years of aesthetic cultivation to achieve its subtle refinement. And Ralph Waldo Emerson's notion of "self-reliance" not only crystallized the pioneering spirit of nineteenth-century America but it also strongly resonated within architectural circles for several generations – and arguably still reverberates in American architecture today. Each idea thus possesses its specific circumstances and points of origin, and to this end we have framed each section of our anthology with a historical overview and provided each entry with an introduction. To further the reader's understanding, we have also suggested a few additional readings in a section at the end of the book.

The decision to include a greater (rather than fewer) number of texts and documents in this anthology as well requires an abbreviated format for each selection and a number of necessary stylistic conventions. The use of simple ellipses, "...", denotes the omission of words or phrases within a sentence. Square brackets, [...], indicate the omission of a sentence, sentences, or several short paragraphs, and they can be employed at the beginning or end of a text as well. Asterisks, ★ ★ ★, refer to the lengthier omission of a paragraph or more, although in some (noted) cases they also appear in the original text. We have left all English texts in their original punctuation, spelling, and style. Books are italicized and the use of quotation marks indicate shorter writings.

The increasing body of texts within the chronological structure reflects not only the growing number of historical documents but also the growing complexity or nuances of the theoretical debate. The aim of this anthology has been to balance the presentation of texts with the always growing richness of ideas, and to provide an introduction to, and an overview of, the subject matter to be reviewed. No anthology is intended to supplant the teaching of architectural theory or to constitute a course in itself; this anthology is most definitely not presented to discourage the reader from turning to the multitude of sources themselves. Anthologies are by nature restrictive, cursory, subjective, even arbitrary in their selection, and always in need of revision. At their best, anthologies provide a framework for ideas and encourage the reader to study the material and its historical context with greater seriousness and depth.

GENERAL INTRODUCTION

Architectural theory has its unique distinctions. It comprises a broad body of ideas and debates, which over many centuries has not only come to form a substantial literary edifice but also one ever more complex and refined in its details and issues. With the articulate engagement of one generation responding to the ideas of another, architectural theory is more often than not contentious and instructive. It is not born in isolation. It reflects the aspirations of emperors and the whims of kings, and again the insights of lay critics and the pride of competing professionals. As an intellectual enterprise, architectural theory draws upon the larger currents of its time – political, social, scientific, philosophical, and cultural – and in this way it often cannot be understood outside of these insinuating forces. As a constructional art, architecture also speaks to the physical world or more generally to human aspirations and values. The study of these ideas is, in its own way, a lucid compendium of human history.

The present volume, which is the first of two, begins with theory in ancient and classical times and concludes in 1870. The different eras within this time span, of necessity, are uneven in their presentation. The earliest records we have of architectural thinking in the West are the lay and religious Hebraic traditions recorded in the Old Testament, which became one of the two cornerstones of the later Christian worldview. The other cornerstone – classicism – is generally taken as synonymous with the Greco-Roman tradition. Although we know aspects of this antique culture extremely well, our knowledge of its architectural dimension is limited to its few surviving monuments and to the treatise of Vitruvius, the lone literary work to come down to us from Roman antiquity. But Vitruvius was operating within a fertile line of theoretical development parallel to and more prolific (in terms of writings devoted to architecture) than that of the Middle East, a tradition of theory that stretches back at least five centuries before him. All of these texts (perhaps hundreds) have unfortunately been lost.

Our textual holdings from Late Roman and medieval times – when the Christian and classical traditions merge into the body of beliefs that we define as Western culture – is scarcely much larger. Nevertheless, its glorious architectural monuments testify to a refined body of theoretical knowledge. It is only with the Renaissance that this dearth of textual evidence begins to be remedied. The production of inexpensive paper, the invention of the printing press, the use of vernacular languages, and the rise of literacy rates – all conspire to make the transmission of ideas more efficient and therefore more abundant. Renaissance writers, at the same time, prided themselves in recovering what they believed to be the lost ideals of classicism. Western theory now plots a relatively straight course (although with interesting regional variations) down to the Enlightenment of the eighteenth century, when secular forces-at-large now openly clash with the religious traditions and political structures inherited from the past. The result is that fascinating shattering of theory along nationalist and "stylistic" lines that we generally subsume under the ambiguous concept of historicism.

In contrast to the often pejorative use of this term with respect to architectural practice, we shall employ the idea of historicism in a positive sense as an attempt to resolve the apparent discrepancy between greater historical understanding (increasingly viewed in absolute and teleological terms) and an emerging modern industrial state (bourgeois life) that tended toward relativism in both historical and cultural terms. The nineteenth century became increasingly time rich in its theoretical possibilities. And what emerges from it, of course, is that worldview of more modest persuasion which we – too narrowly – refer to as modernism.

The concluding line of 1870 may seem arbitrary but it is chosen for several reasons. First the year, or more correctly the years surrounding it, define a time of significant theoretical change. Theory in its four centuries since the Renaissance had been dominated largely by Italian and French writers and was generally "academic" in its bearing. And even though this system and its body of beliefs was tottering well before 1870, academic principles fall into a sharp decline in the last quarter of the nineteenth century, even though classicism as a formal attitude and vocabulary survive. The year, with the defining moment of the Franco-Prussian War, also has symbolic connotations for both Europe and North America. The French defeat not only ushered in for that country (and its proud culture) both economic and military decline, but it also signaled the beginning of cultural parity in the West. Britain, with its proud intellectual traditions, was now confidently pursuing its path of design reforms through the Arts and Crafts Movement. The United States, whose first independent theoretical stirrings appear only in the previous generation, was embarking during its post-bellum years on a period of unparalleled economic and cultural expansion. And the soon to be unified Germany, with its unrivaled system of higher education, had become by 1870 perhaps the dominant player in architectural theory – at least as theory developed in the twentieth century. Cultural identities within the Nordic countries and central Europe, in Austria, Switzerland, Spain, and Italy, were also manifesting themselves around this time. It was thus a period of momentous transformation.

Still another reason for choosing the year 1870 to conclude this volume is to respond to earlier intellectual histories that tended to isolate the twentieth century. This study does not represents a "modernist" view of the world, and indeed it rejects the historiographic notion of a divide proffered by so many twentieth-century historians. Intellectual production is rather a continuous and always evolving process, for architecture is sometimes a closed process frequently circling upon relatively few alternative strategies or ideas. Modernism, if it can be defined at all, is a phenomenon that forms itself over centuries, and whether we trace its roots to the Enlightenment, to the seventeenth century, or to the Renaissance is largely a matter of historical preference. The fact that architectural theory is a closed process should also not be interpreted to mean that it can be understood in and of itself. Indeed, this particular field of ideas can be grasped in its outlines only by taking into account the context of the philosophical, political, and cultural world in which it arises. It is therefore hoped that the broad approach of this volume will bring both an overview and something of substance to architectural curricula and add substance to the teaching of history and theory.

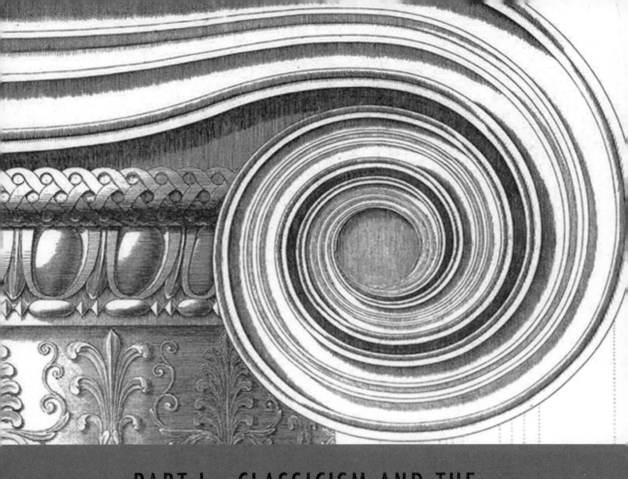

PART I CLASSICISM AND THE RENAISSANCE

A. THE CLASSICAL AND MEDIEVAL TRADITIONS

Introduction

The word "classical" in English, like its Latin counterpart *classicus*, carries with it rich connotations. The Latin word derives from the verb *calare*, "to call," but this meaning in the Late Roman Republic gave way to referring to those "of the first class," as opposed to those of the lower classes. Similar meanings accompanied it until its early English usage in the sixteenth century, when the word more generally came to refer to someone or something of the highest rank or importance, a standard or model to imitate. Around the same time, "classical" also came to be associated with any of the Greek and Roman writers of antiquity who were held up as worthy models for emulation. When we speak of the classical tradition in architecture, we refer to the intellectual and artistic productions of Greek and Roman antiquity, and to the "rediscovery" of this legacy in medieval times, the Renaissance, and in the ensuing centuries.

Classicism in architecture, by happenstance, begins with Vitruvius – or Marcus Vitruvius Pollio (c.85–c.20 BC) as he is sometimes called, although only the middle name is certain. Classicism is synonymous with Vitruvius because, of the dozens of treatises written on architecture in classical times, his is the one to have survived into modern times. Only a few details of the life of this architect, engineer, and scholar are known with certainty. He was born probably in the second decade of the first century BC, and his breadth of knowledge suggests a good liberal education, training with architects, and travel to various parts of Asia. The chapters of his treatise on the design of houses suggest some familiarity with this subject, but sometime around mid-century he was hired into the service of Julius Caesar as a military engineer. Over the next decade he traveled with the conqueror during his campaigns into Gaul and probably Africa, where Vitruvius prepared fortifications and engines of war. After the Ides of March in 44 BC the architect was without a patron, but within a few years he found employment as an engineer under Caesar's adopted son Octavian. His decision proved a wise one, because during the years 42–31 BC the forces of Octavian and those of Marc Anthony were squaring off for the control of Rome – a conflict that ended with the defeat of Anthony and Cleopatra at Actium in 31 BC. Four years later Octavian assumed the honorific title of Augustus Caesar and the Roman Empire was born. The now aged Vitruvius was at this point working hard to complete the treatise on which he had probably worked for many years. He dedicated it to the new Emperor, and shortly thereafter built the one building that he included in his 10 scrolls, the basilica at Fano. His description of this building, of which nothing has survived, would in itself also later shape the idea of classicism. Vitrvuius must have died shortly after completing his treatise in the mid-20s BC.

De architectura, or the text generally referred to as the *Ten Books of Architecture*, embraces many more concerns than what today is considered to fall within the realm of architecture. The last three books deal with water (aqueducts, wells), time-pieces (zodiacs, planets, astrology, sundials), and mechanics (pulleys, screws, catapults, battering rams). The first seven books concern architecture, in both its material, constructional, and theoretical aspects. Perhaps the heart of his treatise is found in Books 3 and 4, in which he presents the proportional rules and description of three types of temples, first and foremost their columns, which later will be construed as "orders." Books 5 and 6 concern other building types, such as basilicas, treasuries, theaters, gymnasia, and dwellings. In Book 1 he presents the six principles of architecture, which are order, arrangement, eurythmy, symmetry, propriety, and economy. A few pages later he reduces these principles to the more famous Vitruvian triad – following a seventeenth-century translation – of commodity, firmness, and delight. Notwithstanding his rules for proportion and symmetry, Vitruvius was not especially dogmatic in his strictures and he allowed the architect considerable latitude in adjusting proportions where the eye deems it necessary. This freedom would be disallowed in later years as proportional rules often came to be seen as sacrosanct canons.

The history of "classicism" in relation to *De architectura* is an interesting one. Limiting the historical importance of these scrolls is the fact that Vitruvius composed them prior to the reign of Augustus, of whom Suetonius once noted that "he found Rome a city of brick and left it a city of marble." Thus many of the major monuments whose ruins still grace the city today were not yet built or even contemplated. And when they later came to be constructed they were not designed to the proportional and design specifications outlined by Vitruvius. Hence his treatise has only a small connection with Roman imperial architecture. Speaking in favor of the treatise of Vitruvius, however, is its relation with the classical past. He was an architect versed not only in such Greek philosophers as Pythagoras, Archimedes, Democritus, Plato, and Aristotle, but also in the work of such contemporaries as Varro and Cicero. Moreover, he makes references to dozens of passages and previous treatises on architecture, the vast majority of which were Greek. Vitruvius's own taste in architecture tended toward the late-Hellenic style, especially the Ionian work of Hermogenes (late third or early second century) and Hermodorus of Salamis (mid-second century). In this way, Vitruvius actually reveals more of the theoretical body of Greek architecture than of the contemporary Roman situation.

The classicism of Vitruvius, however, defines only one foundation stone of the antique tradition upon which Western intellectual development is based; the other derives from the rise and eventual dominance of Christianity in the West. With its roots in Judaism, Christian culture is at least as old as its parallel Hellenistic and Roman counterparts, with which it would become conjoined after Constantine's defeat of Maxentius in AD 312. From his new throne in Constantinople (founded 324–30), Constantine granted religious freedom to all, but himself converted to Christianity, which now aligned its fortunes (at this point a religion still with a small number of followers) with that of the new Empire.

The fates of both the eastern and western Roman empires, however, were not peaceful ones. The Visigoth Alaric captured Rome in 410 (the western empire had moved its capital to Ravenna in 404), and thus began the centuries of the so-called barbarian invasions (actually tribal migrations) that plagued the political stability of Europe well beyond the crowning of Charlemagne as emperor of the Holy Roman Empire in the year 800. Seven-hundred Viking longships camped on the Champ de Mars in 885 and laid siege to Paris for 11 months. As the Byzantine empire fell into serious decline in the eleventh century, both Turks and Mongols pressed into Europe from the east, while only the Pyrenees protected the Franks from Muslim incursions moving up through Spain. Pope Gregory VII declared the supreme legislative and judicial power of the Papacy in 1075, and 40 years later the first of the Crusades was raised to wrest Jerusalem from Islamic control. By the time of the fourth Crusade (1198–1216), the Latin Church had achieved its apogee as a political and military power and essentially unified Europe with its language, law, and theology. Moreover, contacts with Arab scholars had reintroduced the fruits of the Greco-Roman classical tradition into the West. Thus the Gothic period appeared at the moment when a classical cultural renaissance was taking place in Europe; scholars renewed historical interest and the production of books increased dramatically.

Throughout these years the Church's relationship with classicism was nevertheless ambiguous, to say the least. On the one hand classicism bore the marks of paganism, and therefore many of its secular practices (such as art) were often viewed with suspicion. On the other hand there was a genuine interest in recapturing, as it were, the legacy of the past. For instance Vitruvius, whose impact on Roman architecture was very slight, gains considerably in stature in the *Epistles* of Sidonius Apollinarius in the fifth century AD. The oldest existent manuscript of his treatise dates from the ninth century, and from that time forward it was copied and distributed by the monastic route. The Archbishop of Rouen bequeathed a copy of the treatise to his cathedral in 1183 and Vincent of Beauvais quoted Vitruvius on proportions – affirming that *De architectura* was read during Gothic times. Nevertheless, the book of Vitruvius – until the Renaissance – was by no means an influential text, and the major monuments of Romanesque and Gothic times (even with their reminiscences of classical motifs) followed local traditions and the technical knowledge of vaulting that had been evolving since Late Roman times. Symbolism, a prominent feature of Gothic architecture in particular, remained wedded to theological and pedagogical interests. The great monuments of the Middle Ages were extensions of the Church's teachings.

1 VITRUVIUS
from *On Architecture*, Book 1 (c.25 BC)

Vitruvius compiled his 10 "books" (actually scrolls) from a variety of sources, almost entirely Greek. We might therefore see him – like his contemporary Cicero – as a champion of a Greek revival that was prominent in the last years of the Roman Republic. This was a movement among the Roman intelligentsia, in all of the liberal arts, to assimilate and transpose concepts or terminology from Greek theory. The problem inherent in such a process of grafting, as Vitruvius's many interpreters have often pointed out, is that of achieving conceptual clarity and consistency of terms.

Marcus Vitruvius Pollio (c.9–c.20 BC), from Book 1 of *De architectura* [On architecture] (c.25 BC), trans. Morris Hicky Morgan, in *Vitruvius: The Ten Books on Architecture*. New York: Dover, 1960 (orig. 1914), pp. 5, 13–17.

The following passages from the first and second chapters of Book 1 illustrate this problem. After an initial discussion of the areas of education that the aspiring architect should master, Vitruvius identifies the six principles composing the art and science of architecture. But only the last two principles — propriety and economy — are relatively straightforward in their meaning. Order (Greek *taxis*) is the ordering of parts alone and as a whole, and thus implies the concepts of a module and symmetry. Arrangement (Greek *diathesis*), which has also been rendered in English as "design," is similar to order but also adds the idea of aptness of placement. It is also familiar to architects through his discussion of the floor plan, elevation, and perspective. Eurythmy (Latin *eurythmia* is a transliteration of Greek *eurythmos*) and symmetry (Greek *symmetros*; no Latin equivalent) are more elusive. Symmetry, which for Vitruvius is a key concept, is a proper harmony of the parts to each other and to the whole, defining a kind of beauty. Eurythmy, which has also been translated as "proportion," is not dissimilar to order and arrangement, and it suggests the use of numerical ratios. It is also the *visible* coherence of form.

In the next section, after his very broad definition of architecture, Vitruvius reduces architecture to the principles of durability (Latin *firmitas*), convenience (Latin *utilitas*), and beauty (Latin *venustas*). These are the three terms that Henry Wotten translated in 1624 (in a different order) as "commodity, firmness, and delight." The idea of constructing a work in a durable and convenient way is self-evident, and what he means by beauty is made manifest by his invocation of the term "symmetry."

The Education of the Architect

1. The architect should be equipped with knowledge of many branches of study and varied kinds of learning, for it is by his judgement that all work done by the other arts is put to test. This knowledge is the child of practice and theory. Practice is the continuous and regular exercise of employment where manual work is done with any necessary material according to the design of a drawing. Theory, on the other hand, is the ability to demonstrate and explain the productions of dexterity on the principles of proportion.

2. It follows, therefore, that architects who have aimed at acquiring manual skill without scholarship have never been able to reach a position of authority to correspond to their pains, while those who relied only upon theories and scholarship were obviously hunting the shadow, not the substance. But those who have a thorough knowledge of both, like men armed at all points, have the sooner attained their object and carried authority with them. [. . .]

The Fundamental Principles of Architecture

1. Architecture depends on Order (in Greek τάξις), Arrangement (in Greek διάθεσις), Eurythmy, Symmetry, Propriety, and Economy (in Greek οἰκονομία).

2. Order gives due measure to the members of a work considered separately, and symmetrical agreement to the proportions of the whole. It is an adjustment according to quantity (in Greek ποσότης). By this I mean the selection of modules from the members of the work itself and, starting from these individual parts of members, constructing the whole

work to correspond. Arrangement includes the putting of things in their proper places and the elegance of effect which is due to adjustments appropriate to the character of the work. Its forms of expression (in Greek ἰδέαι) are these: groundplan, elevation, and perspective. A groundplan is made by the proper successive use of compasses and rule, through which we get outlines for the plane surfaces of buildings. An elevation is a picture of the front of a building, set upright and properly drawn in the proportions of the contemplated work. Perspective is the method of sketching a front with the sides withdrawing into the background, the lines all meeting in the centre of a circle. All three come of reflexion and invention. Reflexion is careful and laborious thought, and watchful attention directed to the agreeable effect of one's plan. Invention, on the other hand, is the solving of intricate problems and the discovery of new principles by means of brilliancy and versatility. These are the departments belonging under Arrangement.

3. Eurythmy is beauty and fitness in the adjustments of the members. This is found when the members of a work are of a height suited to their breadth, of a breadth suited to their length, and, in a word, when they all correspond symmetrically.

4. Symmetry is a proper agreement between the members of the work itself, and relation between the different parts and the whole general scheme, in accordance with a certain part selected as standard. Thus in the human body there is a kind of symmetrical harmony between forearm, foot, palm, finger, and other small parts; and so it is with perfect buildings. In the case of temples, symmetry may be calculated from the thickness of a column, from a triglyph, or even from a module; in the ballista, from the hole or from what the Greeks call the περίτρητος; in a ship, from the space between the tholepins (διάπηγμα); and in other things, from various members.

5. Propriety is that perfection of style which comes when a work is authoritatively constructed on approved principles. It arises from prescription (Greek θεματισμῷ), from usage, or from nature. From prescription, in the case of hypaethral edifices, open to the sky, in honour of Jupiter Lightning, the Heaven, the Sun, or the Moon: for these are gods whose semblances and manifestations we behold before our very eyes in the sky when it is cloudless and bright. The temples of Minerva, Mars, and Hercules, will be Doric, since the virile strength of these gods makes daintiness entirely inappropriate to their houses. In temples to Venus, Flora, Proserpine, Spring-Water, and the Nymphs, the Corinthian order will be found to have peculiar significance, because these are delicate divinities and so its rather slender outlines, its flowers, leaves, and ornamental volutes will lend propriety where it is due. The construction of temples of the Ionic order to Juno, Diana, Father Bacchus, and the other gods of that kind, will be in keeping with the middle position which they hold; for the building of such will be an appropriate combination of the severity of the Doric and the delicacy of the Corinthian.

6. Propriety arises from usage when buildings having magnificent interiors are provided with elegant entrance-courts to correspond; for there will be no propriety in the spectacle of an elegant interior approached by a low, mean entrance. Or, if dentils be carved in the cornice of the Doric entablature or triglyphs represented in the Ionic entablature over the cushion-shaped capitals of the columns, the effect will be spoilt by the transfer of the peculiarities of the one order of building to the other, the usage in each class having been fixed long ago.

7. Finally, propriety will be due to natural causes if, for example, in the case of all sacred precincts we select very healthy neighbourhoods with suitable springs of water in the places where the fanes are to be built, particularly in the case of those to Aesculapius and to Health, gods by whose healing powers great numbers of the sick are apparently cured. For when their diseased bodies are transferred from an unhealthy to a healthy spot, and treated with waters from health-giving springs, they will the more speedily grow well. The result will be that the divinity will stand in higher esteem and find his dignity increased, all owing to the nature of his site. There will also be natural propriety in using an eastern light for bedrooms and libraries, a western light in winter for baths and winter apartments, and a northern light for picture galleries and other places in which a steady light is needed; for that quarter of the sky grows neither light nor dark with the course of the sun, but remains steady and unshifting all day long.

8. Economy denotes the proper management of materials and of site, as well as a thrifty balancing of cost and common sense in the construction of works. This will be observed if, in the first place, the architect does not demand things which cannot be found or made ready without great expense. For example: it is not everywhere that there is plenty of pitsand, rubble, fir, clear fir, and marble, since they are produced in different places and to assemble them is difficult and costly. Where there is no pitsand, we must use the kinds washed up by rivers or by the sea; the lack of fir and clear fir may be evaded by using cypress, poplar, elm, or pine; and other problems we must solve in similar ways.

9. A second stage in Economy is reached when we have to plan the different kinds of dwellings suitable for ordinary householders, for great wealth, or for the high position of the statesman. A house in town obviously calls for one form of construction; that into which stream the products of country estates requires another; this will not be the same in the case of money-lenders and still different for the opulent and luxurious; for the powers under whose deliberations the commonwealth is guided dwellings are to be provided according to their special needs: and, in a word, the proper form of economy must be observed in building houses for each and every class.

The Departments of Architecture

1. There are three departments of architecture: the art of building, the making of time-pieces, and the construction of machinery. Building is, in its turn, divided into two parts, of which the first is the construction of fortified towns and of works for general use in public places, and the second is the putting up of structures for private individuals. There are three classes of public buildings: the first for defensive, the second for religious, and the third for utilitarian purposes. Under defence comes the planning of walls, towers, and gates, perman-ent devices for resistance against hostile attacks; under religion, the erection of fanes and temples to the immortal gods; under utility, the provision of meeting places for public use, such as harbours, markets, colonnades, baths, theatres, promenades, and all other similar arrangements in public places.

2. All these must be built with due reference to durability, convenience, and beauty. Durability will be assured when foundations are carried down to the solid ground and

materials wisely and liberally selected; convenience, when the arrangement of the apartments is faultless and presents no hindrance to use, and when each class of building is assigned to its suitable and appropriate exposure; and beauty, when the appearance of the work is pleasing and in good taste, and when its members are in due proportion according to correct principles of symmetry.

2 VITRUVIUS
from *On Architecture*, Book 2 (c.25 BC)

Vitruvius devotes almost all of Book 2 of his treatise to a discussion of materials, but he introduces these technical matters with his exposition on the origin of architecture. What this story reveals is the extent of Vitruvius's travels, although it is unclear if he indeed ventured to Spain and Portugal. The vividness of his description of the Phrygians suggests that he visited these parts of central and western Asia Minor, generally what is today Turkey. He also seems to have visited Athens, but the city's most famous monument – the Parthenon – is unfortunately not mentioned in his treatise. This passage also becomes important in the mid-eighteenth century when Marc-Antoine Laugier, who is seeking to overturn the relevance of Vitruvian theory, again draws on the primitive hut to prove that architecture is a rational art.

The Origin of the Dwelling House

1. The men of old were born like the wild beasts, in woods, caves, and groves, and lived on savage fare. As time went on, the thickly crowded trees in a certain place, tossed by storms and winds, and rubbing their branches against one another, caught fire, and so the inhabitants of the place were put to flight, being terrified by the furious flame. After it subsided, they drew near, and observing that they were very comfortable standing before the warm fire, they put on logs and, while thus keeping it alive, brought up other people to it, showing them by signs how much comfort they got from it. In that gathering of men, at a time when utterance of sound was purely individual, from daily habits they fixed upon articulate words just as these had happened to come; then, from indicating by name things in common use, the result was that in this chance way they began to talk, and thus originated conversation with one another.

2. Therefore it was the discovery of fire that originally gave rise to the coming together of men, to the deliberative assembly, and to social intercourse. And so, as they kept coming together in greater numbers into one place, finding themselves naturally gifted beyond the other animals in not being obliged to walk with faces to the ground, but upright and gazing upon the splendour of the starry firmament, and also in being able to do with ease whatever

Marcus Vitruvius Pollio, from Book 2, chapter 1 of *De architectura* [On architecture] (c.25 BC), trans. Morris Hicky Morgan, in *Vitruvius: The Ten Books on Architecture*. New York: Dover, 1960 (orig. 1914), pp. 38–41.

they chose with their hands and fingers, they began in that first assembly to construct shelters. Some made them of green boughs, others dug caves on mountain sides, and some, in imitation of the nests of swallows and the way they built, made places of refuge out of mud and twigs. Next, by observing the shelters of others and adding new details to their own inceptions, they constructed better and better kinds of huts as time went on.

3. And since they were of an imitative and teachable nature, they would daily point out to each other the results of their building, boasting of the novelties in it; and thus, with their natural gifts sharpened by emulation, their standards improved daily. At first they set up forked stakes connected by twigs and covered these walls with mud. Others made walls of lumps of dried mud, covering them with reeds and leaves to keep out the rain and the heat. Finding that such roofs could not stand the rain during the storms of winter, they built them with peaks daubed with mud, the roofs sloping and projecting so as to carry off the rain water.

4. That houses originated as I have written above, we can see for ourselves from the buildings that are to this day constructed of like materials by foreign tribes: for instance, in Gaul, Spain, Portugal, and Aquitaine, roofed with oak shingles or thatched. Among the Colchians in Pontus, where there are forests in plenty, they lay down entire trees flat on the ground to the right and the left, leaving between them a space to suit the length of the trees, and then place above these another pair of trees, resting on the ends of the former and at right angles with them. These four trees enclose the space for the dwelling. Then upon these they place sticks of timber, one after the other on the four sides, crossing each other at the angles, and so, proceeding with their walls of trees laid perpendicularly above the lowest, they build up high towers. The interstices, which are left on account of the thickness of the building material, are stopped up with chips and mud. As for the roofs, by cutting away the ends of the crossbeams and making them converge gradually as they lay them across, they bring them up to the top from the four sides in the shape of a pyramid. They cover it with leaves and mud, and thus construct the roofs of their towers in a rude form of the "tortoise" style.

5. On the other hand, the Phrygians, who live in an open country, have no forests and consequently lack timber. They therefore select a natural hillock, run a trench through the middle of it, dig passages, and extend the interior space as widely as the site admits. Over it they build a pyramidal roof of logs fastened together, and this they cover with reeds and brushwood, heaping up very high mounds of earth above their dwellings. Thus their fashion in houses makes their winters very warm and their summers very cool. Some construct hovels with roofs of rushes from the swamps. Among other nations, also, in some places there are huts of the same or a similar method of construction. Likewise at Marseilles we can see roofs without tiles, made of earth mixed with straw. In Athens on the Areopagus there is to this day a relic of antiquity with a mud roof. The hut of Romulus on the Capitol is a significant reminder of the fashions of old times, and likewise the thatched roofs of temples on the Citadel.

6. From such specimens we can draw our inferences with regard to the devices used in the buildings of antiquity, and conclude that they were similar.

Furthermore, as men made progress by becoming daily more expert in building, and as their ingenuity was increased by their dexterity so that from habit they attained to considerable skill, their intelligence was enlarged by their industry until the more proficient adopted the trade of carpenters. From these early beginnings, and from the fact that nature had not only endowed the human race with senses like the rest of the animals, but had also equipped their minds with the powers of thought and understanding, thus putting all other animals under their sway, they next gradually advanced from the construction of buildings to the other arts and sciences, and so passed from a rude and barbarous mode of life to civilization and refinement.

7. Then, taking courage and looking forward from the standpoint of higher ideas born of the multiplication of the arts, they gave up huts and began to build houses with foundations, having brick or stone walls, and roofs of timber and tiles; next, observation and application led them from fluctuating and indefinite conceptions to definite rules of symmetry. Perceiving that nature had been lavish in the bestowal of timber and bountiful in stores of building material, they treated this like careful nurses, and thus developing the refinements of life, embellished them with luxuries.

3 VITRUVIUS
from *On Architecture*, Book 3 (c.25 BC)

V itruvian theory is sometimes described as anthropomorphic in the sense that he predicates proportional rules on the ratios of the human body. Here, in this explication of the idea of "symmetry" in Book 3, he supplies this theoretical basis for why proportions are important. His description of a man with outstretched limbs, placed within a circle and square, later becomes the basis for various Renaissance sketches, the most famous of which is that of Leonardo da Vinci. This proportional aligning of architecture with the human figure, or more generally with the proportional rules of nature, will become a cornerstone of classical theory.

On Symmetry: In Temples and in the Human Body

1. The design of a temple depends on symmetry, the principles of which must be most carefully observed by the architect. They are due to proportion, in Greek ἀναλογία. Proportion is a correspondence among the measures of the members of an entire work, and of the whole to a certain part selected as standard. From this result the principles of symmetry. Without symmetry and proportion there can be no principles in the design of any temple; that is, if there is no precise relation between its members, as in the case of those of a well shaped man.

2. For the human body is so designed by nature that the face, from the chin to the top of the forehead and the lowest roots of the hair, is a tenth part of the whole height; the open hand from the wrist to the tip of the middle finger is just the same; the head from the chin to

Marcus Vitruvius Pollio, from Book 3, chapter 1 of *De architectura* [On architecture] (c.25 BC), trans. Morris Hicky Morgan, in *Vitruvius: The Ten Books on Architecture*. New York: Dover, 1960 (orig. 1914), pp. 72–3.

the crown is an eighth, and with the neck and shoulder from the top of the breast to the lowest roots of the hair is a sixth; from the middle of the breast to the summit of the crown is a fourth. If we take the height of the face itself, the distance from the bottom of the chin to the under side of the nostrils is one third of it; the nose from the under side of the nostrils to a line between the eyebrows is the same; from there to the lowest roots of the hair is also a third, comprising the forehead. The length of the foot is one sixth of the height of the body; of the forearm, one fourth; and the breadth of the breast is also one fourth. The other members, too, have their own symmetrical proportions, and it was by employing them that the famous painters and sculptors of antiquity attained to great and endless renown.

3. Similarly, in the members of a temple there ought to be the greatest harmony in the symmetrical relations of the different parts to the general magnitude of the whole. Then again, in the human body the central point is naturally the navel. For if a man be placed flat on his back, with his hands and feet extended, and a pair of compasses centred at his navel, the fingers and toes of his two hands and feet will touch the circumference of a circle described therefrom. And just as the human body yields a circular outline, so too a square figure may be found from it. For if we measure the distance from the soles of the feet to the top of the head, and then apply that measure to the outstretched arms, the breadth will be found to be the same as the height, as in the case of plane surfaces which are perfectly square.

4. Therefore, since nature has designed the human body so that its members are duly proportioned to the frame as a whole, it appears that the ancients had good reason for their rule, that in perfect buildings the different members must be in exact symmetrical relations to the whole general scheme. Hence, while transmitting to us the proper arrangements for buildings of all kinds, they were particularly careful to do so in the case of temples of the gods, buildings in which merits and faults usually last forever.

4 VITRUVIUS
from *On Architecture*, Book 4 (c.25 BC)

No book reveals the "Roman" character of *De architectura* better than Book 4, the Preface to which forms this dedication to the Emperor Augustus Caesar. Vitruvius, in his ambition to write a "complete and orderly form of presentation," obviously felt he was setting a historical precedent. Even more enchanting to later generations is his often-repeated discussion of the origin of the three architectural orders: the Doric, Ionic, and Corinthian. These stories are sometimes said to compose the "mythology" of architecture, fables that were eventually discredited by the rational forces of the Western Enlightenment, but once again they demonstrate the anthropomorphic basis of Vitruvian theory. One sentence within this passage that should not be overlooked is his admission that the proportions for both the Doric and Ionic columns changed after some "progress in refinement and delicacy of feeling." Renaissance humanists, operating from a very different aesthetic basis, regarded this

Marcus Vitruvius Pollio, from Book 4, chapter 1 of *De architectura* [On architecture] (c.25 BC), trans. Morris Hicky Morgan, in *Vitruvius: The Ten Books on Architecture*. New York: Dover, 1960 (orig. 1914), pp. 102–7.

remark as a fault of his theory and sought to find hard and fast rules for proportions, ones that would not change over time. In the end, this dispute over the invariability of proportions would eventually lead classical theory into a crisis.

The Origins of the Three Orders, and the Proportions of the Corinthian Capital

1. Corinthian columns are, excepting in their capitals, of the same proportions in all respects as Ionic; but the height of their capitals gives them proportionately a taller and more slender effect. This is because the height of the Ionic capital is only one third of the thickness of the column, while that of the Corinthian is the entire thickness of the shaft. Hence, as two thirds are added in Corinthian capitals, their tallness gives a more slender appearance to the columns themselves.

2. The other members which are placed above the columns, are, for Corinthian columns, composed either of the Doric proportions or according to the Ionic usages; for the Corinthian order never had any scheme peculiar to itself for its cornices or other ornaments, but may have mutules in the coronae and guttae on the architraves according to the triglyph system of the Doric style, or, according to Ionic practices, it may be arranged with a frieze adorned with sculptures and accompanied with dentils and coronae.

3. Thus a third architectural order, distinguished by its capital, was produced out of the two other orders. To the forms of their columns are due the names of the three orders, Doric, Ionic, and Corinthian, of which the Doric was the first to arise, and in early times. For Dorus, the son of Hellen and the nymph Phthia, was king of Achaea and all the Peloponnesus, and he built a fane, which chanced to be of this order, in the precinct of Juno at Argolis, a very ancient city, and subsequently others of the same order in the other cities of Achaea, although the rules of symmetry were not yet in existence.

4. Later, the Athenians, in obedience to oracles of the Delphic Apollo, and with the general agreement of all Hellas, despatched thirteen colonies at one time to Asia Minor, appointing leaders for each colony and giving the command-in-chief to Ion, son of Xuthus and Creusa (whom further Apollo at Delphi in the oracles had acknowledged as his son). Ion conducted those colonies to Asia Minor, took possession of the land of Caria, and there founded the grand cities of Ephesus, Miletus, Myus (long ago engulfed by the water, and its sacred rites and suffrage handed over by the Ionians to the Milesians), Priene, Samos, Teos, Colophon, Chius, Erythrae, Phocaea, Clazomenae, Lebedos, and Melite. This Melite, on account of the arrogance of its citizens, was destroyed by the other cities in a war declared by general agreement, and in its place, through the kindness of King Attalus and Arsinoe, the city of the Smyrnaeans was admitted among the Ionians.

5. Now these cities, after driving out the Carians and Lelegans, called that part of the world Ionia from their leader Ion, and there they set off precincts for the immortal gods and began to build fanes: first of all, a temple to Panionion Apollo such as they had seen in Achaea, calling it Doric because they had first seen that kind of temple built in the states of the Dorians.

6. Wishing to set up columns in that temple, but not having rules for their symmetry, and being in search of some way by which they could render them fit to bear a load and also of a satisfactory beauty of appearance, they measured the imprint of a man's foot and compared this with his height. On finding that, in a man, the foot was one sixth of the height, they applied the same principle to the column, and reared the shaft, including the capital, to a height six times its thickness at its base. Thus the Doric column, as used in buildings, began to exhibit the proportions, strength, and beauty of the body of a man.

7. Just so afterwards, when they desired to construct a temple to Diana in a new style of beauty, they translated these footprints into terms characteristic of the slenderness of women, and thus first made a column the thickness of which was only one eighth of its height, so that it might have a taller look. At the foot they substituted the base in place of a shoe; in the capital they placed the volutes, hanging down at the right and left like curly ringlets, and ornamented its front with cymatia and with festoons of fruit arranged in place of hair, while they brought the flutes down the whole shaft, falling like the folds in the robes worn by matrons. Thus in the invention of the two different kinds of columns, they borrowed manly beauty, naked and unadorned, for the one, and for the other the delicacy, adornment, and proportions characteristic of women.

8. It is true that posterity, having made progress in refinement and delicacy of feeling, and finding pleasure in more slender proportions, has established seven diameters of the thickness as the height of the Doric column, and nine as that of the Ionic. The Ionians, however, originated the order which is therefore named Ionic.

The third order, called Corinthian, is an imitation of the slenderness of a maiden; for the outlines and limbs of maidens, being more slender on account of their tender years, admit of prettier effects in the way of adornment.

9. It is related that the original discovery of this form of capital was as follows. A freeborn maiden of Corinth, just of marriageable age, was attacked by an illness and passed away. After her burial, her nurse, collecting a few little things which used to give the girl pleasure while she was alive, put them in a basket, carried it to the tomb, and laid it on top thereof, covering it with a roof-tile so that the things might last longer in the open air. This basket happened to be placed just above the root of an acanthus. The acanthus root, pressed down meanwhile though it was by the weight, when springtime came round put forth leaves and stalks in the middle, and the stalks, growing up along the sides of the basket, and pressed out by the corners of the tile through the compulsion of its weight, were forced to bend into volutes at the outer edges.

10. Just then Callimachus, whom the Athenians called κατατηξίτεχνος for the refinement and delicacy of his artistic work, passed by this tomb and observed the basket with the tender young leaves growing round it. Delighted with the novel style and form, he built some columns after that pattern for the Corinthians, determined their symmetrical proportions, and established from that time forth the rules to be followed in finished works of the Corinthian order.

5 OLD TESTAMENT
from *I Kings*

Vitruvius died more than two decades before the birth of Christ, and thus he could not have imagined what would become the Judeo-Christian tradition and its eventual assimilation into the Roman Empire. This religious tradition was, in fact, a parallel world existing alongside Greco-Roman antiquity, with similar yet different ties to the various cultures of the Middle East and Egypt. In Hebrew canon, the two Old Testament books of *Kings* formed one volume and constituted one of the eight books of the *Prophets*. Together they compose legendary Jewish history from the time of Ahaziah (c.850 BC) to the release of Jehoiachin from Babylonian imprisonment (c.561 BC). Its author is sometimes said to be Jeremiah, who lived in the late seventh and sixth centuries, although this point has been disputed.

I Kings gains its importance to architectural theory because it contains one of the oldest descriptions of architecture that has survived into modern times. Moreover, it describes the famed Temple of Solomon: the temple built in Jerusalem by King Solomon in the mid-tenth century and destroyed by the Babylonian Nebuchadnezzar in 586 BC. The complex was constructed by Phoenician artisans and its centerpiece was the sanctuary, in front of which stood the two bronze pillars of Yachin and Boaz. The following two passages make clear the importance of costly materials to the chronicler, but equally the importance of numerical proportions (in this case supplied by the Lord himself) to preclassical design. Numeric ratios were thus central not only to the Greco-Roman civilization but also the Judaic and later Christian cultures as well.

Chapter 6

Solomon builds the temple

And it came to pass in the four hundred and eightieth year after the children of Israel were come out of the land of Egypt, in the fourth year of Solomon's reign over Israel, in the month Zif, which *is* the second month, that he began to build the house of the LORD.

2 And the house which king Solomon built for the LORD, the length thereof *was* threescore cubits, and the breadth thereof twenty *cubits*, and the height thereof thirty cubits.

3 And the porch before the temple of the house, twenty cubits *was* the length thereof, according to the breadth of the house; *and* ten cubits *was* the breadth thereof before the house.

4 And for the house he made windows of narrow lights.

5 And against the wall of the house he built chambers round about, *against* the walls of the house round about, *both* of the temple and of the oracle: and he made chambers round about:

6 The nethermost chamber *was* five cubits broad, and the middle *was* six cubits broad, and the third *was* seven cubits broad: for without *in the wall* of the house he made narrowed rests round about, that *the beams* should not be fastened in the walls of the house.

Old Testament, from *I Kings*, chapters 6 and 7 in the King James version of the Holy Bible.

7 And the house, when it was in building, was built of stone made ready before it was brought thither: so that there was neither hammer nor axe *nor* any tool of iron heard in the house, while it was in building.

8 The door for the middle chamber *was* in the right side of the house: and they went up with winding stairs into the middle *chamber*, and out of the middle into the third.

9 So he built the house, and finished it; and covered the house with beams and boards of cedar.

10 And *then* he built chambers against all the house, five cubits high: and they rested on the house with timber of cedar.

11 And the word of the LORD came to Solomon, saying,

12 *Concerning* this house which thou art in building, if thou wilt walk in my statutes, and execute my judgments, and keep all my commandments to walk in them; then will I perform my word with thee, which I spake unto David thy father:

13 And I will dwell among the children of Israel, and will not forsake my people Israel.

14 So Solomon built the house, and finished it.

15 And he built the walls of the house within with boards of cedar, both the floor of the house, and the walls of the ceiling: *and* he covered *them* on the inside with wood, and covered the floor of the house with planks of fir.

16 And he built twenty cubits on the sides of the house, both the floor and the walls with boards of cedar: he even built *them* for it within, *even* for the oracle, *even* for the most holy *place*.

17 And the house, that *is*, the temple before it, was forty cubits *long*.

18 And the cedar of the house within *was* carved with knops and open flowers: all *was* cedar; there was no stone seen.

19 And the oracle he prepared in the house within, to set there the ark of the covenant of the LORD.

20 And the oracle in the forepart *was* twenty cubits in length, and twenty cubits in breadth, and twenty cubits in the height thereof: and he overlaid it with pure gold; and *so* covered the altar *which was of* cedar.

21 So Solomon overlaid the house within with pure gold: and he made a partition by the chains of gold before the oracle; and he overlaid it with gold.

22 And the whole house he overlaid with gold, until he had finished all the house: also the whole altar that *was* by the oracle he overlaid with gold.

23 And within the oracle he made two cher-u-bim *of* olive tree, *each* ten cubits high.

24 And five cubits *was* the one wing of the cherub, and five cubits the other wing of the cherub: from the uttermost part of the one wing unto the uttermost part of the other *were* ten cubits.

25 And the other cherub *was* ten cubits: both the cher-u-bim *were* of one measure and one size.

26 The height of the one cherub *was* ten cubits, and so *was it* of the other cherub.

27 And he set the cher-u-bim within the inner house: and they stretched forth the wings of the cher-u-bim, so that the wing of the one touched the *one* wall, and the wing of the other cherub touched the other wall; and their wings touched one another in the midst of the house.

28 And he overlaid the cher-u-bim with gold.

29 And he carved all the walls of the house round about with carved figures of cher-u-bim and palm trees and open flowers, within and without.

30 And the floor of the house he overlaid with gold, within and without.

31 And for the entering of the oracle he made doors *of* olive tree: the lintel *and* side posts *were* a fifth part *of the wall*.

32 The two doors also *were of* olive tree; and he carved upon them carvings of cher-u-bim and palm trees and open flowers, and overlaid *them* with gold, and spread gold upon the cher-u-bim, and upon the palm trees.

33 So also made he for the door of the temple posts *of* olive tree, a fourth part *of the wall*.

34 And the two doors *were of* fir tree: the two leaves of the one door *were* folding, and the two leaves of the other door *were* folding.

35 And he carved *thereon* cher-u-bim and palm trees and open flowers: and covered *them* with gold fitted upon the carved work.

36 And he built the inner court with three rows of hewed stone, and a row of cedar beams.

37 In the fourth year was the foundation of the house of the LORD laid, in the month Zif:

38 And in the eleventh year, in the month Bul, which *is* the eighth month, was the house finished throughout all the parts thereof, and according to all the fashion of it. So was he seven years in building it.

Chapter 7

The other buildings of Solomon

[. . .]

13 And king Solomon sent and fetched Hiram out of Tyre.

14 He *was* a widow's son of the tribe of Naph-ta-li, and his father *was* a man of Tyre, a worker in brass: and he was filled with wisdom, and understanding, and cunning to work all works in brass. And he came to king Solomon, and wrought all his work.

15 For he cast two pillars of brass, of eighteen cubits high apiece: and a line of twelve cubits did compass either of them about.

16 And he made two chapiters of molten brass, to set upon the tops of the pillars: the height of the one chapiter *was* five cubits, and the height of the other chapiter *was* five cubits:

17 *And* nets of checker work, and wreaths of chain work, for the chapiters which *were* upon the top of the pillars; seven for the one chapiter, and seven for the other chapiter.

18 And he made the pillars, and two rows round about upon the one network, to cover the chapiters there *were* upon the top, with pomegranates: and so did he for the other chapiter.

19 And the chapiters that *were* upon the top of the pillars *were* of lily work in the porch, four cubits.

20 And the chapiters upon the two pillars *had pomegranates* also above, over against the belly which *was* by the network: and the pomegranates *were* two hundred in rows round about upon the other chapiter.

21 And he set up the pillars in the porch of the temple: and he set up the right pillar, and called the name thereof Ja-chin: and he set up the left pillar, and called the name thereof Bo-az.

22 And upon the top of the pillars *was* lily work: so was the work of the pillars finished.

6 OLD TESTAMENT
from *The Book of Ezekiel* (c.586 BC)

Almost contemporary with the writer of *I Kings* was the prophet Ezekiel, a Jewish priest who was carried away to Babylonia in captivity in 597 BC. Four years later he followed his call into the prophetic ministry and soon thereafter began warning his fellow exiles about the impending doom of Jerusalem, which he saw as divine punishment for Hebraic sinfulness. The first 33 chapters of *Ezekiel* were composed before the fall of Jerusalem, but after the city's destruction in 586 Ezekiel turned his prophetic vision to the rebuilding of the city and its holy shrines. In chapters 40 to 42 he speaks of rebuilding the Temple of Jerusalem, now to be constructed on a grander scale equal to the Babylonian temples with which he was familiar. Once again there is a great emphasis on the numerical and mathematical purity of the work (he may indeed have drawn upon *I Kings*), and again there is the great importance he places on symbolism.

Chapter 41

The measuring of the temple

Afterward he brought me to the temple, and measured the posts, six cubits broad on the one side, and six cubits broad on the other side, *which was* the breadth of the tabernacle.

2   And the breadth of the door *was* ten cubits; and the sides of the door *were* five cubits on the one side, and five cubits on the other side: and he measured the length thereof, forty cubits: and the breadth, twenty cubits.

3   Then went he inward, and measured the post of the door, two cubits; and the door, six cubits; and the breadth of the door, seven cubits.

4   So he measured the length thereof, twenty cubits; and the breadth, twenty cubits, before the temple: and he said unto me, This *is* the most holy *place*.

5   After he measured the wall of the house, six cubits; and the breadth of *every* side chamber, four cubits, round about the house on every side.

6   And the side chambers *were* three, one over another, and thirty in order; and they entered into the wall which was of the house for the side chambers round about, that they might have hold, but they had not hold in the wall of the house.

Old Testament, from *The Book of Ezekiel* (c.586 BC), chapter 41, "The Measuring of the Temple," in the King James version of the Holy Bible.

7   And *there was* an enlarging, and a winding about still upward to the side chambers: for the winding about of the house went still upward round about the house: therefore the breadth of the house *was still* upward, and so increased *from* the lowest *chamber* to the highest by the midst.

8   I saw also the height of the house round about: the foundations of the side chambers *were* a full reed of six great cubits.

9   The thickness of the wall, which was for the side chamber without, *was* five cubits: and *that* which *was* left *was* the place of the side chambers that were within.

10   And between the chambers *was* the wideness of twenty cubits round about the house on every side.

11   And the doors of the side chambers *were* toward *the place that was* left, one door toward the north, and another door toward the south: and the breadth of the place that was left *was* five cubits round about.

12   Now the building that *was* before the separate place at the end toward the west *was* seventy cubits broad; and the wall of the building *was* five cubits thick round about, and the length thereof ninety cubits.

13   So he measured the house, a hundred cubits long; and the separate place, and the building, with the walls thereof, a hundred cubits long;

14   Also the breadth of the face of the house, and of the separate place toward the east, a hundred cubits.

15   And he measured the length of the building over against the separate place which *was* behind it, and the galleries thereof on the one side and on the other side, a hundred cubits, with the inner temple, and the porches of the court;

16   The door posts, and the narrow windows, and the galleries round about on their three stories, over against the door, ceiled with wood round about, and from the ground up to the windows, and the windows *were* covered;

17   To that above the door, even unto the inner house, and without, and by all the wall round about within and without, by measure.

18   And *it was* made with cher-u-bim and palm trees, so that a palm tree was between a cherub and a cherub; and *every* cherub had two faces;

19   So that the face of a man *was* toward the palm tree on the one side, and the face of a young lion toward the palm tree on the other side: *it was* made through all the house round about.

20   From the ground unto above the door *were* cher-u-bim and palm trees made, and on the wall of the temple.

21   The posts of the temple *were* squared, *and* the face of the sanctuary; the appearance *of the one* as the appearance *of the other.*

22   The altar of wood *was* three cubits high, and the length thereof two cubits; and the corners thereof, and the length thereof, and the walls thereof, *were* of wood: and he said unto me, This *is* the table that *is* before the LORD.

23   And the temple and the sanctuary had two doors.

24   And the doors had two leaves *apiece*, two turning leaves; two *leaves* for the one door, and two leaves for the other *door.*

25   And *there were* made on them, on the doors of the temple cher-u-bim and palm trees, like as *were* made upon the walls; and *there were* thick planks upon the face of the porch without.

26   And *there were* narrow windows and palm trees on the one side and on the other side, on the sides of the porch, and *upon* the side chambers of the house, and thick planks.

7   NEW TESTAMENT
from *The Revelation of Jesus Christ to Saint John* (c.95 AD)

The book of *Revelation*, also known as the Apocalypse, is the last book to have been incorporated into the canon of the New Testament. It is a work of prophecy, and the author identifies himself as John. Earlier biblical scholars accepted that he was the apostle John, but more recent scholarship suggests that he was a Palestinian Christian priest who fled into exile after the First Jewish Revolt against the Romans in 66–73 AD. The *Revelation* speaks to the Roman persecution of Christians, but more vividly to the second coming of Christ on the day of the Last Judgment. Toward the end of book, after recounting the defeat of Satan, John records his vision of the new earth and the new Jerusalem. The earlier Judaic tradition of numerology and symbolism here takes on a distinct Christian cast. The *Revelation* would become enormously influential during the Christian Middle Ages.

Chapter 21

The new heaven and the new earth

And I saw a new heaven and a new earth: for the first heaven and the first earth were passed away; and there was no more sea.

2   And I John saw the holy city, new Jerusalem, coming down from God out of heaven, prepared as a bride adorned for her husband.

3   And I heard a great voice out of heaven saying, Behold, the tabernacle of God *is* with men, and he will dwell with them, and they shall be his people, and God himself shall be with them, *and be* their God.

4   And God shall wipe away all tears from their eyes; and there shall be no more death, neither sorrow, nor crying, neither shall there be any more pain: for the former things are passed away.

5   And he that sat upon the throne said, Behold, I make all things new. And he said unto me, Write: for these words are true and faithful.

New Testament, from *The Revelation of Jesus Christ to Saint John* (c.95 AD), chapter 21, in the King James version of the Holy Bible.

6   And he said unto me, It is done. I am Alpha and Omega, the beginning and the end. I will give unto him that is athirst of the fountain of the water of life freely.

7   He that overcometh shall inherit all things; and I will be his God, and he shall be my son.

8   But the fearful, and unbelieving, and the abominable, and murderers, and whore-mongers, and sorcerers, and idolaters, and all liars, shall have their part in the lake which burneth with fire and brimstone: which is the second death.

The new Jerusalem

9   And there came unto me one of the seven angels which had the seven vials full of the seven last plagues, and talked with me, saying, Come hither, I will show thee the bride, the Lamb's wife.

10   And he carried me away in the spirit to a great and high mountain, and showed me that great city, the holy Jerusalem, descending out of heaven from God,

11   Having the glory of God: and her light *was* like unto a stone most precious, even like a jasper stone, clear as crystal;

12   And had a wall great and high, *and* had twelve gates, and at the gates twelve angels, and names written thereon, which are *the names* of the twelve tribes of the children of Israel:

13   On the east three gates; on the north three gates; on the south three gates; and on the west three gates.

14   And the wall of the city had twelve foundations, and in them the names of the twelve apostles of the Lamb.

15   And he that talked with me had a golden reed to measure the city, and the gates thereof, and the wall thereof.

16   And the city lieth foursquare, and the length is as large as the breadth: and he measured the city with the reed, twelve thousand furlongs. The length and the breadth and the height of it are equal.

17   And he measured the wall thereof, a hundred *and* forty *and* four cubits, *according to* the measure of man, that is, of the angel.

18   And the building of the wall of it was *of* jasper: and the city *was* pure gold, like unto clear glass.

19   And the foundations of the wall of the city *were* garnished with all manner of precious stones. The first foundation *was* jasper; the second, sapphire; the third, a chalcedony; the fourth, an emerald;

20   The fifth, sardonyx; the sixth, sardius; the seventh, chrysolite; the eighth, beryl; the ninth, a topaz; the tenth, a chrysoprasus; the eleventh, a jacinth; the twelfth, an amethyst.

21   And the twelve gates *were* twelve pearls; every several gate was of one pearl: and the street of the city *was* pure gold, as it were transparent glass.

22   And I saw no temple therein: for the Lord God Almighty and the Lamb are the temple of it.

23   And the city had no need of the sun, neither of the moon, to shine in it: for the glory of God did lighten it, and the Lamb *is* the light thereof.

24   And the nations of them which are saved shall walk in the light of it: and the kings of the earth do bring their glory and honor into it.

25   And the gates of it shall not be shut at all by day: for there shall be no night there.

26   And they shall bring the glory and honor of the nations into it.

27   And there shall in no wise enter into it any thing that defileth, neither *whatsoever* worketh abomination, or *maketh* a lie: but they which are written in the Lamb's book of life.

8   ABBOT SUGER
from *The Book of Suger, Abbot of Saint-Denis* (c.1144)

The onetime village of Saint-Denis (now a part of Paris) holds a particularly important place within architectural history because it is the birthplace of Gothic architecture. The rebuilding of this Carolingian pilgrimage church (originally founded in the late eighth century) is owed to the efforts of Abbot Suger (1081–1151). The church was a shrine to the spiritual apostle of France, and for this reason Charlemagne and his son Pepin, establishing a precedent, were crowned there as kings. It was because of this dual religious and political significance that Suger, a childhood friend of Louis VI, sought to enhance both his friend's political standing (royal power in France at this time was second to that of nobles) and the authority of the Church by enlarging the existing abbey church. The important work of building the new narthex on the western front, containing the first rose window, and the enlarged Gothic choir on the eastern end were largely carried out between 1137 and the church's rededication in 1144. The choir in particular is a masterpiece of structural innovation. With the removal of the traditional walls separating choir chapels in Romanesque churches, Suger and his (unknown) master mason, devising seven radial chapels, created a double ambulatory of pointed arches and vaults supported on slender columns (with quasi-classical capitals), and reinforced the delicacy of the stonework with piers and flying buttresses outside. The curved outside walls of the chapels thus became walls of glass, introducing both abundant light and extreme visual lightness. The new structural solution even achieved the status of a "miracle" when, during construction, a violent storm destroyed many surrounding buildings but left the rib work for the new vaults intact. These passages from Suger's LIBELLUS ALTER DE CONSECRATIONE ECCLESIAE SANCTI DIONYSII relate to the conception and planning of the all-important choir. The importance of geometry and proportions are made evident, as is some of the basic symbolism of the church.

Having thus deliberated with our very devoted brothers – *"Did not our heart burn within us, while he talked with us by the way"* – we decided upon deliberation under God's inspiration ... to respect the stones themselves, sanctified in this way as much as relics. We endeavored to apply ourselves to ennoble this much-needed new [choir] through the beauty of the length and width. Upon reflection, we thus decided to replace the vault, unequal to the higher one that covered the apse containing the bodies of our Patron Saints,

Abbot Suger (c.1081–1151), from *The Book of Suger, Abbot of Saint-Denis* (c.1144), trans. Christina Contandriopoulos from the French translation of the Latin text, ed. and trans. Françoise Gasparri, in *Les Classiques de l'histoire de France*, Vol. 1. Paris: Belles Lettres, 1996, pp. 25–39. Reproduced by permission.

down to the upper level of the crypt, to which it was connected. In this way, a single crypt would offer its top as a pavement to those arriving by the stairs on both sides, and it would allow the visitors on the upper level a view of the relics of saints adorned with gold and precious stone. With perspicacity and with the help of geometrical and arithmetical tools, we also endeavored to make the center of the old church coincide with the center of the new construction by superimposing the upper columns and median arches over those that were built in the crypt; [we managed] also to adapt the proportions of the ancient side aisles to the new ones – except for that remarkable and elegant addition yielding a crown of chapels, because of which the entire [church] would brilliantly shine with the remarkable and uninterrupted light of the dazzling windows illuminating the interior beauty.

[. . .]

Thus at great expense, and thanks to so many workers, we applied ourselves for three years, summer and winter, to the completion of this work . . . In the center [of the building] twelve columns represented the group of twelve Apostles. The second group of the columns represented the same number of prophets in the ambulatory, which suddenly projected the building to another size, according to the Apostle who built spiritually: *"Now therefore,"* he said, *"ye are no more strangers and foreigners, but fellow citizens with the saints, and of the household of God. And are built upon the foundation of the apostles and prophets, Jesus Christ himself being the chief cornerstone; in whom all the building fitly framed together groweth unto a holy temple in the Lord."* In Him, we too applied ourselves to build an edifice materially as tall and with as much fitness as we could, by us spiritually [to become] the house of God in the Holy Spirit.

[. . .]

Here is an event we have thought should not be passed over in silence. When work on the new addition with its capitals and upper arches was reaching the summit of its height, but when the independently constructed main arches were not yet connected to the mass of the vaults, there suddenly arose a terrible, almost intolerable storm. It had accumulations of clouds, pouring rain, and very violent winds, which were severe to the point of shaking not only robust houses but also stone towers and timber donjons. During this storm, on the anniversary of the glorious king Dagobert, the venerable bishop Charles Geoffroy was solemnly celebrating a Mass of thanksgiving at the main altar before the community for the soul of this king. The violence of the opposing winds pushed so hard against these arches, which were not supported by any scaffolding or braced by any prop, that they miserably trembled and oscillated from side to side in such a way that they threatened to fall abruptly into ruin beyond repair. Frightened by the shaking of these arches and roofing, the Bishop frequently extended his hand in that direction in a sign of benediction, and presented with insistence the arm of the old [St.] Siméon, while making the sign of the cross. Thus it became very clear that the collapse [of the construction] was avoided not because of its own strength but only because of God's goodness and the glory of the Saints. Whereas in many places the tempest had caused great damage to many well-built buildings, the storm, held in check by divine force, inflicted no damage at all on these isolated, newly constructed arches tottering in the air.

9 WILLIAM DURANDUS
from *The Symbolism of Churches and Church Ornaments* (1286)

W illiam Durandus was a prominent theorist of canon law in high Gothic times. Born in French Provence, he first studied law at Bologna before teaching canon law at Modena. He was next summoned to Rome by Clement IV, ordained, and given the titular canonries at Beauvais and Chartres. As the secretary to Gregory X, he accompanied him to the Second Council of Lyons in 1274 and later defended papal territories with armies against the Guelphs and Ghibellines. This defense led to his promotion as Bishop of Mende in 1286. Durandus's *Rationale divinorum officiorum* was apparently complete in this year, and this treatise of eight books is still today seen as the most complete authority for thirteenth-century liturgical rites and their symbolism. Book 1, which in 1843 was translated as *The Symbolism of Churches and Church Ornaments*, deals with the symbolism of the church itself and its various parts, and it is evident from this extraordinary excerpt that every architectural component of a Gothic church had its specific meaning or message for the worshippers.

24. The glass windows in a church are Holy Scriptures, which expel the wind and the rain, that is all things hurtful, but transmit the light of the true Sun, that is, God, into the hearts of the faithful. These are wider within than without, because the mystical sense is the more ample, and precedeth the literal meaning. Also, by the windows the senses of the body are signified: which ought to be shut to the vanities of this world, and open to receive with all freedom spiritual gifts.

25. By the lattice work of the windows, we understand the prophets or other obscure teachers of the Church Militant: in which windows there are often two shafts, signifying the two precepts of charity, or because the apostles were sent out to preach two and two.

26. The door of the church is Christ: according to the saying in the Gospel, "I am the door." The apostles are also called doors.

27. The piers of the church are bishops and doctors: who specially sustain the Church of God by their doctrine. These, from the majesty and clearness of their divine message, are called silver, according to that in the Song of Songs. "He made silver columns." Whence also Moses at the entering in of the tabernacle, placed five columns, and four before the oracle, that is, the holy of holies. Although the piers are more in number than seven, yet they are called seven, according to that saying, "Wisdom hath builded her house, she hath hewn out her seven pillars": because bishops ought to be filled with the sevenfold influences of the Holy Ghost: and SS. James and John, as the Apostle testifieth, "seemed to be pillars." The bases of the columns are the apostolic bishops, who support the frame of the whole church. The Capitals of the piers are the opinions of the bishops and doctors. For as the members are directed and moved by the head, so are our words and works governed by their mind. The ornaments of the capitals are the words of Sacred Scripture, to the meditation and observance of which we are bound.

William Durandus (c. 1237–96), from *Rationale divinorum officiorum* (1286), translated in 1843 as *The Symbolism of Churches and Church Ornaments*. The passage used here is from the third edition (London: Gibbings & Co., 1906), pp. 20–2.

28. The pavement of the church is the foundation of our faith. But in the spiritual Church, the pavement is the poor of Christ: the poor in spirit, who humble themselves in all things: wherefore on account of their humility they are likened to the pavement. Again, the pavement, which is trodden under foot, representeth the multitude, by whose labors the Church is sustained.

29. The beams which join together the church are the princes of this world or the preachers who defend the unity of the Church, the one by deed, the other by argument.

B. RENAISSANCE AND BAROQUE IDEALS

Introduction

Although the Renaissance was a much broader intellectual upheaval than can be defined by any one region or humanist perspective, there are ample reasons for giving precedent to the developments of central Italy. The very word "humanist" (*umanista*) first came to be applied there to someone teaching the classical languages and literature, and more specifically to those celebrating the classical authors with their emphasis on human abilities and intellectual accomplishments. Second, the first attempts to revive an architectural language from the imperial Roman past first took place there. Therefore the traditional account of the Italian Renaissance being born in the year 1416 — when the Italian Poggio Bracciolini came upon a Vitruvian manuscript in the Swiss monastery of St. Gall — has a certain symbolic necessity, notwithstanding its anecdotal flavor. The legend also underscores two vitally important points of the fifteenth-century Renaissance. First it was more than an Italic revival of a style on Italian soil; it was a startling revelation of a near-forgotten past. Second, it was a recapturing of ideas that was seen as having momentous consequence for the reformation and reconstitution of artistic principles.

The treatise of Vitruvius indeed became the cornerstone of this classical revival. If some fifteenth-century humanists, such as Leon Battista Alberti, were critical of the Roman's lack of philosophical rigor and eloquence — "his speech such that the Latins might think that he wanted to appear a Greek, while the Greeks would think that he babbled Latin" — this viewpoint altogether disappears by the second quarter of the sixteenth century, by which time a veritable cult of scholars had gathered around the words of this particular classical oracle. One interesting technological innovation furthered this process. Alberti had his manuscript of the mid-fifteenth century copied by hand with limited distribution, that is, precisely around the time that Johann Gutenberg in Strasbourg was perfecting the "tools" of his printing press. The proliferation of the printed word allowed the movement to take shape quickly and reverberate with intellectual developments taking place elsewhere in Europe. The treatises of Vitruvius and Alberti were first printed in 1486. The first illustrated Latin edition of Vitruvius was published by Fra Giocondo in 1511, and the first Italian translation of Cesare Cesariano appeared in 1521. A Vitruvian Academy was founded in Rome in 1542, and seven years later the Venetian Daniel Barbaro began a new, annotated translation of Vitruvius. The great architect Palladio joined with him in preparing the illustrations, and their beautifully crafted edition of 1556 really bespeaks the highpoint of Vitruvian adulation.

Meanwhile, the classical architectural tradition was greatly expanding, as it were, by an ever-widening circle of humanist architects and scholars. The treatises of Alberti, Antonio Filarete, Francesco di Giorgio, Sebastiano Serlio, Palladio, Giacomo Vignola, and Vincenzo Scamozzi were inspired if not modeled on the treatise of Vitruvius, and all attempted to interpret classical principles in a modern Italian way. From its base in Italy, Vitruvian classicism spread northward where it joined with parallel intellectual and cultural movements. Several books of Serlio's treatise first appeared in France, in fact, and the first major annotator of Vitruvius was the Frenchman Guillaume Philander, whose work was published in Rome in 1544, in Paris in the following year. The first French translation of Vitruvius by Jean Martin appeared in 1547, and within a few decades classicism had fully established itself in France through such architects as Philibert de L'Orme and Jacques Androuet du Cerceau. The same is true of the German-speaking states. Walther Hermann Ryff's German translation — *Vitruvius Teutsch* — appeared in 1548, one year after he published his own treatise on classical architecture. Antwerp, then part of the Netherlands, became another important center of Vitruvian publications and classical learning. By the middle of the seventeenth century classicism has more or less insinuated itself into every corner of the Continent and Great Britain. Laurids Lauridsen de Thurah's *Den Danske Vitruvius* (The Danish Vitruvius, 1749), recording a built array of classical buildings in Denmark, testifies to its acceptance in the Nordic countries as well.

The star of Vitruvius only began to dim first with the Mannerism of Michelangelo and then with the gathering currents of the Baroque. However one wishes to characterize this last period — as the late phase of the Renaissance or an era distinct — the fact remains that beyond such new concerns with geometry, movement, and plastic expressiveness lie still the vocabulary of classical motifs and many of its ideals. The spirit of antiquity, in fact, would form an important part of architectural thinking for several centuries to come.

10 ANTONIO DI TUCCIO MANETTI
from *The Life of Brunelleschi* (1480s)

The Italian Renaissance commenced in the first two decades of the fifteenth century, and the first and most illustrious architect of this century was Filippo Brunelleschi (1377–1446), the builder of the Florentine dome. A native of this city, Brunelleschi was originally trained as a goldsmith, although he quickly excelled in other arts. In 1402 he took part in a competition with Lorenzo Ghiberti and Donatello for the design of the new doors of the baptistery of S. Giovanni, a commission won by Ghiberti. In response to this defeat, Brunelleschi and Donatello traveled to Rome for a period, during which time Brunelleschi became the first artist to examine in a serious way the formal and constructional principles of classical Roman architecture — many of whose ruins still lay buried under centuries of debris. He advanced his knowledge of constructional techniques and over the next several years turned his efforts more and more to architecture. He built several classic works of the early Renaissance, including the Hospital of the Innocents (1419), the reconstruction of the church of San Lorenzo (1418–29), and the Pazzi chapel (1425–8). His fame, however, rests chiefly on the dome he constructed for the Florence Cathedral (1417–34), an engineering feat which he was perhaps the only man in fifteenth-century Italy capable of achieving.

Antonio Manetti's biography of Brunelleschi was probably written in the 1480s; Manetti informs us that he met the renowned artist sometime in the mid-1440s, shortly before the master's death, and he devotes nearly half of his biography to describing the controversy surrounding the dome. This selection concerns Brunelleschi's first trip to Rome in 1402 with Donatello, after the two men lost the competition in Florence to Ghiberti. Although Manetti could not have known the details of what he writes, this selection nevertheless provides a good indication of how and why Renaissance artists saw the rediscovery of antiquity as an event of great importance.

Thus left out, Filippo seemed to say: my knowledge was not sufficient for them to entrust me with the whole undertaking; it would be a good thing to go where there is fine sculpture to observe. So he went to Rome where at that time one could see beautiful works in public places. Some of those works are still there, although not many; some have been removed, carried off, and shipped out by various popes and cardinals from Rome and other nations. In studying the sculpture as one with a good eye, intelligent and alert in all things, would do, he observed the method and the symmetry of the ancients' way of building. He seemed to recognize very clearly a certain arrangement of members and structure just as if God had enlightened him about great matters. Since this appeared very different from the method in use at that time, it impressed him greatly. And he decided that while he looked at the sculpture of the ancients to give no less time to that order and method which is in the abutments and thrusts of buildings, [their] masses, lines, and *invenzioni* according to and in relation with their function, and to do the same for the decorations. Thereby he observed many marvels and beautiful things, since for the most part they were built in diverse epochs by very fine masters, who became so through practical experience and through the opportunity to study afforded by the large compensation of the princes and because they were not ordinary men. He decided to rediscover the fine and highly skilled method of

Antonio di Tuccio Manetti (1423–97), from *The Life of Brunelleschi* (1480s), in the *The Life of Brunelleschi by Antonio di Tuccio Manetti*, ed. Howard Saalman, trans. Catherine Enggass. University Park: Pennsylvania State University Press, 1971, pp. 50, 52, 54. © 1971 by Pennsylvania State University Press. Reprinted with permission of Pennsylvania State University Press.

building and the harmonious proportions of the ancients and how they might, without defects, be employed with convenience and economy. Noting the great and complex elements making up these matters – which had nevertheless been resolved – did not make him change his mind about understanding the methods and means they used. And by virtue of having in the past been interested and having made clocks and alarm bells with various and sundry types of springs geared by many diverse contrivances, he was familiar with all or a great number of those contrivances, which helped him a great deal in conceiving different machines for carrying, lifting, and pulling, according to what the exigencies were. He committed some of them to memory and some not, according to how important he judged them to be. He saw ruins – both standing or fallen down for some reason or other – which had been vaulted in various ways. He considered the methods of centering the vaults and other systems of support, how they could be dispensed with and what method had to be used, and when – because of the size of the vault or for other reasons – armatures could not be used. He saw and reflected on the many beautiful things, which as far as is known had not been present in other masters from antique times. By his genius, through tests and experiments, with time and with great effort and careful thought, he became a complete master of these matters in secret, while pretending to be doing something else. He demonstrated that mastery later in our city and elsewhere, as this account will in part make known.

The sculptor Donatello was with him almost all the time during this stay in Rome. They originally went there in agreement about strictly sculptural matters, and they applied themselves constantly to these. Donatello had no interest in architecture. Filippo told him nothing of his ideas, either because he did not find Donatello apt or because he was not confident of prevailing, seeing more every minute the difficulties confronting him. However, together they made rough drawings of almost all the buildings in Rome and in many places beyond the walls, with measurements of the widths and heights as far as they were able to ascertain [the latter] by estimation, and also the lengths, etc. In many places they had excavations made in order to see the junctures of the membering of the buildings and their type – whether square, polygonal, completely round, oval, or whatever. When possible they estimated the heights [by measuring] from base to base for the height and similarly [they estimated the heights of] the entablatures and roofs from the foundations. They drew the elevations on strips of parchment graphs with numbers and symbols which Filippo alone understood.

Since both were good masters of the goldsmith's art, they earned their living in that craft. They were given more work to do in the goldsmiths' shops every day than they could handle. And Filippo cut many precious stones given him to dress. Neither of them had family problems since they had neither wife nor children, there or elsewhere. Neither of them paid much attention to what they ate and drank or how they were dressed or where they lived, as long as they were able to satisfy themselves by seeing and measuring.

Since they undertook excavations to find the junctures of the membering and to uncover objects and buildings in many places where there was some indication, they had to hire porters and other laborers at no small expense. No one else attempted such work or understood why they did it. This lack of understanding was due to the fact that during that period, and for hundreds of years before, no one paid attention to the classical method of building: if certain writers in pagan times gave precepts about that method, such as

Battista degli Alberti has done in our period, they were not much more than generalities. However, the *invenzioni* – those things peculiar to the master – were in large part the product of empirical investigation or of his own [theoretical] efforts.

Returning to the excavations of Filippo and Donato: they were generally called "the treasure hunters" as it was believed that they spent and looked for treasure. They said: The treasure hunters search here today and there tomorrow. Actually they sometimes, although rarely, found some silver or gold medals, carved stones, chalcedony, carnelians, cameos, and like objects. From that in large measure arose the belief that they were searching for treasure.

Filippo spent many years at this work. He found a number of differences among the beautiful and rich elements of the buildings – in the masonry, as well as in the types of columns, bases, capitals, architraves, friezes, cornices, and pediments, and differences between the masses of the temples and the diameters of the columns; by means of close observation he clearly recognized the characteristics of each type: Ionic, Doric, Tuscan, Corinthian, and Attic. As may still be seen in his buildings today, he used most of them at the time and place he considered best.

11   LEON BATTISTA ALBERTI
from *On the Art of Building*, Prologue and Book 1 (1443–52)

Alberti was not only the first great theorist of the Renaissance but he, more than anyone else in this century, personified what came to be known as humanism. He was a man of great classical erudition. Born to a Florentine father-in-exile and to a Genoese mother, he studied Greek and Latin in Padua and earned a doctor of law at the University of Bologna. He seems to have dabbled in the arts in the 1420s, and even considered a literary career before becoming a cleric or secretary, first to Cardinal Carthusian Niccolo Albergati. In 1428 the Florentine ban against the Alberti family was lifted and Leon got to see firsthand early Renaissance works, especially those of Masaccio, Donatello, and Brunelleschi. He responded in 1435 with a treatise on painting, *De pictura*, dedicated to Brunelleschi. By this date Alberti had already traveled to Rome as a secretary to Pope Eugenius IV, where he became the first humanist to prepare a survey of the classical monuments of the city. These archaeological studies formed but a prelude to further classical studies in Rome after 1443, and it was around this time that he began his architectural treatise, in which he now sought to interpret the principles of classical Roman architecture. Around mid-century he also turned his attention to the practice of architecture with a number of important designs, among them the church of San Francesco in Rimini (1450–60), the facades of the Palazzo Rucellai (1450s) and Santa Maria Novella (1458–71) in Florence, and the church of Sant' Andrea in Mantua (begun 1470).

Alberti possessed literary skills in addition to classical learning, and he was rather critical of the talents of Vitruvius. He disliked in particular the architect's conceptual ambiguity and, moreover, he felt that classical theory

Leon Battista Alberti, from Prologue and Book 1 of *De re aedificatoria* [On the art of building] (1443–52) in *On the Art of Building in Ten Books*, trans. Joseph Rykwert, Neil Leach, and Robert Tavernor. Cambridge, MA: MIT Press, 1988, pp. 3, 5–6, 7. © 1988 by The MIT Press. Reprinted with permission of the MIT Press.

had achieved much greater heights of refinement in such writers as Cicero, whose rhetorical concepts he gladly redirected toward architectural theory. Nevertheless, he borrowed the 10-book structure of Vitruvius and even organized his study around the three Vitruvian concepts of durability, convenience, and beauty. As the first Renaissance treatise on architecture, Alberti's effort stands alongside that of Vitruvius as one of the twin pillars of classical theory. The first selection from the opening pages of Book 1 presents a few of the basic definitions of architecture and its general elements of practice. His definition of building as "a form of body" consisting of both matter and lineaments (lines, or more generally design) maps out a philosophical distinction on which his theory of beauty will reside. Matter relates to nature, but the power to wield lineaments (or make designs) resides in the architect's mind.

Before I go any farther, however, I should explain exactly whom I mean by an architect; for it is no carpenter that I would have you compare to the greatest exponents of other disciplines: the carpenter is but an instrument in the hands of the architect. Him I consider the architect, who by sure and wonderful reason and method, knows both how to devise through his own mind and energy, and to realize by construction, whatever can be most beautifully fitted out for the noble needs of man, by the movement of weights and the joining and massing of bodies. To do this he must have an understanding and knowledge of all the highest and most noble disciplines. This then is the architect. [...]

First we observed that the building is a form of body, which like any other consists of lineaments and matter, the one the product of thought, the other of Nature; the one requiring the mind and the power of reason, the other dependent on preparation and selection; but we realized that neither on its own would suffice without the hand of the skilled workman to fashion the material according to lineaments. Since buildings are set to different uses, it proved necessary to inquire whether the same type of lineaments could be used for several; we therefore distinguished the various types of buildings and noted the importance of the connection of their lines and their relationship to each other, as the principal sources of beauty; we began therefore to inquire further into the nature of beauty – of what kind it should be, and what is appropriate in each case. As in all these matters faults are occasionally found, we investigated how to amend and correct them. [...]

Let us therefore begin thus: the whole matter of building is composed of lineaments and structure. All the intent and purpose of lineaments lies in finding the correct, infallible way of joining and fitting together those lines and angles which define and enclose the surfaces of the building. It is the function and duty of lineaments, then, to prescribe an appropriate place, exact numbers, a proper scale, and a graceful order for whole buildings and for each of their constituent parts, so that the whole form and appearance of the building may depend on the lineaments alone. Nor do lineaments have anything to do with material, but they are of such a nature that we may recognize the same lineaments in several different buildings that share one and the same form, that is, when the parts, as well as the siting and order, correspond with one another in their every line and angle. It is quite possible to project whole forms in the mind without any recourse to the material, by designating and determining a fixed orientation and conjunction for the various lines and angles. Since that is the case, let lineaments be the precise and correct outline, conceived in the mind, made up of lines and angles, and perfected in the learned intellect and imagination.

12 LEON BATTISTA ALBERTI
from *On the Art of Building*, Book 6

Alberti's theory of absolute beauty is of paramount importance to Renaissance theory in that it lays an intellectual foundation that will remain largely intact for almost three centuries. The issue of beauty had been problematic for Vitruvius. On the one hand he made allusions to the harmonic ratios of Pythagorean musical theory, suggesting there was a higher cosmic order underlying the judgment of beauty. On the other hand he gave architects the right to vary proportions if the "eye" calls for corrections, or as the arts make progress. Such freedom assumes that judgments of beauty are relative and even subjective – a logical inconsistency unacceptable to Alberti and Renaissance aesthetics. From his classical perspective, Alberti prefers the Platonic belief that there is a higher reality to the physical or phenomenal world, namely Ideas; he accepts as well the Neoplatonic argument that art and architecture can symbolize these higher Ideas through their adherence to universal mathematical laws or harmonic proportions. Beauty is thus the correct mirroring of transcendent Ideas, and – as his reference to a passage of Cicero shows – it is rarely found, even in nature. The mediating element between raw nature (materials) and the ordering lines of the architect is *ornament*. This term possesses a meaning for Alberti quite different than its general meaning today. It is indeed something "attached or additional," but it is not inessential or something that can be dispensed with. Ornament is the correct orchestration of the lineaments of design, the judicious choice of the material, and the polishing and refinement of appearance – in short, the corporal manifestation of those higher Ideas.

Of the three conditions that apply to every form of construction – that what we construct should be appropriate to its use, lasting in structure, and graceful and pleasing in appearance – the first two have been dealt with, and there remains the third, the noblest and most necessary of all.

Now graceful and pleasant appearance, so it is thought, derives from beauty and ornament alone, since there can be no one, however surly or slow, rough or boorish, who would not be attracted to what is most beautiful, seek the finest ornament at the expense of all else, be offended by what is unsightly, shun all that is inelegant or shabby, and feel that any short-comings an object may have in its ornament will detract equally from its grace and from its dignity.

Most noble is beauty, therefore, and it must be sought most eagerly by anyone who does not wish what he owns to seem distasteful. What remarkable importance our ancestors, men of great prudence, attached to it is shown by the care they took that their legal, military, and religious institutions – indeed, the whole commonwealth – should be much embel-lished; and by their letting it be known that if all these institutions, without which man could scarce exist, were to be stripped of their pomp and finery, their business would appear insipid and shabby. When we gaze at the wondrous works of the heavenly gods, we admire the beauty we see, rather than the utility that we recognize. Need I go further? Nature herself,

Leon Battista Alberti, from Book 6 of *De re aedificatoria* [On the art of building] (1443–52) in *On the Art of Building in Ten Books*, trans. Joseph Rykwert, Neil Leach, and Robert Tavernor. Cambridge, MA: MIT Press, 1988, pp. 155–7. © 1988 by The MIT Press. Reprinted with permission of the MIT Press.

as is everywhere plain to see, does not desist from basking in a daily orgy of beauty – let the hues of her flowers serve as my one example.

But if this quality is desirable anywhere, surely it cannot be absent from buildings, without offending experienced and inexperienced alike. What would be our reaction to a deformed and ill-considered pile of stones, other than the more to criticize it the greater the expense, and to condemn the wanton greed for piling up stones? To have satisfied necessity is trite and insignificant, to have catered to convenience unrewarding when the inelegance in a work causes offense.

In addition, there is one particular quality that may greatly increase the convenience and even the life of a building. Who would not claim to dwell more comfortably between walls that are ornate, rather than neglected? What other human art might sufficiently protect a building to save it from human attack? Beauty may even influence an enemy, by restraining his anger and so preventing the work from being violated. Thus I might be so bold as to state: No other means is as effective in protecting a work from damage and human injury as is dignity and grace of form. All care, all diligence, all financial consideration must be directed to ensuring that what is built is useful, commodious, yes – but also embellished and wholly graceful, so that anyone seeing it would not feel that the expense might have been invested better elsewhere.

The precise nature of beauty and ornament, and the difference between them, the mind could perhaps visualize more clearly than my words could explain. For the sake of brevity, however, let us define them as follows: Beauty is that reasoned harmony of all the parts within a body, so that nothing may be added, taken away, or altered, but for the worse. It is a great and holy matter; all our resources of skill and ingenuity will be taxed in achieving it; and rarely is it granted, even to Nature herself, to produce anything that is entirely complete and perfect in every respect. "How rare," remarks a character in Cicero, "is a beautiful youth in Athens!" That connoisseur found their forms wanting because they either had too much or too little of something by which they failed to conform to the laws of beauty. In this case, unless I am mistaken, had ornament been applied by painting and masking anything ugly, or by grooming and polishing the attractive, it would have had the effect of making the displeasing less offensive and the pleasing more delightful. If this is conceded, ornament may be defined as a form of auxiliary light and complement to beauty. From this it follows, I believe, that beauty is some inherent property, to be found suffused all through the body of that which may be called beautiful; whereas ornament, rather than being inherent, has the character of something attached or additional.

This granted, I continue: Anyone who builds so as to be praised for it – as anyone with good sense would – must adhere to a consistent theory; for to follow a consistent theory is the mark of true art. Who would deny that only through art can correct and worthy building be achieved? And after all this particular part concerning beauty and ornament, being the most important of all, must depend on some sure and consistent method and art, which it would be most foolish to ignore. Yet some would disagree who maintain that beauty, and indeed every aspect of building, is judged by relative and variable criteria, and that the forms of buildings should vary according to individual taste and must not be bound by any rules of art. A common fault, this, among the ignorant – to deny the existence of anything they do not understand. I have decided to correct this error; not that I shall attempt (since I would need detailed and extended argument for it) to explain the arts from their origins, by what reasoning they developed, and by what experience they were nourished; let me simply repeat what has been said, that the arts were born of Chance and Observation, fostered by Use and Experiment, and matured by Knowledge and Reason.

13   LEON BATTISTA ALBERTI
from *On the Art of Building*, Book 9

The fullest elaboration of Alberti's theory of beauty, and indeed of his whole architectural conception, comes in Book 9, when he introduces the Ciceronian notion of *concinnitas* or concinnity. In his *Orator* (xxiii), Cicero notes that "words when connected together embellish a style if they produce a certain symmetry (*concinnitas*) which disappears when the words are changed, though the thought remains the same" (Loeb trans.). Concinnity is that perfect harmony or grace that appears when the architect has perfectly composed his design, in such a way that it demonstrates the three qualities of correct number, outline, and position. Number relates to the addition or taking away of parts; outline controls their size and configuration; position adds the criteria of correct placement. Alberti was convinced that in concinnity he had found the "absolute and fundamental rule of Nature" as well as the design secret known to classical antiquity. And like a good Platonist, Alberti next draws upon the numerical ratios of Plato's *Timaeus* to gather the harmonic ratios that should also underlay architecture. Alberti's belief in an absolute numerical scheme for beauty and proportion was his most important contribution to Renaissance theory. Through these passages, architectural beauty now comes to reside principally in proportions.

Now I come to a matter with which we have promised to deal all along: every kind of beauty and ornament consists of it; or, to put it more clearly, it springs from every rule of beauty. This is an extremely difficult inquiry; for whatever that one entity is, which is either extracted or drawn from the number and nature of all the parts, or imparted to each by sure and constant method, or handled in such a manner as to tie and bond several elements into a single bundle or body, according to a true and consistent agreement and sympathy – and something of this kind is exactly what we seek – then surely that entity must share some part of the force and juice, as it were, of all the elements of which it is composed or blended; for otherwise their discord and differences would cause conflict and disunity. This work of research and selection is neither obvious nor straightforward in any other matter, but it is at its most ambiguous and involved in the subject about to be discussed; for the art of building is composed of very many parts, each one, as you have seen, demanding to be ennobled by much varied ornament. Yet we shall tackle the problem to the best of our ability, as we have undertaken. We shall not inquire as to how a sound understanding of the whole might be gained from the numerous parts, but, restricting ourselves to what is relevant, we shall begin by observing what produces beauty by its very nature.

The great experts of antiquity, as we mentioned earlier, have instructed us that a building is very like an animal, and that Nature must be imitated when we delineate it. Let us

Leon Battista Alberti, from Book 9 of *De re aedificatoria* [On the art of building] (1443–52) in *On the Art of Building in Ten Books*, trans. Joseph Rykwert, Neil Leach, and Robert Tavernor. Cambridge, MA: MIT Press, 1988, pp. 301–3. © 1988 by The MIT Press. Reprinted with permission of the MIT Press.

investigate, then, why some bodies that Nature produces may be called beautiful, others less beautiful, and even ugly. Obviously, among those which we count as beautiful all are not such that there is no difference between them; in fact it is precisely where they most differ that we observe them to be infused or imprinted with a quality through which, however dissimilar they are, we consider them equally graceful. Let me give you an example: one man might prefer the tenderness of a slender girl; yet a character in a comedy preferred one girl over all others because she was plumper and more buxom; you, perhaps, might prefer a wife neither so slender of figure as to appear sickly nor so stout of limb as to resemble a village bully, but such that you might add as much to the one as you could take away from the other without impairing dignity. Yet, whichever of the two you prefer, you will not then consider the rest unattractive and worthless. But what it is that causes us to prefer one above all the others, I shall not inquire.

When you make judgments on beauty, you do not follow mere fancy, but the workings of a reasoning faculty that is inborn in the mind. It is clearly so, since no one can look at anything shameful, deformed, or disgusting without immediate displeasure and aversion. What arouses and provokes such a sensation in the mind we shall not inquire in detail, but shall limit our consideration to whatever evidence presents itself that is relevant to our argument. For within the form and figure of a building there resides some natural excellence and perfection that excites the mind and is immediately recognized by it. I myself believe that form, dignity, grace, and other such qualities depend on it, and as soon as anything is removed or altered, these qualities are themselves weakened and perish. Once we are convinced of this, it will not take long to discuss what may be removed, enlarged, or altered, in the form and figure. For every body consists entirely of parts that are fixed and individual; if these are removed, enlarged, reduced, or transferred somewhere inappropriate, the very composition will be spoiled that gives the body its seemly appearance.

From this we may conclude, without my pursuing such questions any longer, that the three principal components of that whole theory into which we inquire are number, what we might call outline, and position. But arising from the composition and connection of these three is a further quality in which beauty shines full face: our term for this is *concinnitas*; which we say is nourished with every grace and splendor. It is the task and aim of *concinnitas* to compose parts that are quite separate from each other by their nature, according to some precise rule, so that they correspond to one another in appearance.

That is why when the mind is reached by way of sight or sound, or any other means, *concinnitas* is instantly recognized. It is our nature to desire the best, and to cling to it with pleasure. Neither in the whole body nor in its parts does *concinnitas* flourish as much as it does in Nature herself; thus I might call it the spouse of the soul and of reason. It has a vast range in which to exercise itself and bloom – it runs through man's entire life and government, it molds the whole of Nature. Everything that Nature produces is regulated by the law of *concinnitas*, and her chief concern is that whatever she produces should be absolutely perfect. Without *concinnitas* this could hardly be achieved, for the critical sympathy of the parts would be lost. So much for this.

If this is accepted, let us conclude as follows. Beauty is a form of sympathy and consonance of the parts within a body, according to definite number, outline, and position, as dictated by *concinnitas*, the absolute and fundamental rule in Nature. This is the main object of the art of building, and the source of her dignity, charm, authority, and worth.

14 IL FILARETE

from Book 1 of his untitled treatise on architecture (1461–3)

The second Renaissance treatise was composed less than a decade after Alberti completed his 10 books and it discloses just how new and foreign classical ideas were to the well-established Gothic building traditions of northern Italy. Averlino's assumed name of Il Filarete means "lover of virtue." He was born in Florence, trained as a bronzesmith, and around 1450 he became involved with architecture. In the first capacity he gained fame for executing a pair of bronze doors for the old church of St. Peter's in Rome (1433–45), which were later reworked into the larger central doors of the new cathedral in 1620. He was also the first architect of the Ospedale Maggiore (great hospital) in Milan (1460–5), now part of the university, which he designed while writing this treatise. The building of brick and richly colored stone brings the Tuscan forms of the Renaissance to Lombardy, but it also retains many of the structural and decorative aspects of the Gothic tradition still very strong in northern Italy.

His treatise makes very much the same point, and it differs from that of Alberti (whom Filarete probably knew personally) in several respects. For one thing, Filarete was not a humanist and did not have the intellectual command of classical sources so evident in Alberti's writings. Second, Filarete did not try to emulate the 10-book structure of Vitruvius. He knew of the latter's treatise, but Filarete was smitten in particular with the work of Brunelleschi. His treatise rather takes the form of a dialogue, essentially a polemic, in which Filarete tries to convince the members of the Sforza family (the rulers of Milan between 1450 and 1535) of the superiority of "ancient art" (classicism) over and above "modern art" (the prevailing Gothic style). Filarete manages to sway Francesco Sforza, in particular, by designing an ideal city called Sforzinda, with its major monuments in the *arte antica*. The first two selections are from Book 1, in which Filarete introduces himself and establishes what he deems to be the proportional basis of the classical style. Taking the proportions of the Doric order back to Adam also underscores the Christian side of this style.

Once I was in a place where a noble and many others were eating. In the course of a conversation about many different things they entered on architecture. One of them said, "It certainly seems to me that you have a high opinion of architecture, yet it doesn't seem as great a thing as many make it out to be. They say you have to know so many kinds of geometry, drawing, and many other things. It seems to me I heard someone speak the other day of a certain Vitruvius and of another who seems to have been named Archimedes. [He said,] "They have written about building, measure, and many other bits of information that one ought to know. I don't search out all these measurements and other things when I have something built. I don't go looking for as many principles of geometry as they advise, and still it comes out all right."

Then one of the others who seemed to speak more seriously said, "Don't talk that way. I think that anyone who wants to construct a building needs to know measure very well and also drawing in order to lay out a large house, a church, or any other sort of building. I do

Il Filarete (Antonio di Piero Averlino) (c.1400–70), from his untitled treatise on architecture (1461–3) in *Filarete's Treatise on Architecture*, 2 vols, ed. and trans. John R. Spencer. New Haven: Yale University Press, 1965, pp. 4–8 (Book I, 1v–2r; 2v–3v). © 1965 by Yale University Press. Reprinted with permission of Yale University Press.

not believe he could do it at all correctly if he does not have drawing, measuring, and the other things. I also believe that anyone who commissions a building should know these things. Nevertheless, do not say that, since it is not my craft, I only know enough to argue about it. I would pay a great deal to find someone who would teach me what it takes and what measure should be used to make a building [well] proportioned, the source of these measurements, and why one reasons and builds in this manner. I would also like to know what their origins are."

On hearing this conversation I stepped forward, because it pertained to my profession and because there was no one else there who practiced it. I said, "Perhaps you will think me presumptuous for attempting to tell you these modes and measures, since other capable men both ancient and modern have written very elegant works about this discipline. For instance, Vitruvius, among others, wrote a worthy treatise on this subject, [as did] Batista Alberti. The latter is one of the most learned men of our times in many disciplines, very skilled in architecture and especially in design which is the basis and means of every art done by the hand. He understands drawing perfectly and he is very learned in geometry and other sciences. He has also written a most elegant work in Latin. For this reason and also because I am not too experienced in letters or in speaking, but rather in other things, I have applied myself. Perhaps I shall seem [to have been] too rash and presumptuous in attempting to describe the modes and measure of building. I do this in Italian and [only] because I am pleased by and experienced in these skills – drawing, sculpture, and architecture – in several other things, and in investigations. At the proper place I shall make mention [of them]. For this reason I am bold enough to think that those who are not so learned will be pleased by it, and that those who are more skilled and learned in letters will read the above-named authors.

Because these matters are a little arduous and difficult to understand, I beg your excellency to be attentive while he listens to my arguments to the same extent that he would if he had ordered his troops to reconquer or defend one of his dearest possessions, and as if letters had been sent from them to him telling that they had reconquered or, better, defended that thing and with no small difficulty had enjoyed a victory over the enemy. To this degree, turn your ears to this. If you do so, I think that it will please you and it will not be at all tedious for me to talk. While enjoying it, you will derive some utility from it.

In order that you can better understand it, I will divide my talk into three parts. The first will recount the origin of measure; the building, its sources, how it ought to be maintained, and the things necessary to construct the building; what one should know about building to be a good architect; and what should be noted about him. The second will narrate the means and the construction for anyone who wants to build a city, its site, and how the buildings, squares, and streets ought to be located so that it will be fine, beautiful, and perpetual according to the laws of nature. The third and last part will tell how to make various forms of buildings according to antique practice, together with things I have discovered or learned from the ancients that are almost lost and forgotten today. From this it will be understood that the ancients built more nobly than we do today." [. . .]

As everyone knows, man was created by God; the body, the soul, the intellect, the mind, and everything was produced in perfection by Him. The body [was] organized and measured and all its members proportioned according to their qualities and measure. He allowed them to produce each other, as is seen in nature. He granted the mind of man [the power] to do various things for his existence and pleasure. As is seen, [some] have more intellect than others, some in one discipline and some in another, some more, some less, according to the way it occurs among men. This is due, many times, to the celestial constellations and to the planets, so that nature produces one who is more industrious than another, as it pleases her. Many times it happens according to the needs of man that through necessity his intellect becomes much more acute in many things and especially in that which he needs most. *As they say, necessity makes man clever.* The first need and necessity of man, after food, was habitation; thus he endeavored to construct a place where he could dwell. From this, then, public and private buildings were derived, as will be seen below.

Since man is made with the measure stated above, he decided to take the measures, members, proportions, and qualities from himself and to adapt them to this method of building. In order that you can understand every part and its source, I will relate to you first of all the measures, members, and proportions of man. When a man is well formed and every member is in harmony with every other, then we say he is well proportioned. You well know that when one has a twisted shoulder and misformed members he is badly proportioned. Of this I will treat more fully in its place. It is true, as Vitruvius says, that in order to understand well this art of building one has to know the seven sciences, or at least participate in them as much as possible.

Let us look briefly at quality and measure and their parts. So far as I understand from the measure of man, there are five qualities. Let us leave aside two of them, because one cannot take true or perfect measure from them. These are dwarfs and overly large men who depart from the normal like the species of giants. Perhaps I should say something about the origin of these giants, according to what I have read. I will not enlarge on it, because I do not believe it; it seems fictional and poetic rather than true history. They say that long ago there were some [women] who gave birth to giants in this manner. There were handsome young men of great stature and whose seed [was brought together] in an indirect manner. There were some large women with whom one of these young men lay. It happened that his seed was received together with that of others who lay with this girl. As a result of this libidinousness she conceived, became pregnant with much seed, and gave birth to many large men. In this way they say giants were born. For this reason they are rarely found and are also a travesty of nature. Even if you should find some, do not take your measure from them. Let us leave them and lay down the three principal ones. They are the following: small, medium, and large men, and from them we will take our measures, proportions, and members. You can say that I too have seen some large men, like Niccolò of Parma, who was with the Emperor Sigismund when he came to Rome to be crowned in the time of Eugene IV. I also saw another in Rome who came from Ascoli in the Marches. He was a man of great size and quite malformed. You speak the truth, because I also saw both of them. Because of their size they were malformed, so let us leave them aside.

Since the large, small, and medium are universal in their proportions, from them we shall take the measure. I believe the ancients took it from them. We shall also take this rule as the best way and explain it part by part in such a way that I believe everyone will be able to understand it. Because we first have this measure from the Greeks – as they had it from Egypt and from others – we shall use their terms. Vitruvius also named them thus, so we shall follow their order, naming these measures, proportions, and qualities Doric, Ionic, and Corinthian, and explaining them as much as we can. Therefore, our first measures will be these – proportion and quality. For the present, we will leave the principal measures of man for another place.

I [will] speak of the three qualities. Their measures are these. The first, which we call Doric, that is, large, they measure with the head. It is nine heads. This quality is called Doric, that is, large. The small one is called Ionic and it is seven heads. The third is called common, or medium, that is, Corinthian, and is eight heads. The two other qualities we will let stand for the reason mentioned above. The origins of these measures [which explain] why the Greeks called them Doric, Ionic, and Corinthian, will be treated in another place. We have begun with the largest as is fitting. First of all, we will begin with the largest. Because it seems fitting that the large things should precede the smaller, we will begin with these. It is to be believed that the inventors of these things must have taken these measures, that is, quality, from the best-formed large men. It is probable that this quality was taken from the body of Adam, because it cannot be doubted that he was handsome and better proportioned than any other [man] who has ever lived, since God formed him. Nature has since transformed [man] into large, small, medium, and other sorts. You can say that the discoverers of these measures did not see Adam. Perhaps they did see him. Perhaps he was even the inventor. This is not known with certainty. We believe that the first inventors, whoever they were, looked at the most worthy and beautiful form, whatever it was. Since Adam's was the most beautiful, as has been stated [above] with various reasons, it is credible that it was taken from him, and [with] his head the first measure was made. They began with the head, which was a worthy thing to do, for the head is the most noble and most beautiful member. They did well, therefore, to begin with it, since it is moreover the most outstanding and most commensurate member and divisible into many various parts. The reason I believe it should be called the first measure and why they divided it into many parts and what its division[s] are will be seen below. They measured the whole man and then composed and divided and increased the measure, and from it all are derived. It seems to me we should treat of these measures as they are found in and derived from their origins.

15   IL FILARETE
from Book 8 of his untitled treatise on architecture

These selections indicate the resistance with which early Florentine artists met as they were attempting to introduce the elements of the classical style to other regions of Italy. Rome, with its antique ruins and the great papal wealth, more quickly embraced the new classicism, and Alberti stands at the beginning of a line of Tuscan classicists (culminating with Michelangelo) who spent much of their time in Rome. Northern Italy, however, was a very different story, as cities such as Milan were only marginally "Italian." Originally a Celtic city, it was

Il Filarete (Antonio di Piero Averlino), from his untitled treatise on architecture (1461–3) in *Filarete's Treatise on Architecture*, 2 vols., ed. and trans. John R. Spencer. New Haven: Yale University Press, 1965, pp. 101–3 (Book VIII, 59r–60r). © 1965 by Yale University Press. Reprinted with permission of Yale University Press.

conquered after much resistance by the ancient Romans, but was one of the first cities overtaken by the so-called barbarian invasions from the north. For much of medieval and early Renaissance times the city was a pawn of the power centers of the north (France and the Habsburg Empire) and the papacy in the south. Architecturally, and as its great cathedral demonstrates, the city was Gothic in its building traditions. Filarete thus had a delicate task before him. As a Tuscan he had to convince this enlightened ruler of Milan how and why the classical style was superior to the Gothic architecture with which he was more familiar. This entailed many arguments, but perhaps the most ingenious is this physiological argument of why the rounded arch is superior to the pointed one.

"My lord, your lordship does not ask a little. I will tell you what I have heard. The arch was discovered when the person who built the first dwelling, either of straw or something else, came to making the door. I think he took a piece of pliable wood, bent it, and thus made a half circle. [Either that] or he tied it to two other perpendicular pieces of wood that he had planted in the place where he had decided the door should be. I think the arch was discovered in the first way. Then someone else made one a little better. He made a circle and cut it in half and then perhaps put it atop two pieces of wood and made a door with a half circle above. The rectangular door was discovered in almost the same way. Someone stuck two pieces of wood in the ground to make an entrance perpendicular to the ground. Then he tied another across them. Perhaps he nailed them or tied them; however he did it, it seems reasonable that this is its origin. It makes no difference whether it was done in one way or another.

"We will now examine their rules and see in what way they are best. [We will also see] how the ancients used them, how they refined them and reduced to rules all these things pertaining to building. Thus, by following their practice, I will [be able to] help anyone who has to build, or to have built, a building and who wishes to follow the ancients and to avoid the notions that are practiced almost everywhere today.

"I freely praise anyone who follows the antique practice and style. I bless the soul of Filippo di ser Brunellesco, a Florentine citizen, a famous and most worthy architect, a most subtle follower of Dedalus, who revived in our city of Florence the antique way of building. As a result no other manner but the antique is used today for churches and for public and private buildings. To prove that this is true, it can be seen that private citizens who have either a church or a house built all turn to this usage, as for example the remodeled house in the Via Contrada that is called Via della Vigna. The entire facade [is] composed of dressed stone and all built in the antique style. This is encouraging to anyone who investigates and searches out antique customs and modes of construction in architecture. If it were not the most beautiful and useful [fashion], it would not be used in Florence, as I said above. Moreover, the lord of Mantua, who is most learned, would not use it if it were not as I have said. The proof of this [is in] a house that he had built at one of his castles on the Po.

"I beg everyone to abandon modern usage. Do not let yourself be advised by masters who hold to such bad practice. Cursed be he who discovered it! I think that only barbaric people could have brought it into Italy. I will give you an example. [There is the same comparison] between ancient and modern architecture [as there is] in literature. That is [there is the same difference] between the speech of Cicero or Virgil and that used thirty or forty years ago. Today it has been brought back to better usage than had prevailed in past times – during at least several hundred years – for today one speaks in prose with ornate language. This has happened solely because they followed the antique manner of Virgil and other worthy men. I give you architecture in the same comparison, for whoever follows antique practice participates precisely in the above comparison, that is, the one on Ciceronian and Virgilian letters. I do not wish to say more, but I beg of your lordship that he at least not use [modern forms] in what he has built. I am quite certain that when you understand drawing a little better you will see that what I say is true."

"It is true that I do not fully understand these differences, but I have seen some things that I like more than others, as for example certain columns, arches, doors, and vaults."

"Which columns do you like most?"

"Some I have seen that appear to be very old. [Some] arches are pointed and some are round; I liked the round ones more than the pointed. I do not know, however, which are better. I have seen some doors that are perfectly square. Others have these small arches and other things that break the square. I preferred the perfectly square. Tell me, which are the ancient and which are better?"

"My lord, your lordship begins to have taste and understanding. The pointed [arches] and the doors, with some impediment in the square that you describe, are these poor modern [examples].

"You have understood the derivation of the arch and the rectangular door. You have heard about their origins. Now understand the [reason] why the round ones are most beautiful, how they should be used, and how they should be constructed according to antique usage.

"The reason round [arches] are more beautiful than pointed. It cannot be doubted that anything which impedes the sight in any way is not so beautiful as that which leads the eye and does not restrain it. Such is the round arch. As you have noticed, your eye is not arrested in the least when you look at a half-circle arch. It is the same when you look at a circle. As you look at it, the eye or, better, the sight, quickly encompasses the circumference at the first glance. The sight moves along, for it has no restraint or obstacle whatsoever. It is the same with the half circle, for as you look at it, the eye, or the sight, quickly runs to the other side without any obstacle, impediment, or other restraint. It runs from one end to the other of the half circle. The pointed is not so, for the eye, or sight, pauses a little at the pointed part and does not run along as it does on the half circle. This is because it departs from its perfection. The pointed is, so to speak, as if you had cut a circle into six parts and then continued one of the pieces in such a way that you would make two circles touching each other. The internal sixth cuts the center of the circle it touches. This, joined to the first circle, will make you two pointed arches by the swinging of the compasses. You can make as many of them [as you want by] draw[ing] circles in this manner. Even though I am teaching this to you, I do not advise you to use it. [I only do it] so you can see that they are neither good nor beautiful. You could perhaps say that pointed [arches] are strong and satisfactory. This is true, but if you make a round arch, that is, a half circle, with a good haunch, it too will be strong. To prove that this is true: I have seen large round arches in Rome that remained strong, especially in the baths, in the Antoniana, and many other buildings. If the Romans had doubted [their strength] at all, they would have made two arches one above the other, but they would never have used any of these pointed [arches]. Since they did not use them, we should not use them.

16 SEBASTIANO SERLIO
from Book 3, *The Complete Works on Architecture and Perspective* (1540)

As the Renaissance movement entered into the sixteenth century, the stylistic battle that had been waged by Alberti, Filarete, and others had largely been won and its theory was now ready to be codified for practicing architects. Fra Giocondo's annotated and illustrated Latin edition of Vitruvius came out in 1511, and Cesare Cesariano's Italian translation of Vitruvius appeared in 1521. The last book proved to be an enormous boon to the Roman's popularity and it led eventually – in 1542 – to the founding of the Vitruvian Academy in Rome. One of the leaders of this Vitruvian revival, the architect who would attempt to translate Vitruvian theory into practical terms, was the Bolognan Sebastiano Serlio.

This architect was originally trained as a painter, but by 1514 he was working in Rome in the Vatican workshop of Bramante. There his principal teacher was the Siennese architect and painter Baldassare Peruzzi (1481–1536), who from 1520 onward was at least partly in charge of the construction of the new church of St. Peter's. It was Peruzzi who conveyed to Serlio a love for classical antiquity, but this period ended in 1527, when the armies of Charles V sacked Rome. Serlio retreated to the north, to the area around Venice, and there he began what amounted to a modest architectural career. He may have designed the villa in Cricoli for Giangiorgio Trissino, the first patron of Palladio. In 1539 he also prepared a design for rebuilding the basilica at Vicenza; the competition was won by Palladio. Serlio by this date had already committed himself to composing an architectural treatise of seven books, the first of which (Book 4) actually appeared in Venice in 1537. Three years later Book 3 was published, and in 1541 Serlio – unable to find a patron in Italy – left for France at the invitation of François I, where he published Books 1, 2, and 5. Book 6 appeared in Lyons in 1551, and the final volume of his literary enterprise, Book 7, appeared posthumously in 1575 in Frankfurt.

Serlio's treatise differs from its predecessors in several important ways. First it was written in Italian for the architect rather than for the educated nobility. It is not especially scholarly or theoretical but is rather heavily illustrated and is intended to be a practical guide in the codification of classical architectural principles. There are books on the principles of geometry and perspective, the orders, churches, and domestic design, all of which make it far-reaching in scope. The selection below is from his third book on Roman antiquities, and it underscores the central dilemma facing Renaissance architects. On the one hand, the text – which refers to the unearthing of the foundations for the Theater of Marcellus in Rome – underscores the fact that Renaissance architects were now aware that the proportional rules given by Vitruvius were not reflected in existing Roman ruins. On the other hand, there was a need to have such a classical authority, and thus the treatise of Vitruvius must be accepted as the "infallible guide and rule." Such allegiance, however, should not be absolute. Like Peruzzi himself in his later years, Serlio was much affected by the Mannerist tendencies of his time, and thus he allowed the architect a certain freedom in interpreting the Roman architect.

...Augustus had this theatre built in the name of his nephew, Marcellus, and hence it is called the Theatre of Marcellus. It is in Rome. Part of it, that is, the external part of the

Sebastiano Serlio (1475–1554), from Book 3 (69v) of *Tutte l'opere d'architettura et prospettiva* [The complete works on architecture and perspective] (1540) in *Sebastiano Serlio on Architecture*, Vol. 1., ed. and trans. Vaughan Hart and Peter Hicks. New Haven: Yale University Press, 1996, p. 136. © 1996 by Yale University Press. Reprinted with permission of Yale University Press.

portico, is to be seen still standing. It is of two Orders only, that is, Doric and Ionic, highly praised work even though the Doric columns do not have their bases or even their collar below, but simply rest upon the pavement of the portico, without anything beneath. Not much was known about the plan of this theatre. However, just recently the noble Roman family, the Massimi, wanted to build a house, the site for which turned out to be above part of this theatre – the said house was designed by that outstanding architect, Baldassare from Siena. While they were excavating the foundations they found the remains of many different parts of the ornamentation of this theatre and clear traces of the ground plan were unearthed. As a result Baldassare deduced the whole from the part uncovered, and thus measured it very carefully and set it in the form which is shown on the following page. Since I happened to be in Rome at the same time, I saw many of those parts of the ornamentation and had an opportunity to measure them, and truly there I found forms as beautiful as any I have ever seen in ancient ruins, especially in the Doric capitals and the imposts of the arches which I thought conformed very closely to the writings of Vitruvius. In, the same way the frieze, the triglyphs and the metopes all corresponded very well. However, even though the Doric cornice was extremely rich in members and highly carved, nonetheless I found it very far from Vitruvian doctrine, very licentious in its members and of such a height that, in proportion to the architrave and frieze, two-thirds of that height would have been enough. Nevertheless I think that modern architects should not err (by err I mean go against Vitruvian precepts) by adducing the licence of this or other ancient things, or be so presumptuous as to carve a cornice or other element in exactly the same proportion that they have seen and measured and then to build it into a work. The fact is that it is not enough to say 'I can do it because the ancients did it' without considering whether the element is otherwise in proportion to the rest of the building. Furthermore, even if the ancient architect was licentious, we must not be so. We should uphold the doctrines of Vitruvius as an infallible guide and rule, provided that reason does not persuade us otherwise, because from the worthy ancients up to our times there has been no one who has written better or more learnedly on architecture than he. If in every other noble art we can see that there is a founder to whom is ascribed so much authority that his pronouncements are given full and perfect trust, who would deny – unless he were very foolhardy and ignorant – that in architecture Vitruvius was at the highest level? Or that his writings (where reason does not dictate otherwise) ought to be sacrosanct and inviolable? Or that we should trust him more than any works by the Romans: although they learned the true order in building from the Greeks, nevertheless later, as conquerors of the Greeks, perhaps some of them became licentious? Certainly, anyone who had seen the wonderful works built by the Greeks – nearly all of which have disappeared, demolished by time and wars – would judge that the Greek works were better by far than those of the Romans. And so all those architects who might condemn the writings of Vitruvius, especially in those parts which can be clearly understood – like the Doric Order which I am discussing – would be architectural heretics, refuting that author who for so many years has been, and still is, approved of by men of discernment.

17 GIACOMO BAROZZI DA VIGNOLA
from Preface to *Rules of the Five Orders of Architecture* (1562)

Building upon the efforts of Serlio was the compendium of Giacomo Barozzi da Vignola. Initially trained as a painter, this artist likely turned to architecture in the 1520s under the influence of Peruzzi and Serlio, although his illustrious career (which would include the design of the Palazzo Farnese in Caprarola and the church of Il Gesù in Rome) would take another two decades to unfold. In 1538 he moved to Rome, and it was there that he became involved with the Vitruvian Academy. It is no doubt from this involvement came his ambition to write a rule book on the orders, in a simpler and easier illustrated format than had previously existed. His *Regola delli cinque ordini* was written during the 1550s, but did not appear until 1562. Its success can be measured by the fact that it became the architect's principal reference book on the orders well down into the twentieth century.

Vignola's rules (modules) are not based on a philological reading of Vitruvius or other sources, but rather on the archaeological study of the most highly regarded Roman models in Rome. It is, moreover, a composite or idealized version of the orders, one also slenderer in its overall proportions than those proposed by either Vitruvius or Serlio. It fully complies with the Renaissance desire to regulate or bring design decisions into a simpler format.

To the Readers

The reason why I was moved to make this little work, good readers, and then to dedicate it (such as it is) to the general service of he who delights in it, I shall briefly explain for clearer understanding.

Having practised the art of architecture for many years in different countries, it has always been a pleasure for me to look at the opinion of as many writers as I could about the practice of ornament, and comparing them with each other and with ancient works still in existence, to try to extract a rule with which I could be content, and which I could be sure would completely satisfy, or at least nearly so, every scholar of this art. And this was solely to serve my own requirements, nor was there any other aim. To do this, leaving aside many things of the writers, where differences of no little consequence are born, and to achieve greater certainty, I decided first to study those ancient ornaments of the five Orders which appear in the antiquities of Rome. And considering all of them carefully and examining their measurements accurately, I found that those which in the general opinion are the most beautiful and appear the most graceful to our eyes also have a certain numerical agreement and proportion which is the least complex: indeed you can measure precisely the large members in all their parts with each minute member. Hence, considering further how much our

Giacomo Barozzi da Vignola (1507–73), from Preface to *Regola delli cinque ordini d'architettura* [Rules of the five orders of architecture] (1562), trans. Richard J. Tuttle in his essay "On Vignola's *Rule of the Five Orders of Architecture*," from *Paper Palaces: The Rise of the Renaissance Architectural Treatise,* ed. Vaughan Hart and Peter Hicks. New Haven: Yale University Press, 1998, pp. 361–2. © 1998 by Yale University Press. Reprinted with permission of Yale University Press.

senses take pleasure in this proportion, and how much the things outside it are unpleasant, as the musicians prove in their science through sensation, I undertook this task many years ago, namely to reduce the said five Orders of architecture to a concise and quick rule which was easy to use, and the method I kept to was as follows. Wishing to put in this rule (by way of example) the Doric Order, I considered that of all the examples of Doric, the one in the Theatre of Marcellus was the most highly praised by everyone. This, then, I took as the basis of the rule for the said Order, that is, determining its principal parts. If some minor member did not entirely obey the numerical proportions (which often happens owing to the work of the stonecutters or other accidents that frequently occur with such details) I accommodated it to my rule not by altering anything of importance but by harmonising this slight licence on the authority of other examples of Doric which are also considered beautiful. From these examples I took other small parts whenever I needed to supplement the one from the Theatre of Marcellus, not as Zeuxis did with the maidens among the Crotons, but rather as my judgment directed. I made this choice for all the Orders, extracting only from ancient works and adding nothing of my own save the distribution of their proportions which were based on simple numbers, using not the *braccia*, or feet, or palms of whatever locality, but an arbitrary measurement called the module, divided into those parts which will be seen from Order to Order in the appropriate place. And I have made an otherwise difficult part of architecture so easy that every ordinary talent, provided he has some enthusiasm for this art, can at a glance and without much bothersome reading, understand the whole and make use of it at opportune moments. And although I was far from interested in publishing this, nevertheless it has been made possible by the entreaties of many friends desiring it, and even more by the generosity of my perpetual lord, the illustrious and most reverend Cardinal Farnese. From him not only have I received the courtesies of his honorable house which have allowed me to work diligently, but he has also given me the means to satisfy my friends and in addition to present to you shortly other, greater things on this subject, if you accept this part in the spirit in which I believe you will. And as it is neither my wish nor my intent to respond here to those objections that I know will be made by some, I leave this task to the work itself which by pleasing the more judicious will lead them to take up my defence. I would only add that should someone judge this a vain effort by saying that one cannot lay down a fixed rule, since, according to the opinion of all and especially of Vitruvius, it is often necessary to enlarge or to diminish the proportions of ornamental members in order to remedy with art where our vision has been deceived by some occurrence, to him I reply that concerning this matter it is necessary to know how much should appear to the eye – this should always be the firm rule which others have proposed to observe – and then proceed in this by certain good rules of perspective, whose practice is fundamental both here and in painting, such that I am sure you will be pleased, [and] I also hope to present that to you soon.

18   PALLADIO
from *The Four Books of Architecture* (1570)

Palladio holds a most exalted place in the history of Renaissance architecture. Generally regarded as the greatest Italian architect of the Renaissance, he is also quite possibly the most influential architect who ever lived – if one dares to count the many allusions to aspects of his style. His numerous buildings across the northeastern Italian landscape compose a virtual Mecca to which every architect yearns or promises to make a pilgrimage. His literary corpus comprises a body of writings both educated and classical in their bearing.

Andrea de Pietro della Gondola was born in Padua in 1508 and at the age of 13 was apprenticed to a stone carver. At 16, however, he broke his contract and moved to nearby Vicenza, where he continued his training in stone-cutting. By the early 1530s he had advanced to the status of master and then set his sights on practicing architecture. This ambition was realized in a dramatic way in 1537, when, as a worker, he became engaged in remodeling the villa of Count Giangiorgio Trissino – a distinguished scholar, dramatist, poet, and humanist. He was invited to join the count's household (which functioned as an academy) and thus began his classical education, which he christened by assuming the name Palladio. Through Trissino, Palladio became familiar with the work of Serlio (whom Trissino knew well), and in addition he met Jacopo Sansovino, Michele Sanmicheli, and Alvise Cornaro. In 1541 Palladio joined Trissino on his first trip (the first of three in the 1540s) to Rome, where he was able to study the ruins of antiquity, in addition to the fruits of the high Renaissance. All of these experiences combined to create one of the best educated and talented architects of the Renaissance.

The theoretical side of Palladio's development was also enhanced with his meeting of Daniele Barbaro around 1550. Barbaro was another prominent humanist who had just returned from a two-year ambassadorship in England. In the countryside of Maser in the 1550s, Palladio designed for Barbaro perhaps the most famous of his grand villas. Since 1547, Barbaro had been involved in preparing a new critical translation of Vitruvius, for which Palladio was encouraged to make the illustrations. The result, which was issued in 1556, was a treatise unsurpassed in the sixteenth century for its beauty and scholarship. This success no doubt encouraged Palladio to compose his own tome on architecture, of which four books appeared in 1570. This heavily illustrated work (consisting largely of classical monuments and his own designs) immediately became one of the great documents of the Renaissance and represents the apogee of fascination with the Vitruvian tradition. The two passages presented here testify to his quintessential classical reasoning. In the first, taken from the opening chapter of Book 1, Palladio re-presents the Vitruvian triad of convenience, duration, and beauty – the last of which is now defined as Vitruvian symmetry. In the second, the Preface to Book 4, Palladio states his belief in absolute beauty or cosmic proportions, which should underlay all good design.

Chapter I: Of the Several Particulars that ought to be Consider'd and Prepar'd before we Begin to Build

Great care ought to be taken, before a building is begun, of the several parts of the plan and elevation of the whole edifice intended to be raised: For three things, according to VITRUVIUS,

Andrea Palladio (1508–80), from *I quattro libri dell'architettura* [The four books of architecture] (1570), trans. Isaac Ware (1738), in *Andrea Palladio: The Four Books of Architecture*, ed. Adolf K. Placzek. New York: Dover Publications, 1965 (reissue), pp. 1, 79–80.

ought to be considered in every fabrick, without which no edifice will deserve to be commended; and these are utility or convenience, duration and beauty. That work therefore cannot be called perfect, which should be useful and not durable, or durable and not useful, or having both these should be without beauty.

An edifice may be esteemed commodious, when every part or member stands in its due place and fit situation, neither above or below its dignity and use; or when the *loggia's*, halls, chambers, cellars and granaries are conveniently disposed, and in their proper places.

The strength, or duration, depends upon the walls being carried directly upright, thicker below than above, and their foundations strong and solid: observing to place the upper columns directly perpendicular over those that are underneath, and the openings of the doors and windows exactly over one another; so that the solid be upon the solid, and the void over the void.

Beauty will result from the form and correspondence of the whole, with respect to the several parts, of the parts with regard to each other, and of these again to the whole; that the structure may appear an entire and compleat body, wherein each member agrees with the other, and all necessary to compose what you intend to form.

★ ★ ★

The Preface *to the* Reader

If upon any fabrick labour and industry may be bestowed, that it may be comparted with beautiful measure and proportion; this, without any doubt, ought to be done in temples; in which the maker and giver of all things, the almighty and supream God, ought to be adored by us, and be praised, and thanked for his continual benefactions to us, in the best manner that our strength will permit. If, therefore, men in building their own habitations, take very great care to find out excellent and expert architects, and able artificers, they are certainly obliged to make use of still much greater care in the building of churches. And if in those they attend chiefly to conveniency, in these they ought to have a regard to the dignity and grandeur of the Being there to be invoked and adored; who being the supream good, and highest perfection, it is very proper, that all things consecrated to him, should be brought to the greatest perfection we are capable of. And indeed, if we consider this beautiful machine of the world, with how many wonderful ornaments it is filled, and how the heavens, by their continual revolutions, change the seasons according as nature requires, and their motion preserves itself by the sweetest harmony of temperature; we cannot doubt, but that the little temples we make, ought to resemble this very great one, which, by his immense goodness, was perfectly compleated with one word of his; or imagine that we are not obliged to make in them all the ornaments we possibly can, and build them in such a manner, and with such proportions, that all the parts together may convey a sweet harmony to the eyes of the beholders, and that each of them separately may serve agreeably to the use for which it shall be appointed. For which reason, although they are worthy to be much commended, who being guided by an exceeding good spirit, have already built temples to the supream God, and still build them; it does not seem, nevertheless, that they ought to remain without some little reprehension, if they have not also endeavoured to make them in the best and most noble form our condition will permit.

Hence, because the antient Greeks and Romans employed the utmost care in building the temples to their Gods, and composed them of the most beautiful architecture, that they might be made with so much greater ornaments, and in greater proportion, as that they might be suitable for the God to whom they were consecrated; I shall shew in this book the form and the ornaments of many antient temples, of which the ruins are still to be seen, and by me have been reduced into designs, that every one may know in what form, and with what ornaments churches ought to be built. And although there is but a small part of some of them to be seen standing above-ground, I nevertheless from that small part, (the foundations that could be seen being also considered) have endeavoured, by conjecture, to shew what they must have been when they were entire. And in this VITRUVIUS has been a very great help to me; because, what I saw, agreeing with what he teacheth us, it was not difficult for me to come at the knowledge of their aspect, and of their form.

But to the ornaments, that is, the bases, columns, capitals, cornices, and such like things, I have added nothing of my own; but they have been measured by me with the utmost attention, from different fragments, found in the places where these temples stood. And I make no doubt, but that they, who shall read this book, and shall consider the designs in it carefully, may be able to understand many places, which in VITRUVIUS are reputed very difficult, and to direct their mind to the knowledge of the beautiful and proportionable forms of temples, and to draw from them various very noble inventions; making use of which in a proper time and place, they may shew, in their works, how one may, and ought to vary, without departing from the precepts of the art, and how laudable and agreeable such variations are.

But before we come to the designs, I shall, as I usually do, briefly mention those advertences, that in building of temples ought to be observed; having also taken them from VITRUVIUS, and from other very excellent men, who have written of so noble an art.

19 JUAN BAUTISTA VILLALPANDO
from *Ezekiel Commentaries* (1604)

Renaissance theory up to this point has been viewed largely as a secular phenomenon, but its biggest supporter in Italy had indeed been the Papacy, which quickly adopted the style as a mark of its universal ecclesiastical authority. What remained for sixteenth-century theory, then, was to forge a more compelling synthesis of classical theory with the biblical elements of the Christian religion. This was the task attempted by Juan Bautista Villalpando. This Spanish Jesuit was a native of Cordoba, and he had been trained in architecture under Juan de Herrera, who was in charge of building the Escorial. After entering the Jesuit order, however, Villalpando

Juan Bautista Villalpando (1552–1608), from *In: Ezekielem Explanationes* [Ezekiel commentaries] (1604), trans. Daniel Pfeiffer, from the Spanish edition, *El tratado de la arquitectura perfecta en la última visión del profeta Ezequiel*, Madrid: Colegio Oficial de Arquitectos, Patrimonio Nacional, 1990, p. 129.

entered the service of the Jesuit Jerónimo Prado, who had begun a commentary on the Old Testament book of *Ezekiel*. One Spanish theologian, Benito Arias Montano, had earlier challenged the authenticity of *Ezekiel's* account, and Prado and Villalpando, in response, started a theological refutation on Montano, in support of the vision of *Ezekiel*. First they had to defend themselves (successfully) against the charge of heresy, but in Rome in 1596 Prado and Villalpando published the first volume of their study. After Prado's death in 1597, Villalpando began the second volume of the commentary, which contains his gloriously illustrated reconstruction of Solomon's Temple. Villalpando's case for the temple rests on two premises. First that the proportions of the temple were absolute and perfect because they were given to Solomon by God himself. Second that the three orders later developed by the Greeks derived from these Solomonic orders, thus squaring Biblical accounts with the classical tradition. The following passage is from the introduction to volume II, in which Villalpando is describing the efforts of Prado and himself to undertake the reconstruction, and their success – as measured by the response of King Philip II and the architect Juan de Herrera.

Because we thought it necessary that the copy should correspond to the example, or that the image should correspond to what it portrays, we reached the conclusion that the prophet with his inner eye saw a certain building complete and perfect in all its details, in which every part responded to the whole in a miraculous way and with incredible artistic skill, proportioned to itself, a building whose facade or aspect had nothing to disturb the mind or the eyes. It had the most solid doors, the widest porticoes, and the most spacious atriums, that is to say, it was a palatial complex sustained by marble columns and a golden roof, adorned at the top with gilded balustrades. Scrupulously he considered the dimensions, the number, order, and proportions of all elements, and such superior things as certain symbols. To his inner eye came the vision of the House of God: its economy, order, and disposition, and the levels and ministries of Christ's Church that were represented by the corresponding ornaments of that building.

Guided only by a certain conjecture, suspecting rather than knowing, we applied our minds and all our knowledge to understanding this unique vision of the prophet. Through the singular blessing of God Almighty we found the power, in large part, to bring this project to a happy conclusion and to give visible form to the temple described by Ezekiel. We no longer have to believe in this vision with only the inner eyes of the mind, but now with the eyes of the body. And we think the diligent reader will be persuaded of the same thing when he reads our commentaries. He will understand that this is the building described by Ezekiel, in which every part follows the measurements of the prophet with no exceptions, where all the rules of perfect architecture are observed, and in which no part deviates from or opposes these rules. As proof, I will offer some unique testimony, which to me at least is quite important. And if everyone finds it as authoritative as I do, I am confident it will convince any adversary that I may have.

This is the testimony of Juan de Herrera, my master and the first architect to the Catholic King Philip II. After viewing our visual reconstruction and its proportions, the dimensions of the parts, its convenience and beauty, its strict use of means, he appreciated just these features and confessed ingenuously to have detected divine intervention in the proportions of the architecture, such that – even if he had only seen the visual evidence and had not read that they were part of the Holy Scriptures – he would have judged that the building could not have been thought up by the human mind but had to be designed by the infinite wisdom of God himself.

This wise and prudent man noted this to me on several occasions and I do not doubt that he did so in front of the Royal Majesty, whose close friend he was. Through his recommendation, and in fact through the approval of the king himself, our modest study was crowned with the greatest benevolence and honors, without which it would scarcely have become known to the public.

If these things seem far-fetched, let us come to the essential aspects and concede those things that are known. This building consists of three parts that are so contrary to one another that they cannot be reduced to a single fabric. Therefore they cannot be reduced to a single visual perspective, since the drawings and figures should present a possible edifice. And Vitruvius judges that these are not the only criteria that should be applied to the art of rendering; he also thinks that visual art should treat those things that can or could exist, which implies that such a building that cannot exist or be represented cannot be reduced to the rule of a graphic description. What, then, does the prophet see:

> Thou son of man, show the house to the house of Israel... the form of the house, and the fashion thereof, and the goings out thereof, and the comings in thereof, and all the forms thereof, and all the ordinances thereof, and all the forms thereof, and all the laws thereof... (Ezekiel, 43.10–11)

20   GEORGIO VASARI
from Preface to *Lives of the Most Eminent Italian Architects, Painters, and Sculptors* (1550, 1568)

Giorgio Vasari, like so many of the sixteenth-century artists, was both a painter and architect. But he possesses one other distinction that makes him truly unique among his peers – he lays claim to being the first art historian of modern times. Vasari was born in Arezzo, educated by the Medici family in Florence, and from the beginning of his career was very much under the spell of Michelangelo, with whom he felt himself privileged to share a friendship. Upon coming of artistic age in the 1540s, he worked mostly as a painter and traveled throughout much of Italy: completing commissions and gathering material for his book. In 1550, under the patronage of Pope Julius III in Rome, he began to turn his attention to architecture, and he renewed this interest when he returned to Florence in 1554 and entered the service of Duke Lorenzo I. Here he designed a number of rooms within the Palazzo Vecchio and built what is considered his masterwork, the Uffizi Gallery (started in 1550). Originally it housed municipal offices, but now it is one of the great museums of Europe.

The two editions of *Le vite* – 1550 and 1568 – almost take the form of two different books. The first edition was drafted in 1546–7 from his travels and research, and it shows the influence of Ghiberti's *Commentaries* (1447–55)

Georgio Vasari (1511–74), from Preface to *Le vite de piu eccellenti architetti, pittori, et scultori italiani* [Lives of the most eminent Italian architects, painters, and sculptors] (1550, 1568), trans. Mrs. Jonathan Foster, in *Lives of the Most Eminent Painters, Sculptors, and Architects*, Vol. 1. London: George Bell and Sons, 1888, pp. 300–3.

and Pliny the Elder's chapters on classical art in Books 34 and 35 of *The Natural History*. It also displays the Ciceronean ambition to elevate historical writing beyond a mere chronicle of events. From the start Vasari intended to add to his first edition, but in the 1560s his rewriting became more extensive as he sought to make his book more historical, more theoretical, and somewhat more impersonal in its tone; he also vastly expanded its earlier length. The Preface to part II of his study relates his historical method and his tripartite scheme of artistic development during the Renaissance. Already in his Preface to part I he had compared a historical period or style (he employs the Italian term *maniera*) to a human being, who is born, grows up to maturity, and becomes old and dies. The three stages or periods of Renaissance development noted in the second Preface are defined not strictly by temporal limits but rather by the artists' views of art. The last two stages evolve, as it were, from the renewed naturalistic footing of the first (achieved by Giotto) in a kind of dialectical manner, with each generation both learning from and correcting the faults of the previous one, while also rediscovering classical norms. Thus Masaccio lifted Renaissance painting into its second phase by perceiving that painters should follow nature as closely as possible, while Brunelleschi did the same for architecture by rediscovering the ancient proportions and the orders. Andrea Mantegna's late second-stage insight that the ancients copied not one model but combined the best of several models to eliminate natural defects allowed the artists of the third state – beginning with Leonardo da Vinci – to achieve productions of unparalleled grace and beauty.

When I first undertook to write these lives, it was not my purpose to make a mere list of the artists, or to give an inventory, so to speak, of their works. Nor could I by any means consider it a worthy end of my – I will not say satisfactory – but assuredly prolonged and fatiguing labours, that I should content myself with merely ascertaining the number, names, and country of the artists, or with informing my reader in what city or borough precisely, their paintings, sculptures, or buildings, were to be found. This I could have accomplished by a simple register or table, without the interposition of my own judgment in any part. But I have remembered that the writers of history, – such of them, that is to say, as by common consent are admitted to have treated their subject most judiciously, – have in no case contented themselves with a simple narration of the occurrences they describe, but have made zealous enquiry respecting the lives of the actors, and sought with the utmost diligence to investigate the modes and methods adopted by distinguished men for the furtherance of their various undertakings. The efforts of such writers have, moreover, been further directed to the examination of the points on which errors have been made, or, on the other hand, by what means successful results have been produced, to what expedients those who govern have had recourse, in what manner they have delivered themselves from such embarrassments as arise in the management of affairs; of all that has been effected, in short; whether sagaciously or injudiciously, whether by the exercise of prudence, piety, and greatness of mind, or by that of the contrary qualities, and with opposite results; as might be expected from men who are persuaded that history is in truth the mirror of human life. These writers have not contented themselves with a mere dry narration of facts and events, occurring under this prince or in that republic, but have set forth the grounds of the various opinions, the motives of the different resolutions, and the character of the circumstances by which the prime movers have been actuated; with the consequences, beneficial or disastrous, which have been the results of all. This is, without doubt, the soul of history. From these details it is that men learn the true government of life; and to secure this effect, therefore, with the addition of the pleasure which may be derived from having past events presented to the view as living and present, is to be considered the legitimate aim of the historian.

Moved by these considerations, I determined, having undertaken to write the history of the noblest masters in our arts, to pursue the method observed by these distinguished writers, so far as my powers would permit; imitating these ingenious men, and desiring, above all things, to honour the arts, and those who labour in them. I have endeavoured, not only to relate what has been done, but to set forth and distinguish the better from the good, and the best from the better, the most distinguished from the less prominent qualities and works, of those who belong to our vocation. I have further sought, with diligence, to discriminate between the different methods, manners, and processes adopted and displayed by the different painters and sculptors, not omitting to notify their various phantasies, inventions, and modes of treatment, all which I have investigated to the best of my ability, that I might the better make known to those who could not pursue the enquiry for themselves, the sources and causes of the different methods, as well as of that amelioration and deterioration of the arts which have been seen to take place at different periods, and by the agency of different persons.

In the First Part of these Lives I have spoken of the nobility and antiquity of these our arts, as at that point of our work was desirable, omitting many remarks by Pliny, and other writers, of which I might have availed myself, if I had not preferred – perhaps in opposition to the opinion of many readers – rather to permit that each should remain free to seek the ideas of others in their original sources. And this I did to avoid that prolixity and tediousness which are the mortal enemies of attention. But on this occasion it appears to me beseeming that I should do what I did not then permit myself – namely, present a more exact and definite explication of my purpose and intention, with the reasons which have led me to divide this collection of Lives into Three Parts.

It is an indubitable fact, that distinction in the arts is attained by one man through his diligent practice; by another, from his profound study; a third seeks it in imitation; a fourth, by the acquirement of knowledge in the sciences, which all offer aid to the arts; others arrive at the desired end by the union of many of these; some by the possession of all united. But as I have sufficiently discoursed, in the lives of various masters, of the modes, processes, and causes of all sorts, which have contributed to the good, the better, or the excellent results of their labours, so I will here discuss these matters in more general terms, and insist, rather, on the qualities which characterize periods, than on those which distinguish individuals. To avoid a too minute inquiry, I adopt the division into three parts, or periods – if we so please to call them – from the revival of the arts, down to the present century, and in each of these there will be found a very obvious difference. In the first, and most ancient, of these periods, we have seen that the three formative arts were very far from their perfection; and that, if it must be admitted that they had much in them that was good, yet this was accompanied by so much of imperfection, that those times certainly merit no great share of commendation. Yet, on the other hand, as it is by them that the commencement was made; as it was they who originated the method, and taught the way to the better path, which was afterwards followed, so, if it were but for this, we are bound to say nothing of them but what is good – nay, we must even accord to them a somewhat larger amount of glory than they might have the right to demand, were their works to be judged rigidly by the strict rules of art.

In the second period, all productions were, obviously, much ameliorated; richer invention was displayed, with more correct drawing, a better manner, improved execution, and more careful finish. The arts were, in a measure, delivered from that rust of old age, and that coarse disproportion, which the rudeness of the previous uncultivated period had left still clinging to them. But who will venture to affirm that there could yet be found an artist perfect at all points? or one who had arrived at that position, in respect of invention, design, and colour, to which we have attained in the present day? Is there any one who has been able so carefully to manage the shadows of his figures, that the lights remain only on the parts in relief? or who has, in like manner, effected those perforations, and secured those delicate results, in sculpture, which are exhibited by the statues and rilievi of our own day? The credit of having effected this is certainly due to the third period only; respecting which it appears to me that we may safely affirm the arts to have effected all that it is permitted to the imitation of nature to perform, and to have reached such a point, that we have now more cause for apprehension lest they should again sink into depression, than ground for hope that they will ever attain to a higher degree of perfection.

21 GEORGIO VASARI
from "Life of Michelangelo" in *Lives of the Most Eminent Italian Architects, Painters, and Sculptors* (1550, 1568)

Several selections in this section have portrayed the sixteenth century as a Vitruvian hymn, in which architecture was made to conform ever more to rules of convenience, proportion, and decorum. Against this tendency marched one artist who took little notice of the Vitruvian tradition. This person was Michelangelo (1475–1564), whom Vasari regarded as an artist of such stature that his unworldly talent could only have been created by divine decree. But the life of Michelangelo is also where the biographer's historical model runs into problems. In Vasari's celebrated passage concerning Michelangelo's design for the new sacristy (Medici Chapel, 1519–34) for the church of San Lorenzo (balancing Brunelleschi's Old Sacristy of 1421–9), he notes that Michelangelo "broke the barriers and chains" that had previously been established by Vitruvius and approved works of classical antiquity. Architecturally, the period of 1520–60 is sometimes called "Mannerist," indicating that architects were not averse to playing with the classical rules and examples laid down by Alberti, Bramante, and others. In Vasari's scenario, Michelangelo's overt violation of classical norms would seem to indicate the acme of this style, from which only the decline of old age can ensue. Vasari's prophecy was, in retrospect, only a little premature. The example of Michelangelo notwithstanding, the Vitruvian phase of the Italian Renaissance would not end until the seventeenth century, with the appearance of such great baroque architects as Giovanni Lorenzo Bernini (1598–1680) and Francesco Borromini (1599–1667).

But to return to Michelagnolo, who had now again repaired to Florence. Losing much time, first in one thing and then in another, he made a model, among other things, for those

Georgio Vasari, from "Life of Michelangelo" in *Le vite de piu eccellenti architetti, pittori, et scultori italiani* [Lives of the most eminent Italian architects, painters, and sculptors] (1550, 1568), trans. Mrs. Jonathan Foster, in *Lives of the Most Eminent Painters, Sculptors, and Architects*, Vol. 5. London: George Bell and Sons, 1888, pp. 270–2.

projecting and grated windows with which are furnished the rooms at the angle of the Palace, in one of which Giovanni da Udine executed the paintings and stucco-work which are so much and so deservedly extolled. He also caused blinds, in perforated copper, to be made by the goldsmith Piloto, but after his own designs, and very admirable they certainly are. Michelagnolo consumed many years, as we have said, in the excavation of marbles; it is true that he prepared models in wax and other requisites for the great undertakings with which he was engaged at the same time, but the execution of these was delayed until the monies, appropriated by the Pontiff for that purpose, had been expended in the wars of Lombardy; and at the death of Leo the works thus remained incomplete, nothing having been accomplished but the foundations of the Façade, and the transport of a great column from Carrara to the Piazza di San Lorenzo.

The death of Pope Leo X. completely astounded the arts and artists, both in Rome and Florence; and while Adrian VI. ruled, Michelagnolo employed himself in the last-named city with the Sepulchre of Julius. But when Adrian was dead, and Clement VII. elected in his place, the latter proved himself equally desirous of establishing memorials to his fame in the arts of sculpture, painting, and architecture, as had been Leo and his other predecessors. It was at this time, 1525, that Giorgio Vasari, then a boy, was taken to Florence by the Cardinal of Cortona, and there placed to study art with Michelagnolo; but the latter having been summoned to Rome by Pope Clement, who had commenced the Library of San Lorenzo; with the New Sacristy, wherein he proposed to erect the marble tombs of his fore-fathers, it was determined that Giorgio should go to Andrea del Sarto, before Michelagnolo's departure; the master himself repairing to the workshop of Andrea, for the purpose of recommending the boy to his care.

Michelagnolo then proceeded to Rome without delay, being much harassed by the repeated remonstrances of Francesco Maria, Duke of Urbino, who complained of the artist greatly; saying that he had received sixteen thousand crowns for the Tomb, yet was loitering for his own pleasure in Florence without completing the same: he added threats, to the effect that if Michelagnolo did not finish his work, he, the Duke, would bring him to an evil end. Arrived in Rome, Pope Clement, who would gladly have had the master's time at his own command, advised him to require the regulation of his accounts from the agents of the Duke, when it seemed probable that they would be found his debtors, rather than he theirs. Thus then did that matter remain; but the Pope and Michelagnolo taking counsel together of other affairs, it was agreed between them that the Sacristy and New Library of San Lorenzo in Florence should be entirely completed.

The master thereupon, leaving Rome, returned to Florence, and there erected the Cupola which we now see, and which he caused to be constructed in various orders. He then made the Goldsmith Piloto prepare a very beautiful ball of seventy-two facettes. While he was erecting his cupola, certain of his friends remarked to him that he must be careful to have his lantern very different from that of Filipp Brunelleschi: to which Michelagnolo replied, "I can make a different one easily; but as to making a better, that I cannot do." He decorated the inside of the Sacristy with four Tombs, to enclose the remains of the fathers of the two Popes, Lorenzo the elder and Giuliano his brother, with those of Giuliano the brother of Leo, and of Lorenzo his nephew. Desiring to imitate the old Sacristy by Filippo Brunelleschi, but with new ornaments, he composed a decoration of a richer and more varied character than had ever before been adopted, either by ancient or modern masters: the beautiful cornices, the capitals, the bases, the doors, the niches, and the tombs themselves, were all very different from those in common use, and from what was considered measure, rule, and order, by Vitruvius and the ancients, to whose rules he would not restrict himself. But this boldness on his part has encouraged other artists to an injudicious imitation, and new fancies are continually seen, many of which belong to *grottesche* rather than to the wholesome rules of ornamentation.

Artists are nevertheless under great obligations to Michelagnolo, seeing that he has thus broken the barriers and chains whereby they were perpetually compelled to walk in a beaten path, while he still more effectually completed this liberation and made known his own views, in the Library of San Lorenzo, erected at the same place. The admirable distribution of the windows, the construction of the ceiling, and the fine entrance of the Vestibule, can never be sufficiently extolled. Boldness and grace are equally conspicuous in the work as a whole, and in every part; in the cornices, corbels, the niches for statues, the commodious staircase, and its fanciful divisions – in all the building, at a word, which is so unlike the common fashion of treatment, that every one stands amazed at the sight thereof.

22 PETER PAUL RUBENS
from Preface to *Palaces of Genoa* (1622)

As the Renaissance style and humanistic principles began to make their way northward in the sixteenth century, interpretations of its forms and meaning often differed from those in the south. The German Walther Ryff not only translated Vitruvius into German in 1548, but in a theoretical text of the preceding year he codified the formulas of Serlio and Cesariano. Hans Blum published the first of the northern "column books" in 1550, *Von den fünff Seülen* (On the five columns), which sought to transmit to his German readers both this "great and useful treasure" of antique principles, first devised in "the time of Solomon," but also which has come north of the Alps only in the last "eight years." To the west, and beginning in 1555, the Flemish artist and Vitruvian scholar Vredeman de Vries began producing his engravings of hypothetical classical designs, which brilliantly captured the range of early northern Renaissance designs. His successor was the incomparable Wendel Dietterlin (c. 1550–99), who in 1593–4 produced his self-styled column book, *Architectura von Ausstheilung, Symmetria und Proportion der fünff Seulen* (Architecture of distribution, symmetry, and proportion of the five columns). It is no column book at all but a highly fanciful visual exploration of the human figures, threatening demons, exotic creatures, and mythological beasts that he associates with the expressive limits of each order.

Nevertheless, one of the most influential of the books introducing the Italian models to the north was that of the painter Peter Paul Rubens (1577–1640). A native of Antwerp, he made his way to Italy in 1600 to serve as a painter at the court of Vincenzo Gonzaga, the Duke of Mantua. During two stays in Rome he read the writings of Serlio and viewed the buildings of Vignola and Carlo Maderno. In 1607 he visited Genoa for seven weeks, where he stayed at the Palazzo Grimaldi and studied the Renaissance palaces of the city. All of this came in handy some years later – in 1615 – when he became involved with designing a Jesuit church in Antwerp. Although the overall design is attributed to Pieter Huyssens, Rubens did considerable work in the interior and (according to Anthony Blunt) was

Peter Paul Rubens (1577–1640), from Preface to *Palazzi di Genova* [Palaces of Genoa] (1622), trans. Harry Francis Mallgrave.

responsible for the Italianate features of the exterior. It is this church to which Rubens also alludes in the preface to his *Palazzi di Genova,* which appeared in 1622. The interesting thing about this brief passage is that the style that Rubens is introducing to his northern colleagues is not the Italian Renaissance but the baroque. The translation is made from the preface to the original edition, written in Italian.

In this small book I give the plans, elevations, and two sections of some palaces that I collected at Genoa, not without trouble and expense, although I had the good luck to avail myself in part of the work of another. [. . .] We see in our country the architecture that is called barbaric or Gothic slowly perishing and disappearing. We see several enlightened men introducing into our country, for its embellishment and decorative glory, a true symmetry that follows the rules of the ancient Greeks and Romans. We find these examples in the magnificent churches built by the Holy Society of Jesus in the towns of Antwerp and Brussels. Because of the dignity of the divine office, we begin to change the temples to a better style.

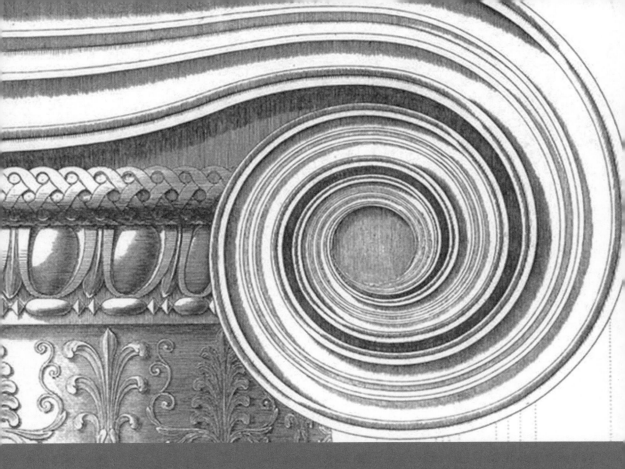

PART II   CLASSICISM IN FRANCE AND BRITAIN

A. FRENCH CLASSICISM: ANCIENTS AND MODERNS

Introduction

The relationship of France and Italy during the Renaissance is defined by the geographical proximity of the two areas and by the interactions of the two cultures. Italy, to begin with, was not a country in any sense of the term. A map of the area at the start of the sixteenth century shows the entire southern half of the Italian peninsula largely under the control of Spain, the republics of the middle region and (an often hostile) Venice composing the Papal States, and parts of Lombardy and Piedmont forming the southern extension of the Holy Roman Empire. France during the same years had geographic borders much smaller than today and was still making its political passage from a monarchy controlled by feudal lords to a centralized state. The religious reformations of the first part of the sixteenth century further complicated this picture. In 1517 Martin Luther nailed his 95 theses on the door of Wittenberg castle's church; in 1529 Henry VIII of England began the process of separating his church from that of Rome; and in 1541 Jean Calvin forcefully assumed control of the city-state of Geneva. Catholic France was thus drawn into alliances and conflicts with the papacy but also into continuous military competition with Britain, Spain, and with the various territorial centers of the Habsburgs. Thus the French monarch Charles VIII initiated the Italian wars in 1494 in pursuit of Naples. Louis XII led a French army south in 1499 in pursuit of Milan, and François I led yet another French army into Italy in 1515 — both to press dynastic claims and to challenge the Habsburgs for control of the Continent. These wars at least served the purpose of cultural exchange. After François's victory at Marignano in 1515 he possessed Milan (for a while), where he became impressed with the splendor of the new Italian residences. Shortly thereafter he invited Leonardo da Vinci to France to design a royal palace at Romorantin (1515–17), and around the same time he began work on his Loire-valley châteaux at Bois (1515–24) and Chambord (begun 1519). The French king especially appreciated the cultural life of Italian humanism and based his own court on its model.

This fascination soon became a trend. The same king, as we have seen, invited Serlio to France in the early 1540s, and Vignola eventually followed. French artists and scholars by this date were also regularly making their way to Italy. Scholarly annotations to the treatise of Vitruvius were published by the Frenchman Guillaume Philander in Rome in 1544, the following year in Paris. In 1547 Jean Martin made the first French translation of Vitruvius, and in 1553 he published a translation of Alberti's treatise. It was a little over a decade later — in 1567 — that the first French treatise of the Renaissance appeared. Its author was the architect Philibert Delorme (c. 1510–70), an almost exact contemporary of Palladio.

Over the next century Renaissance forms became the basis of an emerging French classicism. Architects such as Pierre Lescot (d. 1578), Salomon de Brosse (1571–1626), Jacques Lemercier (1582–1654), and François Mansart (1598–1666) established a refined Renaissance manner of building with a distinct French coloration. The political situation of the country was also changing. The bloody religious wars between Catholics and Calvinists that had wreaked havoc in the last third of the sixteenth century had been brought to a tentative (but not permanent) halt by the Edict of Nantes of 1598, which acknowledged at least the principle of religious toleration. The economic devastation wrought by the strife now slowly came to be repaired over the first half of the seventeenth century, despite the instability the Thirty Years War (1618–48). By the end of this continental conflict, France had succeeded Habsburg Spain as the leading military power on the Continent and was poised for greater things in the cultural field. The architect Louis Le Vau (1612–70) was developing a style of classicism with distinct overtones of the Italian baroque. Painters such as Nicolas Poussin and Claude Lorraine were beginning to rival the efforts of Italian painters. And in 1648 a petition was presented to the 10-year-old Dauphin to create a Royal Academy of Painting and Sculpture. The glorious Age of Louis XIV was poised to begin.

For architecture, French classicism takes its decisive turn in 1671 with the founding of the Royal Academy of Architecture. The Academy was one of several founded by Louis XIV as a way to codify theory and advance the country's standing in the arts. For France these institutions also became a means to define an artistic path independent from that of Italy. French classicism, along every front, now became hostile to the "baroque" turn of the Renaissance, and the various academies advocated a sterner and more rigid interpretation of classicism. The person most responsible for defining this position in architecture was the Academy of Architecture's first director, François Blondel, who in 1674–83 published his two-volume *Cours d'architecture* (Course of architecture). The theory of Vitruvius was central to Blondel's version of classicism, but he nevertheless allowed the Renaissance interpretations of Alberti, Serlio, Vignola, Palladio, and Scamozzi in certain matters. Blondel's view of antiquity and the aesthetic underpinnings of his teachings, however, would not go unchallenged. As in every instance when an institutional authority is set in place, dissenting voices are soon to be heard. Blondel found his protagonist and able opponent in the person of Claude Perrault, a surgeon, scientist, part-time architect, and translator. Squaring off in the 1670s and 1680s — they would initiate the first round of a debate that famously became known as the "quarrel between the Ancients and Moderns." The Renaissance tradition of classicism now came under its first challenge.

23   RENÉ DESCARTES
from *Rules for the Direction of the Mind* (1628)

Renaissance theory, as it became assimilated into France, was predicated on the belief that the arts, like the sciences, participated in the greater order of the universe, in an eternal grammar of mathematical forms, numbers, and relations. This belief, architecturally reinterpreted by Villalpando at the start of the century, was central to Renaissance theory, and it is this belief that will first come under attack in the second half of the seventeenth century. The initial soundings of disquiet, however, are heard not from an architect but rather from the young French mathematician living in Holland, René Descartes. He had spent much of the previous decade traveling around Europe, and was at the time turning from mathematics to philosophy. In embarking on his deductive "system" or method of reasoning — later known as Cartesianism — he, in the late-1620s, compiled a notebook of rules that would guide him through his logical deliberations. The skeptical note voiced in rule 3 — later published as the first principle of his *Discourse on the Method* (1637) — came to be referred to as "Cartesian doubt" and would be widely embraced by scientists intent on advancing knowledge. The implied challenge here to the theories of Plato and Aristotle could be transposed into architecture as skepticism toward the teachings of Vitruvius.

Rule Three

Concerning objects proposed for study, we ought to investigate what we can clearly and evidently intuit or deduce with certainty, and not what other people have thought or what we ourselves conjecture. For knowledge can be attained in no other way.

We ought to read the writings of the ancients, for it is of great advantage to be able to make use of the labours of so many men. We should do so both in order to learn what truths have already been discovered and also to be informed about the points which remain to be worked out in the various disciplines. But at the same time there is a considerable danger that if we study these works too closely traces of their errors will infect us and cling to us against our will and despite our precautions. For, once writers have credulously and heedlessly taken up a position on some controversial question, they are generally inclined to employ the most subtle arguments in an attempt to get us to adopt their point of view. On the other hand, whenever they have the luck to discover something certain and evident, they always present it wrapped up in various obscurities, either because they fear that the simplicity of their argument may depreciate the importance of their finding, or because they begrudge us the plain truth.

René Descartes (1596–1650), from *Regulae ad Directionen Ingenii* [Rules for the direction of the mind] (1628), trans. John Cottingham, Robert Stoothoff, and Dugald Murdoch in *The Philosophical Writings of Descartes*, Vol. I. Cambridge: Cambridge University Press, 1985, p. 13.

But even if all writers were sincere and open, and never tried to palm off doubtful matters as true, but instead put forward everything in good faith, we would always be uncertain which of them to believe, for hardly anything is said by one writer the contrary of which is not asserted by some other. It would be of no use to count heads, so as to follow the view which many authorities hold. For if the question at issue is a difficult one, it is more likely that few, rather than many, should have been able to discover the truth about it. But even if they all agreed among themselves, their teaching would still not be all we need. For example, even though we know other people's demonstrations by heart, we shall never become mathematicians if we lack the intellectual aptitude to solve any given problem. And even though we have read all the arguments of Plato and Aristotle, we shall never become philosophers if we are unable to make a sound judgement on matters which come up for discussion; in this case what we would seem to have learnt would not be science but history.

24 ROLAND FRÉART DE CHAMBRAY
from Preface to *A Parallel of the Ancient Architecture with the Modern* (1650)

I t is within this skeptical context — and as a reaction to the Italian baroque — that we must consider the treatise of Roland Fréart de Chambray (Sieur de Chambray). This diplomat and connoisseur had honed his artistic interests in Italy in the 1630s, where he was close to the circle of painters and savants that had gathered around Poussin. In 1640, while he was accompanying the Paris superintendent of building on a tour of the south, he was asked to write a treatise that would summarize for his countrymen the architectural teachings of antiquity and the Renaissance. He chose to limit his subject to the orders, and to do so in a comparative manner that would pit one example from classical times against several Renaissance examples. He also brought to his study a full classical bearing: a belief in absolute beauty and the importance of geometry (he was also a translator of Euclid) and numerical proportions.

The book, as a result, is a study of contrasts. On the one hand, it is a reining in of French classicism from the dangers of the Italian baroque and an attempt to ground theory once again on Vitruvian or antique principles. On the other hand, Fréart de Chambray — with his recognition that there was no universally accepted proportional system — allowed the modern French architect the same freedom to invent "as the *Antients*," thereby preparing the way for other French departures from Italian taste.

Roland Fréart de Chambray (1606–76), from Preface to *Parallele de l'architecture antique et de la moderne* (1650), trans. John Evelyn in *A Parallel of the Antient Architecture with the Modern*, printed in London by The Roycroft for John Place's shop in Holborn, 1664, pp. 1–3.

Reader,

Before I do altogether resign this *Book* to thy judgement, I advertise thee, that 'twas not my design in compiling it to teach any man, much less yet to satisfie those *Critical* spirits which the World so much abounds with: nor, is the Publique at all beholding to me; I have no thought of obliging it, an envious, and evil Judge: In a word, being nothing inclin'd to give them satisfaction, I have easily gratified my labour with the desir'd success: My principal drift was, First, to satisfie my self, nor has it cost me much trouble; though we sometimes find certain humors that are more averse, and difficult to themselves, then they would prove to others: For my part, I do not so use to treat my self: We have Enemies enough besides; and whatever I were able to do, I expect that men should presently say of me, all that Jealousie does commonly suggest in reproach of Novelty. That being no *Artisan*, it did not become me to prescribe to others the rules of their *Mystery*; That I teach nothing particular and extraordinary here; That the *Books* from whence I have gather'd all that I say being common and much ampler then mine, there was no need to have scumm'd them thus superficially over; That it had been better to have search'd, and produc'd something which the World had not yet seen: That the mind is free, not bound, and that we have as good right to invent, and follow our own *Genius*, as the *Antients*, without rendring our selves their Slaves; since *Art* is an infinite thing, growing every day to more perfection, and suiting it self to the humor of the several *Ages*, and *Nations*, who judge of it differently, and define what is agreeable, every one according to his own mode, with a world of such like vain and frivolous reasonings, which yet leave a deep impression on the minds of certain half-knowing people, whom the practice of *Arts* has not yet disabus'd; and on simple *Workmen*, whose *Trade* dwells all upon their fingers ends onely: but we shall not appeal to such *Arbiters* as these. There are others to be found (though truely very rarely) that having their first studies well founded on the *Principles* of *Geometry* before they adventur'd to work, do afterward easily, and with assurance arrive to the knowledge of the perfection of the *Art*: It is to such onely that I address my self, and to whom I willingly communicate the thoughts which I have had of separating in two branches the *five Orders of Architecture*, and forming a *body* a part of the *Three* which are deriv'd to us from the *Greeks*; to wit, the *Dorique, Ionique,* and the *Corinthian,* which one may with reason call the very flower and perfection of the *Orders*; since they not onely contain whatsoever is excellent, but likewise all that is necessary of *Architecture*; there being but three manners of *Building*, the *Solid,* the *Mean,* and the *Delicate*; all of them accurately express'd in these three *Orders here*, that have therefore no need of the other two (*Tuscan,* and *Composita*) which being purely of *Latine* extraction, and but forrainers in respect to *them*, seem as it were of another *species*; so as being mingl'd, they do never well together, as those to whom I discourse will soon perceive, when they shall have once put off a certain blind respect and reverence, which *Antiquity,* and a long custome (even of the greatest abuses) does commonly imprint in the most part of men, whose judgements they so pre-occupate, that they find it afterwards a difficult matter to undeceive themselves; because they deferr too much, and hardly dare to examine what has been receiv'd by the vulgar approbation for so long a time: Let them but consider, that we find no *antique example* where the *Greek Orders* are employ'd amongst the *Latine*, and that so many ages of ignorance have pass'd over us, especially in the Arts of *Architecture*, and *Painting*, which the Warr, and frequent inundations of *Barbarians* had almost extinguish'd in the very Country of their *Originals*; and which were in a manner new born again but a few years since, when those great Modern *Masters, Michael Angelo,* and *Raphael,* did as it were raise them from the Sepulchers of their antient ruines, under which, these poor *Sciences* lay buri'd; and I shall have fair hopes of their Conversion, and to see them of my opinion. It is the very least of my thoughts to broach *Novelties*; on the contrary, I would (were it possible) ascend even to the very sourse of the *Orders* themselves, and derive from thence the *Images,* and pure *Ideas* of these incomparable *Masters,* who were indeed their first *Inventors,* and be instructed from their own mouths; since doubtless the farther men have wander'd from their *Principles,* transplanting them as it were into a strange soile, the more they are become degenerate, and scarce cognoscible to their very *Authours.* For to say truth, have we at this present any reason in the World to call those *three* by the name of *Orders,* viz. *Dorique, Ionique,* and *Corinthian,* which we daily behold so disfigur'd, and ill treated by the *Workmen* of this age? to speak seriously, remains there so much as a simple *Member,* which has not receiv'd some strange and monstrous alteration? Nay, things are arrived to that pass, that a man shall hardly find an *Architect* who disdains not to follow the best and most approved *examples* of *Antiquity*: Every man will now forsooth compose after his own fansie, and conceives, that to imitate *Them,* were to become an *Apprentise* again; and that to be *Masters* indeed, they must of necessity produce something of new: Poor men that they are, to believe, that in fantastically designing some one kind of particular *Cornice,* or like *Member,* they are presently the *Inventors* of a new *Order,* as if in that onely consisted, what is call'd *Invention*; as if the *Pantheon,* that same stupendious and incomparable Structure (which is yet to be seen at *Rome*) were not the *Invention* of the *Architect* who built it, because he has vary'd nothing from the *Corinthian* Ordinance of which it is intirely compos'd? 'Tis not in the *retail* of the *minuter portions,* that the talent of an *Architect* appears; *this* is to be judg'd from the general distribution of the *Whole* Work. These low and reptile *Souls,* who never arrive to the universal knowledge of the *Art,* and embrace her in all her dimensions, are constrain'd to stop *there,* for want of abilities, incessantly crawling after these poor little things; and as their *studies* have no other objects, being already empty, and barren of themselves; their *Ideas* are so base and miserable, that they produce nothing save *Mascarons,* wretched *Cartouches,* and the like idle and impertinent *Grotesks,* with which they have even infected all our *Modern Architecture.* As for those other to whom Nature has been more propitious, and are indu'd with a clearer imagination, they very well perceive that the true and essential beauty of *Architecture* consists not simply in the minute separation of every member *apart*; but does rather principally result from the *Symmetry* and *Oeconomy* of the *whole,* which is the union and concourse of them all together, producing as 'twere a visible harmony and consent, which those eyes that are clear'd and enlightned by the real Intelligence of *Art,* contemplate and behold with excess of delectation.

25 PAUL FRÉART DE CHANTELOU

from *Diary of the Cavaliere Bernini's Visit to France* (1665)

If the issue of an independent artistic path for France was first suggested by the activities of the various French academies as well as by the treatise of Roland Fréart de Chambray, the matter was given further encouragement by the contentious events surrounding the completion of the Louvre. Louis XIV ascended to the throne in 1661 and three years later he appointed Jean-Baptiste Colbert as his Minister of Finance and Superintendent of Building. Colbert, in turn, initially focused his attention on the completion of the Louvre, which was proposed to be the urban palace of the young king. Work on removing and rebuilding a turreted medieval castle on this site had begun 1557 with Pierre Lescot's design of the pavilion in the southwest corner of the existing square court. In 1624 Jacques Lemercier doubled the length of Lescot's building and added northern and southern wings at each end, which in turn were to be joined by an eastern wing, forming a square with an interior courtyard. As the Dauphin approached the governing age in the late 1650s, the architect Louis Le Vau was given the task of completing the (largely Italianate) work by designing the east wing. He only got as far as laying the foundations in 1664 when the newly appointed Colbert, unhappy with the design, stepped in and halted the project. Colbert solicited various proposals from French and Italian architects, and in December 1664 the king made the decision to appoint the aging Bernini — Italy's greatest artist — as the architect. The Cavaliere undertook the arduous trip by carriage to Paris and arrived on June 1 with much pomp and fanfare. He spent five months finalizing his design for the east wing, while the foundation stone was laid on July 1, 1665.

The civil servant Paul Fréart, the brother of Roland Fréart de Chambray, was given the task of escorting Bernini's entourage into Paris, and during the artist's stay Fréart, who too had been active in Poussin's artistic circle in Rome, recorded in his diary the events that transpired. The following two excerpts convey both the loud acclaim with which Bernini was received, and the bitterness surrounding his departure. Opposition to Bernini's Louvre design seems to have been orchestrated by Colbert, but, as the entry of October 6 shows, it was carried out by Charles Perrault, Colbert's personal secretary, who in an audience with Bernini had the audacity to criticize the final design. Behind this criticism was considerable resentment among French architects at having an Italian brought to France to prepare the design. The project was, in effect, doomed well before Bernini left Paris on October 20, and Colbert would next seek a design more "French" in its overall character.

I June

During the evening one of the minister's servants was sent to look for me. I went over to him, and he told me that the King had chosen me to welcome the Cavaliere Bernini, not in my capacity as maître d'hôtel[1] but as a special emissary to entertain and accompany him

Paul Fréart de Chantelou (1609–94), from *Diary of the Cavaliere Bernini's Visit to France* (1665) in Fréart's *Diary of the Cavaliere Bernini's Visit to France*, ed. Anthony Blunt, trans. Margery Corbett. Princeton: Princeton University Press, 1985, pp. 7–9, 260–2. © 1985 by Princeton University Press. Reprinted by permission of Princeton University Press.

while he was in this country. I said this was a great honor but that it gave me cause for some anxiety; the Ambassador Extraordinary of the Knights of Malta[2] was arriving at court the next day, the King was going to entertain him, and I was solely responsible for the arrangements as I was the only maître d'hôtel at Saint-Germain, both for ordinary and special duties.[3] M. Colbert replied that I must send a note that evening to the other maîtres d'hôtel in waiting to come at once to relieve me, and that I should without further delay, leave very early the next morning.

I then went to see the grand maître,[4] to inform him of this decision, and to take my leave of His Highness. As he was not at home I went to the King's apartments to look for him. There I found the marquis de Bellefonds,[5] the chief maître d'hôtel, and I told him my difficulties. He begged me not to worry, saying that he and M. Sanguin[6] would take over my duties. He added that, while they were having refreshments in the park, the King had asked him whether in his opinion he had not made a very good choice in appointing me, and that he had replied as befitted a good friend.

I had decided to remain so that I could attend the King at dinner, but M. Colbert sent for me again and told me that I must depart for Paris in the morning; I must leave again at midday and travel towards Essonne until I met the Cavaliere who was to dine there. He asked me if I had a coach-and-six; I told him no, whereupon he said, "You must take my brother's[7] I will let him know." He then told me that I should be present at the King's evening toilet, when His Majesty would give me his direct command. I said it was not necessary, that I would write to the maîtres d'hôtel who were in waiting, and would start next day early, which I did.

2 June

I took the carriáge belonging to M. Colbert and started on the road for Essonne. On leaving Juvisy[8] I met the Cavaliere's party. I signalled to his *litter* to stop and got down from my carriage. He had also alighted and I went to greet him addressing him in French. I realized at once that he did not understand a word and I said in Italian that I would not risk making compliments in his tongue, but begged him to get into the carriage that I had brought. His son[9] and Signor Mattia[10] also got out and came up to greet me. Having exchanged civilities, the Cavaliere and I, as well as my nephew, your son,[11] whom I had taken with me, got into M. Colbert's carriage. Once installed I repeated my speech to him in as good Italian as I could muster. I explained to him the King's orders and with what pleasure I had received them, on account of the very great admiration I had always felt for him and for his talent. I reminded him that he had once done me the honor of giving me some of his figure studies which I treasured dearly.[12] I then recalled to him several maxims on the subject of portraiture in marble, which I had heard him express and had carefully remembered because I had always greatly esteemed his opinions; he could judge for himself, therefore, of my eagerness to obey His Majesty's command to meet him and remain with him during his stay in France. He thanked me most courteously, and said that it was a great honor to be asked to serve a king of France; moreover the Pope, his master, had commanded him. Had it not been for these considerations he would still be in Rome. He had heard on all sides that the

King was a great prince with a great heart and a great intelligence, as well as the greatest gentleman in his kingdom. It was this that had chiefly induced him to set out, for he was curious to make his acquaintance and eager to serve him; he only regretted that his gifts were not sufficient to justify the honor done him, nor the high opinion in which he was held. He then turned to the business that had brought him. Beauty in architecture, he declared, as in all else, lay in proportion, the origin of which it might be said was divine; for did it not derive from the body of Adam which not only was shaped by divine hands but was made in the likeness and image of God? The difference between the male and female forms and proportions was the source of the various orders in architecture, and he added many other observations on the same subject, with which we are familiar.[13] [. . .]

6 October

[. . .] When we got back, M. Perrault had arrived. My brother was with us, as he had wished to be present. The Cavaliere opened the conversation by saying that he hoped the foundations would be ready by Saturday for the laying of the foundation stone. M. Perrault replied that the medals would not be ready by that day. The Cavaliere said they could be put under other stones, since he wished to leave by Tuesday as the weather was getting cold; as regards the foundation they should not have to excavate any lower than the foundations of the pavilion, "not more than that," he said, showing his spectacle case. M. Perrault replied that so far they had never had buildings subsiding in Paris. Then he brought forward a number of things on which he wanted enlightenment before the departure of the Cavaliere, all of which seemed trifling matters, such as the arrangement of quarters below, really the business of the maréchal des logis, as the Cavaliere said; it was quite enough if he made a plan for the *piano nobile*, as he had said in the beginning, when he and Signor Mattia were working on it, and he added to M. Perrault, "Every time there is a new pope all the apartments in the Vatican are rearranged, according to the wishes of the new papal officials who want everything changed to suit them." Then M. Perrault brought up the question of the arches in the façade towards the service courtyard, saying that there would be a difficulty in closing them. The Cavaliere took a pencil and showed him how it should be done. I repeated that these were all small difficulties about which there was no urgency; they could be settled in three or four years' time; anyway in the Queen Mother's new apartments there were similar arches for which shutters had been made. He replied that it had caused a lot of trouble. I repeated again that these were all little things that did not matter now, and that everything was clear on the plan. He then told me that he had a notebook with all the difficulties he wanted to bring forward. The Cavaliere had the plans brought in so that he could show him the problems. Whereupon he said there was one thing that required explaining; not only he himself but a hundred others wanted to know why that part of the new wing that runs along the riverside is shorter than the other, it being quite against the laws of symmetry, as each should be in relation to the cupola which is in the center of this façade.[14]

M. Perrault demonstrated what he meant, and from this and from the few words that he understood in spite of knowing little French, the Cavaliere realized he was talking about his work and suggesting there were faults in his design. He told two Italians, who were standing by, to leave the room. Then taking a pencil he said that if he had extended this pavilion to the line of the return of the main block of his façade, it would have been a great error of judgment; it was only necessary for this part of the pavilion to correspond with the other, although it was not so long. He would like M. Perrault to know that it was not for him to make difficulties; he was willing to listen to criticism in what concerned matters of convenience, but only someone cleverer than himself could be permitted to criticize the design; in this respect he was not fit to wipe his boots; anyway the matter did not arise as the designs had been passed by the King; he would complain to the King himself and was going now to M. Colbert to tell him how he had been insulted. M. Perrault, seeing what effect his words had had, was very much alarmed. He begged me to soothe the Cavaliere and to say that he had not wished to be critical of his work, but had merely wanted to have something to reply to those who raised this particular objection. I told the Cavaliere this and added that if he carried things so far, he would ruin the career of a young man, and I was sure that he would not wish to be the cause of his downfall. His son and M. Mattia, who were there, tried to calm him down but without success. He went into the next room saying at one moment he was going to M. Colbert, at the next, he would go to the Nuncio, and meanwhile M. Perrault was beseeching me to tell him that he had not intended to offend him. "To a man like me," the Cavaliere was saying, "whom the Pope treats with attention and to whom he even defers, such usage is a gross insult, and I shall complain of it to the King. If it costs me my life, I intend to leave tomorrow, and I see no reason after the contempt that has been shown me, why I should not take a hammer to the bust. I shall go to see the Nuncio." He seemed to be really going off, and I begged M. Mattia to stop him. He replied it would be better to let him unburden his heart; in the end, this would help to soothe him, and I could rely on him to handle the matter. Signor Paolo was also trying to make excuses for M. Perrault, who had besought him to do so, repeating that what he had said was not intended to offend him. Finally instead of going out they took him upstairs, and my brother and I accompanied M. Perrault as far as M. Colbert's. He said he was going to tell him about the outburst. I told him to be very guarded; it would be as well to know first whether the whole business could be hushed up; it would be better if he mentioned it to no one, and my brother and I would also keep quiet about it, which he entreated us to do.

NOTES

1   That is, one of the royal stewards responsible for serving the King's table.
2   Lomellini, Bailey of the Order of St. John of Jerusalem and Grand Prior of England, who entered Paris on 2 June and took leave of the King on 27 July.
3   Although the multiplication of offices during the minority of Louis XIV had greatly increased the number of stewards in the King's Household – there were 318 in 1660 – only twelve were normally in service during the year, three for each quarter.
4   Henri-Jules de Bourbon (1643–1709), duc d'Enghien, son of the Grand Condé, whom he succeeded as prince de Condé at the latter's death in 1686. From 1660, he was grand maître of France and, as head of the King's Household, was therefore Chantelou's superior.

5 Bernardin Gigault (1630–94), marquis de Bellefonds and Marshal of France (1668). As premier maître d'hôtel du roi (from 1663), he ranked immediately below the grand maître.

6 Jacques Sanguin (d. 1680), seigneur de Livry and, like Chantelou, a maître d'hôtel to the King. In 1676 Sanguin purchased from the marquis de Bellefonds the office of premier maître.

7 Charles-François Colbert (1629–96), later marquis de Croissy, Secretary of State for Foreign Affairs, and Minister of State, who appears in person later in the diary. Having a carriage drawn by six horses placed at his disposal was a mark of the honor being accorded Bernini, and Chantelou rarely forgets to give the number of horses whenever the coach is mentioned.

8 A village about 15 km. south of Paris on the road to Fontainebleau.

9 Paolo Valentino Bernini (1648–1728), trained as a sculptor by his father. Although he became a member of the Accademia di San Luca in 1672, he never seems to have been more than a mediocre artist, who is chiefly documented as an assistant to his father.

10 Mattia de' Rossi (1637–95), an architect and Bernini's longtime assistant to whom Leone Pascoli (*Vite de' pittori, scultori, ed architetti moderni*, Rome, 1730–31, 1, pp. 322–30) dedicated a biography. In 1661 *misuratore* of the Papal Camera, he succeeded Bernini as architect of St. Peter's (1680). In 1672 he became a member of the Accademia di San Luca, which he served as Principe in 1681 and from 1690 to 1693.

11 Roland, son of Jean Fréart de Chantelou, who later became a maître d'hôtel du roi (1675).

12 Chantelou, then secretary to Sublet de Noyers, had been sent to Rome in 1640, in part to bring Poussin back to France. In 1642–3 he was again in Rome, this time to get the Pope's blessing for the gifts being offered by the King and Queen to the Madonna di Loreto in gratitude for the unexpected birth of Louis XIV.

13 In fact, these first comments by Bernini on beauty and proportion repeat traditional Renaissance beliefs that had been formulated from both ancient and mediaeval ideas. See the now classic statements of E. Panofsky, "The History of the Theory of Human Proportions as a Reflection of the History of Styles," in *Meaning in the Visual Arts*, Garden City, NY, 1955, pp. 55–107, and R. Wittkower, *Architectural Principles in the Age of Humanism*, 2d ed., London, 1952. However, as will appear below, Bernini developed a typically Baroque interpretation of proportions on the basis of this inherited foundation.

14 This passage is not altogether easy to interpret, but it appears that Perrault was criticizing the fact that the river façade was not symmetrical, having a much larger pavilion on the right than on the left. Perrault's reference to the dome in the middle of the front is puzzling because in the elevation as engraved this would have disappeared. This almost suggests that even at this late stage Bernini was considering incorporating at least the central pavilion of Le Vau's river front.

26 FRANÇOIS BLONDEL
from "Inaugural Lecture to the Academy of Architecture" (1671)

T he young "Sun King" came into office in 1661 with a vision of himself as a monarch destined for greatness, and he saw France as a modern-day state fated to reign supreme in the arts and sciences. To this end Louis XIV and Colbert set about establishing royal academies to train the country's youth and provide them with the rudiments of greatness. The Academy of Painting and Sculpture was reformed in 1664 with a new constitution mandating formal courses of instruction. A French Academy in Rome was opened in 1666 to reward the most gifted students with advanced schooling. Academies in other fields were founded: Dance (1661), Inscriptions and Belles Lettres (1663), Sciences (1666), and Music (1669). The crowning jewel to this unparalleled educational system was the Royal Academy of Architecture, which opened its doors late in 1671.

The first director of the Academy of Architecture was the 53-year-old François Blondel. He had enjoyed a distinguished career as a military leader, diplomat, engineer, and mathematician, and had been elected to the Academy of Sciences. As the director of the Architectural Academy he was charged with writing a curriculum for the new school (codifying the principles of classical design in line with those taught in the other fine arts) and disseminating these principles to students in two weekly lectures. Vitruvian theory constituted the core of the teachings, but other treatises of the Renaissance could also be consulted on some issues. The perceived excesses of the baroque era were now officially condemned, and an undying faith in absolute beauty and harmonic proportions were other foundation stones of Blondel's academic teachings. His inaugural lecture of 1671 – a formal ceremonial address – itself contains little theory, but it nevertheless conveys the expectations for which the new institution was founded. The passage picks up as Blondel is assuring his student audience of the resources that the crown (both the King and Colbert) have put at their disposal and of the great tasks for which they are to be trained.

No one has had so many advantages or such means to succeed in this endeavor than will you. The King, through the magnitude of his virtue and his actions, fills your heart with vast and grand sentiments. His liberality frees you of those importune troubles that have traditionally plagued the unrelenting self-application that architecture demands.

He provides abundant resources through the quest for rare and precious materials, through the efforts of excellent workers, and by the choice of advantageous building sites. He spares nothing in putting you in a position to immortalize your designs.

Indeed, Messieurs, can we doubt the love that this Prince holds for architecture, when we consider that to oversee his buildings he has chosen this same genius to whom he has entrusted so wisely the most important affairs of the State.

And what fruit has architecture not received from the wisdom of this great man! (I am speaking of the Superintendent of Building) and of his laborious efforts to realize the glorious projects of our invincible Monarch?

François Blondel (1618–86), from "Discours prononcé par Mʳ Blondel a l'ouverture de l'Academie d'Architecture" [Inaugural lecture to the Academy of Architecture] (1671), published at the beginning of the first volume of his *Cours d'architecture* (Paris, 1675), trans. Harry Francis Mallgrave.

Has anyone ever seen building projects that are so grand and useful, so soon, and in so many places at the same time? Have we ever had so many resources and such art to employ in the defense of our frontiers? In the construction of quays and dikes to contain the river beds? In building bridges over rivers? In repairing provincial roads? In excavating ports and constructing sea jetties?

What can I say of that more benevolent enterprise, by this I mean the junctions of the sea, on which Colbert has so happily supported the designs of the King? I mean those naval dockyards at Rochefort, Brest, Marseilles, Toulon, and other places. They yield nothing to those that the Athenians formerly had at Port de Pyrée, nor to those that the Romans had at Ostia and Ravenna, nor even to those that are presently found in Venice, Holland, and Constantinople. What cannot be said, finally, of that prodigious naval fleet, which we have built up into such large numbers?

Is there anything more dazzling to see, anything more luxurious and more sumptuous than what has been made for the royal houses? Or in the admirable construction of that Arch of Triumph, which by the grandeur and magnificence of the work and by the quality of construction surely surpasses everything that has ever been made in this manner.

Messieurs, the viewpoint that I dare to convey in this course of instruction is founded on some of the experience that I have acquired by the study and practice of architecture over a long time. And by the opportunities to employ them, for which I have been honored by service to the crown in every part of the world, which has given me the chance to see and to examine almost every ancient and modern building of reputation in our hemisphere.

Let us therefore work, Messieurs, under so illustrious protection to merit the graces provided for us by the King, and to render ourselves worthy of the tasks for which his Majesty calls us. Let us confer together with good faith and sincerely communicate our ideas for the advancement of architecture. Because to be true architects, it is not enough to have a mediocre understanding of the rules of this excellent art; this qualification demands a conjunction of so many virtues and different kinds of knowledge that an entire lifetime is insufficient to acquire it.

Through our study, work, and manner of noble, generous, and unselfish devotion, let us restore the name of architecture to its ancient luster. And let us make known by our works that this beautiful art was with justice honored among the ancients, where it was held in a scarcely imaginable esteem as far back in time as the Sacred Books. God, after having made that horrible menace for his people to punish them for their impiety, stripped them of his wisdom and abandoned them to their folly; to add to their unhappiness, he even deprived them of their architects.

27 FRANÇOIS BLONDEL
from *Architecture Course* (1675)

The content of Blondel's lectures composed his *Cours d'architecture* (1675–83), which became the first architectural textbook of French academic theory. The director approached his task with a careful, comprehensive, and essentially conservative spirit, yet not in an excessively dogmatic way. As this opening page of the text shows, his definition of architecture and the architect's task was virtually indistinguishable from the conceptions of Vitruvius or Alberti.

Architecture is the art of building well. A good building is one that is solid, commodious, healthy, and pleasing. The first thing that the architect must do is to locate a proper site to place his building, the choice of which is made by good water, clean and pure air, a well-exposed site that is not subject to vapors and gases that render habitations unhealthy or infected. It is for the architect to dispose and to divide his particular spaces in such a way that the parts relate to each other with an agreeable proportion and justness, each being convenient and separated without encumbrance. He must know the nature of the terrain, the stone, wood, lime, and other materials, and employ them with such prudence and care that the foundations will be solid, the walls strong, the wood well-joined, and everything so well laid that nothing contradicts it. Then he must take care to embellish the facades of his building with ornaments that are proper and disposed with regard to the doors, windows, and other parts; in their arrangement they must please and satisfy the eyes that regard them.

28 RENÉ OUVRARD
from *Harmonic Architecture* (1677)

Another aspect of Blondel's teachings was the Neo-Platonic notion – also favored in the Italian Renaissance – that beauty derives principally from proportions, and that architectural proportions, like musical tonalities, emanate from and must reflect the cosmic order of numbers and ratios. This old idea of "harmonic proportions" for architecture was reaffirmed for the French academic system by this book of René Ouvrard. This Oratorian priest was both a friend of Blondel and a music master at Sainte Chapelle, and he was apparently encouraged by the architectural director to write a discourse on this aspect of architectural theory – as Blondel in his textbook refers his students to it. Ouvrard's insistence on the infallibility of these rules was perhaps stated more

François Blondel, from *Cours d'architecture: enseigné dans l'Academie Royale d'Architecture* [Architecture course: instruction at the Royal Academy of Architecture] (Paris: The Author, 1675), trans. Harry Francis Mallgrave.

René Ouvrard (1624–94), from *Architecture harmonique, ou application de la doctrine des proportions de la musique à l'architecture* [Harmonic architecture, or the application of the doctrine of musical proportions to architecture] (1677), trans. Christina Contandriopoulos and Harry Francis Mallgrave, from *La theorie architecturale à l'age classique*, ed. Françoise Fichet, Paris: Pierre Mardaga, 1979, pp. 176–8.

strongly than Blondel himself would do, and they allow the architect no leeway in making "optical adjustments," as Vitruvius had permitted. It is nevertheless a succinct pronouncement of this important cornerstone of academic theory that would later come under strong attack.

There is no precept more universal in the arts than that which prescribes proportion, symmetry, and fitness (or ratio) for the different parts of the same body – and this is especially true in architecture. The masters of this art did not fail to rank this precept among the foremost rules, as Vitruvius did at the beginning of book 1, chapter 22, and in book 3, chapter 1.

But even if architects say that they have to imitate the natural proportions that have been so exactly observed in the fabric of the human body, they seem to heed these rules in practice only in an arbitrary way, as something dependent on the wishes of the designer and not on the principles of art. In effect, when they want to put these rules into use, they have employed other measures and have not regarded the harmony of proportions.

We assume the contrary – that there is an analogy between the proportions of music and architecture, that what displeases the ear in the first art offends the eye in the second art, and that a building cannot be perfect if it does not follow the same rules as composition or the harmonizing of musical chords.

To understand this claim, we must presume here the law of proportions [. . .] of which we will present the basics for those who have not studied this matter [. . .] It is enough to know that all harmonies or possible consonances are contained in the proportional values of the first six numbers, or in multiples of these first six numbers. [. . .]

Those who have not heard of the ratio of proportional numbers with musical sounds may have trouble understanding, for example, that the octave is in the proportion of 1:2, the fifth in the proportion of 2:3. In a few words here, let us say that these proportions have been rendered visible on the instrument called the monochord, where we see that a chord being shortened by one-half makes a sound to the ear one octave higher than the chord at full length. Or that putting one part of the same chord against two other parts creates an octave, while putting two parts of the same chord against three of its parts makes a fifth. Thus we have a right to say that the proportions of an octave are 1:2, and that those of a fifth are 1:3. Similarly, to get the proportion of the fourth, one must divide the chord into seven equal parts, putting three one side and four on the other. And the three parts against the four will make us hear the fourth, because its proportions are 3:4. [. . .]

And just as in music all sounds that are not of these proportions or that do not have these ratios are disagreeable and offensive to the ear, we assume also in architecture that all the dimensions or measures that are not of these proportions, or that do not have these ratios, will offend the eye for lack of agreement. [. . .]

In order to complete this comparison of the sensations of the two senses, it is important to know that in music only the sounds that play together or that one hears at the same time must accord and make a harmony with the others, and not those that follow after or that are not heard at the same time. Similarly in architecture, that which presents itself to the eye at the same time must have these proportions – for example, the casements or windows on a building's facade, or the height and width of the same facade, or at least of each story.

However, sight embraces many more things simultaneously than one is able to hear, and it can perceive simultaneously all the parts of a building's facade. If all of these parts together have their proportions in the ratios that we have said will create a harmony, then the building would be charming and its beauty would make itself felt.

Nevertheless, it is vital that the height and length of the same part have harmonic proportion, that is to say, one of those ratios mentioned above. And if, as we said, all the parts presented from a single vantage point were to have concordant proportions, even if there were no other ornaments, the viewer would sense charms that could even be represented to the ear, as we will see. [...]

29 CLAUDE PERRAULT
annotations to French translation of *The Ten Book of Architecture of Vitruvius* (1673)

A s Blondel was taking control of the architectural curriculum, he would soon be confronted by someone who would directly undermine the academic teachings that he was putting forth. Only a few years earlier, Claude Perrault – the older brother of Colbert's personal secretary Charles – would have been an unlikely opponent. Up to the middle of the 1660s this Cartesian scientist had paid little attention to architecture, and in fact had made his reputation as a surgeon and anatomist, with further interests in botany, geology, mechanics, and physics. Two events would redirect his efforts toward architecture. Sometime toward the end of 1666 Colbert, acting on behalf of Louis XIV, commissioned Perrault to prepare a new French translation of Vitruvius – a project whose completion was no doubt planned for the opening of the Royal Academy of Architecture, where it was to serve as a textbook. In the spring of 1667 Perrault was also appointed to a three-man committee in charge of preparing another design for the east wing of the Louvre, work on which had been suspended since Bernini's departure. Although Perrault joined Louis Le Vau (still the king's first architect) and Charles Le Brun (the king's first painter) on the committee, he later had no qualms about claiming complete credit for the final design of 1668.

The new building of the Louvre was altogether unique within French classical architecture. Instead of a palatial design with load-bearing walls fortified with pilasters (as Bernini had designed), Perrault and the other committee members proposed a colonnaded main story along the eastern front, with the exterior wall recessed behind. The colonnade was also unique in that columns were not regularly spaced but grouped in pairs with a larger spacing between each group – against any accepted antique precedent. An innovative system of iron reinforcing bars (concealed in the columns and ceiling) was also devised (probably by Perrault) to tie the Corinthian colonnade to the recessed wall and entablature; the effect was one of overall lightness and unusually thin visual proportions.

Perrault provided the rationale for the design in a footnote that appeared in his translation of Vitruvius – one of the most important documents of all architectural theory. Throughout the text and in other notes he had repeatedly stressed the flexibility of Vitruvius and his openness to innovation and change. In the particular passage to which this note was attached – where Vitruvius lauds the Hellenistic architect Hermogenes for the innovation of removing the

Claude Perrault (1613–88), annotations to French translation of *Les dix livres d'architecture de Vitruve* [Ten books of architecture of Vitruvius]. Paris: Coignard, 1673, trans. Harry Francis Mallgrave and Christina Contandriopoulos.

inner row of the double range of columns of a dipteral temple (Book 3, ch. 3) — Perrault seizes the occasion to demand the same freedom for French architects. His reference to "a little of the Gothic" in the Louvre design refers not to the decorative or formal language of Gothic architecture, but rather to the structural and visual lightness of Gothic churches. This particular footnote in effect instigates the seventeenth-century quarrel between the "Ancients" and "Moderns." Perrault now defines the "Modern" position, while Blondel will respond by defending the "Ancients."

The taste of our century, or at least of our nation, is different from that of the ancients and perhaps it has a little of the Gothic in it, because we love the air, the daylight, and openness (*dégagemens*). Thus we have invented a sixth manner of disposing of columns, which is to group them in pairs and separate each pair with two intercolumniations. [. . .]

This has been done in imitation of Hermogenes, who in the Eustyle enlarged the middle intercolumniation because it was too narrow for the temple's entrance, and also opened up the Dipteral arrangement, which was choked by the confusion of the two ranges of crowded columns. He invented the Pseudodipteral, eliminating one of the two aisles that the two ranges of columns formed with the wall surrounding the temple. What he did by removing a range of columns in each aisle, we do within a colonnade by removing a column from the middle of two columns and pushing it toward the adjacent column. This manner could be called the Pseudosystyle, by analogy with Hermogenes's Pseudodipteral, or Araeosystyle, because the spacing of some columns is stretched as in the Araeostyle, while others are close together as in the Systyle. Several disapprove of this manner because it has not been authorized by the Ancients. But it is permitted to add something to the inventions of the Ancients by following their example. For if Hermogenes was not faulted for having changed something in architecture, and for not having strictly observed all the precepts of those who preceded him, we can argue that this new manner should not be rejected because it alone has all the advantages that the others have only separately. Because in addition to the beauty of the lively aspect and the ranging of columns that the Ancients liked so much, it has the openness that the moderns look for without sacrificing solidity. Because the single stone of the Ancients' architrave spanning between columns rested only on half a column, it lacked strength. When, however, the architrave lies on a whole column and both the beams and columns are doubled, they have greater strength to support the floors.

This manner has been used with great magnificence on the two large porticos of the Louvre facade [. . .]

30 FRANÇOIS BLONDEL
from *Architecture Course*, Vol. II (1683)

Perrault's insistence on the freedom of modern-day architects to depart from antique precedent certainly called for academic clarification, but Blondel did not respond immediately. When this passage and Perrault's footnote were read at the Architectural Academy in December 1674 (as part of a reading of the entire book), it passed without any comment. But as the Louvre advanced in stages of construction and Perrault became more prominent within the looming debate, a response became imperative. It took the form of an extended censure of Perrault's argument in part III of Blondel's *Cours d'architecture*, which was published in 1683. Blondel, over three entire chapters, contested Perrault on nearly every point. Although an engineer, he was suspicious of the reinforcing iron that had been used in the Louvre colonnade, because the ancients did not have to rely on such contrivances. He questioned the structural advantage of the paired-column solution, and also noted that the Ancients, who knew how to build well, did not resort to such inventions. But his greatest anger was directed to Perrault's almost casual remark that modern-day sensibilities had "a little of the Gothic" in them. Here, he felt, Perrault had clearly crossed the line: not only by departing from antique or Renaissance precedent, but also by invoking false architectural tendencies as a justification for his departure. Blondel believed that the proportions of modern architecture must conform to those of classical times, while the extremely light proportions of the Gothic style should never be emulated. Innovation might be allowed but only in the rarest of circumstances and by an architect of undisputed genius.

I have nothing to say of that love for daylight and openness that he attributes to our nation, because we can admit at the same time that it [our love] still partakes of the Gothic, and in this it is indeed very different from the taste of the Ancients. And when it is said that we must also be allowed to add to the inventions of the Ancients, as Hermogenes was allowed to add to the practices of those who had preceded him, I respond that there is nothing truer. Without doubt it is for the Hermogeneses of the world to produce bold new ideas in every century; they are entitled to correct the defects of others, and their inventions become infallible rules for posterity.

It is also very true that this same reasoning has opened the door at all times to the disorder that is found in architecture and in the other arts. We have almost no workers who do not have a rather good opinion of themselves and who do not believe that they are as equally talented as Hermogenes. Gothic architects only filled their edifices with such impertinences because they believed it was permitted to add to the inventions of the Greeks and Romans. And those ridiculous cartouches, those colorful grotesques, and those extravagant ornaments that are still so pleasing to German [Gothic] architects, in addition to the great scorn that they had for the legitimate measures of the parts of architecture – all came from the conviction that they had as much right to produce novelties and add to the practices of the Ancients as the Ancients had had in creating theirs, and adding to those that had been created by the architects who had preceded them. This would lead me to state unequivocally that necessity requires one to submit oneself to certain rules and stop being capricious if one wants to reestablish beautiful architecture – if this reasoning has not be treated at greater length in another place.

François Blondel, from *Cours d'architecture*, Vol. II (1683), trans. Harry Francis Mallgrave from 1698 Paris edition, part III, p. 235.

31 CLAUDE PERRAULT

from *The Ten Book of Architecture of Vitruvius*, second edition (1684)

Perrault, a Cartesian skeptic and rationalist, wasted little time in joining the battle, now along several fronts. His most succinct response was an expanded footnote to the second edition of his translation of Vitruvius. The nature of the response is again fascinating. On the one hand, he insists that a blind adherence to antique ways would effectively halt all modern innovations (he was a scientist); on the other hand he almost proudly accepts the taint of Blondel's Gothic slur. These were serious words and it would take French theory more than a century to extricate itself from the dilemma posed in these remarks. Entirely new is the argument regarding Gothic structural efficiency, that is, the interior openness and greater daylight allowed by the more slender interior pillars.

Monsieur Blondel in his learned *Leçons d'architecture*, from which he has composed his *Cours*, employs three entire chapters, which are 10, 11, and 12 of the first book of part three, to show that the universal usage seen today for doubling columns is a license that must not be tolerated [...]

The principal objection upon which he leans the most is founded on prejudice and on the false assumption that it is not permitted to depart from the practices of the Ancients, that everything which does not imitate their manners must be bizarre and capricious, and that if this rule is not inviolably protected the door is opened to license, which leads the arts into disorder. But just as this reasoning proves too much it cannot prove anything at all, because it is much more disadvantageous to close the door to beautiful inventions than to open it to those that are so ridiculous that they will destroy themselves. If this rule were in effect, architecture would never have appeared at the time at which we take the inventions of the Ancients, which were new in their time. And it would not be necessary to search for new means to acquire the understanding that we lack, and that we acquire every day in agriculture, navigation, medicine, and the other arts, for the perfection on which the Ancients had worked. [...]

But the greatest reproach that he makes against our Pseudosystyle is to say that it resembles the Gothic. I might hesitate to agree with this fact in my note, but assuming that the Gothic in general (and taking into account everything that composes it) is not the most beautiful style of architecture, I do not think everything in the Gothic must be rejected. The daylight in their buildings and the openness that results are things in which the Gothic people are different from the Ancients, but they are not something for which the Gothic is to be disdained.

Claude Perrault, from *Les dix livres d'architecture de Vitruve* [Ten books of architecture of Vitruvius], second edition (Paris, 1684), pp. 79–80, trans. Harry Francis Mallgrave.

32 CLAUDE PERRAULT

from *Ordonnance for the Five Kinds of Columns after the Method of the Ancients* (1683)

Perrault did not limit his attack on academic authority to the issues thus far noted. A few months before the second edition of his translation of Vitruvius appeared, he published his own architectural treatise relating to the proportioning of column orders. The book grew out of a problem long known to Renaissance architects and raised again by Fréart de Chambray — namely, that architects in both antiquity and in the Renaissance had worked with proportional ratios that were almost never the same. Even the Academy recognized this problem. In 1674 Colbert sent a talented young student, Antoine Desgodetz (1653–1728), to Rome with the missions of making a comprehensive measurement of the principal Roman monuments, in the hope that some classical system might be found. The trip started badly, as Desgodetz and his traveling companion were immediately kidnapped by pirates; yet once ransomed, and after three years of labor, they returned home with disappointing results. No system had been found and, moreover, the measurements published by such notable writers as Serlio and Palladio were filled with errors.

The findings no doubt intrigued the skeptical Perrault. In response, he came up with the "scientific" solution to the problem by collecting the columnar ratios used on buildings in antiquity and Renaissance times, and then calculating the proportional or numerical mean between the extremes. These "mediocre" or average numbers, he argued, should then be accepted by the Academy and all architects should work within their strict limits.

Underlying such a system, however, were two premises that flouted academic theory. First Perrault argued there were no such things as harmonic ratios; that is to say, the eye and ear function on a physiological level in very different ways when perceiving visual and audible harmonies. Second, he insisted that proportions were by no means absolute, but were rather based on custom or habit. He also modified classical theory by suggesting that there were two types of beauty: "positive" and "arbitrary." The former relates only to obvious beauties upon which everyone can agree, such as symmetry, the magnificence of a building, its quality of execution. The latter is a matter of custom, and here — in the realm of relative beauty — is where proportions reside.

The Ancients rightly believed that the proportional rules that give buildings their beauty were based on the proportions of the human body and that just as nature has suited a massive build to bodies made for physical labor while giving a slighter one to those requiring adroitness and agility, so in the art of building, different rules are determined by the different intentions to make a building more massive or more delicate. Now these different proportions together with their appropriate ornaments are what give rise to the different architectural orders, whose characters, defined by variations in ornament, are what distinguish them most visibly but whose most essential differences consist in the relative size of their constituent parts.

Claude Perrault, from *Ordonnance des cinq espèces de colonnes selon la méthode des Anciens* (1683), trans. Indra Kagin McEwen, in *Ordonnance for the Five Kinds of Columns after the Method of the Ancients*. Santa Monica: Getty Publications Program, 1993, pp. 47–8, 49, 50–1. © 1993 by Getty Publications. Reprinted with permission of Getty Publications.

These differences between the orders that are based, with little exactitude or precision, on their proportions and characters are the only well-established matters in architecture. Everything else pertaining to the precise measurement of their members or the exact outline of their profiles still has no rule on which all architects agree; each architect has attempted to bring these elements to their perfection chiefly through the things that proportion determines. As a result, in the opinion of those who are knowledgeable, a number of architects have approached an equal degree of perfection in different ways. This shows that the beauty of a building, like that of the human body, lies less in the exactitude of unvarying proportion and the relative size of constituent parts than in the grace of its form, wherein nothing other than a pleasing variation can sometimes give rise to a perfect and matchless beauty without strict adherence to any proportional rule. A face can be both ugly and beautiful without any change in proportions, so that an alteration of the features – for example, the contraction of the eyes and the enlargement of the mouth – can be the same when one laughs as when one weeps, with a result that can be pleasing in one case and repugnant in the other; whereas, the dissimilar proportions of two different faces can be equally beautiful. Likewise, in architecture, we see works whose differing proportions nevertheless have the grace to elicit equal approval from those who are knowledgeable and possessed of good taste in architectural matters.

One must agree, however, that although no single proportion is indispensable to the beauty of a face, there still remains a standard from which its proportion cannot stray too far without destroying its perfection. Similarly, in architecture, there are not only general rules of proportion, such as those that, as we have said, distinguish one order from another, but also detailed rules from which one cannot deviate without robbing an edifice of much of its grace and elegance. Yet these proportions have enough latitude to leave architects free to increase or decrease the dimensions of different elements according to the requirements occasioned by varying circumstances. It is this prerogative that caused the Ancients to create works with proportions as unusual as those of the Doric and Ionic cornices of the Theater of Marcellus or the cornice of the Facade of Nero, which are all half again as large as they should be according to the rules of Vitruvius. It is also for this very reason that all those who have written about architecture contradict one another, with the result that in the ruins of ancient buildings and among the great number of architects who have dealt with the proportions of the orders, one can find agreement neither between any two buildings nor between any two authors, since none has followed the same rules.

This shows just how ill-founded is the opinion of people who believe that the proportions supposed to be preserved in architecture are as certain and invariable as the proportions that give musical harmony its beauty and appeal, proportions that do not depend on us but that nature has established with absolutely immutable precision and that cannot be changed without immediately offending even the least sensitive ear. For if this were so, those works of architecture that do not have the true and natural proportions that people claim they can have would necessarily be condemned by common consensus, at least by those whom extensive knowledge has made most capable of such discernment. And just as we never find musicians holding different opinions on the correctness of a chord, since this correctness has a certain and obvious beauty of which the senses are readily and even necessarily convinced, so would we also find architects agreeing on the rules capable of perfecting the proportions of architecture, especially when, after repeated efforts, they had apparently explored all the many possible avenues to attaining such perfection. [...]

But we cannot claim that the proportions of architecture please our sight for unknown reasons or make the impression they do of themselves in the same way that musical harmonies affect the ear without our knowing the reasons for their consonance. Harmony, consisting in the awareness gained through our ears of that which is the result of the proportional relationship of two strings, is quite different from the knowledge gained through our eyes of that which results from the proportional relationship of the parts that make up a column. For if, through our ears, our minds [esprit] can be touched by something that is the result of the proportional relationship of two strings without our minds being aware of this relationship, it is because the ear is incapable of giving the mind such intellectual knowledge. But the eye, which can convey knowledge of the proportion it makes us appreciate, makes the mind experience its effect through the knowledge it conveys of this proportion and only through this knowledge. From this it follows that what pleases the eye cannot be due to a proportion of which the eye is unaware, as is usually the case. [...]

In order to judge rightly in this case, one must suppose two kinds of beauty in architecture and know which beauties are based on convincing reasons and which depend only on prejudice. I call beauties based on convincing reasons those whose presence in works is bound to please everyone, so easily apprehended are their value and quality. They include the richness of the materials, the size and magnificence of the building, the precision and cleanness of the execution, and symmetry, which in French signifies the kind of proportion that produces an unmistakable and striking beauty. For there are two kinds of proportion. One, difficult to discern, consists in the proportional relationship between parts, such as that between the size of various elements, either with respect to one another or to the whole, of which an element may be, for instance, a seventh, fifteenth, or twentieth part. The other kind of proportion, called symmetry, is very apparent and consists in the relationship the parts have collectively as a result of the balanced correspondence of their size, number, disposition, and order. We never fail to perceive flaws in this proportion, such as on the interior of the Pantheon where the coffering of the vault, in failing to line up with the windows below, causes a disproportion and lack of symmetry that anyone may readily discern, and which, had it been corrected, would have produced a more visible beauty than that of the proportion between the thickness of the walls and the temple's interior void, or in other proportions that occur in this building, such as that of the portico, whose width is three-fifths the exterior diameter of the whole temple.

Against the beauties I call positive and convincing, I set those I call arbitrary, because they are determined by our wish to give a definite proportion, shape, or form to things that might well have a different form without being misshapen and that appear agreeable not by reasons within everyone's grasp but merely by custom and the association the mind makes between two things of a different nature. By this association the esteem that inclines the mind to things whose worth it knows also inclines it to things whose worth it does not know and little by little induces it to value both equally. This principle is the natural basis for belief, which is nothing but the result of a predisposition not to doubt the truth of something we do not know if it is accompanied by our knowledge and good opinion of the person who assures us of it. It is also prejudice that makes us like the fashions and the patterns of speech that custom has established at court, for the regard we have for the worthiness and patronage of people in the court makes us like their clothing and their way of speaking, although these things in themselves have nothing positively likable, since after a time they offend us without their having undergone any inherent change.

33   JEAN-FRANÇOIS FÉLIBIEN
from Preface to *Historical Survey of the Life and Works of the Most Celebrated Architects* (1687)

In raising the issue of Gothic architecture with respect to the design of the Louvre, Perrault introduced an entirely new element into classical theory – that of structural innovation. He did so not in an accidental way, for on a trip to Bordeaux in 1669 (which he made to examine some Roman-Gallic works) he was struck by the comparative structural efficiencies of several Gothic churches, in particular the thinness and visual lightness of what he termed the *"l'ordre gothique."* This appreciation of Gothic architecture was alien to the classical theory of the Renaissance, which of course regarded the Middle Ages as a period of darkness and artistic barbarity. Slowly this attitude would change. An early sign of this reassessment is the fourth book of the historical survey of Jean-François Félibien, the son of the first secretary to the Architectural Academy, André Félibien. The young architect first distinguishes between the *gothique ancien* and the *gothique moderne*, roughly coinciding with the Romanesque and Gothic periods. Like Perrault, he also appreciates the structural efficiency of the latter, although he terms it "a rather grand excess of delicacy." Such an appraisal prepares the ground for more serious studies of Gothic architecture, which in France will almost always focus on its structural efficiency.

Finally, the fourth book is almost entirely devoted to what one has been able to learn of the particulars related to the architects who appeared in Italy and France from the beginning of the eleventh century until the end of the fourteenth century, and who built most of the ancient churches and the other edifices that are called Gothic or modern.

I felt the need to say something of the different manners of building as the occasion presented itself, that is to say, of the antique manner that was used among the ancient Greeks and Romans, and the Gothic manner, which one assumes to have been introduced by the Goths. The Saracens as well had a particular taste that one calls Arabesque, because in fact the Arabs seem to have been the principal authors.

Antique architecture is nothing other than that of which Vitruvius and his interpreters have spoken. With regard to Gothic buildings, there are no authors who have given any rules: but we notice two kinds of Gothic buildings: ancient and modern. The more ancient have nothing more commendable than their solidity and grandeur. As for the modern, they are of a taste so opposed to that of the ancient Goths, that one can say those who made them

Jean-François Félibien (1658–1733), from Preface to *Recueil historique de la vie et des ouvrages des plus célebres architectes* [Historical survey of the life and works of the most celebrated architects] (1687). Paris: Sebastien Mabre-Cramoisy, trans. Harry Francis Mallgrave.

have applied a rather grand excess of delicacy that equals the ancient's extreme heaviness and coarseness, particularly with regard to the ornaments. It is not difficult to find in France and many other places examples of these two kinds of architecture.

34 CHARLES PERRAULT
from Preface to *Parallel of the Ancients and the Moderns with Regard to the Arts and Sciences* (1688)

The first round of the quarrel of the "Ancients" and "Moderns," exemplified by the dispute between Blondel and Perrault, ended in 1686 with the death of Blondel. Perrault would follow him into posterity in 1688 – like the conscientious scientist that he was – from a fatal infection incurred while dissecting a camel. He was thus still alive to witness the second and better known round of the quarrel that exploded on the afternoon of January 27, 1687, when his brother Charles had his poem, "The Century of Louis the Great," read before a general assembly of the French Academy. The poem, in which Charles lauded the artistic deeds of Louis XIV and compared them favorably with those of the Age of Augustus, created an uproar within the Academy. A contentious debate ensued within literary circles, with Nicolas Boileau-Despreaux, among others, defending the honor of the Ancients.

Charles Perrault, who between 1662 and 1682 had been the personal secretary to Colbert, had held a number of prestigious and influential academic positions. He was a writer of considerable esteem, and in fact wrote many of the fairytales later collected by the Grimm brothers. Charles responded to his critics on this occasion with a four-part Socratic dialogue, *Parallel of the Ancients and the Moderns* (1688–97), in which he remained adamant in defending the right of his age to create its own art apart from the sanction of the past. His central theme is that his era had not only equaled the achievements of antiquity and the Renaissance, but (as progress in the sciences had shown) had even surpassed them.

Nothing is more natural or reasonable than to show the utmost veneration for whatever is possessed of true merit in itself and has the additional merit of age. This sentiment, so right, proper and universal, redoubles the respect that we feel for our ancestors; by virtue of it, laws and customs show themselves still more authoritative and inviolable. But destiny has always decreed that the best things become prejudicial by excess, and this in proportion to their original excellence. Honourable in its inception, this reverence has subsequently become a criminal superstition, at times extending even to idolatry. Princes of extraordinary virtue secured the happiness of their people, and the earth resounded to the fame of their exploits; they were beloved in their lifetime and their memory was revered by posterity. But as time went by, people forgot that these were mere men, and began to offer them incense and sacrifice. The same thing happened to those who first excelled in the arts and sciences.

Charles Perrault (1628–1703), from Preface to *Parallèle des anciens et des modernes en ce qui regarde les arts et les sciences* [Parallel of the ancients and the moderns with regard to the arts and sciences] (1688), trans. Christopher Miller from *Parallèle des anciens et des modernes*, Vol. 1 (Paris: Jean-Baptiste Coignard, 1688) and published in *Art in Theory 1648–1815: An Anthology of Changing Ideas*, ed. Charles Harrison, Paul Wood, and Jason Gaiger. Oxford: Blackwell, 2000. Translation © 2000 by Christopher Miller. Reprinted with permission of Christopher Miller.

The prestige that accrued to their century, and the utility that it derived from their inventions, brought them much glory and renown in their own lifetimes, and their works were admired by posterity, which made of them its greatest delight, and celebrated them in praises boundless and immoderate. Respect for their memory so increased that no taint of human weakness could be attributed to them, and their very faults were deemed sacred. A thing had only to be done or said by these great men to become incomparable, and even today, for certain scholars it is a sort of religion to prefer the least production of the Ancients to the finest works of any modern author. I confess to a sense of injury at this injustice; there seems to me such blind prejudice and ingratitude in the refusal to open one's eyes to the beauty of our century, on which heaven has bestowed a thousand distinctions altogether refused to Antiquity, that I have been unable to restrain a sense of veritable indignation. Of this indignation came the little poem, *The Century of Louis the Great*, which was read to the French Academy when it assembled to thank the Lord for the complete recovery of its august protector. All those present at that illustrious assembly seemed quite satisfied with it, save two or three fanatical admirers of Antiquity, who asserted that it had greatly offended them. It was hoped that their discomfiture might give rise to criticisms such as would disabuse the public; but their sense of offence has boiled away in protest at my attack, and in empty and ill-defined words. [. . .]

So many honourable persons have informed me, with a most tactful and gracious air, that I had, in their eyes, ably defended a bad cause, that I have taken it upon me to state unequivocally, and in prose, that there is nothing in my poem that is not seriously intended. That I am, in short, utterly convinced that, excellent as the Ancients are – on this point there is no disagreement – the Moderns are no whit inferior, and indeed surpass them in many respects. This is a clear statement of my position, which I claim to demonstrate in my dialogues.

35 CHARLES PERRAULT
from "Design of a Portal for the Church of Sainte-Geneviève in Paris" (1697)

In the mid-1670s both Charles and Claude Perrault were involved with a proposal to renovate and enlarge the church of Saint Geneviève in Paris, for which Claude made several drawings. Claude had worked out the structural problems for the colonnade of the Louvre, and at Saint Geneviève he proposed an iron-reinforced colonnaded system for the front porch and nave of the church. For the entrance he sketched – instead of arches – a free-standing colonnade supporting an uninterrupted flat entablature. For the interior, he proposed rows of columns supporting the central nave walls with a false ceiling-vault above. Once again his proposal defied contemporary structural beliefs. Many Christian basilicas and early Renaissance churches had columns between the nave and side

Charles Perrault, from the memorandum "Dessin d'un portail pour l'Église de Sainte-Geneviève à Paris" [Design of a portal for the church of Sainte-Geneviève in Paris] (1697), trans. Harry Francis Mallgrave from *Bulletin monumental*, 115:2 (1957), pp. 94–6.

aisles, but they also had timber roofs. These roofs were both lighter and the lateral forces could be negated by (truss) triangulation. When Alberti, for instance, chose to vault the central nave of Sant' Andrea in Mantua in 1470, he resorted to a series of massive piers and side chapels to resist the lateral (outward) thrust of the vault. Gothic architects had earlier solved the problem by adding flying buttresses to the outside of churches.

The two Perrault brothers, as this memorandum says, believed the problem could be solved by employing the reinforced masonry system that had been used at the Louvre. The use of a tall, slender colonnade (as opposed to heavy piers) recalls Claude's earlier footnote to the translation of Vitruvius, where he notes France's love of daylight and spatial openness. The cited passage begins as Charles Perrault explains how the iron rods were designed at the Louvre. The memorandum was only published in 1957.

If the peristyle of the Louvre were not built, and in a manner more solid than any building in the world, it would be necessary to respond to all of the objections that people made to my brother and myself on the virtual impossibility of having ceilings supported only on columns. We have also been told that it is beautiful in painting but impossible in reality. We no longer fear these objections. The 12-foot ceilings that stand at the Louvre are sufficient for the ceilings of 8 feet that we propose. But because construction might be postponed for a long time and because there are only a few workers left from that time who fully possess this knowledge, I feel obliged to mention here what must be observed in the construction of these peristyles. The drums that compose the shafts of the columns must be pierced for two-thirds the height of the column, and an iron bar from Normandy, two or two-and-a-half inches square, should be placed inside them. This bar must extend above the capital by a foot or a foot-and-a-half, or there about, where its end is looped by another bar of the same thickness, which crosses over to the wall opposite through and through, where it is tied into the church by an iron anchor, which either descends or runs the length of the wall. There should be another transverse bar of the same size as the other that ties the column diagonally to the opposite wall.

[. . .] The peristyle of the Louvre is a beautiful example. It will be good before covering the bars with the second stone course to apply two or three coats of oil to protect them against rust.

36   MICHEL DE FRÉMIN
from *Critical Memoirs of Architecture* (1702)

It did not take long for Perrault's admiration for Gothic structural efficiency to find its way into public discourse, although it is still surprising that the debate was first raised outside, rather than within, the academy's walls. This small tract written by a little-known builder, financial administrator, and engineer, is an interesting interpretation of the argument. Frémin chose the format of 48 (somewhat salty) letters, he tells us at the start of his book, so that his argument can be understood even by people "a little short on intelligence." He eschews the

Michel de Frémin (c. 1631–1713), from *Mémoires critiques d'architecture* [Critical memoirs on architecture] (1702), trans. Christina Contandriopoulos and Harry Francis Mallgrave from a facsimile edition published by Gregg Press, Farnborough, 1967, pp. 26–8, 30–1, 33–4, 37.

idea that architecture is simply a matter of applying columns, and his architectural concerns are largely with practical issues. He makes, however, some very compelling points in his sixth letter, when he compares two Gothic churches (Notre-Dame and Sainte-Chapelle) with two hybrid Gothic/Classical churches (St. Eustache and St. Sulpice). The interior of the two former churches, where the supports are slender Gothic piers, are both spacious in plan and filled with interior daylight. The two latter churches, begun in 1532 and 1645 respectively, are by contrast dark, poorly ventilated, and difficult to move about or find lateral sightlines in because of their massive structural piers. This criticism effectively posed a challenge to architects, as Frémin, like Perrault before him, was not suggesting a return to Gothic forms but rather to lighter proportions for church interiors. The challenge had actually been taken up in part in 1698 by Jules Hardouin Mansart, in his design for the chapel at Versailles; here he employed heavy piers and arcades on the ground story, but at the second level (where the king sat) Mansart used widely spaced Corinthian columns that supported a straight entablature and vaulted ceiling. In this case the ceiling was plaster, not stone, but still he was forced to strengthen his classical work outside with flying buttresses.

Among the public works that are in Paris, I will choose to examine the churches of Nôtre-Dame, Saint Chapelle, Saint Eustache, and Saint Sulpice. [...]

In the building Nôtre-Dame [...] What does this architect do? Respecting the future, he makes a large nave and doubles the floor area by the galleries. With regard to the harmony of the choir, which becomes fuller and more melodious when sound is concentrated, he reduces the vaults of the side aisle relative to their need for light, and in this way he enlarges the high crossing and thereby multiplies the overall daylight. For the spectacle of the Sacrifice, he narrows his pillars to a moderate dimension; he rounds them so as not to block the view by the angles, as they are when the piers are square.

* * *

I will speak of Sainte Chapelle. Again it is a model of true architecture, that is to say, it is a work where the prudent planning of the architect has furnished a number of lessons for building private chapels. This building in its genre is one of the most convenient and most intelligent that there is in Paris. [...]

He makes large windows, knowing that the glass will be painted and that the colors that one will put there will darken the room. He determines that the windows need to be enlarged, so that by the shape of the openings more daylight would come in and it would be brighter. He makes small piers in order to increase the light, thus he treated his work according to the objective and according to the place. He does not fear that gales of wind would come to knock down his work; the buttressing piers assure against this. [...]

This is what I call good and sound architecture, and with the idea that I set out for you, it will be easier to judge works of the same kind. But in order to judge bad architecture, let us take, as I said, the examples of Saint Eustache and Saint Sulpice, whose construction is quite different from the church of Nôtre-Dame and that of the Bernadins. In the mass of piers that are in Saint Eustache, you will find a crudeness that – despite the charity that one must have for one's neighbor – stirs up ill-feeling toward the architect who made the design. What dreadful stiltedness in the vaults of the side aisles, by means of which the crossings of the high vaults are reduced to simple braces! What an enormous mass of stone in the first piers that support the organs, for which more than half of the ground area is taken up by stonework! [. . .]

* * *

Saint Sulpice is another kind of false architecture, which along with Saint-Eustache proves that the massing or piling up of stones do not make a building. It is surprising to see the extent of the distrust of our architects for what they build nowadays. If, as at the church of Petits Pères or at the chapel of. . . they pile up entire quarries in order to support a small pedestal, then tremble lest the work will collapse when they remove their hands. This prejudice is so great and so widespread that as soon as you propose to do any delicate work, you will immediately be assailed by a group of masons who will denounce you. [. . .]

37   JEAN-LOUIS DE CORDEMOY
from *New Treatise on Architecture or the Art of Building* (1706, 1714)

Jean-Louis de Cordemoy was the son of a Cartesian philosopher and historian, and a canon at the church of Saint Jean des Vignes in Soissons. He seems to have had no architectural training, which makes his architectural treatise the first one to be written by a layman. He admired Perrault's design for the Louvre, and was very Perraultian in his demand for the reform of church design — for using columns in church interiors instead of piers and arcades. In this first passage of the two passages presented here, Cordemoy criticizes the church of St. Peter's in Rome because of its massive pier supports. The church of Val-de-Grace in Paris is better, he argues, but it too could be improved with the use of interior columns instead of piers. These remarks evoked a sharp response from Amédée François Frézier (1682–1773), a young architect and engineer, who in a review of Cordemoy's book in 1709 accused Cordemoy of being naive with respect to structural theory, especially with the suggestion that a dome the size of St. Peter's in Rome could be supported on columns. In the second passage from the second edition of Cordemoy's book of 1714, the author responds to Frézier by reiterating his faith in the ancients and his belief that Bramante and Michelangelo took a wrong turn in the Renaissance with their use of piers and pilasters, instead of columns. Cordemoy in this way carries Perrault's ideas into the eighteenth century, and his rationalist perspective would have great appeal to such Enlightenment French theorists as Marc-Antoine Laugier.

One esteems the church of St. Peter's in Rome as the most beautiful piece of architecture that has ever existed in the world, showing to better advantage the grandeur and the sanctity of our religion. For me, I do not have precisely the same idea. Perhaps the vast expanse, the prodigious height of the nave, the boldness and the propriety in the ornamental execution

Jean-Louis de Cordemoy (dates unknown), from *Nouveau traité de toute l'architecture ou l'art de bastir* [New treatise of all architecture or the art of building] (1706, second edition 1714), trans. Harry Francis Mallgrave from a facsimile edition of the 1714 edition published by Gregg Press, Farnborough, 1966, pp. 108–9, 139–40.

have thus far struck the imagination of everyone who has seen it, and they have believed that the other elements in it are equally beautiful.

But in order to evaluate it properly, one has only to cast a glance at the new churches built in France, which make it clear that the ideas that our architects were formed after that of St. Peter's in Rome.

They are practically all made on the same model. They are designed with a large number of very massive arcades, of which the piers on the rear side of the pilasters are also massive. Often, the same arcades that form the crossing also support a round dome of great height. We have never seen anything better since we have had reason to renounce Gothic architecture; we have become accustomed to this kind of beauty.

But if we look at them closely, we will find that these piers are not particularly beautiful. For example the church of Val-de-Grace, which is without doubt the best built, is lighter and better arranged than anything else we have in this genre. Would it not be infinitely more beautiful if, instead of all those useless and ponderous arcades, those pilasters and large piers that occupy so much space and necessarily create gloom, we had placed there columns to carry the rest of the edifice of which they are? Would not its dome have been more beautiful if it were supported by a colonnade, instead of by the square arcades on which it falsely rests?

I think, as do many others, that this work as it is built gives great honor to its architect and to the memory of the great princess who commissioned it. It gives pleasure to all those who come every day to admire it.

Yet I doubt that St. Peter's in Rome would have procured the honor for Michelangelo that has since been accorded this architect were it not for the colonnade that is placed in front of this temple, which renders the entry so agreeable and so majestic. We are convinced that this church would be the most beautiful piece of architecture in the world if one had built it in the taste of that colonnade. The colonnade's inventor [Bernini] was attracted in his design to the taste of the Ancients, who very much loved columns and who utilized them so well. In truth Michelangelo has become esteemed for returning to the taste of ancient architecture, but he would have been even more so if he had retained at the same time what was good in the Gothic, that is to say, the openness and visual tension of the intercolumniation that pleases us so much. [. . .]

★ ★ ★

For the "treatise on stone cutting" that he [Frézier] demands of me once again, it is already found in the excellent portico of the Louvre, of which the architraves have at least 14 feet of span or of length. When M. Perrault showed the design to the king, most of the *connoisseurs* believed that it was more a decoration for a theater than something that could actually be executed. It was nevertheless built in a manner as solid as it is beautiful. And I am persuaded that in following the "treatise on stone cutting" of this capable architect, we could create spans for architraves of 16, 18, or 20 feet without risking anything. Would this distance between columns not be sufficient in a large edifice, such as that of St. Peter's in Rome, and even more so in the Val-de-Grace in Paris, to render them at the same time more open and more magnificent? I therefore insist, despite all of the objections of M. Frézier, that without changing the plan in general or the barrel vault of the two churches, we would have been able to use a peristyle there.

B. BRITISH CLASSICISM AND PALLADIANISM

Introduction

Classicism in Britain during the later stages of the Renaissance shows some parallels, but also some differences, with respect to France and Italy. Throughout the fifteenth century the British Isles were scarcely concerned much with art. They were engaged on the home front with the very formidable issue of England seeking control over Wales, Ireland, and Scotland, and abroad with France and the Hundred Years War (1337–1453). The sixteenth century was again largely taken up with issues of economic expansion and warfare. The biggest event of the first half of the century was the Church of England making its break from the Roman Catholic Church, while one of the most telling events of the second half of the century — after Britain had colonized much of North America — was the British Navy's sinking of the Spanish Armada (1588), which now gave the country control of the seas. Art scarcely had time to catch up. The Tudor buildings of Henry VIII (r. 1509–47), for instance, were entirely Gothic in character, when not derivative of the battlement styles of earlier medieval times. One of the first instances of classical decoration (not building style) is found in the wood-carved screen at King's College, Cambridge (1533–5), presumably the work of Italian artisans. The first building with recognizable classical features (although known only from a drawing) is John Thynne's design for Old Somerset House (1547–52), which was probably based on a French model. Things began to change somewhat in the second half of the century, beginning with the reign of Elizabeth I (r. 1558–1603). The first buildings displaying the Renaissance style – Longleat, Wiltshire (begun 1570), Wollaton Hall, Nottinghamshire (1580–8), and Hardwick Hall, Derbyshire (1590–7) – all show a knowledge of Serlio, probably deriving from texts published in Flanders and France. John Shute's *The First and Chief Groundes of Architecture* (1563) cites not only Serlio but also Vitruvius and Philander. Copies of books by Vredeman de Vries, Wendel Dietterlin, and Hans Blum were also making their way to Britain during these years, and in fact the translation of Blum's *The Booke of Five Columnes of Architecture* (1601) actually precedes by 10 years Robert Peake's production of *The first (-fith) Booke of Architecture, made by Sebastian Serly*.

It was not until the seventeenth century, however, that classicism truly arrived in Britain, and it did so with a certain zest. The first great British classicist was Inigo Jones, who met Scamozzi and discovered the work of Palladio on a trip to Italy in 1613–14. Shortly thereafter, the former British ambassador to Venice, Henry Wotton, compiled his version of classical theory in *The Elements of Architecture* (1624). The major British classicist of the second half of the century was Christopher Wren, who turned to architecture in a serious way only after the Great Fire of London in 1666. Wren's classicism had elements of the baroque in it and, moreover, he occasionally made designs in the Gothic style – an act that would have been almost unthinkable among classicists in France. After yet another round of baroque elements in the work of John Vanbrugh and Nicholas Hawksmoor, classical opposition reformed itself in the first part of the eighteenth century under the guise of a British Palladian movement. In the 1720s Lord Burlington emerged as the leader of this rather strict vision of Palladian classicism, which remained strong until mid-century. Its forces eventually dissipated not so much from without as within. Always an important aspect of British architectural development of the seventeenth century and most of the eighteenth century – with respect to France – was the absence of an official academy to codify the principles of design. This absence cultivated, on the one hand, a rather strict cultural dependence on such imported models as the classicism of Palladio. It also allowed, on the other hand, a certain freedom in design as well as challenges to emerge with regard to classical theory – challenges that would become fully manifest in the mid-eighteenth century.

38 HENRY WOTTON
from *The Elements of Architecture* (1624)

The Renaissance movement in Britain is chiefly owed to the efforts of two men. One is Inigo Jones (1573–1652), a near contemporary of William Shakespeare, who first visited Italy around 1600 as a costume designer and court artist. On a second trip to Italy in 1613, Jones (his interests now turning to architecture) met Vincenzo Scamozzi, visited Palladio's buildings, and purchased a number of his drawings. Jones would go on to have a spectacular career as a classical architect of the first half of the century, beginning with his

Henry Wotton (1568–1639), from the Preface and Part I of *The Elements of Architecture*. London: John Bill, 1624.

Palladian design for London's Banqueting House, in Whitehall (1619–22). The second person to promote Renaissance architecture in Britain was the diplomat Henry Wotton. He had long resided in Italy after James I appointed him to be the ambassador to Venice in 1604, and upon retiring to London in 1624 he quickly wrote *The Elements of Architecture*, which summarized what he believed to be the rudiments of classical architecture. The small book is perhaps best known for the happy translation of the Vitruvian triad as "Commoditie, Firmenes, and Delight," but it is also a solid and scholarly recapitulation of Vitruvian theory augmented with the input of various Renaissance writers, chiefly Alberti, Palladio, and Philibert de l'Orme.

I shall not neede (like the most part of Writers) to celebrate the *Subject* which I deliver. In that point I am at ease. For *Architecture*, can want no commendation, where there are *Noble Men*, or *Noble mindes*; I will therefore spend this *Preface*, rather about those, from whom I have gathered my knowledge; For I am but a gatherer and disposer of other mens stuffe at my best value.

Our principall *Master* is *Vitruvius* and so I shall often call him; who had this felicitie, that he wrote when the *Roman Empire* was neere the pitch; Or at least, when *Augustus* (who favoured his endeavours) had some meaning (if he were not mistaken) to bound the *Monarchie*: This I say was his good happe; For in growing and enlarging times, *Artes* are commonly drowned in *Action*: But on the other side, it was in truth an *unhappinesse*, to expresse himselfe so ill, especially writing (as he did) in a season of the ablest *Pennes*; And his *obscuritie* had this strange fortune; That though he were best practised, and best followed by his owne *Countrymen*; yet after the reviving and repolishing of good *Literature*, (which the combustions and tumults of the *middle Age* had uncivillized) he was best, or at least, first understood by *strangers*: For of the Italians that tooke him in hand, Those that were *Gramarians* seeme to have wanted *Mathematicall* knowledge; and the *Mathematicians* perhaps wanted *Gramer*: till both were sufficiently conjoined, in *Leon-Batista Alberti* the *Florentine*, whom I repute the first learned *Architect*, beyond the *Alpes*; But hee studied more indeede to make himselfe an *Author*, then to illustrate his *Master*. [...]

In *Architecture* as in all other *Operative* arts, the *end* must direct the *Operation*.

The *end* is to build well. Well building hath three Conditions: *Commoditie, Firmenes*, and *Delight*. A common division among the Deliverers of this *Art*, though I know not how, some what misplaced by *Vitruvius* himselfe ... whom I shall be willinger to follow, as a Master of *Proportion*, then of *Methode*.

39 CHRISTOPHER WREN
from Tract I on architecture
(mid-1670s)

Renaissance architecture in Britain in the second half of the seventeenth century is today synonymous with the name of Christopher Wren, who built upon the classicism of Jones. Wren was a man of commanding intelligence, having established his reputation in his early years as a classical scholar, mathematician, founding member of the Royal Society (of science), and as a professor of astronomy at Gresham College in London. His interest in architecture very much grew out of his scientific endeavors. In 1663 he was asked to give structural advice on the remodeling of the old church of St. Paul's Cathedral in London; around the same time he was also asked to prepare designs for two buildings at Oxford. In 1665, in order to enhance his architectural knowledge, Wren made a trip to France, where he was able to meet Bernini, François Mansart, and Louis Le Vau. The great London fire of 1666 essentially mandated his change of profession. He was first appointed to a six-member committee charged with rebuilding the city; in 1669 he was appointed Surveyor General of all new construction. Over the next half century his architectural imprint on London (the new St. Paul's Cathedral and 45 churches), Greenwich (Royal Naval Hospital), Oxford, and Cambridge would become enormous.

Wren published no treatise of his ideas but he composed pages of notes toward that end, which were posthumously published by his son. His theory is an interesting blending of Platonic thought with classical theory, to which he adds the rudiments of a developing British empiricism. The first selection is from Tract I and is notable for his distinction between "natural" and "customary" beauty. It seems to recall Perrault's distinction between positive and arbitrary beauty, except that first category for Wren derives from the mathematical truth of geometry and also encompasses the matter of proportions.

Architecture has its political Use; publick Buildings being the Ornament of a Country; it establishes a Nation, draws People and Commerce; makes the People love their native Country, which Passion is the Original of all great Actions in a Common-wealth. The Emulation of the Cities of *Greece* was the true Cause of their Greatness. The obstinate Valour of the *Jews*, occasioned by the Love of their Temple, was a Cement that held together that People, for many Ages, through infinite Changes. The Care of publick Decency and Convenience was a great Cause of the Establishment of the *Low-countries*, and of many Cities in the World. Modern *Rome* subsists still, by the Ruins and Imitation of the *old*; as does *Jerusalem*, by the Temple of the Sepulchre, and other Remains of *Helena*'s Zeal.

Architecture aims at Eternity; and therefore the only Thing uncapable of Modes and Fashions in its Principals, the *Orders*.

The *Orders* are not only *Roman* and *Greek*, but *Phœnician*, *Hebrew*, and *Assyrian*; therefore being founded upon the Experience of all Ages, promoted by the vast Treasures of all the great Monarchs, and Skill of the greatest Artists and Geometricians, every one emulating each other; and Experiments in this kind being greatly expenceful, and Errors incorrigible,

Christopher Wren (1632–1723), from "Tracts" on architecture (mid-1670s), in *Wren's "Tracts" on Architecture and Other Writings*, ed. Lydia M. Soo. New York: Cambridge University Press, 1998, pp. 153–5 (Tract I).

is the Reason that the Principles of Architecture are now rather the Study of Antiquity than Fancy.

Beauty, Firmness, and Convenience, are the Principles; the two first depend upon the geometrical Reasons of *Opticks* and *Staticks*; the third only makes the Variety.

There are natural Causes of Beauty. Beauty is a Harmony of Objects, begetting Pleasure by the Eye. There are two Causes of Beauty, natural and customary. Natural is from *Geometry*, consisting in Uniformity (that is Equality) and Proportion. Customary Beauty is begotten by the Use of our Senses to those Objects which are usually pleasing to us for other Causes, as Familiarity or particular Inclination breeds a Love to Things not in themselves lovely. Here lies the great Occasion of Errors; here is tried the Architect's Judgment: but always the true Test is natural or geometrical Beauty.

Geometrical Figures are naturally more beautiful than other irregular; in this all consent as to a Law of Nature. Of geometrical Figures, the Square and the Circle are most beautiful; next, the Parallelogram and the Oval. Strait Lines are more beautiful than curve; next to strait Lines, equal and geometrical Flexures; an Object elevated in the Middle is more beautiful than depressed.

Position is necessary for perfecting Beauty. There are only two beautiful Positions of strait Lines, perpendicular and horizontal: this is from Nature, and consequently Necessity, no other than upright being firm. Oblique Positions are Discord to the Eye, unless answered in Pairs, as in the Sides of an equicrural Triangle: therefore *Gothick* Buttresses are all ill-favoured, and were avoided by the Ancients, and no Roofs almost but spherick raised to be visible, except in the Front, where the Lines answer; in spherick, in all Positions, the Ribs answer. Cones and multangular Prisms want neither Beauty nor Firmness, but are not ancient.

Views contrary to Beauty are Deformity, or a Defect of Uniformity, and Plainness, which is the Excess of Uniformity; Variety makes the Mean.

Variety of Uniformities makes compleat Beauty: Uniformities are best tempered, as Rhimes in Poetry, alternately, or sometimes with more Variety, as in Stanza's.

In Things to be seen at once, much Variety makes Confusion, another Vice of Beauty. In Things that are not seen at once, and have no Respect one to another, great Variety is commendable, provided this Variety transgress not the Rules of *Opticks* and *Geometry*.

An Architect ought to be jealous of Novelties, in which Fancy blinds the Judgment; and to think his Judges, as well those that are to live five Centuries after him, as those of his own Time. That which is commendable now for Novelty, will not be a new Invention to Posterity, when his Works are often imitated, and when it is unknown which was the Original; but the Glory of that which is good of itself is eternal.

40 CHRISTOPHER WREN
from Tracts II and IV on architecture (mid-1670s)

W ren's classicism is clearly different from that of France and Italy. He opens "Tract II," for instance, by warning against reducing architecture to "too strick and pedantick" rule-making, which (although essentially Vitruvian) opens the door to a cultural relativism that is similar to that allowed by Perrault. Also unclassical in Wren's thinking is his respect for the Gothic style, which may derive from his own use of this style in such works as Tom Tower, Christ Church, Oxford. Wren's archaeological and scholarly desire to augment the classical inventory of forms with a consideration of Jewish and Egyptian architecture is also somewhat foreign to the more academic approach of the Continent. This catholicity of taste, in fact, would be viewed by eighteenth-century Palladians in Britain as both old-fashioned and hopelessly compromised in its taste.

Modern Authors who have treated of Architecture, seem generally to have little more in view, but to set down the Proportions of Columns, Architraves, and Cornices, in the several Orders, as they are distinguished into *Dorick, Ionick, Corinthian,* and *Composite*; and in these Proportions finding them in the ancient Fabricks of the *Greeks* and *Romans,* (though more arbitrarily used than they care to acknowledge) they have reduced them into Rules, too strict and pedantick, and so as not to be transgressed, without the Crime of Barbarity; though, in their own Nature, they are but the Modes and Fashions of those Ages wherein they were used; but because they were found in the great Structures, (the Ruins of which we now admire) we think ourselves strictly obliged still to follow the Fashion, though we can never attain to the Grandeur of those Works.

Those who first laboured in the Restoration of Architecture, about three Centuries ago, studied principally what they found in *Rome,* above-ground, in the Ruins of the Theatres, Baths, Temples, and triumphal Arches; (for among the *Greeks* little was then remaining) and in these there appeared great Differences; however, they criticised upon them, and endeavoured to reconcile them, as well as they could, with one another, and with what they could meet with in the *Italian* Cities: and it is to be considered, that what they found standing was built, for the most part, after the Age of *Augustus,* particularly, the Arches, Amphitheatres, Baths, &c. The *Dorick* Order they chiefly understood, by examining the Theatre of *Marcellus*; the *Ionick,* from the Temple of *Fortuna Virilis*; the *Corinthian,* from the *Pantheon* of *Agrippa*; the *Composite,* from the triumphal Arch of *Titus,* &c. I have seen among the Collections of *Inigo Jones,* a Pocket-book of *Pyrrho Ligorio*'s, (an excellent Sculptor, and Architect, employed by Pope *Paul* the third, in the building of the *Vatican* Church of *St. Peter* in *Rome,* about the Year 1540) wherein he seemed to have made it his Business, out of the antique Fragments, to have drawn the many different Capitals, Mouldings of Cornices, and Ornaments of Freezes, &c. purposely to judge of the great Liberties of the ancient Architects, most of which had their Education in *Greece.*

Christopher Wren, from "Tracts" on architecture (mid-1670s), in *Wren's "Tracts" on Architecture and Other Writings,* ed. Lydia M. Soo. New York: Cambridge University Press, 1998, pp. 157–8 (Tract II), 188 (Tract IV).

But although Architecture contains many excellent Parts, besides the ranging of Pillars, yet Curiosity may lead us to consider whence this Affectation arose originally, so as to judge nothing beautiful, but what was adorned with Columns, even where there was no real Use of them; as when Half-columns are stuck upon the Walls of Temples, or Basilicæ; and where they are hung-on, as it were, upon the Outside of triumphal Arches, where they cannot be supposed of any Use, but merely for Ornament; as *Seneca* observed in the *Roman* Baths: *Quantum columnarum est nihil sustinentium, sed in ornamentum positarum, impensæ causâ!* It will be to the Purpose, therefore, to examine whence proceeded this Affectation of a Mode that hath continued now at least 3000 Years, and the rather, because it may lead us to the Grounds of Architecture, and by what Steps this Humour of Colonades came into Practice in all Ages.

★ ★ ★

Whatever a mans sentiments are upon mature deliberation it will be still necessary for him in a conspicuous Work to preserve his Undertaking from general censure, and to aim to accommodate his Designs to the Gust of the Age he lives in, though it appears to him less rational.

I have found no little difficulty to bring Persons of otherwise a good Genius, to think anything in Architecture could be better then what they had heard commended by others, and what they had view'd themselves. Many good Gothick forms of Cathedrals were to be seen in our Country, and many had been seen abroad, which they lik'd the better for being not much differing from Ours in England: this humour with many is not yet eradicated, and therefore I judge it not improper to endeavour to reform the Generality to a truer tast in Architecture by giving a larger Idea of the whole Art, beginning with the reasons and progress of it from the most remote Antiquity; and that in short, touching chiefly on some things, which have not been remark'd by others.

41 ANTHONY ASHLEY COOPER
Third Earl of Shaftesbury, from *Characteristics of Men, Manners, Opinions, Times* (1711)

Despite Wren's eclectic success in the second half of the seventeenth century, the stricter classicism of Jones did not entirely lose its following. Upon Jones's death in 1652 his drawings and library were passed on to his capable assistant John Webb (1611–72), who used them to carry out several Palladian designs in the 1650s and 1660s. Interest in Jones also remained high at Oxford, where Dr. Henry Aldrich (1648–1710), the Dean of Christ Church, and Dr. George Clarke (1661–1736), fellow at All Souls College, were fascinated both with Jones

Anthony Ashley Cooper, Third Earl of Shaftesbury (1671–1713), from *Characteristics of Men, Manners, Opinions, Times* (1711) in *Characteristics*, ed. John M. Robertson. London: Grant Richards, 1900, I: pp. 225–9, II: pp. 136–7, II: pp. 267–72.

and with the Palladian ideas that he had espoused. What was lacking for architects, however, was a philosophical foundation on which to ground the Renaissance aesthetics of the Italian master.

This rationale would be supplied by Anthony Ashley Cooper, the Third Earl of Shaftesbury. The grandson of the First Earl of Shaftesbury — famed parliamentarian and foe to Richard Cromwell — the younger Shaftesbury had every advantage in life. He was schooled at home by no less a person than the philosopher John Locke (1632–1704), whose empiricism he would ultimately embellish with his own belief in innate ideas. Next came three years in Italy in the late 1680s to cultivate his aesthetic sensibilities. He followed this travel with five years of private studies, during which time he mastered Greek philosophy. After a brief bout with politics, poor health forced him in the late 1690s to retire to the life of a "virtuoso," that is to say, a gentleman in pursuit of refined or higher aesthetic pleasures. Shaftesbury's philosophy, in fact, can be described as a metaphysical moralism, in that he placed great importance on the inward development of private morality as a means to experience and understand the outward harmony and order of the universe. Higher ideas of truth, beauty, proportions, and goodness are intrinsic or innate values to be cultivated through the moral sense. The following three selections are from three different essays of his *Characteristics*. The first, from his "Advice to an Author" outlines his general aesthetics and indicates his disdain for all that is "Gothic." The second passage, from the dialogue "The Moralists, A Philosophical Rhapsody," briefly articulates his Neo-Platonic views regarding visual forms and proportions. The third passage, which again returns to the theme of the coincidence of beauty and harmony, is extracted from the third of his "Miscellaneous Reflections."

One would imagine that our philosophical writers, who pretend to treat of morals, should far out-do mere poets in recommending virtue, and representing what was fair and amiable in human actions. One would imagine that if they turned their eye towards remote countries (of which they affect so much to speak) they should search for that simplicity of manners and innocence of behaviour which has been often known among mere savages, ere they were corrupted by our commerce, and, by sad example, instructed in all kinds of treachery and inhumanity. 'Twould be of advantage to us to hear the causes of this strange corruption in ourselves, and be made to consider of our deviation from nature, and from that just purity of manners which might be expected, especially from a people so assisted and enlightened by religion. For who would not naturally expect more justice, fidelity, temperance, and honesty from Christians than from Mahometans or mere pagans? But so far are our modern moralists from condemning any unnatural vices or corrupt manners, whether in our own or foreign climates, that they would have vice itself appear as natural as virtue, and from the worst examples would represent to us "that all actions are naturally indifferent; that they have no note or character of good or ill in themselves; but are distinguished by mere fashion, law, or arbitrary decree." Wonderful philosophy! raised from the dregs of an illiterate mean kind, which was ever despised among the great ancients and rejected by all men of action or sound erudition; but in these ages imperfectly copied from the original, and, with much disadvantage, imitated and assumed in common both by devout and indevout attempters in the moral kind.

Should a writer upon music, addressing himself to the students and lovers of the art, declare to them "that the measure or rule of harmony was caprice or will, humour or fashion," 'tis not very likely he should be heard with great attention or treated with real gravity. For harmony is harmony by nature, let men judge ever so ridiculously of music. So is symmetry and proportion founded still in nature, let men's fancy prove ever so barbarous, or their fashions ever so Gothic in their architecture, sculpture, or whatever other designing art. 'Tis the same case where life and manners are concerned. Virtue has the same fixed standard. The same numbers, harmony, and proportion will have place in morals, and are discoverable in the characters and affections of mankind; in which are laid the just foundations of an art and science superior to every other of human practice and comprehension.

This, I suppose therefore, is highly necessary that a writer should comprehend. For things are stubborn and will not be as we fancy them, or as the fashion varies, but as they stand in nature. Now whether the writer be poet, philosopher, or of whatever kind, he is in truth no other than a copyist after nature. His style may be differently suited to the different times he lives in, or to the different humour of his age or nation; his manner, his dress, his colouring may vary; but if his drawing be uncorrect or his design contrary to nature, his piece will be found ridiculous when it comes thoroughly to be examined. For Nature will not be mocked. The prepossession against her can never be very lasting. Her decrees and instincts are powerful and her sentiments inbred. She has a strong party abroad, and as strong a one within ourselves; and when any slight is put upon her, she can soon turn the reproach and make large reprisals on the taste and judgment of her antagonists.

Whatever philosopher, critic, or author is convinced of this prerogative of nature, will easily be persuaded to apply himself to the great work of reforming his taste, which he will have reason to suspect, if he be not such a one as has deliberately endeavoured to frame it by the just standard of nature. Whether this be his case, he will easily discover by appealing to his memory; for custom and fashion are powerful seducers; and he must of necessity have fought hard against these to have attained that justness of taste which is required in one who pretends to follow nature. But if no such conflict can be called to mind, 'tis a certain token that the party has his taste very little different from the vulgar. And on this account he should instantly betake himself to the wholesome practice recommended in this treatise. He should set afoot the powerfullest faculties of his mind, and assemble the best forces of his wit and judgment, in order to make a formal descent on the territories of the heart; resolving to decline no combat, nor hearken to any terms, till he had pierced into its inmost provinces and reached the seat of empire. No treaties should amuse him; no advantages lead him aside. All other speculations should be suspended, all other mysteries resigned, till this necessary campaign was made and these inward conflicts learnt; by which he would be able to gain at least some tolerable insight into himself and knowledge of his own natural principles. [. . .]

★ ★ ★

I allow your expression, said Theocles, and will endeavour to show you that the same pre-conceptions, of a higher degree, have place in human kind. Do so, said I, I entreat you; for so far am I from finding in myself these pre-conceptions of fair and beautiful, in your sense, that methinks, till now of late, I have hardly known of anything like them in Nature. How then, said he, would you have known that outward fair and beautiful of human kind, if such an object (a fair fleshly one) in all its beauty had for the first time appeared to you, by yourself, this morning, in these groves? Or do you think perhaps you should have been unmoved, and have found no difference between this form and any other, if first you had not been instructed?

I have hardly any right, replied I, to plead this last opinion, after what I have owned just before.

Well then, said he, that I may appear to take no advantage against you, I quit the dazzling form which carries such a force of complicated beauties, and am contented to consider separately each of those simple beauties, which taken all together create this wonderful effect. For you will allow, without doubt, that in respect of bodies, whatever is commonly said of the unexpressible, the unintelligible, the I-know-not-what of beauty, there can lie no mystery here, but what plainly belongs either to figure, colour, motion or sound. Omitting therefore the three latter, and their dependent charms, let us view the charm in what is simplest of all, mere figure. Nor need we go so high as sculpture, architecture, or the designs of those who from this study of beauty have raised such delightful arts. 'Tis enough if we consider the simplest of figures, as either a round ball, a cube, or dye. Why is even an infant pleased with the first view of these proportions? Why is the sphere or globe, the cylinder and obelisk preferred; and the irregular figures, in respect of these, rejected and despised?

I am ready, replied I, to own there is in certain figures a natural beauty, which the eye finds as soon as the object is presented to it.

Is there then, said he, a natural beauty of figures? and is there not as natural a one of actions? No sooner the eye opens upon figures, the ear to sounds, than straight the beautiful results and grace and harmony are known and acknowledged. No sooner are actions viewed, no sooner the human affections and passions discerned (and they are most of them as soon discerned as felt) than straight an inward eye distinguishes, and sees the fair and shapely, the amiable and admirable, apart from the deformed, the foul, the odious, or the despicable. How is it possible therefore not to own "that as these distinctions have their foundation in Nature, the discernment itself is natural, and from Nature alone"?

★ ★ ★

'Tis impossible we can advance the least in any relish or taste of outward symmetry and order, without acknowledging that the proportionate and regular state is the truly prosperous and natural in every subject. The same features which make deformity create incommodiousness and disease. And the same shapes and proportions which make beauty afford advantage by adapting to activity and use. Even in the imitative or designing arts (to which our author so often refers) the truth or beauty of every figure or statue is measured from the perfection of Nature in her just adapting of every limb and proportion to the activity, strength, dexterity, life and vigour of the particular species or animal designed.

Thus beauty and truth are plainly joined with the notion of utility and convenience, even in the apprehension of every ingenious artist, the architect, the statuary, or the painter. 'Tis the same in the physician's way. Natural health is the just proportion, truth, and regular course of things in a constitution. 'Tis the inward beauty of the body. And when the harmony and just measures of the rising pulses, the circulating humours, and the moving airs or spirits, are disturbed or lost, deformity enters, and with it, calamity and ruin.

Should not this (one would imagine) be still the same case and hold equally as to the mind? Is there nothing there which tends to disturbance and dissolution? Is there no natural tenour, tone, or order of the passions or affections? No beauty or deformity in this moral kind? Or allowing that there really is, must it not, of consequence, in the same manner imply health or sickliness, prosperity or disaster? Will it not be found in this respect, above all, "that what is beautiful is harmonious and proportionable; what is harmonious and proportionable is true; and what is at once both beautiful and true is, of consequence, agreeable and good?"

Where then is this beauty or harmony to be found? How is this symmetry to be discovered and applied? Is it any other art than that of philosophy or the study of inward numbers and proportions which can exhibit this in life? If no other, who then can possibly have a taste of this kind, without being beholden to philosophy? Who can admire the outward beauties and not recur instantly to the inward, which are the most real and essential, the most naturally affecting, and of the highest pleasure, as well as profit and advantage?

In so short a compass does that learning and knowledge lie on which manners and life depend. 'Tis we ourselves create and form our taste. If we resolve to have it just, 'tis in our power. We may esteem and resolve, approve and disapprove, as we would wish. For who would not rejoice to be always equal and consonant to himself, and have constantly that opinion of things which is natural and proportionable? But who dares search opinion to the bottom, or call in question his early and prepossessing taste? Who is so just to himself as to recall his fancy from the power of fashion and education to that of reason? Could we, however, be thus courageous, we should soon settle in ourselves such an opinion of good as would secure to us an invariable, agreeable, and just taste in life and manners.

42   ANTHONY ASHLEY COOPER
Third Earl of Shaftesbury, from "A Letter Concerning Design" (1712)

I n 1711 Shaftesbury, who was dying of a respiratory illness, left England to spend the final months of his life in Naples. In a letter written to his friend Lord Somers, he made known in a more concrete way his views on the state of the arts and architecture. His negative reference to "one single court-architect" alludes to (the still-living) Wren, and it can be interpreted as Wren's dethronement within certain intellectual circles. Shaftesbury's equally negative reference to "a new palace spoilt" is undoubtedly aimed at the baroque character of Blenheim Palace, designed by John Vanbrugh and Nicholas Hawksmoor between 1705 and 1716. Notwithstanding these criticisms, Shaftesbury is optimistic about the "rising genius of our nation," and to this end he pleads for a national academy to improve the education of artists, similar to the training students receive in France. Such an academy would eventually be instituted, but not until 1768.

[. . .] This in the meantime I can, with some assurance say to your Lordship in a kind of spirit of prophecy, from what I have observed of the rising genius of our nation, That if we live to see a peace any way answerable to that generous spirit with which this war was begun, and carried on, for our own liberty and that of Europe; the figure we are like to make abroad, and the increase of knowledge, industry and sense at home, will render united Britain the principal seat of arts; and by her politeness and advantages in this kind, will shew evidently, how much she owes to those counsels, which taught her to exert herself so resolutely on behalf of the common cause, and that of her own liberty, and happy constitution, necessarily included.

Anthony Ashley Cooper, Third Earl of Shaftesbury, "A Letter Concerning Design" (1712) in *Second Characters or the Language of Forms*, ed. Benjamin Rand. London: Thoemmes Press, 1995 (a reprint of the 1914 edition), pp. 19–24.

I can myself remember the time, when, in respect of music, our reigning taste was in many degrees inferior to the French. The long reign of luxury and pleasure under King Charles the Second, and the foreign helps and studied advantages given to music in a following reign, could not raise our genius the least in this respect. But when the spirit of the nation was grown more free, though engaged at that time in the fiercest war, and with the most doubtful success, we no sooner began to turn ourselves towards music, and enquire what Italy in particular produced, than in an instant we outstripped our neighbours the French, entered into a genius far beyond theirs, and raised ourselves an ear, and judgment, not inferior to the best now in the world.

In the same manner, as to painting. Though we have as yet nothing of our own native growth in this kind worthy of being mentioned; yet since the public has of late begun to express a relish for engravings, drawings, copyings, and for the original paintings of the chief Italian schools (so contrary to the modern French), I doubt not that, in very few years we shall make an equal progress in this other science. And when our humour turns us to cultivate these designing arts, our genius, I am persuaded, will naturally carry us over the slighter amusements, and lead us to that higher, more serious, and noble part of imitation, which relates to history, human nature, and the chief degree or order of beauty; I mean that of the rational life, distinct from the merely vegetable and sensible, as in animals, or plants; according to those several degrees or orders of painting, which your Lordship will find suggested in this extemporary Notion I have sent you.

As for architecture, it is no wonder if so many noble designs of this kind have miscarried amongst us; since the genius of our nation has hitherto been so little turned this way, that through several reigns we have patiently seen the noblest public buildings perish (if I may say so) under the hand of one single court-architect; who, if he had been able to profit by experience, would long since, at our expense, have proved the greatest master in the world. But I question whether our patience is like to hold much longer. The devastation so long committed in this kind, has made us begin to grow rude and clamorous at the hearing of a new palace spoilt, or a new design committed to some rash or impotent pretender.

It is the good fate of our nation in this particular, that there remain yet two of the noblest subjects for architecture; our Prince's Palace and our House of Parliament. For I cannot but fancy that when Whitehall is thought of, the neighbouring Lords and Commons will at the same time be placed in better chambers and apartments, than at present; were it only for majesty's sake, and as a magnificence becoming the person of the Prince, who here appears in full solemnity. Nor do I fear that when these new subjects are attempted, we should miscarry as grossly as we have done in others before. Our State, in this respect, may prove perhaps more fortunate than our Church, in having waited till a national taste was formed, before these edifices were undertaken. But the zeal of the nation could not, it seems, admit so long a delay in their ecclesiastical structures, particularly their metropolitan. And since a zeal of this sort has been newly kindled amongst us, it is like we shall see from afar the many spires arising in our great city, with such hasty and sudden growth, as may be the occasion perhaps that our immediate relish shall be hereafter censured, as retaining much of what artists call the Gothic kind.

Hardly, indeed, as the public now stands, should we bear to see a Whitehall treated like a Hampton Court, or even a new cathedral like St Paul's. Almost every one now becomes concerned, and interests himself in such public structures. Even those pieces too are brought under the common censure, which, though raised by private men, are of such a grandeur and magnificence, as to become national ornaments. The ordinary man may build his cottage, or the plain gentleman his country house according as he fancies: but when a great man builds, he will find little quarter from the public, if instead of a beautiful pile, he raises, at a vast expense, such a false and counterfeit piece of magnificence, as can be justly arraigned for its deformity by so many knowing men in art, and by the whole people, who, in such a conjuncture readily follow their opinion.

In reality the people are no small parties in this cause. Nothing moves successfully without them. There can be no public, but where they are included. And without a public voice, knowingly guided and directed, there is nothing which can raise a true ambition in the artist; nothing which can exalt the genius of the workman, or make him emulous of after fame, and of the approbation of his country, and of posterity. For with these he naturally, as a freeman, must take part: in these he has a passionate concern, and interest, raised in him by the same genius of liberty, the same laws and government, by which his property and the rewards of his pains and industry, are secured to him, and to his generation after him.

Everything co-operates, in such a State, towards the improvement of art and science. And for the designing arts in particular, such as architecture, painting, and statuary, they are in a manner linked together. The taste of one kind brings necessarily that of the others along with it. When the free spirit of a nation turns itself this way, judgments are formed; critics arise; the public eye and ear improve; a right taste prevails, and in a manner forces its way. Nothing is so improving, nothing so natural, so congenial to the liberal arts, as that reigning liberty and high spirit of a people, which from the habit of judging in the highest matters for themselves, makes them freely judge of other subjects, and enter thoroughly into the characters as well of men and manners, as of the products or works of men, in art and science. So much, my Lord, do we owe to the excellence of our national constitution, and legal monarchy; happily fitted for us, and which alone could hold together so mighty a people; all sharers (though at so far a distance from each other) in the government of themselves; and meeting under one head in one vast metropolis; whose enormous growth, however censurable in other respects, is actually a cause that workmanship and arts of so many kinds arise to such perfection.

What encouragement our higher powers may think fit to give these growing arts, I will not pretend to guess. This I know, that it is so much for their advantage and interest to make themselves the chief parties in the cause, that I wish no court or ministry, besides a truly virtuous and wise one, may ever concern themselves in the affair. For should they do so, they would in reality do more harm than good; since it is not the nature of a court (such as courts generally are) to improve, but rather corrupt a taste. And what is in the beginning set wrong by their example, is hardly ever afterwards recoverable in the genius of a nation.

Content therefore I am, my Lord, that Britain stands in this respect as she now does. Nor can one, methinks, with just reason regret her having hitherto made no greater advancement in these affairs of art. As her constitution has grown, and been established, she has in proportion fitted herself for other improvements. There has been no anticipation in the case. And in this surely she must be esteemed wise, as well as happy; that ere she attempted to raise herself any other taste or relish, she secured herself a right one in government. She has now the advantage of beginning in other matters on a new foot. She has her models yet to seek, her scale and standard to form, with deliberation and good choice. Able enough she is at present to shift for herself; however abandoned or helpless she has been left by those whom it became to assist her. Hardly, indeed, could she procure a single academy for the training of her youth in exercises. As good soldiers as we are, and as good horses as our climate affords, our Princes, rather than expend their treasure this way, have suffered our youth to pass into a foreign nation, to learn to ride. As for other academies, such as those for painting, sculpture, or architecture, we have not so much as heard of the proposal; whilst the Prince of our rival nation raises academies, breeds youth, and sends rewards and pensions into foreign countries, to advance the interest and credit of his own. Now if, notwithstanding the industry and pains of this foreign court, and the supine unconcernedness of our own, the national taste however rises, and already shews itself in many respects beyond that of our so highly assisted neighbours; what greater proof can there be of the superiority of genius in one of these nations above the other?

43 COLIN CAMPBELL
Introduction to *Vitruvius Britannicus*, Vol. I (1715)

With Shaftesbury's aesthetics serving as a foundation, a new Palladian movement began to take hold in Britain in the second decade of the century. Two literary enterprises, in particular, popularized the Italian architect and Renaissance classicism in general. Sometime in 1713 or 1714 the Italian architect Giocomo Leoni (1686?–1746) immigrated to England with plans (and plates) for an English translation of Palladio's *Four Books*. Around the same time a group of London booksellers began planning an illustrated book of classical designs by British architects. The two projects were viewed by their originators as contending with each other, and both were timed to coincide with the ascension of King George I. In April 1715 (and shortly before the projected publication date) the architect Colin Campbell was named author of the second project, to be entitled *Vitruvius Britannicus*. Knowing that Leoni's work would shortly appear, he wrote a brief introduction that emphasized the greatness of Palladio – and by extension the equal or even superior talents of his English student Inigo Jones. Campbell likewise seems to have arranged the previously prepared plates in a way that contrasted the modern works of such baroque architects as Thomas Archer and John Vanbrugh with the more restrained classicism of Jones, Campbell, and others. Thus he used the book to launch his own career and become one of the most popular architects in Britain.

The general Esteem that Travellers have for Things that are Foreign, is in nothing more conspicuous than with Regard to Building. We travel, for the most part, at an Age more apt to be imposed upon by the Ignorance or Partiality of others, than to judge truly of the Merit of Things by the Strength of Reason. It's owing to this Mistake in Education, that so many of

Colin Campbell (1676–1729), Introduction to Vol. I of *Vitruvius Britannicus, or the British Architect* (3 vols., 1715–25). New York: Benjamin Blom, 1967 (facsimile edition).

the *British* Quality have so mean an Opinion of what is performed in our own Country; tho', perhaps, in most we equal, and in some Things we surpass, our Neighbours.

I have therefore judged, it would not be improper to publish this Collection, which will admit of a fair Comparison with the best of the *Moderns*. As to the *Antiques*, they are out of the Question; and, indeed, the *Italians* themselves have now no better Claim to them than they have to the Purity of the *Latin*.

We must, in Justice, acknowledge very great Obligations to those Restorers of *Architecture*, which the Fifteenth and Sixteenth Centurys produced in Italy. *Bramante, Barbaro, Sansovino, Sangallo, Michael Angelo, Raphael Urbin, Julio Romano, Serglio, Labaco, Scamozzi*, and many others, who have greatly help'd to raise this Noble Art from the Ruins of Barbarity: But above all, the great *Palladio*, who has exceeded all that were gone before him, and surpass'd his Contemporaries, whose ingenious Labours will eclipse many, and rival most of the Ancients. And indeed, this excellent *Architect* seems to have arrived to a *Ne plus ultra* of his Art. With him the great Manner and exquisite Taste of Building is lost; for the *Italians* can no more now relish the Antique Simplicity, but are entirely employed in capricious Ornaments, which must at last end in the *Gothick*.

For Proof of this Assertion, I appeal to the Productions of the last *Century*: How affected and licentious are the Works of *Bernini* and *Fontana*? How wildly Extravagant are the Designs of *Boromini*, who has endeavoured to debauch Mankind with his odd and chimerical Beauties, where the Parts are without Proportion, Solids without their true Bearing, Heaps of Materials without Strength, excessive Ornaments without Grace, and the Whole without Symmetry? And what can be a stronger Argument, that this excellent Art is near lost in that Country, where such Absurdities meet with Applause?

It is then with the Renowned *Palladio* we enter the Lists, to whom we oppose the Famous *Inigo Jones*: Let the *Banquetting-house*, those excellent Pieces at *Greenwich*, with many other Things of this great Master, be carefully examined, and I doubt not but an impartial Judge will find in them all the Regularity of the former, with an Addition of Beauty and Majesty, in which our *Architect* is esteemed to have out-done all that went before; and when those Designs be gave for *Whitehall*, are published, which I intend in the Second Volume, I believe all Mankind will agree with me, that there is no Palace in the World to rival it.

And here I cannot but reflect on the Happiness of the *British* Nation, that at present abounds with so many learned and ingenious Gentlemen, as Sir *Christopher Wren*, Sir *William Bruce*, Sir *John Vanbrugh*, Mr. *Archer*, Mr. *Wren*, Mr. *Wynne*, Mr. *Talman*, Mr. *Hawksmore*, Mr. *James*, &c. who have all greatly contributed to adorn our Island with their curious Labours, and are daily embellishing it more.

I hope, therefore, the Reader will be agreeably entertained in viewing what I have collected with so much Labour. All the Drawings are either taken from the Buildings themselves, or the original Designs of the Architects, who have very much assisted me in advancing this Work: And I can, with great Sincerity, assure the Publick, That I have used the utmost Care to render it acceptable; and that nothing might be Wanting, I have given the following Explanation to each Figure.

44 NICHOLAS DU BOIS
Translator's Preface to *The Architecture of A. Palladio* (1715)

Sometime in 1714 or early 1715 Leoni became aware of the project for *Vitruvius Britannicus*, and he feared that its focus on British architecture might hamper the sale of his own book. To strengthen his project, Leoni promised on the title page also to include annotations that Inigo Jones had made in his edition of Palladio's *I quattro libri* during his trip of 1613–14 – a promise he was unable to fulfill. Leoni was also interested is distancing his project from that of Campbell, and to this end his translator of Palladio, Nicholas Du Bois, chided the "ingenious Mr. Campbell" for including buildings containing a "ridiculous mixture of Gothick & Roman." Leoni's trilingual publication (Italian, French, and English) was a great success in its early sales, and the architecture of Palladio (some of whose designs Leoni actually sought to improve) now became a touchstone and a focus for a generation of British architects. Buoyed by his success, Leoni next set out to prepare a translation of Alberti's treatise.

One of the most judicious Remarks that have been made upon the Variety of Opinions, which prevail among those Authors, who have written concerning *Architecture*, and given us the proportions of its Orders, is in my judgment, that of *Mons. le Clerc* in a new Treatise lately publish'd by him on that Subject. *If the orders of Columns* (says he) *had real and undisputable beauties, the* Architects, *both Ancient and Modern, would have agreed among themselves about their rules and proportions: but those beauties, being only arbitrary, as not being grounded upon demonstrations, the Authors, who have treated of them, have given us different rules, according to their Taste and Genius.* And indeed, so great is this Variety, that it may be perceiv'd, even in those stately remains of ancient Buildings, which are recommended to us, to this very day, by the greatest Masters, as so many Models. However, if it be true, as *Mons. le Clerc* adds, that *among those several beauties, some are certainly more pleasing and more universally approv'd*; till somebody is so happy, as to be able to demonstrate that such, or such a rule, or proportion, ought to be preferr'd to another, no reasonable Man will scruple to follow those great and noble Ideas, those magnificent Ordinances, those learned and judicious Observations, those just and exact proportions which the most famous *Architects* have left us, and which have gain'd a general applause. Among those great Masters of Civil *Architecture*, *Palladio*, whose Work I have undertaken to translate, is doubtless the most eminent. If therefore the Book of that Learned Man has been admir'd all over *Europe*, tho his *Designs* have only been coursly engrav'd in *Wooden Cuts*; will any one deny that the generous Foreigner, who has spent several years in preparing the *Designs*, from which the following *Cuts* have been engrav'd, makes a very considerable Present to the Publick? No body was certainly better qualified than he, to bestow upon the *Designs* of *Palladio* that gracefulness and strength, which can only be imitated by the *Graver*, with a perfection unknown to the Artists of the XVIth Century. For besides that he is a very good Architect, and has in a particular manner applied himself to the reading of *Palladio*, and studied his method more

Nicholas Du Bois, Translator's Preface to Giocomo Leoni's edition of *The Architecture of A. Palladio; in Four Books, containing A short Treatise of the Five Orders, and the most necessary Observations concerning all Sorts of Buildings.* London, John Watts, 1715.

carefully than that of any other Author; he has also seen most of the Originals of those *Designs* that are in the second, third, and fourth Books of this Work; that is, the Houses, Palaces, Churches, and other Buildings, both publick and private, raised by *Palladio* himself, or designed by him, as being built by other *Architects* for whom he had an Esteem: and as he's an Excellent *Designer*, so he has taken Care to add to all those original *Designs* many Ornaments, which could not appear in *Wooden Cuts*. It would have been no easy thing for him to do this with exactness, had he not seen those Edifices, and made the necessary Observations for that end. Besides, that several faults had crept into the *Italian* Edition; which could not have been so well mended by another hand. Thus the Reader may see how much the Publick is indebted to Mr. *Leoni*.

As for what concerns my own Performance, I was very well pleas'd to find an Opportunity of translating an Author whom I always admir'd: being of Opinion that an intent reading of the two Translations published in this Volume, would very much contribute to fix in my mind the Rules of an Art which has always been my most delightful Study. I was still the more willing to undertake that painful Task, because I had already observ'd that *Monsieur de Chambray's* Translation, tho pretty exact, began to grow obsolete, and that besides many ungrateful expressions (as being now out of use) there are several terms of Art, which have been alter'd with the Language, and which requir'd a greater accuracy. I shall say nothing of the Version made by *Mons. le Muët*, who only translated the first Book. One may very well wonder that so Learned an Architect should have so little regard to the Reputation of his Author, as to lend him his own Notions, by inserting (as he has done in many places) several rules and proportions, which he lik'd, instead of those of his original; under pretence, as he himself says, that the measures and proportions of *Palladio* are *different* from those that *are used* in *France*. Besides, that Translation is so imperfect, and the References from the text to the *Cuts* are so confused and inaccurate, that those who begin to learn Architecture (for whom that Book seems chiefly to have been written) cannot read it with any advantage. I shall pass over in silence another *French* Translation made (according to *Moreri*) by one *Roland Friart*. I never could light on that Version; and therefore I can't judge of it: but it must needs be written in very old *French*, since it was Printed long before that of *Mons. de Chambrai*. However it be, what I have said of the Translation of the first Book of *Palladio* by *Mons. le Müet*, may very well be apply'd to a like Translation in *English*. The Author of which, who, in all probability did not understand the *Italian* Tongue, does altogether depend upon *Mons. le Muet*, and follows him so closely, that he has only translated the first Book, as *Mons. le Muet* did, and even transcrib'd the most palpable faults of the *French* Translator. Besides, in his imitation, he has added so many things of his own, and so much alter'd the work of *Palladio*, that the latter is hardly to be known. Nevertheless, such has always been the Reputation of this great Man, that this last Translation of the most material part of his book, though never so imperfect, or rather unworthy of him, has been reprinted six or seven times.

Every one may rest satisfy'd that the two new Translations publish'd in this Volume, and join'd to the *Italian* Original, are very faithful, and that I have left nothing unattempted to make them as perfect as could be wish'd, and answerable to the Beauty of the *Cuts*, with which they are attended, and which have been engrav'd by the best Masters. But I leave this to the judgment of the Publick. All good Judges must needs own that we wanted a Work of this Nature; and there is no doubt, but it will prove very useful, as much to Architects and

Workmen, as to those who design to build for themselves; since it contains the necessary Rules for raising the plainest Buildings, as well as the most adorn'd. Every body cannot build Palaces, nor enrich their Houses with Columns, Pilasters, and so many other Ornaments of Architecture, which require great charges. But since there are no Houses, tho never so small, without doors and windows, and some of the other parts, first invented by necessity, and then adorn'd that they might be more graceful, it is not more chargeable to make them according to their just proportions, by following the directions of some intelligent Person, than to leave them to the management and discretion of the workmen, who generally mind nothing but what is profitable to them. But as most of those who undertake to build, neglect to make use of any Architect, in order to raise a House, in which they will have none of those Ornaments, as being, in their judgment, either needless, or too expensive; they also neglect the other parts, which are the most material in a building. And because they don't understand the Rules of an Art, that affords those beautiful proportions, which, even in the plainest buildings, do often raise the admiration of the most unskilful, without their knowing the reason of it; they look upon them as inconsiderable things, and frequently prefer their own fancies to the judgment of the most learned and experienc'd Architects: or, at most, they rely upon Workmen, who are often very ignorant, or dare not find fault with any plan, tho never so bad, for fear of displeasing, and so losing their Work. Hence it is that we see so many bungled Houses and so oddly contriv'd, that they seem to have been made only to be admir'd by ignorant Men, and to raise the laughter of those who are sensible of such imperfections. Most of them are like Bird-cages, by reason of the largeness and too great number of windows; or like prisons, because of the Darkness of the rooms, passages and stairs. Some want the most essential part, I mean the *Entablature*, or Cornice; and tho it be the best fence against the injuries of the Weather, it is left out to save charges. In some other Houses, the rooms are so small and strait, that one knows not where to place the most necessary furniture. Others, through the oddness of some new and insignificant ornaments, seem to exceed the *wildest Gothick*. It were an endless thing to enumerate all the absurdities, which many of our Builders introduce every day into their way of building. I shall be contented to apply to them what the ingenious Mr. *Campbell* says of the Architecture of *Boronimi*, in his *Vitruvius Britannicus*, the first part whereos he has newly published with a labour and exactness equal to his skill in Architecture. *They are*, says he, *chimerical beauties, where the Parts are without proportions, solids without their true bearing, heaps of materials without strength, excessive ornaments without grace*. I add, and a ridiculous mixture of *Gothick* and *Roman*, without Judgment, Taste, or *Symmetry*.

I confess that the imperfections observable in our buildings, are often to be ascrib'd to the Caprice and Infatuation of those for whom they are made: but I think it cannot be denied that they do also proceed, in a great measure, from the ignorance and ill taste of the *Designers*, Undertakers, or Builders. Nevertheless, we have good reason to hope, more than ever, that those absurdities will be laid aside, and that the noble and majestick simplicity of the Ancients will prevail again. Many Persons, even among the most illustrious Nobility, begin to relish Architecture. They take delight in learning its most beautiful proportions; and by comparing the buildings of eminent and experienc'd Architects with those that have been rais'd by unskilful Men, they easily perceive what a vast difference there is between the noble productions of the former, and the extravagant performances of the latter. And indeed, they are most concern'd in it: there is hardly any body else that can bear the Charges of a beautiful and perfect Architecture, and undertake those great and stately buildings, wherein the *Work* and the *Matter* seem to contend about the preference, and strive to immortalize the memory of their Masters. Tis therefore very proper for them to be able to judge of the Plans that are propos'd to them.

I hope this Work will meet with a general approbation: if those, who have no skill in Architecture, read it, their curiosity will perhaps move them to learn an Art, which several great Princes did not think unworthy of their application. Those who begin to study Architecture, and whose taste is not come yet to its perfection, will be cur'd of their wrong notions; and finding in this Work a method no less experienc'd than beautiful and safe, they will learn by it to work with good success, and without any fear of being mistaken. As for those Learned Architects, who are better known by the reputation of their works, than by any thing I could say of them, tis not doubted but they will be glad to see *Palladio* come out under a form more suitable to the nobleness of his *Designs*, and the great Esteem the Publick has always had for him.

45 WILLIAM KENT
"Advertisement" to *The Designs of Inigo Jones* (1727)

With the ground prepared by Shaftesbury, Campbell, and Leoni – the Palladian movement in Britain began to flourish in the 1720s. Its intellectual leader was Richard Boyle, Third Earl of Burlington and Fourth Earl of Cork (1694–1753). His rise to prominence also largely defines the Palladian movement in Britain as one inextricably bound with aristocratic pretensions. Born into wealth and high circumstance (George Frideric Handel lived for a while in the Burlington household), Burlington assumed his titles in 1715 shortly after returning from his grand tour of Italy. As a youth he was enthused by Shaftesbury's ideal of a "virtuoso" and his first interests were music, the theater, and the acquisition of paintings. The two books of Leoni and Campbell seemed to have piqued his architectural interest, and shortly after reading them he dismissed his architect James Gibbs, who had been employed in making renovations for Burlington House in Piccadilly. In his place, Burlington hired Campbell, but this relationship would prove to be short-lived, as Burlington detected a lack of classical purity in his style. Burlington left for a second tour of Italy in 1719, this time with the explicit purpose of studying Palladio's architecture at its source. He also purchased all the surviving drawings of the master and, upon returning to London, began to acquire the literary estate and drawings of Inigo Jones. He also moved to his second ancestral estate in Chiswick, renovated the old house, and in 1725 began work on his famed Palladian villa, based on the Villa Rotunda in Vicenza. From this white seat he commanded the movement and those around him by commissioning or financially supporting a score of studies and publications devoted to Palladio, Jones, and aesthetic theory. In one of his first acts, in 1724 he commissioned William Kent to prepare – from the drawings now owned by Burlington – *The Designs of Inigo Jones*, which appeared in two volumes in 1727. Burlington had met the painter Kent in Italy in 1715, and after his second

William Kent (1685–1748), "Advertisement" to *The Designs of Inigo Jones, Consisting of Plans and Elevations for Publick and Private Buildings*, Vol. I (1727).

trip to the south in 1719 he invited him to live in his own households in London and Chiswick. During these years with Burlington, Kent was making a transition from painter to architect and landscape architect, for which he would achieve considerable fame in his own right.

Advertisement

The Character of INIGO JONES is so universally known, that his Name alone will be a sufficient Recommendation of the following Designs; the Originals of which (drawn by himself and Mr. *Webb*) belong to the *Earl of Burlington*.

No better Account can be given of his Life than what Mr. *Webb* hath already done in the Preface of his excellent Defence of that judicious Treatise, entitled, *Stonhenge restor'd*, there being scarce any Materials left, from whence to compile it.

Palladio's Design of the famous Church of *Santo Georgio* at *Venice*, (so deservedly admired by all good Architects) is added to this Work, to shew that as great a Rival as that Restorer of Architecture was to the Antients, his Disciple was in no respect inferior to him.

If the Reputation of this *Great Man* doth not rise in proportion to his Merits in his own Country, 'tis certain, in *Italy*, (which was his School) and other Parts of *Europe*, he was in great esteem; in which places, as well as in *England*, his own Works are his Monument and best Panegyrick; which, together with those of *Palladio*, remain equal Proofs of the Superiority of those two Great Masters to all others.

To this Collection are added Designs of Doors, Windows, Gates, Peers, Chimneys, Insides of Rooms, and Ceilings; as also some few Designs of Buildings by the *Earl of Burlington*. The other Particulars will be shewn in the following Tables annex'd to each Volume.

46 JAMES GIBBS
Introduction to *A Book of Architecture* (1728)

One of the indications of the persuasiveness of Burlington is the influence he exerted on James Gibbs, the architect that he had dismissed in 1715. Born near Aberdeen in Scotland, Gibbs had first studied architecture in Rome at the start of the century under the baroque architect Carlo Fontana (a pupil of Bernini). After returning to Britain in 1708, Gibbs set up his practice, and in 1713 joined the staff of Nicholas Hawksmoor, whose office was charged with building 50 new churches in London. The most famous of Gibbs's designs during these years was for Saint Martin-in-the-Field (1720–6) – where, in a much emulated design, he joined a classical temple front with a lofty, baroque-inspired steeple. Already by this date, however, Gibbs had brought his personal style into line with the early efforts of the Palladian movement, and his designs for Sudbrook Park

James Gibbs (1682–1754), Introduction to *A Book of Architecture, Containing Designs of Buildings and Ornaments* (1728), pp. i–iii.

(1717–28), Down Hall (1720–1), and the Fellows' Building at King's College, Cambridge (1724–49) are fully Palladian in character. He disseminated his designs in *A Book of Architecture* (1728).

Introduction

What is here presented to the Publick was undertaken at the instance of several Persons of Quality and others; and some Plates were added to what was at first intended, by the particular direction of Persons of great Distinction, for whose Commands I have the highest regard. They were of opinion, that such a Work as this would be of use to such Gentlemen as might be concerned in Building, especially in the remote parts of the Country, where little or no assistance for Designs can be procured. Such may be here furnished with Draughts of useful and convenient Buildings and proper Ornaments; which may be executed by any Workman who understands Lines, either as here Design'd, or with some Alteration, which may be easily made by a person of Judgment; without which a Variation in Draughts, once well digested, frequently proves a Detriment to the Building, as well as a Disparagement to the person that gives them. I mention this to caution Gentlemen from suffering any material Change to be made in their Designs, by the Forwardness of unskilful Workmen, or the Caprice of ignorant, assuming Pretenders.

Some, for want of better Helps, have unfortunately put into the hands of common workmen, the management of Buildings of considerable expence; which when finished, they have had the mortification to find condemned by persons of Tast, to that degree that sometimes they have been pull'd down, at least alter'd at a greater charge than would have procur'd better advice from an able Artist; or if they have stood, they have remained lasting Monuments of the Ignorance or Parsimoniousness of the Owners, or (it may be) of a wrong-judged Profuseness.

What heaps of Stone, and even Marble, are daily seen in Monuments, Chimneys, and other Ornamental pieces of Architecture, without the least Symmetry or Order? When the same or fewer Materials, under the conduct of a skilful Surveyor, would, in less room and with much less charge, have been equally (if not more) useful, and by Justness of Proportion have had a more grand Appearance, and consequently have better answered the Intention of the Expence. For it is not the Bulk of a Fabrick, the Richness and Quantity of the Materials, the Multiplicity of Lines, nor the Gaudiness of the Finishing, that give the Grace or Beauty and Grandeur to a Building; but the Proportion of the Parts to one another and to the Whole, whether entirely plain, or enriched with a few Ornaments properly disposed.

In order to prevent the Abuses and Absurdities above hinted at, I have taken the utmost care that these Designs should be done in the best Tast I could form upon the Instructions of the greatest Masters in *Italy*, as well as my own Observations upon the antient Buildings there, during many Years application to these Studies: For a cursory View of those August Remains can no more qualify the Spectator, or Admirer, than the Air of the Country can inspire him with the knowledge of Architecture.

If this Book prove useful in some degree answerable to the Zeal of my Friends in encouraging and promoting the Publication of it, I shall not think my Time mis-spent, nor my Pains ill bestow'd.

47 ROBERT MORRIS
from *An Essay in Defence of Ancient Architecture* (1728)

P erhaps the most prolific writer of the Palladian movement was Robert Morris, whose work also chronicles its rise and decline. Morris was a "kinsman" of the architect Roger Morris (1695–1749), a well-respected Palladian designer who was closely allied with the Earl of Pembroke. Robert Morris was also a native of Twickenham, which suggests a connection to Alexander Pope, whose poetry he often cites. In his dedication to *An Essay in Defence of Ancient Architecture*, he credits first Burlington and then Pembroke and Andrew Fountaine for being "the principal Practitioners and Preservers" of classicism.

The subtitle of Morris's book alludes of course to Fréart de Chambray's earlier work (see ch. 24 above) as well as to the French quarrel of the Ancients and the Moderns. Morris is religiously on the side of the former, and in his writings he emphasizes the necessity of mathematical precision in proportions, symmetry, order, and above all the harmony that is produced where there is a full concordance of parts with one another. This passage from his third chapter relates the conventional history of architectural practice, which declines under the Goths and Vandals but then is resurrected in Renaissance times. His reference to the fact that "no Footsteps of the Grecian Buildings now remain" dates the chronicle prior to the 1750s, when indeed some existing Greek buildings were "rediscovered." Morris is also appreciative of Wren.

Of the Antiquity and General Causes of the Decay of Architecture

As Architecture has no Limits nor Bounds to its Beauties, so likewise its Continuance hitherto has no Determination of Time affixed, from Records, to its Rise and Foundation. Should we trace it back to the suppos'd Time of its first Invention, should we search the greatest Writers of all Ages who have endeavour'd to clear this Point; they so disagree in their Sentiments and Conjectures, that it will be impossible to discover the Certainty of the Time of its primitive Institution. But beyond dispute, the *Grecians* were the first happy Inventers, they extracted the beauteous Ideas of it from rude and unshapen Trees, the Product of Nature, and embellish'd it, by degrees of Perfectness, with those necessary Ornaments, which have been since practised by those of the most sublime Genius's in all Ages. From hence *Rome* herself was furnished with all those excellent Gifts she so anciently enjoy'd; those divine Ideas of moral Virtue and Philosophy, seem to have been first modell'd and fram'd by the Directions and Rules of the ancient *Grecians*: Or whatever else has stamp'd on it the distinguishing Character of Virtue and Beauty, here, and here only had its original Perfections.

As no Footsteps of the *Grecian* Buildings now remain, we must of necessity have recourse to the Antiquities of the *Romans*, who received the Rules and Methods immediately from the

Robert Morris (1701–54), from *An Essay in Defence of Ancient Architecture; or, a Parallel of the Ancient Buildings with the Modern: Shewing the Beauty and Harmony of the Former and the Irregularity of the Latter* (1728). Farnborough: Gregg International Publishers, 1971 (facsimile edition), pp. 19–25.

Grecians. When the just Sense due to Virtue began to decline in the *Grecians*, so did their Nation, Sciences, and Architecture sink, and were over-whelm'd with it in its Ruins; till the industrious Vigilance of the *Romans* transferr'd it to *Rome*, where it continued long in its native Dress, free from all the false Glosses introduced since, in all its natural Innocency it was adorn'd with all the Perfections which Art or Nature were capable of furnishing her with. How beautifully pleasing and perfect are the never-dying Remains of its endless Glories, collected by the indefatigable Care and Industry of *Palladio?* How bold and engaging in the Appearance? How pure and innocent in the Execution, withal mix'd with an Air of Delicacy and Sweetness in the whole Performance. Such are evident Proofs how preferable the Beauties of ancient Architecture are to the illegal Practices of our modern Builders.

Thus long it continued in its primitive Purity till about the fifth Century, when the barbarous Inhumanity of the *Goths* and *Vandals* (who over-run the greatest part of *Christendom*) and the continual Divisions amongst themselves, totally eras'd all the Remains of its Beauties.

But with these was fatally mix'd the most prejudicial and destroying Enemies of it, Novelty and Singleness: Those began to spread and extend themselves, and the soft Infection easily gain'd upon the Minds of the Multitude. Its Professors being so prejudiced and byass'd by Interest and popular Applause, and their own unhappy restless Tempers, and depress'd with the Insensibility of what was truly great and noble; they utterly, nay, shamefully and openly declared against it, rejected its sublime Principles, and treated it with so much malicious Barbarity, that the original Beauties of Architecture were almost extinct and lost. Thus the decaying Principles of Novelty and Singleness were as destroying in their Nature to Art, as all the Barbarism and Ruins of the destructive Wars of the Enemies of the *Romans*; and were more conducive to the Decay of all Sciences, than the unhappy Divisions among themselves.

It may not be unseasonable, in this place, by way of Remark, to explain the true Sense and Intention of those open Enemies to our Subject, by considering, that in nothing we seem more effeminate than by being so blindly fond of every little Novelty offer'd to our view. Some set such an inestimable Value upon any thing which has the least appearance of Novelty, that the most indefatigable Industry is not wanting to attain their Desires of something which has a Correspondency or Resemblance to it in its formal Disposition. Thus are they led insensibly into erroneous Principles by the prejudicial Sentiments of others: A Thirst after every thing which has the Character of Original imprinted on it, is justly, by the Enemies to Art, adapted to the general changeable Dispositions of Mankind; for this reason, such Success always attends those Productions, whose Birth and Appearance is of the latest Date. Singleness is likewise as dangerous in its Tenets, and as prejudicial in its Principles, as the other. Some appear single in their selfish Opinions, by being ever contradictory to the Evidences of Truth and natural Reason: Some there are who appear single in Opinion, only to be continually opposite to the common Judgment of Mankind. Some again, by the Instability of Fortune, a View to Preferment or Favour, or even a publick Applause, appear single in their Judgments, and act reverse to their own Ideas and Sentiments.

Many more Instances of both kinds might be enumerated: But to hasten to my Subject, I shall only observe, that doubtless that which has been by Practice and convincing Arguments from Nature and Reason, prov'd by many in all Ages to be perfect and pure in its Principles, must be preferable to a Novelty directly opposite; and which is spread by one (perhaps) whose Judgment is as short and limited as the Date of the Infection he spreads; and to appear single for the sake of Singleness or Necessity, falls farther short of Perfection, and leaves us no room to imagine that any thing but Folly can be produc'd by those who have the Agreement of no other (skilful) Judgment but their own; and that too so contradictory to Truth and the commonly received Opinion of the opposite Virtue: and where Constraint obliges us to act, we can certainly expect nothing but what is lame and disorder'd.

This has so true a resemblance of our present Condition, that I cannot but believe, that the farther we appear to be from the Centre and Original of Truth, or the Institution of those just and pure Rules prescrib'd by the Ancients in the Perfection of their Sciences, the farther we deviate from the true Path itself, till it leads us at length through so many mystick Ways, and such unsearchable Labyrinths, that we unhappily mistake the fleeting Shadow for the real Substance. But to return again to our Subject.

Architecture, by these uniting Causes, fell a Victim (with its Fellow-Sciences, Painting and Sculpture, & c.) to the sacrilegious *Barbarians*, and lay long buried in the Ashes of Oblivion, till about the latter end of the thirteenth Century, without the least Pity or Affection; till the Love of Virtue encouraged that great Genius *Bramanté*, in the Time of Pope *Julius* II. to revive the Beauties of it, by a due Observation of the ancient Edifices, and the Practice of it in a Conformity to the Rules and Methods he found made use of in the Execution. *Michael Angelo*, *Ligorio*, and many others were great Assistants and Encouragers of the Revival and Practice of it; amongst whom *Palladio* bears away the Palm. How great is his Manner, how elevated his Ideas, and how bold in the Execution, is best discover'd in those noble Productions he left as Examples for our Imitation. He flourish'd with a Grandeur equal to the infinite Beauties of his Studies, which was in the sixteenth Century, and died in the Year 1580.

In them we see the lively Images of Antiquity rising from Heaps of Ruins, where all the Lustre of Beauty and Art conspire to raise our Sentiments and Ideas to that height, that we may easily perceive the immense difference between those ancient beautiful Productions, and the lame and disorder'd Performances of our Moderns. All who have the least Taste of Art, cannot be insensible how great a Degree of Pleasure arises from a bare Reflection of the Imagination alone, in relation to the Nobleness and Grandeur of the former, and the depress'd Ideas of the latter. These, though unregarded by the unthinking part of Mankind, nevertheless cannot detract from the lasting Tokens of their Greatness, where even the most piercing Causes of Decay, nor even Time itself will hardly ever deface their Memory in the Breasts of the Practitioners of ancient Architecture. At length, through various Scenes and Changes, it (being again revived) safely arrived on these distant Shores; yet not so far placed from Nature's Eye are we, but some Notions of Art sprung or at least remain'd in the Breasts of her polite Sons. Barbarity and Ignorance were shook off, and a due Sense of Virtue and Knowledge were placed in their room. Here, in her Infancy (to us) Architecture was nourish'd with a degree of Tenderness and Care, suitably adapted to its Nobleness and Value, cherish'd with an agreeable Fondness, solid, sincere, and naturally apply'd to the real Beauty of the Object itself; first, like true Friendship, it gradually found success in the open Frankness of its Nature; and by its Beauties and engaging Aspects, it at last so far remov'd all its Enemies, that nothing seem'd wanting (except Encouragement for its Professors from

Men of Wealth and Power) to make it appear in such a Degree of Perfection, that it might even vie with the Ancients, in respect of its Correctness; though as yet little appear'd of it dispers'd amongst the *British* Genius's.

But not out of due time arose that Ever-renowned Professor, who traced back all the pleasing Paths of Antiquity in Architecture, with all the Care and industrious vigilance that was possible to give him any Ideas more conducive to Pleasure and Beauty in the Survey, in which his Imagination surpass'd even a Description, his Judgment arriv'd to the most elevated Height of Perfectness, his Soul being aptly fram'd for the reception of all those noble Sciences and Beauties of the Mind, which human Nature can be capable of receiving: He had in himself something peculiar, a fine Manner of introducing those Master-Strokes of Art, which are the more beautiful and pleasing, as they most resemble Nature in the Design and Execution; in short, he has left such lively Representations of a sublime Genius, that none amongst the Worthy but acknowledge him to be an Example fit for our Imitation, and Guide to lead us through the unerring Rules of ancient Architecture: I mean, the *British Palladio*, INIGO JONES.

Not to detract from the just Honour due to that great Genius, but rather to add Lustre to his Name, I must beg leave to remark upon the deserving Character of a Competitor of his, which was Sir CHRISTOPHER WREN. It is not a little conducing to the Justice due to so great and noble a Soul, to see one of so prodigious an Extent of Knowledge as the Latter, guided as it were, or in some measure confirm'd in his Judgment by the Examples of the Former. Behold with what daring Flights of Art he raises his own and Country's Fame! and that too even in his Youth, what he attempted he happily executed. In a word, there's nothing which has imprinted on it the true Character of Great and Noble, but was centred and lodg'd in the Breast of this venerable and worthy Man.

48   ALEXANDER POPE
from *Of False Taste* (1731)

One of Burlington's closest friends was the poet Alexander Pope, who lived for a few years in Chiswick before moving upstream in 1719 to nearby Twickenham. Pope, a poet and translator of Homer, shared Burlington's love for classical literature, and his design of his own garden with a grotto seems to have stirred Burlington's interest in what would later be known as picturesque garden design. The precise circumstances of this somewhat ironic poem written on behalf of Burlington are not well-known, although Pope employs the subtitle "Occasion'd by his Publishing Palladio's Designs of the Baths, Arches, Theatres, etc. of Ancient Rome" – a book on Palladio that Burlington published in Italian in 1730. Pope nevertheless tempers his blandishment of Burlington with the caveat that "Imitating Fools" will also appear to turn the new classical movement into a pedantic exercise.

Alexander Pope (1688–1744), last two verses from *Of False Taste: An Epistle to the Right Honourable Richard Earl of Burlington*, third edition, pp. 13–14. London: L. Gilliver, 1731.

The poem still captures the sense that Britain was experiencing a classical renaissance in both its literary and artistic endeavors. Around 1733 Pope even turned his house into a proper Palladian villa with the addition of a portico.

[...]
I curse such lavish Cost, and little Skill,
And swear, no Day was ever past so ill.

In you, my *Lord*, Taste sanctifies Expence,
For Splendor borrows all her Rays from Sense.
You show us, *Rome* was glorious, not profuse,
And pompous Buildings once were things of use.
Just as they are, yet shall your noble Rules
Fill half the Land with *Imitating Fools*,
Who random Drawings from your Sheets shall take,
And of one Beauty many Blunders make;
Load some vain Church with old Theatric State;
Turn Arcs of Triumph to a Garden-gate;
Reverse your Ornaments, and hang them all
On some patch'd Doghole ek'd with Ends of Wall,
Then clap four slices of Pilaster on't,
And lac'd with bits of Rustic, 'tis a Front:
Shall call the Winds thro' long Arcades to roar,
Proud to catch cold at a *Venetian* door;
Conscious they act a true *Palladian* part,
And if they starve, they starve by Rules of Art.

Yet thou proceed; be fallen Arts thy care,
Erect new Wonders, and the Old repair,
Jones, and *Palladio* to themselves restore,
And be whate'er *Vitruvius* was before:
Till Kings call forth th' Idea's of thy Mind,
Proud to accomplish what such hands design'd,
Bid Harbors open, publick Ways extend,
And Temples, worthier of the God, ascend;
Bid the broad Arch the dang'rous Flood contain,
The Mole projected break the roaring Main;
Back to his bounds their Subject Sea command,
And roll obedient Rivers thro' the Land:
These Honours, Peace to happy *Britain* brings,
These are Imperial Works, and worthy *Kings*.

49 ISAAC WARE

"Advertisement" to *Andrea Palladio: The Four Books of Architecture* (1737)

Another scholar and architect associated with the Burlington circle was Isaac Ware. He was first trained under Thomas Ripley and then worked in the London Office of Works. Toward the end of the 1720s, Ware met the lord and subsequently made several drawings for Burlington's *Fabbriche Antiche* (1730). Next Ware began working on his own version of *Designs of Inigo Jones and Others*, and in the mid-1730s he also began a new translation of Palladio's *Four Books* – both at Burlington's prompting. The latter had long been dissatisfied with Leoni's and Du Bois's edition (especially the changes Leoni had made to Palladio's designs), and in the 1720s in fact he had encouraged James Gibbs to start a new translation of Palladio. Ware's translation, which was dedicated to Burlington, not only had the lord's financial support, but Burlington also revised the text line by line to ensure its accuracy. Leoni's effort of two decades earlier was thus now superseded in a much more demanding classical climate. The book was published by Ware in London in 1737; it has since been reprinted in New York by Dover Publications, 1965.

The works of the famous ANDREA PALLADIO, published by himself at *Venice* in the year 1570. have been universally esteemed the best standard of architecture hitherto extant. The original work written in Italian being very scarce, several have attempted to translate the same into English, and to copy his excellent and most accurate wooden prints on copper plates.

In particular, two persons have published what they honour with the title of PALLADIO's works: The first, and in all respects the best of the two, was done in the year 1721. by Mr. LEONI; who has thought fit not only to vary from the scale of the originals, but also in many places to alter even the graceful proportions prescribed by this great master, by diminishing some of his measures, enlarging others, and putting in fanciful decorations of his own: and indeed his drawings are likewise very incorrect; which makes this performance, according to his own account in the preface, seem rather to be itself an original, than an improvement on PALLADIO.

The other work (published in the year 1735.) is done with so little understanding, and so much negligence, that it cannot but give great offence to the judicious, and be of very bad consequence in misleading the unskilful, into whose hands it may happen to fall.

To do justice therefore to PALLADIO, and to perpetuate his most valueable remains amongst us, are the principal inducements to my undertaking so great and laborious a work; in executing of which, I have strictly kept to his proportions and measures, by exactly tracing all the plates from his originals, and engraved them with my own hands: So that the reader may depend upon having an exact copy of what our author published, without diminution or increase; nor have I taken upon me to alter, much less to correct, any thing that came from the hands of that excellent artist.

From the same motive I have chosen to give a strict and literal translation, that the sense of our author might be delivered from his own words.

Isaac Ware (d. 1766), "Advertisement" to *Andrea Palladio: The Four Books of Architecture* (1737). New York: Dover Publications, 1965 (facsimile edition).

50 ROBERT MORRIS
from "An Essay upon Harmony" (1739)

I n this important explication of the classical notion of harmony, Morris – like Shaftesbury and Burlington before him – co-mingles two very distinct threads of eighteenth-century British aesthetic thought. On the one hand his definition of "Ideal" and "Oral" harmony coincides with conventional Renaissance aesthetics, and in particular with the Albertian notion of concinnity. On the other hand his description of inanimate "Ocular" harmony of nature echoes the relativist aesthetics of association that would play such a major role in the development of picturesque theory. It is particularly apparent in his discussion of "situation," and we will see this particular topic later developed by Morris (see ch. 99 below). A third idea that works its way into these two passages is that of "character," which will take center stage later in the century.

Harmony is that which, in other Words, we express by Symmetry, Order, Exactness, Elegance, Beauty, Propriety, Perfection, and the like; and these Terms are used according to the Difference of the Composition: Briefly it is the nice Assemblage of Parts proportion'd to each other and justly connected together, in one general Form, Structure, or Arrangement.

In Harmony, there are three general Divisions, which may be distinguish'd by the Terms, *Ideal, Oral*, and *Ocular*.

The Ideal ariseth from such Numbers, Parts, or Proportions, which may be revolved in the Mind, and ranged together in Order, by Contemplation. It may arise from an elegant Description, a beautiful Representation, a Flow of eloquent Images; which may be conveyed to us, by Writing, Discourse, &c. Or it may spring from the mental Idea of the divine Nature; his Attributes and Perfections in the Visible, or the Invisible Parts of the Creation.

Oral Harmony ariseth from the just Connection, Analogy, and Agreement of Sounds, the Sympathetick Concurrence of the Parts in Concert to each other, the Variety, and Changes, and Symphony; of Notes and Tones, their rising and faling in due Distance and Proportion, in Strength and Appropriation, or in Language, Eloquence, or Rhetorick. These are the Branches, from which Oral Harmony spring, and of which it is compos'd.

Ocular Harmony is the most pleasing and extensive, and its Perfections arise from a Multitude of Causes.

The General are two, *Nature* and *Art*.

That Ocular Harmony which flows from *Nature* is various, it consists in Things *Animate* and *Inanimate*.

The *Animate* Harmony is in Man, in Birds, Beasts, Fishes, Insects, &c. in infinite Degrees and Forms of Magnitude, Beauty, Propriety, and Perfection.

The *Inanimate* Harmony is in the Prospects of Hills, Woods, Rivers, Vales, &c. Scenes *noble, rural*, and *pleasing*.

Robert Morris, from "An Essay upon Harmony as it Relates Chiefly to Situation and Building." London: T. Cooper, 1739 and Farnborough: Gregg International Publishers, 1971 (facsimile edition), pp. 7–14, 31–2.

The Soul by Sympathy to Scenes of perfect Beauty, of Proportion and Elegance, is insensibly drawn and attracted; the murmuring *Rivulets*, the silent *Grove*, the verdant *Meads*, the particolour'd Gaieties of Nature, have their Charms which Harmoniously please.

The Inanimate consists likewise in the peculiar Form of Mountains, Trees, Stones, &c. in the Variety and Disposition of the Parts of which they are particularly compos'd and in *Colours*.

Ocular *Harmony*, arising from Art, flows from the nice Occurrence and Affinity with *Nature*: Whether it be in copying her, or forming a System of Beauties, which may spring from Fancy; in these, and in every thing Harmonious, one general Observation is to be regarded: The nearer we approach to Nature in Form, Colour, or Number, or from the Nature and Occurrence of Things, the more agreeable will that *Harmony* be.

In *Musick* there is some sympathetick Force, in the Melody of the Sounds, which tremblingly shoots itself through us, a kind of feeling Sensibility of Harmony, which Words cannot describe; which ariseth from the Concurrence and Affinity of Numbers and Sounds, which tally with those *Organs* of Sensation, which Nature implants in Mankind.

The Harmony of Art is very extensive, though it is to be seen in *Sculpture*, in *Painting*, and *Architecture*, in a more distinguish'd Manner, than in other Sciences, because these are practis'd Universal; and the Theory of them is not difficult to attain a Knowledge of: Though, among the Multitude of Professors, *Phidias, Raphael*, and *Palladio* are the only Produce of many Ages; few are Competitors of their Fame, or fewer deserve a Memorial, to perpetuate their Names to Posterity.

That Harmony in *Sculpture*, which best represents *Nature*, which best describes the Form, Composure, and Texture of the Objects which it is intended to be a Pattern of; which figures out the *Beauty, Symmetry*, and *Proportion*, and displays the *Exactness* of the Original, is of all others the most agreeable; and such Representation, as it is most Natural, will also be most *Harmonious*.

In *Painting*, the Fineness of Shades, of Keeping, of Propriety, of Elegance, and Disposition of Beauty, and Exactness in Copy, or Invention, is most just and pleasing, where it more immediately resembles those Beauties which we admire in Nature.

In *Architecture*, the Form, Magnitude, Dress, Decoration and Arrangement; the Fitness and Proportions, as they are most analogous to *Numbers* and *Nature*, are most perfect and agreeable, most beautiful and harmonious.

The Professors of *Sculpture* and *Painting* have long contested the Excellence of those rival Arts: the one claiming the Priority of the other, for these Reasons: The *Sculptors* say, it is more difficult, from rude Matter, to take away the rough Particles, which secrete a beautiful Statue, in a Block of Stone; to give Likeness, and even to represent the Passions, in lifeless Matter, they say this is more difficult than any part of *Painting*.

On the other hand the *Painter* pleads, that he excells the *Sculptor*, who upon a flat Surface can make the Representation of a *Ball*; can preserve Keeping and Distance, can shew an Object near, and afar off, upon the same Plane: can form a Likeness too, and, by his Art, shew the same Image, which the *Sculptor* can; and as for Keeping, and Distance, by Lights and Shades, claim the Pre-eminence.

I shall not here enter into a Disquisition of the Excellence of these great Arts: The *Harmony*, and *Symmetry*, I intend to speak of, is a Compound of *Art* and *Nature*; and which chiefly relates to *Situation*, and *Architecture*, it is the nice Assemblage and Conjunction of

Things applicable and appropriate to each other: It is the Affinity of each Part to the Whole, in the Fineness, Texture, and Composition, so regulated and fitted, that they may appear joint Assistants, to embellish, decorate, and mutually add to each other's Graces.

Architecture is one easy uniform *Harmony*; its Compositions are of a greater Magnitude than the preceding; and Invention is the principal Talent of the Professor: The Painter and the Scultor may, with their own Hands, finish the Performance or Design: The Architect, in the Execution, calls the Assistance of a Number of *Artificers*; among these, many will be unacquainted with *Symmetry* and *Proportion*, with Elegance and Propriety; therefore the greater is his Care to inspect, appropriate, and perfect the Design.

Choice of Situation, of Proportion, Decoration, Materials, and even Artificers, is the Care of the Architect; and in every Branch a Sameness should be blended together, to perfect the Performance; the Situation should be consider'd as it respects the Convenience, Pleasure, or other Advantage of the Spot: The Proportion should be with respect to the Situation; the Dress, Decoration, and Materials should be adapted to the Propriety and Elegance of the *Situation* and *Convenience*; the Artificers Judgments should square and tally with each other; there should be an Affinity of Knowledge, a Sameness of Taste reign through the whole *Class* who are to compleat it; one uniform Sympathy should attract, and be attracted to each other, through the Execution.

* * *

I come now to speak of the Appropriation of Art, as it relates to Building, or Architecture.

Architecture is an Art useful and extensive, it is founded upon Beauty, and Proportion, or Harmony, are the great Essentials of its Composition: It is divided into three Classes, the *Grave*, the *Jovial*, and the *Charming*; the Grave is the Effect of the *Dorian Modus*; the Jovial of the *Ionian*; and the Charming of the *Corinthian*; these are designed to be fitted, and appropriated, to the several Scenes which Art or Nature have produced, in different Situations.

We are to consider the Extent of the Spot, its Beauties and Fertility; what Improvements may be made, in each of these, before the Design can be form'd; agreeable to this, likewise it is necessary, the Genius, and Fortune of the Builder; be consulted, before the Plan is made.

Any of the beforementioned Scenes are capable of having Designs of any Magnitude, appropriated to them; but the Capaciousness of the Spot should be the Standard of it: I mean for such Parts as are intended for Pleasure only: And for such Plantations as are design'd for Delight, it would be necessary the Spot be first planted, and laid out, for the Advantage of intended Beauties, that the several Trees, &c. should come to some Perfection, before the Seat be compleated; the Scenes will be by far less agreeable, if Maturity has not grac'd the Walks, and Avenues and Retreats, before you make it your Residence.

It will be endless, to trace Harmony through all the little Clues and Labyrinths of Planting, and the nice Appropriation of Art, where little Seats, or Temples, for Beauty, Ease, and Retirement, may be placed in them. But of these, no Pattern can give us a more agreeable Idea, than those of Lord *Burlington* at *Cheswick*.

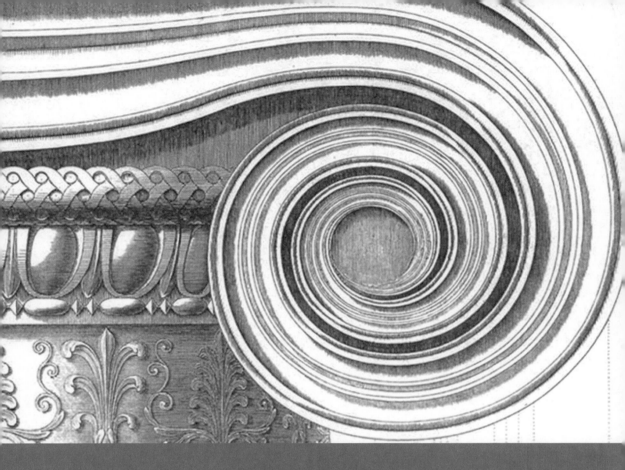

PART III   NEOCLASSICISM AND THE ENLIGHTENMENT

A. EARLY NEOCLASSICISM

Introduction

The classical and Christian traditions that were architecturally mediated during the Renaissance once again come to meet strong resistance in the second half of the eighteenth century. The challenges this time, however, came first not within architectural circles but rather from a more pervasive and commanding cultural upheaval. For this was the period more generally referred to as the Enlightenment: a time of momentous intellectual, political, and social change.

Born of such elusive epithets as reason and toleration, human and scientific progress, political and religious liberty – the Enlightenment is a difficult phenomenon to encapsulate in a few words, but its political consequences can be readily intuited in the American Revolution of 1776 and the French Revolution of 1789. It was a time in which ever widening circles of people became interested in ever broader reaches of history and culture. It was as well a time in which nearly every political, religious, and philosophical idea inherited from the past came under scrutiny. Modern notions of social equality and human freedom were born in the excesses of these times. The first encyclopedias attempted to summarize the depth of human knowledge and make it available to every reader. And reason and human liberty became important touchstones of the new outlook. The sum of what is referred to as the "Western" system of ethical, aesthetic, and legal values here has its modern foundation.

In architectural theory these challenges are generally considered under the term "neoclassicism," which while aptly characterizing a new fascination with Greek antiquity is not especially an appropriate appellation. Classicism, it is true, was once again revisited (this time directly on Greek soil), but it is also now reconstituted in new and surprisingly innovative ways. The hegemony of a single stylistic vocabulary begins to break down, although in a slow and methodical manner. Its former aesthetic grounding in absolute beauty is now severely undercut by art's rather sudden secularization, and even by the new public nature of the widening debate. The desire to expand the formal vocabulary of the designer, while at the same time subjecting design rigorously to the laws of reason, affords new freedoms but at the same time imposes new restraints. To all of these elements one might add the relatively novel idea of a "nation" or national characteristics, and the possibility of a new stylistic synthesis, equal to those attained in Greek, Roman, or Gothic times, becomes pushed beyond the realm of possibility – however much architects might still dream otherwise.

51 JOHANN BERNHARD FISCHER VON ERLACH
from Preface to *Outline for a Historical Architecture* (1721)

Fischer von Erlach was the greatest Austrian architect of the baroque period. Born in Graz and trained in Rome in the late-baroque era of Pietro da Cortona and Domenico Fontana, he returned to the Habsburg capital of Vienna in 1687 and almost immediately gained favor with the imperial crown. Among his many monumental commissions for Vienna were his designs for the Schönbrunn Palace (1696–1711) and the Karlskirche (1715–38) – the last a masterpiece of spatial drama and historical acumen. But Fischer von Erlach was also the author of what is perhaps the most stupendous architectural study ever produced. Despite its early publication date, his *Entwurf einer historischen Architektur* rightfully might be considered the first architectural textbook of the Enlightenment.

This colossal study, started in 1705, consists of five books and features his extraordinary reconstructions of world architecture: from the Temple of Solomon and the Seven Wonders of the ancient world to the architecture of Assyria, India, China, Egypt, Constantinople, Greece, Rome, to mention but a few peoples. Even Stonehenge and modern baroque examples find their way into his visual anthology. The short preface is also of importance, because it defines its author as straddling two eras. As a baroque architect he could not imagine monumental architecture without such basic principles as symmetry. At the same time his cultural relativism, indeed the breadth of his historical scope, seems to be at least a half-century ahead of its time. The "scientific" cast of these remarks is also a feature of the Enlightenment.

In such a way may the present outline of every kind of architecture not only please but also further the sciences and serve the arts. For in historical thinking not everything should be

Johann Bernhard Fischer von Erlach (1656–1723), from Preface to *Entwurf einer historischen Architektur* [Outline for a historical architecture] (1721), pp. 4–5., trans. Harry Francis Mallgrave.

left to the imagination or based on mere descriptions. By consulting illustrations the eyes themselves can draw conclusions and strengthen memory: even if only to gain the chance, exercised in drawings, of comparing the different national tastes (which, as in foods, is also dissimilar in clothing and in architecture) and selecting the best. In this way we can recognize that in architecture, indeed, something can be based on custom not bound by rules . . . that a nation's judgment cannot be contested any more than its taste. Still, in architecture – all variation aside – there are certain general principles that cannot be neglected without evident harm. *Symmetry* is one of them; or, that the weaker must be supported by the stronger, etc. There are also certain conditions that can always be distinguished and that please in every style of building, such as a building's overall size, its attractiveness, and precision in the handling and laying of stone, etc.

52 VOLTAIRE
from *Philosophic Letters on the English* (1733)

If France possesses one godfather of the Enlightenment, it is surely the contentious yet prodigious spirit of Voltaire. A virtual lifetime lived in exile – Voltaire was at home in the salons of kings, queens, and princes, against whom he often could not resist turning his satirical pen. He was a strong supporter of Diderot's encyclopedia project, and when things looked darkest he pleaded with Diderot to bring the project to Potsdam, where Voltaire was enjoying the hospitality of Frederick the Great. In addition to his comedies and other literary works, Voltaire was a prolific historian, and in fact deserves to be named among the Enlightenment's major historians.

His *Lettres philosophiques sur les Anglais* is among the earliest of his published writings. He barely got the book past French censors, and even then it suffered the fate of so many of his writings. It was denounced as heretical in 1734; the publisher was sent to the Bastille; a warrant of arrest was issued for Voltaire himself; and the Parliament of Paris had the book publicly burned by the executioner. Voltaire, however, had already fled Paris for the independent duchy of Lorraine and was living with Émile de Breteuil, the Marquise du Châtelet. If Voltaire's public immorality was not so unusual for this period, the fact that in this book he championed the British Parliament and the notion of political liberty was unique, and therefore was seen as a direct threat to the sovereignty of the French king.

The English Parliament

The members of the English Parliament are fond of comparing themselves, on all occasions, to the old Romans.

Not long since, Mr. Shippen opened a speech in the house of commons with these words: "The majesty of the people of England would be wounded." The singularity of this

Voltaire (François-Marie Arouet, 1694–1778), from *Lettres philosophiques sur les anglais* [Philosophic letters on the English] (1733), trans. William F. Fleming, in *The Works of Voltaire: A Contemporary Version*, Vol. XIX, pp. 5–6. New York: Dingwall-Rock, 1927.

expression occasioned a loud laugh; but this gentleman, far from being disconcerted, repeated the statement with a resolute tone of voice, and the laugh ceased. I must own, I see no resemblance between the majesty of the people of England and that of the Romans, and still less between the two governments. There is in London a senate, some of the members whereof are accused – doubtless very unjustly – of selling their votes, on certain occasions, as was done at Rome; and herein lies the whole resemblance. In other respects, the two nations appear to be quite opposite in character, with regard both to good and to evil. The Romans never knew the terrible madness of religious wars. This abomination was reserved for devout preachers of patience and humility. Marius and Sulla, Cæsar and Pompey, Antony and Augustus, did not draw their swords against one another to determine whether the flamen should wear his shirt over his robe, or his robe over his shirt; or whether the sacred chickens should both eat and drink, or eat only, in order to take the augury. The English have formerly destroyed one another, by sword or halter, for disputes of as trifling a nature. The Episcopalians and the Presbyterians quite turned the heads of these gloomy people for a time; but I believe they will hardly be so silly again, as they seem to have grown wiser at their own expense; and I do not perceive the least inclination in them to murder one another any more for mere syllogisms. But who can answer for the follies and prejudices of mankind?

Here follows a more essential difference between Rome and England, which throws the advantage entirely on the side of the latter; namely, that the civil wars of Rome ended in slavery, and those of the English in liberty. The English are the only people on earth who have been able to prescribe limits to the power of kings by resisting them, and who, by a series of struggles, have at length established that wise and happy form of government where the prince is all-powerful to do good, and at the same time is restrained from committing evil; where the nobles are great without insolence or lordly power, and the people share in the government without confusion.

The house of lords and the house of commons divide the legislative power under the king; but the Romans had no such balance. Their patricians and plebeians were continually at variance, without any intermediate power to reconcile them. The Roman senate, who were so unjustly, so criminally, formed as to exclude the plebeians from having any share in the affairs of government, could find no other artifice to effect their design than to employ them in foreign wars. They considered the people as wild beasts, whom they were to let loose upon their neighbors, for fear they should turn upon their masters. Thus the greatest defect in the government of the Romans was the means of making them conquerors; and, by being unhappy at home, they became masters of the world, till in the end their divisions sank them into slavery.

The government of England, from its nature, can never attain to so exalted a pitch, nor can it ever have so fatal an end. It has not in view the splendid folly of making conquests, but only the prevention of their neighbors from conquering. The English are jealous not only of their own liberty, but even of that of other nations. The only reason of their quarrels with Louis XIV. was on account of his ambition.

53 JACQUES-GABRIEL SOUFFLOT
from "Memoir on Architectural Proportions" (1739)

The first great architect of the Enlightenment in France was Jacques-Gabriel Soufflot. He was born near Auxerre, educated himself for the most part in Rome, and returned to Lyons to begin practice in 1738. During the 1740s his career prospered with commissions for several important buildings, among them the extension of the city's hospital, the Hôtel Dieu (1739–48). As a scholar, he also presented several papers to the Société Royale des Beaux-Arts in Lyons. In general, Soufflot opposed the prevailing trend of rococo design and was seeking an alternative. This search received an unexpected impetus in 1749 when he was asked by Madame de Pompadour, the mistress to Louis XV, to accompany her brother – the future Marquis de Marigny – on his grand tour of Italy. The lengthy sabbatical allowed Soufflot a chance to revisit classical buildings and undertake new studies, the most important of which were the measurements that he, together with Gabriel-Pierre-Martin Dumont, made of the early Greek temples at Paestum. With this, he became the first Frenchman to study authentic Greek buildings. The same trip proved enormously beneficial in another regard. In 1751 Marigny assumed his new post of director of royal buildings in Paris, and he invited Soufflot to the capital to become the municipal architect. Four years later Soufflot received the commission for the grandest building project of eighteenth-century France, the new church of Sainte Geneviève in Paris (replacing the earlier church on which the Perraults had proposed renovations). The task would occupy him for the rest of his life and become the first great monument to French neoclassicism.

The first selection from Soufflot is from a lecture he gave to the Lyons Academy in 1739, and it forms perhaps his first theoretical statement. Two things are of interest. First, he resurrects the Perrault/Blondel dispute and thus places these issues once again on the table. Second, with his youthful support for absolute proportions, he sides with the position of Blondel. This support will later wane when Soufflot, with his design of Sainte Geneviève (1755–80), reverses his earlier position and takes a stand for proportional innovation.

Two of the most able architects of the last century had a most lively dispute on architectural proportions. Their writings on that art, and the superb monuments built from their designs and under their guidance, will stand for posterity (as they do for us) as a measure of their true merit. And it is somewhat difficult to understand how two architects with differing views on such an essential part of their art, have produced things of equal beauty – even if we know well that learned men on occasions, and even too often, possess the bad quality of not wanting to retract something that they have said on one occasion, even if inside they feel they were wrong and are therefore acting contrary to principles to which they declaim. The two learned men of which I wish to speak are M. François Blondel, professor and director of the Royal Academy of Architecture, and M. Perrault, architect of the king. We are indebted to the latter for the well-known translation of Vitruvius and to the former for his learned textbook of architecture, which in my view is sufficient to train a young man in this art of building. In several chapters at the end of this excellent work Blondel asserts and proves, as

Jacques-Gabriel Soufflot (1713–80), from "Mémoire sur les proportions de l'architecture" [Memoir on architectural proportions] (1739), trans. Harry Francis Mallgrave from Michael Petzet (ed.), *Soufflots Sainte-Geneviève und der französische Kirchenbau des 18. Jahrhunderts*. Berlin: Walter de Gruyter, 1961, pp. 131–2.

far as he is able, that architectural proportions are based on natural principles, as they are in the other arts. It is for this reason that we are compelled to feel – even without understanding them – admiration and a liking for the buildings in which they are found, and to form a certain disgust for those buildings where certain proportions are not found, even when these other buildings are superior either in their honesty of execution or in the delicacy of their ornaments.

It is also in the notes to the translation of Vitruvius (Book 4, ch. 1) that M. Perrault announced that architectural proportions are based only on custom and do not have the necessary and convincing positive beauty that surpasses the beauty of other proportions, like the beauty of a diamond surpasses that of a pebble. Instead, positive beauty is found in those works that have additional convincing beauties, such as that of the material or the justness of execution. We approve of the beauty of these proportions because there is nothing more positive than this reason to prefer things by the association or habit that is found almost in all things that please, which one does not believe it a fault to have reflected upon it. He speaks more on proportions in several other places in almost the same terms, and in the end it is easy to find the views of these two men elsewhere in the works that I have cited. I need not say more.

For me, I have always deferred to the sentiments of M. Blondel more so than to those of M. Perrault, at least regarding proportions in general and even with regard to several specific proportions. [. . .]

54 JACQUES GABRIEL SOUFFLOT
from "Memoir on Gothic Architecture" (1741)

Notwithstanding Soufflot's initial reluctance to follow Perrault on the issue of proportions, he shared the latter's respect for the structural ingenuity of Gothic architecture. This very important issue, in fact, never went away after Perrault. Early in the eighteenth century, as we have seen, both Michel de Frémin and Jean-Louis de Cordemoy pressed Perrault's argument further, and others followed suit. In 1736 the architect Ferdinand Delamonce, who would later work with Soufflot on the extension of the Hôtel Dieu, defended the delicacy of Gothic proportions, and in 1738 the engineer Frézier – the one-time opponent of Cordemoy – praised the ingenuity of the Gothic system of vaulting in his structural treatise. Soufflot's "Mémoire sur l'architecture gothique" follows in the same vein. In this lecture he summarizes various dimensional studies he has made of Gothic churches, and at one point concedes that the lightness of Gothic construction is "more ingenious, more daring, and even more difficult than our method of construction." As the following concluding passage makes clear, this admiration for the Gothic structural system does not extend to Gothic forms and ornaments; academic teachings remained firmly and specifically opposed to them. In arguing for the suppression of the entablature above the columns of a church nave, Soufflot is searching for the "right mean" between the heaviness of classical forms and the lightness of Gothic construction. He will later

Jacques-Gabriel Soufflot, from "Mémoire sur l'architecture gothique" (1741), trans. Harry Francis Mallgrave from Michael Petzet (ed.), *Soufflots Sainte-Geneviève und der französische Kirchenbau des 18. Jahrhunderts*. Berlin, Walter de Gruyter, 1961, p. 142.

implement this ambition in his design for the church of Sainte Geneviève, where, as one contemporary commentator noted, he sought "to join under one of the most beautiful forms the lightness of the construction of Gothic edifices with the purity and magnificence of Greek architecture." The partially cited Latin phrase *Omne tulit punctum* [*qui miscuit utile dulci*] is from Horace: "he has gained every vote who blends the useful with the agreeable."

I could provide details of many of the parts that once again tend to make Gothic churches appear grander than our own, but I have only promised an essay and my talk is already too long. All I wish to say in conclusion is that – disregarding entirely the chimerical and bizarre ornaments of the Goths – we are able to profit from a study of the Gothic without giving in to the extreme nature of its proportions. We should be able to find the right mean between their style and our own, which repairs the defect of the first glance and might perhaps let us say to him who should have this good fortune: *Omne tulit punctum.*

This may not happen, I admit, without breaking our rules and without making use of some of those Gothic rules. I risk saying it, but an academy like that in Paris or in Rome, it seems to me, does have the right to make changes in artistic rules that, all prejudice aside, may be both useful and necessary. Learned men have established rules; learned men can assemble to reformulate them.

Vitruvius in his basilica at Fano employed neither a frieze nor a cornice. The ancients also suppressed friezes and cornices in the first order of the Egyptian hall. The Goths, without wanting to imitate them, recognized that these projections break the visual lines and clutter the general contour of their churches; they did not put them in their works although without entirely suppressing them. I believe that we are at least able to give them less projection and greater lightness. Why do we hold to our rules so strictly if, by departing from them, we can give trained eyes (and what is rare, unprejudiced eyes) more satisfaction than by following them? If some barriers avert us from the middle of the road of perfection, we know how to step over them. This liberty, if not being accorded to all architects, should at least be extended to those who through long experience and much prudence have arrived at a profound theory.

55 CARLO LODOLI
from Notes for a projected treatise on architecture (1740s)

One of the characteristics of the Enlightenment was a rationalist willingness to question authority, and in architecture this would mean questioning of the relevance of the teachings of Vitruvius. One of the first individuals to do so was the Franciscan friar Carlo Lodoli. Born in Venice, Lodoli studied in Dalmatia and Rome before moving to Verona in 1715, where he participated in a society of antiquarians well versed in areas of classical learning. Lodoli was a progressive in the sense that he was an admirer of Voltaire, Montesquieu, and

Carlo Lodoli (1690–1761), from Notes for a projected treatise on architecture (c. 1740s), trans. Edgar Kaufmann Jr., from Memmo's *Elementi d'architecturra lodoliana* (Zara, 1834) and first published in *The Art Bulletin* 46:1 (March 1964), pp. 162–4.

Giambattista Vico. Sometime after moving back to Venice in 1730, he opened a private seminar on architectural theory for sons of Venetian nobles. He ran the seminar in a peripatetic fashion until 1748.

Lodoli left no writings of his ideas, but he apparently did leave behind notes for a projected treatise, which were recorded by one of his students, Andrea Memmo (1729–93). Although these notes, actually two different sets of notes, were not published until 1833, they were even then seen as remarkable for the spirit of their functionalist rigor. The following two passages are two outlines for Books 1 and 2 of the projected treatise. Notable in the first is both the opening assault on Vitruvius and the demand for "new forms and new terms" responsive to present needs. Notable in the second is his insistence that "proper function and form are the only two final, scientific aims" of architecture.

Prefatory Discourse

On the Origin and Development of the Building Art. Examination of various hypotheses about the first structures built, in diverse climates and of different materials. Possible difficulties to be overcome in reaching a sensible and correct approach to civil architecture; and remarks on the author's fatal disadvantage in having to reveal the short-sightedness of so many famous practitioners and theorists; architectural systems used up to now.

Book I

I

An impartial, philosophical examination of the chief known [architectural] systems, beginning with the Egyptian, Etruscan, Doric, Ionic, Corinthian, then on to the Composite, and finally the French and Spanish ones. Reasons why no other architectural styles whatever are considered, but only those derivable from Vitruvius, the one authoritative source among the ancients and the late Romans.

Enumeration of the obvious theoretical errors contained in his [Vitruvius's] works.

II

An exposition of the faults, indeed the inadequacies and contradictions of the five orders: blemishes and defects both physical and practical which result, and convincing demonstrations of the wrongfulness [of the orders] when built in stone.

III

About the need for new rules [*instituto*], so that civil architecture shall not remain limited by those effects and memberings, compositions and terminologies, that have been usual up to now; and further, about the resulting necessity for new forms and new terms responsive to the need, as fully as may be necessary to satisfy it completely.

Book II

Prologue

About the new rules, showing the importance of the method which informs them; about the first principles of the theory of reason, and about the theory of experiment and demonstration, with indications of the best writers on geometry for use by architects, as well as on mechanics, statics, stereotomy, and others such as have dealt with arithmetic, design, hydraulics, hydrostatics, physics, etc., together with two new essays on the practical knowledge of the horizontal and vertical compressibility of woods, that is, zilology, and of various stones, that is, lithology [insofar as these materials] exist in the Venetian State, particularly [meant] for the use of unlettered builders, with various remarks on the separate and distinct properties of one and the other material.

Decisive knowledge required for architects, for those who act as architects, or those who build without architectural guidance, and for others who are requested, now and again, to give their opinion on models or on unbuilt buildings, and who [are wont to] rely on their so-called good taste or on knowledge entirely removed from the craft [of building], and who are in search of some solid support.

I

Since civil architecture should take the guise of a science, and should be considered such, and since apparently others have so treated it, one should demand principles that lead with certainty to the fulfillment of those final aims toward which architecture tends, whatever these aims may be, or however many. The integral parts [of architecture] need to be put in order, to be clarified (since so far none of its laws have proven incontrovertible, nor its norms rational and effective in the parts and in the whole).

II

What parts [of architecture] are integral and immutable, capable of being considered primary and demonstrably eternal; and what integral parts may be considered secondary, calling for norms consonant with the unalterable qualities of the primary integral parts.

[...]

Book I

Proem

Definition of civil architecture.
Definition of proper function and form.
—— of soundness
—— of proportion
—— of convenience
—— of ornament

Proper function and form are the only two final, scientific aims of civil architecture. What is meant by one and the other, and why they should be so merged as to become one single thing. Soundness, proportion, and convenience are essential properties of form.

Ornament is not essential but accessory to proper function and form; furthermore, no architectural beauty can be found that does not issue from the truth; cut off, it is no longer harmonious. Authority and habit can never yield more than a borrowed beauty, only such as is relative to unduly vague ideas arising from transitory stimuli and varying from place to place.

Proportion, convenience, and ornament can take shape only through the application of mathematics and physics guided by rational norms.

Book II

The function of a material well suited to building is the repeated and modified effect of this material as it is demonstratively used according to its nature and according to the proposed design; it will always harmonize soundness, proportion, and convenience one with the others.

Form is the indivisible and complete expression resulting from materials employed according to geometric, arithmetic, and optical rules, to reach an intended result.

Architectural soundness is that total and individual strength which arises in buildings from the application of static, physical, and chemical theories to selected materials, simple and composite.

Proportion is that regular correspondence between parts and the whole which should arise in buildings from stereometric and arithmetic theories allied to rational norms, and applied to the shape and dimensions of architectural elevations, members, openings, and spaces [*vasi*].

56 BARON DE MONTESQUIEU
from Preface to *The Spirit of the Laws* (1748)

The Enlightenment hit its stride in the 1750s, but many of its historical premises (and its limitations) are found in this grand historical study of Baron de Montesquieu, a native and long-time resident of Bordeaux. In his early writings he, like Voltaire, was a satirist of the social, political, and ecclesiastical follies of his day, but in this lengthy and mature study of laws and forms of government (numbering 31 books), he — now from a quite moderate position — attempts to analyze the difference between different nations and different cultures. His

Baron de Montesquieu (Charles Louis de Secondat, 1689–1755), from Preface to *L'Esprit des Lois* (1748), trans. Thomas Nugent, in *The Spirit of the Laws*. New York: Hafner Press, 1949, pp. lxvii–lxix. © 1949 by Hafner Publishing Company. Reprinted with permission of The Free Press, a division of Simon & Schuster Adult Publishing Group.

explanation for differences is not so much based on free will or human reason (as would shortly become in vogue) but rather on the premise that human culture, in all of its manifestations, is a product of nature, and specifically of the geographical and climatic conditions under which it is nurtured. Again, this is an early search for the science of history, for an anthropological model under which to evaluate human culture and its various transformations.

I have first of all considered mankind, and the result of my thoughts has been, that amidst such an infinite diversity of laws and manners, they were not solely conducted by the caprice of fancy.

I have laid down the first principles, and have found that the particular cases follow naturally from them; that the histories of all nations are only consequences of them; and that every particular law is connected with another law, or depends on some other of a more general extent.

When I have been obliged to look back into antiquity I have endeavored to assume the spirit of the ancients, lest I should consider those things as alike which are really different, and lest I should miss the difference of those which appear to be alike.

I have not drawn my principles from my prejudices, but from the nature of things.

Here a great many truths will not appear till we have seen the chain which connects them with others. The more we enter into particulars, the more we shall perceive the certainty of the principles on which they are founded. I have not even given all these particulars, for who could mention them all without a most insupportable fatigue?

The reader will not here meet with any of those bold flights which seem to characterize the works of the present age. When things are examined with never so small a degree of extent, the sallies of imagination must vanish; these generally arise from the mind's collecting all its powers to view only one side of the subject, while it leaves the other unobserved.

I write not to censure anything established in any country whatsoever. Every nation will here find the reasons on which its maxims are founded; and this will be the natural inference, that to propose alterations belongs only to those who are so happy as to be born with a genius capable of penetrating the entire constitution of a state.

It is not a matter of indifference that the minds of the people be enlightened. The prejudices of magistrates have arisen from national prejudice. In a time of ignorance they have committed even the greatest evils without the least scruple; but in an enlightened age they even tremble while conferring the greatest blessings. They perceive the ancient abuses; they see how they must be reformed; but they are sensible also of the abuses of a reformation. They let the evil continue, if they fear a worse; they are content with a lesser good, if they doubt a greater. They examine into the parts, to judge of them in connection; and they examine all the causes, to discover their different effects.

Could I but succeed so as to afford new reasons to every man to love his prince; his country, his laws; new reasons to render him more sensible in every nation and government of the blessings he enjoys, I should think myself the most happy of mortals.

Could I but succeed so as to persuade those who command to increase their knowledge in what they ought to prescribe, and those who obey to find a new pleasure resulting from obedience – I should think myself the most happy of mortals.

The most happy of mortals should I think myself could I contribute to make mankind recover from their prejudices. By prejudices I here mean, not that which renders men ignorant of some particular things, but whatever renders them ignorant of themselves.

It is in endeavoring to instruct mankind that we are best able to practice that general virtue which comprehends the love of all. Man, that flexible being, conforming in society to the thoughts and impressions of others, is equally capable of knowing his own nature whenever it is laid open to his view, and of losing the very sense of it when this idea is banished from his mind.

57 JEAN-JACQUES ROUSSEAU
from *Discourse on the Sciences and Arts* (1750)

The Enlightenment in France in the 1750s is often synonymous with two events: Rousseau's literary appearance, and the great encyclopedia project of Denis Diderot and Jean Le Rond D'Alembert. The events were not unrelated, as all three were close friends. Together, however, their critiques conspired to produce a broad attack on the status quo: the king and the aristocracy, the church, education, and art. The political attacks subsequently gathered momentum and ultimately culminated in the French Revolution.

Rousseau never lived to see the storming of the Bastille (politically he much preferred the concept of a small city-state to an international power), but he was always hailed as one of the revolution's intellectual heroes. Born in Geneva, he wandered for much of his youth before arriving in Paris in 1744, where he eventually joined the bohemian circle of Diderot. For some years he worked on a new system of musical notation, but obviously his strengths lay elsewhere. His break came in the summer of 1749 when the Dijon Academy announced an essay competition on the question: "Has the restoration of the sciences and art tended to purify morals?" Rousseau not only won the contest but he also took a position quite contrary to most other competitors by insisting that the advancement of the sciences and arts only leads to national and personal corruption. Here begins his life-long assault on existing social mores. The following excerpt deals with the personal affectation fostered by a cultured society, which stands in contrast to the idealized social vision of earlier times, where – in Rousseau's view – simplicity, honesty, and reason were virtues to be cultivated.

Has the restoration of the sciences and arts tended to purify or corrupt morals? That is the subject to be examined. Which side should I take in this question? The one, gentlemen, that suits an honorable man who knows nothing and yet does not think any the less of himself.

It will be difficult, I feel, to adapt what I have to say to the tribunal before which I appear. How can one dare blame the sciences before one of Europe's most learned Societies, praise ignorance in a famous Academy, and reconcile contempt for study with respect for the truly

Jean-Jacques Rousseau (1712–88), from *Discours sur les sciences et les arts* [Discourse on the sciences and arts] (1750), trans. Roger D. Master and Judith R. Master, in *Jean-Jacques Rousseau: The First and Second Discourses*. New York: St. Martin's Press, 1964, pp. 36–9. © 1969 by Bedford/St. Martin's. Reprinted with permission of Bedford/St. Martin's.

learned? I have seen these contradictions, and they have not rebuffed me. I am not abusing science, I told myself; I am defending virtue before virtuous men. Integrity is even dearer to good men than erudition to the scholarly. What then have I to fear? The enlightenment of the assembly that listens to me? I admit such a fear; but it applies to the construction of the discourse and not to the sentiment of the orator. Equitable sovereigns have never hesitated to condemn themselves in doubtful disputes; and the position most advantageous for one with a just cause is to have to defend himself against an upright and enlightened opponent who is judge of his own case.

This motive which encourages me is joined by another which determines me: having upheld, according to my natural intellect, the cause of truth, whatever the outcome there is a prize which I cannot fail to receive; I will find it at the bottom of my heart.

First Part

It is a grand and beautiful sight to see man emerge from obscurity somehow by his own efforts; dissipate, by the light of his reason, the darkness in which nature had enveloped him; rise above himself; soar intellectually into celestial regions; traverse with giant steps, like the sun, the vastness of the universe; and – what is even grander and more difficult – come back to himself to study man and know his nature, his duties, and his end. All of these marvels have been revived in recent generations.

Europe had sunk back into the barbarism of the first ages. The peoples of that part of the world which is today so enlightened lived, a few centuries ago, in a condition worse than ignorance. A nondescript scientific jargon, even more despicable than ignorance, had usurped the name of knowledge, and opposed an almost invincible obstacle to its return. A revolution was needed to bring men back to common sense; it finally came from the least expected quarter. The stupid Moslem, the eternal scourge of learning, brought about its rebirth among us. The fall of the throne of Constantine brought into Italy the debris of ancient Greece. France in turn was enriched by these precious spoils. Soon the sciences followed letters; the art of writing was joined by the art of thinking – an order which seems strange but which is perhaps only too natural; and people began to feel the principal advantage of literary occupations, that of making men more sociable by inspiring in them the desire to please one another with works worthy of their mutual approval.

The mind has its needs as does the body. The needs of the body are the foundations of society, those of the mind make it pleasant. While government and laws provide for the safety and well-being of assembled men, the sciences, letters, and arts, less despotic and perhaps more powerful, spread garlands of flowers over the iron chains with which men are burdened, stifle in them the sense of that original liberty for which they seemed to have been born, make them love their slavery, and turn them into what is called civilized peoples. Need raised thrones; the sciences and arts have strengthened them. Earthly powers, love talents and protect those who cultivate them.[1] Civilized peoples, cultivate talents: happy slaves, you owe to them that delicate and refined taste on which you pride yourselves; that softness of character and urbanity of customs which make relations among you so amiable and easy; in a word, the semblance of all the virtues without the possession of any.

By this sort of civility, the more pleasant because it is unpretentious, Athens and Rome once distinguished themselves in the much vaunted days of their magnificence and splendor. It is by such civility that our century and our nation will no doubt surpass all times and all peoples. A philosophic tone without pedantry; natural yet engaging manners, equally remote from Teutonic simplicity and Italian pantomime: these are the fruits of the taste acquired by good education and perfected in social intercourse.

How pleasant it would be to live among us if exterior appearance were always a reflection of the heart's disposition; if decency were virtue; if our maxims served as our rules; if true philosophy were inseparable from the title of philosopher! But so many qualities are too rarely combined, and virtue seldom walks in such great pomp. Richness of attire may announce a wealthy man, and elegance a man of taste; the healthy, robust man is known by other signs. It is in the rustic clothes of a farmer and not beneath the gilt of a courtier that strength and vigor of the body will be found. Ornamentation is no less foreign to virtue, which is the strength and vigor of the soul. The good man is an athlete who likes to compete in the nude. He disdains all those vile ornaments which would hamper the use of his strength, most of which were invented only to hide some deformity.

Before art had moulded our manners and taught our passions to speak an affected language, our customs were rustic but natural, and differences of conduct announced at first glance those of character. Human nature, basically, was no better, but men found their security in the ease of seeing through each other, and that advantage, which we no longer appreciate, spared them many vices.

Today, when subtler researches and a more refined taste have reduced the art of pleasing to set rules, a base and deceptive uniformity prevails in our customs, and all minds seem to have been cast in the same mould. Incessantly politeness requires, propriety demands; incessantly usage is followed, never one's own inclinations. One no longer dares to appear as he is; and in this perpetual constraint, the men who form this herd called society, placed in the same circumstances, will all do the same things unless stronger motives deter them. Therefore one will never know well those with whom he deals, for to know one's friend thoroughly, it would be necessary to wait for emergencies – that is, to wait until it is too late, as it is for these very emergencies that it would have been essential to know him.

What a procession of vices must accompany this uncertainty! No more sincere friend-ships; no more real esteem; no more well-based confidence. Suspicions, offenses, fears, coldness, reserve, hate, betrayal will hide constantly under that uniform and false veil of politeness, under that much vaunted urbanity which we owe to the enlightenment of our century. The name of the Master of the Universe will no longer be profaned by swearing, but it will be insulted by blasphemies without offending our scrupulous ears. Men will not boast of their own merit, but they will disparage that of others. An enemy will not be grossly insulted, but he will be cleverly slandered. National hatreds will die out, but so will love of country. For scorned ignorance, a dangerous Pyrrhonism will be substituted. There will be some forbidden excesses, some dishonored vices, but others will be dignified with the name of virtues; one must either have them or affect them. Whoever wants to praise the sobriety of the wise men of our day may do so; as for me, I see in it only a refinement of intemperance as unworthy of my praise as their cunning simplicity.[2]

Such is the purity our morals have acquired. Thus have we become respectable men. It is for literature, the sciences, and the arts to claim their share of such a wholesome piece of work.

I will add only one thought: an inhabitant of some faraway lands who wanted to form a notion of European morals on the basis of the state of the sciences among us, the perfection of our arts, the decency of our entertainments, the politeness of our manners, the affability of our speech, our perpetual demonstrations of goodwill, and that tumultuous competition of men of all ages and conditions who seem anxious to oblige one another from dawn to dark; that foreigner, I say, would guess our morals to be exactly the opposite of what they are.

NOTES

1   Princes always view with pleasure the spread, among their subjects, of the taste for arts of amusement and superfluities which do not result in the exportation of money. For, besides fostering that spiritual pettiness so appropriate to servitude, they very well know that all needs the populace creates for itself are so many chains binding it. Alexander, desiring to keep the Ichthyophagi dependent on him, forced them to give up fishing and to eat foodstuffs common to other peoples; but the American savages who go naked and live on the yield of their hunting have never been subjugated. Indeed, what yoke could be imposed on men who need nothing?

2   "I like," says Montaigne, "to argue and discuss, but only with a few men and for myself. For to serve as a spectacle to the great and to show off competitively one's wit and one's babble is, I find, a very inappropriate occupation for an honorable man." It is the occupation of all our wits, save one.

58   JEAN LE ROND D'ALEMBERT
from "Preliminary Discourse of the Editors" (1751)

Denis Diderot's encyclopedia project, one of the great intellectual monuments to the Enlightenment, had a speckled and difficult history. Diderot was originally hired in 1743 to prepare a French translation of Ephraim Chambers's two-volume *Cyclopaedia*, published in London in 1728. In 1745, when Diderot took over as managing editor, he convinced the French publisher to abandon the earlier work and embark on an entirely new and up-to-date project. The Prospectus of 1750 promised at least 10 volumes and 600 illustrative plates, following the spirit of rigorous logical analysis and scientific methods of reason. The royal academician d'Alembert, who was noted for his work in mathematics and physics, was asked by Diderot to write the philosophical discourse introducing the encyclopedia, as well as various articles related to the sciences. The first two volumes appeared in June 1751 and January 1752, but immediately ran afoul of the law. The French government, operating under rigid censorship laws, objected to the tone of many articles and banned further publication. Through the intercession of the Marquise de Pompadour (the former Madame who had assisted Soufflot) the ban was lifted, and Diderot produced four more volumes between 1753 and 1756, but under strict censorship. The seventh volume of 1759, which had highly controversial articles by Voltaire (Fornication) and d'Alembert (Calvinism), resulted in a royal

Jean Le Rond d'Alembert (1717–83), from "Discours préliminaire des editeurs" [Preliminary discourse of the editors] (1751), trans. Richard N. Schwab, in *Preliminary Discourse to the Encyclopedia of Diderot*. Indianapolis: Bobbs-Merrill, 1963, pp. 3–6.

condemnation and many of the participants fled Paris in fear of arrest (Rousseau had already left the city in 1756). Against governmental strictures, Diderot privately produced another 10 volumes over the next 6 years, and he followed these with 11 volumes of plates. It was the greatest compilation of knowledge ever achieved up to that time, and it became the model for the more specialized encyclopedias of the late eighteenth and nineteenth centuries.

D'Alembert's "Preliminary Discourse," sometimes called the best short introduction to the Enlightenment, is divided into four parts. The first part provides an overview of the project of the encyclopedia, while the second part presents the history of ideas since the Renaissance (including such intellectual heroes as Francis Bacon, René Descartes, John Locke, and Isaac Newton). Part III speaks to the methodology that has been followed, and part IV addresses the particular articles to appear. What is notable throughout is the emphasis placed on reason and the idea of intellectual progress. The following selection from the opening pages underscores the discerning, almost mechanistic metaphysics underlying the outlook of the two editors.

The Encyclopedia which we are presenting to the public is, as its title declares, the work of a society of men of letters. Were we not of their number, we might venture to affirm that they are all favorably known or worthy of being so.[1] But, without wishing to anticipate a judgment which should be made only by scholars, it is at least incumbent upon us, before all else, to remove the objection that could most easily prejudice the success of such a large undertaking as this. We declare, therefore, that we have not had the temerity to undertake unaided a task so superior to our capabilities, and that our function as editors consists principally in arranging materials which for the most part have been furnished in their entirety by others. We had explicitly made the same declaration in the body of the *Prospectus*,[2] but perhaps we should have put it at the beginning of that document. If we had taken that precaution we would doubtless have replied in advance to a large number of gentlemen – and even to some men of letters – who had unquestionably glanced at our *Prospectus*, as their praises attest, but who, nevertheless, have asked us how two persons could treat all the sciences and all the arts.[3] This being the case, the only way of preventing the reappearance of their objection once and for all is to use the first lines of our work to destroy it, as we are doing here. Our introductory sentences are therefore directed solely to those of our readers who will decide not to go further. To the others we owe a far more detailed description of the execution of the *Encyclopedia*, which they will find later in this Discourse, together with the names of each of our colleagues. However, a description so important in its nature and substance must be preceded by some philosophical reflections.

The work whose first volume we are presenting today[4] has two aims. As an *Encyclopedia*, it is to set forth as well as possible the order and connection of the parts of human knowledge. As a *Reasoned Dictionary of the Sciences, Arts, and Trades*, it is to contain the general principles that form the basis of each science and each art, liberal or mechanical, and the most essential facts that make up the body and substance of each.[5] These two points of view, the one of an *Encyclopedia* and the other of a *Reasoned Dictionary*,[6] will thus constitute the basis for the outline and division of our Preliminary Discourse. We are going to introduce them, deal with them one after another, and give an account of the means by which we have tried to satisfy this double object.

If one reflects somewhat upon the connection that discoveries have with one another, it is readily apparent that the sciences and the arts are mutually supporting, and that consequently there is a chain that binds them together. But, if it is often difficult to reduce each particular science or art to a small number of rules or general notions, it is no less difficult to encompass the infinitely varied branches of human knowledge in a truly unified system.[7]

The first step which lies before us in our endeavor is to examine, if we may be permitted to use this term, the genealogy and the filiation of the parts of our knowledge, the causes that brought the various branches of our knowledge into being, and the characteristics that distinguish them. In short, we must go back to the origin and generation of our ideas.[8] Quite aside from the help this examination will give us for the encyclopedic enumeration of the sciences and the arts, it cannot be out of place at the head of a work such as this.

We can divide all our knowledge into direct and reflective knowledge. We receive direct knowledge immediately, without any operation of our will; it is the knowledge which finds all the doors of our souls open, so to speak, and enters without resistance and without effort. The mind acquires reflective knowledge by making use of direct knowledge, unifying and combining it.

NOTES

1 A list of some men who had contributed in one way or another to the first volume of the *Encyclopedia* makes up the last part of the *Discourse*. With each new volume until the final official suppression of the work in 1759, the number of contributors grew in proportion to the enthusiasm for the project among the members of the republic of letters. Very few of the contributors to the first volume of the *Encyclopedia*, except d'Alembert, had achieved a widespread reputation by 1751, and neither Voltaire nor Montesquieu had yet been recruited to the encyclopedic project.

2 D'Alembert's note as follows: "This *Prospectus* was published in the month of November, 1750."

3 Most of that *Prospectus* of November, 1750, which announced the enlarged *Encyclopedia* and invited subscribers, is incorporated into the last part of the *Discourse*. D'Alembert refers to the attacks of the *Journal de Trévoux*. Diderot had promised Father Berthier that d'Alembert would answer all the questions raised in the *Journal*, and many others. See Diderot, *Correspondance*, ed. G. Roth, I, 106.

4 Later editions: "The work which we are beginning (and which we wish to finish). . . ."

5 It is essential to remember throughout this work that the word "science" is by no means restricted to natural science. According to Diderot's definition in the *Encyclopedia*, if the object of a discipline is only *contemplated* from different approaches, the technical collection and disposition of observations relative to that object are called "science." Thus theology, history, and philosophy, as well as physics and mathematics, are sciences. If the object of a discipline is something *executed*, the technical collection and disposition of rules according to which it is executed is called "art." By this definition ethics is an art. See "Art," *Encyclopédie*, I, 713–14.

6 I.e., "Systematic" Dictionary.

7 The rationalist assumption of the unity of knowledge here makes its appearance at the outset of the *Discourse* and, indeed, is the very foundation of the encyclopedic project.

8 A comparison of d'Alembert's wording with the following lines in Condillac's *Essai sur l'origine des connoissances humaines* (*Essay Concerning the Origin of Human Knowledge*, 1746) gives one indication among many of d'Alembert's debt to the work of Condillac throughout the *Discourse*:

> Our first object, which we should never lose from sight, is the study of the human mind – not to discover its nature, but to learn to know its operations, to observe how they are combined and how we ought to use them in order to acquire all the intelligence of which we are capable. It is necessary to go back to the origin of our ideas, to work out their generation,

to follow them to the limits which nature has prescribed for them, and by these means to establish the extent and limits of our knowledge and renew all of human understanding. [*Œuvres philosophiques de Condillac*, ed. Georges Le Roy (Paris, 1947), I, 4.]

Condillac's essay, in turn, was inspired by Locke's great *Essay Concerning Human Understanding* (1690), translated in 1700 into French under Locke's supervision by the Huguenot refugee, Pierre Coste.

59 JACQUES-FRANÇOIS BLONDEL
from "Architecture" in Diderot's *Encyclopedia* (1751)

The article on "Architecture" for Diderot's encyclopedia was written by the relatively young teacher Jacques-François Blondel. Born in Rouen, Blondel had first studied architecture under his uncle Jean-François Blondel, before taking an apprenticeship under the rococo architect Gilles-Marie Oppenord. With his first book of 1737–8, *De la distribution des maisons de plaisance et de la décoration des edifices en général* (On the planning of country houses and the decoration of edifices in general), he showed himself to be a gifted engraver. In 1743 Blondel opened a private architectural school in Paris, which was initially opposed by the Royal Academy of Architecture. With the studio program that he devised, which allowed students a structured progression of courses, the program nevertheless became very successful, and Blondel attracted numerous talented students. In 1755 the Architectural Academy appointed him to the second class, and seven years later Blondel's school was formally incorporated into the Academy. He was at that time the most renowned architectural teacher in France.

For all of his curricular progressiveness, Blondel was quite conservative as a teacher, as the excerpt from this article demonstrates. His historical summary could have been written a century earlier. Moreover, Blondel knew very little of Greek architecture, the whole period between the fall of Rome and the Renaissance (which he labels Gothic) is a virtual historical void, and the ideals of classicism (such as the importance of proportions and the orders) are firmly avowed as academic truths. Its importance is thus in a reverse sense – in that he wrote the essay on the cusp, as it were, of the dramatic changes of the 1750s and 1760s that would challenge so many of these tenets.

Architecture . . . is in general the art of building.

We ordinarily distinguish three kinds: *civil*, which we simply call architecture, *military*, and *naval*. [. . .]

We understand by *civil architecture* the art of designing and constructing buildings for commodity and for the different usages of life, such as sacred edifices, royal palaces, private residences, as well as bridges, public squares, theaters, triumphal arches, etc. [. . .]

In speaking of *civil architecture*, which is our subject, let us say in general that its origin is as ancient as the world; that necessity taught the first men to build huts, tents, and cabins;

Jacques-François Blondel (1705–74), from the entry "Architecture," trans. Harry Francis Mallgrave from a facsimile edition of Diderot's *Encyclopédie, ou Dictionnaire raisonné des sciences, des arts et des métiers*, Vol. 1 (1751). New York: Readex Microprint Corporation, 1969, pp. 616–18.

that because of the times and pressures for selling and buying, as they came together or lived under communal laws, they began to make their lodgings more regular.

The ancient authors credit the Egyptians with having raised the first symmetrical and proportioned buildings; which being done, they say, Salomon appealed to them to build the temple of Jerusalem, although Villalpando assures us that he only brought coppersmiths and silversmiths from Tyre, and that it was God himself who instilled in this king the precepts of *architecture* (what was, according to this author, a very honorable deed for this art). But without entering into this discussion, let us regard Greece as the cradle of good *architecture* [. . .] What inclines us to believe that we are beholden to the Greeks for the proportions of *architecture* are the three orders: the Doric, Ionic, and Corinthian, which we have retained from them. The Romans produced only two others, which are rather imperfect imitations but still useful in our buildings for expressing perfectly the genres of rustic, solid, medium, delicate, and composite *architecture*, known under the names of *Tuscan, Doric, Ionic, Corinthian*, and *Composite*. [. . .] But without speaking here of Greek works, which are very remote from us and of which several celebrated authors have given descriptions, let us pass to a time less distant and speak of the *architecture* of Rome, which attained its highest degree of perfection during the reign of Augustus. Already it began to be neglected under his successor Tiberius, and even Nero, who had an extraordinary passion for the arts despite all the vices that he possessed, did not avail himself of the taste that he had for *architecture*, and chose to display his luxury and vanity with the greatest prodigality, rather than his magnificence. Trajan also evinced much affection for the arts, and despite the decline of *architecture* it was under his reign that Appollodorus raised that famous column which still today in Rome carries the name of this emperor. Finally Severus Alexander also nurtured a love for the arts and *architecture*, but he was unable to prevent them from being swept away with the fall of the Roman Empire, and thus they fell into oblivion from which they were not able to raise themselves for several centuries. During this period the Visigoths destroyed the most beautiful monuments of antiquity and *architecture* found itself reduced to such barbarity that those who practiced it entirely neglected justness of proportions, fitness, and propriety of design, in which resides all the merit of this art.

From that abuse formed a new manner of building, which we call Gothic, and which existed until Charlemagne undertook to reestablish the ancient art. Then France applied itself with some success, encouraged by Hugh Capet, who also had much taste for this science. His son Robert, who succeeded him, had the same inclinations, so that gradually *architecture*, in taking another turn, gave into the opposite excess of becoming too light; the architects of this time made the beauties of their *architecture* consist of a delicacy and a profusion of ornaments unknown until then. It was an excess into which they fell no doubt by opposing the Gothic that had preceded them, or by the taste that they had received from the Arabs and the Moors, who brought this genre into the Meridional areas of France, just as the Vandals and the Goths had brought the heavy taste and Gothic manner to the northern regions.

It is scarcely in the last two centuries that architects of France and Italy have tried to return to the first simplicity, beauty, and proportion of ancient *architecture*; it is also only since this time that our edifices have been executed in imitation, and following the precepts, of antique architecture. Let us point out at this time that civil *architecture* differs with regard to these different epochs and their variations into *antique, ancient, Gothic*, and *modern* manners. It can also be distinguished by its different proportions and its uses, following the different characters of the orders of which we have spoken: *Tuscan, Doric, Ionic, Corinthian,* and *Composite.*

60 CHARLES-ÉTIENNE BRISEUX
from Preface to *Treatise on Essential Beauty in the Arts* (1752)

A nother indication of the academic conservatism still common to the period around 1750 is this short treatise by the architect Charles-Étienne Briseux. Perhaps the most remarkable aspect of this book is that it was written at all, since Briseux was approaching his ninety-second birthday and had therefore witnessed the original debate between the Ancients and the Moderns firsthand. These very issues, for Briseux, were still alive, and this treatise is an attempt to reaffirm the existence of "essential beauty" and harmonic proportions in architecture — even if he admits that as yet no "fixed" proportions have been found. In defending the honor of François Blondel, Briseux blames the skeptical Perrault for nearly everything that has gone wrong in architecture since this time, most especially for the entire rococo period. It is nevertheless a rearguard attempt to save the academic status quo, which would soon meet strong opposition. In this passage Briseux cites a footnote from Perrault's annotations to Vitruvius, and the Preface to which he refers is Perrault's preface to his *Ordonnance for the Five Kinds of Columns.*

The diversity of opinions is advantageous to the sciences and the arts. It hastens their progress by the rivalry that it nurtures; it sheds light on their principles by the examination and discussion that it occasions. But what in these fields is most excellent in its own accord can become prejudicial by an abuse that is only too common. Diversity becomes dangerous when – by a stubborn commitment to it literally, or by the false honor of supporting an odd system – someone resists evidence and inward conviction. This is what happened in a debate that arose between François Blondel and Claude Perrault, the origin of which is as follows.

François Blondel wrote in the fourteenth chapter, part V, of his learned *Cours d'architecture* that we will soon have a work by M. Perrault on the subject of architectural proportions, which may perhaps be excellent coming from him, although in the notes that he made on Vitruvius he appears to hold a viewpoint quite different from this author, when he said that "architectural proportions, which according to the opinion of most architects are something natural, have only been established by a consensus of architects, who have imitated in their works one or another proportion, or who have followed the proportions that leading architects have chosen. It is not at all like having real, convincing, and necessary beauty, which surpass in their beauty other proportions, but only because these proportions are found in works that have other real and convincing beauties, such as found in the material and the correctness of execution, etc."

Charles-Étienne Briseux (1660–1754), from Preface to *Traité du beau essentiel dans les arts* [Treatise on essential beauty in the arts] (1752), trans. Harry Francis Mallgrave from original edition. Paris, 1752, pp. 1–2.

This citation makes it clear that M. Perrault was not then opposed to proportions, but simply that the proportions selected by the leading architects could be substituted for others and varied to infinity and that the choice we make regarding them depends more or less on the taste, experience, and intelligence of those who compose their modulation. If the truth of this viewpoint were in doubt, it should be easy to prove it, just as music does each and every day. This is what eluded M. Blondel, who also accused M. Perrault of an odd and extraordinary line of reasoning. Perrault, out of revenge, then composed a preface of 27 large pages to destroy, or at least to obscure through capricious paradoxes, the learned lectures that Blondel had given in his *Cours d'architecture*.

This preface is remarkable by the mass of contradictions that are found there, and by the continual obscurity that reigns there. It is a bizarre and inconsistent piece, where the author seems to have forgotten himself. But when one's pride is offended, does it not lead him astray? Every day he sacrifices his true interests for his vanity. In such a way Perrault became insensible to proper reasoning, to the testimony of authors, and to the authority of experience in order to maintain that proportions have no part in the beauty of buildings, and that beauty derives only from the material and the correctness of execution.

Still, he often returns to the argument of the preceding citation; the force of truth and his real conviction bring him back there, despite himself. But after clouding and obscuring the true and the evident, he argues that "the reasons for admiring a beautiful work have no other foundation than chance and caprice of the workers, who are not looking for reasons to behave or to fix something for which precision has no importance."

Is it therefore not surprising that such a paradox was able to have had the effect that Perrault himself did not dare to expect, even though he had the boldness to risk it? As a result, the professors of the academy who succeeded Blondel ceased to teach the fundamental principles of architecture. For their students believed them useless and abandoned the principle in order to cling to the accessory, and dazzle the eyes by a confusion of ornaments [. . .]

61   MARC-ANTOINE LAUGIER
from *Essay on Architecture* (1753)

If Briseux in 1752 reiterated what was in essence the old academic position, the rationalist critique of the Abbé Marc-Antoine Laugier that appeared one year later was written very much in the language and spirit of the Enlightenment. Laugier's short polemical book had an extraordinary effect on architectural theory both inside and outside of France, which is surprising in view of the fact that the author was not an architect. It is a masterfully written study, arguably the most important architectural book of the century.

Part of its success had much to do with Laugier's intellectual rearing. He was born in Provence and in 1727 entered a seminary to become a Jesuit. This lengthy process did not conclude until his final vows of 1745, after he

Marc-Antoine Laugier (1713–69), from *Essai sur l'architecture* (1753), trans. Wolfgang and Anni Herrmann, in *An Essay on Architecture*. Los Angeles: Hennessey + Ingalls, 1977, pp. 11–13, 14–15. © 1977 by Hennessey + Ingalls. Reprinted with permission of Hennessey + Ingalls.

completed university studies at Avignon, Lyons, Besançon, and Marseilles. In the same year he was appointed to the Paris church of Saint Sulpice, where he earned distinction for his oratorical skills. Beginning in 1749 he was commanded, on occasions, to Fontainebleu and Versailles to sermonize before the king – a rare honor. He published his *Essai sur l'architecture* anonymously in 1753, and seems by this date already to have been making plans to leave the Jesuits. But his break did not formally come until Easter Sunday of 1754, when – in the midst of a major political crisis – he openly deplored the king's moral indiscretions and political lapses from his pulpit at Versailles. Laugier was immediately recalled by his order to Lyons, where he completed the paperwork for his transfer to the Benedictine order, now as an *abbé*. He soon returned to Paris, where he became active again in literary circles and later would become known for his 12-volume history of the Venetian republic, which appeared between 1759 and 1768. In 1765 he also published another architectural treatise, *Observations sur l'architecture* (Observations on architecture) but by this date his moment in the architectural spotlight had passed.

Laugier's *Essai* of 1753 proved so effective (a second edition appeared in 1755) in part because Laugier was a layman, one with a shrewd eye. His classical knowledge was essentially limited to his personal familiarity with the Maison Carrée, a late-Roman monument in Nîmes. He was, at the same time, a great admirer of the architecture of Perrault, most especially of the east wing of the Louvre. He was also quite familiar with the Perrault/Blondel dispute, as well as Cordemoy's book, and from these few sources he reintroduced the earlier issues that had not been previously resolved – only now within a quite different intellectual framework. In his rationalism he is the first Frenchman to deny the relevance of Vitruvius – "Vitruvius has in effect taught us only what was practiced in his time" – and thus seeks to remove this cornerstone of academic theory since Blondel. In its place he substitutes the notion of "reason": now to be the sole guide for architectural decision-making. From this rationalist spirit comes the logical creation of a primitive hut, and Laugier deduces from it three essential elements (the column, the entablature, and pediment), which will now constitute all that is essential to architecture. Some building parts, such as walls, doors, and windows, are allowed back because they are functionally necessary; all else, however, is simple caprice and therefore a fault. In effect, Laugier, from his purist position, is purging architecture of its rococo excesses. It was a popular prescription because it fell in line with the efforts of a group of talented students of the 1750s, who were also seeking similar reforms.

The first passage is taken from the opening pages of his first chapter and depicts the primitive hut. The second article, regarding the column and entablature, displays his ruthlessly logical method, which he used in subsequent chapters to deprive architecture of nearly all of its baroque motifs.

General Principles of Architecture

It is the same in architecture as in all other arts: its principles are founded on simple nature, and nature's process clearly indicates its rules. Let us look at man in his primitive state without any aid or guidance other than his natural instincts. He is in need of a place to rest. On the banks of a quietly flowing brook he notices a stretch of grass; its fresh greenness is pleasing to his eyes, its tender down invites him; he is drawn there and, stretched out at leisure on this sparkling carpet, he thinks of nothing else but enjoying the gift of nature; he lacks nothing, he does not wish for anything. But soon the scorching heat of the sun forces him to look for shelter. A nearby forest draws him to its cooling shade; he runs to find a refuge in its depth, and there he is content. But suddenly mists are rising, swirling round and growing denser, until thick clouds cover the skies; soon, torrential rain pours down on this delightful forest. The savage, in his leafy shelter, does not know how to protect himself from the uncomfortable damp that penetrates everywhere; he creeps into a nearby cave and, finding it dry, he praises himself for his discovery. But soon the darkness and foul air surrounding him make his stay unbearable again. He leaves and is resolved to make good by his ingenuity the careless neglect of nature. He wants to make himself a dwelling that protects but does not bury him. Some fallen branches in the forest are the right material for his purpose; he chooses four of the strongest, raises them upright and arranges them in a square; across their top he lays four other branches; on these he hoists from two sides yet another row of branches which, inclining towards each other, meet at their highest point. He then covers this kind of roof with leaves so closely packed that neither sun nor rain can penetrate. Thus, man is housed. Admittedly, the cold and heat will make him feel uncomfortable in this house which is open on all sides but soon he will fill in the space between two posts and feel secure.

Such is the course of simple nature; by imitating the natural process, art was born. All the splendors of architecture ever conceived have been modeled on the little rustic hut I have just described. It is by approaching the simplicity of this first model that fundamental mistakes are avoided and true perfection is achieved. The pieces of wood set upright have given us the idea of the column, the pieces placed horizontally on top of them the idea of the entablature, the inclining pieces forming the roof the idea of the pediment. This is what all masters of art have recognized. But take note of this: never has a principle been more fertile in its effect. From now on it is easy to distinguish between the parts which are essential to the composition of an architectural Order and those which have been introduced by necessity or have been added by caprice. The parts that are essential are the cause of beauty, the parts introduced by necessity cause every license, the parts added by caprice cause every fault. This calls for an explanation; I shall try to be as clear as possible.

Let us never lose sight of our little rustic hut. I can only see columns, a ceiling or entablature and a pointed roof forming at both ends what is called a pediment. So far there is no vault, still less an arch, no pedestals, no attic, not even a door or a window. I therefore come to this conclusion: in an architectural Order only the column, the entablature and the pediment may form an essential part of its composition. If each of these parts is suitably placed and suitably formed, nothing else need be added to make the work perfect.

We still have in France a beautiful ancient monument, which in Nîmes is called the *Maison Carrée*. Everybody, connoisseur or not, admires its beauty. Why? Because everything here accords with the true principles of architecture: a rectangle where thirty columns support an entablature and a roof – closed at both ends by a pediment – that is all; the combination is of a simplicity and a nobility which strikes everybody. [. . .]

The Column

(1) The column must be strictly perpendicular, because, being intended to support the whole load, perfect verticality gives it its greatest strength. (2) The column must be free-standing so that its origin and purpose are expressed in a natural way. (3) The column must be round because nature makes nothing square. (4) The column must be tapered from bottom to top in imitation of nature where this diminution is found in all plants. (5) The

column must rest directly on the floor as the posts of the rustic hut rest directly on the ground. All these rules find their justification in our model; all deviations from this model without real necessity must, therefore, be considered as so many faults.

1. Fault: when columns, instead of standing free, are engaged in the wall. The column certainly loses much of its grace when even a small obstacle obscures its outline. I admit that circumstances frequently seem to rule out the use of free-standing columns. People want to live in closed spaces, not in open halls. Therefore, it becomes necessary to fill in the space between the columns and consequently to engage them. In this case, an engaged column will not be regarded as a fault, but as a license sanctioned by necessity. It should, however, always be remembered that any license points to an imperfection and must be used cautiously and only when it is impossible to find a better way. If, therefore, the columns have to be engaged, the degree of engagement should be as small as possible – a quarter at most or even less so that, even when constrained, they retain some quality of the freedom and ease which gives them so much grace. We must avoid getting into the awkward situation where engaged columns have to be employed. It would be best to reserve the use of columns for peristyles where they can be completely free-standing and to omit them altogether whenever necessity compels us to back them onto a wall. After all, even though we have to submit to *bienséance* why should we not disengage the column so that it can be seen in the round? Would the facade of St. Gervais not be improved if the Doric columns were free-standing like those of the upper Orders? Is there anything impossible in this?

62 MARC-ANTOINE LAUGIER
from *Essay on Architecture* (1753)

The column, entablature, and pediment were deemed by Laugier to be the three essential elements of architecture, and this premise carried with it design implications. Columns were to be free-standing, entablatures were to be flat (no arches), and pediments were only appropriate along the short side of a building. What Laugier had in mind as the ideal prototype for architecture was the Roman monument of the Maison Carrée in Nîmes, as well as the east front of the Louvre. In his fourth chapter Laugier turns to the issue of designing churches, and once again he reverts to the arguments of Perrault and Cordemoy by insisting on the use of columns in the nave – instead of arches and piers – to support the vaulted ceiling and roof above. Laugier's model here is the second story of the chapel at Versailles, begun in 1698 by Jules Hardouin Mansart.

Contemporary critics, as with Cordemoy before him, were quick to point out Laugier's lack of structural expertise. What is different now is that Laugier makes his argument precisely at the moment that Soufflot was beginning to think about the design of the church of Sainte Geneviève in Paris, where he too (in 1755) would propose interior columns to support a vaulted nave. Soufflot did so by studying the iron techniques employed at the Louvre, and devising a similar masonry system reinforced with iron bars.

Marc-Antoine Laugier, from *Essai sur l'architecture* (1753), trans. Wolfgang and Anni Herrmann, in *An Essay on Architecture*. Los Angeles: Hennessey + Ingalls, 1977, pp. 100–2, 103–4. © 1977 by Hennessey + Ingalls. Reprinted with permission of Hennessey + Ingalls.

On the Style in Which to Build Churches

Of all buildings churches give architects the best opportunity to display the marvels of their art. Since our churches are meant to receive into their midst a multitude bringing with them the religious image of the God they are going to worship, these churches give the architect scope for working on a large scale and do not in any way restrict the nobility of his concepts. It is surprising that, whereas in any other class there are buildings worthy of admiration, so few of our churches deserve our enlightened interest. For myself, I am convinced that until now we have not developed the right style for this class of building. Our Gothic churches are still the most acceptable. A mass of grotesque ornaments spoils them, and yet, we are awed by a certain air of greatness and majesty. Here we find ease and gracefulness; they only lack simplicity and naturalness. We have rightly renounced the follies of Gothic (*l'architecture moderne*) and have returned to the antique, but it seems we have lost good taste on the way. Moving away from the Gothic architects (*Modernes*) we deserted gracefulness; turning towards the antique we encountered clumsiness; this happened because we have gone half the way. We have halted between two styles, and the result is a new kind of architecture that is only half antique and may make us regret having abandoned Gothic architecture altogether. A simple critical comparison will make this clear.

I enter Notre Dame, the most eminent of our Gothic buildings in Paris, though not by far as beautiful as certain others in the provinces which everybody admires. Nevertheless, at first glance my attention is captured, my imagination is struck by the size, the height and the unobstructed view (*dégagement*) of the vast nave; for some moments I am lost in the amazement that the grand effect of the whole stirs in me. Recovering from the first astonishment and taking note now of the details, I find innumerable absurdities, but I lay the blame for them on the misfortunes of the time. For all that I am still full of admiration when after my thorough and critical examination I return to the middle of the nave and the impression which remains with me makes me say: "How many faults, but how grand!" From there I go to St. Sulpice, the most eminent of all churches we have built in the antique style. It neither strikes me nor impresses me; I find the building to be far below its reputation. I see nothing but thick masses. There are heavy arches set between heavy pilasters of a very heavy and coarse Corinthian Order, and over the whole lies a heavy vault the weight of which makes you fear that the heavy supports may be insufficient. What shall I say of the screen (*jube*) which conceals the main entrance to the church? It is a pretty piece of architecture, but is as little in its proper place as a small house is inside a large one. What shall I say of the main facade? It is an excellent idea which, however, has not come off. M. Servandoni almost reached perfection, yet stopped just short of it. In order to make something out of the facade, the columns should not have been coupled in depth but lengthwise; the enormous Doric cornice of the main entablature, difficult to protect from damage caused by weather, should have been suppressed and the free-standing columns of the first Order repeated in the second, an arrangement that would at least have saved the building from its extreme coarseness. The towers should have been separated from the central part of the facade and been given a less dry and heavy form. [. . .]

I have tried to find if, in building our churches in the good style of classical architecture, there is not a way to give them an elevation and a lightness equal to those of our beautiful Gothic churches. After much thought it seemed to me that not only would it be possible but that it would be much easier for us to succeed in this with the architecture of the Greeks than with all the fretwork of Gothic architecture. By using free-standing columns we will achieve lightness and by setting two Orders one above the other we will reach the required height.

Here is how I should like my idea to be carried out. Let us choose the most common form, that of the Latin cross. I place all around the nave, transept and choir the first Order of isolated columns standing on low socles; they are coupled like those of the portico of the Louvre in order to give more width to the intercolumniations. On these columns I place a straight architrave terminated by an ogee of moderate projection and erect over this a second Order, consisting, like the first one, of free-standing and coupled columns. This second Order has its complete straight entablature and, directly over it without any sort of attic, I erect a plain barrel vault without transverse ribs. Then, around the nave, crossing, and choir I arrange columned aisles which form a true peristyle and are covered by flat ceilings placed on the architraves of the first Order. Beyond this peristyle I arrange chapels with an opening as wide as the intercolumniations. The form of these chapels is a perfect square with four columns in the corners supporting an architrave and flat ceiling. Each chapel has two open and two closed sides. The two which are open are those of the entrances with only a simple grille, and those opposite completely glazed. The two other sides, separating one chapel from the other, are taken up one by the altar, the other by a correspondingly large piece of painting or sculpture. Finally, I have the great vault supported by flying buttresses, based on the walls separating one chapel from the other and abutting on a point just above the capitals of the second Order.

This then is my idea and here are the advantages: (1) A building like this is entirely natural and true; everything is reduced to simple rules and executed according to great principles: no arcades, no pilasters, no pedestals, nothing awkward or constrained. (2) The whole building is extremely elegant and delicate; the plain wall is nowhere to be seen, therefore, nothing is superfluous, nothing is bulky, nothing is offensive. (3) The windows are placed in the most suitable and most advantageous position. All intercolumniations are glazed, above and below. There are no more plain lunettes cutting into the vault as in ordinary churches, but ordinary large windows. (4) The two Orders placed one above the other bring nave, crossing and choir to the height that produces the majestic effect, a height which is in no way irregular and does not require columns of an exorbitant scale. (5) The vault, although a barrel vault, loses all heaviness through this height, especially since it has no transverse ribs which would appear to weigh down heavily. (6) Splendor and magnificence could easily be added to the *dégagement*, simplicity, elegance and dignity of such a building. All it needs is for the different parts to be decorated in good taste.

63 ISAAC WARE
from *A Complete Body of Architecture,* Chapter II (1756)

Whereas the neoclassical movement in France was to some extent a rerun of the issues first raised by Perrault/Blondel dispute, the neoclassical movement in Britain rather emanated from the British tradition of Palladian classicism. This movement remained strong up until 1750, but then began to decline significantly, as other intellectual forces were also coming into play around this time. The British picturesque movement and the empiricist tradition (see part IV below) were in essence contrary to the rules or absolute tenets of Renaissance classicism. Thus in a certain respect, it was easier for British architects – lacking an academic authority – to challenge classical principles than it was for their French counterparts. Isaac Ware is very much a transitional figure in this regard. He was, as we have seen, a prominent member of the earlier Palladian movement, but his one definitive theoretical statement, *A Complete Body of Architecture*, does not appear until 1756 or when Palladianism was clearly on the wane. The idea of harmonic proportions in Britain is now a troubling issue, and if Palladio is not to be dethroned, he is also not to be accepted blindly.

Of the Proportions of the Order

As it was from the works of the antient architects that the several orders were deduced, those who had studied and found their different characters, then became desirous of establishing from the same source their proportions. From the beauties and excellencies they saw in these remains, they took up an almost enthusiastick veneration for the architects who invented them, and from this they fell into an implicit admiration of them which led them into mistakes. Perceiving consummate beauty in what they saw, they sought to build upon that perfection, certain fixed and invariable rules, by the observing of which others might be sure of attaining the same excellence. At first this appeared easy, but when they came to examine more of those works they found the antients themselves had not confined themselves to any such laws; and therefore that it was impossible to build such rules upon their works.

As they became perplexed in studying a variety of antient remains, the young student is confused by reading a variety of authors on the subject. Among a number of the best of these each delivers what he esteems to be the most true and perfect proportion, but in each this differs. All have founded their maxims upon something in the antique, but some having taken in the same order one piece, and some another, those proportions vary extremely; for the antients so varied in their works.

We shall endeavour, in an account of the orders, to set this matter in a more equal light. *Palladio* is understood to be the best and greatest of these authors, we shall therefore deliver

Isaac Ware (d. 1766), from *A Complete Body of Architecture, Adorned with Plans and Elevations, from Original Designs,* printed in London for T. Osborne and J. Shipton, 1756, p. 131 (Chapter II).

his as the general and received authentic proportion in each order; but, upon a general review of the several remains in which that order is preserved, we shall add what is the mean or middle proportion of the several parts, calculating from them all.

The modern architects too strictly and scrupulously follow these antients; they did not so closely or servilely copy one another. They were conscious that beauty in any order was not restrained to an exact proportion of parts: hence they indulged their genius in its regulated flights, and from that liberty produced those several great works in the same order, which are all beautiful, though extremely different one from another. We who tie ourselves down to a severe observance of some one proportion, are but copyists at best; while they, though they preserved the character of the order one after another, yet were each an original. We seem to imagine that but one proportion of features can constitute a beautiful face: they, following where nature led the way, have shown us that very differently proportioned features can constitute beauty, provided a proper harmony be preserved among them.

This may give us an idea of the difference between antient and modern architects: they restrained genius by rules; we propose working by rules in the place of genius: they were in every thing originals, we seem to establish it as a principle, that it is not needful to invent in order to deserve praise.

64 ISAAC WARE
from *A Complete Body of Architecture,*
Chapter IX (1756)

This notion of artistic liberty that Ware so tentatively puts forward early in his treatise becomes more prominent as he nears the end of his lengthy work. This particular chapter of book IX, "Of Retrenching Errors," concerns the appropriateness or inappropriateness of using Italian models in England. It is a virtual British declaration of independence from classical thought – well almost, as Palladio, now not "above error," is still there. The reference near the end of the chapter to a dwarf standing on the shoulders of a giant is an invocation of a metaphor used repeatedly in the seventeenth-century quarrel of the Moderns and Ancients, by such modern supporters as Blaise Pascal and Isaac Newton. It is in fact a compromise to the problem: self-depreciation of the Moderns (dwarfs) who can nevertheless see farther than the giants of the past.

Of Retrenching Errors

If this be the case where the designs are most correct and unexceptionable, much more must it be so where they are liable to exception.

Isaac Ware, from *A Complete Body of Architecture, Adorned with Plans and Elevations, from Original Designs,* printed in London for T. Osborne and J. Shipton, 1756, pp. 694–5 (Chapter IX).

The Custom among English architects has been to observe these too implicitly. To transfer the buildings of Italy right or wrong, suited or unsuited to the purpose, into England; and this, if done exactly, the builder has been taught to consider as merit in his profession. We have pointed out to him a worthier and better plan; let him study those designs, but with some regard to his own Genius. It is not in these he learns the rudiments of the science, though he sees the rules by which he has been taught exemplifyed in them: let him therefore read with more freedom, and regard these structures as they are, as works of great men, but of men: the greatest are not out of the reach of error, nor above improvement.

It was thus the antients studied one another: and thus the science became improved; thus Vitruvius formed his principles; and thus Palladio followed them. The Roman laid down rules which he illustrated by examples; but he did not suppose every thing he saw in the old buildings worthy to be made the principle of a maxim added to the science: and the Italian has shewn in many of his edifices that, altho' he held his master in high reverence, he did not esteem him above error; or think he carried the science beyond improvement.

In studying a design of Palladio's, which which we recommend to the young architect as his frequent practice, let him think, as well as measure. Let him consider the general design and purpose of the building, and then examine freely how far, according to his own judgment, the purpose will be answered by that structure. He will thus establish in himself a custom of judging by the whole as well as by parts; and he will find new beauties in the structure confidered in this light.

He will improve his knowledge and correct his taste by such contemplation; for he will find how greatly the designer thought, and how judiciously he has done many things; which, but for such an examination, would have passed in his mind unnoticed; or at best not understood.

Possibly, when he has thus made himself a master of the author or designer's idea, he will see wherein it might have been improved. Now that he understands the work, he will have a right to judge thus: and what would have been absurdity in one who knew not the science, or presumption in such as had not enough considered the building, will be in him the candid and free use of that knowledge he has attained in the art.

Therefore let him never check these sallies of his fancy; but with due candour, and a modest sense of his own rank in the science, compared with his whose work he studies, let him indulge them freely. Let him consider himself as a dwarf placed upon the giant Palladio's shoulders; as seeing not with his own eyes singly, but with the borrowed light of that great master's; and thus indulge his genius.

Let him commit to paper his thoughts on these subjects; not in words only, but in lines and figures. He will be able to reconsider them at leisure; and thence adopting or condemning his first thought, he will either way improve his judgment, and probably introduce new excellences in his practice.

65 WILLIAM CHAMBERS
from *A Treatise on Civil Architecture* (1759)

Ware is not the name normally associated with the British neoclassical movement. This distinction more generally is given to William Chambers, who – along with Robert Adam – dominates British architecture in the second half of the century. Chambers was actually born in Sweden of parents of Scottish extraction, and in his youth he had the exceedingly rare distinction of making three trips to China and the Far East, while working for the Swedish East India Company. It was during these lengthy periods at sea that he acquired much of his education and the rudiments of architectural theory. In 1749 the 23-year-old world traveler retired from the family business and moved to Paris to study at the private architectural school of Jacques-François Blondel. There he was a classmate of several architects who would become very active in the French neoclassical movement. This period was capped off with four years in Rome, beginning in 1751. There Chambers married an English lady, and after cultivating the friendship of the Prince of Wales and other British aristocrats he moved to London in 1755. Two years later he was appointed architect to the Dowager Princes Augusta, for whom he also served as a tutor to her son, King George III, who ascended the throne in 1760.

A Treatise on Civil Architecture (1759) is an early work in the career of Chambers, and was written in the midst of the revolutionary events of the 1750s. It was originally intended to be a small volume of designs, but Chambers transformed it with a series of commentaries in which he, for his English audience, largely recapitulates the lessons of French theory. But Chambers differs from French academic theory in one important respect: his belief in the relativity of proportions. In forming this view, Chambers had been attracted to the aesthetic ideas of the Irishman Edmund Burke (see chs. 110 and 111 below), especially his argument regarding the relativity of perception. In this first passage concerning the Ovolo of a Doric order, Chambers voices his discomfort with the idea of harmonic relations. The second passage, taken from his chapter "Of Gates, Doors, and Piers," makes the same point, but Chambers now concludes his comment essentially by assuming Perrault's position that proportions are not only relative but should be calculated by taking the mean between two extremes.

Of the Doric Order

De Chambray, in his Parallel, gives three Profiles of the Doric Order; one taken from the Theatre of Marcellus, and the others copied by Pietro Ligorio from various fragments of Antiquity, in and near Rome. Vignola's second Doric Profile bears a near resemblance to the most beautiful of these, and was not improbably collected from the same Antique which Ligorio copied: though it must be owned that Vignola hath, in his composition, far exceeded the original; having omitted the many trivial and insignificant mouldings, with which that is overloaded, and in many respects, amended both its form and proportions.

William Chambers (1723–96), from *A Treatise on Civil Architecture, in which The Principles of that Art are Laid Down, and Illustrated by a Great Number of Plates*, published in London for the author by John Haberkorn, 1759, pp. 17–18, 64.

As this Profile of Vignola's is composed in a greater style, and in a manner more characteristic of the Order, than any other, I have made choice of it for my model; having, in the general form and proportions, adhered strictly to the original; though in particular members I have not scrupled to vary, when observation taught me they might be improved.

Vignola, as appears by the preface to his Orders, imagined that the graceful and pleasing aspect of Architectonic objects, was occasioned by the harmony and simplicity of the relations between their parts; and, in composing his Profiles, he constantly adjusted his measures by these simple affinities, supposing the deviations from them, in his antique originals, to proceed rather from the inaccurate execution of the workmen, than from any premeditated design in the contriver. To this notion may be ascribed many little defects, in the proportions of his mouldings, and minuter members; which, though trifling in themselves, yet, from the smallness of the parts where they happen to be, are of consequence, and easily perceivable by a judicious eye. These I have therefore endeavoured to correct, not only in this, but in others of his Orders; which, from their conformity to the best Antiques, I have in the course of this work chosen to imitate.

It has been already observed, that the real relations, subsisting between dissimilar figures, have no connection with the apparent ones; and it is a truth too evident to require demonstration. No one will deny, for instance, that the Ovolo, in the annexed Doric Cornice, viewed in its proper elevation, will appear much larger than the Capital of the Triglyph under it; though, in reality, they are nearly of the same dimensions: and, if the same Ovolo were placed as much below the level of the spectator's eye, as it is above it in the present case, it is likewise clear that it would appear considerably less than any flat member of the same size. These things being so, a strict attachment to harmonic relations seems to me unreasonable; since what is really in perfect harmony, may in appearance produce the most jarring discord.

Perfect proportion in Architecture, if considered only with regard to the relations between the different objects in a composition, and as far as it relates merely to the pleasure of the sight, seems to consist in this, that those parts, which are either principal or essential, should be so contrived as to catch the eye successively, from the most considerable to the least, according to their degrees of importance in the composition, and impress their images on the mind before it is affected by any of the subservient members; yet that these should be so conditioned, as not to be intirely absorbed by the former, but capable of raising distinct ideas likewise, and such as may be adequate to the purposes for which these parts are designed. The different figures and situations of the parts may, in some degree, contribute toward this effect: for simple forms will operate more speedily than those that are complicated, and such as project will be sooner perceived than those that are more retired. But dimension seems to be the predominant quality; or that which acts most powerfully on the sense: and this, as far as I know, can only be discovered by experience; at least to any degree of accuracy. When therefore any number of parts, arranged in a particular manner, and under particular proportions, excite, in the generality of judicious spectators, a pleasing sensation, it will be prudent on every occasion, where the same circumstances subsist, to observe exactly the same proportions; notwithstanding they may in themselves appear irregular and unconnected.

★ ★ ★

We may look for the origin of many proportions in Architecture in the same source; particularly with relation to objects of real use: and the pleasure or dislike, excited in us at their sight, must, I believe, be ascribed either to prejudice, or to our habit of connecting other ideas with these figures, rather than to any particular charm inherent in them, as some people are apt to imagine. Thus, with regard to elevations, if the breadth be predominant, we are struck with the ideas of majesty and strength; and, if the height predominates, with those of elegance and delicacy: all which occasion pleasing sensations. An excess of the former degenerates into the heavy; and an excess of the latter into the meagre: either of which are equally disgustful. When objects are low, and much extended, we naturally conceive an idea of something mean, abject, and unwieldy: and when they are extremely elevated and narrow, they seem fragile and unstable. Perfect proportion consists in a Medium between these Extremes: which Medium the rules of Architecture tend to fix.

Sometimes too the aptitude of a figure to the purpose it was intended for endears it to us: and what at first only gained our approbation, in time commands our love; as we see men become enamoured of a woman's person, whose mind was at first the only attractive power. But this last is not a general rule; and seldom or ever can happen, either when there is any thing disagreeable in the figure, or any thing remarkably defective or deformed in the person.

66 WILLIAM CHAMBERS
from *A Treatise on the Decorative Part of Civil Architecture* (1791)

In 1759 the young William Chambers stood apart from most of his colleagues in that he believed architectural proportions were relative and unrelated to musical harmonies. Near the end of his career in 1791, when he published the third edition of his earlier treatise, he surprisingly took a different perspective — now seemingly siding with the Ancients and harmonic proportions. Curiously, he did so at a time when this issue of classical theory had all but disappeared and aesthetic relativism had clearly won the day.

Our Saxon and Norman fore-fathers, ultimate corruptors of the almost effaced Roman architecture; sufficiently prove, by the remains of their churches, monasteries, and castles; to what extent barbarism may carry deformity, gloom, unwieldy grandeur, and clumsy solidity. And their successors of the thirteenth century, though following a manner infinitely more scientifick and regular; often carried elegance, lightness, and excessive decoration, far beyond their proper limits: till, in the fifteenth and sixteenth centuries, that manner had its last polish among us; was cleared of its redundancies; improved in its forms; simplified

William Chambers, from *A Treatise on the Decorative Part of Civil Architecture*, third edition. London: Joseph Smeeton, 1791 and New York: Benjamin Blom, 1968 (reissue), p. 107.

and perfected in its decorations: in short, made what it is, in some of the last structures of that stile; the admiration of all enlightened observers.

Amongst the restorers of the ancient Roman architecture, the stile of Palladio is correct and elegant; his general dispositions are often happy; his outlines distinct and regular; his forms graceful: little appears that could with propriety be spared, nothing seems wanting: and all his measures accord so well, that no part attracts the attention, in prejudice to any of the rest.

Scamozzi, in attempting to refine upon the stile of Palladio, has over-detailed, and rendered his own rather trifling; sometimes confused. Vignola's manner, though bolder, and more stately than that of Palladio; is yet correct, and curbed within due limits; particularly in his orders: but in Michael Angelo's, we see licence, majesty, grandeur, and fierce effect; extended to bounds, beyond which, it would be very dangerous to soar.

But whether there be any thing natural, positive, convincing and self amiable, in the proportions of architecture; which, like notes and accord in musick, seize upon the mind, and necessarily excite the same sensations in all; or whether they were first established by consent of the ancient artists, who imitated each other; and were first admired, because accompanied with other real, convincing beauties; such as richness of materials, brilliancy of colour, fine polish, or excellence of workmanship; and were after, only preferred through prejudice or habit; are questions which have much occupied the learned. Those who wish to see the arguments for, and against, these respective notions; are referred to Perrault, Blondel, and other writers upon the subject. To the plurality of students in the profession, it may be sufficient to observe; without attempting to determine in favour of either side; that both agree in their conclusion: the maintainers of harmonick proportions, proving their system, by the measures observed in the most esteemed buildings of antiquity; and the supporters of the opposite doctrine allowing, that as both artists and criticks, form their ideas of perfection, upon these same buildings of antiquity; there cannot be a more infallible way of pleasing, than by imitating that, which is so universally approved.

B. GREECE AND THE CLASSICAL
IDEAL

Introduction

Still another factor affecting architectural theory in the 1750s was the growing awareness of classical Greece — essentially a dramatic "rediscovery" of the country and its architecture. Greece and its ancient culture was certainly long known and appreciated within Western culture, but only in abstraction; educated people had for centuries read and praised the writings of Aristotle, Plato, and the Greek historians. Vitruvius himself had championed Greek theory as the ultimate authority to be emulated, yet up until 1750 Westerners had no accurate image of what constituted Greek architecture or the nuances of its temples. Thus the first detailed drawings of Attic ruins in this decade created a sensation with their formal simplicity and heavier proportions (in relation to Roman works). These images at the same time created a crisis for academic classicism. If classical theory since the

Renaissance had been predicated on Roman forms and models, what would happen to this body of thought if – as some would now argue – Greek forms and proportions were deemed aesthetically superior?

Working hand and hand with these archaeological discoveries were the new and broadening historical perspectives. Greece was "Eastern" in the sense that it was an Ottoman territory, but also because of its known roots and points of contact with the cultures of the Middle East and Egypt. Thus Greece became a doorway to peer back into the past and attempt to discern the stages of historical development. On the basis of these insights, one of the first fruits of the new perspective was the first history of art (by J. J. Winckelmann) and its ambition to stage the development of ancient art.

Still, a third consequence of the rediscovery of Greek architecture were the controversies and debates that ensued. The new-found fashion of "Greek taste" invited a "Roman" response. Thus Giovanni Battista Piranesi, in defending the greatness of Latin culture, was ultimately led to another form of cultural relativism: architectural eclecticism or the architect's right to draw upon different cultures and styles for his creations. If such a position could be considered heretical within academic circles, it also underscores the momentous implications of this new stylistic discovery.

67 JAMES STUART AND NICHOLAS REVETT
from "Proposals for publishing an accurate description of the Antiquities of Athens" (1748)

In book six of his *On the Art of Building in Ten Books*, Leon Battista Alberti began his historical remarks by noting that "Building, so far as we can tell from ancient monuments, enjoyed her first gush of youth, as it were, in Asia, flowered in Greece, and later reached her glorious maturity in Italy." This scenario of ancient architecture achieving its glorious maturity in the Roman Empire became a cornerstone of academic theory between the fifteenth and eighteenth centuries. The French Academy in Rome, which essentially served as a graduate school for France's best students, was founded in that city so that students would have the opportunity to examine the approved monuments of ancient Rome firsthand.

Very little was actually known about Greek architecture, because the country was part of the Ottoman (Turkish) Empire and for centuries had remained nearly inaccessible to Western travelers. Only slowly in the seventeenth and eighteenth centuries did knowledge of Greek art begin to emerge. Colbert arranged an exploration of the Aegean islands in 1673 and it was on this trip that the artist Jacques Carrey made his famous sketches of the Parthenon sculptures (35 sketches have survived), sketches that somewhat remarkably ignored the architecture of the building itself. The Frenchman Jacob Spon and the Englishman George Wheler made a follow-up visit in 1674, but they published a very inaccurate drawing of the building. The Parthenon was still more or less intact at this time, having survived its transformation into a church and later into a mosque. It was housing Turkish powder kegs in 1687 when a Venetian canon shot exploded in the center of building, reducing it to its familiar ruins of columns. When Venice retreated from its short rule of Greece shortly thereafter, the country was again closed to travelers and it was only

James Stuart (1713–88) and Nicholas Revett (1720–1804), from "Proposals for publishing an accurate description of the Antiquities of Athens" (1748) in a footnote to *The Antiquities of Athens*, Vol. I. London: John Haberkorn, 1762, Preface, v.n.

with a relaxation of political tensions a half-century later that travel to Greece once again became possible. The time was now right to explore Greek architecture in a serious way, and this first proposal was put forth toward the end of 1748 by the Englishmen James Stuart and Nicholas Revett.

Stuart was a painter, who had been studying in Rome since 1742. At some point he became interested in Greek antiquity, and on a trip to Sicily in 1748 he discussed the possibility of a trip to Greece with Gavin Hamilton and Nicholas Revett. Hamilton, a noted antiquarian, dropped out of the venture, and Stuart and Revett eventually procured funding for their trip through subscriptions and from the Society of Dilettanti in London. They did not sail out of Venice until January 1751; they arrived in Athens on March 18, where they spent almost two years recording the ruins scattered about Attica. The great historical irony of their well-publicized trip was that Stuart and Revett, after returning to London in 1754, were in no particular hurry to publish their results. The first volume of *The Antiquities of Athens* came out in 1762, but the most important second volume, which contained their careful reconstruction of the Parthenon, was not published until 1788. Thus the honor of being the first to publish a book on Greek architecture fell to a traveler who arrived in Athens after they departed – the Frenchman David Le Roy.

(*a*) This Account of our undertaking, was as follows. Rome 1748. PROPOSALS for publishing an accurate description of the Antiquities of Athens, &c. by James Stuart, and Nicholas Revet.

"There is perhaps no part of Europe, which more deservedly claims the attention and excites the curiosity of the Lovers of polite Literature, than the Territory of Attica, and Athens its capital City; whether we reflect on the Figure it makes in History, on account of the excellent Men it has produced in every Art, both of War and Peace; or whether we consider the Antiquities which are said to be still remaining there, Monuments of the good sense and elevated genius of the Athenians, and the most perfect Models of what is excellent in Sculpture and Architecture."

"Many Authors have mentioned these Remains of Athenian Art as works of great magnificence and most exquisite taste; but their descriptions are so confused, and their measures, when they have given any, are so insufficient, that the most expert Architect could not, from all the Books that have been published on this subject, form a distinct Idea of any one Building these Authors have described. Their writings seem rather calculated to raise our Admiration, than to satisfy our Curiosity or improve our Taste."

"Rome who borrowed her Arts, and frequently her Artificers from Greece, was adorned with magnificent Structures and excellent Sculptures: a considerable number of which have been published, in the Collections of Desgodetz, Palladio, Serlio, Santo Bartoli, and other ingenious Men; and altho' many of the Originals which they have copied are since destroyed, yet the memory, and even the form of them, nay the Arts which produced them, seem secure from perishing; since the industry of those excellent Artists, has dispersed Representations of them through all the polite Nations of Europe."

"But Athens the Mother of elegance and politeness, whose magnificence scarce yielded to that of Rome, and who for the beauties of a correct style must be allowed to surpass her; has been almost entirely neglected. So that unless exact copies of them be speedily made, all her beauteous Fabricks, her Temples, her Theatres, her Palaces, now in ruins, will drop into Oblivion; and Posterity will have to reproach us, that we have not left them a tolerable Idea of what was so excellent, and so much deserved our attention; but that we have suffered the perfection of an Art to perish, when it was perhaps in our power to have retrieved it."

"The reason indeed, why those Antiquities have hitherto been thus neglected, is obvious. Greece, since the revival of the Arts, has been in the possession of Barbarians; and Artists capable of such a Work, have been able to satisfy their passion, whether it was for Fame or Profit, without risking themselves among such professed Enemies to the Arts as the Turks are. The ignorance and jealousy of that uncultivated people may, perhaps, render an undertaking of this sort, still somewhat dangerous."

"Among the Travellers who have visited these Countries, some have been abundantly furnished with Literature, but they have all of them been too little conversant with Painting, Sculpture, and Architecture, to give us tolerable Ideas of what they saw. The Books therefore, in which their Travels are described, are not of such utility nor such entertainment to the Public, as a person acquainted with the practice of these Arts might have rendered them. For the best verbal descriptions cannot be supposed to convey so adequate an Idea, of the magnificence and elegance of Buildings; the fine form, expression, or proportion of Sculptures; the beauty and variety of a Country, or the exact Scene of any celebrated Action, as may be formed from drawings made on the spot, with diligence and fidelity, by the hand of an Artist."

We have therefore resolved to make a journey to Athens; and to publish at our return, such Remains of that famous City as we may be permitted to copy, and that appear to merit our attention; not doubting but a work of this kind, will meet with the Approbation of all those Gentlemen who are lovers of the Arts; and assuring ourselves, that those Artists who aim at perfection, must be more pleased, and better instructed, the nearer they can approach the Fountain-Head of their Art; for so we may call those examples which the greatest Artists, and the best Ages of antiquity have left them.

"We propose that each of the Antiquities which are to compose this Work, shall be treated of in the following manner. First a View of it will be given, faithfully exhibiting the present Appearance of that particular Building and of the circumjacent Country; to this will follow, Architectural Plans and Elevations, in which will be expressed the measure of every Moulding, as well as the general disposition and ordonnance of the whole Building; and lastly will be given, exact delineations of the Statues and Basso-relievos with which those Buildings are decorated. These Sculptures we imagine will be extremely curious, as well on account of their workmanship, as of the subjects they represent. To these we propose adding some Maps and Charts, shewing the general situation and connection of the whole Work. All this perhaps may be conveniently distributed into three folio Volumes, after the following manner."

"The first Volume may contain the Antiquities belonging to the Acropolis, or ancient fortress of Athens; the second those of the City; and the third, those which lye dispersed in different parts of the Athenian Territory: of all which the annexed Catalogue will give a more distinct Idea."

68   ROBERT WOOD AND JAMES DAWKINS
from *The Ruins of Palmyra* (1753)

Greece was not the only land under exploration at this time, as there was a burst of archaeological activity during the 1750s. Greek colonies and Etruscan sites in Italy and Sicily were being investigated, as were other areas of the eastern Mediterranean. In 1750 Robert Wood and James Dawkins set out to explore Asia Minor, Syria, Phoenicia, Palestine, and Egypt. In Athens they even came upon those "two English painters" recording Greek architecture, but took little note of the buildings they saw. Instead, Wood and Dawkins focused their efforts on the sites of two Roman colonies: Baalbek in Lebanon and Palmyra in Syria, the origins of which they rightly found confusing. Palmyra was an ancient city along a trade route high in the desert of Syria, possibly dating back to the sixth century BC. Wood was dubious of the account that it was built on the site where David slew Goliath, but he accepted the biblical story that the city had been founded by Solomon, destroyed by Nebuchadnezzar, and rebuilt in Roman times. This becomes the basis for his brief summary of early artistic development.

How far the taste and manner of the architecture may give any light into the age which produced it, our engravings will put in every person's power to judge for himself; and in forming such judgment, the reader will make what use he thinks proper of the following observations, thrown together, without any view to order.

We thought we could easily distinguish, at Palmyra, the ruins, of two very different periods of antiquity; the decay of the oldest, which are mere rubbish, and incapable of measurement, looked like the gradual work of time; but the later seemed to bear the marks of violence.

There is a greater sameness in the architecture of Palmyra, than we observed at Rome, Athens, and other great cities, whose ruins evidently point out different ages, as much from the variety of their manner, as their different stages of decay. The works done during the republican state of Rome are known by their simplicity and usefulness, while those of the emperors are remarkable for ornament and finery. Nor is it less difficult to distinguish the old simple dorick as Athens from their licentious corinthian of a later age. But at Palmyra we cannot trace so visible a progress of arts and manners in their buildings; and those which are most ruinous seem to owe their decay rather to worse materials, or accidental violence, than a greater antiquity. It is true, there is in the outside of the sepulchral monuments, without the town, an air of simplicity very different from the general taste of all the other buildings, from which, and their singular shape we at first supposed them works of the country, prior to the introduction of the Greek arts; but we found the inside ornamented as the other buildings.

It is remarkable, that except four ionick half columns in the temple of the sun, and two in one of the mausoleums, the whole is corinthian, richly ornamented with some striking beauties, and some as visible faults.

In the variety of ruins we visited in our tour through the east, we could not help observing, that each of the three Greek orders had their fashionable periods: The oldest

Robert Wood (1716–71) and James Dawkins (1717–c.1771), from *The Ruins of Palmyra, otherwise Tedmor, in the Desart.* London, 1753, pp. 15–16.

buildings we saw were dorick; the ionick succeeded, and seems to have been the favourite order, not only in Ionia, but all over Asia Minor, the great country of good architecture, when that art was in it's highest perfection. The corinthian came next in vogue, and most of the buildings of that order in Greece seem posterior to the Romans getting footing there. The composite, and all its extravagancies followed, when proportion was entirely sacrificed to finery and crowded ornament.

Another observation we made in this tour, and which seems to our present purpose, was, that in the progress of architecture and sculpture towards perfection, sculpture arrived soonest at it, and soonest lost it.

The old dorick of Athens is an instance of the first, where the bas-reliefs on the metopes of the temples of Theseus and Minerva, (the first built soon after the battle of Marathon, and the latter in the time of Pericles) shew the utmost perfection that art has ever acquired, though the architecture of the same temples is far short of it, and in many particulars against the rules of Vitruvius, who appears to have founded his principles upon the works of a later age.

That architecture out-lived sculpture we had several instances in Asia Minor, and no where more evident proofs of it, than at Palmyra.

69 JOHANN JOACHIM WINCKELMANN
from *Reflections on the Imitation of Greek Works in Painting and Sculpture* (1755)

Whereas the English and the French provided many of the first travelers to Greece, it was left to a German – one who would never travel to Greece – to attempt to place Greek art within its historical context. Johann Joachim Winckelmann is sometimes called the "father" of modern art history, but he was at the very least the first major historian to ponder what the Greeks achieved artistically. He was born of humble circumstances in the Prussian town of Stendel and pursued a few university studies in the classics in Halle and Jena. After serving as a private tutor and as a school teacher for several years, he was hired by Count von Bünau of Saxony as his librarian. This appointment allowed him access to the count's superb classical library and it allowed him his first contact with classical sculptural works (mostly Roman copies of Greek works), which had been assembled by Electors of Saxony in Dresden. On the basis of these few pieces, Winckelmann composed his first book, *Reflections on the Imitation of Greek Works in Painting and Sculpture*, which appeared in Dresden in 1755. The success of the book encouraged Winckelmann to leave Germany for Italy, where within a few years he would become recognized as the world's foremost authority on Greek art.

Johann Joachim Winckelmann (1717–68), from *Gedanken über die Nachahmung der griechischen Werke in der Mahlerey und Bildhauer-Kunst* (1755), trans. Elfriede Heyer and Roger C. Norton, in *Reflections on the Imitation of Greek Works in Painting and Sculpture*. La Salle: Open Court, 1987. © 1987 by Open Court Publishing Company. Reprinted by permission of Open Court Publishing Company, a division of Carus Publishing Company, Peru, IL.

This particular book thus preceded the later studies that lay behind his great history of ancient art, but many of his later themes are already present here. Foremost is his belief in the superiority of Greek art over that of the Romans, which Winckelmann credited in part to their idealized aesthetic philosophy. Also contributing to this superiority – and here drawing upon Montesquieu – were the moderate Greek climate, the physical beauty of the Greek people, their democratic politics, and above all their highly refined artistic sensibilities, which exalted "noble simplicity and quiet grandeur" over ruder and more vulgar artistic expression. Winckelmann's locution in this regard became a catchphrase for a generation that intensely followed this new artistic discovery.

I.   Natural Beauty

Good taste, which is becoming more prevalent throughout the world, had its origins under the skies of Greece. Every invention of foreign nations which was brought to Greece was, as it were, only a first seed that assumed new form and character here. We are told that Minerva chose this land, with its mild seasons, above all others for the Greeks in the knowledge that it would be productive of genius.

The taste which the Greeks exhibited in their works of art was unique and has seldom been taken far from its source without loss. Under more distant skies it found tardy recognition and without a doubt was completely unknown in the northern zones during a time when painting and sculpture, of which the Greeks are the greatest teachers, found few admirers. [. . .]

The only way for us to become great or, if this be possible, inimitable, is to imitate the ancients. What someone once said of Homer – that to understand him well means to admire him – is also true for the art works of the ancients, especially the Greeks. One must become as familiar with them as with a friend in order to find their statue of Laocoon just as inimitable as Homer. In such close acquaintance one learns to judge as Nicomachus judged Zeuxis' Helena: 'Behold her with my eyes,' he said to an ignorant person who found fault with this work of art, 'and she will appear a goddess to you.'

With such eyes did Michelangelo, Raphael, and Poussin see the works of the ancients. They partook of good taste at its source, and Raphael did this in the very land where it had begun. We know that he sent young artists to Greece in order to sketch for him the relics of antiquity.

The relationship between an ancient Roman statue and a Greek original will generally be similar to that seen in Virgil's imitation of Homer's Nausicaa, in which he compares Dido and her followers to Diana in the midst of her Oreads.

Laocoon was for the artist of old Rome just what he is for us – the demonstration of Polyclitus' rules, the perfect rules of art. [. . .]

In the masterpieces of Greek art, connoisseurs and imitators find not only nature at its most beautiful but also something beyond nature, namely certain ideal forms of its beauty, which, as an ancient interpreter of Plato teaches us, come from images created by the mind alone.

The most beautiful body of one of us would probably no more resemble the most beautiful Greek body than Iphicles resembled his brother, Hercules. The first development of the Greeks was influenced by a mild and clear sky; but the practice of physical exercises from an early age gave this development its noble forms. Consider, for example, a young Spartan conceived by a hero and heroine and never confined in swaddling clothes, sleeping on the ground from the seventh year on and trained from infancy in wrestling and swimming. Compare this Spartan with a young Sybarite of our time and then decide which of the two would be chosen by the artist as a model for young Theseus, Achilles, or even Bacchus. Modelled from the latter it would be a Theseus fed on roses, while from the former would come a Theseus fed on flesh, to borrow the terms used by a Greek painter to characterize two different conceptions of this hero.

The grand games gave every Greek youth a strong incentive for physical exercise, and the laws demanded a ten-month preparation period for the Olympic Games, in Elis, at the very place where they were held. The highest prizes were not always won by adults but often by youths, as told in Pindar's odes. To resemble the god-like Diagoras was the fondest wish of every young man.

Behold the swift Indian who pursues a deer on foot – how briskly his juices must flow, how flexible and quick his nerves and muscles must be, how light the whole structure of his body! Thus did Homer portray his heroes, and his Achilles he chiefly noted as being 'swift of foot'.

These exercises gave the bodies of the Greeks the strong and manly contours which the masters then imparted to their statues without any exaggeration or excess. [. . .]

Moreover, everything that was instilled and taught from birth to adulthood about the culture of their bodies and the preservation, development, and refinement of this culture through nature and art was done to enhance the natural beauty of the ancient Greeks. Thus we can say that in all probability their physical beauty excelled ours by far.

The most perfect creations of nature would, on the other hand, have become only partially and imperfectly known to the artists in a country where nature was hindered by rigid laws, as in Egypt, the reputed home of the arts and sciences. In Greece, however, where people dedicated themselves to joy and pleasure from childhood on, and where there was no such social decorum as ours to restrict the freedom of their customs, the beauty of nature could reveal itself unveiled as a great teacher of artists.

The schools for artists were the gymnasia, where young people, otherwise clothed for the sake of public modesty, performed their physical exercises in the nude. The philosopher and the artist went there – Socrates to teach Charmides, Autolycus, and Lysias; Phidias to enrich his art by watching these handsome young men. There one could study the movement of the muscles and body as well as the body's outlines or contours from the impressions left by the young wrestlers in the sand. The nude body in its most beautiful form was exhibited there in so many different, natural, and noble positions and poses not attainable today by the hired models of our art schools.

Truth springs from the feelings of the heart, and the modern artist who wants to impart truth to his works cannot preserve even a shadow of it unless he himself is able to replace that which the unmoved and indifferent soul of his model does not feel or is unable to express by actions appropriate to a certain sensation or passion.

Many of Plato's dialogues, beginning in the gymnasia of Athens, portray to us the noble souls of these youths and at the same time suggest a uniformity of action and outward carriage developed in these places and in their physical exercises.

The most beautiful young people danced nude in the theaters, and Sophocles, the great Sophocles, was the first who in his youth presented such dramas for his fellow-citizens.

Phryne bathed before the eyes of all the Greeks during the Eleusinian Games, and, as she emerged from the water, became for the artists the prototype of Venus Anadyomene. It is also known that girls from Sparta danced completely naked before the eyes of the young people at certain festive occasions. What might seem strange to us here becomes more acceptable when considering that the early Christians, both men and women, were totally unclothed when they were submersed in the same baptismal font.

Thus every festival of the Greeks was an opportunity for the artists to become intimately acquainted with the beauty of nature. [. . .]

These frequent opportunities to observe nature prompted Greek artists to go still further. They began to form certain general ideas of the beauty of individual parts of the body as well as of the whole – ideas which were to rise above nature itself; their model was an ideal nature originating in the mind alone.

* * *

IV.   Noble Simplicity and Quiet Grandeur

The general and most distinctive characteristics of the Greek masterpieces are, finally, a noble simplicity and quiet grandeur, both in posture and expression. Just as the depths of the sea always remain calm however much the surface may rage, so does the expression of the figures of the Greeks reveal a great and composed soul even in the midst of passion.

Such a soul is reflected in the face of Laocoon – and not in the face alone – despite his violent suffering. The pain is revealed in all the muscles and sinews of his body, and we ourselves can almost feel it as we observe the painful contraction of the abdomen alone without regarding the face and other parts of the body. This pain, however, expresses itself with no sign of rage in his face or in his entire bearing. He emits no terrible screams such as Virgil's Laocoon, for the opening of his mouth does not permit it; it is rather an anxious and troubled sighing as described by Sadoleto. The physical pain and the nobility of soul are distributed with equal strength over the entire body and are, as it were, held in balance with one another. Laocoon suffers, but he suffers like Sophocles' Philoctetes; his pain touches our very souls, but we wish that we could bear misery like this great man.

The expression of such nobility of soul goes far beyond the depiction of beautiful nature. The artist had to feel the strength of this spirit in himself and then impart it to his marble. [. . .]

All movements and poses of Greek figures not marked by such traits of wisdom, but instead by passion and violence, were the result of an error of conception which the ancient artists called *parenthyrsos*.

The more tranquil the state of the body the more capable it is of portraying the true character of the soul. In all positions too removed from this tranquillity, the soul is not in its most essential condition, but in one that is agitated and forced. A soul is more apparent and distinctive when seen in violent passion, but it is great and noble when seen in a state of unity and calm. The portrayal of suffering alone in Laocoon would have been *parenthyrsos*; therefore the artist, in order to unite the distinctive and the noble qualities of soul, showed him in an action that was closest to a state of tranquillity for one in such pain. But in this tranquillity the soul must be distinguished by traits that are uniquely its own and give it a form that is calm and active at the same time, quiet but not indifferent or sluggish.

The common taste of artists of today, especially the younger ones, is in complete opposition to this. Nothing gains their approbation but contorted postures and actions in which bold passion prevails. This they call art executed with spirit, or *franchezza* [sincerity, frankness]. Their favorite term is *contrapposto*, which represents for them the essence of a perfect work of art. In their figures they demand a soul which shoots like a comet out of their midst; they would like every figure to be an Ajax or a Capaneus.

70 ALLAN RAMSAY
from "A Dialogue on Taste" in *The Investigator* (1755)

W inckelmann's book appeared in German in Dresden in 1755, and thus it would take a few years for its ideas to become known throughout Europe. This was not the case with *The Investigator*, published by the Scottish painter Allan Ramsay, which appeared in the same year. Ramsay was a native of Edinburgh and had studied art in London, and by the late 1730s he had emerged as one of Britain's greatest portrait painters. He made his first trip to Italy in 1736–8, but he became an international figure during his second stay in Rome between 1754 and 1757. During this time he formed part of an artistic circle that included the traveler Robert Wood, the architect Robert Adam, and the architect and engraver Giovanni Battista Piranesi. With this standing, his "Dialogue on Taste," with its insistence on the superiority of Greek architecture over that of ancient Rome, would soon create a furor in Rome. In essence it was the first round of a "Greco-Roman" debate that would soon escalate into an international controversy. The two antagonists in this dialogue are Lord Modish, who represents the traditional academic viewpoint; his counterpart is Colonel Freeman, a freethinker who challenges accepted opinions on a variety of topics. The argument presented here is but part of a larger argument on the relativity of judgments of beauty (see ch. 107 below), and begins with Colonel Freeman having just compared architecture, as Fischer von Erlach did earlier, with fashions in clothing.

LORD MODISH.

My dear George, this is a lamentable sinking from architecture to cuffs.

COL. FREEMAN.

I do that, my Lord, in imitation of some great men of our acquaintance, who let themselves down very low in order to rise with the more security. The progress of fashion in dress, and the feelings which are the consequence of that progress, being the most familiar, and having at the same time the quickest revolutions, are of all others the fittest to explain the nature of fashion in general. The fashions in building, tho' more durable than those in dress, are not for that the less fashions, and are equally subject to change. But as

Allan Ramsay (1713–84), from "A Dialogue on Taste" (1755) in the journal *The Investigator* (London, 1762), pp. 37–8.

stones and bricks are more lasting than silk and velvet, and as people do not make up churches and palaces so often as they do coats and capuchines, we must have recourse to history for the knowledge of those changes, which we can learn but very imperfectly from our own proper experience. In history we shall find that every nation received its mode of architecture from that nation which, in all other respects, was the highest in credit, riches, and general estimation. The admiration that attends whatever is great in its dimensions, costly in its materials, and precise in its execution, is, as far as our experience goes, universal; and naturally inclines the mind in favour of any form which accident has combined with those admirable qualities. The Egyptians were the first people we know of who were so rich, and at their ease, as to build with grandeur, cost, and neatness; and from thence inspired the Greeks with a love for those ornaments which their caprice had added to the useful part of architecture. The Greeks, in their turn, becoming for many ages a free, a rich, and a happy people, had an opportunity of practising those arts in many sumptuous buildings; where, beside the invention of arches, and other solid improvements in the art of building, they made many changes, as their fancy led them, upon the Egyptian ornaments. In this state was architecture when it was transplanted to Rome, by a people who, by perpetual wars, had in a short time attained from the meanest origin, to the greatest height of power. Destitute of money, and profoundly ignorant of all the arts of peace, they had never raised any buildings of which they could boast; and no sooner had they an opportunity of considering the Grecian temples and other public works, great in themselves, and set off with all that costly materials and the genius of their excellent painters and sculptors could add to the skill of the mason, but struck with the complex object, they decreed the Greeks to be the only architects in the world, and submitted willingly to receive laws in the arts from those whom their Arms had subdued. Perhaps the philosophy, poetry, and music of Greece, for which they began at the same time to take a relish, served not a little to raise the reputation of the Greeks, and might strengthen their authority in architecture; tho' not necessarily connected with them. An admiration, to a degree of bigotry seized the Roman artists and connoiseurs, and put an effectual stop to any farther change or improvement in architecture. Their sole study was to imitate the Grecian buildings, and the being like or unlike to them became soon the measure of right and wrong. Rules so compiled were committed to writing, and continue to this day, together with some of the antient buildings upon which they were formed, to be the standard of taste all over christendom. Time may possibly produce on it insensible changes, but there is almost nothing which can be imagined to give it a total overthrow, unless Europe should become a conquest of the Chinese.

71 JULIEN-DAVID LE ROY

from *The Ruins of the Most Beautiful Monuments of Greece* (1758)

T he first visual images of Greek architecture, as we noted above, came not from the expedition of Stuart and Revett but from the efforts of David Le Roy. This son of a royal clockmaker had attended the Royal Academy of Architecture in Paris and in 1750 won the prestigious Prix de Rome, which enabled him to spend five years at the French Academy. Midway through his stay there, he heard of Stuart and Revett's trip to Greece and he applied to the French government for official assistance to make his own trip to Athens and sketch the major monuments. He sailed out of Venice in May 1854 aboard a French navy vessel, and first had to go to Constantinople to receive permission from the Ottoman government. He was only in Athens for a little under three months, but he must have worked exceedingly hard to carry out his task of surveying and sketching the principal classical monuments. By July 1854 he was back in Rome, and the following year he returned to Paris to prepare his publication. At this point, at least as far as the French were concerned, it was now a race to publish Le Roy's book before Stuart and Revett could publish their findings. In Paris Le Roy had the assistance of the noted antiquarian Comte de Caylus, as well as the delineators Jean-Joseph Le Lorrain and Philippe La Bas. The finished volume, with its impressive plates of Greek "ruins," appeared in 1758, to high praise within French artistic circles.

Le Roy did more than simply present his visual impressions; he also sought to place them within a historical context. The book was another salvo in the emerging Greco-Roman controversy, and it was the first to buffer the claim for Greece's artistic superiority with powerful visual evidence. In the following passages, taken from his introductory "Discourse on the History of Civil Architecture," Le Roy recasts much of classical history by suggesting that the Greeks were the inventors of everything beautiful in classical architecture, and that the Romans were little more than epigones who were incapable of similar inventive spirit. Such a view was also, in effect, an attack on the French academic system and its long reliance on Roman models. The translation of these four passages picks up at the point where Le Roy turns from Egypt to a consideration of Greece.

The first steps made by the Greeks in architecture were so happy that they never deviated from them, and for this they merit perhaps their greatest praise. Too often reflection spoils the simple productions of the first efforts of genius. They designed their huts with such wisdom that they were able to preserve the form even in their most magnificent temples. Their richest entablatures had no other origin than in the arrangement or spacing of the roof joists that they observed on the sides of the huts, and from the width of the joist they formed the module – first serving to give those parts of the building the necessary dimension for solid construction, but later giving these same parts the forms and grandeur that they must have in order to produce a pleasing effect on the eyes.

Columns seem first to have been used not long after the discovery of the module. Here is what we conjecture on their origin. After the first temples built by the Greeks had become too small for the crowds of people who came to the sacrifice there, the architects probably foresaw that if they built the temples larger, the excessive span of the beams supporting the

Julien-David Le Roy (1724–1803), from *Les Ruines des plus beaux monuments de la Grèce* [The ruins of the most beautiful monuments of Greece]. Paris: H. L. Guerin and L. F. Delatour, 1758, trans. Harry Francis Mallgrave.

roof would bend or weaken the new monuments. Perhaps, as seems more likely, they did not perceive this problem until the larger temples were built. To resolve this problem, they came up with the solution of cutting trunks of trees, arranging them vertically and at equal intervals along the length of the temple. Each column supported at its center the lateral joists and thus relieved the entire structure.

The first rules of proportion were established by the Athenians who crossed over into Asia Minor under the lead of Ion, son of Xuthus. After their conquests they built several temples to the gods. In general they imitated those that they had seen among the Dorians, and for this reason they called them Doric. But then they introduced a refinement: the idea of making the columns resembled the force and beauty of a man's body, which they determined to be six diameters. This first step was without doubt the greatest discovery that has been made in the decorative regard of architecture, and it was the foundation and the basis of all the other discoveries of this type.

After imitating the proportions of the body of a man in the massive proportions of the columns in some of their temples, the Ionians in other buildings easily changed to lighter columns in imitation of the more elegant proportions of the female body. They named this new order Ionic, because they themselves were the inventors. They enriched the columns with bases, and even imitated the women's coiffure in ornamenting the capital. But what served again to distinguish it from the Doric was the novel form that they gave to its entablature. Whereas the Doric was decorated with triglyphs, they simplified the frieze of this order and replaced the wide mutules of the Doric with small dentils. With these last two discoveries they opened a vast field for new reflections and advanced at a rapid pace toward perfection.

Freed from Doric severity, which by placing the columns directly under the triglyphs makes the intercolumniations either too large or too narrow, they devised a variety of intercolumniations for the Ionic order and determined the proportions of columns and entablatures accordingly. Not wanting to limit themselves to general discoveries for this order, the Greeks looked to the history of their country and replaced columns with caryatides or statues representing the women of Caryates, who were punished by the Greeks for betraying their nation in the war with the Persians. They even investigated the nuances of optics, when they noticed that in a temple with a colonnade, those columns at the corners appear the thinnest because they are most surrounded with air. Thus they slightly enlarged them. For the same reason they lightened the columns of the second row, because they receive less light and therefore appear larger. Finally, they enriched the columns of the Ionic order with different fluting from that of the Doric and added several beautiful ornaments to the moldings of the entablature. [. . .]

After these discoveries of the Greeks, they gradually made the two orders more distinct with several beautiful arrangements of temples, and through the different proportions that one must observe in them, it seems that there remained nothing very important to discover in architecture, either with this sort of monument or with regard to the orders. Calimachus, however, in seeing a basket covered with a tile, around which by chance some Acanthus leaves had grown and folded under the angle of the tile, designed the admirable Corinthian capital. But the Greeks, who were only impressed by great things, and who did not accept it as a new order, except for the little enrichment to the capital or the entablature, never regarded the Corinthian order as entirely independent of the other two, and only slightly distinguished it from the Ionic, which in many features it resembled. But they found for it a special character and used it for buildings of the greatest magnificence. Ascending to the most sublime ideas and descending to the most subtle refinements, they fronted Corinthian temples with eight columns, ornamented with the most perfect bas-reliefs and statuary – sculpture always following the progress of architecture. They even acquired an understanding of perspective, whose rules they practiced on the smallest parts of their buildings. On the Doric Temple of Minerva [Parthenon], built by Pericles in Athens, they made the metopes taller than their widths, so that they might appear square at a distance of twice the height of the temple. Eventually the Greeks were able to discover everything in architecture that is beautiful and ingenious, and the Romans, who subjugated them by force of arms, were obliged to recognize the superiority of their intellect. We learn this from the mouths of the Romans.

If the Greeks gave their laws to Italy, they also imposed their arts. Under their first kings the Romans only built monuments in the Tuscan manner, more notable for their size than for their beauty. We do not know if they learned the way of constructing their strong walls directly from the Egyptians, but it seems clear that they took the forms of their temples and the Tuscan order from the Greeks. It is also clear that they found perfection in the arts only when they began to have open trade with the Greeks. In truth, as long as the Republic lasted, the Romans were focused on their plan to make themselves masters of the world, and they never aspired to make admirable things in architecture. Under their emperors, however, they made a great effort to distinguish themselves. They employed the most celebrated Greek architects to build monuments in Rome, Athens, Cyzicus, Palmyra, Baalbec, and in other famous cities of their empire, some of which we still admire for their grandeur and for their beautiful ornaments, although some are too embellished with ornaments. Hadrian prided himself in his great understanding of architecture and distinguished himself above all other emperors by the prodigious number of edifices he built, the chronicle of which he published in the famous Pantheon he built in Athens. He was no less determined to excel than Nero was in music, or Dionysius, the tyrant of Syracuse, in poetry. And just as this last ruler put the poet Philoxenes to death for having criticized his verses, Hadrian had Apollodorus killed for having mocked the Temple of Venus that he had designed. In the end, though, it seems the Romans lacked the creative genius that led the Greeks to so many discoveries. With regard to the orders, they invented nothing of any value. The one invention that they do claim, the Composite order, is only a rather imperfect combination of the Ionic and Corinthian. By increasing the proportions of the columns of the Doric order and multiplying the moldings within its entablature, they perhaps caused it to lose much of the male character that distinguished it in Greece.

72 JULIEN-DAVID LE ROY
from *The Ruins of the Most Beautiful Monuments of Greece* (1758)

After presenting his historical account and providing some general background on the founding of Athens and the Acropolis, Le Roy presents an engraving of the Parthenon, which he calls the Temple of Minerva – the last the Latin name for the Greek goddess Athena. The engraving shows this building from the side, lying amid debris and overgrown vegetation, with its center columns and cella walls destroyed by Venetian canons. What are still present, at least on the parts of the entablature still existent, are the glorious frieze reliefs of Phidias; these were not removed by Lord Elgin and taken to London until the nineteenth century. Le Roy's two-page summary of the temple is somewhat perfunctory and does not really speak of it as one of the great artistic masterpieces of human history. In a second edition of this book, issued in 1770, Le Roy greatly augments this description with artistic information that scholars and antiquarians had been able to piece together over the preceding decade. What follows is therefore the first introduction of this building to the history of Western art – the first solid indication of the greatness of Greek art. Le Roy is off by ten years in recounting the date of its destruction.

The Temple of Minerva, called the Parthenon or the Temple of the Virgin, also the Hecatompedon, is situated in the middle of the rock of the Acropolis, whose height dominates the plain of Athens. We see this superb edifice from a great distance on some of the roads that lead into the city, and we glimpse it from the entrance of the Gulf of Engia. If its grandeur and the whiteness of the marble of which it is built evoke from afar a feeling of admiration, the elegance of its proportions and the beauty of the bas-reliefs that decorate it please us no less when we examine it up close. One sees that Ictinus and Callicrates made every effort to distinguish themselves in architecture by raising this temple to Minerva, who invented this beautiful art. This temple forms a parallelogram in plan, like almost all other Greek and Roman temples. Its length, which is oriented east and west, is 221 feet (not counting the stylobate); its width is 94 feet. It is in the Doric order, peripteral octostyle, that is to say, surrounded by columns detached from the cella or body of the temple, which forms a portico all around and has eight columns at the front. The sides of the body of the temple had two smooth walls, without pilasters between the corners.

The large Doric columns that surround the exterior of the temple are 5 feet, 8 inches in diameter, 32 feet high. There were 46 of these in all. They have no base, but the extremely tall steps that come close to the base of the columns seem to serve this purpose. They support a Doric entablature that is almost one-third of the height of the columns; the metopes of the frieze are decorated with bas-reliefs representing the combat of the Athenians against the Centaurs. On the smooth walls of the body of the temple we find the remnants of a beautiful frieze that ran around it; the figures on the outside appear to represent the sacrifices and the processions of the ancient Athenians. The sculpture of this frieze is shallower in relief than the Centaurs that are on the exterior of the temple, which

Julien-David Le Roy, from *Les Ruines des plus beaux monuments de la Grèce* [The ruins of the most beautiful monuments of Greece]. Paris: H. L. Guerin and L. F. Delatour, 1758, pp. 9–10, trans. Harry Francis Mallgrave.

proves less a different date for these works than the skill of the architects, who gave much more projection to the exterior bas-reliefs because they must be seen at a greater distance. It even seems that they followed this principle in the sculpture that adorns the pediment. The pediments were filled with groups of beautiful marble figures, of which the remnants appear life-size, carved in the round, and marvelously well executed. Pausanias informs us that the birth of Minerva was represented in the pediment of the main facade [. . .]

The Athenians made solemn sacrifices to this divinity in the festivals celebrated in her honor, every three years according to some authors, every five years according to others. In these festivals the elders bearing olive branches proceeded to the sanctuary of the temple and raised the veil that covered the deity, on which was depicted, as some people have reported, her heroic actions. While the ox was being sacrificed to Minerva, a procession encircled the temple, and when the sacrifice was done a trumpet was sounded and a cursor announced the start of the games, from which women were excluded. Minerva was the divinity most respected by the Athenians, and the olive was sacred to her. They crowned her effigies with the branches of this tree, which the Athenians believed to be immortal, and a crown of olives was given to the winners of the Olympic games.

The magnificent Temple of Minerva was long preserved in all of its beauty, even though Athens had many rulers. The Christians who took over this city turned this profane monument into a temple to the true God, and the Turks who followed them changed the building into a mosque. Messrs. Spon and Wheler, during their stay in Attica, had the good fortune to see it in its entirety in 1676. But in 1677 the Proveditor Morosini, leading 8,800 Venetian soldiers, besieged Athens and a bomb fell on the temple. It ignited munitions stored there by the Turks and instantly reduced most of the building to ruin. This General, in his desire to enrich his country with the spoils of this superb monument, again contributed to its ruin. He wanted to remove the statue of Minerva from the pediment, together with her chariot and horses, but to his great regret as well as to ours, he disfigured this masterpiece without succeeding in his task. A part of the group fell to the ground and shattered. Inside the Turks have since built a mosque, surmounted with a low dome, which we see amid the ruins of this temple.

73 JAMES STUART AND NICHOLAS REVETT
from Preface to *The Antiquities of Athens* (1762)

The first volume of Stuart and Revett's book, as we noted earlier, did not contain their reconstructions of the principal Greek monuments; instead, the two authors decided – against their original proposal – to delineate first the smaller classical works in Attica, as well as some temples built during Roman times. But their engravings were nevertheless quite beautiful, almost magical in their "Oriental" character, and in their Preface they provided their own account of their discoveries. If the tone is not as severe in its anti-Roman bias as that of Le Roy,

James Stuart and Nicholas Revett, from Preface to *The Antiquities of Athens*. London: John Haberkorn, 1762, pp. i–v.

Stuart and Revett nevertheless came to the same conclusion with their view that the Athenians attained the highest excellence in sculpture and architecture, while the Romans never quite equaled their accomplishments.

The ruined Edifices of Rome have for many years engaged the attention of those, who apply themselves to the study of Architecture; and have generally been considered, as the Models and Standard of regular and ornamental Building. Many representations of them drawn and engraved by skilful Artists have been published, by which means the Study of the Art has been every where greatly facilitated, and the general practice of it improved and promoted. Insomuch that what is now esteemed the most elegant manner of decorating Buildings, was originally formed, and has been since established on Examples, which the Antiquities of Rome have furnished.

But altho' the World is enriched with Collections of this sort already published, we thought it would be a Work not unacceptable to the lovers of Architecture, if we added to those Collections, some Examples drawn from the Antiquities of Greece; and we were confirmed in our opinion by this consideration principally, that as Greece was the great Mistress of the Arts, and Rome, in this respect, no more than her disciple, it may be presumed, all the most admired Buildings which adorned that imperial City, were but imitations of Grecian Originals.

Hence it seemed probable that if accurate Representations of these Originals were published, the World would be enabled to form, not only more extensive, but juster Ideas than have hitherto been obtained, concerning Architecture, and the state in which it existed during the best ages of antiquity. It even seemed that a performance of this kind might contribute to the improvement of the Art itself, which at present appears to be founded on too partial and too scanty a system of ancient Examples.

For during those Ages of violence and barbarism, which began with the declension, and continued long after the destruction of the Roman Empire, the beautiful Edifices which had been erected in Italy with such great labour and expence, were neglected or destroyed; so that, to use a very common expression, it may truly be said, that Architecture lay for Ages buried in its own ruins; and altho' from these Ruins, it has Phenix-like received a second birth, we may nevertheless conclude, that many of the beauties and elegancies which enhanced its ancient Splendor, are still wanting, and that it has not yet by any means recovered all its former Perfection.

This Conclusion becomes sufficiently obvious, when we consider that the great Artists, by whose industry this noble Art has been revived, were obliged to shape its present Form, after those Ideas only, which the casual remains of Italy suggested to them; and these Remains are so far from furnishing all the materials necessary for a complete Restoration of Architecture in all its parts, that the best collections of them, those published by Palladio and Desgodetz, cannot be said to afford a sufficient variety of Examples for restoring even the three Orders of Columns; for they are deficient in what relates to the Doric and Ionic, the two most ancient of these Orders.

If from what has been said it should appear, that Architecture is reduced and restrained within narrower limits than could be wished, for want of a greater number of ancient Examples than have hither-to been published; it must then be granted, that every such Example of beautiful Form or Proportion, wherever it may be found, is a valuable addition to the former Stock; and does, when published, become a material acquisition to the Art.

But of all the Countries, which were embellished by the Ancients with magnificent Buildings, Greece appears principally to merit our Attention; since, if we believe the Ancients themselves, the most beautiful Orders and Dispositions of Columns were invented in that Country, and the most celebrated Works of Architecture were erected there: to which may be added that the most excellent Treatises on the Art appear to have been written by Grecian Architects.

The City of Greece most renowned for stately Edifices, for the Genius of its Inhabitants, and for the culture of every Art, was Athens. We therefore resolved to examine that Spot rather than any other; flattering ourselves, that the remains we might find there, would excel in true Taste and Elegance every thing hitherto published. How far indeed these Expectations have been answered, must now be submitted to the opinion of the Public.

Yet since the Authorities and Reasons, which engaged us to conceive so highly of the Athenian Buildings, may serve likewise to guard them, in some measure, from the over-hasty opinions and un-unadvised censures of the Inconsiderate; it may not be amiss to produce some of them in this place. And we the rather wish to say something a little more at large on this subject, as it will be at the same time an apology for ourselves, and perhaps the best justification of our undertaking.

After the defeat of Xerxes, the Grecians, secure from Invaders and in full possession of their Liberty, arrived at the height of their Prosperity. It was then, they applied themselves with the greatest assiduity and success to the culture of the Arts. They maintained their Independency and their Power for a considerable space of time, and distinguished themselves by a pre-eminence and universality of Genius, unknown to other Ages and Nations.

During this happy period, their most renowned Artists were produced. Sculpture and Architecture attained their highest degree of excellence at Athens in the time of Pericles, when Phidias distinguished himself with such superior ability, that his works were considered as wonders by the Ancients, so long as any knowledge or taste remained among them. His Statue of Jupiter Olympius we are told was never equalled; and it was under his inspection that many of the most celebrated Buildings of Athens were erected. Several Artists of most distinguished talents were his contemporaries, among whom we may reckon Callimachus an Athenian, the inventor of the Corinthian Capital. After this, a succession of excellent Painters, Sculptors and Architects appeared, and these Arts continued in Greece, at their highest perfection, till after the death of Alexander the Great.

Painting, Sculpture and Architecture, it should be observed, remained all that time in a very rude and imperfect State among the Italians.

But when the Romans had subdued Greece, they soon become enamored of these delightful Arts. They adorned their City with Statues and Pictures, the Spoils of that conquered Country; and, adopting the Grecian Style of Architecture, they now first began to erect Buildings of great Elegance and Magnificence. They seem not however to have equalled the Originals from whence they had borrowed their Taste, either for purity of Design, or delicacy of Execution.

For altho' these Roman Edifices were most probably designed and executed by Grecians, as Rome never produced many extraordinary Artists of her own, yet Greece herself was at that time greatly degenerated from her former excellence, and had long ceased to display that superiority of Genius, which distinguished her in the Age of Pericles and of Alexander. To this a long series of Misfortunes had reduced her, for having been oppressed by the Macedonians first, and afterwards subdued by the Romans, with the loss of her Liberty, that love of Glory likewise, and that sublimity of Spirit which had animated her Artists, as well as her Warriors, her Statesmen, and her Philosophers, and which had formed her peculiar Character, were now extinguished, and all her exquisite Arts languished and were near expiring.

They were indeed at length assiduously cherished and cultivated at Rome. That City being now Mistress of the World, and possessed of unbounded Wealth and Power, became ambitious also of the utmost embellishments which these Arts could bestow. They could not however, tho' assisted by Roman Munificence, reascend to that height of Perfection, which they had attained in Greece during the happy period we have already mentioned. And it is particularly remarkable, that when the Roman Authors themselves, celebrate any exquisite production of Art; it is the work of Phidias, Praxiteles, Myron, Lysippus, Zeuxis, Apelles, or in brief of some Artist, who adorned that happy Period; and not of those, who had worked at Rome, or had lived nearer to their own times than the Age of Alexander.

It seemed therefore evident that Greece is the Place where the most beautiful Edifices were erected, and where the purest and most elegant Examples of ancient Architecture are to be discovered.

74 JOHANN JOACHIM WINCKELMANN
from *History of the Art of Antiquity* (1764)

With the publication of J. J. Winckelmann's *History of the Art of Antiquity* in 1764 – following in the wake of the publications of Le Roy and Stuart & Revett – the third and seemingly final nail had been driven into the coffin of Roman classicism. The learned scholar had made his way to Rome in 1755, where he first worked as a librarian to Cardinal Archinto, and eventually he became the custodian to the library and antiquities collection of Cardinal Alessandro Albino. In this last capacity he also had access to the collections of classical antiquities at the Vatican. It was on the basis of this research that he began writing his history of art in the late 1750s and early 1760s, a book whose encyclopedic breadth owes much in its conception to Montesquieu's legal history. The principal theme of Winckelmann's book is Greek statuary, but Winckelmann's treatment is broad enough to encompass all of the arts within his aesthetic perspective. The first of our selections is taken from the fourth chapter of section 1, and depicts Winckelmann's highly idealized image of the Greek people: healthy, strong, and politically free, bred and nurtured in a perfect climate, enamored with their intellectual capacities and sense of beauty. It was, once again, a clear and attractive vision that enchanted many of the connoisseurs of his generation.

Johann Joachim Winckelmann, from *Geschichte der Kunst des Alterthums* [History of the art of antiquity] (1764), trans. Harry Francis Mallgrave.

Greece achieved its excellence in art in part because of its climate, in part because of constitution and form of government, and in part because of the way of thinking deriving from it. No less important was the respect for artists in Greece, and the use and application of art.

The influence of climate must endue the seed from which art sprouts, and Greece was select soil for this seed. The talent for philosophy that Epicurius wanted to concede solely to the Greeks could with great justification have been claimed for art. Much that we might imagine as ideal was natural for them. Nature, after having passed gradually through the cold and heat, established herself in Greece; here where the temperature is balanced between winter and summer she chose her middle point. And the closer she approaches it the more cheerful and joyous she becomes, and the more generally do we find in her works those spirited and intelligent conformations with distinguished and roseate features. Where nature is less enveloped in clouds and heavy vapors, she precociously gives the body a mature form. She elevates herself with strong creations, especially female ones, and in Greece she also perfected men to the finest degree. The Greeks were conscious of this and, as Polybius says, of their superiority to other peoples generally; among no other people was beauty so highly esteemed as with them. For this reason nothing was concealed that could enhance it, and the artist confronted beauty daily. Beauty was even, as it were, in the service of fame, and we find the most beautiful people recorded in Greek histories. Some were specifically named – as Demetrius Phalereius was for his eyebrows – for beautiful parts of their conformations. Thus there were contests for beauty organized already in the earliest times, such as that arranged by the Arcadian king Cypselus along the banks of the Alpheus in Elia, at the time of the Heraclidae. At the festival of Philesian Apollo, prizes were bestowed on youths for the most exquisite kiss. It was decided by a judge, as was probably also the case in Megara, at the tomb of Diocles. In Sparta, at the temple of Juno on Lesbos, and among the Parrhasians, there were beauty pageants for women.

With regard to the constitution and government of Greece, freedom was the chief reason for their art's superiority. Freedom always had a seat in Greece, even beside the paternal rule of the royal throne, before the enlightenment of reason allowed the people to taste the sweetness of full freedom. Homer calls Agamemnon a shepherd of the people in order to indicate the latter's love and concern for their welfare. Though tyrants later installed themselves, they succeeded only in their own regions and the nation never recognized a lone ruler. Thus one person never had the only right to greatness among his people, or could immortalize himself to the exclusion of others.

In very early times art was used to commemorate a person through his figure, and this path was open to every Greek. Just as the earliest Greeks far preferred natural advantages to learning, so the first rewards were bestowed on physical prowess, and we find – in the thirty-eighth Olympiad – a statue of a Spartan wrestler Eutelides set up in Elis. Presumably this was not the first occasion. In the lesser games at Megara a stone was erected with the name of the victor. Thus the greatest Greek men sought to distinguish themselves in their youth in contests. Chrysippus and Cleanthes were famed in this way before they were known for their philosophy. Plato himself appears as a wrestler in the Isthmian games at Corinth, and in the Pythian games at Sicyon. Pythagoras was a victor at Elis, and he instructed Eurymenes, who was victorious at the same place. Physical prowess was a way to preserve a name even among the Romans, and Papirius, who avenged the Samnites for the shame of the Romans at Furculas Caudinas, is known less for this victory than for his epithet, "the runner," which Homer also gave to Achilles.

A statue in the likeness of a victor, erected on the holiest spot in Greece, was seen and revered by the whole nation, and it was a powerful incentive – no less to fashion it than to achieve the honor of its erection. And no artist of any nation has since had such ample opportunity to display his work, to say nothing of the statues of deities, priests, and priestesses in the temples. Statues were erected to the victors in the great games (following the number of victories) not only at the spot of the games but also in their own lands, and this honor extended as well to other deserving citizens. Dionysius mentions statues of citizens of Cuma in Italy that Aristodemus, the tyrant of this city, ordered to be removed from the temple in which they stood and thrown into unclean places; this happened during the twenty-second Olympiad. Some victors of the first Olympic games, before the arts had flourished, had statues erected long after their deaths to preserve their feats. In the eighteenth Olympiad this honor was conferred on Oibotas, a victor in the sixth Olympiad. It was rare that someone would have his statue commissioned before he was victorious, yet it was done by one individual so confident of his success. To honor a victor, the city of Aegium in Achaea even built a special hall or covered passage to practice gymnastic exercises.

Through freedom the mental attitude of an entire people rose up like a fine branch from a healthy trunk. For just as the human mind accustomed to reflection tends to lift itself higher in a broad field, along an open path, or at the top of a building than in a lowly chamber or any restricted place, so also must the free Greek spirit have been very different in its attitude from that of a subjugated people.

75 JOHANN JOACHIM WINCKELMANN
from *History of the Art of Antiquity* (1764)

Central to Winckelmann's historical view of ancient art is his theory of absolute beauty. This notion for Winckelmann, despite a strong sensual coloration, is ideal in that he argues that a work of sculpture in antiquity was not based on a single model but on the piecing together of the most perfect features from several models. It is also ideal in the sense that rules for it cannot be ascertained. Like the purest water drawn from a spring, its taste is determined as much from the absence of any foreign parts and in the way in which its recognition arises within the human soul without any intermediary concepts. The harmonic quality of its notes is never slurred; instead, its tone is "simple and long sustained." Architecturally this conception of beauty is similar to the Renaissance concept of harmony or concinnity, but without the specific mathematical basis.

Johann Joachim Winckelmann, from *Geschichte der Kunst des Alterthums* [History of the art of antiquity] (1764), trans. Harry Francis Mallgrave.

Beauty, as the highest aim and focus of art, requires some preliminary and general remarks through which I should wish to please myself and the reader, but this is a difficult thing to accomplish in a few pages. Beauty is one of the great mysteries of nature, whose effect we all see and feel, but for which a universal and clear concept of its essence belongs among the undiscovered truths. Were this concept purely geometrical, human judgments on it would not differ and it would be easy to form a consensus on true beauty. Still less would there be men of either unfortunate sensibility or inimical vanity, such that the former would form a false notion of beauty while the latter would refuse a proper conception of it. [. . .]

The wise who have pondered the causes of universal beauty – explored its presence in created things and sought to reach the source of highest beauty – have located it in the perfect harmony of the being with its purpose, and of the parts with each other and with the whole. But as this is synonymous with perfection, of which the human vessel is incapable, our idea of universal beauty remains indefinite. It is formed in us through individual bits of knowledge, which, when correct, are collected and brought together, giving us the highest idea of human beauty. We elevate this the more we raise ourselves above the material. Moreover, as this perfection was given by the Creator to all creatures in the degree suitable to them, and as every concept resides in a cause that must be sought not in the concept but in something else, the cause of beauty cannot be found outside itself, as it exists in all created things. Thus arises the difficulty – because our conceptual knowledge is comparative and beauty cannot be compared with anything higher – of achieving a universal and clear explanation of beauty.

The highest beauty is in God, and the idea of human beauty approaches perfection the more it can be conceived in conformity and harmony with the highest Existence, which we distinguish from matter in our concept of unity and indivisibility. This concept of beauty is like a spirit extracted from matter by fire; it seeks to create a being conforming to the image of the first rational creature sketched in the mind of God. The forms of such an image are simple and uninterrupted, manifold in their unity; thus they are harmonious, like a sweet and pleasing tone produced from the body whose parts are uniform. All beauty is enhanced by unity and simplicity, just as everything we say and do. For what is great in itself is enhanced when expressed and done with simplicity; it will not be narrowly constrained or lose any of its greatness if our mind can survey and measure it with a glance, surround and grasp it with a single concept. Its full greatness is represented just by this conceivability, and the mind is expanded and at the same time elevated by its comprehension. For everything divided that we consider, or everything that we cannot survey at a glance because of the number of assembled parts, loses its greatness, just as the long road is shortened by many objects presented along it, or by many inns in which stops can be made. The harmony that delights the soul resides not in broken, stitched, or slurred notes, but in simple and long-sustained tones. This is why a large palace appears small when overlaid with decoration, and a house seems large when it is simply and elegantly executed. From this unity proceeds another attribute of high beauty – its indeterminateness, that is, its forms are described only by the points and lines that shape beauty, and thus produce a figure that is unique to neither this or that particular person, nor that expresses any one state of mind or sensation of passion, because these would mix foreign tendencies into beauty and disturb the unity. According to this conception, beauty should be like the purest water drawn from the source of the spring; the less taste it has the healthier it is seen to be, because it is cleansed of all foreign parts. Just as the state of happiness – the removal of pain and the pleasure of contentment – is the easiest condition of nature, and the path to it is the straightest and can be maintained without trouble or cost, so also does the idea of the highest beauty appear in the simplest and easiest things, and requires no philosophical knowledge of man, no investigation of the soul and its expression. Yet as – according to Epicurus – there is in human nature no middle point between pain and pleasure, and as the passions are the winds that propel our ship into the sea of life, by which the poet sets sail and the artist elevates himself, so pure beauty alone cannot be the only object of our consideration. We must also place it within the condition of action and emotion, which in art we understand by the word *expression*. We shall therefore treat first the conformation of beauty, and second its expression.

The conformation of beauty is either *individual*, that is, directed to the individual, or it is a selection and combination of beautiful parts from many individuals, which we call *ideal*. Initially the conformation of beauty had to do with individual beauty, that is, with the imitation of a beautiful subject or with the representation of gods. Still in the period of art's flourishing goddesses were modeled on beautiful women, even on those whose favors were common and venal. The gymnasia and other places where naked youths practiced wrestling and other sports, and to which one went to see a beautiful youth – they were the schools where the artists examined the beauty of the human body. The daily opportunity to view the most beautiful naked youths heated the imagination and the beauty of forms became particular and ingrained as mental images. In Sparta even young girls exercised undressed, or nearly so. Also known to Greek artists, as they began to consider the beauty of the two sexes, was a mixed kind of manly youth. It was produced by the removal of the seminal vessels, a licentious practice that Asiatic peoples used on handsome boys in order to inhibit the rapid course of fleeting youth. Among the Ionian Greeks in Asia Minor, the creation of these equivocal beauties was consecrated as a religious practice in the eunuch priests of Cybele.

76 JOHANN JOACHIM WINCKELMANN
from *History of the Art of Antiquity* (1764)

P erhaps the most important contribution that Winckelmann makes to art history is his framework of stylistic evolution. He delineates four stylistic phases for classical art: the Ancient Style, the Grand Style, the Beautiful style, and the Style of the Imitators. Such an organic concept of a style had already been suggested by Vasari, but Winckelmann brings to it a very specific aesthetic and stylistic process of development. Art passes from its initial crude situation to naturalistic imitation, and then elevates itself into the higher plane of ideal beauty. The Grand Style for Winckelmann is still characterized by a certain hardness of features, but this is not a quality to be disdained, as the art of Phidias demonstrates. The Beautiful Style, which for Winckelmann is defined from the period

Johann Joachim Winckelmann, from *Geschichte der Kunst des Alterthums* [History of the art of antiquity] (1764), trans. Harry Francis Mallgrave of Praxiteles (mid-fourth century BC) to that of Lysippus and Apelles (mid-third century BC) achieves a more graceful bearing, but at the same time it borders on excessive refinement and over-elaboration. The fourth phase of classical art, the Art of the Imitators, is by definition a period of decline, and this period includes the entire artistic production of the Romans – a harsh condemnation of Latin culture.

Greek art had, as Scaliger attributed to their poetry, four main periods, and we can even distinguish five. For just as every action or event has five parts or stages – the beginning, progress, rest, decline, and the end, which is the reason for the five scenes or acts in theatrical pieces – so it is with the chronological succession of Greek art. But as the end lies outside of the bounds of art, there are actually only four periods to consider here. The more ancient style lasted until the time of Phidias. Art achieved its greatness through him and the artists of his time, and we can call this next period the grand or high style. Art acquired more grace and favor from the period of Praxiteles to that of Lysippus and Apelles, and this style can be called the beautiful style. Sometime after these artists and their schools, art began to sink into imitation. We can thus define a third style of imitators, which lasted until art gradually listed to its fall. [. . .]

Finally, at the time of full enlightenment and freedom in Greece, art became freer and more elevated. The more ancient style was built on a system consisting of rules that, though taken from nature, later departed from it and became idealistic. The artist worked more from the prescription of these rules than from the nature that was imitated; art had formed its own nature. Those seeking improvement raised themselves above this accepted system and approached the truth of nature. They learned to transform the hard, projecting, and abrupt parts of the figures into flowing contours, to make the violent positions and actions more well-mannered and intelligent, and to display less learning and more beauty, elevation, and grandeur. Through this improvement in art Phidias, Polycletus, Scopas, Alcamenes, and Myron became famous. The style itself can be called the grand style, because – aside from beauty – the intention of the artist seems to have been to achieve grandeur. Here we should distinguish hardness from sharpness in rendering, so that someone will not mistake the sharply drawn indication of the eyebrows that one always sees in the most beautiful forms, for instance, with the unnatural hardness that remained from the more ancient style. For sharpness has its basis in ideas of beauty, as was already noted. [. . .]

After the loss of the works of these great reformers of art, it is impossible to define clearly the insights and characteristics of this high style. Of the style of their successors, which I shall call the *beautiful style*, we can speak with more assurance. For some of the most beautiful figures in antiquity were undoubtedly made in the period in which this style blossomed; and many others of which this cannot be said were at least imitations of them. The beautiful style commences with Praxiteles, and attained its highest splendor with Lysippus and Apelles, the proofs of which will be demonstrated below. It is therefore the style of the period not long before the time of Alexander the Great and his successors.

The chief characteristic distinguishing this style from the high style is *grace*; in this regard the artists just mentioned have the same relation to their predecessors as Guido, among the moderns, has to Raphael. This will become clearer in considering the rendering of this style, and the grace that forms a special part of it. [. . .]

Because the proportions and forms of beauty had been so intensively studied by artists in antiquity, and because the contours of the figures had been so defined that they could not be shifted outwardly or inwardly without error, the idea of beauty could not be driven higher. As art could not go forward, and as in all natural effects a resting point is inconceivable, it had to go backward. The representation of deities and heroes had been fashioned in every possible way and pose, and it was difficult to invent new ones. Thus the path lay open to imitation, which cramps the spirit. And if it is not possible to surpass a Praxiteles or an Apelles, it is difficult to equal them, thus in all times the imitator has remained inferior to the imitated. Art thus followed philosophy, in that *eclectics* or compilers arose among them who, lacking a personal force, sought to combine the individual beauty of many into one. Yet just as eclectics are regarded only as copyists of philosophies of particular schools and have produced little or nothing original, so art could not expect something whole, unique, or harmonious when it took such a path. And just as in compiling excerpts from the great writings of the ancients something gets lost, so through the work of compilers in art the great original works came to be neglected. Imitation advances the lack of personal knowledge, whereby rendering becomes timid. What the artist lacked in knowledge, he tried to obtain by diligence, which displayed itself more and more in details that in flourishing periods of art were omitted or regarded as detrimental to the grand style. Here it is true what Quintilian says – many artists would have made the decorative details of the Jupiter better than Phidias did. By trying to avoid any supposed hardness and to make everything soft and delicate, the parts that were made imposing by previous artists became rounder but dull, charming but insignificant. Corruption has always crept into writing in the very same way; and in renouncing the manly, music has declined like art into the effeminate. The good is often lost in the artificial, because one always wants to make it better.

77 GIOVANNI BATTISTA PIRANESI
from "Observations on the Letter of Monsieur Mariette" (1765)

The efforts of the Scot Ramsey, the Frenchman Le Roy, the Englishmen Stuart and Revett, and the German Winckelmann – all living in Rome – to portray Latin classicism as vastly inferior to Greek classicism quite naturally invited a response. It came in the form of a sustained and spirited defense by Giovanni Battista Piranesi, one of Italy's greatest artists of the eighteenth century. Born in Venice, Piranesi first studied architecture in that city, where he became familiar with the teachings of Carlo Lodoli. In 1740 he moved to Rome and turned his attention to engraving. During this decade and the next he also came into contact with several students at the French Academy in Rome, as well as with other visitors to the city, such as William Chambers, Robert Adam, and Allan Ramsay. He thus witnessed the growing fascination with Greece firsthand. His first response in 1756 took the form of four volumes of engravings, *Le antichità romane* (Roman antiquity), which boasted of the colossal feats of Roman architects and engineers. In 1761 he produced a visual and polemical work, *Della magnificenza ed architettura de'*

Giovanni Battista Piranesi (1720–80), from "*Osservazioni di Gio. Battista Piranesi sopra la Lettre de Monsieur Mariette aux Auteurs de la Gazette Littéraire de l'Europe*" (1765), trans. Caroline Beamish and David Britt, in *Giovanni Battista Piranesi: Observations on the Letter of Monsieur Mariette*. Los Angeles: Getty Publications Program, 2002, pp. 87–9, 95–6. © 2002 by Getty Publications. Reprinted with permission of Getty Publications.

Romane (On the magnificence and architecture of the Romans), which responded more directly to the arguments of Ramsay and Le Roy. Drawing from Vico's earlier defense of the autonomy of Roman civilization, Piranesi now makes the point that the Romans actually inherited their artistic traditions from the Etruscans, and the arts were well advanced prior to their first contacts with the Greeks. And next to the greatness and physical dimension of Roman works, the Greeks were only able to affect an "empty elegance." In 1764 this book was reviewed by the French collector and connoisseur Pierre-Jean Mariette in a French newspaper. In an impolite, even hectoring tone, Mariette sets out to destroy all of Piranesi's statements about Roman history. Mariette not only (incorrectly) claims that the Etruscans (here called Tuscans) were in fact Greek colonists, but he also smugly insists that whatever good architecture the Romans eventually produced had been carried out by Greek slaves. The Greeks, for Mariette, practiced the architecture of "beautiful and noble simplicity" – to use a phrase current at this time – while the Romans practiced a debased architecture of decorative excess.

Piranesi was moved to respond the next year with a three-part polemical and visual refutation, of which the first was a line-by-line response to the points made in Mariette's review. The following two excerpts convey the spirited nature of the debate. In one vertical column Piranesi publishes Mariette's review; beside it he pens his response as "observations" (speaking of himself in the third person).

Observations

A

To Signor Mariette this work is unknown, no *perhaps* about it.

B

To my mind, there is a difference between saying *As far as architecture is concerned, the Romans owe nothing to the Greeks* and saying, as one reads in Piranesi's preface to the published edition of his work, *In the matter of architecture, the Romans owed little or nothing to the Greeks*. Italians understand that the phrase *poco o nulla* [(little or nothing)] is intended to belittle the nature of the debt incurred by the Romans, not to deny that there was any such debt; anyone who has read Piranesi's book knows whether this is true. On *page 93* he demonstrates that Greek architecture conferred no advantage, public or private, on Rome, which had long taken its lead from Etruscan architecture; and that

Monsieur Mariette's Letter

Dear Messieurs, Monsieur Piranesi, the author of a number of works on Roman antiquities that have been reviewed in your pages, has recently published another, which may perhaps be unknown to us,[A] in which he sets out to write a defense of the Romans and to show – contrary to your opinion, which I share – that in the arts, and in architecture in particular, not only does that nation owe nothing to the Greeks[B] but also it is greatly superior to them by virtue of the solidity, the size, and the magnificence of the buildings that formerly adorned its capital city. He contrasts these buildings with those properly pertaining to the Greeks, some vestiges of which are still to be seen in Athens and elsewhere in Greece.[C] He finds none that can bear comparison, in either solidity or size, with the Cloaca Maxima [(sewer system)] of Rome, the foundations of the ancient Capitolium, and the emissarium [(drainage outlet)] of Lago Albano – not to mention sundry other ancient structures built of huge ashlars from the earliest days of the

Greek architecture had been preferred to Etruscan not on merit but out of caprice. There is the *little or nothing* that came to Rome from Greece.

C

In his book, Piranesi makes no comparison with *the buildings properly pertaining to the Greeks, some vestiges of which are still to be seen in Athens and in other parts of Greece.* He does make a comparison with those vestiges, because he has seen them, not *the buildings* of which they formed part.

D

And, in comparing those vestiges with those of ancient Rome, he draws no distinction whatever between what was constructed in that city in *the earliest days of the republic* and what was done later.

E

Which are the plates in Piranesi's work in which he has collected *a considerable number of capitals, bases, column shafts, entablatures, . . . , all varying in shape as well as in the ornaments with which they are laden?* Plates VI, VII, VIII, IX, X, XI, XII, XIII, XIV, XV, XVI, XVII, XVIII, XIX, and XX, I imagine. Now, what does he have to say about all this? *That, these being the things brought into Latium by the Greeks, this would seem to indicate the methods of construction used by the Tuscans* (page 129), *and consequently by the Romans, before they knew the Greeks.* How is it, then, that *these diverse fragments, all varying in shape as well as in the ornaments with which they are laden* are

republic onward[D] that still serve the purpose for which they were first built. The same Monsieur Piranesi has collected a considerable number of capitals, bases, column shafts, entablatures, and so forth. These diverse fragments, which vary in shape as well as in the ornament with which they are laden, furnish him – or so he claims – with convincing proof of the fecundity of the genius of the Romans.[E] That genius, in the opinion of this author, also manifests itself in the size and the scale of the spacious edifices that, though now in ruins, cover vast tracts of land in Rome today. His argument is as follows.

claimed by Piranesi as *convincing proof of the fecundity of the genius of the Romans?* Listen to what he has to say about these architectural members elsewhere in the same work: *Many of these things are likewise to be seen in Rome, either because they were transported there from Greece, or because they were the work of Greek architects; some of these have been collected by me in plates VI, VII, VIII, IX, X, and so on.* So Piranesi, after having made this concession to the Greeks, avails himself of it as convincing proof of the fecundity *of the genius of the Romans?* But on what page, on what line? May Signor Mariette excuse me for saying that by writing such a review of Piranesi's book, he has insulted the public even more than he has offended the author.

How does Piranesi describe the building methods handed on by the Etruscans to the Romans? He says that the Etruscans thought wisely and used little adornment on their architecture. And what does he say of the Greeks? That by dividing their architectural members too much by carving, they achieved too much vain prettiness and too little gravity, *page 101.* That the ornaments in their architecture are for the most part monstrous and run counter to the truth, *ibid.* All which would entitle us to say that the reviewer has not read one word of Piranesi's book. But let us continue.

F

What chicanery! Where exactly, in his book, does Piranesi state that *the more recent buildings of the Romans, laden with ornaments, can be recognized by architectural members of bizarre shape that in no way resemble the same members as invented by the Greeks?* How could he assert such a thing, after having attributed not to the taste of the Romans but to

The earliest buildings of the Romans were built before any communication took place between their nation and that of the Greeks. The more recent buildings are laden with ornaments and can be recognized by architectural members of bizarre shape that in no way resemble the same members as invented by the Greeks.[F] Therefore the Romans borrowed nothing and learned nothing from the Greeks; they owe them neither the science of that of the Greeks these same *architectural members of bizarre shape*, and after having said, as I mentioned above, that these things *are to be seen in Rome, either because they were transported there from Greece, or because they were the work of Greek architects?* It is quite true that Piranesi draws a comparison between the ruins of ancient Greece and the monuments (including the most recent) of ancient Rome, including *the buildings laden with ornament, a considerable number of capitals, bases, column shafts, entablatures, . . . , all varying in their shapes as well as in the ornamentation upon them*; but to what purpose? Here it is: *If anyone*, he says on *page 195, travels to Greece for the purpose of study, what will Greece provide for his instruction? It will not teach him about capitals, because, aside from those of the Erechthion, there are none that bear comparison with Roman capitals; it will not teach him about columns, because there are so many more in Rome of every sort and size; it will not teach him about statues or bas-reliefs – one finds these in Rome in the greatest abundance and elegance, in comparison to those of the Greeks; finally, it will not teach him about work of any other kind, Italy being so chock-full that – as can well be said – to find Greece we should look no further than Italy. Let no one object, at this point, that many of these monuments were taken from the Greeks, or else made by the Romans in the Greek manner; we are trying not to establish the makers of the works in question, whether Greek or Roman, but to determine which is the most appropriate place to learn these arts, Rome or Greece. We have already seen what Rome has to offer to foreign visitors; but what will Greece have to teach those who make their way there, exhausted by the sea crossing, by travel, and by architectural campaigning, if neither the things adduced by us nor ancient or modern architecture can teach them?* Now, such being his

construction and good building practice nor taste in ornamentation.

* * *

P

In his book. Piranesi has asserted (and this I repeat for the last time that the Romans had already been instructed in the arts of peace by the Tuscans. That they (that is, they, the citizens) cultivated those arts after building Rome. That they (the citizens) were excellent in mathematics before they ever came into contact with the Greek arts. That they (they, the citizens) had practiced sculpture and painting before they ever became acquainted with the Greeks. That in matters of construction, once acquainted with the Greeks, they did not adopt the practices of the latter but persevered with their own: that in architecture they (they, the citizens) built things that it had never crossed the minds of the Greeks could be built by a living soul. That very many Romans (that is, of the citizens) were from time to time able architects. That they corrected many of the innumerable defects that they found in the architecture of the Greeks. That they achieved a magnificence equal to that of the Egyptians and the Greeks, and thereafter greater than that of any other nation. What more could the Romans have done to honor the fine arts? What more could they have done, to relieve Signor Mariette of the need to say *that they never had either the leisure or the inclination to distinguish between these arts and the purely mechanical trades?* Did not their emperors, and many illustrious citizens before them, condescend to cultivate the arts and to become practitioners? Nero was a talented painter and sculptor; Hadrian, besides having been an architect, was a painter, as were Severus Alexander, Valentinian, and others, and in Rome they left behind public evidence of their condescension. What more could they have done *to distinguish between these arts and the purely mechanical trades?* Was it their duty *to speak*

They never had either the leisure or the inclination to distinguish between these arts and the purely mechanical trades;[P] they left the cultivation of the arts to mercenary Greeks who, attracted by the promise of gain, did not hesitate to expatriate themselves and to quit a country where, after the Roman conquest, there were undoubtedly fewer opportunities to establish and maintain a reputation. Before long, the arts came to be practiced in Rome exclusively by slaves. People rich enough to keep a large number of slaves purchased them with both profit and utility in mind; they therefore sought out, by preference, slaves with artistic talent.

in praise of those who had cultivated those arts, as [Claude] Perrault says in the preface to his Vitruvius, *giving them a place among the illustrious*. If anyone ventures to deny that they did so, I appeal to the authority of Cossutius, Varro, Pliny, Vitruvius himself, and many other Roman authors. At the same time, the greater part of the practitioners of the fine arts in Rome were slaves. Without wasting time in the attempt to disabuse Signor Mariette of this hasty supposition, I have this to say: Were they slaves because the Romans had decreed that the fine arts were to be practiced only by slaves? Or were they slaves because the slaves were poor and this was a way in which they sought to become rich? Now, in our own time – a time when the fine arts are separated from the purely mechanical trades – who are most of their practitioners? The poor who seek to become rich, or grandees who condescend to practice the arts? If the laws of slavery had not been abolished, even now that these arts are flourishing once more, and have been separated from the purely mechanical trades, how many practitioners would be counted among the slaves! So many that a person who shared Signor Mariette's opinions would say that *the arts are practiced only by slaves*.

Furthermore, if in a country full of persons of taste – as was Greece – *after the Roman conquest, there were undoubtedly fewer opportunities to establish and maintain a reputation,* how could such opportunities have arisen in a country or in a city of men *lacking in taste?* And these men, ignorant and *lacking in taste,* how were they able to choose *slaves with artistic talent?* Perhaps they relied on the praises *that they heard from connoisseurs?* And were those *connoisseurs* Greek or Roman? They were Greek; Signor Mariette has already given us to understand as much. So the Romans purchased Greek slaves, and had them practice the fine arts, not because they knew the value of such slaves or of the works that they created but because those works were appreciated by the Greeks? So they attributed none of the genius to themselves, but to the Greeks? So the Romans *stripped the Greek buildings of their principal ornaments, transported to Rome countless masterpieces of art*, obliged all Greeks *with artistic talent to expatriate themselves*, made slaves of them all, and reduced Greece to a desert, not in order to please themselves but to please the Greeks? If this was the case, why does Signor Mariette say that the Romans *shamelessly stripped the Greek buildings of their principal ornaments?* This was no cause for shame; it was a boon.

78 GIOVANNI BATTISTA PIRANESI
from *Opinions on Architecture* (1765)

The second part of Piranesi's published response of 1765 takes the form of a Socratic dialogue between the characters Protopiro (who represents the classical "rigorists" seeking to simplify and limit ornamentation) and Didascalo (the mouthpiece for Piranesi). It is a dialogue of the greatest importance to architectural theory because it opens up an entirely new line of theoretical development and reflects the crisis of academic theory in the 1760s — a crisis that would continue until the end of the century. Piranesi wrote it when he himself was making his way back into architectural practice, and he now shifts from his earlier archaeological argument into an architectural one. His villain here is actually Laugier and his reform-minded rationalism. In the first part of the dialogue Protopiro has his way, and in the spirit of Laugier he points out the many abuses of contemporary practice with its over-reliance on ornamentation. Didascalo then usurps Protopiro's reformative purism and sarcastically eliminates nearly everything else from architectural usage, leading him to conclude that if Protopiro and Laugier had their way, everyone would once again be living in primitive huts. In short, Didascalo's argument is a defense of the various traditions of architecture, including its baroque tradition, against the simplicity of classicism, and it rallies around the architect's freedom to invent and re-use traditional forms — in short, eclecticism.

> *Protopiro.* I have given you my opinion.
> *Didascalo.* So it is Greece and Vitruvius? Very well: tell me, then, what do columns represent? Vitruvius says they are the forked uprights of huts; others describe them as tree

Giovanni Battista Piranesi, from *Parere su l'Architettura* [Opinions on architecture] (1765), trans. Caroline Beamish and David Britt, in *Giovanni Battista Piranesi: Observations on the Letter of Monsieur Mariette*. Los Angeles: Getty Publications Program, 2002, pp. 105–6, 107–8. © 2002 by Getty Publications. Reprinted with permission of Getty Publications.

trunks placed to support the roof. And the flutes on the columns: what do they signify? Vitruvius thinks they are the pleats in a matron's gown. So the columns stand neither for forked uprights nor for tree trunks but for women placed to support a roof. Now what do you think about flutes? It seems to me that columns ought to be smooth. Therefore, take note: *smooth columns*. The forked uprights and tree trunks should be planted in the earth, to keep them stable and straight. Indeed that is how the Dorians thought of their columns. Therefore they should have no bases. Take note: *no bases*. The tree trunks, if they were used to support the roof, would be smooth and flat on top; the forked props can look like anything you like, except capitals. If that is not definite enough, remember that the capitals must represent solid things, not heads of men, maidens, or matrons, or baskets with foliage around them, or baskets topped with a matron's wig. So take note: *no capitals*. Never fear; there are other rigorists who also call for *smooth columns, no bases, and no capitals*.

As for architraves, you want them to look either like tree trunks placed horizontally across the forked props or like beams laid out to span the tree trunks. So what is the point of the fasciae or of the band that projects from the surface? To catch the water and go rotten? Take note: *architraves with no fasciae and no band*.

What do the triglyphs stand for? Vitruvius says that they represent the ends of the joists of ceilings or soffits. When they are placed at the corners of the building, however, not only do they belie this description but they can never be placed at regular intervals, because they have to be centered over the columns. If they are moved away from the corners, they can then be placed symmetrically only if the building is narrowed or widened with respect to the triglyphs. It is madness that a few small cuts on stone or mortar should dictate the proportions of a building, or that all or some of the due requirements of the building should be sacrificed to them. Thus, the ancient architects cited by Vitruvius held that temples ought not to be built in the Doric manner; better still, the Romans used the Doric without the added clutter. So take note: *friezes without triglyphs*. Now it is your turn, Signor Protopiro, to purge architecture of all the other ornaments that you disparaged just now.

Protopiro. What? Have you finished?

Didascalo. Finished? I have not even started. Let us go inside a temple, a palace, wherever you choose. Around the walls we shall observe architraves, friezes, and cornices adorned with those features that you just described as standing for the roof of a building – triglyphs, modillions, and dentils. And when those features are absent, and the friezes and cornices are smooth, even then the architraves and friezes will seem to support a roof and the cornices seem to be the eaves. These eaves, however, will drip rain inside the temple, the palace, or basilica. So the temple, the palace, or the basilica will be outside, and the outside inside, will they not? To rectify such anomalies, such travesties of architecture, take note: *internal walls of buildings with no architraves, friezes, and cornices*.

And then, on these cornices, which stand for eaves, vaults are erected. This is an even worse impropriety than those *episkēnia* on the roofs that we discussed a little while ago and that Vitruvius condemns.

Therefore take note: *buildings with no vaults*.

Let us observe the walls of a building from inside and outside. These walls terminate in architraves and all that goes with them above; below these architraves, most often we find engaged columns or pilasters. I ask you, what holds up the roof of the building? If the wall, then it needs no architraves; if the columns or pilasters, what is the wall there for? Choose,

Signor Protopiro, Which will you demolish? The walls or the pilasters? No answer? Then I will demolish the whole lot. Take note: *buildings with no walls, no columns, no pilasters, no friezes, no cornices, no vaults, no roofs*. A clean sweep. [...]

Didascalo. You would like me to agree with you that the architectural manners laid down by Vitruvius are rational? That they imitate truth?

Protopiro. Rational – highly rational – by comparison with the unbridled license that prevails in construction today.

Didascalo. Aha! Rational by comparison with current practice? And so, if we leave current practice out of it, your rationality disappears at once. The critics, who never let up, will still want the last word; deprive them of the wide scope for indignation that present-day practice affords them, and they will soon turn against the little that you and your friends are prepared to accept. Then, go ahead and say that extremes are dangerous, that too much rigor is really abuse; all the same, the manners in which you build will be judged just as they were or might have been judged when first invented. You call me excessively severe, on the grounds that I am going too far by taking you back to huts in which people have no desire to live; but you would yourselves be condemned for monotonous buildings that people would detest just as much.

Protopiro. Monotonous?

Didascalo. Yes, monotonous, architecturally always exactly the same. As architects, you think yourselves extraordinary, but you would soon become utterly ordinary. When your simple manners of building were first established, why did the successors of those who established them soon begin to find different ways of decorating their buildings? Was it for want of the capacity to equal their predecessors? Surely not, since they had been trained as their pupils; and, all around them, they could see an architecture that was simple enough to be easy to reproduce.

Protopiro. I am not saying that we should do nothing but follow those early manners of building. I don't blame the successors of those first architects for wanting to innovate. But I do blame them for the quality of their innovations, and I blame all those architects who have vied with each other ever since in devising more and more of them.

Didascalo. I suppose you mean architects like [Gian Lorenzo] Bernini and [Francesco] Borromini, and all those others who have failed to bear in mind that ornament must derive from the components of architecture. But, in criticizing them, whom do you think you criticize? You criticize the greatest architect who ever was or ever will be. You criticize the experience of all those many practitioners who from the moment when this kind of architecture was first invented until it was buried beneath the ruins always worked in this way; and the experience of those many who ever since this kind of architecture was first revived have been and are unable to work in any other way. You criticize the very spirit that invented the architecture that you praise; the spirit that, seeing the world still unsatisfied, has found itself obliged to seek variety by the very same ways and means that you dislike. Now if, over the centuries, among all those countless practitioners, the experience of the totality of architecture to date has failed to produce what you are looking for, then how can we avoid concluding that, if everything you dislike were removed from architecture, we would be left with buildings of unendurable monotony? What word other than foolish can we apply to those who flatter themselves that they are destined to find in this art something that has never been found in all these centuries? All the more foolish, in that they cannot even salve their own self-esteem by finding what they are looking for.

79 GIOVANNI BATTISTA PIRANESI
from "An Apologetical Essay in Defence of the Egyptian and Tuscan Architecture" (1769)

Piranesi's final say in the matter – one of the more audacious architectural statements of the eighteenth century – was presented in a trilingual publication published in 1769, whose English title is *Divers Manners of Ornamenting Chimneys and All Other Parts of Houses*. The book is for the most part a series of drawings displaying decorative designs for mantelpieces; attached to it, however, is Piranesi's "Apologetical Essay in Defence of the Egyptian and Tuscan Architecture." The argument is now exceedingly simple: the architect should be able to borrow from any or every style (including the Greek, Egyptian, Roman, and Etruscan), mix these borrowings, as well as invent new forms. His only limitation should be his acquired taste.

What I pretend by the present designs is to shew what use an able architect may make of the ancient monuments by properly adapting them to our own manners and customs. I propose shewing the use that may be made of medals, cameos, intaglios, statues, bassorelieves, paintings, and such like remains of antiquity, not only by the critics and learned in their studies, but likewise by the artists in their works, uniting in an artful and masterly manner all that is admired and esteemed in them: whoever has the least introduction into the study of antiquity must plainly see how large a field I have by this laid open for the industry of our artists to work upon: and such as have not that advantage will easily comprehend it on casting an eye over the following plates. I flatter my self that the great and serious study, I have made upon all the happy remains of ancient monuments, has enabled me to execute this useful, and if I may be allowed to say it, even necessary project. The study of Architecture, having been carried by our ancestors to the highest pitch of perfection, Seems now on the decline, and returning again to barbarism. What irregularities in columns, in architraves, in pediments, in cupolas; and above all what extravagance in ornaments! one would think that ornaments are used in works of architecture, not to embellish them, but to render them ugly. I know indeed that in this the caprice of those, for whom the buildings are made, has often more part then the architect who makes the design.

A military man will have arms and instruments of war every where, wether they be proper or not. A sea-faring man will have ships, Tritons, Dolphins, and shells. An antiquarian will have nothing but ruins of ancient Temples, broken Columns, Statues of Gods, and Emperours. Let them have their will, for no curb ought to be put on such caprices of men, but then let them be executed according the rules of art. Let Tritons and fish be placed on chimneys, if it be so required, but let them not so cover the frame as entirely to hide it, or take away its character. Let the architect be as extravagant as he pleases, so he destroy not architecture, but give to every member its proper character. Let the artist be free to drape a

Giovanni Battista Piranesi, from "An Apologetical Essay in Defence of the Egyptian and Tuscan Architecture" (1769) in *Divers Manners of Ornamenting Chimneys*. Rome: Generoso Salomoni, 1769, pp. 2–3, 32–3.

statue, or figure in painting as he likes best, let him adjust the folds and garments with the greatest variety he is able; but let it be always so that it may appear an human body and not a block covered with drapery. Let all the variety of graces be given to architecture that can be desired, but let them be such as agree with it. This the ancients had in view: we ought to follow their manner, and observe the kinds of ornaments used by them, the manner in which they disposed them to make them harmonise with the whole, and the modifications by which the Egyptian and Tuscan manners were adapted to another species of architecture. But this knowledge is not to be acquired but by a long frequenting of the ruins and remains of ancient buildings. And I am sorry that the want of this study has deprived even the greatest men of a certain abundance of Ideas; whence many of their works are wanting in that uniformity of character and stile, which so much pleases. Some who excelled in the great parts of architecture, are wanting In the small ones; others have boldly raised themselves, and shewed the greatness of this genius in the daring flights they have taken in imitation of the ancients, but they have not always been able to sustain themselves, but have lost sight of the antique, to give themselves up to the bad taste of the times in which they lived. Who for instance is more noble than Palladio, when the question is concerning works of magnificence? yet this great man is not equally happy in the internal ornaments of houses, which either shew a poverty of ideas, or a want of knowledge, hence there is a sameness in the doors, windows, and chimneys; or there is no correspondance and the thread is broken, as may be seen in the pannels of the ceilings, which do not correspond with the external design, and are far from the good taste of the ancients.

★ ★ ★

I might add much more in praise of the ancient Tuscans, and of our Italy, which was not so much indebted to the Greeks, as some may perhaps imagine: but it is now time to put an end to this argument. I flatter my self that, by what I have hitherto said, I have at the same time vindicated the Egyptian, and Tuscan architecture from those undeserved aspersions which they lye under, and justified my self for having in these designs united the Grecian with the Egyptian and Tuscan manners. The law which some people would impose upon us of doing nothing but what is Grecian, is indeed very unjust. [. . .] The human understanding is not so short and limited, as to be unable to add new graces, and embellishments to the works of architecture, if to an attentive and profound study of nature one would likewise join that of the ancient monuments. Whoever thinks that these are exhausted, and that nothing more is to be discovered in them is very much mistaken. No, this vein is not yet exhausted; new pieces are daily dug out of the ruins, and new things présent themselves to us, capable of fertilizing, and improving the ideas of an artist, who thinks, and reflects. Rome is certainly the most fruitful magazine of this kind, and notwithstanding that several Nations strive which shall most enrich themselves with our spoils, the arts will here have helps, which they will scarcely find elsewhere. The Roman school, founded upon these monuments, will continue to be the mother of good taste, and perfect design, which are the distinctive marks of her superiority over all others, and which bring such a number of hopeful youths from different nations into her bosom, there to learn the perfection of design.

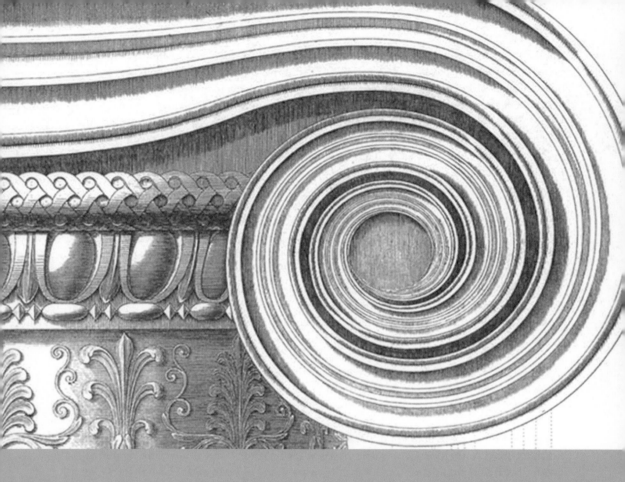

C.   CHARACTER AND EXPRESSION

Introduction

Still another dimension of the crisis of theory in the second half of the eighteenth century can be found in discussions relating to the well-established academic notions of expression or character. For painting the rules in this regard go back to a lecture given to the Academy of Painting and Sculpture of 1668 by Charles Le Brun, entitled "The Expression of the Passions." Le Brun's principal concern was with individual expressions in historical paintings, and he drew upon both classical and modern sources to devise rules for finding the proper expression. For the arts the rhetorical concept of decorum, for instance, translated into a theory of literary styles or musical modes, such as Phrygian, Dorian, Aeolian, and Lydian. The architectural parallels to these styles, of course, were the Doric, Ionic, and Corinthian orders. Such an approach was first strengthened in the mid-eighteenth century at the hands of Germain Boffrand and Jacques-François Blondel, but with the push of Soufflot and others for lighter proportions and less detailing on the one hand, and with the heavier proportions of Greek architecture on the other hand, these rules and their meanings were suddenly destabilized. Architects now began to see the idea of character in more abstract terms, as well as the possibility for expressions beyond the earlier range of characters. Hence we have a direction of theory in the last several decades of the eighteenth century that proffered different approaches to the idea of character and alternative modes of expression. For instance, in the theory of A. C. Quatremère de Quincy, character is now viewed as a multifaceted concept with quasi-organic and anthropological dimensions, while with the formal explorations of Claude-Nicolas Ledoux the idea of character transposes itself into a formal symbolism that came to be known as *architecture parlante* or "speaking architecture."

80 GERMAIN BOFFRAND
from *Book of Architecture* (1745)

The decade of the 1750s began a period of architectural experimentation in which many of the academic rules, canons, and forms established over the preceding century were openly reconsidered. For the idea of character, the starting point in terms of classical theory was the treatise of Germain Boffrand, perhaps the most important French architect of the first half of the eighteenth century. Born in the era of Perrault and Blondel, he was a student of Jules Hardouin Mansart in the 1690s, where he learned the highly ornate, rococo style first used at Versailles. Likewise, his chateaux and Parisian residences of the first half of the eighteenth century were renowned for their elaborate interiors. In the 1740s, as Boffrand was withdrawing from practice, he began assembling a monograph of his designs, which he prefaced with an essay entitled "Principles Derived from Horace's *Art of Poetry*." It was based on a lecture he had presented to Royal Academy in 1734, and in it he – like Le Brun before him – attempted to draft architectural rules of character from the body of classical theory. His method was to take passages from Horace's work (italicized in the text) and replace the literary terms with architectural terms. He then adds a short paragraph of explanation. What is notable in his endeavor is his attempt to expand the idea of character beyond its three major modalities related to the three primary orders. Boffrand now considers the idea of character in more subtle ways, such as in the curve of a molding or other nuances of detailing. He thus brings this old idea of character or expression to the fore, where it will find new currency over the next several decades.

So close is the affinity between science and art that the principles of the one are the principles of the other. All the divisions of mathematics are closely allied; geometry is the foundation of all the sciences, and the study of one subject adds new knowledge to the other. Painting, sculpture and poetry are sisters: the first two address the eye, the third the ear. Music paints the various incidents of Nature; it expresses and arouses the tenderest and the most violent passions. Architecture, although its object may seem to be no more than the use of material, falls into a number of genres, in which its component parts are so to speak

Germain Boffrand (1667–1754), from *Livre d'architecture* (1745), trans. David Britt in *Book of Architecture Containing the General Principles of the Art*, ed. and introduced by Caroline van Eck. Aldershot: Ashgate Publishing, 2003, pp. 21–2, 28–9, 35, 36, 39. © 2003 by Ashgate Publishing Ltd. Reprinted with permission of Ashgate Publishing Ltd.

brought to life by the different characters that it conveys to us. Through its composition a building expresses, as if in the theatre, that the scene is pastoral or tragic; that this is a temple or a palace, a public building destined for a particular purpose or a private house. By their planning, their structure and their decoration, all such buildings must proclaim their purpose to the beholder. If they fail to do so, they offend against expression and are not what they ought to be. [. . .]

Elegance and grace in a building consist in putting everything in its place, and leaving out all that ought not to be there.

Inside a building, do not use ornaments that ought only to be on the outside. Arrange every room as best suits the master of the house, with the dimensions and decoration becoming to its use; take care to keep your most precious ornaments in reserve, and find the right places for them as you progress.

Much care is called for in using new words.

The profiles of mouldings, and the other members that compose a building, are in architecture what words are in a discourse. All edifices are made up of only three sorts of line: straight, concave and convex. These three also compose all the mouldings that enter into profiles. Be wary of introducing new mouldings, and use them only where appropriate. [. . .]

It is not enough for a building to be handsome; it must be pleasing, and the beholder must feel the character that it is meant to convey; so that it must appear cheerful where it is intended to communicate joy, and serious and melancholy where it is meant to instil respect or sadness.

If you are setting out to build a music room, or a salon in which to receive company, it must be cheerful in its planning, in its lighting, and in its manner of decoration. If you want a mausoleum, the building must be suited to its use, and the architecture and decoration must be serious and sad; for Nature makes us susceptible to all these impressions, and a unified impulse never fails to touch our feelings. [. . .]

The Muses taught the Greeks the art of speaking well.

It was they who first erected beautiful buildings; their works are our models; their proportions have been applauded and adopted by most nations, and have been handed down to us. From those proportions we cannot depart without relapsing into barbarism – as several nations have done, either because they had no knowledge of them or because, with the presumption that commonly attends on ignorance and folly, they wanted to be free of them.

Precisely observed, those principles leave vast scope for genius in the composition of buildings. Genius may exercise itself in any number of ways, but by those principles it must be sustained; and in the absence of genius those same principles decline into aridity and inanition.

81 ÉTIENNE BONNOT DE CONDILLAC
from *Essay on the Origin of Human Knowledge* (1746)

Boffrand's theory of character permitted architectural forms to be considered primarily for their expressive possibilities, rather than for some adherence to a stylistic canon. Another influence that would shortly come into play in this regard was the empiricism of John Locke, which bypassed the classical issue of proportions by giving primacy to the senses (see chapters 92 and 101 below). The translator of Lockean theory in France was Étienne Bonnot de Condillac, a friend of both Diderot and Rousseau, who also composed several articles for the Encyclopedia. Condillac's *Essay on the Origins of Human Knowledge* is the first great philosophical text of the French Enlightenment and it shares many of the ideas of the encyclopedists. A few years earlier Voltaire had pointed to Locke's ideas as an alternative system to the metaphysics of René Descartes and Nicolas Malebranche, which were based on the existence of a few innate ideas. Condillac departs from Descartes by more systematically interpreting Locke's thought from a strict psychological perspective. What he will ultimately argue (in his *Traité des sensations*, 1754) is that all human understanding, including the emotions and the reasoning of the intellect, are dependent solely on the five senses – a theory known as sensationalism. But in this book, as these two selections demonstrate, he does not go quite so far. While he reduces human understanding to sensations, which he calls our "first thoughts," he accepts Locke's thesis of "connection" or "association of ideas" and thus still allows "reflection" to enter the process of human understanding. With or without this allowance, the result is a relativist aesthetics, that is, all judgments are inherently subjective in nature. If we substitute the idea of a building for his discussion of human physiognomy, we can also see how such a model of association might also be applied to architecture.

§1 Whether we raise ourselves, to speak metaphorically, into the heavens or descend into the abyss, we do not go beyond ourselves; and we never perceive anything but our own thought. Whatever the knowledge we have, if we wish to trace it to its origin, we will in the end arrive at a first simple thought, which has been the object of the second, which has been the object of the third, and so on. It is this order of thoughts we must explore if we wish to know the ideas we have of things.

§2 It would be useless to inquire into the nature of our thoughts. The first reflection on oneself is enough to convince us that we have no means of conducting that inquiry. We are conscious of our thought; we distinguish it perfectly from all that it is not; we even distinguish among all our thoughts, each from every other, and that is sufficient. If we stray from that, we stray from something that we know so clearly that it cannot lead us into any error.

§3 Let us consider a man at the first moment of his existence. His soul first has different sensations, such as light, colors, pain, pleasure, motion, rest – those are his first thoughts.

§4 Let us follow him in the moments when he begins to reflect on what these sensations occasion in him, and we shall find that he forms ideas of the different operations of his soul, such as perceiving and imagining – those are his second thoughts.

Étienne Bonnot de Condillac (1714–80), from *Essai sur l'origine des connaissances humaines* (1746), trans. Hans Aarsleff in *Essay on the Origin of Human Knowledge*. Cambridge: Cambridge University Press, 2001, pp. 11–12, 56.

Thus, according to the manner in which external objects affect us, we receive different ideas via the senses, and, further, as we reflect on the operations which the sensations occasion in our soul, we acquire all the ideas which we would not have been able to receive from external objects.

§5 Thus the sensations and operations of the soul are the materials of all our knowledge, materials that are employed by reflection as it explores the relations they contain by making combinations of them. But the whole success depends on the circumstances we pass through. The most favorable are those that provide us with the greatest number of objects that may exercise our reflection. The great circumstances in which those who are destined to govern mankind find themselves constitute, for example, an occasion to form very extensive views; and those which continually repeat themselves in the world at large produce the sort of disposition we call natural because, since they are not the fruit of study, we cannot identify the causes that produce them. Let us conclude that there are no ideas that have not been acquired: the first come directly from the senses, the others from experience and increase in proportion to the capacity for reflection.

★ ★ ★

§80 In general the impressions we have in different circumstances make us connect ideas we are no longer able to separate. In our dealings with other human beings, for instance, we imperceptibly connect ideas of certain turns of mind and character with the most notable outward aspects. That is why people with a marked physiognomy please or displease us more than others, for the physiognomy is merely a collection of features to which we have connected ideas that do not come to life unless they are accompanied by pleasure or dislike. Thus it is not surprising that we judge other people by their physiognomy and that we sometimes even at first sight find them off-putting or attractive.

Owing to these connections, we often feel excessive attraction to some people, while we are altogether unjust to others. That is because what strikes us in our friends as well as our enemies naturally connects with the agreeable or disagreeable sentiments they have raised in us; and furthermore, because the shortcomings of the former always borrow something agreeable from what we find most amiable in them, just as the better qualities of the latter seem infected by their defects. For these reasons these connections have an enormous influence on our conduct. They nourish our love or our hate, arouse our esteem or contempt, excite our approval or resentment, and produce the sympathies, antipathies, and all the bizarre inclinations we often find it so hard to account for. I believe I have read somewhere that Descartes always had a liking for the squint-eyed because the first woman he fell in love with had this defect.

82 JULIEN-DAVID LE ROY

from *History of the Arrangement and Different Forms that the Christians Have Given to Their Churches* (1764)

After his large work on Greece had appeared in 1758, Le Roy's future was assured. Toward the end that year he presented a copy of the book to Jacques-François Blondel, acting on behalf of the Academy of Architecture, and by the end of the year Le Roy was elected to the second class of that august body of architects. In 1762 he became an adjunct professor of history at the Academy. And by 1764 he had joined forces with Soufflot in preparing the way for the domed church of Sainte Geneviève in Paris (now the Panthéon). Soufflot, as we have noted, had sought to marry classical forms with the structural lightness of the Gothic style, and he was most intrigued with the idea of replicating the visual effect of the colonnade with the flat lintel that Perrault had employed at the Louvre. To this end, he worked from a Greek-cross plan for the large church and used freestanding Corinthian columns with smaller domed nave vaults. He also fronted the church with a colossal porch of columns (four deep), again surmounted with a flat lintel and pediment. For the church's dedication in 1764, Le Roy wrote his small study of Christian churches, which attempts to justify Soufflot's design by showing it to be the latest development in the drive toward perfection in church design.

Le Roy's history is important in a historiographic sense in that he was first to trace the genealogy of church designs with a comparative plate of different plans and sections drawn at the same scale. It is very important for aesthetic theory, because in the third article or chapter of his study, Le Roy pauses to reflect on the psychological effect of viewing rows of columns or colonnades. This reflection on architectural sensations certainly owes something to Condillac, but it also advances the idea that architecture can indeed be considered beyond the limits of its classical vocabulary — that is, simply as forms, lights, and shadows that have certain aesthetic qualities in themselves. Most of this chapter was later incorporated verbatim into the second edition of *Les Ruines des plus beaux monuments de la Grece* of 1770.

Whatever the cause of the sensations that architecture inspires, it is undoubtedly the nature, force, or quantity of those sensations that prompts our judgment of those buildings that come to our attention. Often when the fine proportions of the parts of a building attract the eye, we traverse it from end to end, we observe all its parts and its details with a delight almost equal to that inspired by the most beautiful sights in nature. Sometimes, again, the grandeur of the divisions of the exterior or the interior of a building, the relief of its parts, the great space that it occupies, and its prodigious height produce a strong impression on the soul. Again, a multitude of small and disparate objects offered all at once to the eye affords us a multiplicity of mild sensations; while a small number of large objects presented

Julien-David Le Roy, from *Histoire de la disposition et des formes differentes que les chréstiens ont données à leur temples, depuis le Règne de Constantin le Grand, jusqu'à nous* [History of the arrangement and different forms that the Christians have given to their churches from the reign of Constantine the Great until today] (1764), trans. David Britt, in *The Ruins of the Most Beautiful Monuments of Greece*. Los Angeles: Getty Publications Program, 2003, pp. 368, 372–3 (excerpts). © 2003 by Getty Publications. Reprinted with permission of Getty Publications.

from new aspects multiply the pleasing or strong sensations that we receive from the most beautiful decorations.

These three qualities – the pleasantness, the strength, and the variety of the sensations conveyed to us by architecture – though rarely combined in a single building, are the causes that make architecture beautiful. We shall show how they are to be found in peristyles in particular and how some peristyles reveal more of these qualities than others.

* * *

Run your eye along the full extent of the colonnade of the Louvre while walking the length of the row of houses opposite; stand back to take in the whole; then come close enough to discern the richness of its soffit, its niches, its medallions; catch the moment when the Sun's rays add the most striking effects by picking out certain parts while plunging others in shadow: how many enchanting views are supplied by the magnificence of the back wall of this colonnade combined in a thousand different ways with the pleasing outline of the columns in front of it and with the fall of the light! The rich variety of this spectacle appears to its greatest advantage when we compare it with the riverside elevation. Try to find new views in that array of pilasters, which are set at very much the same intervals as the columns of the peristyle; you will see, in contrast, only a kind of frigid and monotonous ornament that even sunlight, which brings all nature to life, can hardly change.

Even after several hours, the spectator will not exhaust the prospects afforded by the colonnade of the Louvre; indeed, new ones will appear at every hour of the day. Every new position of the Sun causes the shadows of the columns or of the soffit they support to fall on different parts of the wall; just as every change in its altitude will cause their shadows to rise or fall against the back of the colonnade.

This last-named source of variety in colonnades, born of the effects of light, is almost enough in itself, when they are well situated and built in good climates. There, lit by sunlight through almost every hour of the day, they have less need of richly decorated rear walls to hold the spectator's attention. In contrast, in those countries where the sky is always overcast, nature supplies less animation; and the architect must draw on other resources for the variety that will cause his colonnades to give constant pleasure. By enriching the walls behind them, he succeeds in overcoming the monotony that might arise when their decorations are uniformly lit.

To these general remarks on the beauty of the views that colonnades offer to the spectator who sees them from different angles, we shall add some important and detailed reflections concerning his perceptions on seeing them from a great distance, on drawing close, and on walking beneath them.

When we want to appreciate a colonnade as a whole, we are obliged to stand well back, in order to embrace the whole mass of it; then our movements make little apparent change in the positions of the discrete solids of which it is composed. As we come closer, our view alters. The mass of the building as a whole escapes us, but we are compensated by our closeness to the columns; as we change position, we create changes of view that are more striking, more rapid, and more varied. But if we enter beneath the colonnade itself, an entirely new spectacle offers itself to our eyes: every step we take adds change and variety to the relation between the positions of the columns and the scene outside the colonnade, whether this be a landscape, or the picturesque disposition of the houses of a city, or the magnificence of an interior.

These two last classes of beauty, born of the spectator's closeness to the columns of the colonnade, are characteristic of the colonnade as it is used in interiors. Inside a temple or a church, however large, the spectator generally takes in almost the entire volume of the space at a glance; and, as he is always standing very close to a number of rows of columns, and as the walls that he sees beyond are commonly far richer and more complicated than those of external colonnades, his slightest movements produce the most striking changes in his view of the interior. In short, so universal is the beauty derived from such colonnades that it would remain apparent even if their constituent pillars were not superb Corinthian columns but mere trunks of trees, cut off above the roots and below the springing of the boughs; or if they were copied from those of the Egyptians or the Chinese; or even if they represented no more than a confused cluster of diminutive Gothic shafts or the massive, square piers of our porticoes.

The effect of these supports is indeed enhanced or diminished by their form, by the number of them within a set space, by their relationship to the intervals that separate them, by their varying distances from the backgrounds from which they project, and above all by the quantity of divisions created in the backgrounds. They compel us to vary the proportions of the principal parts of the interior according to the form and spacing of the pillars that mark its divisions; and their general effect, combined with other causes that we shall now examine, may tend to make those interiors seem either smaller or larger than they are.

83 JACQUES-FRANÇOIS BLONDEL
from *Course of Architecture* (1771)

I n 1762 Jacques-François Blondel was appointed a professor at the Royal Academy of Architecture, where he was now required to give regular lectures. These became the basis for his definitive text of theory, the *Cours d'architecture* or course on architecture, which he published in nine volumes between 1771 and 1777. Once again, Blondel in his teachings tended to be conservative. He emphasized the importance of studying and learning from the masterpieces of architectural history. He stressed reason and taste in the process of design. But he also gave new importance to the issue of character, which in the end constituted a very flexible and open-ended approach to design. This may help to explain his great popularity as a teacher, even among students who would boldly challenge the academic conventions of the day. Blondel begins his section on character by laying down some general rules, and then goes on to define – over some 30 pages – these "imperceptible nuances," in which he distinguishes such styles or characters as the manly, firm, virile, elegant, delicate, rustic, feminine, mysterious, and grand.

After having spoken of the numerous members of architecture and of the sculptural ornaments related to architecture, let us offer some new and no less interesting observations. They are concerned with the manner of recognizing – with regard to our French edifices – the true beauties that are widespread in the most celebrated examples and the

Jacques-François Blondel, from *Cours d'architecture, ou traité de la décoration, distribution & construction des bâtiments* [Course of architecture, or treatise on the decoration, distribution and construction of buildings]. Paris: Chez Desaint, 1771, pp. 373–4, 411–12, 419–20, trans. Harry Francis Mallgrave.

mediocrities of which some others are not always exempt. Let us give the precise idea that is produced in the imagination of the spectators by the different architectural members that we have come to define. Finally, let us discuss the different means by which we choose to assemble them in our productions: methods that are able to lead to those imperceptible nuances that the ignorant cannot perceive, that the artist sees and that the enlightened amateur applauds. Do not doubt that it is by the assistance of these imperceptible nuances that we are able to make a real distinction in the design of two buildings of the same genre, but which nevertheless should announce themselves differently: preferring in one a style sublime, noble, and elevated; in the other a character naive, simple, and true. Distinct and particular expressions that are never confused or synonymous, that need to be felt and later discussed, they contribute more than one ordinarily imagines in assigning to each building the character that is proper to it.

★ ★ ★

On the Difference between a Character Male, Firm, or Virile in Architecture

One imagines by a male architecture that which, without being heavy, preserves in its arrangement a character of firmness matched to the grandeur of the lines and to the genre of the building; it is that which is simple in its general composition, discreet in its forms, and sparse in the details of its ornaments. It is that which announces itself by rectilinear plans, by right angles, by projecting bodies that throw large shadows; it is that which is designed for public markets, fairs, hospitals, and for military buildings in particular. It should be composed of beautiful masses in which one is careful to avoid mixing small, puny, and large parts within the ensemble. Often when one tries to make masculine architecture, one makes it with heavy, massive, material; one takes the word for the thing. One tries to make something new, and one reverts to the heaviness of the beautiful productions of Michelangelo, Le Brun, or Le Pautre, without suspecting that the de Brosses, the Hardouin Mansarts, and the François Blondels have left us immortal examples in this genre, in the composition, grandeur, and solidity of the Luxembourg Palace, in the stables and the orangerie of Versailles, in the triumphal arch of St. Denis. They are admirable productions that incontestably must serve as authorities for the arrangement of the different edifices that require the male character of which we wish to speak.

★ ★ ★

On the Feminine Genre in Architecture

One calls architecture feminine in those cases in which the expression displays the proportions of the Ionic order; where the expression is more naive, more charming, less robust than that of the Doric order. Thus the feminine order must be conveniently and judiciously placed in the decoration of buildings. Taken in a bad sense, feminine architecture will be that which, instead of being virile – in keeping with the genre that the edifice seems to demand – presents a contrary Ionic order; it is true but much less suitable than the precedent because of the usage and the particular purpose of the building. Once again, taken in a bad sense, one again calls architecture feminine when, instead of indicating some rectilinear body (as the style of architecture will be solid), it offers some fore-buildings composed of sinuous parts. The building will thus display an uncertainty in the masses and in the details that one intends to admire, and for this reason feminine architecture must be rejected in all military monuments, in all the edifices raised to the glory of heroes, for princely lodgings, etc. But it can be applied suitably to the exterior decoration of a country pleasure house, of a petit Trianon, in the interiors of a queen's apartments, in those of an empress, in baths, fountains, and other edifices consecrated to maritime or terrestrial divinities, of which one has derived the dedication from sacred or profane history.

84 NICOLAS LE CAMUS DE MÉZIÈRES
from *The Genius of Architecture* (1780)

Blondel's system of classifying building characters was taken to the next stage of development by Nicholas Le Camus de Mézières, the designer of the famed Halle au Blé (1763–7) in Paris. Le Camus also wrote on several topics but he is known principally for this one book, two-thirds of which is little more than a room-by-room analysis of the French *hôtel* or residence. But serving as a preface to this study is his theory of character, in which Le Camus de Mézières again brings the sensationalism of Condillac into architecture, when speaking of the psychological experience of moving through space and how all of the senses can be exploited in a successful design. The defense of Ouvrard's theory of harmonic proportions against the attack of Perrault is almost an oddity at this late date, and it points to one of several contradictions in French theory in these pre-revolutionary years.

No one has yet written on the analogy of the proportions of Architecture with our sensations; we find only scattered fragments, superficial and, as it were, set down by chance.

These may be regarded as diamonds in their rude covering, which require the aid of Art to assume their full splendor.

This is a new subject; and we offer this study as no more than a sketch, with a view to inciting more fortunate spirits to take up the same point of view and to compose on this topic a finished Work worthy of the enlightened age in which we live.

Hitherto it has been customary to work in accordance with the proportions of the five Orders of Architecture, used in the ancient Buildings of Greece and Italy: this is a priceless model, and we cannot do better. But how many Artists have employed these Orders

Nicolas Le Camus de Mézières (1721–89), from *Le génie de l'architecture; ou, l'analogie de cet art avec nos sensations* [The genius of architecture; or, the analogy of that art with our sensations] (1780), trans. David Britt, in *The Genius of Architecture*. Santa Monica: Getty Publications Program, 1992, pp. 69–70, 73–4. © 1992 by Getty Publications. Reprinted with permission of Getty Publications.

mechanically, without taking the opportunity to combine them into a whole with a character all its own, capable of producing certain sensations; they have not been inspired by the analogy and relation of those proportions with the affections of the soul.

We sometimes see examples of Architecture that surprise and impress, but leave the judgment uncertain: there remains something to be desired. Why is this so? Because these are the offspring of caprice: good taste may prevail in them, and they may bear the marks of genius; but we find, on inspecting them, that the execution is uncertain, and that the true principles of Art have been mistaken or neglected. At the same time, there are the happy creations of those men of genius who are the wonder of their age: let us take these works as our models. Let us discuss them with reasoned application, distinguish the causes of their effect on our souls, and in this way establish our principles.

Our purpose is to enlarge upon these causes through our Observations on the most remarkable Buildings, those that have most impressed us, in accordance with the sensations that we have ourselves experienced. Nature and art will jointly guide us; theirs is the path that we intend to follow; we shall count ourselves fortunate if this undertaking does not exceed our strength.

Occupied with such observations since my youth, my zeal has sustained itself by fixing my attention upon the works of nature. The more closely I have looked, the more I have found that every object possesses a character, proper to it alone, and that often a single line, a plain contour, will suffice to express it. The faces of the lion, the tiger, and the leopard are composed of lines that make them terrible and strike fear into the boldest hearts. In the face of a cat, we discern the character of treachery; meekness and goodness are written on the features of a lamb; the fox has a mask of cunning and guile: a single feature conveys their character. The celebrated Le Brun,[1] whose talents do honor to his country, has proved the truth of this principle through his characterization of the passions; he has expressed the various affections of the soul, and has rendered joy, sadness, anger, fury, compassion, etc., in a single line.

Similarly, in inanimate objects, it is their form that makes some pleasing to us, others unpleasing. A flower charms the eye: a gentle sympathy attracts us, and the disposition of its parts delights us. Why should not the productions of the Art that forms my theme enjoy the same advantages? A structure catches the eye by virtue of its mass; its general outline attracts or repels us. When we look at some great fabric, our sensations are of contradictory kinds: gaiety in one place, despondency in another. One sensation induces quiet reflection; another inspires awe, or maintains respect, and so on.

What are the causes of these various effects? Let us try to distinguish them. Their existence is in no doubt; and this becomes still more apparent if we combine Painting and Sculpture with Architecture. Who can resist this threefold magic, which addresses almost all the affections and sensations known to us?

★ ★ ★

But let us leave this digression and say only that a close affinity exists between colors and sounds, that they move the passions to an equal degree, and that they produce the same effects. At the sight of a fine building, the eyes enjoy a pleasure as sweet as any that the ears can receive from the sublime art of sounds. Music, the divine Art that enchants us, bears the closest relation to Architecture. The consonances and the proportions are the same. The City of Thebes, or so legend has it, was built to the strains of Amphion's lyre: a fiction that teaches us, at least, that the Ancients felt how intimately Architecture was allied to harmony, which is none other than the combination of different parts to form a concordant whole.

Architecture is truly harmonic. The ingenious M. Ouvrard, Master of the Music at the Sainte-Chapelle and one of the ablest musicians of the age of Louis XIV, proves it so in the most victorious manner in his Treatise.[2] To sustain his system, he shows that the dimensions of Solomon's Temple are related by the harmonic numbers; these dimensions conform to those that Scripture has given us and Villalpanda has so finely elucidated.[3] He does not stop at this one Building: he has applied his principles to several ancient Buildings and to all the precepts of Vitruvius; a number of pleasing works, all marked with the seal of genius, have come from his pen. All cavils against his systems have been in vain. M. Perrault[4] was in the wrong when he wrote that there should be no fixed proportions and that taste alone must decide; that genius must have its flights; that too many and too strict rules seemed to circumscribe it and, as it were, to make it barren.

NOTES

1   Charles Le Brun, who died in Paris in 1690, was first Painter to Louis XIV and has left the Public a characterization of the passions, simply drawn in line.
2   *Architecture harmonique; ou, Application de la doctrine des proportions de la Musique à l'Architecture* [Harmonic architecture; or, Application of the doctrine of musical proportions to architecture].
3   Juan Bautista Villalpanda, an able Jesuit and a native of Cordova, Author of a learned Commentary on Ezekiel, in three volumes *in folio*, which is particularly esteemed for its description of the City and Temple of Solomon. He died in 1608.
4   Claude Perrault, of whom Boileau speaks so frequently in his Satires, and who died in Paris in 1688, has left us a Translation and a learned Commentary on Vitruvius. His were the Designs for the Porte Saint-Bernard, the Observatory, and the famous Colonnade of the Louvre. This celebrated Artist commenced with the study of Medicine; he was a Doctor of the Paris Faculty.

85   NICOLAS LE CAMUS DE MÉZIÈRES
from *The Genius of Architecture* (1780)

In this excerpt from the beginning of Le Camus's chapter on "Exterior Decoration" another influence with regard to character is making itself felt: the idea of the "sublime" as it was developing in British aesthetic theory. Le Camus in fact dedicated his book to Claude-Henri Watelet (1718–86), the author of the *Essai sur les jardins* (Essay on gardens, 1774) – one of the first French texts to discuss British garden theory. This passage may also owe something to Thomas Whateley's *Observations on Modern Gardening* (1870; see chapter 114 below), which

Nicolas Le Camus de Mézières (1721–89), from *Le génie de l'architecture; ou, l'analogie de cet art avec nos sensations* [The genius of architecture; or, the analogy of that art with our sensations] (1780), trans. David Britt, in *The Genius of Architecture*. Santa Monica: Getty Publications Program, 1992, pp. 93–5. © 1992 by Getty Publications. Reprinted with permission of Getty Publications.

was translated into French in 1771. Le Camus is analyzing building forms, as Le Roy had suggested, entirely from the point of view of the emotions they invoke within us.

True harmony in Architecture depends on the consonance between the masses and between the various parts. The style and the tone must be relative to the character of the whole, and the whole must be founded on nature, on the kind of Building that is to be built, and on its purpose.

The part of Architecture that we call by the name of fitness is defined and may be learned not so much by the study of rules as by a perfect understanding of the manners and customs of the age and country in which one lives. Even so, let us essay some general laws, which taste will develop and experience confirm. This will, moreover, be the subject of reflections that will lead us toward perfection by an easier path.

Let us begin with the masses of the building. Their proportion, their mutual relation, gives rise to the sound ensemble, elegant arrangement, and delightful harmony, without which nothing can satisfy.

To this end, all excessively small parts must be avoided; they create confusion, consonance is destroyed, and there is no proportion left; or the proportion is nebulous and doubtful and fails to produce the desired effect. It is an established principle that there can be no proportion between incommensurable quantities and that good proportions in general are founded on correct, immediate, and apprehensible relations. Permit yourself no lapses; for any neglect of the principles of union leads to confusion; it offends the eyes, as the ears are offended by a false note in music. The true Artist pays the closest attention to this; if he be an accurate observer, he will discern in every form the marks that distinguish it from every other; he will understand that if he wishes his building to set a calm and gentle scene, he must combine masses that do not differ too widely; he will see that they must not have too much variety and relief and that the prevailing tone must be one of tranquility and majesty; the contrasts of light and shade must be well regulated, for any excess of either would be harmful. Nothing better conveys the character of mildness than shadows that become less dense as they grow longer.

In a building of a kind in which more harshness is called for, the succession will be less regular, and the transitions more frequent.

If a building is to be marked by simplicity, too many divisions will be avoided. Another, where no pretension to elegance is wanted, may still be rendered notable by the use of numerous masses and divisions to create an effect of richness and profusion. An air of vivacity and gaiety may be imparted by similar means: stringcourses and cornices provide enhancement and variety.

The harsh effects produced by excessive relief, the unduly strong impressions caused by contrasts of light and shade, all, in short, that seems to spring from immoderate effort, disturbs the enjoyment of a scene intended only for amusement and pleasure.

The majestic character, even at its calmest, is never languid. In a building of this sort, a happy mean prevails: harmony must be found in every part; magnificent objects, grand in their dimensions and in their style, suffice to fill and satisfy the soul; it is only where these are too few that recourse may be had to those ornaments that are proper and relative to beautiful Architecture. These are riches that may be employed; but much art is needed, together with great tact and unfailing prudence.

Terror is the effect of magnitude combined with power. The terror inspired by a natural scene may be likened to that which springs from a scene in a play; the soul is powerfully moved, but its sensations are pleasurable only when they partake of terror without repugnance. The resources of Art may be used to render these sensations more lively. The aim is to amplify those objects whose character is in their size and to give added vigor to those distinguished by power; take care to accentuate those that convey terror, while dispensing scattered hints of sadness. Projecting bays may be employed; recessions terminating in a dim obscurity, into which the eye can scarcely penetrate, will be a great resource. Where the occasion arises, afford a glimpse of some distant, vague, and indeterminate vista, in which no object meets the eye. Nothing could be more terrible; the soul stands amazed; it trembles. The stately, bold masses on which the eye first rested have prepared the soul for such a sensation. Even the majesty of the Ocean itself scarcely mitigates its measureless vastness; to become a pleasing prospect, it requires a shore, a cape, or an island in the middle distance. These varied objects give shape and life to the whole.

This genre of the terrible is enhanced by suitable ornaments; but observe that these accessories, though they may serve to designate the character, will do nothing to convey the expression. This bears the stamp of nobler qualities, which nothing can replace.

Great size is indispensable to the genre of the terrible, just as stately and clear-cut masses are the province of majesty.

When we are on the banks of a river, the motion of the water in itself numbs our senses and lulls us to sleep; a quicker motion rouses us and animates us. When carried to excess, this rapidity alarms our senses; it becomes a torrent whose noise, force, and impetuosity inspire terror, a sensation closely allied to the sublime, whether as a cause or as an effect.

Such is the progression of our sensations: the proportion between one part and the whole determines the natural placing of an object, indicates its kind, and supplies the style appropriate to every scene.

It is impossible to pay too much attention to the masses in a building, to their intended effect in elevation, and to the greater or lesser degree of light that may result; the shadows must temper the light, and the light must temper the shadows. In this principle, success resides; here alone *true beauty* is to be found; this is a subject of great importance, which has yet to receive due attention. If only this can be considered and discussed, the truth will come to light, and the greatest benefits will ensue. This observation, we repeat, is essential. Even the most intelligent Architect can hope to succeed only by adapting his design to the exposure of the Sun to the principal parts of his building. Like the skillful Painter, he must learn to take advantage of light and shade, to control his tints, his shadings, his nuances, and to impart a true harmony to the whole. The general tone must be proper and fitting; he must have foreseen the effects and be as careful in considering all the parts as if he had to show a picture of them.

Just as in a play a single action occupies the stage, similarly in a building the unity of character must be observed, and this truth must capture the imagination by presenting itself to the eye.

Never depart from fitness and decorum in relation to the genre to which the intended building belongs.

86 JEAN-LOUIS VIEL DE SAINT-MAUX
from *Letters on the Architecture of the Ancients and the Moderns* (1787)

Little is known of this architect and writer, other than he was a younger brother of the more famous architect Charles-François Viel (1745–1819). The significance of these letters is that they reveal another side of French architectural theory in the closing years of the Ancien Régime. Viel de Saint-Maux was a caustic critic of the Vitruvian tradition and of the French Academy. In a footnote to one letter, he refers to Jacques-François Blondel as "the Charlatan of architecture," and he was equally dismissive of Paris's most celebrated architect, Claude-Nicholas Ledoux, whom he accuses of plagiarism. He faults modern practice for lacking a "distinctive character," and this freemason counters with a highly symbolic interpretation of architecture. In reviewing ancient architecture, he devotes much of his discussion to the still little-known architecture of India, Japan, China, Babylonia, and Persia. He underscores the cosmogony, cosmology, and fertility rituals originally giving rise to the range of symbolic forms. Whereas Laugier had earlier interpreted the pediment as based on an imitation of the rustic hut, Viel de Saint-Maux views the triangle as the near universal symbol of the Supreme Being in ancient religions. Architecture for him thus functions in an entirely expressive and intensely symbolic manner.

Filled with these ideas and persuaded that architecture must have an origin more true, more noble, and more useful than what is attributed to it, I have searched to find it and to discard everything that has until now prevented us from making this discovery. I have wanted to penetrate those very motives that had persuaded the Greeks and the Romans to cover the primordial ideas with a veil, out of which arose, at its origin, the art of architecture.

It is in the temples related to cults that ancient architecture developed all of its richness and achieved its greatest heights. It is therefore relative to that which the cult requires that one must analyze this art; then and only then will we arrive at its august origin. It is by not having done this that we have substituted great errors for truth. We have supposed, for example, that these temples were primarily intended for sacrificing victims; as proof we point to the heads of bulls with which they were decorated. But if these edifices were only conceived as sacred butcher's houses, why were their soffits and their vaults adorned with astronomical objects? Why did these temples everywhere present symbols relating to the health and the subsistence of man? What relations did all of these things have with the animal sacrifices? What could have caused such astonishing and irrational disparities?

★ ★ ★

The origin of what has been attributed to the different parts of buildings is worthy of these silly ideas. The base of a column, it has been said, represents ropes; the column's shaft is derived from a trunk or a piece of wood that supports the structure of our garrets; the capital, according to some of us, is an assemblage of iron hoops or cords with which tree

Jean-Louis Viel de Saint-Maux, from *Lettres sur l'architecture des anciens et celles des modernes* [Letters on the architecture of the ancients and the moderns] (1787), trans. Harry Francis Mallgrave from facsimile edition. Geneva: Minkoff Reprint, 1974, pp. 7–8, 10–13, 16–18.

trunks were tied. According to others, it is a large shelf forcefully placed atop the pretended trunk, and in this ridiculous system the cornice becomes an awning.

That which we call ornament in each order has a no more distinguished origin. Some plants, they say, grew between the cords and the wood that formed either the base or the capital. One found these plants to be a marvelous ornament, and they were imitated in marble when more durable edifices were built. Is this not indulging oneself in calumny and disparaging these buildings and those who invented the different parts? In some way is it not stripping antiquity of any merit?

★ ★ ★

It [the classical temple] is a masterpiece that honored and really honors the human race. Its sublime origin, to the great astonishment of those who claim to be the wisest in these matters, is agriculture itself and the cult that was behind it. It is thus a *speaking poem*; in its ensemble it was how the ancients instructed themselves, as in a book – not only in matters of primitive theogony but also of the combinations of their cosmogony. In a word, in its full complement it was that which came to reunite all knowledge and it was refined by ingenious allegories and emblems that one was not able to misinterpret. It was not simply a base or a capital of so many modules that they assessed for this type of monument, but rather objects relating to agricultural science, of which the column revealed its interesting origin. The entablature retraced the history of the godsend: the happy influences of the sun on the fecundity of the soil. It came about because of the gratitude of man, which completed this *ex voto* or theological construction.

Although we believe that this genius was manifested only in the sculpture of ancient monuments, sometimes a rough stone produced the same effect. The appearance of the edifice, its ensemble and elevation, also offered the ideas that they wanted to transmit to posterity by constructing them.

In ancient temples everything is open to analysis, everything presents some symbols and mysterious types; everywhere we discover the great attributes of the divinity. In effect, the temple celebrates only the marvels of creation, the perpetual miracles of *fertility*, structural feats, the laws of movement, etc. On temple walls we even find geographic maps of the known world with the different revolutionary epochs that had passed. We also find represented there lessons for tilling the soil, the annual seasons, and the orbit of the sun, under the guise of characters or under the form of the country's production. These same seasons – the sun itself – have always been considered as the attributes of the divinity; thus, the people became enlightened, diligent, and grateful.

87   A. C. QUATREMÈRE DE QUINCY
from *Methodical Encyclopedia* (1788)

T he most extensive exposition on the notion of character in the late eighteenth century was that presented by Antoine Chrysosthôme Quatremère de Quincy, whose ideas on this and other issues would later have an enormous impact on architectural thinking. Born in Paris, he first studied law before switching his interest to sculpture. He did not win the *grand prix* but traveled to the south in 1776, where he remained until 1784. During his stay he befriended the grand-prix winning painter Jacques-Louis David, met Piranesi and Canova, and visited the classical sites at Pompei, Paestum, and Sicily. Upon returning to France he wrote a competition essay on Egyptian architecture in 1785, for which he won a prize. Shortly thereafter, he was commissioned to write an architectural encyclopedia, the first volume of which (*Abajour* to *Colonne*) he completed in 1788. This 52 page essay on "Character" was written a little more than a decade after Blondel had presented his elaborate discussion of this concept, but Quatremère de Quincy takes the idea an entirely different direction. It is much broader and at the same time more grounded in his rational vision of classical architecture, which was opposed to what he regarded as the expressionist excesses of the day — for instance, the fanciful visions of Claude-Nicholas Ledoux. The article opens with an etymological discussion of the Greek term "character," which literally means "a mark or figure traced on stone, metal, paper, or any other material with the chisel, the burin, the brush, the pen, or any other instrument." Quatremère de Quincy next distinguishes between physical character and moral character, and it is here that the first of our two passages commences. After these rather general remarks on the three kinds of each character, Quatremère goes off, over many more pages, to analyze architectural character with respect to these distinctions and to the climatic, racial, national, and personal variables affecting character. In essence it is largely an anthropological consideration of character, although underlain with Quatremère de Quincy's own classical preferences.

A More Precise Definition of the Word Character

This first definition of *character* leads us to another more precise distinction, and one very important for understanding the nuances of this word.

One must recognize, be it physical or moral, three kinds of *character*: *essential character*, *distinctive* or *accidental character*, and *relative character*.

In a physical sense, essential *character* is the type by which nature makes its works recognizable; it is that complex indication of large traits that constitute above all the general divisions of the three kingdoms of nature, especially the distinctions of different classes of being, of the proper nuances of species, of gender, of age, and of all the apparent and grandly impressed exterior marks that oppose the confusion of one species with another. Distinctive or accidental *character* is that which depends on all the particular accidents, on all the varieties of development that a multitude of visible or invisible causes impress on the same species, following the diversity of their circumstances, thus on individuals of a

A. C. Quatremère de Quincy (1755–1849), from *Encyclopédie méthodique: architecture*. Paris: Panckouke, 1788, pp. 478–9, 500, trans. Harry Francis Mallgrave.

same species, following the diversity of elements that modify their forms, and of the influences that have some effect on them. Relative *character* is a most particular indication of faculties relative to different genres of properties of which nature has endowed certain species or certain individuals, and which makes known for what use they are especially destined.

In a moral sense, essential character resides in the uniformity of general habits that form the particular instinct of each species of being, and that always indicates in a constant way their inclinations, their dominant tastes, and their tendencies, which – adhering to nature even in their organization – can never be averted by accidental causes. Distinctive *character* is that in which the particular accidents of organization, circumstances, social institutions, and all exceptions that are in the same order of nature render appropriate to such or such individual, or to such or such part of the same species. Indeed it is only a local or momentary modification of essential *character*. Relative *character* is the stamp or the particular development of certain analogous qualities to such or such an end, and to such or such a manner of being, and that indicates what is appropriate to such or such a being; it denotes a correlation between how one appears and what is appropriate.

These distinctions and definitions have clarified for us the different acceptances of the word *character* and we will see that these different meanings, which usage so often confuses, respond precisely to the established distinctions.

Significations and Acceptances of the Word Character

In speaking of the same object, the same being, or the same work, one says that it has some *character*, it has a *character*, or it has its *character*. They are not the same thing, although in ordinary language they are misused. As we will see – and especially with works of art – something can have some *character* or a *character* without having its *character*.

When one says something about an object, it has some *character*, or rather, there is some *character* in it that one is able to express by some manner of speaking, whether the indefinable something of greatness, strength, or importance that one is always at pains to determine. In this accepted sense of *character*, one is able to say *character par excellence*, that of force, which is how I have defined *essential character* – that is, these traits energetically articulate what is taken for the essence of something.

Thus in a physical sense when you say this man has some *character*, it is as if you say this man is conformed in such a way that his traits are very striking and pronounced, which distinguishes him in very distinct ways from the traits of a woman or of an infant. It is in this sense that a mature man has more *character* than a young man. The man who has no *character* will be he whose traits are little or badly developed, and thus his equivocal conformation approaches more the rotundity of the infant or the softness of the woman. When one says in a moral sense that a man has some character, it is as if one says this man has some habits strongly pronounced, and particularly those that constitute the moral essence of a man. This kind of *character* especially resides in force, gravity, seriousness, severity, inflexibility, in short, in all the qualities that depart from playfulness, grace, and the frivolity that constitutes the *character* of age or gender, that is to say, having none of it.

Thus in this sense, *some character* signifies *character par excellence, character* of force or the essential.

When one uses this word in its second acceptance, as when one says that this object or that being has *a character*, one simply speaks of those infinite nuances that modify all the objects of the same genre, all the individuals of a species. Let me explain.

We have seen that *character*, in its etymology, signifies only a mark or distinctive sign of something. We have seen that essential *character*, which one expresses by *some character*, refers to the indicative marks of essential qualities that constitute in an energetic and pronounced manner the large distinctions of nature. Now when you say that a being physically has *a character*, you are no longer speaking of these large distinctions, but of the individual nuances more or less distinct in each being of the same species. It is as if you say he has a distinctive sign, which indicates faculties strong or weak, large or small, but which are unique to him. Although each being in reality has a configuration distinct from others, and therefore a *character*, you only use this expression when a particular modification is more expressly marked. For example in speaking of physiognomy, each man has his own; but one says that a man has a physiognomy when his offers something rather remarkable apart from the commonality of physiognomies. A being thus has *a character* when one observes in him an individual modification that differs in a striking way from others. There are a large number of people who are similar in exterior conformation, of whom one might say that among them there is a *character*. When one speaks of a man in a moral sense and says that he has a *character*, one understands that the genre of his formed habits is distinct in its nuances from other men, without having to explain of what nature they are. One may speak of a particular combination of tastes, of inclinations, or remark on his moral organization as very distinct from others. In this sense one is able to have a *character* without having *some character*. There are some men who have both; there are many more, especially in urban societies, who have neither one nor the other.

Thus under this acceptance, *character* conveys of a person no particular relation of such or such quality, such or such property; it is as if one simply says this person has a sign that distinguishes him from others. *Character* then relates to that which I have called *distinctive character*.

When one says that an object or a being has *its character*, especially when one joins it with the word *appropriate* (and it is always this that one understands even when one suppresses this epithet), one wants to say that such an object or such a being carries within him the indicative mark of that which is appropriate. This acceptance carries the idea of propriety for something, or for some use.

Thus in this third usage, when you say that a man physically has his appropriate *character* it supposes that you already understand the faculties with which he is gifted, and that you find an exact correlation between what he is and what he seems. Suppose a man capable of some kind of force, of address, of exercise, of swiftness. You say that he has *his appropriate character* when his proportions, his conformation, his musculature, etc. appear to conform to the use to which he is destined by nature, and you are capable of understanding what is proper. In a moral sense, you say that a man has *his appropriate character* when his habits or his moral conformation correspond to the place, the state, the profession, the manner of being for which he seems born, and for which he has accepted. One understands, without necessarily explaining it, that one applies the word *character* in this last sense when one says of a warrior, of an artisan, of a poet, of a master, of a slave that he has his *character*. It is as if one says the development of his moral qualities indicate that he is appropriate to what he is, to what he does.

Thus *character*, when one speaks of *his appropriate character*, never says that the *character* that one has is proper in itself, but that it is appropriate to the use for which it is formed. And this is what I call *relative character*.

★ ★ ★

Essential Character, or of Force and Grandeur

[. . .] The energetic expression of force and all the sentiments that derive from this essential virtue depend in particular on the same expression of the essence of architecture, or on the types that brought it into being. Therefore, of the three accepted orders that architecture is rightly deemed to have, the Doric order has the most character. It is the primitive order in which the expression of carpentry and of the constitutive types of art are expressed and rendered with the most force and evidence. It is for this reason that Greek architecture, where this expression essentially dominates, has more *character* than Roman architecture, in which the characteristic impression of these types begins to disappear and become confused. It is for this reason that modern architecture will always have lost some *character* – to the extent that this faithful imitation of the type of carpentry has been effaced and altered to the point of becoming unrecognizable. Do you want to restore this characteristic virtue to your works? Then always have your eyes fixed on the real or ideal model that has brought architecture into being. All the constitutive parts of your edifices should articulate the intention for making them, and as much as possible conform to the parts of the models of which they represent. Never lose sight of their origin, the needs that served as a motive for their shapes, in short, the reality of the objects that you necessarily render – in some way – as the image. This primitive model for which you are merely the copyist will deter you from all those bizarre compositions and details that lessen and weaken the appearance and the effects of buildings. It will save you from these equivocal and bastard forms that leave the mind uncertain of their usefulness, from those weak and indecisive forms of which no design or no motif seems to have made itself felt. It will especially save you from all those nonsensical forms and ornaments that work in a contrary sense to the necessary forms of construction, setting up a perpetual lie between the appearance and reality of objects.

88 ÉTIENNE-LOUIS BOULLÉE
from *Architecture, Essay on Art* (c.1794)

Between 1760 and 1789 French architecture enjoyed a most creative period. Part of its success had to do with an unprecedented building boom initiated by the crown and city government. Part also had to do with a loss of authority within the academic system, the new knowledge of Greece, and the general desire to experiment with new aesthetic ideas. A third and very important component of the formal innovation also had to do with the quality of young architects who emerged. Joining Soufflot as his generation's most gifted designer were a number of highly talented architects, among them Pierre Contant d'Ivry, Jacques Gabriel, Marie-Joseph Peyre, Charles De Wailly, Jacques-Denis Antoine, Jacques Gondoin, and Claude-Nicolas Ledoux.

Étienne-Louis Boullée was a prominent member of this professional generation. In his early years he was known principally as the architect of a number of elegant townhouses, beginning with the Hôtel Alexandre (1763–6) and culminating with the grand Hôtel de Brunoy (1774–9) along the Champs-Elysées. But he was also highly regarded as a teacher and elevated to the first class of the Architectural Academy in 1780. Two years later, he resigned from his official governmental offices and devoted himself to painting and to architectural theory. In the first regard – for which today he is most famous – he produced a bevy of "visionary" and highly imaginative designs, of which over 100 drawings still survive. In the second regard, as a theorist, he composed an explanatory essay, which he planned to publish with his drawings. The French Revolution interrupted these plans and it was only in 1957 that his essay was published, although it was widely known in its day.

Boullée considers character in a way different from Quatremère de Quincy, and in fact his ideas derive very much from the substance of his drawings. On the one hand he was very skeptical of Vitruvius (whom he regards as little more than a technician), the issues of the Blondel/Perrault dispute, and academic culture itself. He was also a sensationalist in his aesthetics and spoke of architecture as poetry, by which he meant a kind of poetry composed of symmetry, regularity, varied form, and character. This first selection of passages outlines what is essentially a theory of volumes under the play of light; its expression is its character.

In my search to discover the properties of volumes and their analogy with the human organism, I began by studying the nature of some irregular volumes.

What I saw were masses with convex, concave, angular or planimetric planes, etc., etc. Next I realized that the various contours of the planes of these volumes defined their shape and determined their form. I also perceived in them the confusion (I cannot say variety) engendered by the number and complexity of their irregular planes.

Weary of the mute sterility of irregular volumes, I proceeded to study regular volumes. What I first noted was their regularity, their symmetry and their variety; and I perceived that that was what constituted their shape and their form. What is more, I realized that regularity alone had given man a clear conception of the shape of volumes, and so he gave them a definition which, as we shall see, resulted not only from their regularity and symmetry but also from their variety.

Étienne-Louis Boullée (1728–99), from *Architecture, Essai sur l'art* [Architecture, essay on art] (c.1794), edited and annotated at the Bibliothèque Nationale in Paris by Helen Rosenau, trans. Sheila de Vallée, published in *Boullée & Visionary Architecture*, New York: Harmony Books, 1976, pp. 86, 87, 89.

An irregular volume is composed of a multitude of planes, each of them different and, as I have observed above, it lies beyond our grasp. The number and complexity of the planes have nothing distinct about them and give a confused impression.

How is it that we can recognize the shape of a regular volume at a glance? It is because it is simple in form, its planes are regular and it repeats itself. But since we gauge the impression that objects make on us by their clarity, what makes us single out regular volumes in particular is the fact that their regularity and their symmetry represent order, and order is clarity.

It is obvious from the above remarks that man had no clear idea of the shape of volumes before he discovered the concept of regularity.

Once I had observed that the shape of a regular volume is determined by regularity, symmetry and variety, then I understood that proportion is the combination of these properties.

By the proportion of a volume, I mean the effect produced by its regularity, its symmetry and its variety. Regularity gives it a beautiful shape, symmetry gives it order and proportion, variety gives it planes that diversify as we look at them. Thus the combination and the respective concord which are the result of all these properties, give rise to volumetric harmony. [...]

What then is the primary law on which architectural principles are based?

Let us consider an example of Architecture that has been imperfectly observed and lacks proportion. This will certainly be a defect but the defect will not necessarily be such an eyesore that we cannot bear to look at the Building; and nor will it necessarily have the same effect on our eyes that a discord has on our ears.

In architecture a lack of proportion is not generally very obvious except to the eye of the connoisseur. It is thus evident that although proportion is one of the most important elements constituting beauty in architecture, it is not the primary law from which its basic principles derive. Let us try, therefore, to discover what it is impossible not to admit in architecture, and that from which there can be no deviation without creating a real eyesore.

Let us imagine a man with a nose that is not in the middle of his face, with eyes that are not equidistant, one being higher than the other, and whose limbs are also ill-matched. It is certain that we would consider such a man hideous. Here we have an example that can readily be applied to the subject under discussion. If we imagine a Palace with an off-centre front projection, with no symmetry and with windows set at varying intervals and different heights, the overall impression would be one of confusion and it is certain that to our eyes such a building would be both hideous and intolerable.

It is easy for the reader to surmise that the basic rule and the one that governs the principles of architecture, originates in regularity and also that any deviation from symmetry in architecture is as inconceivable as failing to observe the rules of harmony in music. [...]

Character

Let us consider an object. Our first reaction is, of course, the result of how the object affects us. And what I call character is the effect of the object which makes some kind of impression on us.

To give a building character is to make judicial use of every means of producing no other sensations than those related to the subject. In order to understand what I mean by the character or expected effect of different objects, let us take a look at some of the beauties of nature and we shall see that we are forced to express ourselves in accordance with the effect they have on our senses.

What a charming spectacle delights our eyes! What an agreeable day! How pleasant it is! The image of a good life extends over the whole Earth! Nature is bedecked with the charms of youth and is a work of love! Sweet harmony reigns over all our impressions on such a delightful day; and its charm intensifies the colours and our senses are drunk with their freshness, their delicate nuances, their smooth, rich tones. What a pleasure it is to run our eyes over all these things and how agreeable they are; their adolescent forms have a *je ne sais quoi* that emphasizes the smooth flowing curves that barely indicate their presence and adds new charms. The beauty of their elegant proportions lends them grace and unites in them all things that have the gift of pleasing us!

But summer comes and forces a change of mood. The glorious light makes us drunk with joy and our sense of wonder has no limits. This pleasure is truly divine! What pure happiness we feel in the bottom of our hearts at this spectacle! What ecstasy! No, we cannot possibly give expression to it!

At this season nature's work is done; everything is the image of perfection; everything has acquired a clearly defined form that is full-blown, accurate and pure. Outlines are clear and distinct; their maturity gives them noble, majestic proportions; their bright, vivid colours have acquired all their brilliance. The earth is decked out with all its riches and lavishes them on our gaze. The depth of the light enhances our impressions; its effects are both vivid and dazzling. All is radiant! The God of day seems to inhabit the earth. Nature is adorned with a multitude of beautiful things and offers us a splendid vista of magnificence.

But autumn has already taken the place of summer and raises our spirits with new pleasures; it is a time of fulfilment; spring had already awakened our desire for it. The earth, still adorned with Flora's dazzling gifts, is now covered with Pomona's treasures. How varied are the images! How gay and smiling! Bacchus and the gentle Goddess of Folly have taken over the earth. The God of mirth, the spirit of our pleasures, makes our hearts drunk with joy! It is as if the Goddess wanted to give pleasure to the God by disguising the earth. Colours are mixed, variegated, mottled. Forms are picturesque and have the appealing attraction of novelty; variety had added to their spice and the play of light and shadow produces countless surprise effects which are all delightful.

But fine days are superseded by the dark winter season. What a sad time! The torch of heaven has disappeared! Darkness is all around us! Hideous winter comes and chills our hearts! It is brought by the weather! Night follows in its wake, unfurls her sombre shades over the earth and spreads darkness everywhere. The shining crystal of the ocean is already tarnished by the blast of the north wind. What remains of the pleasant forest are no more than skeletons and nature is in mourning. The image of the good life has faded to be succeeded by that of death! Everything has lost its brilliance and colour, forms sag, outlines are hard and angular and to our eyes the denuded earth resembles an all-embracing tomb!

Oh, Nature! How true it is that you are the book of books, universal knowledge! No, we can do nothing without you! But although each year you begin again the most interesting and instructing course of study that exists, how few men pay attention to your lessons and know how to benefit from them!

It follows from these remarks occasioned by the seasons of the year that to create something beautiful we must, as in nature, ensure that the general impression given is gentle; colours must be soft and muted, their shades delicate; shapes must be flowing with light, elegant proportions.

The art of making things agreeable stems from Good Taste.

Good Taste is a delicate, aesthetic discernment with regard to objects that arouse our pleasure. It is not enough to simply put before us objects that give us pleasure. It is when we choose among them that our pleasure is aroused and we feel delight in the depths of our being.

Let us concentrate on architecture and we shall see that here Good Taste consists of providing more delicacy than opulence, more subtlety than strength, more elegance than ostentation. Thus it is grace that is indicative of Good Taste.

We have observed that during the summer season the whole of nature is bathed in light which produces the most magnificent effects; that this life-giving light was diffused over an extraordinary multitude of objects all with the most beautiful forms, all shining with the brilliance of the brightest colours, all of them developed to the full; and that the result of this beautiful assembly was a vista of magnificent splendour.

As in nature, the art of giving an impression of grandeur in architecture lies in the disposition of the volumes that form the whole in such a way that there is a great deal of play among them, that their masses have a noble, majestic movement and that they have the fullest possible development. The arrangement should be such that we can absorb at a glance the multiplicity of the separate elements that constitute the whole. The play of light on this arrangement of volumes should produce the most widespread, striking and varied effects that are all multiplied to the maximum. In a large ensemble, the secondary components must be skilfully combined to give the greatest possible opulence to the whole; and it is the auspicious distribution of this opulence that produces splendour and magnificence.

89 ÉTIENNE-LOUIS BOULLÉE
from *Architecture, Essay on Art* (c.1794)

Perhaps the most famous of Boullée's visionary designs is his cenotaph for Isaac Newton, a gigantic spherical monument dedicated to his theories and lit by apertures cut into the upper portion of the vault. It plays perfectly into Boullée's symbolism of forms and exploitation of mysterious sources of light. These two excerpts are followed by concluding remarks to his essay, entitled "Summary Reflections on the Art of Teaching Architecture."

Étienne-Louis Boullée, from *Architecture, Essai sur l'art* [Architecture, essay on art] (c.1794), edited and annotated at the Bibliothèque Nationale in Paris by Helen Rosenau, trans. Sheila de Vallée, published in *Boullée & Visionary Architecture*, New York: Harmony Books, 1976, pp. 107, 115.

Sublime mind! Prodigious and profound genius! Divine being! Newton! Deign to accept the homage of my feeble talents! Ah! If I dare to make it public, it is because I am persuaded that I have surpassed myself in the project which I shall discuss.

O Newton! With the range of your intelligence and the sublime nature of your Genius, you have defined the shape of the earth; I have conceived the idea of enveloping you with your discovery. That is as it were to envelop you in your own self. How can I find outside you anything worthy of you? It was these ideas that made me want to make the sepulchre in the shape of the earth. In imitation of the ancients and to pay homage to you I have surrounded it with flowers and cypress trees. [. . .]

The form of the interior of this monument is, as you can see, that of a vast sphere. The centre of gravity is reached by an opening in the base on which the Tomb is placed. The unique advantage of this form is that from whichever side we look at it (as in nature) we see only a continuous surface which has neither beginning nor end and the more we look at it, the larger it appears. This form has never been utilized and it is the only one appropriate to this monument, for its curve ensures that the onlooker cannot approach what he is looking at; he is forced as if by one hundred different circumstances outside his control, to remain in the place assigned to him and which, since it occupies the centre, keeps him at a sufficient distance to contribute to the illusion. He delights in it, without being able to destroy the effect by wanting to come too close in order to satisfy his empty curiosity. He stands alone and his eyes can behold nothing but the immensity of the sky. The tomb is the only material object.

The lighting of this monument, which should resemble that on a clear night, is provided by the planets and the stars that decorate the vault of the sky. The arrangement of the planets corresponds to nature. These planets are in the shape of and resemble funnel-like openings which transpierce the vaulting and once inside assume their form. The daylight outside filters through these apertures into the gloom of the interior and outlines all the objects in the vault with bright, sparkling light. This form of lighting the monument is a perfect reproduction and the effect of the stars could not be more brilliant.

It is easy to imagine the natural effect that would result from the possibility of increasing or decreasing the daylight inside the monument according to the number of stars. It is also easy to imagine how the sombre light that would prevail in this place would favour the illusion.

★ ★ ★

Summary Reflections on the Art of Teaching Architecture

I have long meditated on the profession I teach and I have concentrated on devising methods for accelerating its progress.

It seemed to me that the manner in which architecture was taught was in some respects defective and for this reason I decided to try and find a more suitable method than the usual one.

Man can only learn by proceeding from the simple to the complicated. The first Lesson that painters give their Students is how to draw eyes. Language teachers do not begin their lessons by demonstrating the richness of a language to their students. Why then do

Architects make their Students begin by drawing the ['five' erased] orders of Architecture which constitute all the opulence of this art?

Let us proceed with order, so that the methods we are proposing follow from all that can be obtained by a method that will favour the study of this great Art.

Let us first ascertain what we mean and what architecture should incorporate. Let us give a definition! It is the art of bringing any building to perfection. What does this perfection consist of? A building can be considered perfect when its decoration corresponds to the kind of building to which it is applied and when its layout corresponds to its function.

In the light of this explanation, if we want to proceed methodically with our teaching, we should place in front of a new student the most simple building in existence such as the country cabin mentioned by Vitruvius.

Since evidence is based on what strikes us most, we should make the student draw the façade of the cabin, and then make him familiar with a plan by showing him how to draw one. In the same way, the section and cross-section of the Cabin will teach him the art of combining interior and exterior.

After this Cabin he will progress successively to buildings that are a little more complicated and finally to an apartment building. Why? Because the dividing up it necessitates requires special techniques which will teach him good organization and will shape his understanding.

After making a beginning with this practical teaching, it is necessary to develop his concept of the artistic side, properly so called.

The theory of volumes will serve to demonstrate that the basic principles of his art are established in nature. And by applying these volumes to art, he will learn to recognize Poetry.

What does this Poetry consist of? It lies in the art of creating perspectives through the effect of volumes. But what causes the effects of volumes? It is their mass. And so it is the mass of these volumes that gives rise to our sensations. Without doubt. And it is the effect that they have on our senses that has enabled us to give them appropriate names and to distinguish massive forms from delicate ones, etc., etc. Again it is the various sensations that we experience that make us realize that volumes that drag on the ground make us sad; those that surge up into the heavens delight us; that we find gentle volumes pleasant whereas those that are angular and hard we find repugnant.

The examples taken from art that the teacher places before his students will make this even more evident.

As a result of this method the student will become a student of nature for he will be forced to recognize that this is the source of beauty in art.

90 CLAUDE-NICOLAS LEDOUX

from *Architecture Considered in Relation to Art, Morals, and Legislation* (1804)

C laude-Nicolas Ledoux was the most famous and indeed the most gifted architect of his generation. No one better represents the dynamic energy of this era, and no one more seriously challenged the boundaries of classicism in both built and visionary works. But his life and his career were not always filled with happy moments; in fact he was arrested during the infamous Reign of Terror in 1793–4 and nearly lost his head on the guillotine. Forced into retirement after his release, he wrote this apologia of his career to vindicate his reputation. He published the first of four projected volumes two years before his sudden paralysis and death.

Ledoux's career falls into two well-defined phases. He was born in the province of Champagne and moved to Paris in the first half of the 1750s to study at the private school of Jacques-François Blondel. Ledoux entered private practice in the early 1760s, where he quickly established his reputation as the fashionable designer for aristocratic townhouses for the city's elite. In 1771 his interests shifted when he was given a government post as the inspector of saltworks for the eastern province of Franche-Comté. Between 1775–80, he built the small factory community at Arc-et-Senans, where he first explored an abstract, geometric, and rustic classicism that he simultaneously pursued in ideal designs for the city of Chaux. His building of the (hated) Paris toll houses between 1784–9 allowed another outlet for his experiments in reducing the classical language – at times to the point of pure abstraction – but they at the same time made him a very unpopular figure in revolutionary France. Ledoux's only published work, *L'architecture considérée sous le rapport de l'art, des moeurs, et de la legislation*, was started in 1780 and conceived as a collection of plates that brought together his utopian designs for the city of Chaux with his various built works at the saline. The project with its magnificent plates grew in his mind during the 1780s, but the French Revolution of 1789 stalled the project. In the meantime Ledoux expanded upon the idea with a highly ornate allegorical foreword and introduction to his architectural fantasies. These introductory pieces are the closest Ledoux came to defining his theoretical outlook. The theory of sensationalism composes one base of his theory. Another is the inclusion of "morals" (*moeurs*) and "legislation" in the book's title, which – after his harrowing experience in prison – underscores his overall didactic or social-regulative conception of practice. Also prominent in his thinking is the role that freemasonry plays in his highly charged symbolism of forms. Critics of his work – especially of the rhetorical power of forms and ornamental elements – characterized his approach as *architecture parlante* or "speaking architecture." The selection of passages from the introduction discusses architecture as the art most useful in shaping the morality and happiness of the human race. It is a utopian and utilitarian conception, certainly moderated by the social consciousness of the French Revolution.

Let nations raise the trumpet that sounds a general call to this beneficent competition! The architect will be prompt in coming, and his active and generous hand will pour forth to society the treasures for which he will be paid only with his ashes. Like the dew that brilliantly nourishes our fields, which is no longer celebrated after it has fertilized the

Claude Nicolas Ledoux (1736–1806), from *L'architecture considérée sous le rapport de l'art, des moeurs et de la legislation* [Architecture considered in relation to art, morals, and legislation]. Paris: C. F. Patris, 1802, pp. 9–12, trans. Harry Francis Mallgrave.

abundant harvest of grain, his works will be reimbursed only through the immortality of his name.

Posterity will conserve and honor his memory. In his works – propagators of art – it will admire the great principles. The entire falsified amalgam, the particular fruit of circumstances, will disappear.

There, as with an elementary textbook, these principles will develop with their different results, everything will be confirmed by experience.

We will find there a series of simple and positive ideas, benevolent principles of the operations of genius; in the men fated to follow these tracks, it will powerfully assist their judgment in the choice of means and in the reasoning used to do it.

Note those immutable rules that have been collected there.

The salutary effect of the wind, the most favorable site must always precede and determine the manner and order of construction; we must build according to the temperature.

The dependence that too long perpetuated the vices of the conception will count for nothing, and we will not subordinate the favor of the site to comply with a usage that is considered dangerous.

We will not separate the unity of the thought from the variety of forms, laws of fitness, propriety, or economy. Unity, a type of beauty – *omnis porro pulchritudinis est* – resides in the relation of the masses to the details or the ornaments, in uninterrupted lines that do not allow the eye to be distracted by harmful accessories.

Variety gives to each building the physiognomy that is proper to it. It multiplies and changes this physiognomy according to the adjacent situations and to the planes leading to the horizon, and a satisfied desire in fact hatches a thousand others.

Fitness, which values richness and disguises adversity, will subordinate ideas to the localities, will reassemble the different needs with suitable and inexpensive exteriors.

Propriety will offer us the analogy of proportions and ornaments; it will indicate at first glance the motive of the construction and its use.

Economy of materials will deceive us about the real cost, thanks to the enchanting illusion that tricks the eye by the prudent combinations of art.

We will not forget symmetry; imbibed from nature it contributes to solidity and establishes parallel relations that do not exclude the picturesque, I say further, the bizarre that it must reject.

Who can neglect taste? To which we owe so many enjoyments, or the method specific to every idea.

Taste demonstrates what is good or bad of he who exercises it. True taste is without all mannerisms; it is not, as one believes, attached to the fugitive wings of the arbitrary or founded in fantastic conventions. It is the produce of an exquisite discernment which nature has placed in its favorite minds.

Method offers infinite meanings; it teaches us to connect the simplest things with the complex; it gives us the means to draw logical consequences.

Who has not experienced the despotism of beauty? That unexpected and thoughtless sympathy that commands our admiration and forces our senses into its empire. [. . .]

Decoration is the expressive character, more or less simple, more or less compound, that we give to each edifice. It distinguishes the altars that play for eternity with the Supreme Being, from the fragile palace that transitory power sustains. It breathes life into surfaces, immortalizes them with the imprint of every sensation and passion. It modifies the irregularities of fate, humbles presumptuous opulence, and relieves timid misfortune. It blackens ignorance, promotes knowledge, and in its just apportionment it gives to nations the luster that makes them shine, while plunging into barbarity those ungrateful or careless peoples who neglect its favors. This artful coquette, supported by the sweet arts of civilization, plays every role; it is alternatively severe or facile, sad or gay, calm or carried away. Her deportment is imposing or seductive; she is jealous of everyone, and supports neither the neighbor who offends her nor the comparison that would destroy her charms. Always surrounded by desires that group themselves within her rays, she isolates herself from the world. In her methodical retreat, she accentuates her rhythms with equal movements.

91 JOHN SOANE
from Royal Academy Lectures on Architecture (V and XI; 1812–15)

What Ledoux's formal innovations represented for French architecture in the last years of the eighteenth century, John Soane's designs did for British architecture. Soane was in fact a close student of French theory. Born the son of a builder, he slowly worked his way up through the generally aristocratic nature of the British profession. After apprenticeships with George Dance and Henry Holland, he won the gold medal at the Royal Academy in 1776 and with this stipend he traveled to France and Italy. There he saw the work of Ledoux, Boullée, and Goindoin, and in Italy met Piranesi a few months before his death. In his early career, Soane mostly focused on renovations and additions to country estates as well as to publishing his designs. His fame came in 1792, when he was appointed architect to the Bank of England. There, from the existing complex of buildings in London, he carved out a series of extraordinary halls and courtyards that were much admired. Three years later, in 1795, he gained an associate membership to the Royal Academy in Britain, and seven years later was elevated to the first class, where he occupied the vacant chair of the late William Chambers. In 1806 he successfully lobbied for the professorship of architecture, for which he was required to give an annual cycle of lectures.

Soane possessed a quiet, intense, and somewhat withdrawn personality, and in his architectural tastes he combined both his liking for French theory and design with the formal exuberance that British picturesque theory allowed. He was thus a classicist but at the same time rather unclassical in his personal preferences. In his lectures he paid homage to such well-worn phrases as "good taste" and "sound judgment," but he also stressed the need for character and expression – indeed freedom – in architectural design. In this regard he was more an eclectic in his tastes than a pedagogue, and he was a firm upholder of the concept of *architecture parlante* in the French tradition. The first of these two excerpts, where he praises the "bold flights of irregular fancy" of the English baroque architect John Vanbrugh, speaks to the exuberance with which Soane himself approached design. The second excerpt succinctly encompasses his notion of character, which again owes something to French theory.

John Soane (1753–1837), from Royal Academy Lectures on Architecture (V and XI; 1812–15) in *Sir John Soane: Enlightenment Thought and the Royal Academy Lectures*, ed. David Watkin. London: Cambridge University Press, 1996, pp. 563, 648.

Contemporary with Sir Christopher Wren was Sir John Vanbrugh whose numerous and extensive works show the versatility of his talents: and, if he wanted the grace and elegance of Palladio, he possessed in an eminent degree the powers of invention.

His works are full of character, and his outlines rich and varied: and although few of his compositions show any great knowledge of classical correctness, yet the mausoleum in the park at Castle Howard executed by his pupil, and the Temple of Concord and Victory at Stowe[1] are proofs that he occasionally felt the force of the simplicity of the ancients, whilst his house at Whitehall, in spite of the alterations and additions it has undergone, shows that he had the power of making small things interesting. His great work is Blenheim. The style of this building is grand and majestically imposing, the whole composition analogous to the war-like genius of the mighty hero for whom it was erected. The great extent of this noble structure, the picturesque effect of its various parts, the infinite and pleasing variety, the breaks and contrasts in the different heights and masses, produce the most exquisite sensations in the scientific beholder, whether the view be distant, intermediate, or near.

The delightful scenery on first entering this noble park, the immense sheet of water, which so entrancingly enriches the landscape, the princely palace, the great Column, and that magnificent feature, the Bridge, taken altogether produce the very climax of excellence.

It was once, sarcastically, said that the Bridge at Blenheim designated the ambitious mind of the Duke of Marlborough, whilst the rivulet beneath (alluding to what it was originally) indicated the smallness of his liberality. Such were the observations of a peevish satirist. How unlike the noble-minded Bolingbroke who, being asked his opinion of the Duke's failings, replied, with all the feelings of a great mind that 'he was so fully impressed with the good qualities of the Hero of Blenheim that he could not recollect that he had any faults.'[2]

It is impossible to contemplate the works of Sir John Vanbrugh without feeling those emotions which the happy efforts of genius alone can produce. In his bold flights of irregular fancy, his powerful mind rises superior to common conceptions, and entitles him to the high distinctive appellation of the Shakespeare of architects. To try the works of such an artist by the strict rules of Palladian tameness would be like judging the merits and mighty darings of the immortal bard by the frigid rules of Aristotle.

★ ★ ★

So requisite did the ancients consider this attention to distinctive character to make a perfect and beautiful composition, that even in the very steps to their buildings they regarded it. Those to the temples of the early Doric order were of larger dimensions, both as to rise and tread than those which were afterwards used when the Doric order became less massive. In like manner the steps to the temples of the Ionic order were still less, and upon the same principle those of the Corinthian were lower in their rise and narrower in the tread.

Too much attention cannot be given to produce a distinct character in every building, not only in the great features but in the minor details likewise: even a moulding, however diminutive, contributes to increase or lessen the character of the assemblage of which it forms a part.

Character is so important that all its most delicate and refined modifications must be well understood and practised with all the fine feelings and nice discrimination of the artist. He who is satisfied with heaping stone upon stone, may be a useful builder, and increase his fortune. He may raise a convenient house for his employer, but such a man will never be an artist, he will not advance the interests or credit of the art, nor give it importance in public estimation. He will neither add to its powers to move the soul, or to speak to the feelings of mankind.

Notwithstanding all that has been urged to the contrary, be assured my young friends, that architecture in the hands of men of genius may be made to assume whatever character is required of it. But to attain this object, to produce this variety, it is essential that every building should be conformable to the uses it is intended for, and that it should express clearly its destination and its character, marked in the most decided and indisputable manner. The cathedral and the church; the palace of the sovereign, and the dignified prelate; the hotel of the nobleman; the hall of justice; the mansion of the chief magistrate; the house of the rich individual; the gay theatre, and the gloomy prison; nay even the warehouse and the shop, require a different style of architecture in their external appearance, and the same distinctive marks must be continued in the internal arrangements as well as in the decorations. Who that looks at the interior of St. Martin's church, and observes its sash-windows and projecting balconies at the east end, but is inclined rather to imagine himself in a private box in an Italian theatre than in a place of devotion?

Without distinctness of character, buildings may be convenient and answer the purposes for which they were raised, but they will never be pointed out as examples for imitation nor add to the splendour of the possessor, improve the national taste, or increase the national glory.

NOTES

1   The design of the Temple of Concord and Victory at Stowe is now attributed to Richard Grenville and Giambattista Borra, not to Vanbrugh.
2   This seems to be a paraphrase of a passage in Bolingbroke's essay on Marlborough in *The Craftsman*, no. 252, Saturday 1 May 1731.

PART IV   THEORIES OF THE PICTURESQUE AND THE SUBLIME

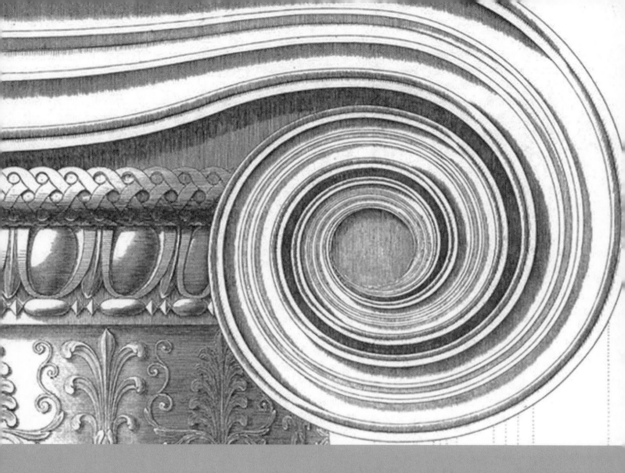

A.   SOURCES OF THE PICTURESQUE

Introduction

E ighteenth-century British architectural theory, while always taking heed of artistic developments in France, at the same takes a very different tack. To understand why and how this divergence of ideas came about, it is important to understand the different philosophical basis of Anglo-Saxon thought as well as unique circumstances affecting it, such as its novel ideas regarding garden design. If French philosophical traditions are often characterized as rationalist and deductive (a reliance on reason, conclusions deduced from preestablished premises), British philosophy is often said to be empirical or inductive. Empiricism, in its most general sense, argues that sensory or practical experience has primacy in human knowledge (over that of reflective reason). In its purest form, it opposes the notion of "innate ideas," as espoused by such earlier philosophers as Descartes, and it argues that the mind is essentially a blank slate (*tabula rasa*) at birth, one that subsequently fills out, as it were, by the recordings of the senses. The strict dependence of all mental states on sensations (and the mental "associations" they give rise to) is known as "sensationalism," yet not all empiricists are sensationalists. John Locke, for instance, emphasized the primacy of sense experience, but he also argued that the mind's reflections on its own mental operations were another source of ideas.

Empiricism, by its very premises, stands in opposition to the aesthetic norms of classicism. When Alberti argued that judgments of beauty were formed from "a reasoning faculty that is inborn in the mind," he was equating beauty with universal and innate ideas essentially of divine origin; objects are beautiful to the extent to which they mirror perfectly these preordained ideas. When Winckelmann insisted that Greek artists had attained the most perfect beauty possible, he too was establishing an idealized norm against which all subsequent artistic efforts should be measured. Empirical thought, however, essentially deprives art of any such norms. As we are born without innate ideas of beauty, we can only make judgments of beauty from the sensations of pleasure or displeasure that arise from the objects we contemplate. When we try to penetrate the cause of this pleasure or displeasure, we can only point to certain attributes or qualities associated with objects and our perception of them – often culturally ingrained. Therefore some empiricists argue that judgments of beauty are relative or lack any other standards than our own subjectivity, while others argue that the correctness of these judgments, while intrinsically subjective, is universal because people share common experiences and judgments as human beings.

We can see how these philosophical distinctions might translate into architectural theory by considering garden design. One might view a Renaissance or French classical garden and judge it beautiful, because nature is arrayed in a mathematical order and displays such attributes as symmetry, regularity, and hierarchy of forms. These attributes are aesthetic premises that the gardener brings to the design in the desire to create something beautiful. Someone else, however, might come upon a natural stream or wooded glen and judge it beautiful precisely because it lacks such attributes. Here the judgment is made intuitively on the scene or "picture" one sees, and not on the presence of preconceived mathematical rules. The development of the so-called English garden exploited nature in the latter sense, and as we shall see this innovation in garden design also carries with it major aesthetic implications.

92 JOHN LOCKE
from *An Essay Concerning Human Understanding* (1690)

Although several earlier thinkers – such as William Ockham (c.1285–1347), Francis Bacon (1561–1626), and Thomas Hobbes (1588–1679) – developed models of empirical thought, John Locke was the first modern philosopher to raise it into a coherent and logical system. A friend of Robert Boyle and Isaac Newton, Locke originally studied scholastic philosophy at Oxford in the 1650s, but chose medicine and science as a profession. He became an avid defender of civil and religious freedom, and this interest attracted him in 1666 to the politician Lord Anthony Ashley Cooper, later the first Earl of Shaftesbury. The next year Locke moved into the lord's household as both his physician and personal secretary; he tutored Ashley's children, among them the third Earl of Shaftesbury. Locke's political sympathies proved dangerous, however. When the first Earl of Shaftesbury fell from power in 1675, Locke was forced to join him in exile in Paris. And although Locke returned with Ashley to London

John Locke (1632–1704), from *An Essay Concerning Human Understanding* (1690), ed. Alexander Campbell Fraser. New York: Dover, 1959, Vol I: pp. 37–8, 121–4.

four years later, another charge of insurrection in 1682 led both men once again into political exile, this time to the Netherlands. It was here in Holland (as with Descartes earlier) that Locke wrote the first draft of *An Essay Concerning Human Understanding*, which he published shortly after his return to England in 1689. The two passages below, taken from the beginning of Books 1 and 2, outline his system. Book 1 opens with his rejection of innate ideas, which Locke follows by arguing that all ideas (knowledge) come from sensation (the senses) and reflection (mental operations). The remainder of the two books, as well as Books 3 and 4, develop in great detail the arguments for and implications of such a model.

No Innate Speculative Principles

1. It is an established opinion amongst some men,[1] that there are in the understanding certain *innate principles*; some primary notions, κοιναὶ ἔννοιαι, characters, as it were stamped upon the mind of man; which the soul receives in its very first being, and brings into the world with it.[2] It would be sufficient to convince unprejudiced readers of the falseness of this supposition, if I should only show (as I hope I shall in the following parts of this Discourse) how men, barely by the use of their natural faculties,[3] may attain to all the knowledge they have, without the help of any innate impressions; and may arrive at certainty, without any such original notions or principles. For I imagine any one will easily grant that it would be impertinent to suppose the ideas of colours innate in a creature to whom God hath given sight, and a power to receive them by the eyes from external objects: and no less unreasonable would it be to attribute several truths to the impressions of nature, and innate characters, when we may observe in ourselves faculties fit to attain as easy and certain knowledge of them as if they were originally imprinted on the mind. [. . .] the constant impressions[4] which the souls of men receive in their first beings, and which they bring into the world with them, as necessarily and really as they do any of their inherent faculties.

3. This argument, drawn from universal consent, has this misfortune in it, that if it were true in matter of fact, that there were certain truths wherein all mankind agreed, it would not prove them innate, if there can be any other way shown how men may come to that universal agreement, in the things they do consent in, which I presume may be done.[5]

4. But, which is worse, this argument of universal consent, which is made use of to prove innate principles, seems to me a demonstration that there are none such: because there are none to which all mankind give an universal assent. I shall begin with the speculative, and instance in those magnified principles of demonstration, 'Whatsoever is, is,' and 'It is impossible for the same thing to be and not to be'; which, of all others, I think have the most allowed title to innate.

★ ★ ★

Of Ideas in General, and their Original

1. Every man being conscious to himself that he thinks; and that which his mind is applied about whilst thinking being the *ideas* that are there,[6] it is past doubt that men have in

their minds several ideas, – such as are those expressed by the words *whiteness, hardness, sweetness, thinking, motion, man, elephant, army, drunkenness*, and others: it is in the first place then to be inquired, *How he comes by them?*

I know it is a received doctrine, that men have native ideas, and original characters, stamped upon their minds in their very first being. This opinion I have at large examined already; and, I suppose what I have said in the foregoing Book will be much more easily admitted, when I have shown whence the understanding may get all the ideas it has; and by what ways and degrees they may come into the mind; – for which I shall appeal to every one's own observation and experience.

2. Let us then suppose the mind to be, as we say, white paper,[7] void of all characters, without any ideas: – How comes it to be furnished? Whence comes it by that vast store which the busy and boundless fancy of man has painted on it with an almost endless variety? Whence has it all the *materials* of reason and knowledge?[8] To this I answer, in one word, from EXPERIENCE.[9] In that all our knowledge is founded; and from that it ultimately derives itself. Our observation employed either, about external sensible objects, or about the internal operations of our minds perceived and reflected on by ourselves, is that which supplies our understandings with all the *materials* of thinking.[10] These two are the fountains[11] of knowledge, from whence all the ideas we have, or can naturally have, do spring.

3. First, our Senses, conversant about particular sensible objects, do convey into the mind several distinct perceptions[12] of things, according to those various ways wherein those objects do affect them. And thus we come by those *ideas* we have of *yellow, white, heat, cold, soft, hard, bitter, sweet*, and all those which we call sensible qualities; which when I say the senses convey into the mind, I mean, they from external[13] objects convey into the mind what produces there those perceptions. This great source of most of the ideas we have, depending wholly upon our senses, and derived by them to the understanding, I call SENSATION.[14]

4. Secondly, the other fountain from which experience furnisheth the understanding with ideas is, – the perception of the operations of our own mind within us, as it is employed about the ideas it has got; – which operations, when the soul comes to reflect on and consider, do furnish the understanding with another set of ideas, which could not be had from things without. And such are *perception, thinking, doubting, believing, reasoning, knowing, willing*, and all the different actings of our own minds; – which we being conscious of, and observing in ourselves, do from these receive into our understandings as distinct ideas as we do from bodies affecting our senses. This source[15] of ideas every man has wholly in himself; and though it be not sense, as having nothing to do with external objects, yet it is very like it, and might properly enough be called *internal sense*.[16] But as I call the other Sensation, so I call this REFLECTION, the ideas it affords being such only as the mind gets by reflecting on its own operations within itself. By reflection then, in the following part of this discourse, I would be understood to mean, that notice which the mind takes of its own operations, and the manner of them, by reason whereof there come to be ideas of these operations in the understanding.[17] These two, I say, viz. external material things, as the objects of SENSATION, and the operations of our own minds within, as the objects of REFLECTION, are to me the only originals from whence all our ideas take their beginnings. The term *operations* here I use in a large sense, as comprehending not barely the actions of the mind about its ideas, but some

sort of passions arising sometimes from them, such as is the satisfaction or uneasiness arising from any thought.

NOTES

1   Locke does not name the 'men' of 'innate principles' whose 'opinion' he proceeds to criticise; nor does he quote their words in evidence of what *they* intended by the opinion. He says (ch. ii. § 15) that after he had argued out objections to the 'established opinion,' his attention was directed to the arguments in its defence in the *De Veritate* of Lord Herbert, which thereupon he proceeds to controvert. From the first, Descartes, with whose writings he was early familiar, was probably in his view. According to Descartes there are three sources of ideas: 'Entre ces idées, *les unes semblent être nées avec moi*; les autres être étrangères et venir de dehors; et les autres être faites et inventées par moi-même.' (*Méd*. iii. 7.) But even the 'idées nées avec moi' of Descartes were not regarded by him as in consciousness until 'experience' had evoked them from latency – a position which Locke's argument always fails to reach. Though Locke nowhere names More, Hale, or Cudworth, he might have found expressions of theirs which, on a superficial view, appear to countenance the *sort* of innateness which he attributes to the 'established opinion.' See Hume's *Inquiry concerning Human Understanding*, in Note A, on 'innate ideas,' and Locke's 'loose sense of the word idea.'

2   The impossibility of resolving the intellectual necessities, which govern and constitute knowledge and existence, into transitory data of sense; or of explaining, by means of nature and its evolutions, the spiritual elements in human experience, which connect man with the supernatural, the infinite, the divine – has suggested that those elements, presupposed by experience, must have been *innate*, or born with the mind; thus potentially belonging to it, antecedently to all acquired knowledge. This hypothesis has found expression in many forms; and it has waxed or waned, as the spiritual or the sensuous was most developed in the consciousness of the philosopher or of the age. Locke assails it in its crudest form, in which it is countenanced by no eminent advocate; according to which the ideas and principles which ultimately constitute knowledge are supposed to be held *consciously*, from birth, or even before it, in every human mind, being thus 'stamped' on us from the beginning, and 'brought into the world' with us. It is easy to refute this; for it can be shown that there are no principles of which all men are aware as soon as they are born, or even in which all mankind are agreed when they are adult. That data of experience are needed, to awaken what must otherwise be the slumbering potentialities of man's spiritual being; and that human knowledge is the issue of sense when sense is combined with latent intellect, is an interpretation of the 'established opinion,' which Locke does not fairly contemplate.

3   Locke recognises the *innateness* of 'faculties' in calling them 'natural'; but without examining whether any, and if so what, ideas and judgments are (consciously or unconsciously) presupposed in a rational exercise of the innate faculties.

4   'Constant impressions,' i. e. of which there is a conscious impression in all human beings from birth, and about which all, even infants and idiots, are agreed.

5   Conscious consent on the part of every human being cannot be alleged on behalf of any abstract principle, as Locke is easily able to show. There is no proposition which some one has not been found to deny. A better criterion of the supernatural or divine, in man and in the universe, than this of 'universal consent,' which Locke makes so much of, is found, when it is shown, – that the full and adequate exercise of our faculties in experience necessarily presupposes principles of which the mass of mankind may be only dimly conscious, or wholly unconscious. Locke ignores the main issue; and when he explains his meaning is found nearer than he supposes to those who hold the innateness of reason in experience. He acknowledges innateness of faculty. Also that knowledge

involves and is based upon what is self-evident is a prominent lesson of the Fourth Book. 'That there can be any knowledge without self-evident propositions,' he assures Stillingfleet that he is so far from denying, 'that I am accused by your lordship for requiring more such in demonstration than you think necessary' (*Third Letter*, p. 264). 'I contend for the usefulness and necessity of self-evident propositions in all certainty, whether of intuition or demonstration' (p. 286). 'I make self-evident propositions necessary to certainty, and found all knowledge or certainty in them' (p. 340).

6 Cf. Introd. § 8. It must be remembered that 'ideas,' as treated of in the Second Book, are not regarded as *cognitions* (the subject reserved for the Fourth Book), but as phenomena considered in abstraction from affirmation and denial, truth and falsehood, as simple apprehensions in short. And he here asks, in the 'historical plain method,' under what conditions the phenomena of real existence begin to appear, and gradually multiply, in new combinations, in a human understanding?

7 'White paper' might suggest that we are originally void of ideas or appearances of which there is *consciousness*; but not necessarily void of *latent capacities* and *their intellectual implicates*. He means by the metaphor that we are all born ignorant of every thing.

8 Assuming, then, that the human mind is at first ignorant of everything, – what, he asks, is the explanation of the state in which adult human understanding may now be found, with its often rich stores of varied and elaborated ideas?

9 'Experience.' The ambiguity of this term is a main source of the controversies which the *Essay* has occasioned. Locke did not see that *innateness* (in a different meaning) and *experience* are not contradictories, but are really two different ways of regarding the possessions of the understanding. 'Our attitude towards the philosophy of Experience must entirely depend upon the meaning we put into the term experience. . . . The point on which issue should be joined is, – the identification of Experience with *mere* sense. If we prove that this is not so, and that, on the contrary, mere sense is an abstraction, impossible *in rerum natura*, Experientialism is at once shorn of all its supposed terrors.' (Seth, *Scottish Philosophy*, pp. 142, 3.) What Locke argues for is, that, *in respect of the time of its manifestation in the conscious life of each man*, no knowledge that he possesses can *precede* awakening of intellectual life into (at first dim and imperfect) exercise through impressions on the senses. He thus makes our adult understanding of things the issue of the exercise of the faculties in 'experience'; but he does not get in sight of Kant's question, or try to disengage the elements of reason through which a *scientific* or *intelligible* experience is itself possible, – the problem of the next great critique of a human understanding of the universe.

10 But the '*materials* of thinking' presuppose, for their conversion into scientific experience, *intellectual conditions*, which conditions Locke either leaves in the background, or mixes up with the 'materials,' i. e. with those gradually accumulated data without which our notions would be empty, and our common terms meaningless.

11 The *exordium* of knowledge, back to which the *contents* of all our concepts may be traced, and apart from which they would be empty; not its *origo*, or the elements in the intellectual products that are found, after critical analysis of its logical constitution. Locke means by 'origin,' 'exordium,' which alone has relation to his 'historical' method. The acquired contents of our real knowledge, he goes on to show, must be either ideas of the qualities of matter, or ideas of the operations of mind.

12 Here *perception* is virtually equivalent to *idea* – but regarded from the point of view of the apprehensive act, not of the phenomena apprehended. For the three cognate meanings of 'perception' in the *Essay*, see ch. xxi. § 5, the second and third of these being those only which 'use allows us' to attribute to the 'understanding.' In its third meaning 'perception' plays a great part in the Fourth Book.

13 'External objects,' i. e. extra-organic objects.

14 This is one of Locke's definitions of *sensation*, which he here treats as incapable of analysis – passive impression of extra-organic phenomena upon the organism. Cf. § 23; also ch. xix. § I.

15 These metaphorical terms, 'source,' 'fountain,' 'channel,' which he employs here and elsewhere, are ambiguous. Is their equivalent *exordium* or *origo*? The former alone is properly within the scope of the 'historical plain method' of psychology: the critical analysis which finds intellectual necessities presupposed in the operations of mind belongs to metaphysical philosophy, to which Locke's historical method is inadequate, if 'reflection' is limited to *contingent ideas* of 'internal sense.'

16 That Locke applies the term *sense* to 'perception of the operations of our own mind,' seems to confine 'reflection' to empirical apprehension of mental states. But his use of this term is not conclusive on the point. Reid and Hamilton, along with many other philosophers, call the *a priori* or Common Reason a sense – the 'Common Sense.'

17 Whether *reflection* should be interpreted in the *Essay* empirically or intellectually, is a primary question for the interpreter, since on the answer depends whether it includes *reflex consciousness of reason proper*, with the judgments therein necessarily presupposed as conditions of our having more in experience than the momentary data. The alternative was not contemplated by Locke.

93 WILLIAM TEMPLE
from "Upon the Gardens of Epicurus; or, of Gardening, in the Year 1685" (1692)

I deas of far-reaching consequence are not always presented in formal and well-reasoned treatises. Diaries, personal correspondence, and travel accounts on occasions not only provide novel speculations but they also often summarize succinctly aesthetic proclivities of the age. This small essay by William Temple, written in 1685 during a period of great colonial expansion, is a case in point. Temple, a close friend of Jonathan Swift, built a successful career as a diplomat under Charles II, but in 1681 he quit his missions for the king and retired to his country estate in Surrey to devote himself to letters. Here he also focused much of his attention on his garden, which he ponders both from the point of view of his worldly travels and the gardens of antiquity. What is of great importance to his deliberations, however, is his flirtation with non-Western aesthetic values: in this case, with the aesthetics of the Chinese garden. Much of this essay will prove to be of little consequence, but this particular passage, following his discussion of Moor Park, will reverberate throughout the eighteenth century and help give rise to a "picturesque" aesthetics. To put the essay into perspective, the reader should also note that it was written during the period in which the quintessential formal garden of Versailles was being planned and executed.

This was Moor Park when I was acquainted with it, and the sweetest place, I think, that I have seen in my life, either before or since, at home or abroad; what it is now I can give little account, having passed through several hands that have made great changes in gardens as

William Temple (1628–99), from "Upon the Gardens of Epicurus; or, of Gardening in the Year 1685" (1692), in *Five Miscellaneous Essays by Sir William Temple*, ed. Samuel Holt Monk. Ann Arbor: University of Michigan Press, 1963, pp. 29–30.

well as houses; but the remembrance of what it was is too pleasant ever to forget, and therefore I do not believe to have mistaken the figure of it, which may serve for a pattern to the best gardens of our manner, and that are most proper for our country and climate.

What I have said of the best forms of gardens is meant only of such as are in some sort regular; for there may be other forms wholly irregular, that may, for aught I know, have more beauty than any of the others; but they must owe it to some extraordinary dispositions of nature in the seat, or some great race of fancy or judgment in the contrivance, which may reduce many disagreeing parts into some figure, which shall yet upon the whole be very agreeable. Something of this I have seen in some places, but heard more of it from others who have lived much among the Chineses; a people whose way of thinking seems to lie as wide of ours in Europe, as their country does. Among us, the beauty of building and planting is placed chiefly in some certain proportions, symmetries, or uniformities; our walks and our trees ranged so as to answer one another, and at exact distances. The Chineses scorn this way of planting, and say a boy that can tell an hundred may plant walks of trees in straight lines, and over against one another, and to what length and extent he pleases. But their greatest reach of imagination is employed in contriving figures, where the beauty shall be great, and strike the eye, but without any order or disposition of parts that shall be commonly or easily observed: and though we have hardly any notion of this sort of beauty, yet they have a particular word to express it, and where they find it hit their eye at first sight, they say the *sharawadgi* is fine or is admirable, or any such expression of esteem. And whoever observes the work upon the best India gowns, or the painting upon their best screens or porcelains, will find their beauty is all of this kind (that is) without order. But I should hardly advise any of these attempts in the figure of gardens among us; they are adventures of too hard achievement for any common hands; and though there may be more honour if they succeed well, yet there is more dishonour if they fail, and it is twenty to one they will; whereas in regular figures it is hard to make any great and remarkable faults.

94 JOHN VANBRUGH
from Letter to the Duchess of Marlborough (1709)

The predominant architectural direction of the first half of the eighteenth century in Britain, as we have seen, was the neo-Palladian movement that attempted to resurrect the aesthetics of absolute beauty as defined by Renaissance classicism. Alongside this development, however, were baroque sensibilities of the seventeenth century that had not fully subsided, and that found a natural outlet in what can only be described as an early phase of stylistic eclecticism. The various stylistic works of the architects Nicholas Hawksmoor (1661–1736) and John

John Vanbrugh (1664–1726), Letter to the Duchess of Marlborough (June 11, 1709) in *The Complete Works of Sir John Vanbrugh*, Vol. 4, ed. Geoffrey Webb. London: The Nonesuch Press, 1928, pp. 29–30.

Vanbrugh illustrate these tendencies. Both have ties back to the classical and baroque architecture of Christopher Wren, and both collaborate at the start of the century on two of Britain's late-baroque masterpieces, Castle Howard (1699–1712) and Blenheim Palace (1705–25). But even the stylistic freedom of this formal vocabulary did not satisfy the expressive yearnings of the two men. Hawksmoor was perhaps at his scenographic best as an architect with his design for All Souls College, Oxford (1718–25), which combined classical interiors with the exterior Gothic forms of a pinnacled roofline with bold romantic towers. Vanbrugh, also a playwright by profession, celebrated his succession to Wren as Surveyor to Greenwich Hospital in 1716 by constructing nearby his medieval "Vanbrugh Castle," replete with a crenellated gateway and a false "Nunnery."

While overseeing the construction of Blenheim Palace in 1709, Vanbrugh was also engaged in making changes to the grounds – a large, partially wooded estate outside of Oxford. The Duchess instructed him to remove the ruins of the "Old Manour" and chapel existing on the site. Vanbrugh responded with this letter, in which he argued for the preservation of these ruins for their historical "Affections," but also for the "Variety" that they provide the landscape, when mixed "Promiscuously" with untamed nature. Here is another early manifestation of a picturesque aesthetic, in this case a sensibility relying not on classical rules but on ideas or impressions "that the best of Landskip Painters can invent." Note the response by someone on the Duchess's staff.

June 11th.—1709

There is perhaps no one thing, which the most Polite part of Mankind have more universally agreed in; than the Value they have ever set upon the Remains of distant Times Nor amongst the Severall kinds of those Antiquitys, are there any so much regarded, as those of Buildings; Some for their Magnificence, or Curious Workmanship; And others; as they move more lively and pleasing Reflections (than History without their Aid can do) On the Persons who have Inhabited them; On the Remarkable things which have been transacted in them, Or the extraordinary Occasions of Erecting them. *As I believe it cannot be doubted, but if Travellers many Ages hence, shall be shewn The Very House in which so great a Man Dwelt, as they will then read the Duke of Marlborough in Story; And that they Shall be told, it was not only his Favourite Habitation, but was Erected for him by the Bounty of the Queen And with the Approbation of the People, As a Monument of the Greatest Services and Honours, that any Subject had ever done his Country: I believe, tho' they may not find Art enough in the* Builder, to make them *Admire the Beauty of the Fabrick* they will find Wonder enough in the Story, to make 'em pleas'd with the Sight of it.

I hope I may be forgiven, if I make some faint Application of what I say of Blenheim, to the Small Remains of ancient Woodstock Manour.

It can't indeed be said, it was Erected on so Noble nor on So justifiable an Occasion, But it was rais'd by One of the Bravest and most Warlike of the English Kings; And tho' it has not been Fam'd, as a Monument of his Arms, *it has been tenderly regarded* as the Scene of his Affections. Nor amongst the *Multitude of People who come daily to View what is raising to the Memory of the Great Battle of Blenheim; Are there any that do not run eagerly to See* what Ancient Remains are to be found. of Rosamonds Bower. *It may perhaps be worth some Little Reflection Upon what may be said, if the Very footsteps of it Are no more to be found.*

But if the Historicall Argument Stands in need of Assistance; there is Still much to be said on Other Considerations.

That Part of the Park which is Seen from the North Front of the New Building, has Little Variety of Objects Nor dos the Country beyond it Afford any of Vallue, It therefore Stands in Need of all the helps that can be given, which are only Five; Buildings, And Plantations

These rightly dispos'd will indeed Supply all the wants of Nature in that Place. And the Most Agreable Disposition is to Mix them: in which this Old Manour *gives so happy an Occasion* for; that were the inclosure filld with Trees (principally Fine Yews and Hollys) Promiscuously Set to grow up in a Wild Thicket. So that all the Building left, (which is only the Habitable Part and the Chappel) might Appear in Two Risings amongst 'em, it wou'd make One of the Most Agreable Objects that the best of Landskip Painters can invent. And if on the Contrary this Building is taken away; there then remains nothing but an Irregular, Ragged Ungovernable Hill, the deformitys of which are not to be cured *but by a Vast Expence; And that at last will only remove an Ill Object* but not produce a good One, whereas to finish the present Wall for the Inclosures, to forme the Sloops and make the Plantation (which is all that is now wanting to Compleat the Whole Designe) wou'd not Cost Two Hundred pounds.

I take the Liberty to offer this Paper with a Picture to Explain what I endeavour to Describe, That if the Present Direction for destroying the Building, shou'd happen hereafter to be Repented of, I may not be blam'd for Neglecting to set in the truest Light I cou'd, a Thing that Seem'd at least to me so very Matteriall,

J VANBRUGH

[*Endorsed by Duchess of M., tho' not in her hand.*]

This paper has something ridiculous in it to preserve the house for himself, ordered to be pulled down; but I think there is something material in it concerning the occasion of building Blenheim.

95 ANTHONY ASHLEY COOPER
Third Earl of Shaftesbury, from ''The Moralists'' (1709)

The concurrence of classical ideals with the early development of picturesque aesthetics is perhaps no better demonstrated than in the opinions of the third Earl of Shaftesbury. In part II (chapter 42) we saw his ''Letter Concerning Design,'' in which he both castigated the ''Gothic'' works of Wren and Vanbrugh and called for the founding of a national academy of architecture and art – presumably to be based on classical principles of design. Yet in his Platonic dialogue ''The Moralists,'' written a few years earlier, Shaftesbury voiced a very different side of his thought: his love for wild nature untamed by the straight rule of the human hand. This philosophical homily, revised and published in 1709, recounts a number of discussions relating to Shaftesbury's theistic vision of ethical and aesthetic harmony. His preference for unkempt nature over the ''formal mockery of princely gardens'' would become widely quoted over the next several decades, in fact become etched into British eighteenth-century consciousness.

Anthony Ashley Cooper, Third Earl of Shaftesbury, from ''The Moralists'' (1709) in *Characteristics of Men, Manners, Opinions, Times, etc.,* (orig. 1711), ed. John M. Robertson. New York: E. P. Dutton & Co., 1900, Vol. II: pp. 124–5.

Methinks, said he, Philocles (changing to a familiar voice), we had better leave these unsociable places whither our fancy has transported us, and return to ourselves here again in our more conversable woods and temperate climates. Here no fierce heats nor colds annoy us, no precipices nor cataracts amaze us. Nor need we here be afraid of our own voices whilst we hear the notes of such a cheerful choir, and find the echoes rather agreeable and inviting us to talk.

I confess, said I, those foreign nymphs (if there were any belonging to those miraculous woods) were much too awful beauties to please me. I found our familiar home-nymphs a great deal more to my humour. Yet for all this, I cannot help being concerned for your breaking off just when we were got half the world over, and wanted only to take America in our way home. Indeed, as for Europe, I could excuse your making any great tour there, because of the little variety it would afford us. Besides that, it would be hard to see it in any view without meeting still that politic face of affairs which would too much disturb us in our philosophical flights. But for the western tract, I cannot imagine why you should neglect such noble subjects as are there, unless perhaps the gold and silver, to which I find you such a bitter enemy, frighted you from a mother-soil so full of it. If these countries had been as bare of those metals as old Sparta, we might have heard more perhaps of the Perus and Mexicos than of all Asia and Africa. We might have had creatures, plants, woods, mountains, rivers, beyond any of those we have passed. How sorry am I to lose the noble Amazon! How sorry —

Here, as I would have proceeded, I saw so significant a smile on Theocles's face that it stopped me, out of curiosity, to ask him his thought.

Nothing, said he; nothing but this very subject itself. Go on – I see you'll finish it for me. The spirit of this sort of prophecy has seized you. And Philocles, the cold indifferent Philocles, is become a pursuer of the same mysterious beauty.

'Tis true, said I, Theocles, I own it. Your genius, the genius of the place, and the Great Genius have at last prevailed. I shall no longer resist the passion growing in me for things of a natural kind, where neither art nor the conceit or caprice of man has spoiled their genuine order by breaking in upon that primitive state. Even the rude rocks, the mossy caverns, the irregular unwrought grottos and broken falls of waters, with all the horrid graces of the wilderness itself, as representing Nature more, will be the more engaging, and appear with a magnificence beyond the formal mockery of princely gardens. . . . But tell me, I entreat you, how comes it that, excepting a few philosophers of your sort, the only people who are enamoured in this way, and seek the woods, the rivers, or seashores, are your poor vulgar lovers?

Say not this, replied he, of lovers only. For is it not the same with poets, and all those other students in nature and the arts which copy after her? In short, is not this the real case of all who are lovers either of the Muses or the Graces?

96 JOSEPH ADDISON
from *The Spectator* (1712)

Close to the circle of Shaftesbury was the gifted essayist and poet Joseph Addison. Like Shaftesbury, Addison devoted much of his life to politics and political writings, but beginning in 1709 he became active with his friend and former classmate, Richard Steele, in founding the semipolitical journal *Tatler*. When this enterprise folded in 1711, Addison and Steele combined to start the daily journal *The Spectator*, which ran only from March 1711 to December 1712. Despites the brevity of its run, it was a highly successful literary paper that fulfilled its pledge to bring "Philosophy out of Closets and Libraries, Schools and Colleges, to dwell in Clubs and Assemblies, at Tea-tables, and in Coffee-houses" (*Spectator* no. 10). In the summer of 1712, Addison prepared a series of 11 essays entitled "Pleasures of the Imagination," which summarized his aesthetic views regarding the various arts and nature. Much of what we have previously seen in parcel is here consolidated in these highly influential essays: Lockean empiricism applied to aesthetics, Shaftesbury's fondness for untamed nature, but also much more. In his essay of June 23, for instance, he makes the important distinction between "Greatness, Novelty, or Beauty," the first term of which would later be conceptualized under the notion of the "sublime." In his following essay of June 25, he follows William Temple in discussing Chinese garden design, which serves as a veritable manifesto for developing the idea of the picturesque garden. Addison was, above all, a master of English prose.

Saturday, June 21, 1712.

Avia Pieridum peragro loca, nullius ante
Trita solo; juvat integros accedere fonteis;
Atque haurire: —*Lucr.*

Our Sight is the most perfect and most delightful of all our Senses. It fills the Mind with the largest Variety of Ideas, converses with its Objects at the greatest Distance, and continues the longest in Action without being tired or satiated with its proper Enjoyments. The Sense of Feeling can indeed give us a Notion of Extension, Shape, and all other Ideas that enter at the Eye, except Colours; but at the same time it is very much streightned and confined in its Operations, to the number, bulk, and distance of its particular Objects. Our Sight seems designed to supply all these Defects, and may be considered as a more delicate and diffusive kind of Touch, that spreads it self over an infinite Multitude of Bodies, comprehends the largest Figures, and brings into our reach some of the most remote Parts of the Universe.

It is this Sense which furnishes the Imagination with its Ideas; so that by the Pleasures of the Imagination or Fancy (which I shall use promiscuously) I here mean such as arise from visible Objects, either when we have them actually in our View, or when we call up their Ideas in our Minds by Paintings, Statues, Descriptions, or any the like Occasion. We cannot indeed have a single Image in the Fancy that did not make its first Entrance through the Sight; but we have the Power of retaining, altering and compounding those Images, which we have once received, into all the varieties of Picture and Vision that are most agreeable to

Joseph Addison (1672–1719), from *The Spectator* (1712), reprinted in *The Spectator*. London: George Routledge & Sons, 1868, pp. 593–5 and 597–8.

the Imagination; for by this Faculty a Man in a Dungeon is capable of entertaining himself with Scenes and Landskips more beautiful than any that can be found in the whole Compass of Nature.

There are few Words in the *English* Language which are employed in a more loose and uncircumscribed Sense than those of the *Fancy* and the *Imagination*. I therefore thought it necessary to fix and determine the Notion of these two Words, as I intend to make use of them in the Thread of my following Speculations, that the Reader may conceive rightly what is the Subject which I proceed upon. I must therefore desire him to remember, that by the Pleasures of the Imagination, I mean only such Pleasures as arise originally from Sight, and that I divide these Pleasures into two Kinds: My Design being first of all to Discourse of those Primary Pleasures of the Imagination, which entirely proceed from such Objects as are [before our] Eye[s]; and in the next place to speak of those Secondary Pleasures of the Imagination which flow from the Ideas of visible Objects, when the Objects are not actually before the Eye, but are called up into our Memories, or formed into agreeable Visions of Things that are either Absent or Fictitious.

The Pleasures of the Imagination, taken in the full Extent, are not so gross as those of Sense, nor so refined as those of the Understanding. The last are, indeed, more preferable, because they are founded on some new Knowledge or Improvement in the Mind of Man; yet it must be confest, that those of the Imagination are as great and as transporting as the other. A beautiful Prospect delights the Soul, as much as a Demonstration; and a Description in *Homer* has charmed more Readers than a Chapter in *Aristotle*. Besides, the Pleasures of the Imagination have this Advantage, above those of the Understanding, that they are more obvious, and more easie to be acquired. It is but opening the Eye, and the Scene enters. The Colours paint themselves on the Fancy, with very little Attention of Thought or Application of Mind in the Beholder. We are struck, we know not how, with the Symmetry of any thing we see, and immediately assent to the Beauty of an Object, without enquiring into the particular Causes and Occasions of it.

A Man of a Polite Imagination is let into a great many Pleasures, that the Vulgar are not capable of receiving. He can converse with a Picture, and find an agreeable Companion in a Statue. He meets with a secret Refreshment in a Description, and often feels a greater Satisfaction in the Prospect of Fields and Meadows, than another does in the Possession. It gives him, indeed, a kind of Property in every thing he sees, and makes the most rude uncultivated Parts of Nature administer to his Pleasures: So that he looks upon the World, as it were in another Light, and discovers in it a Multitude of Charms, that conceal themselves from the generality of Mankind.

There are, indeed, but very few who know how to be idle and innocent, or have a Relish of any Pleasures that are not Criminal: every Diversion they take is at the Expence of some one Virtue or another, and their very first Step out of Business is into Vice or Folly. A Man should endeavour, therefore, to make the Sphere of his innocent Pleasures as wide as possible, that he may retire into them with Safety, and find in them such a Satisfaction as a wise Man would not blush to take. Of this Nature are those of the Imagination, which do not require such a Bent of Thought as is necessary to our more serious Employments, nor, at the same time, suffer the Mind to sink into that Negligence and Remissness, which are apt to accompany our more sensual Delights, but, like a gentle Exercise to the Faculties, awaken them from Sloth and Idleness, without putting them upon any Labour or Difficulty.

We might here add, that the Pleasures of the Fancy are more conducive to Health, than those of the Understanding, which are worked out by Dint of Thinking, and attended with too violent a Labour of the Brain. Delightful Scenes, whether in Nature, Painting, or Poetry, have a kindly Influence on the Body, as well as the Mind, and not only serve to clear and brighten the Imagination, but are able to disperse Grief and Melancholy, and to set the Animal Spirits in pleasing and agreeable Motions. For this Reason Sir *Francis Bacon*, in his Essay upon Health, has not thought it improper to prescribe to his Reader a Poem or a Prospect, where he particularly dissuades him from knotty and subtile Disquisitions, and advises him to pursue Studies that fill the Mind with splendid and illustrious Objects, as Histories, Fables, and Contemplations of Nature.

I have in this Paper, by way of Introduction, settled the Notion of those Pleasures of the Imagination which are the Subject of my present Undertaking, and endeavoured, by several Considerations, to recommend to my Reader the Pursuit of those Pleasures. I shall, in my next Paper, examine the several Sources from whence these Pleasures are derived.

Monday, June 23, 1712.

Divisum sic breve fiet Opus. —Mart.

I shall first consider those Pleasures of the Imagination, which arise from the actual View and Survey of outward Objects: And these, I think, all proceed from the Sight of what is *Great, Uncommon*, or *Beautiful*. There may, indeed, be something so terrible or offensive, that the Horror or Loathsomeness of an Object may over-bear the Pleasure which results from its *Greatness, Novelty*, or *Beauty*; but still there will be such a Mixture of Delight in the very Disgust it gives us, as any of these three Qualifications are most conspicuous and prevailing.

By *Greatness*, I do not only mean the Bulk of any single Object, but the Largeness of a whole View, considered as one entire Piece. Such are the Prospects of an open Champain Country, a vast uncultivated Desart, of huge Heaps of Mountains, high Rocks and Precipices, or a wide Expanse of Waters, where we are not struck with the Novelty or Beauty of the Sight, but with that rude kind of Magnificence which appears in many of these stupendous Works of Nature. Our Imagination loves to be filled with an Object, or to grasp at any thing that is too big for its Capacity. We are flung into a pleasing Astonishment at such unbounded Views, and feel a delightful Stillness and Amazement in the Soul at the Apprehension[s] of them. The Mind of Man naturally hates every thing that looks like a Restraint upon it, and is apt to fancy it self under a sort of Confinement, when the Sight is pent up in a narrow Compass, and shortned on every side by the Neighbourhood of Walls or Mountains. On the contrary, a spacious Horizon is an Image of Liberty, where the Eye has Room to range abroad, to expatiate at large on the Immensity of its Views, and to lose it self amidst the Variety of Objects that offer themselves to its Observation. Such wide and undetermined Prospects are as pleasing to the Fancy, as the Speculations of Eternity or Infinitude are to the Understanding. But if there be a Beauty or Uncommonness joined with this Grandeur, as in a troubled Ocean, a Heaven adorned with Stars and Meteors, or a spacious Landskip cut out into Rivers, Woods, Rocks, and Meadows, the Pleasure still grows upon us, as it rises from more than a single Principle.

Every thing that is *new* or *uncommon* raises a Pleasure in the Imagination, because it fills. the Soul with an agreeable Surprize, gratifies its Curiosity, and gives it an Idea of which it was not before possest. We are indeed so often conversant with one Set of Objects, and tired out with so many repeated Shows of the same Things, that whatever is *new* or *uncommon* contributes a little to vary human Life, and to divert our Minds, for a while, with the Strangeness of its Appearance: It serves us for a kind of Refreshment, and takes off from that Satiety we are apt to complain of in our usual and ordinary Entertainments. It is this that bestows Charms on a Monster, and makes even the Imperfections of Nature [please] us. It is this that recommends Variety, where the Mind is every Instant called off to something new, and the Attention not suffered to dwell too long, and waste it self on any particular Object. It is this, likewise, that improves what is great or beautiful, and makes it afford the Mind a double Entertainment. Groves, Fields, and Meadows, are at any Season of the Year pleasant to look upon, but never so much as in the Opening of the Spring, when they are all new and fresh, with their first Gloss upon them, and not yet too much accustomed and familiar to the Eye. For this Reason there is nothing that more enlivens a Prospect than Rivers, Jetteaus, or Falls of Water, where the Scene is perpetually shifting, and entertaining the Sight every Moment with something that is new. We are quickly tired with looking upon Hills and Vallies, where every thing continues fixed and settled in the same Place and Posture, but find our Thoughts a little agitated and relieved at the Sight of such Objects as are ever in Motion, and sliding away from beneath the Eye of the Beholder.

But there is nothing that makes its Way more directly to the Soul than *Beauty,* which immediately diffuses a secret Satisfaction and Complacency through the Imagination, and gives a Finishing to any thing that is Great or Uncommon. The very first Discovery of it strikes the Mind with an inward Joy, and spreads a Chearfulness and Delight through all its Faculties. There is not perhaps any real Beauty or Deformity more in one Piece of Matter than another, because we might have been so made, that whatsoever now appears loathsome to us, might have shewn it self agreeable; but we find by Experience, that there are several Modifications of Matter which the Mind, without any previous Consideration, pronounces at first sight Beautiful or Deformed. Thus we see that every different Species of sensible Creatures has its different Notions of Beauty, and that each of them is most affected with the Beauties of its own Kind. This is no where more remarkable than in Birds of the same Shape and Proportion, where we often see the Male determined in his Courtship by the single Grain or Tincture of a Feather, and never discovering any Charms but in the Colour of its Species.

Wednesday, June 25, 1712.

Alterius sic
Altera poscit opem res et conjurat amicè. —Hor.

If we consider the Works of *Nature* and *Art,* as they are qualified to entertain the Imagination, we shall find the last very defective, in Comparison of the former; for though they may sometimes appear as Beautiful or Strange, they can have nothing in them of that Vastness and Immensity, which afford so great an Entertainment to the Mind of the Beholder. The one may be as Polite and Delicate as the other, but can never shew her self so August and Magnificent in the Design. There is something more bold and masterly in the rough careless Strokes of Nature, than in the nice Touches and Embellishments of Art. The Beauties of the most stately Garden or Palace lie in a narrow Compass, the Imagination immediately runs them over, and requires something else to gratifie her; but, in the wide Fields of Nature, the Sight wanders up and down without Confinement, and is fed with an infinite variety of Images, without any certain Stint or Number. For this Reason we always find the Poet in Love with a Country-Life, where Nature appears in the greatest Perfection, and furnishes out all those Scenes that are most apt to delight the Imagination. [. . .]

But tho' there are several of these wild Scenes, that are more delightful than any artificial Shows; yet we find the Works of Nature still more pleasant, the more they resemble those of Art: For in this case our Pleasure rises from a double Principle; from the Agreeableness of the Objects to the Eye, and from their Similitude to other Objects: We are pleased as well with comparing their Beauties, as with surveying them, and can represent them to our Minds, either as Copies or Originals. Hence it is that we take Delight in a Prospect which is well laid out, and diversified with Fields and Meadows, Woods and Rivers; in those accidental Landskips of Trees, Clouds and Cities, that are sometimes found in the Veins of Marble; in the curious Fret-work of Rocks and Grottos; and, in a Word, in any thing that hath such a Variety or Regularity as may seem the Effect of Design, in what we call the Works of Chance.

If the Products of Nature rise in Value, according as they more or less resemble those of Art, we may be sure that artificial Works receive a greater Advantage from their Resemblance of such as are natural; because here the Similitude is not only pleasant, but the Pattern more perfect. The prettiest Landskip I ever saw, was one drawn on the Walls of a dark Room, which stood opposite on one side to a navigable River, and on the other to a Park. The Experiment is very common in Opticks. Here you might discover the Waves and Fluctuations of the Water in strong and proper Colours, with the Picture of a Ship entering at one end, and sailing by Degrees through the whole Piece. On another there appeared the Green Shadows of Trees, waving to and fro with the Wind, and Herds of Deer among them in Miniature, leaping about upon the Wall. I must confess, the Novelty of such a Sight may be one occasion of its Pleasantness to the Imagination, but certainly the chief Reason is its near Resemblance to Nature, as it does not only, like other Pictures, give the Colour and Figure, but the Motion of the Things it represents.

We have before observed, that there is generally in Nature something more Grand and August, than what we meet with in the Curiosities of Art. When therefore, we see this imitated in any measure, it gives us a nobler and more exalted kind of Pleasure than what we receive from the nicer and more accurate Productions of Art. On this Account our *English* Gardens are not so entertaining to the Fancy as those in *France* and *Italy*, where we see a large Extent of Ground covered over with an agreeable mixture of Garden and Forest, which represent every where an artificial Rudeness, much more charming than that Neatness and Elegancy which we meet with in those of our own Country. It might, indeed, be of ill Consequence to the Publick, as well as unprofitable to private Persons, to alienate so much Ground from Pasturage, and the Plow, in many Parts of a Country that is so well peopled, and cultivated to a far greater Advantage. But why may not a whole Estate be thrown into a kind of Garden by frequent Plantations, that may turn as much to the Profit, as the Pleasure of the Owner? A Marsh overgrown with Willows, or a Mountain shaded with Oaks, are not only more beautiful, but more beneficial, than when they lie bare and unadorned. Fields of Corn make a pleasant Prospect, and if the Walks were a little taken care of that lie between them, if the natural Embroidery of the Meadows were helpt and improved by some small Additions of Art, and the several Rows of Hedges set off by Trees and Flowers, that the Soil was capable of receiving, a Man might make a pretty Landskip of his own Possessions.

Writers who have given us an Account of *China*, tell us the Inhabitants of that Country laugh at the Plantations of our *Europeans*, which are laid out by the Rule and Line; because, they say, any one may place Trees in equal Rows and uniform Figures. They chuse rather to shew a Genius in Works of this Nature, and therefore always conceal the Art by which they direct themselves. They have a Word, it seems, in their Language, by which they express the particular Beauty of a Plantation that thus strikes the Imagination at first Sight, without discovering what it is that has so agreeable an Effect. Our *British* Gardeners, on the contrary, instead of humouring Nature, love to deviate from it as much as possible. Our Trees rise in Cones, Globes, and Pyramids. We see the Marks of the Scissars upon every Plant and Bush. I do not know whether I am singular in my Opinion, but, for my own part, I would rather look upon a Tree in all its Luxuriancy and Diffusion of Boughs and Branches, than when it is thus cut and trimmed into a Mathematical Figure; and cannot but fancy that an Orchard in Flower looks infinitely more delightful, than all the little Labyrinths of the [more] finished Parterre. But as our great Modellers of Gardens have their Magazines of Plants to dispose of, it is very natural for them to tear up all the beautiful Plantations of Fruit Trees, and contrive a Plan that may most turn to their own Profit, in taking off their Evergreens, and the like Moveable Plants, with which their Shops are plentifully stocked.

97 ROBERT CASTELL
from *The Villas of the Ancients Illustrated* (1728)

The parallel development of English Palladianism and aesthetic relativism even continues in the 1720s within the circle of Lord Burlington. In 1718 the poet Alexander Pope, who had been a close friend to Addison, leased a villa along the banks of the Thames near Twickenham and began altering his garden, based on the premise that "all gardening is landscape painting." Pope's new style, especially his artificial grotto and serpentine paths, may have encouraged Burlington, sometime after 1725, to relax the formal garden around his Palladian villa at Chiswick, which was still under construction. Burlington's change of direction was also certainly influenced by a book being written (at least in part under his aegis) by Robert Castell, of whom we know very little. His book, *The Villas of the Ancients Illustrated*, is a scholarly attempt to reconstruct the gardens at Pliny's villas at Laurentinum and Tuscum, but Castell in his reasoning goes much further, as in theory he attempts to square classical theory with a still evolving knowledge of Chinese gardens. He does so by establishing three stages of development for the Roman garden. The first stage consisted of little more than selecting a pleasing site; in the second stage a classical symmetry

Robert Castell (d. 1729), from *The Villas of the Ancients Illustrated*, printed by the author, 1728, pp. 116–18.

and order was sought. This phase, Castell goes on to argue, was superseded by a third and more refined stage whereby gardening "consisted in a close Imitation of Nature" that exploited the attribute of visual irregularity. In essence, he formulates or constructs a classical source for picturesque landscape design.

Before any Notice be taken of that Part that lay beyond the *Hippodrome*, which is the only *Roman* Garden whose Description is come down to us, it may not be improper to enquire into the first Rise of Gardens, and of what they at first consisted, by which a Judgment may be the better passed on this before us. The Invention of this Art seems to have been owing to the first Builders of *Villas*, who were naturally led to search for the most beautiful Places in which to build them; but as it was hardly possible to meet with any, that within the Compass designed for the Pleasure of the *Villa*, should contain every thing that was compleatly agreeable, it was necessary to supply by Care and Industry whatever was wanting in the natural Face of the Country: but at first they aimed at nothing further than the Disposition of their Plantations, for by the small Knowledge we can arrive at, in the Gardens of the first Ages, they seem to have been no more than select, well-water'd Spots of Ground, irregularly producing all sorts of Plants and Trees, grateful either to the Sight, Smell, or Taste, and refreshed by Shade and Water: Their whole Art consisting in little more than in making those Parts next their *Villas* as it were accidentally produce the choicest Trees, the Growth of various Soils, the Face of the Ground suffering little or no Alteration; the Intent of Gardens being within a fixt Compass of Ground, to enjoy all that Fancy could invent most agreeable to the Senses. But this rough Manner, not appearing sufficiently beautiful to those of a more regular and exact Taste, set them upon inventing a Manner of laying out the Ground and Plantations of Gardens by the Rule and Line, and to trim them up by an Art that was visible in every Part of the Design. By the Accounts we have of the present Manner of Designing in *China*, it seems as if from the two former Manners a Third had been formed, whose Beauty consisted in a close Imitation of Nature; where, tho' the Parts are disposed with the greatest Art, the Irregularity is still preserved; so that their Manner may not improperly be said to be an artful Confusion, where there is no Appearance of that Skill which is made use of, their *Rocks, Cascades,* and *Trees,* bearing their natural Forms. In the Disposition of *Pliny*'s Garden, the Designer of it shews that he was not unacquainted with these several Manners, and the Whole seems to have been a Mixture of them all Three. In the *Pratulum* Nature appears in her plainest and most simple Dress; such as the first Builders were contented with about their *Villas,* when the Face of the Ground it self happened to be naturally beautiful. By the Care used in regulating the turning and winding Walks, and cutting the Trees and Hedges into various Forms, is shewn the Manner of the more regular Gardens; and in the *Imitatio Ruris,* he seems to hint at the third Manner, where, under the Form of a beautiful Country, *Hills, Rocks, Cascades, Rivulets, Woods, Buildings,* &c. were possibly thrown into such an agreeable Disorder, as to have pleased the Eye from several Views, like so many beautiful Landskips; and at the same time have afforded at least all the Pleasures that could be enjoy'd in the most regular Gardens. The main Body of this Garden was disposed after the Second of these three Manners; through its winding Paths One as it were accidentally fell upon those Pieces of a rougher Taste, that seem to have been made with a Design to surprize those that arrived at them, through such a Scene of Regularities, which (in the Opinion of some) might appear more beautiful by being near those plain Imitations of Nature, as Lights in Painting are heightened by Shades. The Intent of this Garden (besides pleasing the Eye, being to afford Shade and Coolness in the hotter Season of the Year) required it to be well stockt with Trees and Water; which last we may suppose took its seeming natural Course through the rougher Parts of the Garden, and in the regular appeared in a more artful Disposition; as did also the Trees, which both here and in those Parts on the *South* Side, or Front of the *Villa*, were cut into unwarrantable Forms, if the Ornaments of Gardens are allow'd to be only Imitations of Nature's Productions; for it cannot be supposed that Nature ever did or will produce Trees in the Form of Beasts, or Letters, or any Resemblance of Embroidery, which Imitations rather belong to the Statuary, and Workers with the Needle than the Architect; and tho' pleasing in those Arts, appear monstrous in this.

98 BATTY LANGLEY
from *New Principles of Gardening* (1728)

Langley's book, which appeared in the same year as Castell's classical history, testifies to how widely the new approach to garden design was spreading by this date. Langley, even though he lived in nearby Twickenham, was not connected with the Burlington circle at Chiswick; in fact, he was a defender of the eclectic tradition of Hawksmoor and Vanbrugh and he vehemently opposed the severity of the new classicism that was taking root. Langley was a prolific writer on architecture and garden design. He is perhaps best known for his *Ancient Architecture* (1742), in which he played to the emerging interest in Gothic forms by codifying five Gothic "orders." As a son of a gardener, however, he was perhaps more at home with garden design. His *New Principles of Gardening* (1728) is a landmark text in the sense that it is the first attempt to define the principles of the new style. In the Introduction, he – following Addison – decries the "stiff, regular Garden" and suggests instead that one imitate nature "with the greatest Accuracy that can be" (pp. v–vi). He goes on to place great emphasis on the quality of the visual experience of the garden, especially its novelty and unaffected irregularity. The excerpt presented here is toward the end of the book, where he attempts to summarize the new principles of design. His suggestions for the exploitation of dales, streams, canals, grottos, and serpentine meanders would within a few years become standard features of the English garden.

Of the Disposition of Gardens in General

On this very Point depends the whole Beauty or Ruin of a Garden, and therefore every Gentleman should be very cautious therein; I must needs confess, that I have often been surprized to see that none of our late and present Authors did ever attempt to furnish Gentlemen with better Plans and Ideas thereof, than what has hitherto been practised.

Batty Langley (1696–1751), from *New Principles of Gardening* (1728). Farnborough: Gregg International Publishers, 1971 (facsimile edition), pp. 193–5.

The End and Design of a good Garden, is to be both profitable and delightful; wherein should be observed, that its Parts should be always presenting new Objects, which is a continual Entertainment to the Eye, and raises a Pleasure of Imagination.

If the Gentlemen of *England* had formerly been better advised in the laying out their Gardens, we might by this Time been at least equal (if not far superior) to any Abroad.

For as we abound in good Soil, fine Grass, and Gravel, which in many Places Abroad is not to be found, and the best of all Sorts of Trees; it therefore appears, that nothing has been wanting but a noble Idea of the Disposition of a Garden. I could instance divers Places in *England*, where Noblemen and Gentlemens Seats are very finely situated, but wretchedly executed, not only in respect to disproportion'd Walks, Trees planted in improper Soils, no Regard had to fine Views, &c. but with that abominable Mathematical Regularity and Stiffness, that nothing that's bad could equal them.

Now these unpleasant forbidding Sort of Gardens, owe their Deformity to the insipid Taste or Interest of some of our Theorical Engineers, who, in their aspiring Garrets, cultivate all the several Species of Plants, as well as frame Designs for Situations they never saw: Or to some Nursery-Man, who, for his own Interest, advises the Gentleman to such Forms and Trees as will make the greatest Draught out of his Nursery, without Regard to any Thing more: And oftentimes to a Coxcomb, who takes upon himself to be an excellent Draughtsman, as well as an incomparable Gardener; of which there has been, and are still, too many in *England*, which is witness'd by every unfortunate Garden wherein they come. Now as the Beauty of Gardens in general depends upon an elegant Disposition of all their Parts, which cannot be determined without a perfect Knowledge of its several Ascendings, Descendings, Views, &c. how is it possible that any Person can make a good Design for any Garden, whose Situation they never saw?

To draw a beautiful regular Draught, is not to the Purpose; for altho' it makes a handsome Figure on the Paper, yet it has a quite different Effect when executed on the Ground: Nor is there any Thing more ridiculous, and forbidding, than a Garden which is regular; which, instead of entertaining the Eye with fresh Objects, after you have seen a quarter Part, you only see the very same Part repeated again, without any Variety.

And what still greatly adds to this wretched Method, is, that to execute these stiff regular Designs, they destroy many a noble Oak, and in its Place plant, perhaps, a clumsey-bred Yew, Holley, &c. which, with me, is a Crime of so high a Nature, as not to be pardon'd.

There is nothing adds so much to the Pleasure of a Garden, as those great Beauties of Nature, *Hills and Valleys*, which, by our *regular Coxcombs*, have ever been destroyed, and at a very great Expence also in Levelling.

For, to their great Misfortune, they always deviate from Nature, instead of imitating it.

There are many other Absurdities I could mention, which those *wretched Creatures* have, and are daily guilty of: But as the preceding are sufficient to arm worthy Gentlemen against such Mortals, I shall at present forbear, and instead thereof, proceed to General Directions for laying out Gardens in a more grand and delightful Manner than has been done before. But first observe,

That the several Parts of a beautiful Rural Garden, are *Walks, Slopes, Borders, Open 'Plains, Plain Parterres, Avenues, Groves, Wildernesses, Labyrinths, Fruit-Gardens, Flower-Gardens, Vineyards, Hop-Gardens, Nurseries, Coppiced Quarters, Green Openings*, like Meadows: Small Inclosures of *Corn, Cones of Ever-Greens,* of *Flowering-Shrubs,* of *Fruit-Trees,* of *Forest-Trees,* and mix'd together: *Mounts, Terraces,* Winding *Valleys, Dales, Purling Streams, Basons, Canals, Fountains, Cascades, Grotto's, Rocks, Ruins, Serpentine Meanders, Rude Coppies, Hay-Stacks, Wood-Piles, Rabbit* and *Hare-Warrens, Cold Baths, Aviaries, Cabinets, Statues, Obelisks, Manazeries, Pheasant* and *Partridge-Grounds, Orangeries, Melon-Grounds, Kitchen-Gardens, Physick* or *Herb-Garden, Orchard, Bowling-Green, Dials, Precipices, Amphitheatres,* &c.

99   ROBERT MORRIS
from *Lectures on Architecture* (1736)

By the 1730s the new English garden movement was clearly taking shape. The first significant representative of the new trend was William Kent (1685–1748), a painter whom Lord Burlington had lured back from Italy in 1715. During the mid-1720s Kent was commissioned by Burlington to write a book on Inigo Jones, and by the end of this decade he was assisting Burlington in redesigning his own garden. Kent would also turn to architecture (as a classicist) in the 1730s, but at the same time he gained considerable renown for his relaxed or informal garden designs, first manifesting itself in his masterpieces at Stowe (1731–5) and Rousham (beginning in 1737). Kent left no literary record of his ideas of garden design, but we can gain an insight into his design sensitivities by turning to another contemporary book by Robert Morris.

The latter, as we have already seen, was at least loosely connected with the Burlington circle, and in his classical theory he places great emphasis on the notion of harmony. In his *Lectures on Architecture*, however, we have the emerging "picturesque" side of his thought, which Morris obviously felt to be fully consistent with classicism. Again, many of the elements of later British theory are evident here: the preference for rural living, for convenience of the plan (over beauty), for the prospect of gardens from the house, and for a freer treatment of nature as a painter might arrange a landscape painting. There are, however, still echoes of the classical tradition as well, such as the preference for a classical design of the residential seat, embellished with the three Greek orders (depending on the characteristics of the landscape). The lecture is thus an interesting transitional piece between the earlier classicism and mature picturesque theory, in which geometric and symmetric architecture and the informal garden are regarded as complementary features. The great emphasis on the situation, however, presages the later step of seeking to make the design of the house also more "picturesque."

When I speak of Situation, it must not be suppos'd that I mean proper Choice of it in Towns or Cities, where every *Order* is promiscuously perform'd, and, perhaps, in the same Pile of Building; but I would be understood, such Situations which are the proper Choice of Retirements, where a Sameness should be preserv'd between *Art* and *Nature*.

Convenience is certainly the first Thing to be consider'd in Choice of Situation; what Supplies of Water, of Provision, of Carriage, &c. can easily and speedily be attain'd: For without these principal and necessary Conveniences, for the Support of little Commonwealths of Families, a Structure would soon be deserted, and left a Residence only for the Fowls of the Air to retire to, from the Inclemencies of the Seasons, and a Place of Repose.

Robert Morris, from *Lectures on Architecture* (1734–6). Farnborough: Gregg International Publishers, 1971 (facsimile edition), pp. 63–70.

But it is at the same time to be observ'd, such Situations which produce such Supplies, are not difficult to be found: And, perhaps, with the Additions of a healthy and fertile Soil, uninterrupted Vistas and Avenues, an agreeable River, or some opening Lawn, or at least a distant Groupe of Hills and Vales diminishing from the Eye by a pleasing Gradation: I say such an agreeable Spot of Ground, where Nature wantons in Luxuriancy, is the first Care of a Builder; and by a proper Design compos'd to blend Art and Nature together, must consequently render it the Delight of the Inhabitant, and give an unspeakable Pleasure to the Eye of every Beholder.

A Person who builds on such a useful and delightful Glebe, must doubtless not only agreeably improve that *Fortune* which Providence has supplied him with, but likewise perpetuate his Judgment to his Posterity; it must render his Off-spring a Happiness and Pleasure, which gives a true Relish to Life. But he who, on the contrary, lays the Foundation of his Fabrick on a barren or unpleasant Soil, or on a bleak Wild which Nature seems to have deserted, is, consequently, only perpetuating his Folly to future Ages.

But it is to be observ'd, that every one that builds has not an equal Felicity in the Opportunity of chusing a fine Situation; therefore some must fall into little Errors and Inconveniences: But it were better to have an ill-shap'd Hand or Leg, than to have none. Therefore Conveniency must he preferr'd to Beauty; and the fine Prospect, the opening Lawns, the distant Views, must give way to a more healthy, a more temperate, or more convenient *Soil*.

I might here descend to shew you by what Methods you must proceed to distinguish a healthy Soil, such as by the Complexion of the Inhabitants, the Health of Cattle, and even by the Soundness of *Stones* and *Trees*, are known; and in the choice of *Water*, concerning its Goodness, by being in running Streams, not stagnated, muddy, or leaving any Sediment in the Vessel, its Remoteness from Lakes or Ponds of Water, &c. But as this would divert your Thoughts from the Application of Buildings, to a proper Situation; I shall refer it to another *Lecture*, or to *Alberti*, or *Andrea Palladio*, who has said what is necessary on this Subject, in his first and second Books of *Architecture*.

As Nature requires a Sameness, when Art is made use of to add Lustre to her Beauty; so Art never more agreeably pleases us, than when she has a Resemblance of Nature: Therefore, by a kind of Sympathy and Attraction, when both are blended or mingled together, so as to be preserv'd without starting into Extreams, they must necessarily give that Pleasure to the Senses, which alone can flow from the nice Hand and Skill of the Designer.

In this, I think, our modern Way of planning Gardens is far preferable to what was us'd 20 Years ago, where, in large Parterres, you might see Men, Birds, and Dogs, cut in Trees; or, perhaps, something like the Shape of a Man on Horseback – (pardon this Digression.) – In *Architecture* Men have fell into Methods equally absurd. In some Places, may be seen little Boys supporting a Burden of a Monument that had been the Labour of 10 or 12 Persons to place there; or a *Corinthian* Column set in a Fish-pond, and a *Tuscan* at the Entrance of a Summer-house. I say, such Inconsistencies in Nature always hurt the Imagination, and we view such Objects with more Pain and Surprize than any Pleasure they can possibly give us.

A champaign open Country, requires a noble and plain Building, which is always best supplied by the *Dorick* Order, or something analogous to its Simplicity. If it have a long extended View, it were best to range the Offices in a Line with the Building; for at distant Views it fills the Eye with a majestick Pleasure. A Situation near the Sea requires the same, or rather a Rusticity and Lowness: The Vapours of the Sea, by its saline Qualities, expand themselves some Distance, and always are a decaying Principle; and with the boisterous Winds which blow from it, must, consequently, require a Power forcible enough to withstand its corrosive Quality.

The chearful Vale requires more Decoration and Dress; and if the View be long, or some adjacent River runs near it; the *Ionick* Order is the most proper; where Nature seems to *wanton* in Dress, and is gay in *Verdure*, she requireth Art to assist and embellish her, and the Liveliness of the *Ionick* Order can deck and garnish the Glebe. If the Spot be an Ascent, and some distant Hills or Wood environ the back Part, (in which I suppose the Front a South Aspect) then a few Ornaments may be scatter'd in proper Parts, to give it an enlivening Variety; – but Care must be had not to use Superfluity. If it be on an Eminence, and surrounded with Woods, the principal Avenues should be spacious: *Portico's* give a grateful Pleasure to us in the View, and more so, if the Front is not contracted by the Avenue, nor continue too near it, to take off the proper Shades and keeping of Design.

The *Ionick* Order is of the three *Greek* Orders the most applicable to Situations of various Kinds; and if I say her Measures and Proportions more pleasingly attract the Eye, it is not without Reason: The Parts are analogous to Nature, in which she has been so nicely pois'd between the Rusticity of the *Dorick* and the Luxuriancy of the *Corinthian*, that I am more apt to believe the *Ionick* Order was invented as a Mean between the *Dorick* and the *Corinthian*, than that the *Ionick* was in so beautiful Proportion before the *Corinthian* Order was invented.

The silent *Streams*, the gay, the wanton *Scene*, requires the *Corinthian* Order; where Nature is gilded with lively Landskips, where the Verdure is blended with Flowers, which she decks herself with, and where the party-colour'd Painting of some opening Lawn garnishes her in all her Pride; then the *Architect* must have Recourse to Fancy, must mingle his Flowers with Nature, his Festoons of Fruits, &c. must deck the Fabrick, and be Nature in every thing but Lavishness; the same Chain of Similitude should run through the Design, rising from one Degree of Dress to another, still preserving the Consistency of the Parts with the Whole, and keeping that *Mediocrity* in Ornament which the Nature of the Design requires.

100 WILLIAM CHAMBERS
from *Designs of Chinese Buildings* (1757)

This first book by the architect William Chambers voices a sub-theme lurking in the background of picturesque theory – the Chinese garden. This book of Chambers owes everything to the circumstances of his early years, the three trips to China and the Orient in the 1740s. This fascination with China later found an outlet when, during his architectural training in Paris, he met the Prince of Wales. As the story goes, the latter encouraged him to design a Chinese building for the garden at Kew, and Chambers indeed built a "House of Confuscius" there in the

William Chambers, from *Designs of Chinese Buildings, Furniture, Dresses, Machines, and Utensils,* published by the author, 1757. New York: Benjamin Bloom, 1968 (reissue), pp. 14–18.

early 1750s, even before the architect had settled in England. After moving to London in 1755, as architect to Princess Augusta, Chambers further transformed the gardens at Kew. The gardens today are still best known for the 10-story Great Pagoda, laid out by Chambers in 1761. Chambers published all of his designs for Kew in his *Plans, Elevations, Sections, and Perspective Views of the Gardens and Buildings at Kew in Surry* (1763), and he would also later publish *A Dissertation on Oriental Gardening* (1772). His *Designs of Chinese Buildings* is an earlier book, and it captures Chambers at the moment when he was most attracted to what he regarded as the Chinese style. The passages are from the chapter, "Of the Art of Laying Out Gardens among the Chinese."

The gardens which I saw in China were very small; nevertheless from them, and what could be gathered from Lepqua, a celebrated Chinese painter, with whom I had several conversations on the subject of gardening, I think I have acquired sufficient knowledge of their notions on this head.

Nature is their pattern, and their aim is to imitate her in all her beautiful irregularities. Their first consideration is the form of the ground, whether it be flat, sloping, hilly, or mountainous, extensive, or of small compass, of a dry or marshy nature, abounding with rivers and springs, or liable to a scarcity of water; to all which circumstances they attend with great care, chusing such dispositions as humour the ground, can be executed with the least expence, hide its defects, and set its advantages in the most conspicuous light.

As the Chinese are not fond of walking, we seldom meet with avenues or spacious walks, as in our European plantations: the whole ground is laid out in a variety of scenes, and you are led, by winding passages cut in the groves, to the different points of view, each of which is marked by a seat, a building, or some other object.

The perfection of their gardens consists in the number, beauty, and diversity of these scenes. The Chinese gardeners, like the European painters, collect from nature the most pleasing objects, which they endeavour to combine in such a manner, as not only to appear to the best advantage separately, but likewise to unite in forming an elegant and striking whole.

Their artists distinguish three different species of scenes, to which they give the appellations of pleasing, horrid, and enchanted. Their enchanted scenes answer, in a great measure, to what we call romantic, and in these they make use of several artifices to excite surprize. Sometimes they make a rapid stream, or torrent, pass under ground, the turbulent noise of which strikes the ear of the new-comer, who is at a loss to know from whence it proceeds: at other times they dispose the rocks, buildings, and other objects that form the composition, in such a manner as that the wind passing through the different interstices and cavities, made in them for that purpose, causes strange and uncommon sounds. They introduce into these scenes all kinds of extraordinary trees, plants, and flowers, form artificial and complicated ecchoes, and let loose different sorts of monstrous birds and animals.

In their scenes of horror, they introduce impending rocks, dark caverns, and impetuous cataracts rushing down the mountains from all sides; the trees are ill-formed, and seemingly torn to pieces by the violence of tempests; some are thrown down, and intercept the course of the torrents, appearing as if they had been brought down by the fury of the waters; others look as if shattered and blasted by the force of lightning; the buildings are some in ruins, others half-consumed by fire, and some miserable huts dispersed in the mountains serve, at once to indicate the existence and wretchedness of the inhabitants. These scenes are generally succeeded by pleasing ones. The Chinese artists, knowing how powerfully contrast operates on the mind, constantly practise sudden transitions, and a striking opposition of forms, colours, and shades. Thus they conduct you from limited prospects to extensive views; from objects of horrour to scenes of delight; from lakes and rivers to plains, hills, and woods; to dark and gloomy colours they oppose such as are brilliant, and to complicated forms simple ones; distributing, by a judicious arrangement, the different masses of light and shade, in such a manner as to render the composition at once distinct in it's parts, and striking in the whole.

Where the ground is extensive, and a multiplicity of scenes are to be introduced, they generally adapt each to one single point of view: but where it is limited, and affords no room for variety, they endeavour to remedy this defect, by disposing the objects so, that being viewed from different points, they produce different representations; and sometimes, by an artful disposition, such as have no resemblance to each other.

In their large gardens they contrive different scenes for morning, noon, and evening; erecting, at the proper points of view, buildings adapted to the recreations of each particular time of the day: and in their small ones (where, as has been observed, one arrangement produces many representations) they dispose in the same manner, at the several points of view, buildings, which, from their use, point out the time of day for enjoying the scene in it's perfection.

As the climate of China is exceeding hot, they employ a great deal of water in their gardens. In the small ones, if the situation admits, they frequently lay almost the whole ground under water; leaving only some islands and rocks: and in their large ones they introduce extensive lakes, rivers, and canals. The banks of their lakes and rivers are variegated in imitation of nature; being sometimes bare and gravelly, sometimes covered with woods quite to the water's edge. In some places flat, and adorned with flowers and shrubs; in others steep, rocky, and forming caverns, into which part of the waters discharge themselves with noise and violence. Sometimes you see meadows covered with cattle, or rice-grounds that run out into the lakes, leaving between them passages for vessels; and sometimes groves, into which enter, in different parts, creeks and rivulets, sufficiently deep to admit boats; their banks being planted with trees, whose spreading branches, in some places, form arbours, under which the boats pass. These generally conduct to some very interesting object; such as a magnificent building, places on the top of a mountain cut into terrasses; a casine situated in the midst of a lake; a cascade; a grotto cut into a variety of apartments; an artificial rock; and many other such inventions.

Their rivers are seldom streight, but serpentine, and broken into many irregular points; sometimes they are narrow, noisy, and rapid, at other times deep, broad, and slow. Both in their rivers and lakes are seen reeds, with other aquatic plants and flowers; particularly the *Lyen Hoa*, of which they are very fond. They frequently erect mills, and other hydraulic machines, the motions of which enliven the scene: they have also a great number of vessels of different forms and sizes. In their lakes they intersperse islands; some of them barren, and surrounded with rocks and shoals; others enriched with every thing that art and nature can furnish most perfect. They likewise form artificial rocks; and in compositions of this kind the Chinese surpass all other nations. The making them is a distinct profession; and there are at Canton, and probably in most other cities of China, numbers of artificers constantly employed in this business. The stone they are made of comes from the southern coasts of China. It is of a bluish cast, and worn into irregular forms by the action of the waves. The

Chinese are exceeding nice in the choice of this stone; insomuch that I have seen several Tael given for a bit no bigger than a man's fist, when it happened to be of a beautiful form and lively colour. But these select pieces they use in landscapes for their apartments: in gardens they employ a coarser sort, which they join with a bluish cement, and form rocks of a considerable size. I have seen some of these exquisitely fine, and such as discovered an uncommon elegance of taste in the contriver. When they are large they make in them caves and grottos, with openings, through which you discover distant prospects, They cover them, in different places, with trees, shrubs, briars, and moss; placing on their tops little temples, or other buildings, to which you ascend by rugged and irregular steps cut in the rock.

When there is a sufficient supply of water, and proper ground, the Chinese never fail to form cascades in their gardens. They avoid all regularity in these works, observing nature according to her operations in that mountainous country. The waters burst out from among the caverns, and windings of the rocks. In some places a large and impetuous cataract appears; in others are seen many lesser falls. Sometimes the view of the cascade is intercepted by trees, whose leaves and branches only leave room to discover the waters, in some places, as they fall down the sides of the mountain. They frequently throw rough wooden bridges from one rock to another, over the steepest part of the cataract; and often intercept it's passage by trees and heaps of stones, that seem to have been brought down by the violence of the torrent.

In their plantations they vary the forms and colours of their trees; mixing such as have large and spreading branches, with those of pyramidal figures, and dark greens, with brighter, interspersing among them such as produce flowers; of which they have some that flourish a great part of the year. The Weeping-willow is one of their favourite trees, and always among those that border their lakes and rivers, being so planted as to have it's branches hanging over the water. They likewise introduce trunks of decayed trees, some-times, erect, and at other times lying on the ground, being very nice about their forms, and the colour of the bark and moss on them.

Various are the artifices they employ to surprize. Sometimes they lead you through dark caverns and gloomy passages, at the issue of which you are, on a sudden, struck with the view of a delicious landscape, enriched with every thing that luxuriant nature affords most beautiful. At other times you are conducted through avenues and walks, that gradually diminish and grow rugged, till the passage is at length entirely intercepted, and rendered impracticable, by bushes, briars, and stones: when unexpectedly a rich and extensive prospect opens to view, so much the more pleasing as it was less looked for.

Another of their artifices is to hide some part of a composition by trees, or other intermediate objects. This naturally excites the curiosity of the spectator to take a nearer view; when he is surprised by some unexpected scene, or some representation totally opposite to the thing he looked for. The termination of their lakes they always hide, leaving room for the imagination to work; and the same rule they observe in other compositions, wherever it can be put in practice.

B. TOWARD A RELATIVIST AESTHETICS

Introduction

These implications of empiricism, combined with the development of the English garden, become more visible at mid-century, as British theory enters the flowering phase of its Enlightenment. The crucial texts in this regard appear, almost entirely, along a philosophical front. Locke's philosophical successors, George Berkeley and David Hume, had advanced more elaborate empirical models, which now began to consider the foundation of aesthetic beliefs. Various writers, among them Edmund Burke, began to see the "new" aesthetics as a distinct alternative to Continental rationalism and its theory of beauty, while at the same time many European intellectuals – such as Voltaire, Condillac, and Diderot – became much attracted to British theory as a way to ground their aesthetic ideas within more scientifically rigorous and modern systems. Also of crucial importance here is the almost sudden elevation of the idea of the "sublime" to aesthetic importance: now a concept having a different yet equal importance to the idea of the "beautiful." This expansion of aesthetic enjoyment into other areas in itself allows an alternative vision of what constitutes pleasing aesthetic sensations. The period around mid-century is a rich and productive time of conceptual innovation. In the third quarter of the century, a recognizable relativist aesthetics not only takes hold but in Britain largely overtakes the absolute underpinnings of classicism.

101   JOHN LOCKE
from *An Essay Concerning Human Understanding*, fourth edition (1700)

As such exotic phenomena as the Chinese garden were affecting British aesthetic thought, philosophers were also more directly approaching the issue of relative beauty. Once again the line of development can be traced back to John Locke. In his *Essay* he never addressed the question of beauty and proportions directly, but in a chapter added to the fourth edition of his work in 1700, "On the Association of Ideas," he provides a way to consider the problem of beauty within the philosophical system he had set out. The world, he argues, is perceived through the senses, and these sensations spark ideas; these ideas are then mentally associated with other ideas, from which we derive our like or dislike of things we experience. This chain reaction of ideas is actually philosophically close to Perrault's notion of "custom," in that certain proportions are pleasing to our senses not because of any inherent mathematical properties but because we have become habituated to them and their associations are found to be pleasing. But there is one crucial distinction inherent to Locke's argument, and this is the increasing emphasis that he places on sensation and the mental stimulation that is derived from it. This theory of association will become the cornerstone of eighteenth-century British aesthetics, and it will be applied not only to the "associations" connected with the perception of beauty, but also with such concepts as the sublime and the picturesque. On the Continent, as we have already seen, it also dovetails with the expanding architectural notion of "character."

5.   Some of our ideas have a *natural* correspondence and connexion one with another: it is the office and excellency of our reason to trace these, and hold them together in that union and correspondence which is founded in their peculiar beings. Besides this, there is another connexion of ideas wholly owing to *chance* or *custom*. Ideas that in themselves are not all of kin, come to be so united in some men's minds, that it is very hard to separate them; they always keep in company, and the one no sooner at any time comes into the understanding, but its associate appears with it; and if they are more than two which are thus united, the whole gang, always inseparable, show themselves together.[1]

6.   This strong combination of ideas, not allied by nature,[2] the mind makes in itself either voluntarily or by chance; and hence it comes in different men to be very different, according to their different inclinations, education, interests, &c. *Custom* settles habits of thinking in the understanding, as well as of determining in the will, and of motions in the body: all

John Locke, from *An Essay Concerning Human Understanding* (fourth edition, 1700), ed. Alexander Campbell Fraser. New York: Dover, 1959, Vol. I, ch. XXXIII, pp. 529–33.

which seems to be but trains of motions in the animal spirits, which, once set a going, continue in the same steps they have been used to; which, by often treading, are worn into a smooth path, and the motion in it becomes easy, and as it were natural. As far as we can comprehend thinking, thus ideas seem to be produced in our minds; or, if they are not, this may serve to explain their following one another in an habitual train, when once they are put into their track, as well as it does to explain such motions of the body.[3] A musician used to any tune will find that, let it but once begin in his head, the ideas of the several notes of it will follow one another orderly in his understanding, without any care or attention, as regularly as his fingers move orderly over the keys of the organ to play out the tune he has begun, though his unattentive thoughts be elsewhere a wandering. Whether the natural cause of these ideas, as well as of that regular dancing of his fingers be the motion of his animal spirits, I will not determine, how probable soever, by this instance, it appears to be so: but this may help us a little to conceive of intellectual habits, and of the tying together of ideas.

7. That there are such associations of them made by custom, in the minds of most men, I think nobody will question, who has well considered himself or others; and to this, perhaps, might be justly attributed most of the sympathies and antipathies observable in men, which work as strongly, and produce as regular effects as if they were natural; and are therefore called so, though they at first had no other original but the accidental connexion of two ideas, which either the strength of the first impression, or future indulgence so united, that they always afterwards kept company together in that man's mind, as if they were but one idea.[4] I say most of the antipathies, I do not say all; for some of them are truly natural, depend upon our original constitution, and are born with us; but a great part of those which are counted natural, would have been known to be from unheeded, though perhaps early, impressions, or wanton fancies at first, which would have been acknowledged the original of them, if they had been warily observed. A grown person surfeiting with honey no sooner hears the name of it, but his fancy immediately carries sickness and qualms to his stomach, and he cannot bear the very idea of it; other ideas of dislike, and sickness, and vomiting, presently accompany it, and he is disturbed; but he knows from whence to date this weakness, and can tell how he got this indisposition. Had this happened to him by an over-dose of honey when a child, all the same effects would have followed; but the cause would have been mistaken, and the antipathy counted natural.

8. I mention this, not out of any great necessity there is in this present argument to distinguish nicely between natural and acquired antipathies; but I take notice of it for another purpose, viz. that those who have children, or the charge of their education, would think it worth their while diligently to watch, and carefully to prevent the undue connexion of ideas in the minds of young people. This is the time most susceptible of lasting impressions; and though those relating to the health of the body are by discreet people minded and fenced against, yet I am apt to doubt, that those which relate more peculiarly to the mind, and terminate in the understanding or passions, have been much less heeded than the thing deserves: nay, those relating purely to the understanding, have, as I suspect, been by most men wholly overlooked.

9. This wrong connexion in our minds of ideas in themselves loose and independent of one another, has such an influence, and is of so great force to set us awry in our actions, as

well moral as natural, passions, reasonings, and notions themselves, that perhaps there is not any one thing that deserves more to be looked after.

10. The ideas of goblins and sprites have really no more to do with darkness than light: yet let but a foolish maid inculcate these often on the mind of a child, and raise them there together, possibly he shall never be able to separate them again so long as he lives, but darkness shall ever afterwards bring with it those frightful ideas, and they shall be so joined, that he can no more bear the one than the other.

11. A man receives a sensible injury from another, thinks on the man and that action over and over, and by ruminating on them strongly, or much, in his mind, so cements those two ideas together, that he makes them almost one; never thinks on the man, but the pain and displeasure he suffered comes into his mind with it, so that he scarce distinguishes them, but has as much an aversion for the one as the other. Thus hatreds are often begotten from slight and innocent occasions, and quarrels propagated and continued in the world.

12. A man has suffered pain or sickness in any place; he saw his friend die in such a room: though these have in nature nothing to do one with another, yet when the idea of the place occurs to his mind, it brings (the impression being once made) that of the pain and displeasure with it: he confounds them in his mind, and can as little bear the one as the other.

13. When this combination is settled, and while it lasts, it is not in the power of reason to help us, and relieve us from the effects of it. Ideas in our minds, when they are there, will operate according to their natures and circumstances. And here we see the cause why time cures certain affections, which reason, though in the right, and allowed to be so, has not power over, nor is able against them to prevail with those who are apt to hearken to it in other cases. The death of a child that was the daily delight of its mother's eyes, and joy of her soul, rends from her heart the whole comfort of her life, and gives her all the torment imaginable: use the consolations of reason in this case, and you were as good preach ease to one on the rack, and hope to allay, by rational discourses, the pain of his joints tearing asunder. Till time has by disuse separated the sense of that enjoyment and its loss, from the idea of the child returning to her memory, all representations, though ever so reasonable, are in vain; and therefore some in whom the union between these ideas is never dissolved, spend their lives in mourning, and carry an incurable sorrow to their graves.

14. A friend of mine knew one perfectly cured of madness by a very harsh and offensive operation. The gentleman who was thus recovered, with great sense of gratitude and acknowledgment owned the cure all his life after, as the greatest obligation he could have received; but, whatever gratitude and reason suggested to him, he could never bear the sight of the operator: that image brought back with it the idea of that agony which he suffered from his hands, which was too mighty and intolerable for him to endure.

NOTES

1   So far from trying to explain reason, by means of 'association of ideas,' Locke here expressly contrasts the 'natural' or rational relations of things with that connexion among ideas which is gradually generated, by their accidental coexistences and sequences in the mental experience of

individuals. 'Inseparable' association, in an individual experience, is thus distinguished from intrinsic necessity of reason, and also from objective causality.

2   Again Locke opposes association of phenomena according to the reason that is in nature – what he elsewhere calls 'the visible agreement that is in the ideas themselves' – to those associations which issue from 'the prevailing custom of the individual mind joining them together.' See *Conduct of the Understanding*, § 41.

3   Locke thus makes little of those physiological 'explanations' of the associations among our ideas that refer them to motions in the nerves, which have played so large a part in materialistic psychology since Hartley. The cause therein supposed to explain why ideas, when often united, are apt ever after to keep company, in the individual mind in which they were so united, is alleged to be certain motions in the nerves; 'ideas' themselves being our *feeling* of those motions, and thus dependent for their order upon mechanical causes.

4   The connexions thus formed, by accidents in the history of the individual, and so in unreason, give rise to Bacon's idols of the human mind, which fail to correspond to the objective connexions in nature that express Ideas of the Divine Mind. The complex ideas of substances that possess *our* minds thus come to be at cross purposes with the substances themselves, as they exist in the intelligible system of nature.

102   JOSEPH ADDISON
from *The Spectator* (1712)

In the essay by Addison of June 23, which we cited in the last section, we saw him make the distinction between the "Great, Uncommon, or Beautiful." If the Chinese garden represents for him an example of the uncommon, here architecture is considered under the mental association of "greatness" – later to be renamed the sublime. This is a pivotal essay with respect to eighteenth-century aesthetic theory. Not only will the idea of the "sublime" eventually emerge as a major aesthetic category alongside "beauty," but Addison's discussion of this idea with respect to architecture will also help to displace architectural theory's former preoccupation with beauty and proportions. One could very well argue, for instance, that the so-called visionary architecture of the late-eighteenth century – seen in the spectacular drawings of Boullée – has its starting point in this particular essay.

Thursday, June 26, 1712.

> *Adde tot egregias urbes, operumque laborem.*
> Virg.

Having already shewn how the Fancy is affected by the Works of Nature, and afterwards considered in general both the Works of Nature and of Art, how they mutually assist and compleat each other, in forming such Scenes and Prospects as are most apt to delight the

Joseph Addison, from *The Spectator* (June 26, 1712), reprinted in *The Spectator*. London: George Routledge & Sons, 1868, pp. 598–600.

Mind of the Beholder, I shall in this Paper throw together some Reflections on that Particular Art, which has a more immediate Tendency, than any other to produce those Pleasures of the Imagination, which have hitherto been the Subject of this Discourse. The Art I mean is that of Architecture, which I shall consider only with regard to the Light in which the foregoing Speculations have placed it, without entring into those Rules and Maxims which the great Masters of Architecture have laid down, and explained at large in numberless Treatises upon that Subject.

Greatness, in the Works of Architecture, may be considered as relating to the Bulk and Body of the Structure, or to the *Manner* in which it is built. As for the first, we find the Ancients, especially among the Eastern Nations of the World, infinitely superior to the Moderns.

Not to mention the Tower of *Babel*, of which an old Author says, there were the Foundations to be seen in his time, which looked like a spacious Mountain; what could be more noble than the Walls of *Babylon*, its hanging Gardens, and its Temple to *Jupiter Belus*, that rose a Mile high by Eight several Stories, each Story a Furlong in Height, and on the Top of which was the *Babylonian* Observatory; I might here, likewise, take Notice of the huge Rock that was cut into the Figure of *Semiramis*, with the smaller Rocks that lay by it in the Shape of Tributary Kings; the prodigious Basin, or artificial Lake, which took in the whole *Euphrates*, 'till such time as a new Canal was formed for its Reception, with the several Trenches through which that River was conveyed. I know there are Persons who look upon some of these Wonders of Art as Fabulous, but I cannot find any [Ground] for such a Suspicion, unless it be that we have no such Works among us at present. There were indeed many greater Advantages for Building in those Times, and in that Part of the World, than have been met with ever since. The Earth was extremely fruitful, Men lived generally on Pasturage, which requires a much smaller number of Hands than Agriculture: There were few Trades to employ the busie Part of Mankind, and fewer Arts and Sciences to give Work to Men of Speculative Tempers; and what is more than all the rest, the Prince was absolute; so that when he went to War, he put himself at the Head of a whole People: As we find *Semiramis* leading her [three] Millions to the Field, and yet over-powered by the Number of her Enemies. 'Tis no wonder, therefore, when she was at Peace, and turned her Thoughts on Building, that she could accomplish so great Works, with such a prodigious Multitude of Labourers: Besides that, in her Climate, there was small Interruption of Frosts and Winters, which make the Northern Workmen lie half the Year Idle. I might mention too, among the Benefits of the Climate, what Historians say of the Earth, that it sweated out a Bitumen or natural kind of Mortar, which is doubtless the same with that mentioned in Holy Writ, as contributing to the Structure of *Babel. Slime they used instead of Mortar.*

In *Egypt* we still see their Pyramids, which answer to the Descriptions that have been made of them; and I question not but a Traveller might find out some Remains of the Labyrinth that covered a whole Province, and had a hundred Temples disposed among its several Quarters and Divisions.

The Wall of *China* is one of these Eastern Pieces of Magnificence, which makes a Figure even in the Map of the World, altho' an Account of it would have been thought Fabulous, were not the Wall it self still extant.

We are obliged to Devotion for the noblest Buildings that have adorn'd the several Countries of the World. It is this which has set Men at work on Temples and Publick Places of Worship, not only that they might, by the Magnificence of the Building, invite the Deity to reside within it, but that such stupendous Works might, at the same time, open the Mind to vast Conceptions, and fit it to converse with the Divinity of the Place. For every thing that is Majestick imprints an Awfulness and Reverence on the Mind of the Beholder, and strikes in with the Natural Greatness of the Soul.

In the Second place we are to consider *Greatness of Manner* in Architecture, which has such Force upon the Imagination, that a small Building, where *it* appears, shall give the Mind nobler Ideas than one of twenty times the Bulk, where the Manner is ordinary or little. Thus, perhaps, a Man would have been more astonished with the Majestick Air that appeared in one of [*Lysippus's*] Statues of *Alexander*, tho' no bigger than the Life, than he might have been with Mount *Athos*, had it been cut into the Figure of the Hero, according to the Proposal of *Phidias*, with a River in one Hand, and a City in the other.

Let any one reflect on the Disposition of Mind he finds in himself, at his first Entrance into the *Pantheon* at *Rome*, and how his Imagination is filled with something Great and Amazing; and, at the same time, consider how little, in proportion, he is affected with the Inside of a *Gothick* Cathedral, tho' it be five times larger than the other; which can arise from nothing else, but the Greatness of the Manner in the one, and the Meanness in the other.

I have seen an Observation upon this Subject in a *French* Author, which very much pleased me. It is in Monsieur *Freart's* Parallel of the Ancient and Modern Architecture. I shall give it the Reader with the same Terms of Art which he has made use of. *I am observing* (says he) *a thing which, in my Opinion, is very curious, whence it proceeds, that in the same Quantity of Superficies, the one Manner seems great and magnificent, and the other poor and trifling; the Reason is fine and uncommon. I say then, that to introduce into Architecture this Grandeur of Manner, we ought so to proceed, that the Division of the Principal Members of the Order may consist but of few Parts, that they be all great and of a bold and ample Relievo, and Swelling; and that the Eye, beholding nothing little and mean, the Imagination may be more vigorously touched and affected with the Work that stands before it. For example; In a Cornice, if the Gola or Cynatium of the Corona, the Coping, the Modillions or Dentelli, make a noble Show by their graceful Projections, if we see none of that ordinary Confusion which is the Result of those little Cavities, Quarter Rounds of the Astragal and I know not how many other intermingled Particulars, which produce no Effect in great and massy Works, and which very unprofitably take up place to the Prejudice of the Principal Member, it is most certain that this Manner will appear Solemn and Great; as on the contrary, that it will have but a poor and mean Effect, where there is a Redundancy of those smaller Ornaments, which divide and scatter the Angles of the Sight into such a Multitude of Rays, so pressed together that the whole will appear but a Confusion.*

Among all the Figures in Architecture, there are none that have a greater Air than the Concave and the Convex, and we find in all the Ancient and Modern Architecture, as well in the remote Parts of *China*, as in Countries nearer home, that round Pillars and Vaulted Roofs make a great Part of those Buildings which are designed for Pomp and Magnificence. The Reason I take to be, because in these Figures we generally see more of the Body, than in those of other Kinds. There are, indeed, Figures of Bodies, where the Eye may take in two Thirds of the Surface; but as in such Bodies the Sight must split upon several Angles, it does not take in one uniform Idea, but several Ideas of the same kind. Look upon the Outside of a Dome, your Eye half surrounds it; look up into the Inside, and at one Glance you have all the Prospect of it; the entire Concavity falls into your Eye at once, the Sight being as the Center that collects and gathers into it the Lines of the whole Circumference: In a Square Pillar, the Sight often takes in but a fourth Part of the Surface: and in a Square Concave, must move up and down to the different Sides, before it is Master of all the inward Surface. For this Reason, the Fancy is infinitely more struck with the View of the open Air, and Skies, that passes through an Arch, than what comes through a Square, or any other Figure. The Figure of the Rainbow does not contribute less to its Magnificence, than the Colours to its Beauty, as it is very poetically described by the Son of *Sirach: Look upon the Rainbow, and praise him that made it; very beautiful it is in its Brightness; it encompasses the Heavens with a glorious Circle, and the Hands of the* [most High] *have bended it.*

Having thus spoken of that Greatness which affects the Mind in Architecture, I might next shew the Pleasure that arises in the Imagination from what appears new and beautiful in this Art; but as every Beholder has naturally a greater Taste of these two Perfections in every Building which offers it self to his View, than of that which I have hitherto considered, I shall not trouble my Reader with any Reflections upon it. It is sufficient for my present Purpose, to observe, that there is nothing in this whole Art which pleases the Imagination, but as it is Great, Uncommon, or Beautiful.

103   JEAN BAPTISTE DU BOS
from *Critical Reflections on Poetry, Painting, and Music* (1719)

Although born in Beauvais and schooled in theology in Paris, the Abbé du Bos traveled widely within Europe and in fact met Locke while visiting England. He knew also the ideas of Shaftesbury and Addison, and like them he was a man of letters and critic of the arts. This book, first published in 1719 in France, was popular for a growing class of dilettanti for whom he attempted to serve as a guide to these matters. In his introduction, du Bos promises to "explain the origin of that pleasure which we receive from poems and paintings," that is to say, to instruct the reader as to "the nature of his own sentiments, how they rise and are formed within him." These sentiments are different from the logical workings of human reason, he argues, and indeed du Bos's contribution to eighteenth-century theory lies in the importance that he attaches to human passions or feelings as the primary vehicle for aesthetic enjoyment. Here, in fact, is the counterpoint to Addison's discussion of "greatness" with respect to architecture, only now applied to poetry and painting.

Since the most pleasing sensations that our real passions can afford us, are balanced by so many unhappy hours that succeed our enjoyments, would it not be a noble attempt of art to endeavour to separate the dismal consequences of our passions from the bewitching pleasure we receive in indulging them? Is it not in the power of art to create, as it were, beings of a new nature? Might not art contrive to produce objects that would excite artificial

Jean-Baptiste du Bos (1670–1742), from *Critical Reflections on Poetry, Painting, and Music* (orig. 1719), trans. Thomas Nugent from the fifth edition of du Bos's work. London: John Nourse, 1748, pp. 21–8.

passions, sufficient to occupy us while we are actually affected by them, and incapable of giving us afterwards any real pain or affliction?

An attempt of so delicate a nature was reserved for poetry and painting. I do not pretend to say, that the first painters and poets, no more than other artists, whose performances may not perhaps be inferior to theirs, had such exalted ideas, or such extensive views, upon their first sitting down to work. The first inventers of bathing never dreamt of its being a remedy proper for the curing of certain distempers; they only made use of it as a kind of refreshment in sultry weather, though afterwards it was discovered to be extreamly serviceable to human bodies in several disorders: In like manner, the first poets and painters had nothing more in view perhaps, than to flatter our senses and imagination; and in labouring with that design, they found out the manner of exciting artificial passions. The most useful discoveries in society, have been commonly the effect of hazard: Be that as it will, those imaginary passions which poetry and painting raise artificially within us, by means of their imitations, satisfy that natural want we have of being employed.

Painters and poets raise those artificial passions within us, by presenting us with the imitations of objects capable of exciting real passions. As the impression made by those imitations is of the same nature with that which the object imitated by the painter or poet would have made; and as the impression of the imitation differs from that of the object imitated only in its being of an inferior force, it ought therefore to raise in our souls a passion resembling that which the object imitated would have excited. In other terms, the copy of the object ought to stir up within us a copy of the passion which the object itself would have excited. But as the impression made by the imitation is not so deep as that which the object itself would have made; moreover, as the impression of the imitation is not serious, inasmuch as it does not affect our reason, which is superior to the illusory attack of those sensations, as we shall presently explain more at large: Finally, as the impression made by the imitation affects only the sensitive soul, it has consequently no great durability. This superficial impression, made by imitation, is quickly therefore effaced, without leaving any permanent vestiges, such as would have been left by the impression of the object itself, which the painter or poet hath imitated.

The reason of the difference between the impression made by the object, and that made by the imitation, is obvious. The most finished imitation hath only an artificial existence, or a borrowed life; whereas the force and activity of nature meet in the object imitated. We are influenced by the real object, by virtue of the power which it hath received for that end from nature. *In things which we propose for imitation*, says Quintilian, *there is the strength and efficacy of nature, whereas in imitation there is only the weakness of fiction.*

Here then we discover the source of that pleasure which poetry and painting give to man. Here we see the cause of that satisfaction we find in pictures, the merit whereof consists in setting before our eyes such tragical adventures, as would have struck us with horror, had we been spectators of their reality. For as Aristotle in his Poetics says, *Tho' we should be loth to look at monsters, and people in agony, yet we gaze on those very objects with pleasure when copied by painters; and the better they are copied, the more satisfaction we have in beholding them.*

The pleasure we feel in contemplating the imitations made by painters and poets, of objects which would have raised in us passions attended with real pain, is a pleasure free from all impurity of mixture. It is never attended with those disagreable consequences, which arise from the serious emotions caused by the object itself.

A few examples will illustrate, better than all my arguments, an opinion, which, methinks, I can never set in too clear a light. The massacre of the innocents must have left most gloomy impressions in the imaginations of those, who were real spectators of the barbarity of the soldiers slaughtering the poor infants in the bosom of their mothers, all imbrued with blood. Le Brun's picture, where we see the imitation of this tragical event, moves indeed our humanity, but leaves no troublesome idea in our mind; it excites our compassion, without piercing us with real affliction. A death like that of Phædra, a young princess expiring in the midst of the most frightful convulsions, and accusing herself of the most flagitious crimes, which she has endeavoured to expiate with poison; such a death, I say, as that, would be one of the most frightful and most disagreable objects. We should be a long time before we could get rid of the black and gloomy ideas which such a spectacle would undoubtedly imprint in our imagination. The tragedy of Racine, wherein the imitation of that event is represented, touches us most sensibly, without leaving any permanent seed of affliction. We are pleased with the enjoyment of our emotion, without being under any apprehension of its too long continuance. This piece of Racine draws tears from us, though we are touched with no real sorrow; for the grief that appears is only, as it were, on the surface of our heart, and we are sensible, that our tears will finish with the representation of the ingenious fiction that gave them birth.

104 FRANCIS HUTCHESON
from *An Inquiry into the Original of our Ideas of Beauty and Virtue* (1725)

The philosophical argument of whether the sensation of beauty is absolute, relative, or a combination of both was largely fought out in the second decade of the eighteenth century. And as with the parallel or complementary acceptance of classical and (an emerging) picturesque aesthetics in architecture, the solutions were initially composite or hybrid. Shaftesbury, with his "moral" sense theory, had been the first to attempt to graft aspects of Lockean metaphysics onto a classical framework of goodness and harmony, and this too was the approach of Francis Hutcheson, a Scottish philosopher who taught both in Dublin and Glasgow. His *Inquiry into the Original of Our Ideas of Beauty and Virtue* (1725) was the most comprehensive attempt up to this time to apply the Lockean system of sensation to the subject of beauty, while at the same time retaining the morality explicit in Shaftesbury's arguments. Hutcheson, in fact, sides more with the latter in defining the perception of beauty as an "internal sense," that is to say, an innate sense of harmony that is evoked in thinking about certain natural or manmade objects. Hence his ultimate formulation – and one that we have seen earlier – is that beauty is both absolute and relative, with the one crucial distinction being that absolute beauty is not a quality of the object but rather a feature of the human mind. While ingenious as a solution, such a result would soon come under critical scrutiny.

To make the following Observations understood, it may be necessary to premise some Definitions, and Observations, either universally acknowledg'd, or sufficiently prov'd by

Francis Hutcheson (1694–1746), from *An Inquiry into the Original of Our Ideas of Beauty and Virtue in Two Treatises,* fourth edition (1738, orig. 1725). London: D. Midwinter et al., 1738, pp. 1–2, 4–6, and 8–10.

many Writers both antient and modern, concerning our Perceptions called Sensations, and the Actions of the Mind consequent upon them.

Art.I. Those Ideas which are rais'd in the Mind upon the Presence of external Objects, and their acting upon our Bodys, are call'd Sensations. We find that the Mind in such Cases is passive, and has not Power directly to prevent the Perception or Idea, or to vary it at its Reception, as long as we continue our Bodys in a State fit to be acted upon by the external Object.

II. When two Perceptions are intirely different from each other, or agree in nothing but the general Idea of Sensation, we call the Powers of receiving those different Perceptions, different Senses. Thus Seeing and Hearing denote the different Powers of receiving the Ideas of Colours and Sounds. And altho' Colours have great Differences among themselves, as also have Sounds; yet there is a greater Agreement among the most opposite Colours, than between any Colour and a Sound: Hence we call all Colours Perceptions of the same Sense. All the several Senses seem to have their distinct Organs, except Feeling, which is in some Degree diffus'd over the whole Body.

III. The Mind has a Power of compounding Ideas, which were receiv'd separately; of comparing Objects by means of the Ideas, and of observing their Relations and Proportions; of enlarging and diminishing its Ideas at Pleasure, or in any certain Ratio, or degree; and of considering separately each of the simple Ideas, which might perhaps have been impress'd jointly in the Sensation. This last Operation we commonly call Abstraction. [. . .]

★ ★ ★

VIII. The only Pleasure of Sense, which many Philosophers seem to consider, is that which accompanys the simple Ideas of Sensation: But there are far greater Pleasures in those complex Ideas of Objects, which obtain the Names of Beautiful, Regular, Harmonious. Thus every one acknowledges he is more delighted with a fine Face, a just Picture, than with the View of any one Colour, were it as strong and lively as possible; and more pleas'd with a Prospect of the Sun arising among settled Clouds, and colouring their Edges, with a starry Hemisphere, a fine Landskip, a regular Building, than with a clear blue Sky, a smooth Sea, or a large open Plain, not diversified by Woods, Hills, Waters, Buildings: And yet even these latter Appearances are not quite simple. So in Musick, the Pleasure of fine Composition is incomparably greater than that of any one Note, how sweet, full, or swelling soever.

IX. Let it be observ'd, that in the following Papers, the Word Beauty is taken for the Idea rais'd in us, and a Sense of Beauty for our Power of receiving this Idea. Harmony also denotes our pleasant Ideas arising from Composition of Sounds, and a good Ear (as it is generally taken) a Power of perceiving this Pleasure.

In the following Sections, an Attempt is made to discover "what is the immediate Occasion of these pleasant Ideas, or what real Quality in the Objects ordinarily excites them."

X. It is of no Consequence whether we call these Ideas of Beauty and Harmony, Perceptions of the External Senses of Seeing and Hearing, or not. I should rather choose to call our Power of perceiving these Ideas, an INTERNAL SENSE, were it only for the Convenience of distinguishing them from other Sensations of Seeing and Hearing, which Men may have without Perception of Beauty and Harmony. It is plain from Experience, that many Men have, in the common Meaning, the Senses of Seeing and Hearing perfect enough; they perceive all the Simple Ideas separately, and have their Pleasures; they distinguish them from each other, such as one Colour from another, either quite different, or the stronger or fainter of the same Colour, when they are plac'd beside each other, altho' they may often confound their Names when they occur apart from each other, as some do the Names of Green and Blue: they can tell in separate Notes the higher, lower, sharper or flatter, when separately sounded; in Figures they discern the Length, Breadth, Wideness of each Line, Surface, Angle; and may be as capable of hearing and seeing at great Distances as any Men whatsoever: And yet perhaps they shall find no Pleasure in Musical Compositions, in Painting, Architecture, natural Landskip; or but a very weak one in comparison of what others enjoy from the same Objects. This greater Capacity of receiving such pleasant Ideas we commonly call a fine Genius or Taste: In Musick we seem universally to acknowledge something like a distinct Sense from the External one of Hearing, and call it a good Ear; and the like Distinction we should problably acknowledge in other Objects, had we also got distinct Names to denote these Powers of Perception by. [...]

★ ★ ★

XIV. Hence it plainly appears, "that some Objects are immediately the Occasions of this Pleasure of Beauty, and that we have Senses fitted for perceiving it; and that it is distinct from that Joy which arises upon Prospect of Advantage." Nay, do not we often see Convenience and Use neglected to obtain Beauty, without any other Prospect of Advantage in the beautiful Form, than the suggesting the pleasant Ideas of Beauty? Now this shews us, that however we may pursue beautiful Objects from Self-love, with a View to obtain the Pleasures of Beauty, as in Architecture, Gardening, and many other Affairs; yet there must be a Sense of Beauty, antecedent to Prospects even of this Advantage, without which Sense these Objects would not be thus advantageous, nor excite in us this Pleasure which constitutes them advantageous. Our Sense of Beauty from Objects, by which they are constituted good to us, is very distinct from our Desire of them when they are thus constituted: Our Desire of Beauty may be counter-balanc'd by Rewards or Threatnings, but never our Sense of it; even as Fear of Death may make us desire a bitter Potion, or neglect those Meats which the Sense of Taste would recommend as pleasant; but cannot make that Potion agreeable to the Sense, or Meat disagreeable to it, which was not so antecedently to this Prospect. The same holds true of the Sense of Beauty and Harmony; that the Pursuit of such Objects is frequently neglected, from Prospects of Advantage, Aversion to Labour, or any other Motive of Interest, does not prove that we have no Sense of Beauty, but only that our Desire of it may be counter-balanc'd by a stronger Desire.

XV. Had we no such Sense of Beauty and Harmony, Houses, Gardens, Dress, Equipage, might have been recommended to us as convenient, fruitful, warm, easy; but never as beautiful: And yet nothing is more certain, than that all these Objects are recommended under quite different Views on many Occasions: 'Tis true, what chiefly pleases in the Countenance, are the Indications of Moral Dispositions; and yet were we by the longest Acquaintance fully convinc'd of the best Moral Dispositions in any Person, with that Countenance we now think deform'd, this would never hinder our immediate Dislike of the Form, or our liking other Forms more: And Custom, Education, or Example could never give us Perceptions distinct from those of the Senses which we had the Use of before, or recommend Objects under another Conception than grateful to them. But of the Influence of Custom, Education, Example, upon the Sense of Beauty, we shall treat below.

XVI. Beauty, in Corporeal Forms, is either Original or Comparative; or, if any like the Terms better, Absolute, or Relative: Only let it be observ'd, that by Absolute or Original Beauty, is not understood any Quality suppos'd to be in the Object, which should of itself be beautiful, without relation to any Mind which perceives it: For Beauty, like other Names of sensible Ideas, properly denotes the Perception of some Mind; so Cold, Hot, Sweet, Bitter, denote the Sensations in our Minds, to which perhaps there is no Resemblance in the Objects, which excite these Ideas in us, however we generally imagine otherwise. The Ideas of Beauty and Harmony being excited upon our Perception of some primary Quality, and having relation to Figure and Time, may indeed have a nearer Resemblance to Objects, than these Sensations, which seem not so much any Pictures of Objects, as Modifications of the perceiving Mind; and yet were there no Mind with a Sense of Beauty to contemplate Objects, I see not how they could be call'd Beautiful. We therefore by Absolute Beauty understand only that Beauty which we perceive in Objects without Comparison to any thing external, of which the Object is suppos'd an Imitation, or Picture; such as that Beauty perceiv'd from the Works of Nature, artificial Forms, Figures. Comparative or Relative Beauty is that which we perceive in Objects, commonly considered as Imitations or Resemblances of something else.

105 GEORGE BERKELEY
from the "Third Dialogue" of *Alciphron* (1732)

The first sustained criticism of Hutcheson's position came from the pen of the Irishman George Berkeley, a Bishop in the Anglican Church of Ireland. Berkeley was a native of Kilkenny, a Fellow of Trinity College in Dublin, who first laid the ground for his idealist philosophical system (we know not the world but only our ideas of it) in *Towards a New Theory of Vision* (1709) and *Principles of Human Knowledge* (1710). While fully accepting Lockean empiricism, he in fact strengthened it by discounting Locke's belief in abstract ideas and thereby placing even greater emphasis on the perceptual side of experience on the one hand, and human reasoning (the mental operations of sifting through perceptual data) on the other. In his late dialogue *Alciphron* – actually written in Rhode Island – Berkeley criticizes the innate or "internal sense" of Hutcheson (Alciphron's argument in the dialogue), and counters with his contention (articulated by Euphranor) that since utility or fitness is a necessary component of beauty, the perception of the latter is a mental judgment arrived at through the reasoning of the mind, and is not a product of the sensation or perception in itself. Beauty is therefore relative and logical, not absolute or innate.

8. *Euph.* What you now say is very intelligible: I wish I understood your main principle as well.

George Berkeley (1685–1753), from the "Third Dialogue" of *Alciphron, or the Minute Philosopher in Seven Dialogues* (1732), in *Alciphron, or the Minute Philosopher in Focus*, ed. David Berman. London: Routledge, 1993, pp. 65–71.

Alc. And are you then in earnest at a loss? Is it possible you should have no notion of beauty, or that having it you should not know it to be amiable – amiable, I say, in itself and for itself?

Euph. Pray tell me, Alciphron, are all mankind agreed in the notion of a beauteous face?

Alc. Beauty in humankind seems to be of a mixed and various nature; forasmuch as the passions, sentiments, and qualities of the soul, being seen through and blending with the features, work differently on different minds, as the sympathy is more or less. But with regard to other things is there no steady principle of beauty? Is there upon earth a human mind without the idea of order, harmony, and proportion?

Euph. O Alciphron, it is my weakness that I am apt to be lost in abstractions and generalities, but a particular thing is better suited to my faculties. I find it easy to consider and keep in view the objects of sense: let us therefore try to discover what their beauty is, or wherein it consists; and so, by the help of these sensible things, as a scale or ladder, ascend to moral and intellectual beauty. Be pleased then to inform me, what is it we call beauty in the objects of sense?

Alc. Everyone knows beauty is that which pleases.

Euph. There is then beauty in the smell of a rose, or the taste of an apple?

Alc. By no means. Beauty is, to speak properly, perceived only by the eye.

Euph. It cannot therefore be defined in general that which pleaseth?

Alc. I grant it cannot.

Euph. How then shall we limit or define it?

Alciphron, after a short pause, said that beauty consisted in a certain symmetry or proportion pleasing to the eye.

Euph. Is this proportion one and the same in all things, or is it different in different kinds of things?

Alc. Different, doubtless. The proportions of an ox would not be beautiful in a horse. And we may observe also in things inanimate, that the beauty of a table, a chair, a door, consists in different proportions.

Euph. Doth not this proportion imply the relation of one thing to another?

Alc. It doth.

Euph. And are not these relations founded in size and shape?

Alc. They are.

Euph. And, to make the proportions just, must not those mutual relations of size and shape in the parts be such as shall make the whole complete and perfect in its kind?

Alc. I grant they must.

Euph. Is not a thing said to be perfect in its kind when it answers the end for which it was made?

Alc. It is.

Euph. The parts, therefore, in true proportions must be so related, and adjusted to one another, as that they may best conspire to the use and operation of the whole?

Alc. It seems so.

Euph. But the comparing parts one with another, the considering them as belonging to one whole, and the referring this whole to its use or end, should seem the work of reason: should it not?

Alc. It should.

Euph. Proportions, therefore, are not, strictly speaking, perceived by the sense of sight, but only by reason through the means of sight.

Alc. This I grant.

Euph. Consequently, beauty, in your sense of it, is an object, not of the eye, but of the mind.

Alc. It is.

Euph. The eye, therefore, alone cannot see that a chair is handsome, or a door well proportioned.

Alc. It seems to follow; but I am not clear as to this point.

Euph. Let us see if there be any difficulty in it. Could the chair you sit on, think you, be reckoned well proportioned or handsome, if it had not such a height, breadth, wideness, and was not so far reclined as to afford a convenient seat?

Alc. It could not.

Euph. The beauty, therefore, or symmetry of a chair cannot be apprehended but by knowing its use, and comparing its figure with that use; which cannot be done by the eye alone, but is the effect of judgment. It is, therefore, one thing to see an object, and another to discern its beauty.

Alc. I admit this to be true.

9. *Euph.* The architects judge a door to be of a beautiful proportion, when its height is double of the breadth. But if you should invert a well-proportioned door, making its breadth become the height, and its height the breadth, the figure would still be the same, but without that beauty in one situation which it had in another. What can be the cause of this, but that, in the forementioned supposition, the door would not yield convenient entrances to creatures of a human figure? But, if in any other part of the universe there should be supposed rational animals of an inverted stature, they must be supposed to invert the rule for proportion of doors; and to them that would appear beautiful which to us was disagreeable.

Alc. Against this I have no objection.

Euph. Tell me, Alciphron, is there not something truly decent and beautiful in dress?

Alc. Doubtless, there is.

Euph. Are any likelier to give us an idea of this beauty in dress than painters and sculptors, whose proper business and study it is to aim at graceful representations?

Alc. I believe not.

Euph. Let us then examine the draperies of the great masters in these arts: how, for instance, they use to clothe a matron, or a man of rank. Cast an eye on those figures (said he, pointing to some prints after Raphael and Guido, that hung upon the wall): what appearance do you think an English courtier or magistrate, with his Gothic, succinct, plaited garment, and his full-bottomed wig; or one of our ladies in her unnatural dress, pinched and stiffened and enlarged, with hoops and whale-bone and buckram, must make, among those figures so decently clad in draperies that fall into such a variety of natural, easy, and ample folds, that cover the body without encumbering it, and adorn without altering the shape?

Alc. Truly I think they must make a very ridiculous appearance.

Euph. And what do you think this proceeds from? Whence is it that the eastern nations, the Greeks, and the Romans, naturally ran into the most becoming dresses; while our

Gothic gentry, after so many centuries racking their inventions, mending, and altering, and improving, and whirling about in a perpetual rotation of fashions, have never yet had the luck to stumble on any that was not absurd and ridiculous? Is it not from hence that, instead of consulting use, reason, and convenience, they abandon themselves to irregular fancy, the unnatural parent of monsters? Whereas the ancients, considering the use and end of dress, made it subservient to the freedom, ease, and convenience of the body; and, having no notion of mending or changing the natural shape, they aimed only at showing it with decency and advantage. And, if this be so, are we not to conclude that the beauty of dress depends on its subserviency to certain ends and uses?

Alc. This appears to be true.

Euph. This subordinate relative nature of beauty, perhaps, will be yet plainer, if we examine the respective beauties of a horse and a pillar. Virgil's description of the former is –

> *Illi ardua cervix,*
> *Argutumque caput, brevis alvus, obesaque terga,*
> *Luxuriatque toris animosum pectus.*[1]

Now, I would fain know whether the perfections and uses of a horse may not be reduced to these three points: courage, strength, and speed; and whether each of the beauties enumerated doth not occasion or betoken one of these perfections? After the same manner, if we inquire into the parts and proportions of a beautiful pillar, we shall perhaps find them answer to the same idea. Those who have considered the theory of architecture tell us, the proportions of the three Grecian orders were taken from the human body, as the most beautiful and perfect production of nature. Hence were derived those graceful ideas of columns, which had a character of strength without clumsiness, or of delicacy without weakness. Those beautiful proportions were, I say, taken originally from nature, which, in her creatures, as hath been already observed, referreth them to some end, use, or design. The *gonfiezza* also, or swelling, and the diminution of a pillar, is it not in such proportion as to make it appear strong and light at the same time? In the same manner, must not the whole entablature, with its projections, be so proportioned, as to seem great but not heavy, light but not little; inasmuch as a deviation into either extreme would thwart that reason and use of things wherein their beauty is founded, and to which it is subordinate? The entablature, and all its parts and ornaments, architrave, frieze, cornice, triglyphs, metopes, modiglions, and the rest, have each a use or appearance of use, in giving firmness and union to the building, in protecting it from the weather and casting off the rain, in representing the ends of beams with their intervals, the production of rafters, and so forth. And if we consider the graceful angles in frontispieces, the spaces between the columns, or the ornaments of their capitals, shall we not find, that their beauty riseth from the appearance of use, or the imitation of natural things, whose beauty is originally founded on the same principle? which is, indeed, the grand distinction between Grecian and Gothic architecture; the latter being fantastical, and for the most part founded neither in nature nor in reason, in necessity nor use, the appearance of which accounts for all the beauty, grace, and ornament of the other.

Cri. What Euphranor hath said confirms the opinion I always entertained, that the rules of architecture were founded, as all other arts which flourished among the Greeks, in truth, and nature, and good sense. But the ancients, who, from a thorough consideration of the grounds and principles of art, formed their idea of beauty, did not always confine themselves strictly to the same rules and proportions; but, whenever the particular distance, position, elevation, or dimension of the fabric or its parts seemed to require it, made no scruple to depart from them, without deserting the original principles of beauty, which governed whatever deviations they made. This latitude or licence might not, perhaps, be safely trusted with most modern architects, who in their bold sallies seem to act without aim or design; and to be governed by no idea, no reason, or principle of art, but pure caprice, joined with a thorough contempt of that noble simplicity of the ancients, without which there can be no unity, gracefulness, or grandeur in their works; which of consequence must serve only to disfigure and dishonour the nation, being so many monuments to future ages of the opulence and ill taste of the present; which, it is to be feared, would succeed as wretchedly, and make as mad work in other affairs, were men to follow, instead of rules, precepts, and morals, their own taste and first thoughts of beauty.

Alc. I should now, methinks, be glad to see a little more distinctly the use and tendency of this digression upon architecture.

Euph. Was not beauty the very thing we inquired after?

Alc. It was.

Euph. What think you, Alciphron, can the appearance of a thing please at this time, and in this place, which pleased two thousand years ago, and two thousand miles off, without some real principle of beauty?

Alc. It cannot.

Euph. And is not this the case with respect to a just piece of architecture?

Alc. Nobody denies it.

Euph. Architecture, the noble offspring of judgment and fancy, was gradually formed in the most polite and knowing countries of Asia, Egypt, Greece, and Italy. It was cherished and esteemed by the most flourishing states and most renowned princes, who with vast expense improved and brought it to perfection. It seems, above all other arts, peculiarly conversant about order, proportion, and symmetry. May it not therefore be supposed, on all accounts, most likely to help us to some rational notion of the *je ne sais quoi* in beauty? And, in effect, have we not learned from this digression that, as there is no beauty without proportion, so proportions are to be esteemed just and true, only as they are relative to some certain use or end, their aptitude and subordination to which end is, at bottom, that which makes them please and charm?

Alc. I admit all this to be true.

NOTE

1   [That is: 'He has a proud neck, a finely chiselled head, a short belly, well-rounded flanks, and his fiery chest ripples with muscles' (Virgil, *Georgics*, III, line 79 ff.)]

106 DAVID HUME
from *A Treatise of Human Nature* (1739–40)

The Scottish philosopher David Hume holds an exalted place in British thought, in both positive and negative senses. On the one hand, he is regarded as the last of the triumvirate of major British empiricists – following Locke and Berkeley – and the one who brought the system to completion. On the other hand, his insistence that philosophy cannot go beyond human experience led him into a skepticism that caused later thinkers, such as Immanuel Kant, to reformulate entirely the problem of human knowledge and perception.

Within his portfolio of ideas, *A Treatise of Human Nature* is an early work, begun when he was still in his teens and completed at the age of 29. The inspiration for his treatment of the theme of beauty are the two books of du Bos and Hutcheson. But Hume clearly takes the problem of beauty in a new direction. Like his two predecessors, he assumes beauty to be a special "power" of objects that provokes certain sensations in our minds – a "form" that produces pleasure – but he gives it as well a more relative cast. Not only are certain forms pleasing in some animals and not in others (suggesting a necessary utilitarian or functional component to beauty), but he will also argue that the sensation of beauty is, in effect, relative to our own level of experience. What, for Hume, prevents the relative nature of aesthetic judgments from falling into pure subjectivity is simply the argument that there is a universal psychological make-up to the human mind, and that we can train our minds to acquire those higher gleanings of beauty.

Of Beauty and Deformity

Whether we consider the body as a part of ourselves, or assent to those philosophers, who regard it as something external, it must still be allow'd to be near enough connected with us to form one of these double relations, which I have asserted to be necessary to the causes of pride and humility. Wherever, therefore, we can find the other relation of impressions to join to this of ideas, we may expect with assurance either of these passions, according as the impression is pleasant or uneasy. But *beauty* of all kinds gives us a peculiar delight and satisfaction; as *deformity* produces pain, upon whatever subject it may be plac'd, and whether survey'd in an animate or inanimate object. If the beauty or deformity, therefore, be plac'd upon our own bodies, this pleasure or uneasiness must be converted into pride or humility, as having in this case all the circumstances requisite to produce a perfect transition of impressions and ideas. These opposite sensations are related to the opposite passions. The beauty or deformity is closely related to self, the object of both these passions. No wonder, then, our own beauty becomes an object of pride, and deformity of humility.

But this effect of personal and bodily qualities is not only a proof of the present system, by shewing that the passions arise not in this case without all the circumstances I have requir'd,

David Hume, from *A Treatise of Human Nature* (1739–40). Amherst, NY: Prometheus Books, 1992, pp. 298–9.

but may be employ'd as a stronger and more convincing argument. If we consider all the hypotheses, which have been form'd either by philosophy or common reason, to explain the difference betwixt beauty and deformity, we shall find that all of them resolve into this, that beauty is such an order and construction of parts, as either by the *primary constitution* of our nature, by *custom*, or by *caprice*, is fitted to give a pleasure and satisfaction to the soul. This is the distinguishing character of beauty, and forms all the difference betwixt it and deformity, whose natural tendency is to produce uneasiness. Pleasure and pain, therefore, are not only necessary attendants of beauty and deformity, but constitute their very essence. And indeed, if we consider, that a great part of the beauty, which we admire either in animals or in other objects, is deriv'd from the idea of convenience and utility, we shall make no scruple to assent to this opinion. That shape, which produces strength, is beautiful in one animal; and that which is a sign of agility in another. The order and convenience of a palace are no less essential to its beauty, than its mere figure and appearance. In like manner the rules of architecture require, that the top of a pillar shou'd be more slender than its base, and that because such a figure conveys to us the idea of security, which is pleasant; whereas the contrary form gives us the apprehension of danger, which is uneasy. From innumerable instances of this kind, as well as from considering that beauty like wit, cannot be defin'd, but is discern'd only by a taste or sensation, we may conclude, that beauty is nothing but a form, which produces pleasure, as deformity is a structure of parts, which conveys pain; and since the power of producing pain and pleasure make in this manner the essence of beauty and deformity, all the effects of these qualities must be deriv'd from the sensation; and among the rest pride and humility, which of all their effects are the most common and remarkable.

107 ALLAN RAMSEY
from "Dialogue on Taste" in *The Investigator* (1755)

The translation of Hume's empirical skepticism into architectural terms did not take too many years. It was soon voiced by the Scottish painter Allan Ramsey, whom we saw earlier in the spirited dispute over the superiority of Greek art over Roman art in classical times. His "Dialogue on Taste" (1755), in fact, defines a landmark in architectural theory because it is the first clear articulation of relativist aesthetics.

Ramsay and Hume, in fact, were the best of friends. In 1754 the two men (together with Adam Smith, Alexander Gerard, and Robert Adam, among others) founded the Select Society of Edinburgh, a debating forum that became the cornerstone of what is generally referred to as the Scottish Enlightenment. The following year the Select Society offered a prize for the best essay on the problem of "taste." Ramsay was the first of the participants to publish his views (the next two entries follow from the same contest), which he actually wrote during a 9-month stay in Edinburgh in 1754. And rather than being a formal essay, it takes the form of a dialogue in which the defender of the classical tradition (Lord Modish) is pitted against a free-thinking modernist (Colonel Freeman), who is said to

Allan Ramsey, from "A Dialogue on Taste" (1755) in the journal *The Investigator* (London, 1762), pp. 32–5.

have been modeled on the character of Hume. The work is intentionally provocative in its comparison of architectural taste with clothing fashions and cookery.

Col. FREEMAN.

The fame, my Lord, that I should say to a good taste in dress or cookery, that, abstracted from health and conveniency, which are the objects of reason, it is one of those tastes which custom, a second nature, has bestowed upon us; and is so much mere taste that it can never, with any propriety, become a matter of dispute or comparison. To insist upon one form of dress, or one form of building, being in itself more beautiful than another, must appear to a philosopher entering upon as sensless a controversy, as the pretending that one dish was in itself more palatable than another, and that he who preferred the one had a better taste than he who preferred the other.

Lord MODISH.

But sure, Colonel, there are rules for the beauties of architecture, and not the smallest ornament of a base or cornish without its settled proportion.

Col. FREEMAN.

Were that strictly the case, my Lord, we should call it knowledge or judgment in architecture, not taste; for, as far as these rules go, no taste is required, either good or bad. An Artist may, by a Palladian receipt alone, without any taste, form a very elegant Corinthian pillar; as a cook, without any palate, and by the help of the *housewife's vade mecum* only, makes an unexceptionable dish of *beef a la daube*. These rules are plainly no more than the analysis of certain things which custom has rendered agreeable; but do not point out to us any natural standard of beauty or flavour, by which such things, whether pillars or dishes, could have been originally contrived to answer the purpose of pleasing. I should be exceedingly glad to hear a reason why a Corinthian capital clapt upon its shaft upside-down should not become, by custom, as pleasing a spectacle as in the manner it commonly stands. I know this would be look'd upon as a sort of blasphemy by some of our dilettanti; but so is every opinion, however reasonable, which opposes what is by custom established in any country. Perhaps there are countries in the world where my capital is so much in taste, that their virtuosi would be surprized to hear that there was any nation so absurd as to put the volutes uppermost. At least there is no imagination of that sort so odd that some similar experience is not sufficient to justify and render probable.

Lord MODISH.

How then came the present fashion (since you will have it to be no better) of architecture to be so universally embraced?

Col. FREEMAN.

It's universality, my Lord, does not extend beyond Christendom; and, if it should become the taste of the whole universe, the same means, which have procured it a reception among us, will account for its further progress, without our giving ourselves the trouble of searching for any standard in nature for its recommendation. It is the nature of all fashions (I except only those of a religious kind) to take their rise from the sovereign will and pleasure of the rich and powerful. Men in such circumstances are known from thence to acquire a presumption, which naturally induces them to take the lead in every thing; while those very circumstances which engage them to indulge their caprices, enable them at the same time to render those caprices respectable. As for instance, let a man of ordinary rank or figure appear in publick in a coat whose cuffs are triangular, when the mode is square; and there is no doubt he will meet with many to despise, but none to imitate him. Let the same be tried by a man blest with title, riches, youth, and all the trappings of prosperity; let the sleeve be of velvet, curiously embroidered, and part of a suit of cloaths in all other respects fashionable and rich, the triangle will then be found to meet with a quite different reception, and tho' feeble in itself, will be so powerfully seconded by, being incorporated with, the title, the embroidery, the coach, and the footman, as to become part of the august idea of his grace; and so far from being able to render him ridiculous, will receive a share of respect by being part of him; and from being tolerable, will soon become an object of imitation, especially to the persons who are the most intimate with him and his cloaths. The more those imitations encrease, the more the sensation of their beauty is confirmed; till, in a short time, all other cuffs but the triangular are detestable. City taylors bribe his Lordship's valet de chambre to let them take it's shape and proportions; and here is, at last, a precise rule established.

108   ALEXANDER GERARD
from *An Essay on Taste* (1756)

The winner of the Select Society's essay competition of 1755 was Alexander Gerard. A precocious child and professor of the classics, philosophy, and the sciences, Gerard was teaching at Marischal College in Aberdeen in 1756 when he wrote this essay. It is a highly structured and somewhat classically conceived work that draws upon many of the discussions of the previous 30 years. The faculties of the human mind for Gerard are four: the external senses, memory, judgment, and imagination. Taste resides in the last faculty, and Gerard follows both Hutcheson and Hume in viewing imagination as an "inner sense," which he now reduces to the sensations (tastes) of novelty, sublimity, beauty, imitation, harmony, ridicule, and virtue. The following two excerpts are taken from his chapters on "grandeur and sublimity" and "beauty." The philosophical and psychological problem he is addressing is really how or why certain objects evoke or suggest certain ideas in the mind. The distinction between sublimity (greatness) and beauty in aesthetic thought, which had been suggested by Addison earlier in the century, had been more recently addressed by John Baillie in *An Essay on the Sublime* (1747). It would soon have a more comprehensive treatment at the hands of Edmund Burke. Gerard's discussion of "proportion" also underscores the central architectural dilemma with regard to relative beauty.

Grandeur or sublimity gives us a still higher and nobler pleasure, by means of a sense appropriated to the perception of it; while meanness renders any object to which it adheres,

Alexander Gerard (1728–95), from *An Essay on Taste* (1756, published 1759), facsimile edition published by Walter J. Hipple for the Scholars' Facsimiles & Reprints, Gainesville, 1963, pp. 11–14 and 33–5.

disagreeable and distasteful. Objects are sublime, which possess *quantity,* or amplitude, and *simplicity,* in conjunction.

Considerable *magnitude,* or largeness of extension, in objects capable of it, is necessary to produce sublimity. It is not on a small rivulet, however transparent, and beautifully winding; it is not on a narrow valley, though variegated with flowers of a thousand pleasing hues; it is not on a little hill, though cloathed with the most delightful verdure, that we bestow the epithet *sublime*: but on the Alps, the Nile, the ocean, the wide expanse of heaven, or the immensity of space uniformly extended without limit or termination.

We always contemplate objects and ideas with a disposition similar to their nature. When a large object is presented, the mind expands itself to the extent of that object, and is filled with one grand sensation, which totally possessing it, composes it into a solemn sedateness, and strikes it with deep silent wonder and admiration: it finds such a difficulty in spreading itself to the dimensions of its object, as enlivens and invigorates its frame: and having overcome the opposition which this occasions, it sometimes imagines itself present in every part of the scene which it contemplates; and from the sense of this immensity, feels a noble pride, and entertains a lofty conception of its own capacity.

Large objects can scarce indeed produce their full effect, unless they are also *simple,* or made up of parts in a great measure similar. Innumerable little islands scattered in the ocean, and breaking the prospect, greatly diminish the grandeur of the scene. A variety of clouds, diversifying the face of the heavens, may add to their beauty, but must take from their grandeur.

Objects cannot possess that largeness which is necessary for inspiring a sensation of the sublime, without simplicity. Where this is wanting, the mind contemplates, not one large, but many small objects; it is pained with the labour requisite to creep from one to another; and is disgusted with the imperfection of the idea with which, even after all this toil, it must remain contented. But we take in with ease one entire conception of a simple object, however large: in consequence of this facility, we naturally account it one: the view of one single part suggests the whole, and enables fancy to extend and enlarge it to infinity, that it may fill the capacity of the mind. [. . .]

★ ★ ★

Proportion consists not so much in relations of the parts precisely measurable, as in a general aptitude of the structure to the end proposed: which experience enables us instantaneously to perceive, better than any artificial methods can determine it. Its influence on beauty is therefore derived from *fitness,* a principle which will be illustrated presently.

A very small disproportion in any of the members of the human body produces deformity. The least deviation, in the productions of the fine arts, from the natural harmony of the parts, always occasions a blemish.

There is another kind of *proportion,* at least not wholly dependent on utility, which is preserved in the appearances of things, when none of the parts are so small, in respect of one another, and of the whole, as to disappear through their smallness, while we contemplate the whole; and when none of them are so large, that, when we fix our view on them, we cannot distinctly perceive at the same time their relation to the whole, and to the other parts. Figures, the sides of which are very numerous, lose a great part of the beauty which would arise from this variety, by the want of proportion between the sides and the diameter.

Works in the Gothic taste, crowded with minute ornaments, fall as much short of perfect beauty, by their disproportion, as by their deviation from simplicity.

As nothing gives us greater pleasure than what leads us to form a lofty conception of our own faculties, so nothing is more disagreeable than what reminds us of their imperfection. On this account it is, that the want of this kind of proportion disgusts us. It leads us to entertain a low, and consequently ungrateful, opinion of our capacity, by rendering it impossible to form one entire distinct conception of the object. The variety of its parts may amuse us, and keep us from attempting to comprehend the whole; and then, especially if it be joined with uniformity, it will yield us some degree of pleasure, and constitute an inferior and imperfect species of beauty. But still proportion is necessary for perfecting the beauty and fully gratifying a correct and improved taste.

Thus the absence of any one of these ingredients, the want either of uniformity, of variety, or of proportion, diminishes the beauty of objects: but where all of them are in a great measure wanting, deformity must prevail. Figures may be desirable or valuable on other accounts; but without these qualities they cannot be beautiful.

109   DAVID HUME
from "Of the Standard of Taste"
(1757)

Hume's contribution to the problem of taste was his essay "Of the Standard of Taste," which he published in 1757 as the fourth of his *Four Dissertations*. Again it derives from his earlier empirical system in which "Beauty is no quality in things themselves: It exists merely in the mind which contemplates them; and each mind perceives a different beauty." And thus for Hume the matter became the question of whether there are in fact any rules behind these judgments of taste concerning beauty, or whether we each live only in our own solipsistic world, that is, a private and subjective space unknown to each other. The great diversity of opinions in matters of taste, Hume argues, speaks to the latter proposition, but at the same time over centuries a consensus has generally formed regarding the superiority of one work of art over another. If this consensus cannot be found within the rules of artistic composition (which Hume rejects), then it must reside in the universality of the human mind – the mind rightly formed to allow just these "tender and delicate" emotions of beauty to arise.

But though all the general rules of art are founded only on experience and on the observation of the common sentiments of human nature, we must not imagine, that, on every occasion, the feelings of men will be conformable to these rules. Those finer emotions of the mind are of a very tender and delicate nature, and require the concurrence of many favourable circumstances to make them play with facility and exactness, according to their general and established principles. The least exterior hindrance to such small springs, or the

David Hume, from "Of the Standard of Taste" (1757) in a facsimile edition of *Four Dissertations*, ed. John Immerwahr. Bristol: Thoemmes Press, 1995, pp. 212–17.

least internal disorder, disturbs their motion, and confounds the operation of the whole machine. When we would make an experiment of this nature, and would try the force of any beauty or deformity, we must choose with care a proper time and place, and bring the fancy to a suitable situation and disposition. A perfect serenity of mind, a recollection of thought, a due attention to the object; if any of these circumstances be wanting our experiment will be fallacious, and we shall be unable to judge of the catholic and universal beauty. The relation, which nature has placed betwixt the form and the sentiment, will at least be more obscure; and it will require greater accuracy to trace and discern it. We shall be able to ascertain its influence not so much from the operation of each particular beauty, as from the durable admiration, which attends those works, that have survived all the caprices of mode and fashion, all the mistakes of ignorance and envy.

The same *Homer*, who pleased at *Athens* and *Rome* two thousand years ago, is still admired at *Paris* and at *London*. All the changes of climate, government, religion, and language have not been able to obscure his glory. Authority or prejudice may give a temporary vogue to a bad poet or orator; but his reputation will never be durable or general. When his compositions are examined by posterity or by foreigners, the enchantment is dissipated, and his faults appear in their true colours. On the contrary, a real genius, the longer his works endure, and the more wide they are spread, the more sincere is the admiration which he meets with. Envy and jealousy have too much place in a narrow circle; and even familiar acquaintance with his person may diminish the applause due to his performances: But when these obſtructions are removed, the beauties, which are naturally fitted to excite agreeable sentiments immediately display their energy; and while the world endures, they maintain their authority over the minds of men.

It appears then, that amidst all the variety and caprices of taste, there are certain general principles of approbation or blame, whose influence a careful eye may trace in all operations of the mind. Some particular forms or qualities, from the original structure of the internal fabric, are calculated to please, and others to displease; and if they fail of their effect in any particular instance, it is from some apparent defect or imperfection in the organ. A man in a fever would not insist on his palate as able to decide concerning flavours; nor would one, affected with the jaundice, pretend to give a verdict with regard to colours. In each creature, there is a sound and a defective state; and the former alone can be supposed to afford us a true standard of taste and sentiment. If in the sound state of the organs, there be an entire or a considerable uniformity of sentiment among men, we may thence derive an idea of the perfect and universal beauty; in like manner as the appearance of objects in day-light to the eye of a man in health is denominated their true and real colour, even while colour is allowed to be merely a phantasm of the senses.

Many and frequent are the defects in the internal organs, which prevent or weaken the influence of those general principles, on which depends our sentiment of beauty or deformity. Though some objects, by the structure of the mind, be naturally calculated to give pleasure, it is not to be expected, that in every individual the pleasure will be equally felt. Particular incidents and situations occur, which either throw a false light on the objects, or hinder the true from conveying to the imagination the proper sentiment and perception.

One obvious cause, why many feel not the proper sentiment of beauty, is the want of that *delicacy* of imagination, which is requisite to convey a sensibility of those finer emotions. This delicacy every one pretends to: Every one talks of it; and would reduce every kind of taste or sentiment to its standard. But as our intention in this dissertation is to mingle some light of the understanding with the feelings of sentiment, it will be proper to give a more accurate definition of delicacy, than has hitherto been attempted. And not to draw our philosophy from too profound a source, we shall have recourse to a noted story in *Don Quixote*.

'Tis with good reason, says *Sancho* to the squire with the great nose, that I pretend to have a judgment in wine: This is a quality hereditary in our family. Two of my kinsmen were once called to give their opinion of a hogshead, which was supposed to be excellent, being old and of a good vintage. One of them tastes it; considers it, and after mature reflection pronounces the wine to be good, were it not for a small taste of leather, which he perceived in it. The other, after using the same precautions, gives also his verdict in favour of the wine; but with the reserve of a taste of iron, which he could easily distinguish. You cannot imagine how much they were both ridiculed for their judgment. But who laughed in the end? On emptying the hogshead, there was found at the bottom, an old key with a leathern thong tied to it.

110 EDMUND BURKE
from *A Philosophical Inquiry into the Origin of our Ideas of the Sublime and Beautiful* (1757)

The aesthetic development that can be traced through the writings of Addison, Hutcheson, and Hume comes to a head in this most important book of Edmund Burke, the Irish statesman, political writer, and essayist. This book appeared in 1757 only a few months after Hume's essay, and in fact Burke seems to have held back the introductory essay of his book, "On Taste," until the second edition of 1759, in order to respond more fully to Hume's position. Burke also notes in the preface of 1757 that he had actually finished the manuscript in 1753. Whatever the case, Burke's solution would eclipse the efforts of his contemporaries and largely chart the direction of British aesthetic theory for the remainder of the century.

Much of the reason for the book's success lies in its simple ambition. If Hume had attempted to salvage judgments of taste by arguing, in essence, that they could be justly displayed only by people of superior or purified imagination, Burke takes a more systematic or scientific approach. He believes that there are indeed "some invariable and certain laws" underlying judgments of taste, which he defines as "that faculty or those faculties of the mind, which are affected with, or which form a judgment of, the works of imagination and the elegant arts." His approach is to describe more comprehensively the range of emotions that are evoked by objects as well as to eliminate many of the vestiges of classical theory, such as the connection of fitness or utility with aesthetic judgments

Edmund Burke (1729–97), from *A Philosophical Inquiry into the Origin of our Ideas of the Sublime and Beautiful* (1757) in *The Works of Edmund Burke*, Vol. I, London: G. Bell & Sons, 1913, pp. 118–22.

(which requires the intervention of reason). It is in the last regard that this first selection from his study is presented. Appearing under the heading "Proportion Not the Cause of Beauty in the Human Species," this passage is a masterpiece of Burkean prose that cuts to the chase by quickly disposing of all classical conceptions. Note, for instance, his use of the famous Renaissance and Vitruvian image of a man standing in a square — how he not only rejects its relevance but also exploits its meaning to strengthen his own comments on architecture and garden design.

There are some parts of the human body that are observed to hold certain proportions to each other; but before it can be proved that the efficient cause of beauty lies in these, it must be shown, that wherever these are found exact, the person to whom they belong is beautiful: I mean in the effect produced on the view, either of any member distinctly considered, or of the whole body together. It must be likewise shown, that these parts stand in such a relation to each other, that the comparison between them may be easily made, and that the affection of the mind may naturally result from it. For my part, I have at several times very carefully examined many of those proportions, and found them hold very nearly or altogether alike in many subjects, which were not only very different from one another, but where one has been very beautiful, and the other very remote from beauty. With regard to the parts which are found so proportioned, they are often so remote from each other, in situation, nature, and office, that I cannot see how they admit of any comparison, nor consequently how any effect owing to proportion can result from them. The neck, say they, in beautiful bodies, should measure with the calf of the leg; it should likewise be twice the circumference of the wrist. And an infinity of observations of this kind are to be found in the writings and conversations of many. But what relation has the calf of the leg to the neck; or either of these parts to the wrist? These proportions are certainly to be found in handsome bodies. They are as certainly in ugly ones; as any who will take the pains to try may find. Nay, I do not know but they may be least perfect in some of the most beautiful. You may assign any proportions you please to every part of the human body; and I undertake that a painter shall religiously observe them all, and notwithstanding produce, if he pleases, a very ugly figure. The same painter shall considerably deviate from these proportions, and produce a very beautiful one. And indeed it may be observed in the master-pieces of the ancient and modern statuary, that several of them differ very widely from the proportions of others, in parts very conspicuous and of great consideration; and that they differ no less from the proportions we find in living men, of forms extremely striking and agreeable. And after all, how are the partisans of proportional beauty agreed amongst themselves about the proportions of the human body? Some hold it to be seven heads; some make it eight; whilst others extend it even to ten; a vast difference in such a small number of divisions! Others take other methods of estimating the proportions, and all with equal success. But are these proportions exactly the same in all handsome men? or are they at all the proportions found in beautiful women? Nobody will say that they are; yet both sexes are undoubtedly capable of beauty, and the female of the greatest; which advantage I believe will hardly be attributed to the superior exactness of proportion in the fair sex. Let us rest a moment on this point; and consider how much difference there is between the measures that prevail in many similar parts of the body, in the two sexes of this single species only. If you assign any determinate proportions to the limbs of a man, and if you limit human beauty to these proportions, when you find a woman who differs in the make and measures of almost every part, you must conclude her not to be beautiful, in spite of the suggestions of your imagination; or, in obedience to your imagination, you must renounce your rules; you must lay by the scale and compass, and look out for some other cause of beauty. For if beauty be attached to certain measures which operate from a *principle in nature*, why should similar parts with different measures of proportion be found to have beauty, and this too in the very same species? But to open our view a little, it is worth observing, that almost all animals have parts of very much the same nature, and destined nearly to the same purposes; a head, neck, body, feet, eyes, ears, nose, and mouth; yet Providence, to provide in the best manner for their several wants, and to display the riches of his wisdom and goodness in his creation, has worked out of these few and similar organs and members, a diversity hardly short of infinite in their disposition, measures, and relation. But, as we have before observed, amidst this infinite diversity, one particular is common to many species: several of the individuals which compose them are capable of affecting us with a sense of loveliness; and whilst they agree in producing this effect, they differ extremely in the relative measures of those parts which have produced it. These considerations were sufficient to induce me to reject the notion of any particular proportions that operated by nature to produce a pleasing effect; but those who will agree with me with regard to a particular proportion, are strongly prepossessed in favour of one more indefinite. They imagine, that although beauty in general is annexed to no certain measures common to the several kinds of pleasing plants and animals; yet that there is a certain proportion in each species absolutely essential to the beauty of that particular kind. If we consider the animal world in general, we find beauty confined to no certain measures: but as some peculiar measure and relation of parts is what distinguishes each peculiar class of animals, it must of necessity be, that the beautiful in each kind will be found in the measures and proportions of that kind; for otherwise it would deviate from its proper species, and become in some sort monstrous: however, no species is so strictly confined to any certain proportions, that there is not a considerable variation amongst the individuals; and as it has been shown of the human, so it may be shown of the brute kinds, that beauty is found indifferently in all the proportions which each kind can admit, without quitting its common form; and it is this idea of a common form that makes the proportion of parts at all regarded, and not the operation of any natural cause: indeed a little consideration will make it appear, that it is not measure, but manner, that creates all the beauty which belongs to shape. What light do we borrow from these boasted proportions, when we study ornamental design? It seems amazing to me, that artists, if they were as well convinced as they pretend to be, that proportion is a principal cause of beauty, have not by them at all times accurate measurements of all sorts of beautiful animals to help them to proper proportions, when they would contrive anything elegant; especially as they frequently assert that it is from an observation of the beautiful in nature they direct their practice. I know that it has been said long since, and echoed backward and forward from one writer to another a thousand times, that the proportions of building have been taken from those of the human body. To make this forced analogy complete, they represent a man with his arms raised and extended at full length, and then describe a sort of square, as it is formed by passing lines along the extremities of this strange figure. But it appears very clearly to me, that the human figure never supplied the architect with any of his ideas. For, in the first place, men are very rarely seen in this strained posture; it is not natural to them; neither is it at all becoming. Secondly, the view of the human figure so disposed, does not naturally suggest the idea of a square, but rather of a cross; as that large space between the arms and the ground must be filled with something before it can make anybody think of a square. Thirdly, several buildings are by no means of the form of that particular square, which are notwithstanding planned by the best architects, and produce an effect altogether as good, and perhaps a better. And certainly nothing could be more unaccountably whimsical, than for an architect to model his performance by the human figure, since no two things can have less resemblance or analogy, than a man and a house, or temple: do we need to observe, that their purposes are entirely different? What I am apt to suspect is this: that these analogies were devised to give a credit to the works of art, by showing a conformity between them and the noblest works in nature; not that the latter served at all to supply hints for the perfection of the former. And I am the more fully convinced, that the patrons of proportion have transferred their artificial ideas to nature, and not borrowed from thence the proportions they use in works of art; because in any discussion of this subject they always quit as soon as possible the open field of natural beauties, the animal and vegetable kingdoms, and fortify themselves within the artificial lines and angles of architecture. For there is in mankind an unfortunate propensity to make themselves, their views, and their works, the measure of excellence in everything whatso-ever. Therefore, having observed that their dwellings were most commodious and firm when they were thrown into regular figures, with parts answerable to each other; they transferred these ideas to their gardens; they turned their trees into pillars, pyramids, and obelisks; they formed their hedges into so many green walls, and fashioned their walks into squares, triangles, and other mathematical figures, with exactness and symmetry; and they thought, if they were not imitating, they were at least improving nature, and teaching her to know her business. But nature has at last escaped from their discipline and their fetters; and our gardens, if nothing else, declare we begin to feel that mathematical ideas are not the true measures of beauty. And surely they are full as little so in the animal as the vegetable world. For is it not extraordinary, that in these fine descriptive pieces, these innumerable odes and elegies, which are in the mouths of all the world, and many of which have been the entertainment of ages, that in these pieces which describe love with such a passionate energy, and represent its object in such an infinite variety of lights, not one word is said of proportion, if it be, what some insist it is, the principal component of beauty; whilst, at the same time, several other qualities are very frequently and warmly mentioned? But if proportion has not this power, it may appear odd how men came originally to be so prepossessed in its favour. It arose, I imagine, from the fondness I have just mentioned, which men bear so remarkably to their own works and notions; it arose from false reasonings on the effects of the customary figure of animals; it arose from the Platonic theory of fitness and aptitude. For which reason, in the next section, I shall consider the effects of custom in the figure of animals; and afterwards the idea of fitness: since, if proportion does not operate by a natural power attending some measures, it must be either by custom, or the idea of utility; there is no other way.

111 EDMUND BURKE

from *A Philosophical Inquiry into the Origin of our Ideas of the Sublime and Beautiful* (1757)

s the title of Burke's book shows, the primary intention of his investigation is to elevate the notion of the "sublime" to an aesthetic category equal to the idea of the "beautiful." This is, once again, an anticlassical approach to aesthetics from the start, in the sense that beauty is central to all classical conceptions of art. In Vitruvian theory, for instance, it was named as one of the three essential principles of good design. It is also an anticlassical approach in that in divorcing beauty from such traditional concepts as proportion, fitness, perfection, and virtue, Burke must define it anew on the basis of sensations alone. Thus he comes to define beauty as arising from the object's qualities: smallness, smoothness, gradual variation, delicacy, clean and fair but not especially strong colors. Beauty is therefore inherent in things and is not, as Berkeley argued, a construct of the mind. These qualities or attributes of beauty are visual sensations; therefore the idea of beauty in the mind is caused by the body's neurological responses to objects rather than by mental operations. Hence, the play of the association of ideas gives way in this instance to a physiological explanation.

Alongside the notion of the beautiful, there is now also the aesthetic category of the sublime. What is its cause? Burke's answer of "pain or danger" may at first seem startling, but what he is really referring to is the exhilarating emotion of danger that a mountain climber might feel in standing on the edge of a cliff and surveying the world far below him, or the painful emotion of isolation that someone might experience in staring out into the vast expanse of the ocean. Burke goes to speak of the passions roused by the sublime over many pages; he begins his treatment with the emotions of terror, obscurity, power, privation (vacuity, darkness, solitude, and silence). The second excerpt below picks up the discussion with the notion of "vastness," and continues through to his discussion of "Light in Building." The architectural implications, when not explicitly stated, are fully transparent; the architect might in some instances now seek to exploit the emotions of the sublime rather than those of the beautiful.

Of The Sublime

Whatever is fitted in any sort to excite the ideas of pain and danger, that is to say, whatever is in any sort terrible, or is conversant about terrible objects, or operates in a manner analogous to terror, is a source of the *sublime;* that is, it is productive of the strongest emotion which the mind is capable of feeling. I say the strongest emotion, because I am satisfied the ideas of pain are much more powerful than those which enter on the part of pleasure. Without all doubt, the torments which we may be made to suffer are much greater in their effect on the body and mind, than any pleasures which the most learned voluptuary could suggest, or than the liveliest imagination, and the most sound and exquisitely sensible

Edmund Burke, from *A Philosophical Enquiry into the Origin of our Ideas of the Sublime and Beautiful* (1757) in *The Works of Edmund Burke*, Vol. I, London: G. Bell & Sons, 1913, pp. 74–5, 100–8.

body, could enjoy. Nay, I am in great doubt whether any man could be found, who would earn a life of the most perfect satisfaction, at the price of ending it in the torments, which justice inflicted in a few hours on the late unfortunate regicide in France. But as pain is stronger in its operation than pleasure, so death is in general a much more affecting idea than pain; because there are very few pains, however exquisite, which are not preferred to death: nay, what generally makes pain itself, if I may say so, more painful, is that it is considered as an emissary of this king of terrors. When danger or pain press too nearly, they are incapable of giving any delight, and are simply terrible; but at certain distances, and with certain modifications, they may be, and they are, delightful, as we every day experience. The cause of this I shall endeavour to investigate hereafter. [...]

Vastness

Greatness of dimension is a powerful cause of the sublime. This is too evident, and the observation too common, to need any illustration: it is not so common to consider in what ways greatness of dimension, vastness of extent or quantity, has the most striking effect. For certainly, there are ways and modes, wherein the same quantity of extension shall produce greater effects than it is found to do in others. Extension is either in length, height, or depth. Of these the length strikes least; an hundred yards of even ground will never work such an effect as a tower an hundred yards high, or a rock or mountain of that altitude. I am apt to imagine likewise, that height is less grand than depth; and that we are more struck at looking down from a precipice, than looking up at an object of equal height; but of that I am not very positive. A perpendicular has more force in forming the sublime, than an inclined plane; and the effects of a rugged and broken surface seem stronger than where it is smooth and polished. It would carry us out of our way to enter in this place into the cause of these appearances; but certain it is they afford a large and fruitful field of speculation. However, it may not be amiss to add to these remarks upon magnitude, that, as the great extreme of dimension is sublime, so the last extreme of littleness is in some measure sublime likewise: when we attend to the infinite divisibility of matter, when we pursue animal life into these excessively small, and yet organized beings, that escape the nicest inquisition of the sense; when we push our discoveries yet downward, and consider those creatures so many degrees yet smaller, and the still diminishing scale of existence, in tracing which the imagination is lost as well as the sense; we become amazed and confounded at the wonders of minuteness; nor can we distinguish in its effects this extreme of littleness from the vast itself. For division must be infinite as well as addition; because the idea of a perfect unity can no more be arrived at, than that of a complete whole, to which nothing may be added.

Infinity

Another source of the sublime is *infinity;* if it does not rather belong to the last. Infinity has a tendency to fill the mind with that sort of delightful horror, which is the most genuine effect and truest test of the sublime. There are scarce any things which can become the objects of our senses, that are really and in their own nature infinite. But the eye not being able to perceive the bounds of many things, they seem to be infinite, and they produce the same effects as if they were really so. We are deceived in the like manner, if the parts of some large object are so continued to any indefinite number, that the imagination meets no check which may hinder its extending them at pleasure.

Whenever we repeat any idea frequently, the mind, by a sort of mechanism, repeats it long after the first cause has ceased to operate. After whirling about, when we sit down, the objects about us still seem to whirl. After a long succession of noises, as the fall of waters, or the beating of forge-hammers, the hammers beat and the water roars in the imagination long after the first sounds have ceased to affect it; and they die away at last by gradations which are scarcely perceptible. If you hold up a straight pole, with your eye to one end, it will seem extended to a length almost incredible. Place a number of uniform and equi-distant marks on this pole, they will cause the same deception, and seem multiplied without end. The senses, strongly affected in some one manner, cannot quickly change their tenor, or adapt themselves to other things; but they continue in their old channel until the strength of the first mover decays. This is the reason of an appearance very frequent in madmen; that they remain whole days and nights, sometimes whole years, in the constant repetition of some remark, some complaint, or song; which having struck powerfully on their disordered imagination in the beginning of their phrensy, every repetition reinforces it with new strength; and the hurry of their spirits, unrestrained by the curb of reason, continues it to the end of their lives.

Succession and Uniformity

Succession and *uniformity* of parts are what constitute the artificial infinite. 1. *Succession;* which is requisite that the parts may be continued so long and in such a direction, as by their frequent impulses on the sense to impress the imagination with an idea of their progress beyond their actual limits. 2. *Uniformity;* because if the figures of the parts should be changed, the imagination at every change finds a check; you are presented at every alteration with the termination of one idea, and the beginning of another; by which means it becomes impossible to continue that uninterrupted progression, which alone can stamp on bounded objects the character of infinity.[1] It is in this kind of artificial infinity, I believe, we ought to look for the cause why a rotund has such a noble effect. For in a rotund, whether it be a building or a plantation, you can nowhere fix a boundary; turn which way you will, the same object stil seems to continue, and the imagination has no rest. But the parts must be uniform, as well as circularly disposed, to give this figure its full force; because any difference, whether it be in the disposition, or in the figure, or even in the colour of the parts, is highly prejudicial to the idea of infinity, which every change must check and interrupt, at every alteration commencing a new series. On the same principles of succession and uniformity, the grand appearance of the ancient heathen temples, which were generally oblong forms, with a range of uniform pillars on every side, will be easily accounted for. From the same cause also may be derived the grand effect of the aisles in many of our own old cathedrals. The form of a cross used in some churches seems to me not so eligible as the parallelogram of the ancients;

at least, I imagine it is not so proper for the outside. For, supposing the arms of the cross every way equal, if you stand in a direction parallel to any of the side walls, or colonnades, instead of a deception that makes the building more extended than it is, you are cut off from a considerable part (two-thirds) of its *actual* length; and to prevent all possibility of progression, the arms of the cross, taking a new direction, make a right angle with the beam, and thereby wholly turn the imagination from the repetition of the former idea. Or suppose the spectator placed where he may take a direct view of such a building, what will be the consequence? The necessary consequence will be, that a good part of the basis of each angle formed by the intersection of the arms of the cross, must be inevitably lost; the whole must of course assume a broken, unconnected figure; the lights must be unequal, here strong, and there weak; without that noble gradation, which the perspective always effects on parts disposed uninterruptedly in a right line. Some or all of these objections will lie against every figure of a cross, in whatever view you take it. I exemplified them in the Greek cross, in which these faults appear the most strongly; but they appear in some degree in all sorts of crosses. Indeed there is nothing more prejudicial to the grandeur of buildings, than to abound in angles; a fault obvious in many; and owing to an inordinate thirst for variety, which, whenever it prevails, is sure to leave very little true taste.

Magnitude in Building

To the sublime in building, greatness of dimension seems requisite; for on a few parts, and those small, the imagination cannot rise to any idea of infinity. No greatness in the manner can effectually compensate for the want of proper dimensions. There is no danger of drawing men into extravagant designs by this rule; it carries its own caution along with it. Because too great a length in buildings destroys the purpose of greatness, which it was intended to promote; the perspective will lessen it in height as it gains in length; and will bring it at last to a point; turning the whole figure into a sort of triangle, the poorest in its effect of almost any figure that can be presented to the eye. I have ever observed, that colonnades and avenues of trees of a moderate length, were, without comparison, far grander, than when they were suffered to run to immense distances. A true artist should put a generous deceit on the spectators, and effect the noblest designs by easy methods. Designs that are vast only by their dimensions, are always the sign of a common and low imagination. No work of art can be great, but as it deceives; to be otherwise is the prerogative of nature only. A good eye will fix the medium betwixt an excessive length or height, (for the same objection lies against both,) and a short or broken quantity; and perhaps it might be ascertained to a tolerable degree of exactness, if it was my purpose to descend far into the particulars of any art.

Infinity in Pleasing Objects

Infinity, though of another kind, causes much of our pleasure in agreeable, as well as of our delight in sublime, images. The spring is the pleasantest of the seasons; and the young of most animals, though far from being completely fashioned, afford a more agreeable sensation than the full-grown; because the imagination is entertained with the promise of something more, and does not acquiesce in the present object of the sense. In unfinished sketches of drawing, I have often seen something which pleased me beyond the best finishing; and this I believe proceeds from the cause I have just now assigned.

Difficulty

Another source of greatness is *Difficulty*. When any work seems to have required immense force and labour to effect it, the idea is grand. Stonehenge, neither for disposition nor ornament, has anything admirable; but those huge rude masses of stone, set on end, and piled each on other, turn the mind on the immense force necessary for such a work. Nay, the rudeness of the work increases this cause of grandeur, as it excludes the idea of art and contrivance; for dexterity produces another sort of effect, which is different enough from this.

Magnificence

Magnificence is likewise a source of the sublime. A great profusion of things, which are splendid or valuable in themselves, is *magnificent*. The starry heaven, though it occurs so very frequently to our view, never fails to excite an idea of grandeur. This cannot be owing to the stars themselves, separately considered. The number is certainly the cause. The apparent disorder augments the grandeur, for the appearance of care is highly contrary to our idea of magnificence. Besides, the stars lie in such apparent confusion, as makes it impossible on ordinary occasions to reckon them. This gives them the advantage of a sort of infinity. In works of art, this kind of grandeur, which consists in multitude, is to be very courteously admitted; because a profusion of excellent things is not to be attained, or with too much difficulty; and because in many cases this splendid confusion would destroy all use, which should be attended to in most of the works of art with the greatest care; besides, it is to be considered, that unless you can produce an appearance of infinity by your disorder, you will have disorder only without magnificence. There are, however, a sort of fireworks, and some other things, that in this way succeed well, and are truly grand. There are also many descriptions in the poets and orators, which owe their sublimity to a richness and profusion of images, in which the mind is so dazzled as to make it impossible to attend to that exact coherence and agreement of the allusions, which we should require on every other occasion. I do not now remember a more striking example of this, than the description which is given of the king's army in the play of Henry the Fourth:

> – All furnished, all in arms,
> All plumed like ostriches that with the wind
> Baited like eagles having lately bathed:

As full of spirit as the month of May,
And gorgeous as the sun in Midsummer,
Wanton as youthful goats, wild as young bulls.
I saw young Harry with his beaver on
Rise from the ground like feathered Mercury;
And vaulted with such ease into his seat,
As if an angel dropped from the clouds
To turn and wind a fiery Pegasus.

In that excellent book, so remarkable for the vivacity of its descriptions, as well as the solidity and penetration of its sentences, the Wisdom of the Son of Sirach, there is a noble panegyric on the high priest Simon the son of Onias; and it is a very fine example of the point before us:

How was he honoured in the midst of the people, in his coming out of the sanctuary! He was as the morning star in the midst of a cloud, and as the moon at the full; as the sun shining upon the temple of the Most High, and as the rainbow giving light in the bright clouds: and as the flower of roses in the spring of the year, as lilies by the rivers of waters, and as the frankincense tree in summer; as fire and incense in the censer, and as a vessel of gold set with precious stones; as a fair olive tree budding forth fruit, and as a cypress which groweth up to the clouds. When he put on the robe of honour, and was clothed with the perfection of glory, when he went up to the holy altar, he made the garment of holiness honourable. He himself stood by the hearth of the altar, compassed with his brethren round about; as a young cedar in Libanus, and as palm trees compassed they him about. So were all the sons of Aaron in their glory, and the oblations of the Lord in their hands, &c.

Light

Having considered extension, so far as it is capable of raising ideas of greatness; *colour* comes next under consideration. All colours depend on *light*. Light therefore ought previously to be examined; and with its opposite, darkness. With regard to light, to make it a cause capable of producing the sublime, it must be attended with some circumstances, besides its bare faculty of showing other objects. Mere light is too common a thing to make a strong impression on the mind, and without a strong impression nothing can be sublime. But such a light as that of the sun, immediately exerted on the eye, as it overpowers the sense, is a very great idea. Light of an inferior strength to this, if it moves with great celerity, has the same power; for lightning is certainly productive of grandeur, which it owes chiefly to the extreme velocity of its motion. A quick transition from light to darkness, or from darkness to light, has yet a greater effect. But darkness is more productive of sublime ideas than light. Our great poet was convinced of this; and indeed so full was he of this idea, so entirely possessed with the power of a well-managed darkness, that in describing the appearance of the Deity, amidst that profusion of magnificent images, which the grandeur of his subject provokes him to pour out upon every side, he is far from forgetting the obscurity which surrounds the most incomprehensible of all beings, but

> – With majesty of *darkness* round
> Circles his throne. –

And what is no less remarkable, our author had the secret of preserving this idea, even when he seemed to depart the farthest from it, when he describes the light and glory which flows from the Divine presence; a light which by its very excess is converted into a species of darkness.

> *Dark* with excessive *light* thy skirts appear.

Here is an idea not only poetical in a high degree, but strictly and philosophically just. Extreme light, by overcoming the organs of sight, obliterates all objects, so as in its effect exactly to resemble darkness. After looking for some time at the sun, two black spots, the impression which it leaves, seem to dance before our eyes. Thus are two ideas as opposite as can be imagined reconciled in the extremes of both; and both, in spite of their opposite nature, brought to concur in producing the sublime. And this is not the only instance wherein the opposite extremes operate equally in favour of the sublime, which in all things abhors mediocrity.

Light in Building

As the management of light is a matter of importance in architecture, it is worth inquiring, how far this remark is applicable to building. I think then, that all edifices calculated to produce an idea of the sublime, ought rather to be dark and gloomy, and this for two reasons; the first is, that darkness itself on other occasions is known by experience to have a greater effect on the passions than light. The second is, that to make an object very striking, we should make it as different as possible from the objects with which we have been immediately conversant; when therefore you enter a building, you cannot pass into a greater light than you had in the open air; to go into one some few degrees less luminous, can make only a trifling change; but to make the transition thoroughly striking, you ought to pass from the greatest light, to as much darkness as is consistent with the uses of architecture. At night the contrary rule will hold, but for the very same reason; and the more highly a room is then illuminated, the grander will the passion be.

NOTE

1   Mr. Addison, in the Spectators concerning the pleasures of imagination, thinks it is because in the rotund at one glance you see half the building. This I do not imagine to be the real cause.

112 LORD KAMES
from *Elements of Criticism* (1762)

The innovative aspects of Burke's arguments for the beautiful and the sublime can also be judged by the contemporary account of beauty and sublimity by Lord Kames, who was born Henry Home. Kames was another figure of the Scottish Enlightenment and a member of the Select Society of Edinburgh. He labored over the writing of *Elements of Criticism* throughout the 1750s and thus was able to incorporate many of the insights put forth in this decade. The starting point for his system, however, was older, and thus the study owes more to Shaftesbury than to Hume. The result is a curious mixture of old and new ideas. Kames defines beauty, for instance, as both *intrinsic* (the object of sensation without mental reflection; the beauty of a river, for instance) and *relative* (an object when seen in relation to utility and goodness). He accepts the notion of the sublime, but – following Addison – defines it simply as the experience of dimension or grandeur. Toward the end of his lengthy study he also turns his attention to the landscape and to architecture. In the first regard he disapproves of the stiffness and artificiality of regular designs, except very near the house. In the second regard he allows regularity in monumental architectural works and irregularity in more utilitarian structures, such as dwellings. Kames wants to have it both ways. For example, he can defend the idea of proportion and criticize Perrault for trying to ground ratios in custom, yet he can admit to the aesthetic pleasure of employing the Gothic style in such rough and uncultivated regions as Scotland.

It provokes a smile to find writers acknowledging the necessity of accurate proportions, and yet differing widely about them. Laying aside reasoning and philosophy, one fact, universally allowed, ought to have undeceived them, that the same proportions which are agreeable in a model, are not agreeable in a large building; a room 40 feet in length, and 24 in breadth and height, is well proportioned; but a room 12 feet wide and high, and 24 long, approaches to a gallery.

Perrault, in his comparison of the ancients and moderns, is the only author who runs to the opposite extreme; maintaining, that the different proportions assigned to each order of columns are arbitrary, and that the beauty of these proportions is entirely the effect of custom. This betrays ignorance of human nature, which evidently delights in proportion as well as in regularity, order, and propriety. But, without any acquaintance with human nature, a single reflection might have convinced him of his error, That if these proportions had not originally been agreeable, they could not have been established by custom.

To illustrate the present point, I shall add a few examples of the agreeableness of different proportions. In a sumptuous edifice, the capital rooms ought to be large, for otherwise they will not be proportioned to the size of the building; and, for the same reason, a very large room is improper in a small house. But in things thus related, the mind requires not a precise or single proportion, rejecting all others; on the contrary, many different proportions are made equally welcome. In all buildings accordingly, we find rooms of different proportions equally agreeable, even where the proportion is not influenced by utility. With respect to the height of a room, the proportion it ought to bear to the length and breadth is arbitrary; and

Lord Kames, (Henry Home, 1696–1782), from *Elements of Criticism* (1762). London: Vernor and Hood, 1805 (eighth edition), pp. 370–4.

it cannot be otherwise, considering the uncertainty of the eye as to the height of a room when it exceeds 17 or 18 feet. In columns, again, even architects must confess, that the proportion of height and thickness varies betwixt eight diameters and ten, and that every proportion between these extremes is agreeable. But this is not all. There must certainly be a farther variation of proportion depending on the size of the column: a row of columns 10 feet high, and a row twice that height, require different proportions; the intercolumniations must also differ according to the height of the row.

Proportion of parts is not only itself a beauty, but is inseparably connected with a beauty of the highest relish, that of concord or harmony; which will be plain from what follows. A room, of which the parts are all finely adjusted to each other, strikes us with the beauty of proportion. It strikes us at the same time with a pleasure far superior: the length, the breadth, the height, the windows, raise each of them separately an emotion: these emotions are similar; and though faint when felt separately, they produce in conjunction the emotion of concord or harmony, which is extremely pleasant. On the other hand, where the length of a room far exceeds the breadth, the mind, comparing together parts so intimately connected, immediately perceives a disagreement or disproportion which disgusts. But this is not all: viewing them separately, different emotions are produced; that of grandeur from the great length, and that of meanness, or littleness, from the small breadth, which, in union, are disagreeable by their discordance. Hence it is, that a long gallery, however convenient for exercise, is not an agreeable figure of a room: we consider it, like a stable, as destined for use, and expect not that in any other respect it should be agreeable.

Regularity and proportion are essential in buildings destined chiefly, or solely, to please the eye, because they produce intrinsic beauty. But a skilful artist will not confine his view to regularity and proportion: he will also study congruity, which is perceived when the form and ornaments of a structure are suited to the purpose for which it is intended. The sense of congruity dictates the following rule, That every building have an expression corresponding to its destination: a palace ought to be sumptuous and grand; a private dwelling neat and modest; a play-house gay and splendid; and a monument gloomy and melancholy.[1] A Heathen temple has a double destination: It is considered chiefly as a house dedicated to some divinity; and, in that respect, it ought to be grand, elevated, and magnificent: it is considered also as a place of worship; and, in that respect, it ought to be somewhat dark or gloomy, because dimness produces that tone of mind which is suited to humility and devotion. A Christian church is not considered to be a house for the Deity, but merely a place of worship: it ought, therefore, to be decent and plain, without much ornament. A situation ought to be chosen low and retired; because the congregation, during worship, ought to be humble and disengaged from the world. Columns, besides their chief service of being supports, may contribute to that peculiar expression which the destination of a building requires: columns of different proportions serve to express loftiness, lightness, &c. as well as strength. Situation, also, may contribute to expression; conveniency regulates the situation of a private dwelling-house; but, as I have had occasion to observe, the situation of a palace ought to be lofty.

And this leads to a question, Whether the situation, where there happens to be no choice, ought, in any measure, to regulate the form of the edifice? The connection between a large house and the neighbouring fields, though not intimate, demands however some congruity. It would, for example, displease us to find an elegant building thrown away upon a wild uncultivated country: congruity requires a polished field for such a building: and besides the pleasure of congruity, the spectator is sensible of the pleasure of concordance from the similarity of the emotions produced by the two objects. The old Gothic form of building seems well suited to the rough uncultivated regions where it was invented: the only mistake was, the transferring this form to the fine plains of France and Italy, better fitted for buildings in the Grecian taste; but by refining upon the Gothic form, every thing possible has been done to reconcile it to its new situation. The profuse variety of wild and grand objects about Inverary demanded a house in the Gothic form; and every one must approve of the taste of the proprietor, in adjusting so finely the appearance of his house to that of the country where it is placed.

NOTE

1 A house for the poor ought to have an appearance suited to its destination. The new hospital in Paris for foundlings errs against this rule; for it has more the air of a palace than of an hospital. Propriety and convenience ought to be studied in lodging the indigent; but in such houses splendour and magnificence are out of all rule. For the same reason, a naked statue or picture, scarce decent anywhere, is in a church intolerable. A sumptuous charity-school, besides its impropriety, gives the children an unhappy taste for high living.

113   ROBERT AND JAMES ADAM
from Preface to *The Works in Architecture of Robert and James Adam* (1773–8)

The final member of the Edinburgh Select Society to be considered in this section is Robert Adam, who with his younger brother James, would go on to become one of Britain's most successful neoclassical architects of the third quarter of the eighteenth century. Robert Adam was very much a central figure within the artistic excitement of the 1750s in both Britain and Italy. He was a close friend of David Hume, and when he left Scotland for his grand tour of Italy in 1754 he was accepted into the circle of Ramsay in Rome, and thus became a friend of Piranesi as well. Adam was also attracted to the circle of students at the French Academy in Rome. In the summer of 1757 Adam traveled to Spalatro (in Croatia) to record the ruins of Diocletian's Palace, and thus he contributed the archaeological flurry of this decade. James Adam, who followed Robert to the south, also regularly corresponded with Lord Kames, and in 1762 spoke to Kames about the possibility of writing a discourse on "sentimental" architecture, that is, espousing an architecture appealing principally to the senses and feelings rather than to classical rules.

Robert Adam (1728–92) and James Adam (1732–94), from Preface to *The Works in Architecture of Robert and James Adam, Esquires* (1773–8), ed. Robert Oresko. London: Academy Editions, 1975 (facsimile edition), pp. 45–7.

Near the end of the 1750s the two brothers set up their practice in London and began to build a highly successful architectural practice in what is now known simply as the "Adam style." In contrast to the severity of some Greek classicists, the Adam brothers took their inspiration from the more permissive eclectic outlook of Piranesi, from the lighter decorative styles of Pompeii and Herculaneum, and – most importantly – from the baroque propensities of John Vanbrugh, who for the past half-century had been much out of favor. Effectively, the Adam brothers resurrected his reputation by outfitting his designs with the new aesthetic principles. Their preface to the first volume of *Works in Architecture of Robert and James Adam* constitutes their lone theoretical statement, and it is only in the footnotes that we find an articulation of their ideas. It is not unfair to call the "Adam style" a classical and baroque-inspired picturesque style, influenced (as the footnote on "Movement" suggests) by the innovations in landscape design. The actual term "picturesque" is still a decade or two away from widespread use, but the Adams brothers allude to it in their reference to composing "like a picture."

Some apology may, perhaps, be requisite, for giving to the world a book of architecture, after so many works of this kind have been published in Italy, France and England during the tow last centuries.

The novelty and variety of the following designs, will, we flatter ourselves, not only excuse, but justify our conduct, in communicating them to the world. – We have not trod in the path of others, nor derived aid from their labours. In the works which we have had the honour to execute, we have not only met with the approbation of our employers, but even with the imitation of other artists, to such a degree, as in some measure to have brought about, in this country; a kind of revolution in the whole system of this useful and elegant art. These circumstances induced us to hope, that to collect and engrave our works would afford both entertainment and instruction.

To enter upon an enquiry into the state of this art in Great Britain, till the late changes it has undergone, is no part of our present design. We leave that subject to the observation of the skilful; who we doubt not, will easily perceive, within these few years, a remarkable improvement in the form, convenience, arrangement, and relief of apartments; a greater movement (A) and variety, in the outside composition, and in the decoration of the inside, an almost total change.

The massive entablature (B), the ponderous compartment ceiling (C), the tabernacle frame, almost the only species of ornament (D) formerly known, in this country, are now universally exploded, and in their place, we have adopted a beautiful variety of light mouldings, gracefully formed, delicately enriched and arranged with propriety and skill. We have introduced a great diversity of ceilings, freezes, and decorated pilasters, and have added grace and beauty to the whole, by a mixture of grotesque (E) stucco, and painted ornaments, together with the flowing rainceau (F), with its fanciful figures and winding foliage. [...]

(A) **Movement** *is meant to express, the rise and fall, the advance and recess, with other diversity of form, in the different parts of a building, so as to add greatly to the picturesque of the composition. For the rising and falling, advancing and receding, with the convexity and concavity, and other forms of the great parts, have the same effect in architecture, that hill and dale, fore-ground and distance, swelling and sinking have in lanscape: That is, they serve to produce an agreeable and diversified contour, that groups and contrasts like a picture, and creates a variety of light and shade, which gives great spirit, beauty and effect to the composition.*

It is not always that such variety can be introduced into the design of any building but where it can be attained without encroaching upon its useful purposes, it adds much to its merit, as an object of beauty and grandeur.

The effect of the height and convexity of the dome of St. Peter's, contrasted with the lower square front, and the concavity of its court, is a striking instance of this sort of composition. The college and church des quatre nations at Paris, is though small, another of the same kind; and with us, we really do not recollect any example of so much movement and contrast, as in the south front of Kedleston house in Derbyshire, one of the seats of the Right Honourable Lord Scarsdale, of which building we shall have occasion to speak more at large hereafter.

We cannot however allow ourselves to close this note without doing justice to the memory of a great man, whose reputation as an architect, has been long carried down the stream by a torrent of undistinguishing prejudice and abuse.

Sir John Vanburgh's genius was of the first class; and, in point of movement, novelty and ingenuity, his works have not been exceeded by any thing in modern times. We should certainly have quoted Blenheim and Castle Howard as great examples of these perfections, in preference to any work of our own, or of any other modern architect; but unluckily for the reputation of this excellent artist, his taste kept no pace with his genius, and his works are so crouded with barbarisms and absurdities, and so borne down by their own preposterous weight, that none but the discerning can separate their merits from their defects. In the hands of the ingenious artist, who knows how to polish and refine and bring them into use, we have always regarded his productions, as rough jewels of inestimable value.

[. . .]

(E) By **grotesque** is meant that beautiful light stile of ornament used by the ancient Romans, in the decoration of their palaces, baths and villas. It is also to be seen in some of their amphitheatres, temples and tombs; the greatest part of which being vaulted and covered with ruins, have been dug up and cleared by the modern Italians, who for these reasons, give them the name of grotte, which is perhaps a corruption of the Latin Criptæ, a word borrowed from the Greeks, as the Romans did most of their terms in architecture; and hence the modern word grotesque, and the English word grotto, signifying a cave.

In the times of Raphael, Michael Angelo, Julio Romano, Polidoro, Giov. d'Udine, Vasari, Zuchero and Algardi, there is no doubt but there was much greater remains of the grotte, than what are now to be seen, and in imitation of them, were decorated the loggias of the Vatican, the villas Madama, Pamsili, Caprarola, the old palace at Florence; and indeed whatever else is elegant or admirable in the finishings of modern Italy. The French, who till of late never adopted the ornaments of the ancients, and jealous as all mankind are of the reputation of their national taste, have branded those ornaments with the vague and fantastical appellation of arabesque, a stile which, though entirely distinct from the grotesque, has, notwithstanding, been most absurdly and universally confounded with it by the ignorant.

This classical stile of ornament, by far the most perfect that has ever appeared for inside decorations, and which has stood the test of many ages, like other works of genius, requires not only fancy and imagination in the composition, but taste and judgement in the application; and when these are happily combined, this gay and elegant mode is capable of inimitable beauties.

Vitruvius with great reason condemns an over licentiousness in compositions of this kind, and blames the painters of his time for introducing monstrous extravagancies. We mean not to vindicate *any thing that deserves suchs appellations but surely in light and gay compositions, designed merely to amuse, it is not altogether necessary to exclude the whimsical and the bisarre.*

(F) **Rainçeau**, *apparently derived from rain, an old French word, signifying the branch of a tree. This French term is also used by the artists of this country, to express the winding and twisting of the stalk or stem of the acanthus plant; which flowing round in many graceful turnings, spreads its foliage with great beauty and variety, and is often intermixed, with human figures, animals and birds, imaginary or real; also with flowers and fruits.*

This gay and fanciful diversity of agreeable objects, well composed, and delicately executed in stucco of painting, attains a wonderfull power of pleasing.

We hope this minute explanation of these terms will be excused. It is intended to supply in some measure a geneal deficiency which we have found upon this subject, in all the encyclopedias and technical dictionaries.

C.   CONSOLIDATION OF PICTURESQUE THEORY

Introduction

The elements of a picturesque aesthetics had been bandied about for nearly a century, and it is in the last years of the eighteenth century that they were brought together into a coherent theory. It is in fact the first great success of relativist aesthetics. Picturesque theory is often considered exclusively in relation to landscape design, but in fact it has much broader aesthetic implications. For one thing, the relativist basis of picturesque theory will dovetail nicely not only with the demise of proportional and stylistic norms but also with the emergence of historicist and eclectic tendencies. Second, picturesque theory will also in some cases merge quite seamlessly with classical theory, such as we find in the melding of classical and baroque (picturesque) sensibilities in the work and thought of John Soane. And picturesque theory as well opens the door to further conceptual development. Arguably, the culmination of picturesque theory is found not in the eighteenth century but in the aesthetics of John Ruskin, whose influence was preeminent in the English-speaking world in the second half of the nineteenth century. Thus the roots for the displacement of classical ideals in architectural theory are surprisingly complex in both their structure and design implications.

114 THOMAS WHATELY
from *Observations on Modern Gardening* (1770)

The term "picturesque" originally came into the English language in the early eighteenth century through its Italian and French usage of "like or having the elements of a picture." In 1768 the critic William Gilpin, in his *An Essay on Prints*, defined it as "a term expressive of that peculiar kind of beauty, which is agreeable in a picture." Over the last 30 years of the century, however, the term became transformed and gained a new and somewhat different meaning. One of the books that contributed to this development was Thomas Whately's *Observations of Modern Gardening* (1770).

Whately was a Shakespearean scholar, a parliamentarian, and above all a supporter of Lancelot "Capability" Brown (1716–83), who was England's most sought-after garden designer in the third quarter of the century. Brown in his designs preferred to work solely with the elements of nature – with rolling landscapes, partially open vistas, and especially with water (formed by damming creeks) – and Whately in his treatise codifies these elements and principles, which he divides into his five "materials" of landscape design: ground, wood, water, rocks, and buildings. Whately's theory of gardening is essentially a theory of character, and in fact his book, as we have already noted (see chapter 85 above), was translated into French and was influential in France. But it is also important in Britain as the first attempt to define the term "picturesque" as a landscape principle, that is, in terms other than relating to painting. The two passages selected here underscore the connection of the notion of the picturesque with theories of expression or character. In the first he is speaking of the use of buildings or mock structures in landscape design – a practice he prefers to be limited, but which is nevertheless important for the different characters that may be evoked by the designer. In the second passage, under the heading "Of Picturesque Beauty," he defines the new concept in terms of nature, although still with a reference to painting.

XLII. To enumerate the several buildings which may be used for convenience, or distinction, as ornaments, or as characters, would lead me far from my subject into a treatise of architecture; for every branch of architecture furnishes, on different occasions, objects proper for a garden; and different species may meet in the same composition; no analogy exists between the age and the country, whence they are borrowed, and the spot they are applied to, except in some particular instances; but in general, they are naturalized to a place of the most improved cultivated nature by their effects; beauty is their use; and they are consistent with each other, if all are conformable to the style of the scene, proportioned to its extent, and agreable to its character. On the other hand, varieties more than sufficient for

Thomas Whately (d. 1772), from *Observations on Modern Gardening* (1770). New York and London: Garland Publishing, Inc., 1982 (facsimile edition), pp. 127–32, 146–50.

any particular spot, enough for a very extensive view, may be found in every species; to each also belong a number of characters: the Grecian architecture can lay aside its dignity in a rustic building; and the caprice of the Gothic is sometimes not incompatible with greatness; our choice therefore may be confined to the variations of one species, or range through the contrasts of many, as circumstances, taste, or other considerations shall determine.

The choice of situations is also very free; circumstances which are requisite to particular structures, may often be combined happily with others, and enter into a variety of compositions; even where they are appropriated, they may still be applied in several degrees, and the same edifice may thereby be accommodated to very different scenes: some buildings which have a just expression when accompanied with proper appendages, have none without them; they may therefore be characters in one place, and only objects in another. On all these occasions, the application is allowable, if it can be made without inconsistency; a hermitage must not be close to a road, but whether it be exposed to view on the side of a mountain, or concealed in the depth of a wood, is almost a matter of indifference, that it is at a distance from publick resort is sufficient: a castle must not be sunk in a bottom; but that it should stand on the utmost pinnacle of a hill, is not necessary; on a lower knole, and backed by the rise, it may appear to greater advantage as an object; and be much more important to the general composition: a tower,

Bosomed high in tufted trees,

has been selected by one of our greatest poets as a singular beauty; and the justness of his choice has been so generally acknowledged, that the description is become almost proverbial; and yet a tower does not seem designed to be surrounded by a wood; but the appearance may be accounted for; it does sometimes occur; and we are easily satisfied of the propriety, when the effect is so pleasing. Many buildings, which from their splendor best become an open exposure, will yet be sometimes not ill bestowed on a more sequestered spot, either to characterise or adorn it; and others, for which a solitary would in general be preferred to an eminent situation, may occasionally be objects in very conspicuous positions. A Grecian temple, from its peculiar grace and dignity, deserves every distinction; it may, however, in the depth of a wood, be so circumstanced, that the want of those advantages to which it seems entitled, will not be regretted. A happier situation cannot be devised, than that of the temple of Pan, at the south lodge on Enfield Chace.[1] It is of the usual oblong form, encompassed by a colonade; in dimensions, and in style, it is equal to a most extensive landskip; and yet by the antique and rustic air of its Dorick columns without bases; by the chastity of its little ornament, a crook, a pipe, and a scrip, and those only over the doors; and by the simplicity of the whole, both within and without, it is adapted with so much propriety to the thickets which conceal it from the view, that no one can wish it to be brought forward, who is sensible to the charms of the Arcadian scene which this building alone has created. On the other hand, a very spacious field, or sheep-walk, will not be disgraced by a cottage, a Dutch barn, or a hay-stack; nor will they, though small and familiar, appear to be inconsiderable or insignificant objects. Numberless other instances might be adduced to prove the impossibility of restraining particular buildings to particular situations, upon any general principles; the variety in their forms is hardly greater than in their application.

XLIII. To this great variety must be added the many changes which may be made by the means of *ruins*; they are a class by themselves, beautiful as objects, expressive as characters, and peculiarly calculated to connect with their appendages into elegant groupes: they may be accommodated with ease to irregularity of ground, and their disorder is improved by it; they may be intimately blended with trees and with thickets, and the interruption is an advantage; for imperfection and obscurity are their properties; and to carry the imagination to something greater than is seen, their effect. They may for any of these purposes be separated into detached pieces; contiguity is not necessary, nor even the appearance of it, if the relation be preserved; but straggling ruins have a bad effect, when the several parts are equally considerable. There should be one large mass to raise an idea of greatness, to attract the others about it, and to be a common centre of union to all: the smaller pieces then mark the original dimensions of one extensive structure; and no longer appear to be the remains of several little buildings.

All remains excite an enquiry into the former state of the edifice, and fix the mind in a contemplation on the use it was applied to; besides the characters expressed by their style and position, they suggest ideas which would not arise from the buildings, if entire. The purposes of many have ceased; an abbey, or a castle, if complete, can now be no more than a dwelling; the memory of the times, and of the manners, to which they were adapted, is preserved only in history, and in ruins; and certain sensations of regret, of veneration, or compassion, attend the recollection: nor are these confined to the remains of buildings which are now in disuse; those of an old mansion raise reflections on the domestic comforts once enjoyed, and the ancient hospitality which reigned there. Whatever building we see in decay, we naturally contrast its present to its former state, and delight to ruminate on the comparison. It is true that such effects properly belong to real ruins; but they are produced in a certain degree by those which are fictitious; the impressions are not so strong, but they are exactly similar; and the representation, though it does not present facts to the memory, yet suggests subjects to the imagination: but in order to affect the fancy, the supposed original design should be clear, the use obvious, and the form easy to trace; no fragments should be hazarded without a precise meaning, and an evident connection; none should be perplexed in their construction, or uncertain as to their application. Conjectures about the form, raise doubts about the existence of the ancient structure; the mind must not be allowed to hesitate; it must be hurried away from examining into the reality, by the exactness and the force of the resemblance.

★ ★ ★

Of Picturesque Beauty

XLVII. But regularity can never attain to a great share of beauty, and to none of the species called *picturesque*; a denomination in general expressive of excellence, but which, by being too indiscriminately applied, may be sometimes productive of errors. That a subject is recommended at least to our notice, and probably to our favour, if it has been distinguished by the pencil of an eminent painter, is indisputable; we are delighted to see those objects in the reality, which we are used to admire in the representation; and we improve upon their intrinsic merit, by recollecting their effects in the picture. The greatest beauties of nature will often suggest the remembrance; for it is the business of a landskip painter to select them; and his choice is absolutely unrestrained; he is at liberty to exclude all objects which may hurt the composition; he has the power of combining those which he admits in the most agreable manner; he can even determine the season of the year, and the hour of the day, to shew his landskip in whatever light he prefers. The works therefore of a great master, are fine exhibitions of nature, and an excellent school wherein to form a taste for beauty; but still their authority is not absolute; they must be used only as studies, not as models; for a picture and a scene in nature, though they agree in many, yet differ in some particulars, which must always be taken into consideration, before we can decide upon the circumstances which may be transferred from the one to the other.

In their *dimensions* the distinction is obvious; the same objects on different scales have very different effects; those which seem monstrous on the one, may appear diminutive on the other; and a form which is elegant in a small object, may be too delicate for a large one. Besides, in a canvass of a few feet, there is not room for every species of variety which in nature is pleasing. Though the characteristic distinctions of trees may be marked, their more minute differences, which however enrich plantations, cannot be expressed; and a multiplicity of enclosures, catches of water, cottages, cattle, and a thousand other circumstances, which enliven a prospect, are, when reduced into a narrow compass, no better than a heap of confusion. Yet, on the other hand, the principal objects must often be more diversified in a picture than in a scene; a building which occupies a considerable portion of the former, will appear small in the latter, when compared to the space all around it; and the number of parts which may be necessary to break its sameness in the one, will aggravate its insignificance in the other. A tree which presents one rich mass of foliage, has sometimes a fine effect in nature; but when painted, is often a heavy lump, which can be lightened only by separating the boughs, and shewing the ramifications between them. In several other instances the object is frequently affected by the proportion it bears to the actual, not the ideal, circumjacent extent.

Painting, with all its powers, is still more unequal to some subjects, and can give only *a faint, if any, representation* of them; but a gardiner is not therefore to reject them; he is not debarred from a view down the sides of a hill, or a prospect where the horizon is lower than the station, because he never saw them in a picture. Even when painting exactly imitates the appearances of nature, it is often weak in conveying the *ideas* which they excite, and on which much of their effect sometimes depends. This however is not always a disadvantage; the appearance may be more pleasing than the idea which accompanies it; and the omission of the one may be an improvement of the other; many beautiful tints denote disagreable circumstances; the hue of a barren heath is often finely diversified; a piece of bare ground is sometimes overspread with a number of delicate shades; and yet we prefer a more uniform verdure to all their variety. In a picture, the several tints which occur in nature may be blended, and retain only their beauty, without suggesting the poverty of the soil which occasions them; but in the reality, the cause is more powerful than the effect; we are less pleased with the sight, than we are hurt by the reflection; and a most agreable mixture of colours may present no other idea than of dreariness and sterility.

On the other hand, *utility* will sometimes supply the want of beauty in the reality, but not in a picture. In the former, we are never totally inattentive to it; we are familiarised to the marks of it; and we allow a degree of merit to an object which has no other recommendation. A regular building is generally more agreable in a scene than in a picture; and an adjacent platform, if evidently convenient, is tolerable in the one; it is always a right line too much in the other. Utility is at the least an excuse, when it is real; but it is an idea never included in the representation.

Many more instances might be alledged to prove, that the subjects for a painter and a gardiner are not always the same; some which are agreable in the reality, lose their effect in the imitation; and others, at the best, have less merit in a scene than in a picture. The term picturesque is therefore applicable only to such objects in nature, as, after allowing for the differences between the arts of painting and of gardening, are fit to be formed into groupes, or to enter into a composition, where the several parts have a relation to each other; and in opposition to those which may be spread abroad in detail, and have no merit but as individuals.

NOTE

1   A villa belonging to Mr. Sharpe, near Barnet, in Middlesex.

115   HORACE WALPOLE
from "The History of the Modern Taste in Gardening" (1771)

Another early theorist of the picturesque garden was Horace Walpole, who was certainly one of the more interesting figures of the eighteenth century. The fifth son of the first Earl of Oxford (Robert Walpole), he was blessed with education, inherited wealth, and a parliamentary career, but his true passions were his literary endeavors and the continual refurbishing of his country estate. In 1748 he purchased a small house in Twickenham, which he named Strawberry Hill, and began a series of additions over the next several decades that were remarkable, if only for the fact that they were first attempt to revive the Gothic style simply for its picturesque qualities (see chapters 140 and 141 below). He also surrounded his estate with a "natural" garden, and among the many volumes emanating from his pen is this history of gardening, which he printed at his own press in 1771, as the last volume of his *Anecdotes of Painting in England*.

Walpole was a scholar and man of letters, and it is not surprising that he begins his study with such examples as the Garden of Eden, the labyrinth described by Aesop, and the garden of Alcinous as described by Homer in the *Odyssey*. What is novel, however, is the attention he devotes to the development of the English Garden in the

Horace Walpole (1717–97), from "The History of the Modern Taste in Gardening" (1771) in *Horace Walpole: Gardenist*, ed. Isabel Wakelin Urban Chase. Princeton: Princeton University Press, 1943, pp. 25–9.

eighteenth century, whose roots he discerns in Milton, William Temple, and the latter's references to Chinese gardens. These sources for Walpole crystallized in the second quarter of the century with the "new style" of gardening, which he attributes largely to the genius of William Kent. In his view, the key invention prompting this new style was the "Ha! Ha!" – a manmade ravine or sunken fence designed not to be visible from afar. For Walpole it permitted not only an unbounded view of nature but also the ability to mold what was now seen as unspoiled natural landscape.

But the capital stroke, the leading step to all that has followed, was [I believe the first thought was Bridgman's] the destruction of walls for boundaries, and the invention of fossès – an attempt then deemed so astonishing, that the common people called them Ha! Ha's! to express their surprize at finding a sudden and unperceived check to their walk.

One of the first gardens planted in this simple though still formal style, was my father's at Houghton. It was laid out by Mr. Eyre, an imitator of Bridgman. It contains three-and-twenty acres, then reckoned a considerable portion.

I call a sunk fence the leading step, for these reasons. No sooner was this simple enchantment made, than levelling, mowing and rolling, followed. The contiguous ground of the park without the sunk fence was to be harmonized with the lawn within; and the garden in its turn was to be set free from its prim regularity, that it might assort with the wilder country without. The sunk fence ascertained the specific garden, but that it might not draw too obvious a line of distinction between the neat and the rude, the contiguous out-lying parts came to be included in a kind of general design: and when nature was taken into the plan, under improvements, every step that was made, pointed out new beauties and inspired new ideas. At that moment appeared Kent, painter enough to taste the charms of landscape, bold and opinionative enough to dare and to dictate, and born with a genius to strike out a great system from the twilight of imperfect essays. He leaped the fence, and saw that all nature was a garden. He felt the delicious contrast of hill and valley changing imperceptibly into each other, tasted the beauty of the gentle swell, or concave scoop, and remarked how loose groves crowned an easy eminence with happy ornament, and while they called in the distant view between their graceful stems, removed and extended the perspective by delusive comparison.

Thus the pencil of his imagination bestowed all the arts of landscape on the scenes he handled. The great principles on which he worked were perspective, and light and shade. Groupes of trees broke too uniform or too extensive a lawn; evergreens and woods were opposed to the glare of the champain, and where the view was less fortunate, or so much exposed as to be beheld at once, he blotted out some parts by thick shades, to divide it into variety, or to make the richest scene more enchanting by reserving it to a farther advance of the spectator's step. Thus selecting favourite objects, and veiling deformities by screens of plantation; sometimes allowing the rudest waste to add its foil to the richest theatre, he realised the compositions of the greatest masters in painting. Where objects were wanting to animate his horizon, his taste as an architect could bestow immediate termin-ation. His buildings, his seats, his temples, were more the works of his pencil than of his compasses. We owe the restoration of Greece and the diffusion of architecture to his skill in landscape.

But of all the beauties he added to the face of this beautiful country, none surpassed his management of water. Adieu to canals, circular basons, and cascades tumbling down marble steps, that last absurd magnificence of Italian and French villas. The forced elevation of cataracts was no more. The gentle stream was taught to serpentize seemingly at its pleasure, and where discontinued by different levels, its course appeared to be concealed by thickets properly interspersed, and glittered again at a distance where it might be supposed naturally to arrive. Its borders were smoothed, but preserved their waving irregularity. A few trees scattered here and there on its edges sprinkled the tame bank that accompanied its mæanders; and when it disappeared among the hills, shades descending from the heights leaned towards its progress, and framed the distant point of light under which it was lost, as it turned aside to either hand of the blue horizon.

Thus dealing in none but the colours of nature, and catching its most favourable features, men saw a new creation opening before their eyes. The living landscape was chastened or polished, not transformed. Freedom was given to the forms of trees; they extended their branches unrestricted, and where any eminent oak, or master beech had escaped maiming and survived the forest, bush and bramble was removed, and all its honours were restored to distinguish and shade the plain. Where the united plumage of an ancient wood extended wide its undulating canopy, and stood venerable in its darkness, Kent thinned the foremost ranks, and left but so many detached and scattered trees, as softened the approach of gloom and blended a chequered light with the thus lengthened shadows of the remaining columns.

Succeeding artists have added new master-strokes to these touches; perhaps improved or brought to perfection some that I have named. The introduction of foreign trees and plants, which we owe principally to Archibald duke of Argyle, contributed essentially to the richness of colouring so peculiar to our modern landscape. The mixture of various greens, the contrast of forms between our forest-trees and the northern and West-Indian firs and pines, are improvements more recent than Kent, or but little known to him. The weeping-willow and every florid shrub, each tree of delicate or bold leaf, are new tints in the composition of our gardens. The last century was certainly acquainted with many of those rare plants we now admire. The Weymouth pine has long been naturalized here; the patriarch plant still exists at Longleat. The light and graceful acacia was known as early; witness those ancient stems in the court of Bedford-house in Bloomsbury-square; and in the bishop of London's garden at Fulham are many exotics of very ancient date. I doubt therefore whether the difficulty of preserving them in a clime so foreign to their nature did not convince our ancestors of their inutility in general; unless the shapeliness of the lime and horse-chesnut, which accorded so well with established regularity, and which thence and from their novelty grew in fashion, did not occasion the neglect of the more curious plants.

But just as the encomiums are that I have bestowed on Kent's discoveries, he was neither without assistance or faults. Mr. Pope undoubtedly contributed to form his taste. The design of the prince of Wales's garden at Carlton-house was evidently borrowed from the poet's at Twickenham. There was a little of affected modesty in the latter, when he said, of all his works he was most proud of his garden. And yet it was a singular effort of art and taste to impress so much variety and scenery on a spot of five acres. The passing through the gloom from the grotto to the opening day, the retiring and again assembling shades, the dusky groves, the larger lawn, and the solemnity of the termination at the cypresses that lead up to his mother's tomb, are managed with exquisite judgement; and though lord Peterborough assisted him

> To form his quincunx and to rank his vines,

those were not the most pleasing ingredients of his little perspective.

116 WILLIAM CHAMBERS
from *A Dissertation on Oriental Gardening* (1772)

Earlier we saw excerpts from William Chambers's *Designs of Chinese Buildings, Furniture, Dresses, Machines, and Utensils* (1757), which prompted interest in Britain in all things Chinese (see chapter 100). Chambers's *Dissertation on Oriental Gardening*, however, did not appear until a decade later, and by this time the novelty of China had to some extent worn off. What is interesting here is also the change or evolution in the viewpoint of Chambers himself. He is still attracted to aspects of Chinese gardens (which he had not visited since the 1740s), but it is an attraction now moderated by events that have taken place in Britain. These few pages are generally interpreted to be an attack on the overly "natural" landscape designs of Capability Brown – those praised by Whately. Chambers wants to define a middle path between the developing idea of a picturesque garden and the geometric gardens still popular on the Continent. It is a mediation, however, that would fail to take hold.

Amongst the Chinese, Gardening is held in much higher esteem, than it is in Europe; they rank a perfect work in that Art, with the great productions of the human understanding; and say, that its efficacy in moving the passions, yields to that of few other arts whatever.

Their Gardeners are not only Botanists, but also Painters and Philosophers, having a thorough knowledge of the human mind, and of the arts by which its strongest feelings are excited. It is not in China, as in Italy and France, where every petty Architect is a Gardener; neither is it as in another famous country, where peasants emerge from the melon grounds to commence professors; so Sganarelle, the faggot-maker, laid down his hatchet to turn physician. In China, Gardening is a distinct profession, requiring an extensive study; to the perfection of which few arrive. The Gardeners there, far from being either ignorant or illiterate, are men of high abilities, who join to good natural parts, most ornaments that study, travelling, and long experience can supply them with: it is in consideration of these accomplishments only that they are permitted to exercise their profession; for with the Chinese the taste of Ornamental Gardening is an object of legislative attention, it being supposed to have an influence upon the general culture, and consequently upon the beauty of the whole country. They observe, that mistakes committed in this Art, are too important

William Chambers, from *A Dissertation on Oriental Gardening*. W. Griffin, 1772, pp. 11–17.

to be tolerated, being much exposed to view, and in a great measure irreparable; as it often requires the space of a century, to redress the blunders of an hour.

The Chinese Gardeners take nature for their pattern; and their aim is to imitate all her beautiful irregularities. Their first consideration is the nature of the ground they are to work upon: whether it be flat or sloping; hilly or mountainous; small or of considerable extent; abounding with springs and rivers, or labouring under a scarcity of water; whether woody or bare, rough or even, barren or rich; and whether the transitions be sudden, and the character grand, wild or tremendous; or whether they be gradual, and the general bent placid, gloomy or chearful. To all which circumstances they carefully attend; choosing such dispositions as humour the ground, hide its defects, improve or set off its advantages, and can be executed with expedition, at a moderate expence.

They are also attentive to the wealth or indigence of the patron by whom they are employed; to his age, his infirmities, temper, amusements, connections, business and manner of living; as likewise to the season of the year in which the Garden is likely to be most frequented by him: suiting themselves in their composition to his circumstances, and providing for his wants and recreations. Their skill consists in struggling with the imperfections and defects of nature, and with every other impediment; and in producing, in spite of every obstacle, works that are uncommon, and perfect in their kind.

Though the Chinese artists have nature for their general model, yet are they not so attached to her as to exclude all appearance of art; on the contrary, they think it, on many occasions, necessary to make an ostentatious shew of their labour. Nature, say they, affords us but few materials to work with. Plants, ground and water, are her only productions: and though both the forms and arrangements of these may be varied to an incredible degree, yet have they but few striking varieties, the rest being of the nature of changes rung upon bells, which, though in reality different, still produce the same uniform kind of jingling; the variation being too minute to be easily perceived.

Art must therefore supply the scantiness of nature; and not only be employed to produce variety, but also novelty and effect: for the simple arrangements of nature are met with in every common field, to a certain degree of perfection; and are therefore too familiar to excite any strong sensations in the mind of the beholder, or to produce any uncommon degree of pleasure.

It is indeed true that novelty and variety may both be attained by transplanting the peculiarities of one country to another; by introducing rocks, cataracts, impending woods, and other parts of romantic situations, in flat places; by employing much water where it is rare; and cultivated plains, amidst the rude irregularities of mountains: but even this resource is easily exhausted, and can seldom be put in practice, without a very great expence.

The Chinese are therefore no enemies to strait lines; because they are, generally speaking, productive of grandeur, which often cannot be attained without them: nor have they any aversion to regular geometrical figures, which the say are beautiful in themselves, and well suited to small compositions, where the luxuriant irregularities of nature would fill up and embarrass the parts they should adorn. They likewise think them properest for flower gardens, and all other compositions, where much art is apparent in the culture; and where it should therefore not be omitted in the form.

Their regular buildings they generally surround with artificial terrasses, slopes, and many flights of steps; the angles of which are adorned with groupes of sculpture and vases, intermixed with all sorts of artificial waterworks, which, connecting with the architecture, serve to give it consequence, and add to the gaiety, splendor, and bustle of the scenery.

Round the main habitation, and near all their decorated structures, the grounds are laid out with great regularity, and kept with great care: no plants are admitted that intercept the view of the buildings; nor no lines but such as accompany the architecture properly, and contribute to the general good effect of the whole composition: for they hold it absurd to surround an elegant fabric with disorderly rude vegetation; saying, that it looks like a diamond set in lead; and always conveys the idea of an unfinished work. When the buildings are rustic, the scenery which surrounds them is wild; when they are grand, it is gloomy; when gay, it is luxuriant: in short, the Chinese are scrupulously nice in preserving the same character through every part of the composition; which is one great cause of that surprizing variety with which their works abound.

117 WILLIAM GILPIN
from *Observations on the River Wye* (1782)

We saw earlier Whately's use of the term "picturesque" in reference to pictorial composition. William Gilpin also defined the word in 1768 as "expressive of that peculiar kind of beauty, which is agreeable in a picture." By 1782, the time when Gilpin published the first of his many guidebooks to scenic sites in England, Scotland, and Wales, the word had now acquired a somewhat different meaning. Gilpin was an enthusiast of nature. In the 1760s and 1770s he had undertaken numerous excursions to scenic areas, both by hiking and by canoe, and with words and painted aquatints he recorded his impressions. He subtitled his book about the River Wye, in southern Wales, as "Relative Chiefly to Picturesque Beauty." In explaining the purpose of his study, he expounded upon the aesthetic principles to be gleaned: "that of not barely examining the face of a country; but of examining it by the rules of picturesque beauty; that of not merely describing; but of adapting the description of natural scenery to the principles of artificial landscape; and of opening the sources of these pleasures, which are derived from the comparison." Gilpin's various guidebooks were quite popular as a series and they helped to popularize the notion of a picturesque aesthetic. The passage reprinted here follows his general description of the river and focuses – from a canoe – on that section of the river surrounding Goodrich Castle.

Having thus analyzed the Wye, and considered separately its constituent parts – the *steepness* of its banks – its *mazy* course – the *ground, woods*, and *rocks*, which are its native ornaments – and the *buildings*, which still farther adorn its natural beauties; we shall now take a view of

William Gilpin (1724–1804), from *Observations on the River Wye*. London: R. Blamire, 1782, pp. 15–22.

some of those delightful scenes, which result from the *combination* of all the picturesque materials.

I must however premise, how ill-qualified I am to do justice to the banks of the Wye, were it only from having seen them under the circumstance of a continued rain; which began early in the day, before one third of our voyage was performed.

It is true, scenery *at hand* suffers less under such a circumstance, than scenery at *a distance*; which it totally obscures.

The picturesque eye also, in quest of beauty, finds it almost in every incident, and under every appearance of nature. Her works, and all her works, must ever, in some degree, be beautiful. Even the rain gave a gloomy grandeur to many of the scenes; and by throwing a veil of obscurity over the removed banks of the river, introduced, now and then, something like a pleasing distance. Yet still it hid greater beauties; and we could not help regretting the loss of those broad lights, and deep shadows, which would have given so much lustre to the whole; and which, ground like this, is in a peculiar manner adapted to receive.

The first part of the river from Ross, is tame. The banks are low; and there is scarce an object worth attention, except the ruins of *Wilton-castle*, which appear on the left, shrouded with a few trees. But the scene wants accompaniments to give it grandeur.

The bank however soon began to swell on the right, and was richly adorned with wood. We admired it much; and also the vivid images reflected from the water; which were continually disturbed, as we sailed past them; and thrown into tremulous confusion, by the dashing of our oars. A disturbed surface of water endeavouring to collect its scattered images; and restore them to order, is among the *pretty* appearances of nature.

We met with nothing, for some time, during our voyage, but these grand woody banks, one rising behind another; appearing, and vanishing, by turns, as we doubled their several capes. But though no particular objects marked and characterized these different scenes; yet they afforded great variety of beautiful perspective views, as we wound round them; or stretched through the reaches, which they marked out along the river.

The channel of no river can be more decisively marked, than that of the Wye. *Who hath divided a water-course for the flowing of rivers?* faith the Almighty in that grand apostrophe to Job on the works of creation. The idea is happily illustrated here. A nobler *water-course* was never *divided* for any river, than this. Rivers, in general, pursue a devious course along the countries, through which they flow; and form a channel for themselves by constant fluxion. But, here and there, we see a channel marked out with such precision; that it appears as if originally intended only for the bed of a river.

After sailing four Miles from Ross, we came to *Goodrich-castle*; where a very grand view presented itself; and we rested on our oars to examine it. A reach of the river, forming a noble bay, is spread before the eye. The bank, on the right, is steep, and covered with wood; beyond which a bold promontory shoots out; crowned with a castle, rising among the trees.

This view, which is one of the grandest on the river, I should not scruple to call *correctly picturesque*; which is seldom the character of a purely natural scene.

Nature is always great in design; but unequal in composition. She is an admirable colourist; and can harmonize her tints with infinite variety, and inimitable beauty: but is seldom so correct in composition, as to produce an harmonious whole. Either the fore-ground, or the background, is disproportioned: or some awkward line runs across the piece: or a tree is ill-placed: or a bank is formal: or something, or other is not exactly what it should be. The case is, the immensity of nature is beyond human comprehension. She works on a *vast scale*; and, no doubt, harmoniously, if her schemes could be comprehended. The artist, in the mean time, is confined to a *span*. He lays down his little rules therefore, which he calls the *principles of picturesque beauty*, merely to adapt such diminutive parts of nature's surfaces to his own eye, as come within its scope.

Hence therefore, the painter, who adheres strictly to the *composition* of nature, will rarely make a good picture. His picture must contain *a whole*: his archetype is but *a part*.

In general however he may obtain views of such parts of nature, as with the addition of a few trees; or a little alteration in the foreground, (which is a liberty, that must always be allowed) may be adapted to his rules; though he is rarely so fortunate as to find a landscape completely satisfactory to him. In the scenery indeed at Goodrich-castle the parts are few; and the whole is a very simple exhibition. The complex scenes of nature are generally those, which the artist finds most refractory to the rules of composition.

In following the course of the Wye, which makes here one of its boldest sweeps, we were carried almost round the castle, surveying it in a variety of forms. Many of these retrospects are good; but, in general, the castle loses, on this side, both its own dignity, and the dignity of its situation.

The views *from* the castle, were mentioned to us, as worth examining: but the rain was now set in, and would not permit us to land.

As we leave *Goodrich-castle*, the banks, on the left, which had hitherto contributed less to entertain us, began now principally to attract our attention; rearing themselves gradually into grand steeps; sometimes covered with thick woods; and sometimes forming vast concave slopes of mere verdure; unadorned, except here and there, by a straggling tree: while the flocks, which hung browsing upon them, seen from the bottom, were diminished into white specks.

The view at *Rure-dean-church* unfolds itself next; which is a scene of great grandeur. Here, both sides of the river are steep, and both woody; but in one the woods are intermixed with rocks. The deep umbrage of the forest of Dean occupies the front; and the spire of the church rises among the trees. The reach of the river, which exhibits this scene, is long; and, of course, the view, which is a noble piece of natural perspective, continues some time before the eye: but when the spire comes directly in front, the grandeur of the landscape is gone.

The *stone-quarries*, on the right, from which the bridge of Bristol was built; and, on the left, the furnaces of *Bishop's-wood*, vary the scene, though of no great importance in themselves.

For some time, both sides of the river continue steep and beautiful. No particular object indeed characterizes either: but nature always characterizes her own scenes. We admire the infinite variety, with which she *shapes* and *adorns* these vast concave, and convex forms. We admire also that *varied touch*, with which she expresses every object.

Here we see one great distinction between *her* painting, and that of all her *copyists*. Artists universally are *mannerists* in a certain degree. Each has his particular mode of forming particular objects. His rocks, his trees, his figures are cast in one mould: at least they possess only a *varied sameness*. Rubens's figures are all full-fed: Salvator's, spare, and long-legged.

The artist also discovers as little variety in filling up the surfaces of bodies, as he does in delineating their forms. You see the same touch, or something like it, universally prevail, though applied to different objects.

In every part of painting, except execution, an artist may be assisted by the labours of those, who have gone before him. He may improve his skill in composition, in light and shade, in perspective, in grace and elegance; that is, in all the scientific parts of his art: but with regard to execution, he must set up on his own stock. A *mannerist*, I fear, he must be. If he get a manner of his own, he *may* be an agreeable mannerist: but if he copy another's, he *will certainly* be a formal one. The more closely he copies nature, the better chance he has of being free from this general defect.

118   JOSHUA REYNOLDS
from *Discourses on Art* (1786)

This passage from the thirteenth discourse of the painter Joshua Reynolds is notable in two respects. First Reynolds – following Addison – elevates gardening to an art form, and one that plays specifically to the imagination. Second, in his architectural comments, Reynolds's high regard for the genius of John Vanbrugh helps to resurrect the reputation of this baroque architect and will prove enormously influential. Reynolds, who was the founding president of the very classical Royal Academy, was far from a picturesque theorist, but on occasions his words and ideas speak otherwise. His applause for painterly effects in architecture, his appreciation for the irregularities of Gothic architecture (not to mention "those Asiatick Buildings"), and his fondness for intricacy and variety of effects – all play into the development of the emerging picturesque aesthetic and would sway a younger generation.

So also Gardening, as far as Gardening is an Art, or entitled to that appellation, is a deviation from nature; for if the true taste consists, as many hold, in banishing every appearance of Art, or any traces of the footsteps of man, it would then be no longer a Garden. Even though we define it, "Nature to advantage dress'd," and in some sense it is such, and much more beautiful and commodious for the recreation of man; it is however, when so dress'd, no longer a subject for the pencil of a Landskip-Painter, as all Landskip-Painters know, who love to have recourse to Nature herself, and to dress her according to the principles of their own Art; which are far different from those of Gardening, even when conducted according to the most approved principles, and such as a Landskip-Painter himself would adopt in the disposition of his own grounds, for his own private satisfaction.

I have brought together as many instances as appear necessary, to make out the several points which I wished to suggest to your consideration in this Discourse; that your own thoughts may lead you further in the use that may be made of the analogy of the Arts, and of the restraint which a full understanding of the diversity of many of their principles ought to impose on the employment of that analogy.

The great end of all those arts is, to make an impression on the imagination and the feeling. The imitation of nature frequently does this. Sometimes it fails, and something else succeeds. I think therefore the true test of all the arts, is not solely whether the production is

Joshua Reynolds (1723–92), from *Discourses on Art* (1786), ed. Robert R. Wark. New Haven: Yale University Press, 1959, pp. 240–4.

a true copy of nature, but whether it answers the end of art, which is to produce a pleasing effect upon the mind.

It remains only to speak a few words of Architecture, which does not come under the denomination of an imitative art. It applies itself, like Musick (and I believe we may add Poetry,) directly to the imagination, without the intervention of any kind of imitation.

There is in Architecture, as in Painting, an inferior branch of art, in which the imagination appears to have no concern. It does not however acquire the name of a polite and liberal art, from its usefulness, or administering to our wants or necessities, but from some higher principle: we are sure that in the hands of a man of genius it is capable of inspiring sentiment, and of filling the mind with great and sublime ideas.

It may be worth the attention of Artists, to consider what materials are in their hands, that may contribute to this end; and whether this art has it not in its power to address itself to the imagination with effect, by more ways than are generally employed by Architects.

To pass over the effect produced by that general symmetry and proportion, by which the eye is delighted, as the ear is with musick, Architecture certainly possesses many principles in common with Poetry and Painting. Among those which may be reckoned as the first, is, that of affecting the imagination by means of association of ideas. Thus, for instance, as we have naturally a veneration for antiquity, whatever building brings to our remembrance ancient customs and manners, such as the Castles of the Barons of ancient Chivalry, is sure to give this delight. Hence it is that *towers and battlements* are so often selected by the Painter and the Poet, to make a part of the composition of their ideal Landskip; and it is from hence in a great degree, that in the buildings of Vanbrugh, who was a Poet as well as an Architect, there is a greater display of imagination, than we shall find perhaps in any other; and this is the ground of the effect which we feel in many of his works, notwithstanding the faults with which many of them are justly charged. For this purpose, Vanbrugh appears to have had recourse to some principles of the Gothick Architecture; which, though not so ancient as the Grecian, is more so to our imagination, with which the Artist is more concerned than with absolute truth.

The Barbarick splendour of those Asiatick Buildings, which are now publishing by a member of this Academy, may possibly, in the same manner, furnish an Architect, not with models to copy, but with hints of composition and general effect, which would not otherwise have occurred.

It is, I know, a delicate and hazardous thing, (and as such I have already pointed it out,) to carry the principles of one art to another, or even to reconcile in one object the various modes of the same Art, when they proceed on different principles. The sound rules of the Grecian Architecture are not to be lightly sacrificed. A deviation from them, or even an addition to them, is like a deviation or addition to, or from, the rules of other Arts, fit only for a great master, who is thoroughly conversant in the nature of man, as well as all combinations in his own Art.

It may not be amiss for the Architect to take advantage *sometimes* of that to which I am sure the Painter ought always to have his eyes open, I mean the use of accidents; to follow when they lead, and to improve them, rather than always to trust to a regular plan. It often happens that additions have been made to houses, at various times, for use or pleasure. As such buildings depart from regularity, they now and then acquire something of scenery by this accident, which I should think might not unsuccessfully be adopted by an Architect, in an original plan, if it does not too much interfere with convenience. Variety and intricacy is a beauty and excellence in every other of the Arts which address the imagination; and why not in Architecture?

The forms and turnings of the streets of London, and other old towns, are produced by accident, without any original plan or design; but they are not always the less pleasant to the walker or spectator, on that account. On the contrary, if the city had been built on the regular plan of Sir Christopher Wren, the effect might have been, as we know it is in some new parts of the town, rather unpleasing; the uniformity might have produced weariness, and a slight degree of disgust.

I can pretend to no skill in the detail of Architecture. I judge now of the art, merely as a Painter. When I speak of Vanbrugh, I mean to speak of him in the language of our art. To speak then of Vanbrugh in the language of a Painter, he had originality of invention, he understood light and shadow, and had great skill in composition. To support his principal object, he produced his second and third groups or masses; he perfectly understood in *his* Art what is the most difficult in ours, the conduct of the back-ground, by which the design and invention is set off to the greatest advantage. What the back-ground is in Painting, in Architecture is the real ground on which the building is erected; and no Architect took greater care than he that his work should not appear crude and hard: that is, it did not abruptly start out of the ground without expectation or preparation.

This is a tribute, which a Painter owes to an Architect who composed like a Painter; and was defrauded of the due reward of his merit by the Wits of his time, who did not understand the principles of composition in poetry better than he; and who knew little, or nothing, of what he understood perfectly, the general ruling principles of Architecture and Painting. His fate was that of the great Perrault; both were the objects of the petulant sarcasms of factious men of letters; and both have left some of the fairest ornaments which to this day decorate their several countries; the façade of the Louvre, Blenheim, and castle Howard.

119 JOHN SOANE
from *Plans, Elevations, and Sections of Buildings* (1788)

Prior to Soane's association with the Royal Academy in 1795, he was an architect in private practice. And like many architects of his day, he sought commissions from potential clients by publishing examples of his work. This process began in 1778, shortly after he left Italy, with his *Designs in Architecture*, which consisted of hypothetical and whimsical designs. As he began to acquire clients in the 1780s, he amassed sufficient built works to publish his *Plans, Elevations and Sections of Buildings* in 1788. His clients during this decade were mostly gentlemen

John Soane, from *Plans, Elevations, and Sections of Buildings Erected in the Counties of Norfolk, etc.* (1788). Farnborough: Gregg International Publishers, 1971 (facsimile edition), pp. 8–11.

of sufficient affluence to build a country house or add to an existing one. He prefaced this book with some observations on architecture, in which he stresses the duties and responsibilities of architects. Toward the end of his remarks, however, he turns to the question of ornament, and here – with his comments on the Gothic style and his concern with the natural setting of the house – we see the influence of both Reynolds (whose lectures he attended) and picturesque thought making their way into architectural consciousness. Soane, as we have seen (see chapter 91 above), was trained as a neoclassical architect, but with his interest in character and almost eccentric fascination with ruins, he is very much an architect at the forefront of emerging baroque and picturesque sensibilities.

Ornaments are to be cautiously introduced; those ought only to be used that are simple, applicable and characteristic of their situations: they must be designed with regularity and be perfectly distinct in their outlines; the Doric members must not be mixed with the Ionic, nor the Ionic with the Corinthian, but such ornaments only should be used, as tend to shew the destination of the edifice, as assist in determining its character, and for the choice of which the architect can assign satisfactory reasons.

The ancients with great propriety decorated their temples and altars with the sculls of victims, rams heads and other ornaments peculiar to their religious ceremonies; but when the same ornaments are introduced in the decoration of English houses, they become puerile and disgusting.

After the authors and works already mentioned it would be as useless as presumptuous to enter into any detail relating to the elements and orders of architecture; the lovers of the arts will consult with pleasure and profit the parallel of the ancient architecture with the modern, written in French by Roland Freart and translated by Evelyn, a work of great learning and merit.

The ingenuity of mankind has hitherto produced only three distinct orders of architecture, and perhaps never will invent more, unless such attempts as are shewn in ''A Proposition for a ''New Order of Architecture'' can be considered as increasing the number; yet the Gothic architecture being entirely distinct in all its parts from the Grecian orders gives us some reason to hope.

By Gothic architecture I do not mean those barbarous jumbles of undefined forms in modern imitations of Gothic architecture: but the light and elegant examples in many of our cathedrals, churches, and other public buildings, which are so well calculated to excite solemn, serious and contemplative ideas, that it is almost impossible to enter such edifices without feeling the deepest awe and reverence. King's College Chapel at Cambridge, is a glorious example of the wonderful perfection of Gothic architecture; there is a boldness and mathematical knowledge peculiar to this edifice, which claims our earnest attention and admiration, which excites us to the pursuit of geometrical knowledge, and reminds us of the high opinion the ancients had of geometry.

In this country are the most and best examples of Gothic architecture, in its various stages of rise, progress and decline; it is therefore to be hoped some ingenious artist will find a patron of sufficient taste and fortune to employ his talents and preserve from destruction, by accurate drawings and models, the mouldering remains of Gothic genius and grandeur. [...]

Ideal designs have been treated, by an ingenious author, with great contempt: certainly those that have been executed are more to be relied on, as they must have been better considered and digested, for without practical knowledge theory is of little worth; the artist conversant in the practice of building, must have often met with difficulties after he had made drawings of every part, and attentively considered the whole design.

It is impossible to compose one design adapted to every situation, an eminence and a valley require a different stile of architecture; an edifice in an open country should consist of large and simple parts, while the peaceful valley, and silent stream admit of more delicacy and ornament. The difference in manner of living, and the different ideas of convenience, comfort and elegance, render the attempt at forming one plan for every situation still more impracticable.

In composing the following designs I have been more anxious to produce utility in the plans than to display expensive architecture in the elevations; the leading objects were to unite convenience and comfort in the interior distributions, and simplicity and uniformity in the exterior; to collect together some designs of houses and other buildings already executed, in which attention has been paid to the locality, to the different ideas of comfort and convenience, and to the stile of living of the several possessors. If the public should judge as favourably of them as the individuals for whom they have been executed, I shall flatter myself that my time has not been misapplied, nor my endeavours useless.

120   UVEDALE PRICE
from *Essays on the Picturesque* (1794)

The actual consolidation of picturesque theory took place in the 1790s and was tackled by three individuals: a landscape architect and two exceptional writers. The gardener was Humphry Repton, a disciple of Brown; the two promulgators of picturesque theory were Uvedale Price and Richard Payne Knight.

Price was the first to put his ideas into print and his three-volume study is not only monumental in size but also in ambition, as he seeks to elevate the notion of the picturesque to an aesthetic category equal to the headings of the beautiful and the sublime. In this regard this book follows directly upon Burke's *A Philosophical Inquiry into the Origin of our Ideas of the Sublime and Beautiful*, of which Price was a keen admirer. And Price, like his mentor, was a parliamentarian, a man of enormous wealth, and a classical scholar. He was also a lover of art and possessed an especial affinity for the landscape paintings of Claude Lorraine, Nicolas Poussin, and Jean-Antoine Watteau. What is more, Price attempted to put his picturesque theories into practice on his own estate – Foxley – in Herefordshire, where he allowed a certain "neatness" only in those areas surrounding the house.

In spirit, *Essays on the Picturesque* is closer to the natural and rough picturesque sensibilities of Gilpin than to the more refined garden tradition that had evolved from the hands of Capability Brown, who had died in 1783. Price is in fact highly critical of the tradition of Brown because he feels that his formulaic use of serpentine driveways, walks, and ponds was not only monotonous but also substituted an artificial informality for the earlier formality of geometric designs. Price prefers nature untamed – trees with natural undergrowth and accidental effects. The following passages are from chapters 3 and 4 of the first volume, where Price first compares the idea of the picturesque with Burke's conception of the beautiful and the sublime. Price wants to posit the picturesque as a

Uvedale Price (1747–1829), from *Essays on the Picturesque, as Compared with the Sublime and the Beautiful*, Vol. I (1794). J. Mawman, 1810, pp. 43–53, 87–92.

middle "station between beauty and sublimity." The (anticlassical) association of the picturesque with ruins and with Gothic architecture also falls in with a trend that was hastening the Gothic Revival in Britain.

The principles of those two leading characters in nature, the sublime and the beautiful, have been fully illustrated and discriminated by a great master; but even when I first read that most original work, I felt that there were numberless objects which give great delight to the eye, and yet differ as widely from the beautiful, as from the sublime. The reflections which I have since been led to make, have convinced me that these objects form a distinct class, and belong to what may properly be called the picturesque.

That term, as we may judge from its etymology, is applied only to objects of sight; and indeed in so confined a manner, as to be supposed merely to have a reference to the art from which it is named. I am well convinced, however, that the name and reference only are limited and uncertain, and that the qualities which make objects picturesque, are not only as distinct as those which make them beautiful or sublime, but are equally extended to all our sensations by whatever organs they are received; and that music (though it appears like a solecism) may be as truly picturesque, according to the general principles of picturesqueness, as it may be beautiful or sublime, according to those of beauty or sublimity.

But there is one circumstance particularly adverse to this part of my essay; I mean the manifest derivation of the word picturesque. The Italian *pittoresco* is, I imagine, of earlier date than either the English or the French word, the latter of which, *pittoresque*, is clearly taken from it, having, no analogy to its own tongue. *Pittoresco* is derived, not like picturesque, from the thing painted, but from the painter; and this difference is not wholly immaterial. The English word refers to the performance, and the objects most suited to it: the Italian and French words have a reference to the turn of mind common to painters; who, from the constant habit of examining all the peculiar effects and combinations, as well as the general appearance of nature, are struck with numberless circumstances, even where they are incapable of being represented, to which an unpractised eye pays little or no attention. The English word naturally draws the reader's mind towards pictures; and from that partial and confined view of the subject, what is in truth only an illustration of picturesqueness, becomes the foundation of it. The words sublime and beautiful have not the same etymological reference to any one visible art, and therefore are applied to objects of the other senses: sublime indeed, in the language from which it is taken, and in its plain sense, means high, and therefore, perhaps, in strictness, should relate to objects of sight only; yet we no more scruple to call one of Handel's chorusses sublime, than Corelli's famous *pastorale* beautiful. But should any person simply, and without any qualifying expressions, call a capricious movement of Scarlatti or Haydn *picturesque*, he would, with great reason, be laughed at, for it is not a term applied to sounds; yet such a movement, from its sudden, unexpected, and abrupt transitions, – from a certain playful wildness of character and appearance of irregularity, is no less analogous to similar scenery in nature, than the concerto or the chorus, to what is grand or beautiful to the eye.

There is, indeed, a general harmony and correspondence in all our sensations when they arise from similar causes, though they affect us by means of different senses; and these causes, as Mr. Burke has admirably pointed out, can never be so clearly ascertained when we confine our observations to one sense only.

I must here observe, and I wish the reader to keep it in his mind, that the inquiry is not in what sense certain words are used in the best authors, still less what is their common, and vulgar use, and abuse; but whether there be certain qualities, which uniformly produce the same effects in all visible objects, and, according to the same analogy, in objects of hearing and of all the other senses; and which qualities, though frequently blended and united with others in the same object or set of objects, may be separated from them, and assigned to the class to which they belong.

If it can be shewn that a character composed of these qualities, and distinct from all others, does universally prevail; if it can be traced in the different objects of art and of nature, and appears consistent throughout, – it surely deserves a distinct title; but with respect to the real ground of inquiry, it matters little whether such a character, or the set of objects belonging to it, be called beautiful, sublime, or picturesque, or by any other name, or by no name at all.

Beauty is so much the most enchanting and popular quality, that it is often applied as the highest commendation to whatever gives us pleasure, or raises our admiration, be the cause what it will. Mr. Burke has given several instances of these ill-judged applications, and of the confusion of ideas which result from them; but there is nothing more ill-judged, or more likely to create confusion, if we at all agree with Mr. Burke in his idea of beauty, than the mode which prevails of joining together two words of a different, and in some respects of an opposite meaning, and calling the character by the title of Picturesque Beauty.

I must observe, however, that I by no means object to the expression itself; I only object to it as a general term for the *character*, and as comprehending every kind of scenery, and every set of objects which look well in a picture. That is the sense, as far as I have observed, in which it is very commonly used; consequently, an old hovel, an old cart horse, or an old woman, are often, in that sense, full of picturesque *beauty*; and certainly the application of the last term to such objects, must tend to confuse our ideas: but were the expression restrained to those objects only, in which the picturesque and the beautiful are mixed together, and so mixed, that the result, according to common apprehension, is beautiful; and were it never used when the picturesque (as it no less frequently happens) is mixed solely with what is terrible, ugly, or deformed, I should highly approve of the expression, and wish for more distinctions of the same kind.

In reality, the picturesque not only differs from the beautiful in those qualities which Mr. Burke has so justly ascribed to it, but arises from qualities the most diametrically opposite.

According to Mr. Burke, one of the most essential qualities of beauty is smoothness: now as the perfection of smoothness is absolute equality and uniformity of surface, wherever that prevails there can be but little variety or intricacy; as, for instance, in smooth level banks, on a small, or in open downs, on a large scale. Another essential quality of beauty is gradual variation; that is (to make use of Mr. Burke's expression) where the lines do not vary in a sudden and broken manner, and where there is no sudden protuberance: it requires but little reflection to perceive, that the exclusion of all but flowing lines cannot promote variety; and that sudden protuberances, and lines that cross each other in a sudden and broken manner, are among the most fruitful causes of intricacy.

I am therefore persuaded, that the two opposite qualities of roughness,[1] and of sudden variation, joined to that of irregularity, are the most efficient causes of the picturesque.

This, I think, will appear very clearly, if we take a view of those objects, both natural and artificial, that are allowed to be picturesque, and compare them with those which are as generally allowed to be beautiful.

A temple or palace of Grecian architecture in its perfect entire state, and with its surface and colour smooth and even, either in painting or reality is beautiful; in ruin it is picturesque. Observe the process by which time, the great author of such changes, converts a beautiful object into a picturesque one. First, by means of weather stains, partial incrustations, mosses, &c. it at the same time takes off from the uniformity of the surface, and of the colour; that is, gives a degree of roughness, and variety of tint. Next, the various accidents of weather loosen the stones themselves; they tumble in irregular masses, upon what was perhaps smooth turf or pavement, or nicely trimmed walks and shrubberies; now mixed and overgrown with wild plants and creepers, that crawl over, and shoot among the fallen ruins. Sedums, wall-flowers, and other vegetables that bear drought, find nourishment in the decayed cement from which the stones have been detached: birds convey their food into the chinks, and yew, elder, and other berried plants project from the sides; while the ivy mantles over other parts, and crowns the top. The even, regular lines of the doors and windows are broken, and through their ivy-fringed openings is displayed in a more broken and picturesque manner [. . .]

Gothic architecture is generally considered as more picturesque, though less beautiful than Grecian; and upon the same principle that a ruin is more so than a new edifice. The first thing that strikes the eye in approaching any building, is the general outline, and the effect of the openings: in Grecian buildings, the general lines of the roof are strait; and even when varied and adorned by a dome or a pediment, the whole has a character of symmetry and regularity. But symmetry, which, in works of art particularly, accords with the beautiful, is in the same degree adverse to the picturesque; and among the various causes of the superior picturesqueness of ruins compared with entire buildings, the destruction of symmetry is by no means the least powerful.

In Gothic buildings, the outline of the summit presents such a variety of forms, of turrets and pinnacles, some open, some fretted and variously enriched, that even where there is an exact correspondence of parts, it is often disguised by an appearance of splendid confusion and irregularity. [. . .]

★ ★ ★

According to Mr. Burke, the passion caused by the great and sublime in *nature*, when those causes operate most powerfully, is astonishment; and astonishment is that state of the soul, in which all its motions are suspended with some degree of horror: the sublime also, being founded on ideas of pain and terror, like them operates by stretching the fibres beyond their natural tone. The passion excited by beauty, is love and complacency; it acts by relaxing the fibres somewhat below their natural tone, and this is accompanied by an inward sense of melting and languor. I have heard this part of Mr. Burke's book criticized, on a supposition that pleasure is more generally produced from the fibres being stimulated, than from their being relaxed. To me it appears, that Mr. Burke is right with respect to that pleasure which is the effect of beauty, or whatever has an analogy to beauty, according to the principles he has laid down.

If we examine our feelings on a warm genial day, in a spot full of the softest beauties of nature, the fragrance of spring breathing around us – pleasure then seems to be our natural state; to be received, not sought after; it is the happiness of existing to sensations of delight only; we are unwilling to move, almost to think, and desire only to feel, to enjoy. In pursuing the same train of ideas, I may add, that the effect of the picturesque is curiosity; an effect, which, though less splendid and powerful, has a more general influence. Those who have felt the excitement produced by the intricacies of wild romantic mountainous scenes, can tell how curiosity, while it prompts us to scale every rocky promontory, to explore every new recess, by its active agency keeps the fibres to their full tone; and thus picturesqueness when mixed with either of the other characters, corrects the languor of beauty, or the tension of sublimity. But as the nature of every corrective, must be to take off from the peculiar effect of what it is to correct, so does the picturesque when united to either of the others. It is the coquetry of nature; it makes beauty more amusing, more varied, more playful, but also,

"Less winning soft, less amiably mild."

Again, by its variety, its intricacy, its partial concealments, it excites that active curiosity which gives play to the mind, loosening those iron bonds, with which astonishment chains up its faculties.[2]

Where characters, however distinct in their nature, are perpetually mixed together in such various degrees and manners, it is not always easy to draw the exact line of separation: I think, however, we may conclude, that where an object, or a set of objects are without smoothness or grandeur, but from their intricacy, their sudden and irregular deviations, their variety of forms, tints, and lights and shadows, are interesting to a cultivated eye, they are simply picturesque. Such, for instance, are the rough banks that often inclose a bye-road, or a hollow lane: imagine the *size* of these banks, and the *space* between them to be increased, till the lane, becomes a deep dell; the coves, large caverns; the peeping stones, hanging rocks, so that the whole may impress an idea of awe and grandeur; – the sublime will then be mixed with the picturesque, though the *scale* only, not the *style* of the scenery would be changed. On the other hand, if parts of the banks were smooth and gently sloping; or if in the middle space the turf were soft and close-bitten; or if a gentle stream passed between them, whose clear, unbroken surface reflected all their varieties – the beautiful and the picturesque, by means of that softness and smoothness, would then be united.

I may here observe, that as softness is become a *visible* quality as well as smoothness, so also, from the same kind of sympathy, it is a principle of beauty in many visible objects: but as the hardest bodies are those which receive the highest polish, and consequently the highest degree of smoothness, there must be a number of objects in which smoothness and softness are for that reason incompatible. The one however is not unfrequently mistaken for the other, and I have more than once heard pictures, which were so smoothly finished that they looked like ivory, commended for their softness.

The skin of a delicate woman, is an example of softness and smoothness united; but if by art a higher polish be given to the skin, the softness, and in that case I may add the beauty, is destroyed. Fur, moss, hair, wool, &c. are comparatively rough; but they are soft, and yield to pressure, and therefore take off from the appearance of hardness, and also of edginess. A stone or rock, when polished by water, is smoother, but less soft than when covered with moss; and upon this principle, the wooded banks of a river have often a softer general effect, than the bare, shaven border of a canal. There is the same difference between the grass of a pleasureground mowed to the quick, and that of a fresh meadow; and it frequently happens, that continual mowing destroys the verdure, as well as the softness. So much does excessive attachment to one principle destroy its own ends.

NOTES

1   I have followed Mr. Gilpin's example in using roughness as a general term; he observes, however, that, "properly speaking, roughness relates only to the *surface* of bodies; and that when we speak of their *delineation* we use the word ruggedness." In making roughness, in this general sense, a very principal distinction between the beautiful and the picturesque, I believe I am supported by the general opinion of all who have considered the subject, as well as by Mr. Gilpin's authority.
2   This seems to be perfectly applicable to tragicomedy, and is at once its apology and condemnation. Whatever relieves the mind from a strong impression, of course weakens that impression.

121   RICHARD PAYNE KNIGHT
from "Postscript" to *The Landscape,* second edition (1795)

Nothing establishes the parameters of a theoretical direction better than a timely debate, and this Postscript to a poem first published in 1794 defines an interesting split already apparent within the picturesque movement. The first direction had been set out by Price — first in his reliance on the philosophical structure of Burke in establishing the notion of the picturesque and second with his coupling of the picturesque with the passion of "curiosity." Price's excoriation of the landscape tendencies of Brown, however, prompted a defense of the latter's ideas by his disciple Humphrey Repton, as promulgated in his "A Letter to Uvedale Price, Esq." (1794). Price would shortly respond in kind, but before doing so Repton would find his work as well as that of Brown attacked on a second front in a poem of Richard Payne Knight published in 1794, *The Landscape, A Didactic Poem in Three Books.*

Knight was the son of a wealthy Shropshire mine owner and ironmaster and a friend and neighbor of Uvedale Price. Upon coming of age in 1772 he used a portion of his fortune to build his crenellated Downton Castle in Herefordshire, which — after Walpole's endeavor — was one of the early forays into medieval revivalism. Also in the 1770s he made two trips to Italy to examine classical ruins, in particular the Greek monuments at Paestum and on Sicily. Upon returning home he was accepted as a member of the Society of Dilettanti, entered Parliament, and later settled into the life of a private collector and scholar.

In the 1790s, however, Knight's interests turned to landscape theory. In the first edition of *The Landscape,* he had attacked both Brown and Repton for their unnatural or affected approaches to landscape gardening. Knight was from the old school in the sense that he wanted to elevate landscape design into an art akin to its sister art of

Richard Payne Knight (1751–1824), from "Postscript" to the second edition of *The Landscape, a Didactic Poem in Three Books* (second edition, 1795). London: W. Bulmer, 1795 and Farnborough: Gregg International Publishers, 1972 (facsimile edition), pp. 98–104.

landscape painting; he also shared Price's fondness for a rougher or less tamed nature. In the second edition of his poem, in which he reflected on Repton's response to Price's earlier criticisms, Knight adds a Postscript to make his own points of difference more transparent. But what is not apparent is the fact that Knight was already beginning to become dissatisfied with the picturesque model of Price — differences that he would specifically address in a later book (see chapter 124 below).

Postscript to the Second Edition

Before I take leave of Mr. Repton, who has so gallantly stood forth the champion of the present system of rural decoration, I beg to assure him that whatever contempt I may have expressed in the course of my supplementary remarks to this Edition, of his professional principles and opinions, I most sincerely return the compliment, which he has been so obliging as to pay me in his Letter to Mr. Price; and furthermore to inform him, that I had not only great pleasure in his conversation, but conceived from it a much higher idea of those professional principles and opinions, than I have found verified in his works.

My acquaintance with him commenced many years ago, on his being employed to lay out a small, but romantic place, near to my own, in the fate of which I was of course much interested, and consequently dreaded the approach of a professed improver. When, however, I found that improver to be a man of liberal education, conversant (in some degree at least) with almost every branch of polite literature, and skilled in the art of design, which he executed with equal taste and facility, my fears were suddenly changed into the most pleasing expectations, which were still heightened and confirmed when I heard him launch out in praise of picturesque scenery, and declare that he had sought the principles of his art, not in the works of Kent or Brown, but in those of the great landscape painters; whose different styles he professed to have studied with care and attention, in order to employ them as occasion required, and thus to merit the new title which he had assumed, of *Landscape Gardener*.

It had long been my favourite wish that such a person would apply himself to this profession, and rescue it from the hands of mere gardeners, nurserymen, and mechanics; and when I found this favourite wish so unexpectedly gratified, my exultation was such, that I immediately communicated it to Mr. Price, and others of my friends, whom I knew to be equally interested in the cause of picturesque beauty. But alas! my triumph was of short duration: – the plans of improvement which he produced for the place abovementioned instantly undeceived me; and he will do me the justice to allow, that I did not, through any affected delicacy, or hypocritical politeness, conceal my disappointment from him; but when he did me the honour to consult me on his plans, communicated to him in writing my disapprobation of the greatest part of what he proposed doing, in as plain terms as common civility would admit of, and founded on such reasons as had guided me in all my own works of this kind. He will also recollect that he then declared himself to be convinced by these reasons, such as they were; and that he furthermore did me the honour (and I really esteem it as such) of requesting my assistance in reviewing the ground, and forming a plan more suitable to its natural character; with which request I should have been, on all accounts, happy to comply, but the sudden death of the owner put an entire stop to the business.

Since that time I have not had the pleasure of much of Mr. Repton's conversation; but I have had the misfortune to see many of his performances designed and executed exactly after Mr. Brown's receipt, without any attention to the natural, or artificial character of the country, or the style of the place. In his Letter, too, to Mr. Price, he has avowedly become the patron and defender of this system, and professedly abandoned the school of the painter for that of the gardener; he having, as he says, *found, after mature consideration, and more practical experience, that there is not so great an affinity betwixt painting and gardening as his enthusiasm for the picturesque had originally led him to fancy* (p. 5). I, it seems, had the good fortune first to enjoy his conversation, when this original enthusiasm for the picturesque was in its full vigour; and the ill fortune to become first acquainted with his works just as it was gone off, and he was animated with all the zeal of a new proselyte for the adverse system. In some respects, however, he has deviated from both; for I believe he is the first who ever thought of giving grandeur of character to a place, by hanging the family arms of the proprietor on the sign-post of a neighbouring inn, or emblazoning them on the neighbouring milestones (I beg pardon), I should say, *stones with distances upon them*. Neither Mr. Brown, *nor any of the tasteless herd of his followers*, ever thought of this happy expedient; though there is in the Spectator a story of an improving publican, who put the portrait of his old master Sir Roger de Coverley upon his sign, which may derogate from its claim to originality. The old knight, however, it is added (knowing nothing I suppose of the true principles of grandeur and sublimity), thought it tended more to throw ridicule on his person than give dignity to his possessions, and therefore had it turned into a Saracen's head: but this is supposed to have happened in a barbarous age of the art, when all its modern wonders of clumps, belts, and shrubberies were unknown.

I do not mean at present to enter into any further detailed criticisms of any particular performances, either of Mr. Brown or Mr. Repton, whatever I may do hereafter; for I still maintain, that the avowed principles and practice of every public professor, who devotes his talents to the public for pay, whether he professes law, medicine, painting, or gardening, are proper subjects for public discussion; nor can I consider the written opinion, for which the lawyer has received a fee, or the plan and explanation, for which the landscape gardener has been paid his bill, as private manuscripts, belonging to their respective authors, and which it is therefore unfair to quote.

I assure Mr. Repton, however, that I will never follow the example which he has set, in his Letter to Mr. Price, of endeavouring to involve speculative differences of opinion, upon subjects of mere elegant amusement, with the nearest and dearest interests of humanity; and thus to engage the popular passions of the times in a dispute, which I am certain that he, as well as every other candid and liberal man, will, upon more mature reflection, wish to keep entirely free from them. To say that his own system of rural embellishment resembles the British constitution, and that Mr. Price's and mine resemble the Democratic tyranny of France, is a species of argument which any person may employ, on any occasion, without being at any expence either of sense or science; whence it has been the constant weapon of controversy with those who have no other.

> Qui meprise Cotin, n'estime point son roi;
> Et n'a, selon Cotin, ni Dieu, ni foi, ni loi.

Could I presume that he would take my advice on a general principle, as he once did in a particular application of his art, we might yet avoid any further difference; and I assure him, that I do not mean (as advisers generally do) to impose my own opinions upon him, and bid him renounce his own; but merely to recommend to him the renewal of a course of study, which I fear he abandoned before he had made much progress in it. Let him for a while quit the school of Mr. Brown, and return to that of the great masters in landscape painting, whose lessons will not make such a savage of him as he seems to apprehend, nor teach him to injure either the health, comfort, or convenience of himself or his employers. Picturesque circumstances, as I can prove to him by many examples, may be preserved even close to a house, without sacrificing, or even diminishing, the *health*, I suppose he means *healthiness, cheerfulness, or comfort of a country residence* (ibid. p. 5 and 6.); and walks perfectly clean and commodious may be made through the wildest forest scenery, without derogating at all from its natural character. I will even go farther; and assert that there is scarcely any external circumstance, which can contribute to the convenience of a dwelling, but may at the same time be so contrived as to be a real embellishment. Even the straight walls, alleys, and espaliers of a kitchen garden, may be so disposed as to have such an effect. At Arundel castle, there is one within the peribolus of that venerable structure, which certainly adds to its picturesque beauty; and it was with the utmost pleasure that I learned that the noble proprietor had, with that genuine good taste which soars above all local and temporary fashions, determined to preserve it amidst the extensive alterations and improvements which he is now making there. Even Mr. Repton, before he had entirely abandoned the school of the painters for that of Mr. Brown, appears to have agreed with me on this point. The place above-mentioned, which he was employed to lay out in my neighbourhood, is situated on an eminence, commanding a very rich distance, terminated by bold and high mountains; but in the front of the house is a kitchen garden, bounded by a common, over which the proprietor had no power, it being in a different manor. Mr. Brown, in this case, would have turned the garden into a little lawn, surrounded by a sunk fence, a belt of low shrubs, and a serpentine gravel walk; and, if permission could have been obtained for more extensive improvements, would have cleared the common of its fern and heath, and have dotted it with clumps. Mr. Repton, at that time, acted upon better principles, at least in this instance, and therefore determined to let the old garden remain; justly observing, that it served better both as a skreen to the common, and a foreground to the distance, than any thing which he could substitute in so limited a space. Whether his taste has been since vitiated by habit, or whether he found by experience that the public taste had been previously so vitiated, that professional prudence obliged him to comply with it, I shall not presume to inquire: his Letter to Mr. Price seems to imply the former; but the reception which his plans of this place met with from the proprietor, incline me to suspect the latter. The preservation of the kitchen garden, though the only part of them which would have pleased a landscape painter, was the only part which did not please that gentleman; who, though a man of sense and information, had never turned his attention to the subject, and therefore only employed an improver, to be like the rest of the world, and have his grounds laid out in the newest fashion; according to which, he knew that the kitchen garden ought to be remote, or at least concealed from the house.

Though in writing upon landscape, I have confined my remarks to picturesque decoration, I agree with Mr. Repton, that it is the business of a practical landscape gardener to exercise his profession upon a more enlarged plan, and to take domestic convenience as well as rural embellishment into his consideration. He must therefore, in order to be perfect in it, join the taste of the artist to the skill of the mechanic; but as he also justly observes, and as has often been justly observed before, *a little knowledge is a dangerous thing*: it engenders conceit and pedantry, and makes men arrogant in the display of what they neither know the principles nor the use. I remember a country clockmaker, who being employed to clean a more complex machine than he had been accustomed to, very confidently took it to pieces; but finding, when he came to put it together again, some wheels of which he could not discover the use, very discreetly carried them off in his pocket. The simple artifice of this prudent mechanic always recurs to my mind, when I observe the manner in which our modern improvers repair and embellish old places: not knowing how to employ the terraces, mounds, avenues, and other features which they find there, they take them all away, and cover the places which they occupied with turf. It is a short and easy method of proceeding; and if their employers will be satisfied with it, they are not to be blamed for persevering in it, as it may be executed by proxy as well as in person; and, like Dr. Sangrado's system of physic, be learned in an hour as completely as in an age, and be applied to all cases as skilfully and effectually by the common labourer or journeyman, as by the great professor himself. All that I entreat is, that they will not at this time, when men's minds are so full of plots and conspiracies, endeavour to find analogies between picturesque composition and political confusion; or suppose that the preservation of trees and terraces has any connection with the destruction of states and kingdoms.

122   HUMPHRY REPTON
from *Sketches and Hints on Landscape Gardening* (1795)

S hortly after Knight's Postscript had appeared, Repton responded to the attacks of Price and Knight with his *Sketches and Hints on Landscape Gardening*. The book, in fact, had been completed in manuscript form before the texts of the other two men had been published, but a delay by the artists who were preparing Repton's engravings had postponed the appearance of the book. Thus Repton had sat with manuscript in hand as he followed the attacks on his theory and design by Price and Knight, and he decided to respond by adding a few pages to his lengthy book in an appendix.

In his youth, Humphry Repton had none of the financial and educational advantages of his two protagonists. After failing in several endeavors at earning a living, he turned to landscape gardening in 1788 at the age of 36. He became immediately successful — in part through his careful study and emulation of the work of Capability Brown. His success was due as well to his natural aptitude for drawing and watercolors, and his approach as a designer was innovative in that he was one of the first gardeners to sit down at the site and sketch his overall conceptions. His

Humphry Repton (1752–1818), from *Sketches and Hints on Landscape Gardening* (1795), from the 1890 edition of *Sketches and Hints*, entitled *The Landscape Gardening and Landscape Architecture of the Late Humphry Repton*. Farnborough: Gregg International Publishers, 1969 (facsimile edition), pp. 111–14.

book of 1795 speaks to gardening theory only in the most general terms, but it is a worthy essay expounding his picturesque and other principles. Note how in this excerpt from the appendix, he responds to Price and Knight by incorporating the notion of the picturesque fully into his garden theory, coupling the idea with such effects as "intricacy" and "association."

I will allow that there is a shade of difference betwixt the opinions of Mr. *Price* and Mr. *Knight*, which seems to have arisen from the different characters of their respective places; *Foxley* is less romantic than *Downton*, and therefore Mr. Price is less extravagant in his ideas, and more willing to allow some little sacrifice of picturesque beauty to neatness, near the house; but by this very concession he acknowledges, that real *comfort*, and his ideas of *picturesqueness*, are incompatible. In short, the mistake of both these gentlemen arises from their not having gone deep enough in the inquiry, and not having carefully traced, to all its sources, that pleasure which the mind receives from landscape gardening; for although picturesque effect is a very copious source of our delight, it is far from being the only one.

After sedulously endeavouring to discover other causes of this pleasure, I think it may occasionally be attributed to each of the following different heads; which I have enumerated in my *Red Book* of Warley, near Birmingham, a seat of Samuel Galton, Esquire.

Sources of Pleasure in Landscape Gardening

I. *Congruity*; or a proper adaptation of the several parts to the whole; and that whole to the character, situation, and circumstances of the place and its possessor.

II. *Utility.* This includes convenience, comfort, neatness, and everything that conduces to the purposes of habitation with elegance.

III. *Order.* Including correctness and finishing; the cultivated mind is shocked by such things as would not be visible to the clown: thus, an awkward bend in a walk, or lines which ought to be parallel, and are not so, give pain; as a serpentine walk through an avenue, or along the course of a straight wall or building.

IV. *Symmetry;* or that correspondence of parts expected in the front of buildings, particularly Grecian; which, however formal in a painting, require similarity and uniformity of parts to please the eye, even of children. So natural is the love of order and of symmetry to the human mind, that it is not surprising it should have extended itself into our gardens, where nature itself was made subservient, by cutting trees into regular shapes, planting them in rows, or at exact equal distances, and frequently of different kinds in alternate order.

These first four heads may be considered as generally adverse to picturesque beauty; yet they are not, therefore, to be discarded: there are situations in which the ancient style of gardening is very properly preserved: witness the academic groves and classic walks in our universities; and I should doubt the taste of any improver, who could despise the congruity, the utility, the order, and the symmetry of the small garden at Trinity college, Oxford, because the clipped hedges and straight walks would not look well in a picture.

V. *Picturesque Effect.* This head, which has been so fully and ably considered by Mr. Price, furnishes the gardener with breadth of light and shade, forms of groups, outline, colouring, balance of composition, and occasional advantage from roughness and decay, the effect of time and age.

VI. *Intricacy.* A word frequently used by me in my *Red Books*, which Mr. Price has very correctly defined to be, "that disposition of objects, which, by a partial and uncertain "concealment, excites and nourishes curiosity."

VII. *Simplicity;* or that disposition of objects which, without exposing all of them equally to view at once, may lead the eye to each by an easy gradation, without flutter, confusion, or perplexity.

VIII. *Variety.* This may be gratified by natural landscape, in a thousand ways that painting cannot imitate; since it is observed of the best painters' works, that there is a sameness in their compositions, and even their trees are all of one general kind, while the variety of nature's productions is endless, and ought to be duly studied.

IX. *Novelty.* Although a great source of pleasure, this is the most difficult and most dangerous for an artist to attempt; it is apt to lead him into conceits and whims, which lose their novelty after the first surprise.

X. *Contrast* supplies the place of novelty, by a sudden and unexpected change of scenery, provided the transitions are neither too frequent nor too violent.

XI. *Continuity.* This seems evidently to be a source of pleasure, from the delight expressed in a long avenue, and the disgust at an abrupt break between objects that look as if they ought to be united; as in the chasm betwixt two large woods, or the separation betwixt two pieces of water; and even a walk, which terminates without affording a continued line of communication, is always unsatisfactory.

XII. *Association.* This is one of the most impressive sources of delight; whether excited by local accident, as the spot on which some public character performed his part; by the remains of antiquity, as the ruin of a cloister or a castle; but more particularly by that personal attachment to long known objects, perhaps indifferent in themselves, as the favourite seat, the tree, the walk, or the spot endeared by the remembrance of past events: objects of this kind, however trifling in themselves, are often preferred to the most beautiful scenes that painting can represent, or gardening create: such partialities should be respected and indulged, since true taste, which is generally attended by great sensibility, ought to be the guardian of it in others.

XIII. *Grandeur.* This is rarely picturesque, whether it consists in greatness of dimension, extent of prospect, or in splendid and numerous objects of magnificence; but it is a source of pleasure mixed with the sublime: there is, however, no error so common as an attempt to substitute extent for beauty in park scenery, which proves the partiality of the human mind to admire whatever is vast or great.

XIV. *Appropriation.* A word ridiculed by Mr. Price as lately coined by me, to describe extent of property; yet the appearance and display of such extent is a source of pleasure not to be disregarded; since every individual who possesses anything, whether it be mental endowments, or power, or property, obtains respect in proportion as his possessions are known, provided he does not too vainly boast of them; and it is the sordid miser only who enjoys for himself alone, wishing the world to be ignorant of his wealth. The pleasure of appropriation is gratified in viewing a landscape which cannot be injured by the malice or bad taste of a neighbouring intruder: thus an ugly barn, a ploughed field, or any obtrusive object which disgraces the scenery of a park, looks as if it belonged to another, and therefore robs the mind of the pleasure derived from appropriation, or the unity and continuity of unmixed property.

XV. *Animation;* or that pleasure experienced from seeing life and motion; whether the gliding or dashing of water, the sportive play of animals, or the wavy motion of trees; and particularly the playsomeness peculiar to youth, in the two last instances, affords additional delight.

XVI. And lastly, the *seasons*, and times of day, which are very different to the gardener and the painter. The noontide hour has its charms; though the shadows are neither long nor broad, and none but a painter or a sportsman will prefer the sear and yellow leaves of autumn to the fragrant blossoms and reviving delights of spring, "the youth of the year."

123   UVEDALE PRICE
from "An Essay on Architecture and Buildings as connected with Scenery" (1798)

In 1798 Price supplemented a new edition of his *Essays on the Picturesque* with an essay on architecture, which is notable in that it is one of the first attempts to apply the notion of the picturesque to architectural design. The little-known essay is important in several other respects, and in fact it should be considered a landmark of architectural thought.

Three selections draw out aspects of Price's overall argument. He does more than simply reiterate the earlier remarks of Reynolds regarding Vanbrugh, but — over more than 20 pages — turns these few comments into a full-fledged paean to the genius of Vanbrugh, in which his "fantastic style" is precisely what is to be admired for its picturesque singularity. Such a viewpoint, as well as his underlying eclecticism, again underscores a decline of classical theory in Britain in the wake of the picturesque onslaught. In the second passage Price succinctly defines the picturesque in relation to beauty. And in the third passage, perhaps owing more to Walpole than to anyone else, Price squarely aligns the idea of picturesque beauty with convenience and asymmetry of plan. This again will eventually become a mainstay of British architectural theory in the nineteenth century.

Sir Joshua Reynolds is, I believe, the first who has done justice to the architecture of Vanbrugh, by shewing that it was not a mere fantastic style, without any other object than that of singularity, but that he worked on the principles of painting, and has produced the most painter-like effects. It is very possible that the ridicule thrown on Vanbrugh's buildings by some of the wittiest men of the age he lived in, though not the best judges of art, may in no slight degree have prevented his excellencies from being properly attended to; for what has been the subject of keen and amusing redicule, will seldom become the object of study, or imitation. It appears to me that at Blenheim, Vanbrugh conceived and executed a

Uvedale Price, from "An Essay on Architecture and Buildings as connected with Scenery" (1798) from *Essays on the Picturesque*, Vol II. J. Mawman, 1810, pp. 211–14, 258–60, 265–9.

very bold and difficult design; that of uniting in one building, the beauty and magnificence of Grecian architecture, the picturesqueness of the Gothic, and the massive grandeur of a castle; and that in spite of the many faults with which he is very justly reproached, he has formed, in a style truly his own, a well-combined whole, a mansion worthy of a great prince and warrior. His first point seems to have been massiveness, as the foundation of grandeur. Then, to prevent that mass from being a lump, he has made various bold projections of various heights, which from different points serve as foregrounds to the main building. And, lastly, having probably been struck with the variety of outline against the sky in many Gothic and other ancient buildings, he has raised on the top of that part, where the slanting roof begins in many houses of the Italian style, a number of decorations of various characters. These, if not new in themselves, have at least been applied and combined by him in a new and peculiar manner; and the union of them gives a surprising splendour and magnificence, as well as variety, to the summit of that princely edifice. There is a point on the opposite side of the lake, whence it is seen in full glory, and with its happiest accompaniments. The house, the lake, and the rich bank of the garden, may be so grouped with some of the trees that stand near the water and hang over it, and so framed amidst their stems and branches, as to exclude all but the choicest objects, and whoever catches that view towards the close of the evening, when the sun strikes on the golden balls and pours his beams through the open parts, gilding every rich and brilliant ornament, will think he sees some enchanted palace. But let those decorations be changed for the summit of any of the most celebrated houses built since the time of Vanbrugh, such as Fonthill, or Keddlestone, in which (if I may trust to my recollection, and to the designs) the edge of a slanting roof, with scarcely any other break but that of detached chimnies, forms the outline against the sky – however the sun might illuminate such a summit, the spectator would no longer think of Alcina or Armida.

I have already disclaimed all knowledge of architecture as a science, and have professed my intention of treating of it chiefly as connected with scenery: after what I have said of Vanbrugh, it is highly necessary to renew that declaration. Few persons, I believe, have in any art been guilty of more faults, though few, likewise, have produced more striking effects. As an author, and an architect, he boldly set rules at defiance, and in both those characters, completely disregarded all purity of style; yet, notwithstanding those defects, Blenheim and Castle Howard, the Provoked Wife and the Relapse will probably be admired, as long as the English nation or language shall continue to exist.

★ ★ ★

I have shewn in an early part of my first Essay, how time and decay convert a beautiful building into a picturesque one, and by what process the change is operated. That the character of every building must be essentially changed by decay, is very apparent; and, likewise, that the alteration must be in proportion as the original character or design is obliterated by that decay: a building, however, does not immediately change its original character, but parts with it by degrees; and seldom, perhaps, loses it entirely. It will probably be acknowledged, that a beautiful building is in its most beautiful state, when the columns are in every part round and smooth, the ornaments entire, and the whole design of the artist in every part complete. If this be granted, then from the first moment that the smoothness, the symmetry, the design of such a building suffers any injury, it is manifest that its beauty is thereby diminished: and it may be observed, that there is a state of injury and decay, in which we only perceive and lament the diminution of beauty, without being consoled for it by any other character. In proportion as the injury increases, in proportion as the embellishments that belong to architecture, the polish of its columns, the highly finished execution of its capitals and mouldings, its urns and statues, are changed for what may be called the embellishments of ruins, for incrustations and weather stains, and for the various plants that spring from, or climb over the walls – the character of the picturesque prevails over that of the beautiful; and at length, perhaps, all smoothness, all symmetry, all trace of design are totally gone. But there may still remain an object which attracts notice. Has it then no character when that of beauty is departed? is it ugly? is it insipid? is it merely curious? Ask the painter, or the picturesque traveller; they never abandon a ruin to the mere antiquary, till none but an antiquary would observe it. Whatever then has strong attractions as a visible object, must have a character; and that which has strong attractions for the painter, and yet is neither grand nor beautiful, is justly called picturesque.

⋆ ⋆ ⋆

The most picturesque *habitable* buildings, are old castles which were originally formed for defence as well as habitation: they in general consist of towers of different heights, and of various outworks and projections; particularly where the abruptness and irregularity of the ground, has in a manner forced the architect to adopt the same irregularity in the shapes and heights of his building. It is not improbable that many of those old castles owe the extreme picturesqueness of their appearance, to their having been built at different times, just as occasion required; for by those means, as we well know, a number of common houses become picturesque, the separate parts of which have nothing of that character. Why are they so? Because they are built of various heights, in various directions, and because those variations are sudden and irregular. Architects, like painters, (or to speak more justly, like men of genius and observation in every art,) have in many cases taken advantage of the effects of accident, and have converted the mere shifts of men who went the nearest way to work, into sources of beauty and decoration. An irregular room, for instance, detached from the body of the house, with a low covered passage to it, may have given to architects the idea of pavillions, connected with the house by arcades, or colonnades; but in the use which they have made of these accidents, they have proceeded according to the genius of their own art. That of painting admits, and often delights in irregularity: architecture, though, like other arts, it studies variety, yet it must in general consider that variety as subject to symmetry, especially in buildings on a large scale, and highly decorated; a symmetry not always ostentatiously displayed, but still to be traced through the whole design. In transferring something of the variety and picturesque effect of irregular buildings to regular architecture, the architect proceeds no further than the buildings themselves: but the painter, from having observed the effect of trees among the irregular parts of old houses, may, in his pictures, have been induced to add them in correspondent situations to regular pieces of architecture, though he may not have seen them so placed in reality. The mere architect would not place them there; but it is from the joint labours of the two artists, that the improver must form himself.

Some of the most striking and varied compositions, both in painting and in nature, are those where the more distant view is seen between the stems, and across and under branches of large trees; and where some of those trees, are very near the eye. But where trees are so disposed, a house with a regular extended front could not be built, without destroying together with many of the trees, the greatest part of such well composed pictures. Now, if the owner of such a spot, instead of making a regular front and sides, were to insist upon having many of the windows turned towards those points where the objects were most happily arranged, the architect would be forced into the invention of a number of pictur-esque forms and combinations, which otherwise might never have occurred to him; and would be obliged to do what so seldom has been done – accommodate his building to the scenery, not make that give way to his building.

Many are the advantages, both in respect to the outside and the inside, that might result from such a method. In regard to the first, it is scarcely possible that a building formed on such a plan, and so accompanied, should not be an ornament to the landscape, from whatever point it might be viewed. Then the blank spaces that would be left where the aspect suddenly changed (which by the admirers of strict regularity would be thought incurable blemishes) might, by means of trees and shrubs, or of climbing plants trained about wood or stone work, be transformed into beauties; which, at the same time that they were interesting in the detail, would very essentially contribute to the rich effect of the whole.

I am well convinced, that such a disposition of the outside would suggest to an artist of genius, no less varied and picturesque effects within; and that the arrangement of the rooms, would oftentimes be at least as convenient as in a more uniform plan. I am, likewise, convinced, that a house of that kind would not be admired by men of a picturesque taste only; for I have had occasion to observe, that men of a different turn are often struck with a certain appearance of irregularity in the distribution of a house, and in the shapes of the rooms; and even to conceive an idea of comfort from it.

124 RICHARD PAYNE KNIGHT
from *An Analytical Inquiry into the Principles of Taste* (1805)

By the end of the 1790s Price and Knight were diverging to some extent in their viewpoints, and in response Knight composed his own psychological exposition of the new aesthetics. Knight differs from his friend not in his appreciation for and acceptance of picturesque effects, but rather in his explanation of how such feelings come about. He rejects the argument of Burke and Price who, in positing the aesthetic categories of the sublime and the picturesque, tied their sensations to the neurological reactions of the eye to characteristics of the objects themselves. Reverting to a Humean position, Knight now insists that all "perceptions" of beauty, sublimity, and picturesqueness are mental states created simply and only by the mind itself, that is, by the mind's process of associating ideas. The eye can discern only color and light, and the mind does the rest. Thus these finer perceptions of things sublime or picturesque are not universal categories of objects but acquired tastes, such as when the

Richard Payne Knight, from *An Analytical Inquiry into the Principles of Taste* (second edition). London: Luke Hansard, 1805, pp. 220–5.

musician learns to tune an instrument. Such categories of beauty or the picturesque lack firm and hard rules because taste, in the end, is a mental habit and is culturally conditioned.

Knight brings the same skepticism to his consideration of architecture, which in theory he now takes in a startling direction. He begins with what is essentially a critique of both neoclassical (which he calls Grecian) and Gothic designs for country houses. If the former are too rigid and severe in their design principles, the latter unfortunately evoke the ideas of those "barbarous structures" of the middle ages, whose heavily ornamented interiors were dark and gloomy within. By contrast, he points to the design of his own castle at Downton, where he combined the simpler medieval forms of the castle with refined Grecian ornaments throughout its interiors. Therefore his solution for architecture is actually one of a free eclecticism, similar to that of Piranesi, in which the architect should be guided first and foremost by convenience, comfort, and overall painterly effects. Again the architect Vanbrugh is exalted as the proper model to be emulated.

97. Some few attempts have lately been made to adapt the exterior forms of country-houses to the various character of the surrounding scenery, by spreading them out into irregular masses: but as our ideas of irregularity, in buildings of this kind, have been habitually associated with those of the barbarous structures of the middle ages, a mistaken notion of congruity has induced us to exclude from them, every species of ornament, or scale of proportion, not authorized by the rude and unskilful monuments of those times: as if that, which is, at once, convenient and elegant, needed any authority to justify its use; or a house, that is picturesque without, must, from a principle of congruity, be heavy, clumsy, and gloomy within. It has already been observed that the architecture of the Gothic castles, as they are called, is of Grecian or Roman origin: but, if it were not, there could be no impropriety in employing the elegancies of Grecian taste and science, either in the external forms and proportions, or interior decorations of houses built in that style: for, surely, there can be no blamable inconsistency in uniting the different improvements of different ages and countries in the same object; provided they are really improvements, and contribute to render it perfect.

98. It is now more than thirty years since the author of this inquiry ventured to build a house, ornamented with what are called Gothic towers and battlements without, and with Grecian ceilings, columns, and entablatures within; and though his example has not been much followed, he has every reason to congratulate himself upon the success of the experiment; he having at once, the advantage of a picturesque object, and of an elegant and convenient dwelling; though less perfect in both respects than if he had executed it at a maturer age. It has, however, the advantage of being capable of receiving alterations and additions in almost any direction, without any injury to its genuine and original character.

99. In all marked deviations from the ordinary style of the age and country, in which we live, the great difficulty is to avoid the appearance of trick and affectation; which seem to be, in some degree, inseparable from buildings made in imitation of any obsolete or unusual style: for, as the execution, as well as the design of almost every age and country, has a particular character, these imitations are scarcely ever in perfect harmony and congruity throughout; but generally proclaim themselves, at first sight, to be mere counterfeits; which, how beautiful soever to the eye, necessarily excite unpleasant ideas in the mind. A house may be adorned with towers and battlements, or pinnacles and flying buttresses; but it should still maintain the character of a house of the age and country in which it is erected;

and not pretend to be a fortress or monastery of a remote period or distant country: for such false pretensions never escape detection; and, when detected, necessarily excite those sentiments, which exposed imposture never fails to excite.

100. Rustic lodges to parks, dressed cottages, pastoral seats, gates, and gateways, made of unhewn branches and stems of trees, have all necessarily a still stronger character of affectation; the rusticity of the first being that of a clown in a pantomime, and the simplicity of the others that of a shepherdess in a French opera. The real character of every object of this kind must necessarily conform to the use, to which it is really appropriated; and if attempts be made to give it any other character, it will prove, in fact, to be only a character of imposture: for to adapt the genuine style of a herdsman's hut, or a ploughman's cottage, to the dwellings of opulence and luxury, is as utterly impossible, as it is to adapt their language, dress, and manners to the refined usages of polished society.

101. The best style of architecture for irregular and picturesque houses, which can now be adopted, is that mixed style, which characterizes the buildings of Claude and the Poussins: for as it is taken from models, which were built piece-meal, during many successive ages; and by several different nations, it is distinguished by no particular manner of execution, or class of ornaments; but admits of all promiscuously, from a plain wall or buttress, of the roughest masonry, to the most highly wrought Corinthian capital: and, in a style professedly miscellaneous, such contrasts may be employed to heighten the relish of beauty, without disturbing the enjoyment of it by any appearance of deceit or imposture. In a matter, however, which affords so wide a field for the licentious deviations of whim and caprice, it may be discreet always to pay some attention to authority; especially when we have such authorities as those of the great landscape painters above mentioned; the study of whose works may at once enrich and restrain invention.

102. In choosing a situation for a house of this kind, which is to be a principal feature in a place, more consideration ought to be had of the views towards it, than of those fromwards it: for, consistently with comfort, which ought to be the first object in every dwelling, it very rarely happens that a perfect composition of landscape scenery can be obtained from a door or window; nor does it appear to me particularly desirable that it should be; for few persons ever look for such compositions, or pay much attention to them, while within doors. It is in walks or rides through parks, gardens, or pleasure grounds, that they are attended to and examined, and become subjects of conversation; wherefore the seats, or places of rest, with which such walks and rides are accommodated, are the points of sight, to which the compositions of the scenery ought to be principally adapted. To them, picturesque fore-grounds may always be made or preserved, without any loss of comfort or violation of propriety: for that sort of trim neatness, which both require in grounds immediately adjoining a house, is completely misplaced, when employed on the borders of a ride or walk through a park or plantation. If the house be the principal object or feature of the scene from these points of view, the middle ground will be the properest situation for it; as will clearly appear from the landscapes of the painters above cited: this is also the situation, which considerations of domestic comfort will generally point out; as being the middle degree of elevation, between the too exposed ridges of the hills, and the too secluded recesses of the vallies. In any position, however, above the point of sight, such objects may be happily placed; and contribute to the embellishment of the adjoining scenery: but there are scarcely any buildings, except bridges, which will bear being looked

down upon; a foreshortening from the roof to the base being necessarily awkward and ungraceful.

103. Sir John Vanbrugh is the only architect, I know of, who has either planned or placed his houses according to the principle here recommended; and, in his two chief works, Blenheim and Castle Howard, it appears to have been strictly adhered to, at least in the placing of them. The views from the principal fronts of both are bad, and much inferior to what other parts of the grounds would have afforded; but the situations of both, as objects to the surrounding scenery, are the best that could have been chosen; and both are certainly worthy of the best situations, which, not only the respective places, but the island of Great Britain could afford.

125   JOHN SOANE
from Royal Academy Lectures on Architecture, V, VIII, and XI (1812–15)

S oane was an architect with complex and eclectic literary tastes, as we know from his notes and transcriptions from books contained in his large private library. He had studied Knight's book very carefully and was drawn to certain ideas, while also rejecting others. He was attracted as well to Knight's aesthetic sensitivities regarding the nuances of the beautiful and the picturesque, his concern for sensitively placing a building within a landscape, and his desire to achieve varied and picturesque effects. And from Reynolds he had acquired his keen appreciation for the works of Vanbrugh. In an earlier passage (chapter 91 above), we even saw the influence of the French idea of "character" on his own thinking.

But Soane was also a classical architect by training, as well as a professor at the Royal Academy. His lectures, in a refreshing way, are thus filled with contradictions and inconsistencies, as these following excerpts indicate. On the one hand, he can praise the "bold flights of irregular fancy" of Vanbrugh; on the other hand, he can argue that Knight had simply gone too far in his espousal of eclecticism, because this lack of stylistic inconsistency would only wreak havoc with young designers who had yet to acquire an advanced taste. And for all of Soane's high regard for the effects of the Gothic style, he in fact did not want to see this style resurrected in his day. In his own architecture he remained a neoclassicist with scarcely concealed picturesque sympathies.

Contemporary with Sir Christopher Wren was Sir John Vanbrugh whose numerous and extensive works show the versatility of his talents: and, if he wanted the grace and elegance of Palladio, he possessed in an eminent degree the powers of invention.

His works are full of character, and his outlines rich and varied: and although few of his compositions show any great knowledge of classical correctness, yet the mausoleum in the

John Soane, from Royal Academy Lectures on Architecture (V, VIII, XI; 1812–15) in *Sir John Soane: Enlightenment Thought and the Royal Academy Lectures*, ed. David Watkin. London: Cambridge University Press, 1996, pp. 563, 600, 645–6.

park at Castle Howard executed by his pupil, and the Temple of Concord and Victory at Stowe[1] are proofs that he occasionally felt the force of the simplicity of the ancients, whilst his house at Whitehall, in spite of the alterations and additions it has undergone, shows that he had the power of making small things interesting. His great work is Blenheim. The style of this building is grand and majestically imposing, the whole composition analogous to the war-like genius of the mighty hero for whom it was erected. The great extent of this noble structure, the picturesque effect of its various parts, the infinite and pleasing variety, the breaks and contrasts in the different heights and masses, produce the most exquisite sensations in the scientific beholder, whether the view be distant, intermediate, or near.

The delightful scenery on first entering this noble park, the immense sheet of water, which so entrancingly enriches the landscape, the princely palace, the great Column, and that magnificent feature, the Bridge, taken altogether produce the very climax of excellence.

It was once, sarcastically, said that the Bridge at Blenheim designated the ambitious mind of the Duke of Marlborough, whilst the rivulet beneath (alluding to what it was originally) indicated the smallness of his liberality. Such were the observations of a peevish satirist. How unlike the noble-minded Bolingbroke who, being asked his opinion of the Duke's failings, replied, with all the feelings of a great mind that 'he was so fully impressed with the good qualities of the Hero of Blenheim that he could not recollect that he had any faults.'[2]

It is impossible to contemplate the works of Sir John Vanbrugh without feeling those emotions which the happy efforts of genius alone can produce. In his bold flights of irregular fancy, his powerful mind rises superior to common conceptions, and entitles him to the high distinctive appellation of the Shakespeare of architects. To try the works of such an artist by the strict rules of Palladian tameness would be like judging the merits and mighty darings of the immortal bard by the frigid rules of Aristotle.

★ ★ ★

From a want of attention to character and this feeling of propriety, the ferme ornée, the cottage, the hermitage, instead of being confined to retired situations, are sometimes placed contiguous to the approaches into great cities. Instead of being composed of two or three rooms of moderate dimensions, as their titles import, they often form large buildings. Their external appearance, likewise, instead of being distinguished by uniform simplicity or even rusticity, are frequently plastered to resemble the most delicate stone, with a portico in the centre to protect a fine mahogany door and sash window, whilst the interior is completed in the most finished style, with the most elegant, fashionable and expensive furniture of every kind. And lastly, that such structures should not be mistaken, or passed unnoticed, letters conspicuously large announce that this is a ferme ornée, this a cottage, this a hermitage.

Architectural inconsistency does not stop here. A celebrated writer on the principles of taste tells us that he 'ventured to build a house, ornamented with Gothic towers, battlements, pinnacles, and flying buttresses, without, and Grecian columns and entablatures, within,'[3] and although this example, the author adds, has not been much followed, he has every reason to congratulate himself on the success of the experiment, he having at once an elegant and convenient dwelling, though less perfect than if he had executed it at a more mature age.

Under the sanction of this and such-like examples with their Gothic towers, battlements, pinnacles, flying buttresses, Grecian ceilings, columns, and entablatures, we have innovations of a still more dangerous tendency, calculated to destroy all relish, even for the finer efforts of Gothic architecture, so happily and successfully displayed in some of our ancient structures, the beauties of which, if felt, are certainly not often transferred into modern buildings.

From the same causes we see in many modern buildings called Gothic, not only the improvements and changes made in different Gothic edifices in different ages and under peculiar circumstances, blended together in the exterior of the same building, but likewise without any attention to priority of invention.

The advocates for the mixture of the works of different ages and styles justify this manner of building from the examples of our ancient cathedrals. Some of those edifices, from their great extent, occupied several ages in their completion, and consequently were under the influence of different opinions and feelings, the architects frequently introducing such variations and improvements, as they observed in other works subsequently raised.

★ ★ ★

In these buildings the general feeling is the same: the same insipidity and want of variety is apparent in a greater or lesser degree, both in outline and in decoration. In many, even of those constructed with stone and decorated with the orders of architecture, the doors and windows are sunk in plain square recesses without any relief, whilst in the Gothic buildings we constantly see the most picturesque, fanciful, and ingenious play in the outline, and a variety and breadth of effect in the decoration of the subordinate parts. Words of explanation are unnecessary: the drawings sufficiently show how poor these modern examples appear when viewed together with the Gothic. The door of the Gothic church is noble and full of effect, and gives an idea of strength and dignity; the door of the nobleman's palace is mean and trifling. The Gothic window is of the same superior design. Every part is equally studied and superior to the modern window with which it is contrasted.

These considerations, amongst many other more important motives, will lead the architect to a study of the Gothic buildings for effect, as well as with respect to construction.

Having shown the general style of the composition of the exteriors of different houses, the interiors of which abound with comforts and conveniences (however destitute their outsides may be of taste and architectural effect), candour itself must admit that the frequent repetitions of such buildings as these examples must be extremely tiresome, and finally disgusting. The numbers of them, either constructed or to be met with in books of ideal designs, are such as no person could imagine without looking closely into the subject; whilst the number of those wherein any character and variety are to be met with, is comparatively small indeed.

Having shown different fronts of houses finished with a pediment in the centre of each, very different from the practice of the ancients, I shall now offer two specimens of elevations more congenial to first principles.

The house of the volatile and witty Sir John Vanbrugh at Whitehall was on so limited a scale that it excited the mirth and derision of the contemporary wits. Their criticisms, however, were not just; even Swift, with all his antipathy, or rather jealousy, of Vanbrugh, was compelled to say, speaking of this very house,

> '... 'tis owned by all,
> Thou'rt well contrived, tho' thou are small.'[4]

The front, however small, contains the same number of general divisions, and at least as much variety of outline as the magnificent Palladian mansion in Piccadilly of the late Lord Burlington. The straight line which terminates each of these buildings accords most admirably with the general style and features of the architecture, and this indication of a flat roof or terrace will always succeed wherever quietness of character is aimed at, and the building is viewed at a small distance or confined with projecting wings.

This is not, however, the general character of Sir John Vanbrugh's architecture who, for invention, has had no equal in this country. Boldness of fancy, unlimited variety, and discrimination of character mark all his productions. He had all the fire and power of Michael Angelo and Bernini, without any of the elegant softness and classical delicacy of Palladio and his followers. The young architect, by studying the picturesque effects of his works, will learn to avoid the dull monotony of minor artists, and learn to think for himself and acquire a taste of his own. Having spoken of this great architect in the first course of lectures, I shall present to your observation some of his designs to exemplify what I have advanced.

These works are inimitable examples of the power of variety of outline to please. A building to please must produce different sensations from each different point of view. These effects will never be completely attained without variety in heights as well as in the projections. It is chiefly the inequalities of height which produce that prodigious play and movement in the outline, and make the edifice important in very distant points of view, and more so as we approach nearer to it; and finally it still improves upon us when we are sufficiently close to perceive all its parts in detail. Such was the manner in which our forefathers designed their buildings, such was the effect they frequently produced.

Many other examples besides these might be selected, but time will not permit, and indeed these, I trust, will be found sufficient for the information of the student, and for the illustration of what I have advanced. I must add, however, that every building, notwithstanding its front being extensive and rich, without these varieties in the heights, will always, when viewed at a distance, be regarded as a heavy, uninteresting lump.

Too great a variety of parts and movement in the exteriors of buildings, as well as in their plans, is to be avoided as much as monotony. Variety may be carried to excess by too many breaks and divisions: by a repetition of curves and undulating forms running into each other without proper repose, the general effect is weakened, and the whole becomes confused instead of producing that movement and variety which creates the most pleasing sensations and gives the spectator an interest in the work before him. A composition overcharged, although it may please the ignorant, will not fail to make the judicious grieve. [...]

NOTES

1 The design of the Temple of Concord and Victory at Stowe is now attributed to Richard Grenville and Giambattista Borra, not to Vanbrugh.

2 This seems to be a paraphrase of a passage in Bolingbroke's essay on Marlborough in *The Craftsman*, no. 252, Saturday 1 May 1731.

3 Richard Payne Knight on Downton Castle in his *Analytical Inquiry into the Principles of Taste* (1805), 4th edn, 1808, p. 223.

4 Jonathan Swift, 'Vanbrug's House: Built from the Ruins of Whitehall that was Burnt', lines 115–16, in *The Complete Poems*, Harmondsworth 1983, p. 99.

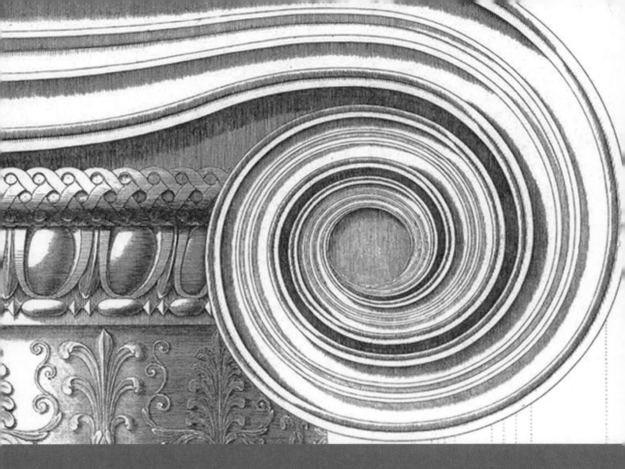

PART V   THE RISE OF HISTORICISM IN THE NINETEENTH CENTURY

A. CHALLENGES TO CLASSICISM IN FRANCE, 1802–34

Introduction

The classical architecture tradition of France that had been created in 1671 came to a rude halt on the night of August 16, 1793, when the doors of the Royal Academy of Architecture were sealed by political revolutionaries. A few months later, and quite symbolically, the Ecole Polytechnique was created nearby to train corps of military engineers and scientists. Still, the need for an architectural school did not disappear. Napoleon, who assumed power in 1799 in a *coup d'état*, toyed with its re-creation in 1803, but this interest subsided with his focus on European military conquest. It was only after he met his Waterloo and the royal lineage of the Bourbon kings was restored to power in 1816 that the newly reconstituted Académie des Beaux-Arts, from which sprang the Ecole des Beaux-Arts, was officially opened. Its director was someone we have already seen — Antoine Chrysosthôme Quatremère de Quincy — who after his early encyclopedic efforts had gone on to become both a revolutionary and a royalist. Over his new dominion he now attempted to re-impose the principles and teachings of the academic classicism upon which he was raised. His efforts in the end would not be successful, as increasingly in the 1820s his version of classicism once again came under attack. There were a multitude of reasons for this failure, not the least of which was the deteriorating political situation in France. After the political revolution of 1830 once again swept away the Bourbon line, classicism itself was in a certain sense deposed – although not entirely. At the same time no clear theoretical or stylistic alternative emerged to take its place, and architectural practice quickly fractured into competing stylistic schools.

This phenomenon is generally known as historicism, a term that has been applied in various ways and is sometimes wrongly equated with eclecticism. In its broadest sense in architecture, historicism is simply the use of historical motifs in design. With this very general meaning, the architecture of the Renaissance or the neoclassicism of the eighteenth century could be called historicist, in that in both periods employed stylistic motifs from earlier times. The meaning of historicism as it is generally applied to the nineteenth century, however, is somewhat more limited. It refers not to a particular style but rather to an attitude or approach to design related to an ever-expanding knowledge of history. If classical systems of thought were in essence normative in their values, historicist practice in the nineteenth century was relative at its core, but a relativism with strong values. Some proponents of Gothic architecture, for instance, argued that returning to this style would improve or elevate the morals of society, while others looked to the rationality and efficiencies of its structural logic. Similar arguments were also attached to the other historical styles, but these various options for a correct path should not in any way detract from the seriousness of a much expanded and increasingly complex architectural debate. Not only was widening historical knowledge affecting architectural practice, but also the Industrial Revolution and the social or class upheaval that it was presaging. All in all, historicism in the nineteenth century is inseparable from the myriad of issues surrounding the creation of modern democratic nations suited to the new economic realities of the industrial world. Within this arena of competing social and economic forces, traditional architectural values and technology clash in a way that they never did before. Thus the most frequently voiced question raised throughout the nineteenth century is what style can best represent the new social and political ideals, what style can serve as the basis for evolving a new and future style? And the better architects of each generation were exceptionally creative in their responses.

126 JEAN-NICOLAS-LOUIS DURAND
from *Précis of the Lectures on Architecture* (1802)

The French Revolution of 1789, at first blush, created not a new political order but social instability. The "Declaration of the Rights of Man" that was issued by revolutionary decree in 1789 gave way in the next few years to a series of provisional governments and increasingly to political anarchy. This social turmoil culminated in the summer of 1793 in the "Reign of Terror" of Maximilien Robespierre, during which over 20,000 victims lost their heads on the guillotine. Not only did new construction cease altogether, but the aristocratic

Jean-Nicolas-Louis Durand (1760–1834), from *Précis des leçons d'architecture données à l'École Royale Polytechnique* (1802–5), trans. David Britt, in *Précis of the Lectures on Architecture*. Los Angeles: Getty Publications Program, 2000, pp. 83–5. © 2000 by Getty Publications. Reprinted with permission of Getty Publications.

affectations of classical architecture — monumentality for its own sake — had now become hated things of the past. Economy became the architectural catchphrase of the day.

The effect of the Revolution on practice can also be gauged by the career and ideas of Jean-Nicolas-Louis Durand. This one-time student of Boullée had placed second in the Grand-Prix competitions of 1779 and 1780, visited Italy, and returned to France to begin a career sometime in the mid-1780s. If his first years of practice were undistinguished, he would gain some fame in the 1794 when he, together with Jean-Thomas Thibault, won a competition for a "Temple of Equality," an event sponsored by the revolutionary government. In the same year Durand was hired as a draftsman at the newly founded Ecole Royale Polytechnique. Three years later he was promoted to assistant professor and charged with teaching a course on architecture to these engineers. It was this course of lectures that he published between 1802 and 1805, and offered his reformist ideas to the world.

Durand's course is notable, above all, for its novel compositional and graphic techniques. The student is presented with a sheet of grid paper, on which the principal spaces of the building can be blocked out. From a series of typological facades, floor plans, porches, vestibules, staircases, elevations, and roof shapes, the student can then pick and choose, as it were, the elements composing the design of the building. To further assist the student, Durand prepared a series of prototypical designs for libraries, justice ministries, museums, colleges, and hospitals. Never before had architecture been reduced to such a closed syntactic system, inherently devoid of stylistic or historical interests.

Durand's lectures were also novel with respect to classical theory. Although trained as a classicist, he excoriates the Vitruvian tradition and sharply criticizes as well the ideas of Marc-Antoine Laugier and Quatremère de Quincy — who had both argued that architecture finds its prototype in the primitive hut. After exploding these two "myths," Durand next takes issue with the belief that the principal aim of architecture is to please, that is, to find beauty through the addition of ornaments. His contrary functionalist formulation is that the two guiding principles of architecture should be fitness to purpose and economy of means. Such a view not only turns classical theory (and its use of ornaments) on its head, but it also characterizes a theory conceived in the anti-aristocratic fervor of revolutionary times. And even though Durand's thesis was not influential when first published (these remarks were lectures given to military engineers), its publication became significant in the late-1820s as the classical tradition once again came under challenge.

But is it true that the principal aim of architecture is to please and that decoration is its principal concern? In the passage by Laugier, quoted above, it will be seen that the author, for all his curious prejudices, is forced to acknowledge that this art owes its origins to necessity alone and that it has no other goal than public and private utility. How could he ever have imagined otherwise, even if we suppose that the builder of the hut, the alleged prototype of all architecture, was capable of conceiving the idea of decoration? Surely, the idea of his needs, and of the means proper to satisfy them, would have presented itself first, and would indeed have banished all other ideas? Is it reasonable to suppose that, left alone to defend himself from the inclement weather and from the fury of wild beasts, needing to provide himself with many advantages that he had always lacked, the builder of the shelter gave a moment's thought to making it an object to delight his eye? Is it any more reasonable to suppose that men in society, with a host of new ideas and, consequently, a host of new needs to satisfy, adopted decoration as the principal concern of architecture?

Some writers, who have sustained and elaborated the hut theory with all conceivable ingenuity, will object that we have been speaking of mere building; that in this respect architecture is no more than a manual trade; and that it never merited the name of art until the nations, having attained the height of wealth and luxury, undertook to adorn the buildings that they had erected. But here we appeal to these authors themselves. Was it after the Romans attained the height of wealth and luxury, covering their buildings with moldings, entablatures, and so forth, that they produced their best architecture? The Greeks were far less wealthy; and is not their architecture, in which such objects are so few in number, preferable to the architecture of the Romans? These same authors readily admit as much; indeed, they go so far as to say that the Greek is the only architecture worthy of the name. Now, Greek architecture, which they admire, and which deserves to be generally admired, never took pleasure as its aim or decoration as its object. Of course, care and purity are apparent in its execution; but is not care essential for solidity? In some buildings, sculptural ornaments are to be found; but the others are, for the most part, totally devoid of them, and are none the less highly esteemed. Is it not clear that such ornaments are not essential in architecture? And when architecture does use them, do they not show that it cannot aspire to give pleasure by virtue of the intrinsic beauty of its proportions and its forms? And even if some forms are found that do not directly spring from need, do not the differences that appear in them, from one building to the next, prove that the Greeks attached no importance whatever to architectural decoration?

Whether we consult reason or examine the monuments, it is evident that pleasure can never have been the aim of architecture; nor can architectural decoration have been its object. Public and private utility, the happiness and the protection of individuals and of society: such is the aim of architecture. Whether it be accorded or denied the name of art, it will nonetheless deserve to be practiced, and the means to its end will deserve to be examined; and this we shall now do.

We shall find, on looking into the matter, that, in all ages and in all places, all of men's thoughts and actions have sprung from two principles alone: love of comfort and dislike of all exertion. Accordingly, whether building their own private dwellings in isolation, or erecting public buildings in society, men inevitably sought (1) to derive from their buildings the greatest possible advantage, consequently making them as fit as possible for their purpose; and (2) to build them in the way that would in early times be the least laborious and later – when money had become the price of labor – the least costly.

Thus, fitness and economy are the means that architecture must naturally employ, and are the sources from which it must derive its principles: the only principles that can guide us in the study and exercise of the art.

First, if a building is to be fit for its purpose, it must be solid, salubrious, and commodious.

It will be solid: if the materials employed in its construction are of good quality and intelligently disposed; if the building rests on good foundations; if its principal supports are sufficient in number, placed perpendicularly for greater strength, and equally spaced so that each may support an equal portion of the load.

It will be salubrious: if it is situated in a wholesome place; if the floor or pavement is raised above the soil and protected from humidity; if there are walls to fill the intervals between the supports that form its skeleton, and to protect the internal parts from heat and from cold; if those walls are pierced by openings permeable to air and light; if all the openings in the internal walls correspond to each other and to the external openings, thus promoting the renewal of the air; if a covering shelters it from rain and sun in such a way that the edge of this covering, projecting beyond the walls, throws the water away from them; and if its exposure is to the south in cold countries, or to the north in hot countries.

Finally, it will be commodious: if the number and size of all its parts, their form, situation, and arrangement, are in the closest possible relation to its purpose.

So much for fitness; now for economy.

If a given area demands less length of perimeter when bounded by the four sides of a square than when bounded by those of a parallelogram, and less still when bounded by the circumference of a circle; if the square form is superior in symmetry, in regularity, and in simplicity to that of the parallelogram, and inferior to that of a circle: it will be readily supposed that the more symmetrical, regular, and simple a building is, the less costly it becomes. It is hardly necessary to add that, since economy demands the utmost simplicity in all necessary things, it absolutely forbids all that is unnecessary.

Such are the general principles that must have guided reasonable men, everywhere and in every age, when they came to erect buildings; and such are the principles that governed the design of the most universally and justly admired of ancient buildings, as will later become apparent.

It will be argued that, since there are buildings that are rightly admired, or rightly despised, it follows that there must be beauties and defects in architecture; that it must pursue the former and avoid the latter; and thus that it is capable of giving pleasure; that, if such is not its principal aim, it must at least attempt to blend the agreeable with the useful.

So far from denying that architecture can give pleasure, we maintain that it cannot but give pleasure, where it is treated in accordance with its true principles. Has not nature associated pleasure with the satisfaction of our needs, and are not our keenest pleasures the satisfactions of our most pressing needs? Such an art as architecture, which immediately satisfies so many of our needs, which places us in a position to satisfy all the others with ease, which defends us against the seasons, and which leads us to enjoy all the gifts of nature: an art, indeed, to which all the other arts owe their very existence: how could it fail to give us pleasure?

Certainly, the grandeur, magnificence, variety, effect, and character that are observed in buildings are all beauties, all causes of the pleasure that we derive from looking at them. But where is the need to run after such things, if a building is disposed in a manner fitted to its intended use? Will it not differ sensibly from another building intended for some other use? Will it not naturally possess a character – and, what is more, a character of its own? If all of the parts of the building, being intended for different uses, are disposed as they should be, will they not inevitably differ? Will not the building afford variety? And if the same building is disposed in the most economical, that is to say, the simplest manner, will it not appear as grand and as magnificent as it is possible to be? Undoubtedly, it will, because the eye will embrace the greatest number of its parts at one glance. Again, where is the need to chase after all those partial beauties?

127 A. C. QUATREMÈRE DE QUINCY
from *On Egyptian Architecture* (1803)

Shortly after he completed the first volume of the his architectural encyclopedia, Quatremère de Quincy found his life thrown into disarray. He initially supported the cause and was even elected to the provisional legislative assembly, but in 1793 he was accused of being a royalist, fled Paris, and was arrested. After his release he was later charged with another crime and – after fleeing to Germany – condemned to death *in absentia*. With Napoleon's general amnesty of 1800 he returned to France, and in 1804 was he elected to the Académie des Inscriptions et Belles-Lettres. In 1816 he was named to the powerful post of permanent director of the resurrected Académie des Beaux-Arts.

Quatremère de Quincy's *mémoire* on Egyptian architecture of 1785 thus stands at the very beginning of his literary production. It was not published until 1803 and then under a different title and with some notable points of evolution in his thinking. Its leading premise – the superiority of Greek classicism to all other styles – remains the same. The premise is supported on the one hand by the Biblical chronological framework, and on the other hand by the most recent anthropological research. According to the Book of Genesis, Noah had three sons, Shem, Ham, and Japheth, whose descendants spread out over the earth and formed the cultural stocks of Africa, the Orient, and Europe. Quatremère de Quincy aligned these three human stocks with the three modes of living of hunters (also fishermen), shepherds, and farmers, and also with the three primitive architectural "types" of caves, tents, and huts. In the passage below, Quatremère de Quincy not only insists on the superiority of the Greek "cabin" or hut over and above the formal possibilities of caves and tents, but he also makes the argument that the genius of Greek architecture (hence European classical architecture) lies precisely in this happy fiction of transposing the logic of wooden forms into stone. This passage thus marks the beginning of his effort to reinterpret classicism in light of contemporary anthropological and historical investigations.

Recall that at the beginning of this essay we made mention of the three principle types from which have derived the different architectures known to us. These three types are the tent, the subterranean cave (*souterrains*), and the hut or carpentry.

If we analyze these three models of the building art and the implications of their imitation, we are easily persuaded that the model of Greek architecture is the richest in its combinations and it is that which best joins the advantage of solidity with the charm of variety.

It appears, in effect, that the cave must present for art a model so finite, so complete, that its imitation has nothing to add to it or go beyond it. With tents, which compose the type for Chinese architecture, architecture too has many small things to imitate. This model, moreover, lacks solidity, which might be the reason that the architecture that imitates it will also lack this most important quality, whose appearance is as necessary as reality.

Extreme heaviness and extreme lightness were the necessary consequences of the two imitative systems of Egypt and China. There is too little to imitate in the first model, or

A. C. Quatremère de Quincy, from *De l'architecture égyptienne considérée dans sa origine, ses principes et son goût, et comparé sous le même rapports à l'Architecture Greque* [On Egyptian architecture considered in its origins, its principles, and its taste, and compared on the same points with Greek architecture]. Paris: Barrois l'Aîné et Fils, 1803. pp. 239–42, trans. Harry Francis Mallgrave.

better said, there is nothing to imitate there; it offers neither a transposition of forms nor a change of material. In the second type, imitation is also simply futile because the material of the model is too far removed from the kind that the copy uses. There is too much of the positive in one and too much of the fictive in the other.

Let us observe again that in the subterranean cave there necessarily rules a monotony of forms and unity of behavior that lead architecture to adopt the perpetual repetition of the same parts; it becomes a source of tediousness, that is to say, of uniformity. Tents, for their part, too easily yield to every caprice and they convey to art the greatest variability of forms, and thus inspire bizarre details incompatible with the simplicity and common sense of the order that one requires of architecture for it to be able to satisfy both taste and reason.

Carpentry, on the contrary, being both solid and light, or susceptible to becoming more or less one and the other, was the happiest medium for architecture. Wood, as [Francesco] Algarotti has observed, was the material most capable of furnishing the art with the greatest number of profiles, modifications, and ornaments of every kind. Anyone who studies the matter will easily see that wood contains the germ of all the parts that give rise to utility and beauty.

Caves offered everywhere and in every sense only cold and smooth surfaces. Nothing about them, as we have seen, presents either the reality or the idea of joining parts, of relationships, divisions, or proportions. The very objects that art imagined in order to overcome monotony (being alien to the principle that created them) – nothing in the decoration of this architecture was found necessary or based on reason. No rules could be submitted to a determined order that, in its essence, had only been the product of caprice.

This is not the case with the principle of carpentry. Everywhere it produces projections, forced divisions, distributions of members, necessary relationships of parts with other parts, bodies advancing and receding, and sources of effects, variety, and pleasure in architectural combinations. Art is forced to embellish such a model; it is subjected to a reasoned use of objects and of parts, which can no longer be either transposed or decomposed by the genius of decoration without the pleasure of imitation and the effects that derive from it being altered.

Moreover, it is evident that from the first rough idea of this architecture, or even to arrive at that stage, there was needed calculation, intelligence, a reasoned disposition of forces and resistances, an agreement on the equilibrium of forces, and diverse understanding that had to open the path by which this art was raised to the extent that we now know. One can therefore affirm that only the school of carpentry was able to make architecture a reasoned art.

The transposition of wood into stone is also the principal cause of the pleasure that we receive from Greek architecture, and this pleasure is similar to that for which we are so eager in the other imitative arts. [...]

I have already said that detractors of this metamorphosis can be found. There are some critics who fault the system in which architecture is limited to imitating primitive wooden constructions. They object to the fact that stone represents another material; they complain that in some way marble has been reduced to a subordinate role, obliged to reproduce the appearance of poor, wretched cabins. They would prefer that each material imbibe from itself and from its own proper constitution the principles of its forms and of its taste. It is to ask almost what we have seen, for what has occurred in the development of Egyptian architecture.

However, it has already been noted that stone left to itself, or in copying itself (which is the same thing), presents no forms to the mind, no system for art, no pleasure of imitation for the eye, no logic – by means of which architecture is able to have mastered that kind of sixth sense that is attributed particularly to mankind, and which one is able to call the *imitative sense*. To want to take away from architecture the type that sets the rule for its inventions, is to reduce it almost to a non-art.

In effect, it will take little to recognize that the essence of architecture, and in large part the means by which it pleases us, is in raising this agreeable fiction, this ingenious mask, which, in association with the other arts, permits them to appear on its stage and furnishes architecture with an occasion to rival them as well.

128 CHRISTIAN LUDWIG STIEGLITZ
from *Archaeology of the Architecture of the Greeks and Romans* (1801)

The classical view of beauty articulated by Quatremère de Quincy in the last years of the eighteenth century very much followed in the idealistic formalistic tradition that J. J. Winckelmann had fashioned from the white marble works of Greek sculpture. In such a conception the essence of beauty resides in form. Ornamentation and other effects, such as color, were at best secondary, and in fact Winckelmann even made the argument that the whiter the piece of sculpture, the more beautiful it was because whiteness reflects the greatest number of the sun's rays and thus reveals the form more readily to the eye. Form in sculpture translates into proportions in architecture, which of course had been the academic position regarding beauty for centuries. And the images of Greek temples displayed by David Le Roy and Stuart and Revett — many of which had also been constructed of white marble — popularized the image of Greek classicism as one of gleaming white temples often placed within dramatic hilltop settings. Enthusiasm for Greek art and architecture also enjoyed a renewal around 1800, as a number of British travelers visited Greece to continue earlier archaeological investigations. Foremost among these men was Thomas Bruce, the seventh Earl of Elgin, who was installed as a British Envoy Extraordinary at Porte in 1799. Soon thereafter he hatched his plan to purchase (from the residing Turkish authority) and remove the sculptural frieze from the Parthenon and sell the panels to the British Museum. Although the artistic merits of these sculptural works was at first disputed, once they reached London (and were bathed in an acid bath to remove all foreign substances) they soon became regarded as the masterpieces of the Periclean Age.

The following passage by the German archaeologist Christian Ludwig Stieglitz summarizes perfectly the classical historian's view of Greek architecture at the turn of the nineteenth century. It is essentially Winckelmannian in its high regard for the unparalleled superiority of Greek art. The parallel perfection of Greek architecture resides above all else in order, symmetry, and good proportions. Decorations were always secondary and tastefully moderated. This vision defines what came to be known as the "white view" of Greek antiquity, a view that would soon be undermined by archaeological discoveries.

Christian Ludwig Stieglitz (1756–1836), from *Archaologie der Baukunst der Griechen und Römer* [Archaeology of the architecture of the Greeks and Romans] (1801), pp. 258–61, trans. Harry Francis Mallgrave.

Until now we have spoken of what is essential to architecture; now we want to turn to what belongs to its ornamentation.

Works of architecture receive their beauty through beautiful form, which in this art, as in the other fine arts to which it is related, is evoked by order and symmetry, by propriety and good proportions. A building can therefore only be called beautiful when all its parts are constructed and joined in a normal position and order, when they compose a symmetry, when they relate to one another and to the whole and have both a grandeur and proportions pleasing to the eye, and when the arrangement of these parts and the whole is suited to the character of the building. If everything that gives the building a beautiful form is taken into account, then it will certainly create the proper effect and make a pleasing impression. Decoration should be added only in order to enhance form, to avoid too much simplicity from which monotony arises, and to give the whole greater multiplicity. We achieve such thorough embellishments or ornaments that are joined to the essential parts of a building and serve as their adornment.

The urge to decorate an object lies deep in the human soul, for even barbarous and uncivilized peoples have a feeling for it. [. . .]

We find therefore that the earliest peoples known to us – the Indians and the Egyptians – applied decorations to their buildings. They took their inspiration from nature, which in abundance offered a number of beautiful and unassuming objects. In the beginning they imitated only the adornments of the meadows and forests, and took plants, leaves, foliage, flowers, and fruit for decorations; eventually they learned to portray men and animals. Usually affixed and arranged without taste, these ornaments could only have been badly designed, because art at that time still stood at the lowest stages of its subsequent perfection. Soon, however, art raised itself among the Greeks and their cultivation of it influenced the adornment of buildings. Their decorations became more tastefully arranged and were worked out with as much precision and care as the main parts of the buildings. In addition, the Greeks not only strove to make the decorations beautiful, they also in all situations took into account the character of the building and the type of construction to which ornaments were applied, in order to give each part the most suitable decorations.

129 A. C. QUATREMÈRE DE QUINCY
from *The Olympian Jupiter* (1814)

The wave of archaeological investigation around the turn of the eighteenth century soon created problems for the "white" image of Greek art. As early as the 1750s, in fact, Stuart and Revett had noted that the Temple of Theseus (Hephaesteum) in Athens had been "enriched with painted ornament, which appears to be as ancient as the Building itself," but they made no further comment. Three separate British travelers to Greece around 1800 – William Leake, William Wilkins, and Edward Dodwell – also noted "various colors" applied to parts of

A. C. Quatremère de Quincy, from *Le Jupiter olympien, ou l'art de la sculpture antique considérée sous un nouveau point de vue* [The Olympian Jupiter, or the art of antique sculpture considered from a new point of view]. Paris: Firmin Didot, 1814, pp. viii, 36, trans. Harry Francis Mallgrave.

temples, but again these findings were assumed to be minor decorative embellishments tastefully applied to secondary architectural members, while the principal architectural masses were white. A more serious challenge came about with a remarkable discovery in 1811. A team of architects that included Charles Robert Cockerell, Haller von Hallerstein, and Peter Oluf Brønsted unearthed the pedimental sculptures of the Temple of Aphaea on the island of Aegina — all of which were painted, although the paint quickly oxidized when exposed to air. The next year, when excavating the Arcadian temple ruins at Bassae, a team headed by O. M. Baron von Stackelberg again found traces of paint on the frieze statuary, which was significant in that the marble temple was built at the beginning of the Periclean Age.

Against this mounting evidence of painted antique statuary, there was a philological problem that had long haunted Winckelmann's history of Greek antiquity. His theory of ideal beauty had been founded on such marble works as the Apollo Belvedere and Laocoön — both of which he knew only from Roman copies in marble. The second-century (AD) Greek writer Pausanias, however, had regarded such works as the statues of Zeus in the temple at Olympia and that of Athena in the Parthenon as the masterpieces of antiquity. The problem here was that these were not marble works but statues wrought of gold and ivory, in which these two materials in their colors emulated cloth and skin. Neoclassical critics had frowned upon the lack of artistic purity of these works, arguing that they represented a taste foreign to (a superior) Greek sensitivity, that they were inferior to works in marble or bronze because they mixed two materials in one composition, that the material extravagance of these works falsely swayed people as to their artistic value, and that they violated the formal essence of this art.

Against such issues, Quatremère de Quincy published *Le Jupiter olympien* in 1814, which he regarded as an addendum to Winckelmann's great historical study. He proposes to explain how and why color came to be applied to ancient statuary, and he begins by tracing the impulse for color back to the most primitive sculptural traditions — wooden idols painted and dressed with actual materials. From this practice, he argues, emerged a tradition for using color in Greek statuary, which over time became a fundamental part of the Greek artistic psyche and survived down to the time of Pericles. Color was therefore central to Greek sculpture for reasons of tradition and style. What is most interesting of Quatremère de Quincy's image of Greek polychromy is the subtlety of his image. In the second of these two passages he compares the process of employing gold and ivory to that of engraving cameos; hence the colors are not strident or overwhelming (painted), but subdued and moderate.

If Winckelmann gave a great impulse to the study of antiquity, if by the unique synthetic conception of his work he showed the ensemble and the life in the decomposed parts of the art of the ancients, it must also be said that, as a historian, he had the great disadvantage of all of those who treat things past. The plan of his history had to suffer from two sorts of gaps: those objects that time had destroyed, and those that one day should be restored. His successors, as the result of new discoveries, had to be richer in facts and materials that he did not have. Thus this history, which has the honor of being the first to be conceived and carried out, ought to be considered less as a complete body than as a monument whose plan is susceptible to new additions, and whose attending stones call for continual supplements.

★ ★ ★

The precious stones of the ancients, which we call *cameo* when the subjects are in relief, ordinarily offer in the various colors of their layers, as we know, a kind of imitation of natural tones and tint of objects, whether a horse, draperies, crowns, or other accessories. These accidents were particularly studied, and they gave to the inventions of engraving a merit that also enhanced the value. It is true that in this genre there is a price that depends on the rarity itself. The nuances of the stone especially elicit their charms when art exploits those things that nature gives them. What one likes in these works is a sort of painting without being colored, that is to say, of being colored without being painted, it offers finally the appearance and not the reality of illusion. And here precisely is what we see as generally constituting the spirit and the taste of polychrome sculpture; it is of a kind that colored cameos offer us in small: the system of variety that we will recognize as having been that of most grand monuments, a system that, born of imitation without art, succeeded in forgetting the vice of its origin.

130   CHARLES ROBERT COCKERELL
from "On the Aegina Marbles" (1819)

C ockerell, who had made the most problematic discovery of painted Greek statuary, returned to England in 1817 and two years later published this report of his findings to a journal. One of the issues with these discoveries was that the residues of the paint on the statues, once exposed to the air and sunlight, quickly evaporated. His report is important for historical reasons, but also for the fact that here he employs some of the arguments of Quatremère de Quincy to justify the use of paint on sculptural works. As a footnote to this report, the statues he unearthed, now without their paint, were restored by the Danish sculptor Berthel Thorwaldsen in Rome and sold to the Bavarian crown; they are now displayed in the Glyptothek in Munich. Cockerell himself would later return to the practice of architecture, succeed John Soane as the professor at the Royal Academy, and become one of Britain's leading classical architects.

In the temple of Ægina, we have a very remarkable, and very ancient example of the practice which prevailed among the Greeks, of painting their sculpture; for the style and execution of the colours found on the statues and ornaments of the temple, prove that they cannot be of any other date than the original construction.

The particular notes on the statues, will shew the various portions of them which were painted; in order to relieve the statues, the tympanum of the pediment was of a clear light blue: large portions of the colour was still seen on the fragments as we raised them from the ground.

The moulding, both under and over the cornice, was painted; the leaf was red and white, and the superior moulding of the cornice was painted in encaustic; the colours being on marble, and more exposed, had long disappeared, but the relief in which the part so covered, was found, indicated very perfectly its outline.

In considering a custom which appears so extraordinary to us, it must be recollected, that although the Greek buildings were grand in conception and idea, their scale was small; hence they required a greater nicety and delicacy in the execution: the colours served as the means of distinguishing the several parts, and heightening the effect by a delicate variety of tones, so as to relieve what might otherwise be inanimate or monotonous. To paint white marble, or other stone exposed to the open air, appears very singular to us, but there are

Charles Robert Cockerell (1788–1863), from "On the Aegina Marbles" from *Journal of Science, Literature, and Art* VI (1819), pp. 340–1.

many considerations not obvious to our northern ideas and prejudices, which must be taken into the account. In Greece, the mildness of the climate, and purity of the atmosphere rendered works of finished execution much more secure from degradation; and admitted refinements of sculpture and painting, that would be thrown away and lost in a northern climate, the inhabitants of which finding little enjoyment in the open air, are obliged to lavish upon their interior apartments, those luxuries of sculpture and ornament which the ancients, passing a great part of their time in their fine atmosphere, or under the shade of porticos, bestowed upon the exterior of their building.

131   WILLIAM KINNARD
annotations to Stuart and Revett's *Antiquities of Athens*, second edition (1825)

Although Quatremère de Quincy's *Le Jupiter olympien* was written to explain the use of color on Greek statuary, the fact that similar justifications for color could be applied to architecture was not lost to architects and archaeologists. In 1816 another large contingent of British architects and archaeologists, led by William Kinnard, set off for Athens with the intention of producing a new edition of Stuart and Revett's book, which was now to be annotated with up-to-date footnotes. In volume II of this new edition, which appeared in 1825, Kinnard addresses the issue of polychromy with respect to the Parthenon. Stuart and Revett, as we have noted, had recorded traces of painted decorations on the monument, but now a more comprehensive examination of the work – in light of the new interest in polychromy – had revealed far more extensive traces of paint than had been noticed before. The following passages are from footnotes that appear in the volume, and again follow upon the argument of Quatremère de Quincy in justifying polychromy originally because of the use of poor materials. By the time that polished marble had been introduced for monuments, polychromy – as this explanation goes – had now become sanctioned by years of practice and was an integral part of Greek artistic consciousness.

A remarkable decoration of this temple, as well as others, of the Age of Pericles was the painting, the remains of which are still distinctly perceptible on various parts of the building, of a character correspondent with early Grecian ornament; and, in the same places, where the colors have fled, the outlines of the ornament graved on the marble, still indicate the place of their application. The nearest parts painted now perceptible to the eye, are the capitals of the antae; the taenia and regula of the external architrave; the fascia underneath the mutules; the fascia, and ogee beneath it over the frieze within the peristylium; the fascia

William Kinnard, annotations to Stuart and Revett's *The Antiquities of Athens,* second edition (1825).

and moulding above it within the posticum; the frieze of the posticum; the raking bed-mouldings, and cymatium of the pediment. [. . .]

The sculptures were originally painted – that enrichment, having probably, as discovered at the temple of Aegina, a light-blue ground, and the naked figures and draperies distinguished by tints, and their attributes, armour, and the contiguous shields, and inscriptions sparkling with gilding. The external walls of the cella may have been adorned with heroic paintings. [. . .]

The polished columns of white marble with their architrave, triglyphs, and the chief part of the cornice, may therefore have been thus relieved in a manner agreeable to the eye, in so sunny an atmosphere, by the enrichment and combination with the colours and gilding judiciously applied.

Color was doubtless originally introduced on the edifices of the primitive Eastern nations, as in China, both to protect from atmosphere, and to correct the repulsive appearance of the mean materials used in early building: for timber, burnt clay, and soft and porous stone, were the substances progressively adopted in architectural design, which was first exercised only on sacred edifices. Afterwards, when temples were raised of white and polished marble, it may have been deemed still necessary to conform to the impression derived from colour, associated with the appearance of former religious structures. On that account both polychrome ornaments and gilding may have been therefore introduced on this temple, as well as to cause the edifice to correspond in richness with the gorgeously decorated colossus it enshrined; but here, at this epoch, as in the adoption of every other ancient accessory belonging to the arts and religion of their ancestors, the Athenians were guided by purer principles of design. The taste for polychrome or colored edifices was thus derived by the Greeks from Egypt and the East.

132 OTTO MAGNUS VON STACKELBERG
from *The Temple of Apollo at Bassae in Arcadia* (1826)

The classical site at Bassae, in Arcadia, which had been visited by Cockerell in 1811, was the site of excavation the next year by a team of archaeologists led by the Russian Baron von Stackelberg. Twice this explorer had nearly died of typhoid while traveling in Greece, and on one occasion was kidnapped by pirates and held for ransom. But at Bassae he made a major discovery by excavating over 100 feet of the temple's frieze – a building that was credited historically to Ictinus, the architect of the Parthenon, and therefore nearly contemporary with it. Again the marbles showed clear signs of paint, although once again the paint vaporized when exposed to air. In Stackelberg's lavish monograph of the temple of 1826 he noted its painted forms in great detail but also placed

Otto Magnus von Stackelberg (1787–1837), from *Der Apollotempel zu Bassae in Arcadien und die daselbst ausgegrabenen Bildwerke* [The temple of Apollo at Bassae in Arcadia and the carvings excavated there] (1826), pp. 33–4, trans. Harry Francis Mallgrave.

polychromy within a larger context of the picturesque landscape and ruddy Greek spirit. His comments are an indication of just how strong the classical ideal and respect for Greek art was in the 1820s, even though the earlier "white" image of its beauty was being radically transformed. Note also the expansion of color usage beyond simple painted decorations and its connection with an entire style of living remote from the North.

Color, even today indispensable to all Southern peoples to enliven the architectural masses, was used by the Greeks on the greatest architectural masterworks of the Periclean Age, both Doric and Ionic, as seen on Theseum, the Parthenon, the Temple of Minerva Polias, and the Propyläen, where colors were even applied to the exterior building decorations. In addition, several examples of memorials, Greek vase paintings, and frescoes from Pompeii demonstrate the universality of painted decorations on architectural works themselves. The mild climate favored this use, and the Doric temple appeared much more richly decorated than one might imagine. Since the already noted excavation on Aegina, interest in this subject has become animated, and the most recent investigations of Sicilian temples have led to the same conclusion. When the color applied to those temple ruins has remained in a fresh condition, the manner of its use has become clearer. Individual moldings were decorated with color, and color was also applied to the recesses of the completely painted primary masses. Typically, there were two colors applied decoratively to the white ground-color: scarlet red and sky blue. It is noteworthy that the same two colors have also frequently been found on Egyptian buildings and were regarded as sacred colors. Often gilding was applied to buildings, which complements, enhances, and unites all colors. In the above-mentioned Aeginan temple, it was found that the pedimental field against which the colored statues stood was painted blue, the enclosing moldings with a kind of leaf-work, the fluting similarly, alternating red and blue with white borders. The gable cornice and the upper and lower surfaces of the moldings of the main cornice were also painted with the same colors. On Athenian and Sicilian buildings, traces of similar ornaments have been found, again in the same colors as found on the cornices of Egyptian monuments. The gutter molding and the antefix were decorated merely with a painted flower decoration. The undersides of the mutules beneath the corona were a bright blue, the spaces or gaps in between a (viae) red color, and the fascia white. Blue was again applied to the triglyphs, and red was applied as the running band along the taenia. The egg-and-dart motifs generally alternate in these colors; the border of the eggs is white, however.

Greek forms in general have a special charm, as do the decorations, implements, etc., which lend an infectious youth to their art. The parallel with natural forms in terms of functionality, inner relationships, stability, necessity – all become utilized in these masterworks of architec-ture. Following the natural principle of organic formation, the essence of Doric architecture is based on a character of purposeful construction. In contrast to Nordic, Gothic, or Roman-esque architecture – which through audacious and artistic combinations seeks to exceed the limits of the possible in order to express the incomprehensible and the effusiveness of spiritual foreboding – the Southern manner of building, in service to a sensuous religion, strives to attain the logic and clarity of nature's perfection. If therefore the Greeks in their best period especially preferred this manner of building temples sanctified by religion and tradition, they also revealed to the artist the path to architecture's ideal.

133 JACQUES IGNACE HITTORFF
from "Polychrome Architecture Among the Greeks" (1830)

The reference that Stackelberg made to the recent discoveries of polychromy made in Sicily alludes to archaeological excavations undertaken in the 1820s, and especially to those of the German/French architect J. I. Hittorff. The beginning of the Greek war of independence from Ottoman rule in 1821 had suddenly made travel to Greece very dangerous. Architects and archaeologists were forced to turn to other areas of the ancient world, chief of which were the Greek colonies of Sicily.

Hittorff was an architect of considerable talent. Although he was born in Cologne, he took advantage of Napoleon's incorporation of the west bank of the Rhine into France to gain acceptance into the Ecole des Beaux-Arts in 1811, and 7 years later he succeeded his mentor François Joseph Bélanger in state office as one of two *architects pour les fêtes et ceremonies*. He rapidly gained a reputation as a fashionable designer and frequented the salon circles of the capital where the polychrome question was a frequent topic of discussion. In 1822 he decided to try and make his own discovery and took leave from his practice to travel to Rome. There he heard of the unearthing of some painted metopes in Sicily by the Englishmen William Harris and Samuel Angell, and he immediately set out to examine these sites. On the acropolis of Selinus, and employing 19 workmen to excavate, he found fragments of a small temple that he construed as the "Temple of Empedocles." Back in Rome, and later in Paris, he prepared his "reconstruction" of the temple, but he presented nothing significant of his findings until the evening of April 3, 1830. There in the main hall of the Academie des Beaux-Arts – in an atmosphere electric with the tension of the pending political revolution – he displayed brilliant polychrome drawings of this temple, in which every part, including the columns and walls of the cella, was decorated with bold and brilliant color. He had gone much further than anyone before him in his polychrome image, and in fact he insisted he had discovered the universal "system" for ancient polychromy. Such a contention would ignite a spirited polychrome debate across Europe in which various architects, archaeologists, and historians participated. The fact that Hittorff made his restoration from only a few small pieces of the temple, and incorporated various classical and nonclassical motifs from elsewhere, only helped to fuel this controversy.

The researches and the discoveries that I have made with regard to the antique monuments of Sicily, and the studies and investigations of the antiquities of Greece since the beginning of the nineteenth century, have been very fruitful in producing new and interesting results and in confirming that colors were applied to Hellenic monuments in every epoch. The principal goal of my work in the restitution of the Temple of Empedocles, through the mustering of numerous facts and supporting evidence, has been to establish that there was a *system* for polychrome architecture among the Greeks. Within the ensemble of their architectural creations, color was one of the most appropriate means for adding the charm of an elegant beauty to the majestic character of their temples – always the poetic prerogative of this nation and of their divinities. We have come to see that the system applied to the edifices

Jacques Ignace Hittorff (1792–1867), from the lecture "De l'architecture polychrôme chez les Grecs, ou restitution complete du temple d'Empédoclés, dans l'acropolis de Sélinute" [Polychrome architecture among the Greeks, or complete restitution of the temple of Empedocles on the acropolis of Selinus] (April 3, 1830), trans. Harry Francis Mallgrave from *Annals de L'Institut de Correspondence Archéologique*, Vol. 2. Paris, 1830, pp. 263–4.

raised under the purest atmosphere, illuminated by the most beautiful sunlight, surrounded by brilliant vegetation and by the freshness and brightness of the colors, had been the only means at the disposal of the artist for putting the work of art in harmony with the inexhaustible richness of nature. The use of this system, reproduced here in its entirety on a monument of antiquity, does not in any way detract from the perfection and beauty of Greek works of art. My object has therefore been to envision Greek polychrome architecture in conjunction with its use as a means of preserving their monuments, as a consequence and necessity of this system, as a practice entirely identical with that of colored statuary, as a special embellishment intended for monuments, and as a way of accommodating the local use of historical painting on temples and the buildings of antiquity. This union of sculpture and architecture offered the indispensable elements or complement for most antique temples and public buildings; it was the means of admitting that the most beautiful and the most important architectural works of antiquity (which without these effects were already raised almost to the point of sublimity) drew their powerful overall effect from the alliance of the three arts. When this simultaneous impression was discovered, the senses and the mind – through human genius, talent, and science – were able to produce at a glance the most pleasing and the most impressive effects.

134   GOTTFRIED SEMPER
from *Preliminary Remarks on Polychrome Architecture and Sculpture in Antiquity* (1834)

Hittorff was rather quickly branded an "extremist" for his polychrome views, and he was soon joined in this camp by a young German architect which would eventually make a big name for himself. Gottfried Semper was studying architecture in Paris when Hittorff gave his controversial address, and shortly thereafter he himself began his tour of the South in search of a polychrome discovery. He first traveled to Sicily where, interestingly, he was unable to confirm the "system" of Hittorff. The excitement of the search, nevertheless, enticed him to press onward to Greece, which was still in the midst of civil war. In Athens, after being pressed into diplomatic service on behalf of the Bavarian crown, he erected a makeshift scaffold around parts of the Parthenon and the Temple of Theseus and scraped numerous paint samples off the walls. Back in Rome in 1833, and through the auspices of the Archeological Institute, he began to prepare drawings for a proposed folio on polychromy. The large volume never appeared (in part because he embarked on a successful architectural practice), but in 1834 Semper published a polemical pamphlet announcing the proposed book and calling attention to his findings: *Preliminary Remarks on Polychrome Architecture and Sculpture in Antiquity*. Here he reaffirms the colorful images presented by

Gottfried Semper (1803–79), from *Vorläufige Bemerkungen über bemalte Architectur und Plastik bei den Alten* [Preliminary remarks on polychrome architecture and sculpture in antiquity] (1834), trans. Harry Francis Mallgrave and Wolfgang Herrmann, in *Gottfried Semper: The Four Elements of Architecture and Other Writings*. New York: Cambridge University Press, 1989, pp. 58–60, 65–6. © 1989 by Cambridge University Press. Reprinted with permission of Cambridge University Press.

Stackelberg and Hittorff, and now presents Greek polychromy as "the" great artistic synthesis of the arts achieved during the golden age.

What should not be overlooked in these increasingly colorful images of the past is that the issue of polychromy for this younger generation of architects was only partly an issue of archaeology; it was just as importantly a means to challenge the aesthetic tenets of classicism. Architects around 1830 were beginning to look for a more expressive system or way of practicing their art. The basis of the "white" view of Winckelmann and the Greek neoclassicism of Quatremère de Quincy had clearly collapsed at this point.

Let us now take the opportunity to assess the objections and doubts of the skeptics concerning polychromy in antiquity.

Very few any longer deny the existence of paint on antique monuments, because the corroborating testimony of travelers cannot reasonably be refuted. Yet that the ancients should have covered all their monuments with color, especially those built of white marble, that the *Greeks* could have been so tasteless – this they deny. Forced to affirm the existence of painted traces, they deny their authenticity and assign them to a later and more barbaric time. Of those who halfheartedly make a polychrome concession to architecture, very few admit that Greek sculpture was also painted.

First, with regard to the authenticity of the paint, the perception of an artist's practiced eye can soon persuade us *that the painted decorations on Greeks monuments, in character and execution, are in the most perfect harmony with the sculptural decorations and with the whole in general*. The colors of the Temple of Theseus, of the Parthenon – how beautiful they are! Indeed, from what other times than in the best period of Attic art could formations of such exquisite, exact, and sensitive design, of such harmonious color arrangements have arisen? What is more, the paint in both material composition and manner of treatment is easy to distinguish from the Christian coats of paint, often found directly alongside.[1]

Yet critics call them barbaric and do not concede that the Greeks could have covered such delicately shaped profiles with paint. On the contrary, the monuments have become monochrome through barbarism. All periods of high artistic accomplishment agree in the disputed principle of polychromy. The Greeks, the Moors, the Normans, the Byzantines and pre-Goths, even the Gothic masters themselves practiced it.[2] How harsh and unfair it is to reproach such times as barbaric because their views of art deviate from our own! Is it really not possible that *we* could be in error? Would it not be fair to think of the possibility, at least, that what appears to us bizarre, glaring, gaudy, and glittering would no longer be so if we looked at it with less stupid eyes?

In a bright, consuming southern light and strongly tinted environment, the effect of refraction on well-ordered tones of color placed next to one another is so mild that the colors do not offend the eye but soothe it. The secret lies in arranging the colors in such a way as not to harm each other. The recently excavated walls at Pompeii show how adept the ancients were in applying the brilliantly pure colors. And indeed, we begin to become accustomed to them. The ancients in their decoration knew no subdued, half-tones of color. The blending and mixing took place not on the palette but on the wall, through the juxtaposition of variegated and graceful decorations that at a certain distance appear to the eye as intermixed, but that always retain a tender playfulness that has such a charming effect. [...]

These observations might convince those who only admire the *pure forms* of antiquity that color studies are necessary for a better understanding of these forms. They are the key. Without them the coherence of the whole cannot be seen. Likewise, many secrets of antique sculpture would become clear if we were able to restore their *painted* effects.

Once we have established through various observations that certain forms in architecture are a sculptural alternative to ornaments painted on their surface, we can then conclude with reasonable certainty that where these same forms are found in other combinations, they were originally decorated in a similar way – even if every trace of the painted decoration has been washed away with time.

The form of the Greek egg-and-dart molding appears in various combinations on all Doric, Ionic, and Corinthian monuments. Its surface was completely painted, decorated mostly with blue eggs separated by red arrowheads. Now, the form of the echinus on the Doric capital presents exactly the same curvature that is unique to the egg-and-dart molding. Am I not justified, therefore, in assuming that this echinus was originally decorated in a similar way, even if actual traces of this kind have not been found? The echinus had to have been decorated; the whole, if dressed everywhere with rich decoration, would have suffered no unadorned place. Should its name not be suggestive of its decorative manner? Contemporary and later Doric capitals contain the same sculptural ornament, for example, at Samos and on the caryatids of the Minerva Polias.

If we can make similar inferences and analogies our guide in cases where observation fails us, it would be easier to trace the connection and to compose a system of ancient temple decoration. In addition to the painting, the metal ornaments, gilding, tapestrylike draperies, balachins, curtains, and movable implements must not be forgotten. From the beginning the monuments were designed with all these things in mind, even for the surroundings – the crowds of people, priests, and the processions. The monuments were the scaffolding intended to bring together these elements on a common stage. The brilliance that fills the imagination when trying to visualize those times makes the imitations that people have since fancied and imposed on us seem pale and stiff.

NOTES

1   The Greeks seem to have used a siliceous solution in their marble paint. The color crust on marble temples has the appearance of a hard vitreous enamel a half-millimeter thick. Certainly the thickness and brittleness of the color coating demanded that the whole monument be covered with it; otherwise the color very quickly would have peeled off around the edges. The places where the monument was supposed to appear white were by no means left bare, but were covered with a white paint.
2   They not only furnished the Gothic churches with richly colored decorations, but even tinted the ray of sunlight that penetrated the stained glass windows.

135 LÉON VAUDOYER
excerpts from three letters of 1829, 1830, and 1831

As the elements of the polychrome controversy were taking shape in the second half of the 1820s, the classical teachings of the Ecole des Beaux-Arts were taking a hit along another front – from some of the school's most talented students. What in fact was transpiring was a growing student rebellion. The battleground was not in Paris but at the French Academy in Rome, where the *grand prix* winners at the Ecole des Beaux-Arts were awarded five years of additional study. The leader of the protesting "Romantics" was Henri Labrouste (1801–75), later the designer of the Bibliothèque Ste-Geneviève and Bibliothèque Nationale. In 1824 he won the grand prix, and for his fourth-year restoration project of 1828, he chose a classical theme – the temples at Paestum – but used the restoration for polemical purposes. In the text accompanying his drawings, he reversed the accepted chronology of the monuments (in which column proportions had moved from squatter proportions to leaner and more refined profiles) and argued that the Greek colonists moved away from the Greek ideal by following local, material, and cultural conditions specific to the Italian landscape and cultural conditions. In other words, there was no growing perfection of classical architecture but quite the reverse. When the drawings were displayed back in Paris in the summer of 1829 they created a furor, in which Quatremère de Quincy publicly censored the director of the French Academy, Horace Vernet, for his lack of control over students. The situation, widely reported in the French press, only gained in intensity in the following year.

Another of the dissenting students in Rome was Léon Vaudoyer, who had won the *grand prix* in 1826. His participation in the student unrest was significant because he was the son of the respected architect and academician Antoine-Laurent-Thomas Vaudoyer (1756–1846), who in his letters was urging his son to refrain from activities that would harm the institution of the Ecole des Beaux Arts. The excerpts from three letters over three years convey some of the issues in dispute. The first, written in response to the controversy back in Paris, discloses how severely Quatremère de Quincy's academic authority had been eroded. In the second letter the younger Vaudoyer calls for a "little revolution," in keeping with the changing trends in the other arts. And in the third letter, written to his former teacher and friend Hippolyte Lebas (1782–1867), Vaudoyer makes his plea for a contemporary and rational architecture fitted to the socialist ideals of his generation. The influence of the teachings of Claude-Henri Saint Simon was making itself felt (see the next chapter).

Léon Vaudoyer to A.-L.-T. Vaudoyer, July 20, 1829

The Institute with its old-fashioned ideas can decide whatever it wants. But we will always place ourselves above it and the century marches on despite the old prejudices and wet blankets who don't want anyone to do things differently than they do. [. . .] The perennial, boring Mr. Quatremère will continue to discourse forever and this has thrown much disfavor on the Academy of Fine Arts; you need someone to wake you up. And certainly not Mr. Raoul Rochette who is another bumbler who doesn't know anything about architecture and talks incessantly, which isn't what it takes to be an antiquarian.

Léon Vaudoyer (1803–72), excerpts from three letters of 1829, 1830, and 1831 in *Léon Vaudoyer: Historicism in the Age of Industry*, ed. Barry Bergdoll. Cambridge, MA: MIT Press, 1994, pp. 293n.47, 296n.92, 294–5n.61.

The war I'm talking about isn't dangerous. It's only a matter of taste and as you know in matters of taste it is difficult to prove who is right; in fact this war in architecture is no different from that now being waged in literature between Victor Hugo and the classicists or even that in painting. Why shouldn't architecture have its own little revolution? That's natural enough, and one is led there naturally by today's conditions. A civilization's architecture should take its character from 1. its institutions, 2. its usages, 3. its climate, 4. from the nature of materials, etc. [...] thus the architecture of 1830 cannot be the same as that of 1680 when Versailles was built by making people die of starvation and poverty. The luxury of a despot is superbly impressive. But the well-being of an entire nation wisely governed is much more satisfying. And thus with the greatest wisdom we are led today to return architecture to more truthful expression, more in harmony with the ideas of our time.

Léon Vaudoyer to H. Lebas, May 28, 1831

I agree with you that it is natural enough for a generation to seek to do things differently from the last generation, and that often innovation undermines quality, since too often in order to do something differently it is quite enough to do it less well, which is much easier than to do it better; it is this craze which ties everything to the tides of fashion where ideas are forever in flux and where true principles are sometimes lost from sight ... M. Percier ... gave a new impetus to architecture and it was thought that the beautiful had truly been found, but it simply can't be found! Then prevailing ideas changed, and the constitutional system gave us a spirit of inquiry, reasoning, and of frugality. We began to believe that it wasn't enough to have superlative taste in composing, in the perfect adjustment of ornamentation, and to draw them perfectly, to load our monuments with figures, with bas-relief sculpture, and the like, in order to make architecture. But that is precisely where things were in the Ecole a few years ago and this system was soon taken to extremes by the least talented ... all under the influence of the Professor of architecture, Mr. B[altard] ... and it is obvious that we began to stray into exaggeration and the disadvantages of an architecture created originally for entirely different needs made us lose sight of precious principles of rationality, of solidity, and even of appropriateness. This evil had to come to an end and I think it has been reached and that we have come to understand that our political and social institutions demand an intelligent and rational architecture, easily, simply, and economically realizable. [...] In order to strip the rich monuments of the Empire of all their adornments and to find underneath them the Nude we have plunged ourselves into the study of republican and Greek monuments which have no other ornament than the purity of their forms and their simplicity. [...] So just what is this architecture that has been called Romantic, why I'm not too sure? It is an architecture that seeks to return to true principles, which requires that every form be determined by reason and by need, which seeks to respect the nature of materials, and which, finally, seeks to place the art of architecture in harmony with this century. Is that really such a fault? [...] To reach that goal it seemed necessary to study these monuments of an early period, without of course overlooking those of other epochs. Is it not after all logical if you want to know the true meaning of a word to refer to its etymology? I am well aware that one can go astray in this new approach; and that is why it is necessary to benefit from the experience of enlightened people by asking for their advice in order to develop these new ideas all the while taking advantage of established ideas.

136 ÉMILE BARRAULT
from *To Artists* (1830)

When the European Congress of Vienna in 1815 reimposed the old monarchy on France after the defeat of Napoleon, political opposition within France appeared on several fronts. One contending social theorist was Claude-Henri Saint-Simon (1760–1825). Beginning in 1816, he called for a social revolution and new socialist system of government based on the tools of industrial production. At the top of this meritocracy, in which women would participate fully, he proposed an elite of scientists, artists, and industrialist-artisans, who would guide social production and progress. In 1825 Olinde Rodrigues, one of Saint-Simon's leading disciples, called for the creation of an "avant-garde" of artists to work consciously to direct humanity toward the new social and religious order. The means of carrying out this political mandate were further explicated in Emile Barrault's manifesto of 1830.

Saint-Simonian theory, in its early phase, saw human development as evolutionary and cyclical, broken into a series of "organic" and "critical" epochs. Within Western civilization, early Greece and the Gothic Middle Ages formed the two principal "organic" epochs; each had provided stylistic models for architecture, and in the succeeding "critical" periods these models were refined and eventually overdone. Within this overriding chronology, the French revolution was deemed to be the last event of the medieval era, and thus the stage was set for the start of a new and creative organic epoch. The influence of the ideas of Saint-Simon was reaching its apogee around 1830, and it was this ideological fervor, for instance, that was prompting Vaudoyer's call for a "little revolution." With the political overthrow of Charles X in the summer of 1830, the Saint-Simonians believed that the Promised Land was indeed now within sight. This (short-lived) enthusiasm is reflected in Barrault's book, which appeared in 1830, and this disciple again stresses the important role reserved for artists in forming this new society; for architecture, it means the creation of a new style with new social and religious meanings.

The decadence of the arts is evident. The indifference of the public toward their productions testifies to this sad truth, and the efforts of artists to resuscitate the arts attests to it even more. Everyone today, on every possible occasion, strives to be poetic; such remedies demonstrate the malady.

The day has arrived when we, in the midst of such diverse opinion, must likewise voice ours. We have come neither to prescribe a literary code nor to comment on the violation of established rules; we shall not attempt to defend or combat or mediate Aristotle, Boileau, or Schlegel. We speak not in the name of those who hold the scepter of criticism or who aspire to found the science of aesthetics. Our mission is higher and, if we will accomplish it in its

Émile Barrault (1799–1869), from *Aux Artistes: du passé et de l'avenir des beaux-arts* [To artists: of the past and future of the fine arts]. Paris: Alexandre Mesnier Libraire, 1830, pp. 9–10, 12–18, trans. Harry Francis Mallgrave.

august simplicity, let us repeat to artists the words of Saint-Simon, our master: "Love God and humanity; love them like they want now to be loved, and this sacred love, in warming the heart, will enhance your genius!" Here is the divine poetic that we offer in our turn. [...]

Faithful to the method according to which we observe the march of science and industry and applying it to the study of the arts, let us begin by recognizing that history from Greek antiquity until the present day presents in turn two distinct epochs: *organic* and *critical*. Characteristics of the first are found in polytheism and in the Middle Ages; those of the second in the interregnum that follows each of these social periods. The history of the arts, envisioned within the same series of facts, must offer us successively two corresponding epochs.

In initially glancing at these periods of world history, we first note that a shameful obscurity seems to be the lot of organic epochs; a glorious glow, on the contrary, is cast on the critical epochs by the four immortal centuries. In the former, it is said, there ruled a frightful barbarity; in the latter only poetry and eloquence. In the critical epochs, the arts were freely developed and they hastened the progress of humanity, and in everything called for the pleasures of the heart and of the imagination. Finally, words have been exhausted on the succession of these two epochs and always to the advantage of the second – with comparisons of the dawn dissipating the night, of awakening superseding the dream, of childbirth appearing after a period of sterility. So that, for those who study the arts and their influence, the organic epochs are seen as the time of darkness, of inertia, of impotence. But should we hasten to conclude that their rule is fatal to the arts, while those of the critical epochs give them life? Then from where comes our present deterioration?

This prejudice against the organic epochs can undoubtedly be explained by their coincidence with the large barbarian invasions into Greece, as well as into Rome, with the formation or renewal of languages, and finally by the necessary interruption or retardation, owing to circumstances, of the long apprenticeship required in all the arts for technical perfection. But is it therefore true that poetry, stifled under such obstacles, cannot raise itself to glory? What! When societies have the same beliefs, are directed by the same principles, and are driven by the same feelings, the spring of emotions is dried up and the arts are stricken with sterility! But if, wracked by an anxious intensity, they strive to regain their stride, if the ground on which they walk trembles or is filled with debris, then poetry is simply reborn, as on favorable and privileged terrain. What does tend to work to the detriment of organic epochs, however, is a critical epoch. Impartiality must commence on the day that the course of the organic epoch is complete.

And first, what is poetry? It is the power to move someone. What are the fine arts? They are the various expressions of this power. All the arts thus have their poetry; it is their secret soul. And it does not necessarily reside in a correct and pure form, but in the tangible influence that it exerts on us.

Now let us turn our attention first to the architecture of the two organic epochs that we will consider. The evidence that these buildings convey to us is scarcely open to challenge because they are able to move everyone who regards them. Moreover, these buildings acquire their great value by their duration, which often allows us to contemplate them as a sincere expression of an organic epoch in all of its vigor. Indeed after an order of ideas and feelings formed in the world for moving beyond the shelter of the first ancient temples, architecture – called upon to offer a more dignified sanctuary – seemed supremely confident, eternal, and powerfully inspired. Today, in order to forestall the scorn of future antiquarians, we take care to place some medals or contemporary money in the foundations of our buildings. And while with the first stone we seal in advance the glory of its ruins; the explanation of its use is not read in the facade but often remains a secret buried in a footing. But when, in times more distant, this practice did not exist, we almost always find in the digging of the foundations a public consensus; to the eyes of successive generations, they were a sure sign of the destiny attached to the edifice ready to be raised. The edifice appears as some kind of built omen itself and this was visible to all. The peculiarity of the monuments of the religious epoch was that they were intended to be a sign. Polytheism has bequeathed to us in the debris of the cyclopean constructions that have survived so many revolutions the idea of colossal forms that polytheism instilled in them. The vast churches of the Middle Ages, with their towers and slender spires, again place before us the spectacle of both grandeur in general plan and profusion of details. From any perspective – how these monuments again appear full and impress our imagination! They impress us by their tall proportions, and popular traditions, which often ascribe them to giants or to a race of more vigorous men, are the poetic expression of this human redoubling of forces that derives from this continuity of unanimous efforts determined by a common belief. They impress us finally by the profound sentiment of their destination. We easily recognize in the temples constructed in pagan times the faithful representation of that religion that scarcely touches the heart but speaks more to the senses. It honors the divinity by a magnificent deployment of forces. Atlas, or Hercules, supporting the vault of the sky, is emblematic of this architecture. And in viewing Gothic edifices, whose audacious architecture seems to send our glance, our prayers, and our hopes all the way to heaven – can we defend ourselves against such pious fervor? Do we not experience an emotion of religious sadness when we visit these interiors, where the daylight passing through the stained glass and penetrating deeply into the vaults invites meditation, and yet the silence seems able to be interrupted without profanation only by grave and sacred words? Now look at the edifices of the irreligious epoch. Elegance, purity, and grace are their merits, even higher proportions. The Tower of Babel – raised with passion and success as long as men spoke the same language, broken off and unfinished by the confusion of language – truly symbolizes the impotency of critical epochs to construct such vast and sublime monuments. Even if someone perhaps attained a material grandeur, the absence of significant feeling will always be noticed there.

137 VICTOR HUGO
from *The Hunchback of Notre-Dame* (1832)

An avid onlooker to the rebellious proceedings at the French Academy in Rome was the Romantic novelist Victor Hugo. The writer had long opposed the vestiges of classicism in France and he, like many of his generation, was an enthusiast for Gothic architecture. The outlet for his beliefs was his novel *The Hunchback of Notre-Dame*, which he started in 1828. After some delays and under a tight deadline, Hugo submitted the novel to the publisher in mid-January 1831, but with some missing chapters. The question of why they were not included, or when or whether they were actually written, will perhaps never be answered, but it seems clear that in the fall or early winter of 1830 Hugo sought out Labrouste, who had just returned triumphantly from Rome, for his comments on chapters relating to architecture. The most important of these, "Ceci tuera cela" (This will kill that), first appeared in the revised edition of the book in 1832. The chapter is an excursus on a medieval conversation between Archdeacon Claude Frollo and King Louis XI in disguise, in which Frollo, in referring to a book on his desk and the Cathedral of Notre Dame outside his window, makes the comment that "this" (the book) will kill "that" (architecture). His reasoning is that prior to the printing press architecture had always been the primary social vehicle for recording the deeds and knowledge of human civilization, and this art form reached its apotheosis in medieval times with the great Gothic Cathedrals, whose works of art served as epistles to inform the parishioners of church doctrines. This role for architecture ended with the invention of the printing press, because the book was an easier, less expensive, and a more effective way to communicate knowledge. Thus all post-Gothic architecture for Hugo – including the recent return to classicism at the Academy – had been on a downward slope with regard to its meaning, and architecture was increasingly being stripped of its monumental purpose for being. The following passage speaks of this decline, and can be read as a pessimistic response to the utopian enthusiasm of the Saint-Simonians, as well as to the belief that a new organic architecture can be created.

With the emancipation of the arts, thought, too, is everywhere set free. The freethinkers of the Middle Ages had already made gaping wounds in the side of Catholicism. The sixteenth century ripped asunder religious unity. Before the printing press, the Reformation would have been but a schism; printing made it a revolution. Take away the press and heresy is paralyzed. Be it fatal or providential, Gutenberg is the precursor of Luther.

However, when the sun of the Middle Ages has completely set, when the light of the Gothic genius has gone out forever over the horizon of art, architecture, too, becomes more and more pale, colorless, and lifeless. The printed book, that gnawing worm in the structure, sucks its blood and eventually devours it. It droops, withers, wastes away before your very eye. It becomes shabby, poor, of no account. It no longer expresses anything, not even the art of another time. Architecture left to itself, abandoned by the other arts, because human thought has deserted it, must employ the artisan in default of the artist. Plain glass replaces stained glass; the stone mason, the sculptor. Farewell to the vital juices, to originality, to life, and to intelligence. Like a lamentable beggar of the studios, it drags itself from copy to copy. Michelangelo, doubtless aware of its demise in the sixteenth century, made one last despairing attempt to save it. That

Victor Hugo (1802–85), from *Notre-Dame de Paris* (1832), trans. Walter J. Cobb, in *The Hunchback of Notre-Dame*. Signet, 1964, pp. 184–5. © 1965 by Walter J. Cobb. Used by permission of Dutton Signet, a division of Penguin Group (USA) Inc.

titan of the world of art piled the Pantheon on the Parthenon, and so made Saint Peter's of Rome, a gigantic work that deserved to remain unique, the last expression of architectural originality, the signature of a great artist at the bottom of a colossal register in stone thus closed. But when Michelangelo was dead, what then did this wretched architecture do, this architecture which only survived as a specter, as a shadow? It copied Saint Peter's in Rome; it parodied it. This impulse to imitate became a mania – something to weep over.

Henceforth each century has its Roman Saint Peter's. In the seventeenth century, it was the Val-de-Grâce; in the eighteenth, Sainte-Geneviève. Every country has its Saint Peter's. London has hers; St. Petersburg, hers; Paris has two or three. A paltry legacy, the last drivels of a great but decrepit art, was falling into second childhood before dying.

If, instead of characteristic monuments, such as we have just mentioned, we examine art in general from the sixteenth to the eighteenth century, we would at once observe the same phenomenon of decrepitude and decay. From Francis II the dressing of the edifice is effaced more and more and so lets the geometric design show through, like the bony framework of an emaciated invalid. The graceful lines of art give way to the cold, inexorable lines of geometry. A structure is no longer a structure; it is a polyhedron. Architecture, however, painfully tries to hide this nudity. Hence the Greek pediment set over the Roman pediment, and vice versa. It is forever the Pantheon on the Parthenon, Saint Peter's at Rome. Such are the brick houses with stone corners during the time of Henry IV; to wit, the Place Royale and the Place Dauphine. Such are the churches during the reign of Louis XIII, heavy, squat, top-heavy, laden down with a dome like a hump. Thus, too, the Mazarin architecture, the bad Italian *pasticcio* of the Quatre-Nations, the palaces of Louis XIV, long court barracks, stiff, cold, boring. Such are, lastly, the buildings of Louis XV, with chicory leaves and vermicelli ornaments, and all the warts and fungi which disfigure that aged, toothless, and debased coquette. From Francis II to Louis XV the disease progressed in geometric ratio. Art becomes nothing but skin clothing bones. It dies miserably.

138   GOTTFRIED SEMPER
from *Preliminary Remarks on Polychrome Architecture and Sculpture in Antiquity* (1834)

The German Semper was not only trained at a private architectural atelier in France, but on his tour of the south, beginning in 1830, he traveled with a number of French students and thus shared their revolutionary enthusiasm that a new social and architectural era was dawning. Here, in the manifesto-like Preface to his pamphlet on polychromy, he voices dissatisfaction with the current state of affairs and affirms at the same time the desire of his generation to create an architecture better suited to the social needs of the time. Interestingly, there

Gottfried Semper, from *Vorläufige Bemerkungen über bemalte Architectur und Plastik bei den Alten* [Preliminary remarks on polychrome architecture and sculpture in antiquity] (1834), trans. Harry Francis Mallgrave and Wolfgang Herrmann, in *Gottfried Semper: The Four Elements of Architecture and Other Writings.* New York: Cambridge University Press, 1989, pp. 46–7. © 1989 by Cambridge University Press. Reprinted with permission of Cambridge University Press.

are two targets of his scorn. One is the design method proposed by Durand, "in the manner of a knitting pattern or chessboard, on which the plans of buildings arrange themselves quite mechanically." The second is historicism in general, and the work of Leo von Klenze in particular. The reference to the "organic life" of Greek art has unmistakable Saint-Simonian overtones. Like Labrouste, Semper would later employ Renaissance-inspired design elements to fashion his vision of a style better suited to the times.

One blames the architecture of our time for lagging behind its sisters in the footrace of the arts, for no longer being consistent with needs that require a totally new and, so it seems, advantageous arrangement of things for art. Unfortunately, this harsh reproach cannot be refuted entirely. Conscious of its guilt and pressured by its creditors, an almost bankrupt architecture seeks relief and recovery by introducing into circulation two kinds of paper currencies. The first are Durand's assignats, which this chancellor of the exchequer of failed ideas has put into circulation. They consist of blank sheets that are divided into many squares in the manner of a knitting pattern or chessboard, on which the plans of buildings arrange themselves quite mechanically. (See Durand's work: *Précis des leçons d'architecture*, etc.)

Who still doubts their sterling value? – since without a second thought we can gather the most heterogeneous things under one umbrella, everything the ancients threw together so higgledy-piggledy. With them, the first-year polytechnical student in Paris becomes a complete architect within six months: riding schools, baths, theaters, dance salons, and concert halls almost spontaneously assemble themselves on his grids into one plan and carry off the great academic prize. Following such rigid principles, entire cities like Mannheim and Karlsruhe are laid out.

The second paper currency that comes into use no less in the general want of ideas is transparent tracing paper. Through this magical expedient we become absolute masters of ancient, medieval, and modern times. The young artist traverses the world, crams his notebooks full of pasted-on tracings of every kind, then returns home with the cheerful expectation (taking care to show his specimens to the right connoisseur) that soon he will receive the commission for a Walhalla à la Parthénon, a basilica à la Monréale, a boudoir à la Pompeii, a palace à la Pitti, a Byzantine church, or even a bazaar in the Turkish taste! What miracles result from this invention! Thanks to it our major cities blossom forth as true *extraits de mille fleurs*, as the quintessence of all lands and centuries, so that in our pleasant delusion we forget in the end to which century we belong!

Yet, joking aside, do we benefit by all of this? We desire art; we are given numbers and rules. We desire the new; we are given something even older and more remote from the needs of our time. We should understand these needs and arrange them from the point of beauty, and not see beauty simply where the fog of a distant time and place has shrouded our eyes. So long as we grasp at every old tatter and our artists sneak off into corners to draw bare subsistence from the moss of the past, there is no prospect for a productive artistic life.

Art knows only one master – the need. It degenerates when it follows the whim of artists, even more so when it obeys powerful patrons of art. Its proud determination can indeed raise a Babylon, a Persepolis, or a Palmyra from the desert sands, whose regular streets, mile-wide squares, stately halls and palaces impatiently await in their sad emptiness the population that the despotic ruler was unable to conjure. The organic life of Greek art is not its work; it flourished only on the soil of need and under the sun of freedom.

139   LÉONCE REYNAUD
from "Architecture" in the *New Encyclopedia* (1834)

The most eloquent exposition of an advancing Saint-Simonian position regarding architecture is that presented by the architect Léonce Reynaud in his article "Architecture," written for the *Encyclopédie nouvelle*. Reynaud had long had connections with dissident groups. He had originally enrolled at the Ecole Polytechnique in 1821 but was shortly thereafter expelled on the suspicion that he belonged to an anarchist organization. A few years later he enrolled at the Ecole des Beaux-Arts, but never competed for the *grand prix*. Instead, in 1828, he traveled at his own expense to the French Academy in Rome, where – as Robin Middleton has surmised – he made known the ideas of Saint-Simon to Labrouste and Vaudoyer. By 1832 Reynaud was part of a circle of intellectuals led by Pierre Leroux, who in 1831 had taken over the *Revue encyclopédie* and (together with Léonce's brother Jean) planned to turn it into a new encyclopedia project predicated on Saint-Simonian principles. Léonce Reynaud wrote the entry "Architecture" toward the end of 1834.

The article is innovative and important to theory for a number of reasons. First, his conclusion that no architectural system or style from the past has any claim on present-day design is of course a firm rejection of the classical theory of Quatremère de Quincy as well as the belief that any style can be privileged. Second, Reynaud moves beyond the cyclical historical view of the Saint-Simonians by arguing that architecture, instead of moving up and down between organic and critical cycles, marches as a progressive evolution, following the science of building techniques (materials and structure), while still reflecting the changing beliefs and aspirations of the society at large. At the conclusion of this excerpt, in fact, he embarks on a historical survey – beginning with Celtic, Egyptian, Etruscan, and Greek constructional systems – to demonstrate architecture's technological advances toward more slender proportions. A third innovative feature of this article is its very rationalism itself. Styles may represent larger social ideas, but in a real way their forms are determined by materials and the ingenuity of their structural systems. Such a position would not only influence such young architects as Eugène-Emmanuel Viollet-le-Duc (see chapter 204 below), but may also indicate the first instance of Germanic theory influencing French thought (see part V, section C, below).

In summary, architecture is an art on which science and industry immediately have considerable influence, because they must be its means of existence and a part of its expression. And it is precisely this dependence on the material and on the laws that govern it – this triple imprint of art, science, and industry – from which architecture draws its particular character. And it for this reason that its productions in different epochs have truly dominated those of the other arts. There exists, in effect, a certain relation between the

Léonce Reynaud, from the entry "Architecture" in *Encyclopédie nouvelle* (1834), trans. Harry Francis Mallgrave from facsimile edition. Geneva: Slatkine Reprints, 1991.

practices, knowledge, and feelings of humanity and the different periods of human development. This relation constitutes a sublime and mysterious harmony that is marked on all the works of the human hand; but even though we are aware of it, we cannot always read it in each thing. Architecture, however, has the ability to summarize and exhibit it clearly. Feelings, knowledge, and customs are translated into our edifices through decoration and proportions, through the nature and use of the materials, and through the number and the distribution of the parts. In addition, the richness and grandeur of monuments represent the power and industry of the nation that has raised them. In the same way the distribution must conform to the exigencies of customs, the methods of construction must be those that are indicated by science, the proportions and the mode of decoration proceed naturally from feelings and the taste of the epoch, and the architecture system that results from these factors will have the privilege and the power to represent society and all of its forces. It will address itself to all the faculties of man; it will be, in a certain way, an admirable encyclopedia. It will harmoniously bring together everything into a synthesis.

But it is clear that human beings are able to believe in the representation of a grand synthesis only insofar as they are themselves conscious of this synthesis – in a word, a general science is necessary for the establishment of a complete system of architecture. Therefore architecture has had its grand character of truth and general harmony only in religious epochs, and in each religious synthesis we have always seen a corresponding system of architecture that has been the symbol and material realization of it. We have continually seen as well these systems developing together and dying together. The ruins of one seem to exist only to affirm the past power and irrevocable overthrow of the other. It is in such epochs that architecture attains its high degree of perfection in religious monuments; it is for these periods that it seems to have been created, and it is from religious monuments that a style descends to other building types. Therefore, all science and poetry come from a known God and they aspire to represent him. Nations happily consecrate the riches and the forces that they have at their command in order to honor a principle or popularize a moral idea for which they have faith and love. Monuments consecrated to the divinity are magnificent expressions of the people's feelings; they respond to such imperious needs and they are indispensable. For if one is unable to conceive of a social religion without ritual, one can no more conceive it without architecture. Without doubt, some precepts of morals are able to be formulated and diffused by spoken poetry. Painting and sculpture are able to present them well: under seductive forms they take pleasure in retracing the consonant actions to the necessities of the association. But it is important to demonstrate that all these manifestations of feelings aspire toward a unique goal. It requires a line of reconciliation for all those people summoned by the same idea; it requires a vessel in which the voice of the orator or the poet can reverberate, and into which works of painting and sculpture would harmoniously be inserted. Architecture creates this edifice, and this creation is only great to the extent that it implicitly understands all the others, and inspires and directs them.

It follows that the architecture of a nation is able to achieve a very great perfection when the painting and sculpture of this nation are little more than in their infancy. Thus was the case in India and ancient Egypt, with the Arabs, and in the Middle Ages. Conversely, one can cite some epochs in which paintings and statues are true works of art, while the monuments are little more than piles of stone and no longer speak to the imagination of man or satisfy his material needs. It is not that architecture, by the development that it acquires, stifles or saps the life of the other arts and prevents them from being productive, as one of our poets has claimed, who has devoted some eloquent pages to the exposition of his particular conceptions on art. In Greece, for example, all of the arts marched in parallel and all arrived at the same time at their highest degree of perfection. But it is that painters, poets, and sculptors are able to reveal and make themselves understood in all times, while it requires a complete social organization for an architect to manifest the power of his art. The works of the painters and sculptors aspire to more diverse and special expressions; they are more individualized. Those of the architect are only able to render ideas or general feelings that belong more to their epoch than to the architect. They are in large part determined by the techniques used for introducing light into a building, while the works of the other arts are fully independent of these methods. In other words, painting and sculpture belong exclusively to art, while architecture depends at the same time on art and science.

This point is important; because if, in fact, every system of architecture corresponds to a certain stage of human science and derives from it, it follows directly that none of the past systems can be considered as having absolute value because science is essentially variable and progressive. Therefore no architectural system that had somewhere else been artistically perfected is able to serve as a definite model or formally impose its laws on us. Such considerations, drawing exclusively on the goal and means of art, have led us to establish this intimate relation between architecture and science.

Let us now demonstrate the correctness of our conclusion by proving that the different architectures that have succeeded have been in effect – with regard to science – in a state of continual progress. Just as science has only been able to exercise its immediate effect on the material alone, in architecture we need only to review the different modes of construction. But what has been the goal of scientific activity? Evidently this: to obtain the desired result with the least possible effort. In such a way a system of construction will be progressive every time that it covers a given space, and the number or dimensions of its supports are lessened, or when it is able to do so with materials of an easier extraction, transport, or use.

B.   THE GOTHIC REVIVAL IN BRITAIN, GERMANY, AND FRANCE

Introduction

Stalking classical theory for more than a half century — between 1770 and 1830 — had been a slowly developing Gothic Revival movement. And while its first signs appear in Britain in isolated instances in the eighteenth century, it becomes by the nineteenth century very much a Europe-wide movement. What also distinguishes it are the very distinct colorations it takes on — both over time and within each country. In Britain, as we have seen, its roots are at least sympathetic with the rise of picturesque aesthetics. At the start of the nineteenth century in Britain, Gothic architecture becomes a subject of great historical fascination. By the time that Charles Barry won the competition for the new Parliament building with his Gothic design in 1836, however, the Gothic cause had become in some quarters a religious crusade, and in others an idea closely identified with Britain's national heritage. In the German states it follows a somewhat similar path in that it was always called the *altdeutsch* or "Old-German" style. Its starting point as an idea lies in the Romantic period of Johann Wolfgang Goethe, and its consolidation as a movement takes place in 1815 with the defeat of Napoleon, where it now becomes the most prominent symbol of the cause of Germany's unification of a country. In France the movement passes from its historical stage of the 1820s and 1830s — where the conservation and restoration of medieval monuments became prominent issues — to both a nationalist and reformist cause. In the last regard theorists such as Eugène-Emmanuel Viollet-le-Duc embraced it as supremely rational and logical methods of construction, with important lessons for what they could bring to present-day practice — thereby bringing to a culmination the rationalist tradition established by Perrault and Soufflot. The Gothic Revival movement as a whole, then, has no single identifiable theme.

140 HORACE WALPOLE
from Letter to H. Zouch (1759)

Gothic architecture was a style that never entirely fell out of practice in Great Britain, and thus there were ample historical precedents for its revival in the eighteenth century. Classical architects such as Christopher Wren and Nicholas Hawksmoor had both designed Gothic buildings. Alexander Pope, James Gibbs, and William Kent — all active in the Palladian circle of Lord Burlington — had as well a fascination with Gothic architecture. And in 1742 Batty Langley published his *Ancient Architecture*, which delineated five Gothic orders and even suggested a parity of this style with classicism. Interest in Gothic took a very different turn around the mid-eighteenth century, however, in large part through the efforts of Horace Walpole. In 1748 he purchased his estate, Strawberry Hill, at Twickenham, and over the next quarter of a century transformed the manor into a complex of Gothic buildings with increasing attention to their archaeological accuracy. His desire to authenticate genuine Gothic details brought him to the realization in the late 1750s that a comprehensive history of "our architecture" was needed — a task he hoped to share with William Cole and the architect James Essex. Although the collaborative project never got off the ground, Walpole at the start of this letter of 1759 sets out his plan.

Arlington Street, March 15, 1759

You judge very rightly, Sir, that I do not intend to meddle with accounts of *religious* houses; I should not think of them at all unless I could learn the names of any of the architects, not of the founders. It is the history of our architecture I should search after, especially of the beautiful Gothic. I have by no means digested the plan of my intended work; the materials I have ready in great quantities in Vertue's MSS. But he has collected little with regard to our architects, except Inigo Jones.[1] As our painters have been very indifferent, I must to make the work interesting, make it historical; I would mix it with anecdotes of patrons of the arts; and with dresses and customs from old pictures, something in the manner of Montfaucon's antiquities of France.[2] I think it capable of being made a very amusing work, but I don't know whether I shall ever bestow the necessary time on it.[3] At present, even my press is at a stop; my printer,[4] who was a foolish Irishman, and who took himself for a genius, and who

Horace Walpole, from Letter to H. Zouch (March 15, 1759), in *The Yale Edition of Horace Walpole's Letters*, Vol. XVI, ed. W. S. Lewis. New Haven: Yale University Press, 1952, p. 27.

grew angry that I thought him extremely the former, not the least of the latter, has left me, and I have not yet fixed upon another.

NOTES

1 Inigo Jones (1573–1652). Vertue's numerous jottings on Jones fill three columns of entries in the index to his notebooks (*Vertue Notebooks* vi. 127–9).
2 Bernard de Montfaucon (1655–1741), author of *Les Monuments de la monarchie française*, 5 vols, 1729–33.
3 Although the *Anecdotes* go beyond Vertue's collections, HW did not carry out his intention of expanding them in the manner of Montfaucon. In Feb. 1762 he began a new project, which he called 'Collections for a History of the Manners, Customs Habits, Fashions, Ceremonies, etc., of England,' in which he was encouraged by Lord Bute and others. The project was ultimately carried out by Richard Gough in his *Sepulchral Monuments in Great Britain*, 1786, in the Preface to which (and again at i. 36) he acknowledges his indebtedness to HW.
4 William Robinson, HW's printer 1757–9. He left 5 March 1759 (*Journal of the Printing-Office* 8).

141   HORACE WALPOLE
from *A Description of the Villa of Horace Walpole at Strawberry Hill* (1774)

Strawberry Hill at Twickenham was first popularized by visitors and by word of mouth, but it became an especially well-known manor in Britain through the guidebooks that Walpole published in 1774 and 1778, describing its buildings and their contents. His additions to the initial house had been extensive. In 1754 he added a library, five years later the very Gothic Holbein room; in the 1760s and 1770s he built a Gallery, the Round Tower, and Beauclerk Tower. Not only were the architectural details modeled from authentic Gothic examples in Britain, but Walpole filled each room with eclectic collections that often featured Gothic specimens. By the time that the architect James Wyatt finished a new grouping of Gothic offices near the manor in 1790 (to a design of James Essex), Strawberry Hill had done much to advance the cause of Gothic architecture in Britain.

It will look, I fear, a little like arrogance in a private man to give a printed description of his villa and collection, in which almost every thing is diminutive. It is not, however, intended for public sale, and originally was meant only to assist those who should visit the place. A farther view succeeded; that of exhibiting specimens of Gothic architecture, as collected from standards in cathedrals and chapel-tombs, and showing how they may be applied to

Horace Walpole, from *A Description of the Villa of Horace Walpole at Strawberry Hill* (1774) in *The Works of Horatio Walpole, Earl of Orford*, Vol II. London: G. O. and J. Ribonson, 1798, pp. 395–8.

chimney-pieces, ceilings, windows, balustrades, loggias, &c. The general disuse of Gothic architecture, and the decay and alterations so frequently made in churches, give prints a chance of being the sole preservatives of that style.

Catalogues raisonnés of collections are very frequent in France and Holland; and it is no high degree of vanity to assume for an existing collection an illustration that is allowed to many a temporary auction – an existing collection – even that phrase is void of vanity. Having lived, unhappily, to see the noblest school of painting that this kingdom beheld, transported almost out of the fight of Europe, it would be strange fascination, nay, a total insensibility to the pride of family, and to the moral reflections that wounded pride commonly feels, to expect that a paper fabric and an assemblage of curious trifles, made by an insignificant man, should last or be treated with more veneration and respect than the trophies of a palace deposited in it by one of the best and wisest ministers that this country has enjoyed.

Far from such visions of self-love, the following account of pictures and rarities is given with a view to their future dispersion. The several purchasers will find a history of their purchases; nor do virtuosos dislike to refer to such a catalogue for an authentic certificate of their curiosities. The following collection was made out of the spoils of many renowned cabinets; as Dr. Meade's, lady Elizabeth Germaine's, lord Oxford's, the duchess of Portland's, and of about forty more of celebrity. Such well-attested descent is the genealogy of the objects of virtù – not so noble as those of the peerage, but on a par with those of race-horses. In all three, especially the pedigrees of peers and rarities, the line is often continued by many insignificant names.

The most considerable part of the following catalogue consists of miniatures, enamels, and portraits of remarkable persons. The collection of miniatures and enamels is, I believe, the largest and finest in any country. His Majesty has some very fine, the duke of Portland more; in no other is to be seen, in any good preservation, any number of the works of Isaac and Peter Oliver. The large pieces by the latter, in the royal collection, faded long ago by being exposed to the sun and air. Mons. Henery at Paris, and others, have many fine pieces of Petitot. In the following list are some most capital works of that master, and of his only rival Zincke. Raphael's missal is an unique work in miniature of that monarch of painting; and the book of psalms by Julio Clovio the finest specimen extant of illumination. The drawings and bas-reliefs in wax, by lady Diana Beauclerc, are as invaluable as rare.

To an English antiquary must be dear so many historic pictures of our ancient monarchs and royal family; no fewer than four family-pieces of Henry V, VI, VII, and VIII. of queen Mary Tudor and Charles Brandon; of the duchess of Suffolk and her second husband; and that curious and well-painted picture of Charles II. and his gardener. Nor will so many works of Holbein be less precious to him, especially Zucchero's drawings from his Triumphs of Riches and Poverty.

To virtuosos of more classic taste, the small busts of Jupiter Serapis in basaltes, and of Caligula in bronze, and the silver bell of Benvenuto Cellini, will display the art of ancient and modern sculpture – how high it was carried by Greek statuaries, appears in the eagle.

To those who have still more taste than consists in mere sight, the catalogue itself will convey satisfaction, by containing a copy of madame du Deffand's letter in the name of madame de Sevigné; not written in imitation of that model of letter-writers, but composed of more delicacy of thought and more elegance of expression than perhaps madame de Sevigné herself could have attained. The two ladies ought not to be compared – one was all natural ease and tenderness – the other charms by the graces of the most polished style, which, however, are less beautiful than the graces of the wit they clothe.

Upon the whole, some transient pleasure may even hereafter arise to the peruser of this catalogue. To others it may afford another kind of satisfaction, that of criticism. In a house affecting not only obsolete architecture, but pretending to an observance of the *costume* even in the furniture, the mixture of modern portraits, and French porcelaine, and Greek and Roman sculpture, may seem heterogeneous. In truth, I did not mean to make my house so Gothic as to exclude convenience, and modern refinements in luxury. The designs of the inside and outside are strictly ancient, but the decorations are modern.[1] Would our ancestors, before the reformation of architecture, not have deposited in their gloomy castles antique statues and fine pictures, beautiful vases and ornamental china, if they had possessed them? – But I do not mean to defend by argument a small capricious house. It was built to please my own taste, and in some degree to realize my own visions. I have specified what it contains: could I describe the gay but tranquil scene where it stands, and add the beauty of the landscape to the romantic cast of the mansion, it would raise more pleasing sensations than a dry list of curiosities can excite: at least the prospect would recall the good humour of those who might be disposed to condemn the fantastic fabric, and to think it a very proper habitation of, as it was the scene that inspired, the author of the Castle of Otranto.

NOTE

1   And the mixture may be denominated, in some words of Pope, *A Gothic Vatican of Greece and Rome.*

142   JOHANN WOLFGANG VON GOETHE
from "On German Architecture"
(1772)

Gothic architecture had also remained very much alive in many pockets of Germany, a largely rural country still divided politically and culturally, and still unaffected by industrialization. The renewed interest in Gothic architecture around the turn of the eighteenth century, largely associated with the German Romantic movement, springs from this essay written by a youthful Goethe at the beginning of his *Sturm und Drang* (storm and stress) period. Goethe, of course, would become one of the most widely read and influential German writers over the lengthy course of his lifetime. Born in Frankfurt-on-Main, he attended Leipzig University in the mid-1760s

Johann Wolfgang von Goethe (1749–1832), from "Von deutscher Baukunst" [On German architecture] (1772), trans. John Gage, in *Goethe on Art.* London: Scolar Press, 1980, pp. 106–8. © 1980 by John Gage. Reprinted with permission of John Gage.

and there cultivated his interest in literature and art (he was an avid reader of Winckelmann). An illness forced him back home, and his father, who disapproved of his wish to be a writer, sent him to the (then German) town of Strasbourg to study law. There his interest in medieval times was piqued by the writer Johann Gottfried Herder, a few years his elder, and by the great Gothic cathedral or minster in this city, the work in part of the architect Ervin von Steinbach. This essay serves as a personal and heartfelt tribute to Steinbach and the quasi-mystical spirit of Gothic architecture, which Goethe believed to represent the intensive feelings of the German people. But interestingly, this essay and its feelings would represent only a temporary pause in Goethe's intellectual development, as the poet would later develop a keen appreciation for Greek classicism. Nevertheless, this essay was widely admired by German Romantic writers and philosophers, and it strongly influenced the course of Romantic thought.

The first time I went to the Minster, my head was full of the common notions of good taste. From hearsay I respected the harmony of mass, the purity of forms, and I was the sworn enemy of the confused caprices of Gothic ornament. Under the term Gothic, like the article in a dictionary, I threw together all the synonymous misunderstandings, such as undefined, disorganized, unnatural, patched-together, tacked-on, overloaded, which had ever gone through my head. No less foolish than the people who call the whole of the foreign world barbaric, for me everything was Gothic that did not fit my system, from the lathe-turned gaudy dolls and paintings with which our *bourgeois gentilshommes* decorate their homes to the sober remains of early German architecture, on which, on the pretext of one or two daring curlicues, I joined in the general chorus: 'Quite smothered with ornament!' And so I shuddered as I went, as if at the prospect of some mis-shapen, curly-bristled monster.

How surprised I was when I was confronted by it! The impression which filled my soul was whole and large, and of a sort that (since it was composed of a thousand harmonizing details) I could relish and enjoy, but by no means identify and explain. They say it is thus with the joys of heaven, and how often have I gone back to enjoy this heavenly-earthly joy, and to embrace the gigantic spirit of our ancient brothers in their works. How often have I returned, from all sides, from all distances, in all lights, to contemplate its dignity and his magnificence. It is hard on the spirit of man when his brother's work is so sublime that he can only bow and worship. How often has the evening twilight soothed with its friendly quiet my eyes, tired-out with questing, by blending the scattered parts into masses which now stood simple and large before my soul, and at once my powers unfolded rapturously to enjoy and to understand. Then in hinted understatements the genius of the great Master of the Works revealed itself to me. 'Why are you so surprised?' he whispered to me. 'All these shapes were necessary ones, and don't you see them in all the old churches of my city? I have only elevated their arbitrary sizes to harmonious proportions. How the great circle of the window opens above the main door which dominates the two side ones: what was otherwise but a hole for the daylight now echoes the nave of the church! How, high above, the belfry demands the smaller windows! All this was necessary, and I made it beautiful. But ah! if I float through the dark and lofty openings at the side that seem to stand empty and useless, in their strong slender form I have hidden the secret powers which should lift those two towers high in the air – of which, alas! only one stands mournfully there, without its intended decoration of pinnacles, so that the surrounding country would pay homage to it and its regal brother.'

143 FRANÇOIS RENÉ CHATEAUBRIAND
from *The Genius of Christianity* (1802)

S imilar to the impressions of Goethe, although founded on very different circumstances, were those of the Viscount de Chateaubriand, as published in his literary masterpiece *Génie du christianisme*. This son of a nobleman first studied for the priesthood, but then enlisted in the army. In the early 1790s he was in the United States planning a search for the northwest passage. The "Reign of Terror," in the meantime, had greatly affected his family. His brother lost his head on the guillotine; his wife, mother, two sisters were imprisoned. Chateaubriand thus spent the years 1794–9 in exile in London, but he returned to Paris with Napoleon's amnesty of 1800. The *Génie du christianisme* was largely written by this date, and it appeared in 1802 almost simultaneously with Napoleon's reestablishment of Catholicism in France. Chateaubriand's style is generally considered to be a transition from classicism to romanticism in France; it is a luxurious literary style composed with the eye of a painter and with an evident depth of poetic emotion. Again, it is one of the first attempts in France (outside of the earlier structural appreciation) to speak of Gothic architecture in a positive way, and – as with Goethe's essay – its full impact would manifest itself only some decades later. The chapter is a Romantic *tour-de-force*.

Gothic Churches

Every thing ought to be in its proper place. This is a truth become trite by repetition; but without its due observance there can be nothing perfect. The Greeks would not have been better pleased with an Egyptian temple at Athens than the Egyptians with a Greek temple at Memphis. These two monuments, by changing places; would have lost their principal beauty; that is to say, their relations with the institutions and habits of the people. This reflection is equally applicable to the ancient monuments of Christianity. It is even curious to remark how readily the poets and novelists of this infidel age, by a natural return toward the manners of our ancestors, introduce dungeons, spectres, castles, and Gothic churches, into their fictions, – so great is the charm of recollections associated with religion and the history of our country. Nations do not throw aside their ancient customs as people do their old clothes. Some part of them may be discarded; but there will remain a portion, which with the new manners will form a very strange mixture.

In vain would you build Grecian temples, ever so elegant and well-lighted, for the purpose of assembling the *good people* of St. Louis and Queen Blanche, and making them adore a *metaphysical God*; they would still regret those *Notre Dames* of Rheims and Paris, – those venerable cathedrals, overgrown with moss, full of generations of the dead and the ashes of their forefathers; they would still regret the tombs of those heroes, the Montmorencys, on which they loved to kneel during, mass, to say nothing of the sacred fonts to which they

François René Chateaubriand, from *Le génie du christianisme* (1802), trans. Charles I. White, in *The Genius of Christianity; or the Spirit and Beauty of the Christian Religion*. Baltimore: John Murphy, 1856, pp. 384–7.

were carried at their birth. The reason is that all these things are essentially interwoven with their manners; that a monument is not venerable, unless a long history of the past be, as it were, inscribed beneath its vaulted canopy, black with age. For this reason, also, there is nothing marvellous in a temple whose erection we have witnessed, whose echoes and whose domes were formed before our eyes. God is the eternal law; his origin, and whatever relates to his worship, ought to be enveloped in the night of time.

You could not enter a Gothic church without feeling a kind of awe and a vague sentiment of the Divinity. You were all at once carried back to those times when a fraternity of cenobites, after having meditated in the woods of their monasteries, met to prostrate themselves before the altar and to chant the praises of the Lord, amid the tranquillity and the silence of night. Ancient France seemed to revive altogether; you beheld all those singular costumes, all that nation so different from what it is at present; you were reminded of its revolutions, its productions, and its arts. The more remote were these times the more magical they appeared, the more they inspired ideas which always end with a reflection on the nothingness of man and the rapidity of life.

The Gothic style, notwithstanding its barbarous proportions, possesses a beauty peculiar to itself.[1]

The forests were the first temples of the Divinity, and in them men acquired the first idea of architecture. This art must, therefore, have varied according to climates. The Greeks turned the elegant Corinthian column, with its capital of foliage, after the model of the palm-tree.[2] The enormous pillars of the ancient Egyptian style represent the massive sycamore, the oriental fig, the banana, and most of the gigantic trees of Africa and Asia.

The forests of Gaul were, in their turn, introduced into the temples of our ancestors, and those celebrated woods of oaks thus maintained their sacred character. Those ceilings sculptured into foliage of different kinds, those buttresses which prop the walls and terminate abruptly like the broken trunks of trees, the coolness of the vaults, the darkness of the sanctuary, the dim twilight of the aisles, the secret passages, the low doorways, – in a word, every thing in a Gothic church reminds you of the labyrinths of a wood; every thing excites a feeling of religious awe, of mystery, and of the Divinity.

The two lofty towers erected at the entrance of the edifice overtop the elms and yew-trees of the churchyard, and produce the most picturesque effect on the azure of heaven. Sometimes their twin heads are illumined by the first rays of dawn; at others they appear crowned with a capital of clouds or magnified in a foggy atmosphere. The birds themselves seem to make a mistake in regard to them, and to take them for the trees of the forest; they hover over their summits, and perch upon their pinnacles. But, lo! confused noises suddenly issue from the top of these towers and scare away the affrighted birds. The Christian architect, not content with building forests, has been desirous to retain their murmurs; and, by means of the organ and of bells, he has attached to the Gothic temple the very winds and thunders that roar in the recesses of the woods. Past ages, conjured up by these religious sounds, raise their venerable voices from the bosom of the stones, and are heard in every corner of the vast cathedral. The sanctuary re-echoes like the cavern of the ancient Sibyl; loud-tongued bells swing over your head, while the vaults of death under your feet are profoundly silent.

NOTES

1 Gothic architecture, as well as the sculpture in the same style, is supposed to have been derived from the Arabs. Its affinity to the monuments of Egypt would rather lead us to imagine that it was transmitted to us by the first Christians of the East; but we are more inclined to refer its origin to nature.

2 Vitruvius gives a different account of the invention of the Corinthian capital; but this does not confute the general principle that architecture originated in the woods. We are only astonished that there should not be more variety in the column, after the varieties of trees. We have a conception, for example, of a column that might be termed *Palmist*, and be a natural representation of the palm-tree. An orb of foliage slightly bowed and sculptured on the top of a light shaft of marble would, in our opinion, produce a very pleasing effect in a portico.

144 FRIEDRICH VON SCHLEGEL
from *Notes on a Trip Through the Netherlands* (1806)

Among the best-known German Romantic writers to appear at around the turn of the nineteenth century was Friedrich Schlegel. Originally trained in law, Schlegel soon turned his attention to literary matters, and two of his early scholarly studies were devoted to Greece and Rome. But Schlegel also came to epitomize the German Romantic spirit. In 1799 he joined his brother August, a leading literary theorist and teacher, in Jena – a town that during this time counted among its faculty such great minds as the philosophers Friedrich von Schelling and G. W. F. Hegel. Friedrich Schlegel's own incendiary personality, however, was prone to controversy, and in 1802 the critic moved to Paris to edit the journal *Europa* and commence his Oriental studies. The French Revolution and its aftermath would also play heavily upon Schlegel's development. Napoleon would conquer and pillage most of the German lands, and this forced occupation naturally engendered a strong reaction of nationalism among the German-speaking populations.

In 1803 Schlegel, while still living in Paris, was visited by Sulpiz Boisserée, the foremost antiquarian of German Gothic architecture. Together, the two men undertook an extensive tour of the medieval buildings and art works in France, Flanders, the Rhineland, and Switzerland in 1804–5. Schlegel's nationalism is apparent in many of these descriptions, but his preference for calling Gothic architecture (by which he means both the Romanesque and Gothic styles) "German" or "Romantic" derives more from the belief that the Gothic style, like its name suggests, was Germanic in origin. This misconception was not unusual, as many British writers of this period also believed that the style had originated on their native soil. Nevertheless, Schlegel's very sympathetic description of Gothic works, such as of the spire at Cambrai (between Amiens and the Belgian border), would help to popularize the style with many of his contemporaries, who now longed to know their medieval past.

Friedrich von Schlegel (1772–1829), from *Briefen auf einer Reise durch die Niederlande, Rheingegenden, die Schweiz und einen Teil von Frankreich* [Notes on a trip through the Netherlands, the Rhine country, Switzerland, and a part of France] (1806), trans. E. J. Millington, in *The Aesthetic and Miscellaneous Works of Frederick von Schlegel*. London: H. G. Bohn, 1849, pp. 154–8.

The route from Paris to the Netherlands is monotonous, uncultivated, and little attractive; indeed, with the exception of the old provinces of Burgundy and Normandy, the interior of France is not particularly favoured by nature. We easily understand why her people have always aimed at foreign conquest; and, indeed, during the last century and a half, she has succeeded in annexing the most beautiful and cultivated portions of Europe to her territories. It seems, in fact, doubtful whether the soil in the old provinces, which would require the utmost diligence and labour for its proper cultivation, could produce sufficient to maintain a population, who have never deserved to be numbered among the most hard-working and industrious of mankind. The rapid increase of population, during the early part of French history, constrained that people to seek foreign possessions, like those innumerable hordes which migrate continually from the barren plains of central Asia, in search of more fertile regions.

In approaching Cambray, my eyes were long fixed upon a marvellous object, which I was able to follow along the windings of the road, for the space of half an hour. It was the spire of a Gothic tower, of such delicate tracery and openwork, as to appear transparent; it stands upon a hill, and is the sole remaining relic of the cathedral, which was purchased during the reign of terror as a national property, and paid for in assignats; the marble of the monuments and pavement must alone have more than repaid the cost of purchase.

Wonderful style of architecture! springing from the highest story of the tower, it seems to pierce the clouds like a transparent obelisk, or pyramid of open tracery! more pointed and slender than the one, it is less so than the other, and formed of slender shafts, clustering together, with various flowers and crockets, it terminates at length in a slender spire and finial.

The design of most Gothic towers is similar, although very few of them have ever been finished.

I have a decided predilection for the Gothic style of architecture; and when I am so fortunate as to discover any monument, however ruined or defaced, I examine every portion of it with unwearied zeal and attention, for it appears to me that from a neglect of such study the deep meaning and peculiar motive of Gothic architecture is seldom fully arrived at.

It unites an extreme delicacy and inconceivable skill in mechanical execution, with the grand, the boundless, and infinite, concentrated in the idea of an entire Gothic fabric; a rare and truly beautiful combination of contrasting elements, conceived by the power of human intellect, and aiming at faultless perfection in the minutest details, as well as in the lofty grandeur and comprehensiveness of the general design.

No art ought ever to be permitted to encroach upon its sister arts. The ancient classic monuments at Athens, Pæstum, and Girgenti would undoubtedly, if seen in their native clime, excite feelings of veneration, in the same manner as the feeble designs and gigantic works of Egyptian, Persian, or Indian antiquity inspire wonder and astonishment. But what with us is usually styled Grecian art is merely a copy, a soulless imitation of the period when Greek art was in its decline, and an agreeable but most unmeaning symmetry had replaced that grandeur of soul and expression which had too long been lost.

The Gothic may possibly be styled in the next work on architecture the German style, from its having been common among all the nations of ancient Germany, and the grandest, heretofore called Gothic, edifices in Italy, France, and even in Spain, being also the work of German architects. This old Teutonic architecture certainly requires some effort of the mind to penetrate its unfathomable obscurity. It flourished most in the Netherlands, and appears to have attained there its highest perfection, scarcely a town in Brabant being without one or more remarkable monuments of that art.

However, the general title of "Gothic Architecture," if that great national name be taken in its widest sense, for the old Christian and romantic style of the middle ages, from Theodoric down to the present time, is decidedly the most appropriate, and must ever be retained. I may remark also that the apparently arbitrary epithet of Romantic, applied to Mediæval poetry, so completely expresses the prevalence of fancy in that art, that it seems impossible to exchange it for any other term equally significant and appropriate.

The Burgundians, Vandals, and some portion of the people of the Netherlands, having been originally Gothic tribes, that people may be considered founders of the Christian kingdoms of France, southern Germany, Italy, and Spain; whence, extending to the Scandinavian north, they took root in, and exercised dominion over, the whole of the south of Russia, and the countries of Poland and Hungary. The term Gothic is, therefore, historically appropriate to that collective body of all nations who derive their origin from the same root as the Dutch and Germans. The Goths brought into Europe that overwhelming influx of German people and German ideas with which the history and social customs of the west, as well as the taste and style of its poetry, have ever since remained strongly imbued.

The objections urged by some few critics to the use of the term Gothic, arise from an imperfect comprehension of its grand and universal signification. It may be possible to discover and explain the influence exercised by German genius on the works of other countries, but we cannot possibly call a style of architecture, which flourished throughout all the lands once possessed by the Goths, from the most extreme east to the farthest west of Christendom, the German, as this exclusive epithet would only apply to that German fatherland which has been separated from the other states since the time of King Conrad, and would confine the term to boundaries much too limited; or, on the other hand, to call this peculiar style of architecture the Teutonic, would lead us too far back into antiquity, yet obscure as regards the art.

The terms "Old Saxon," and "Decorated Norman," seem very appropriately employed in England, as they indicate two grand epochs of the international history of that country, but they are not equally well suited to the rest of Europe. Old Saxon may, indeed, be applicable to Germany, in which country the rise of this peculiar style may be referred to the time of the old Saxon emperors; and also because Cologne, in which the most magnificent works of this as well as of a later period are to be found, was one of the most important towns of old Saxony. Still the epithet is too confined to apply to the whole Christian west comprehended under the Roman dynasty, and the greater part of which became German through the Gothic conquests.

No particular examples are needed in support of the assertion, that the first rude elements of Christian architecture were of Greek or Roman origin. Still that redundant and vigorous fancy, which constituted the peculiar charm of Christian ecclesiastical architecture, is unquestionably Gothic.

The rise of this principle, founded on a peculiar sentiment of nature pervading both architecture and all other imitative arts, is first found among the Goths, and from them it spread gradually on all sides, its progress and dominion being sufficiently attested by the architectural remains at Ravenna and elsewhere. Of the two epochs of Gothic art, one may properly be called early Christian, on account of the religious ideas therein developed; and the second, termed by the English Decorated Norman, I should rather style Romantic, because every element of vigorous architectural fancy then first received its full development.

145 JOSEPH GÖRRES
from "The Cathedral in Cologne" (1814)

The combative journalist and writer Joseph Görres was a man of many causes. As a youth he was a supporter of the French Revolution, but then became disenchanted with the French following their occupation of the west bank of the Rhine in 1794, even more so with Napoleon's creation of the Confederation of the Rhine in 1806 (incorporating much of western and southern Germany in France). The years 1813–15, however, changed everything. On the heels of the Emperor's crushing defeat at Leipzig in October 1813, Napoleon began a retreat that – with his abdication – would eventually take him to the island of Elba. The Congress of Vienna opened in September 1814, where the issue of a national German "Confederation" of states – addressed here by Görres – was first proposed by the European powers as a hedge against French aggression. Napoleon's escape from Elba in March 1815 complicated political matters, and, following Waterloo, the Congress of Vienna eventually decided to place Catholic Rhineland under the administrative control of Lutheran Prussia. Görres thus became an ardent supporter of Rhinish autonomy and religious freedom.

Central to Catholic Rhineland was the unfinished Cologne Cathedral. The massive Gothic structure (second only to Milan Cathedral in size) had been started in 1248, largely on the model of Amiens, and the eastern choir was roofed in 1322. Work on other parts of the church lagged, however, and was suspended in 1560 with only one western tower less than half finished. When the French occupied the city in 1794 they turned the enclosed choir into a warehouse and ransacked the city of most of its artistic treasures. With Napoleon's defeat, the unfinished cathedral thus became a symbol of German occupation and political liberation. This event coincided with the discovery in 1814 by Georg Moller of a partial drawing of the west elevation (it had been stored in a Cologne archive but removed by the French to a barn in Darmstadt). When Sulpiz Boisserée shortly thereafter found the other half of the drawing in a Paris art shop, the complete design intensified national feelings toward resuming work on the cathedral. Görres and Boisserée would lead the crusade for completing the monument, although it would take several decades to be successful. It was not until 1842, in fact, that work on the cathedral did resume.

There is much public debate today on how large memorials should be erected to the time. The colossal column should be roused from its thousand-year rest and be transplanted to the battlefield on the Elbe. Solemn temples should be raised there, large waterways should be cut through Germany, and the Rhine River should entertain statues and columns on all of its islands. The impulse is good and the intention praiseworthy, but if we were to pool our meager resources to carry it out then in the end we will have once again only imitated the

Joseph Görres (1776–1848), from "Der Dom in Köln" [The cathedral at Cologne] (1814), trans. Harry Francis Mallgrave from the *Rheinischer Merker*, 151 (Nov. 20, 1814), pp. 125–7.

French, as we also unconsciously did when we recently renamed the squares of our cities in our best desire to honor our great men. If we are to act as Germans, then we should first direct the force that in vain might be spent on external matters back toward ourselves. Let the idea within us shine more and more on our inward selves and warm us. Let us bring the lamp of one to the other, so that it might also illuminate it. Let us shape ourselves like the artist shapes bronze and stone. And if we then shape ourselves correctly and close ranks under one will, then our people themselves will become a shining commemorative column, where as yet none in history has stood. If the inner self only claims its due, then it may in part direct itself to exterior matters, and life can happily manifest itself in forms and images playfully taken from nature, whereas now it must still anxiously and slavishly struggle after them. Best of all, however, we can then turn to the past, not to satisfy our vanity, but to complete and perfect what the past – because of the all-too-powerful immensity of the idea – left incomplete. We will then regard the past as a sacred legacy passed down to later generations to complete.

Such a legacy is the Cathedral in Cologne. And if German honor once again rears up within us, we could not honorably find a more splendid work to begin, that is, until we bring it to its end and completely finish the building. The idea of the master sadly hovers over this cathedral; he laments it from heaven. But every generation has the body of its unfilled past, and thus it hovers, half spirit and half incarnate, like the dead or unborn around a powerful mass; the body cannot dissolve itself and return, or even give birth, and thus it endures a thousand-year sojourn on earth. Like an eternal reproach, the building stands before us and the artist is resentful for the fact that so many lifetimes could not bring to realization the ideas that he alone, a weak mortal man, nurtured in his spirit. A curse was even placed on it when the workmen abandoned it, allowing the angry spirit to take refuge in it. So long has Germany lived in shame and humiliation, the price of our own discord and peculiar arrogance; it will remain so until our people return to the idea that we renounced in chasing after selfishness, and until we, with a true fear of God, again become fit in a genuinely true sense, with the unified spirit and modest self-denial needed to be able to execute such works and . . . to realize what a generation, which we again want to be like, had begun. Certainly Kotzebue, Weinbrenner, Wiebeking, and others who have occupied themselves with making plans for memorials will not devise something more beautiful, more proper, and more glorious than this most artistic and most simple cathedral that stands before us. In its deteriorating state of incompletion, in its abandonment, it has become a symbol of Germany after the confusion of tongues and ideas. It will therefore also become a symbol of the new Reich that we will build. The period of anarchy that lay between the break and the resumption will be looked upon as if no harm took place, and we will begin in fact again with the image of where it was when the last of the good times left off. It is like a solemn vow of the father that we are obliged to carry out. If the forces of Germany join together for its completion then we can easily bring to a conclusion what would far exceed the severest efforts of a city or a province. We should not blithely and cheerfully assume the task, like an object of idle chatter, as we have become accustomed with such things up to now; no, we should seriously reflect on the time and resources needed, and then, when the execution is assured, strive assiduously to bring it to completion. It is not the work of a single generation, nor can it display a sense of poverty. Therefore we hereby present the proposal only to stimulate debate and recommend the project for the future deliberation of the nation.

146 GEORG MOLLER
from *Monuments of German Architecture* (1815–21)

ollowing his discovery of the partial west elevation of the Cologne Cathedral in 1814, Moller quickly established his credibility on another level in the following year – by publishing the first volume of his historical investigation of medieval architecture. The publication of the *Denkmähler* is important on several counts. Moller, to begin with, was an architect trained under the classicist Friedrich Weinbrenner in Karlsruhe, and his two major commissions of the 1820s (the Ludwigskirche in Darmstadt and the Theater in Mainz) are, respectively, classical and Renaissance in their formal vocabulary. His interest in Gothic architecture was thus primarily that of a historian, and indeed he does not advocate building in this style but rather understanding the nuances of its origin and development. And even though his book was focused almost entirely on German medieval works, he does speak of Gothic works in France and England, and therefore is one of the first individuals to see the Gothic style as an international phenomenon maturing almost simultaneously across northern Europe in the thirteenth century. It is perhaps for this reason that his discussion of the origin of the Gothic style was first translated into English in 1824, and his larger book in 1836 – thus making Moller's study highly influential in England. Moller still sees the Gothic style as primarily a German creation, but at the same time he is rightly dubious of almost all prior historical speculation regarding the style and its dating, and argues that historians must be very scrupulous in this regard. His book thus stands at the beginning of the long line of works devoted to Gothic architecture over the next several decades.

In order to judge correctly of the internal credibility of statements concerning the history of architecture, the buildings to which they refer must not be considered singly, but in connexion with earlier, contemporary, and later works. But above all, the history of the art is never to be separated from the history of the nation, whose fate it shares alike in its progress and in its decay. Architecture, whose application, more than that of any other art, depends on outward contingencies, developes itself but slowly and gradually. The creations of the greatest genius are constantly modified by the influence of the time to which he belongs, so that the best and most perfect work can be considered only as the result of the progressive improvement of several generations; and an accurate comparison of a series of architectural works combined with a diligent study of history, points out the only safe road on which the development of the different styles of architecture is to be pursued. After the principal periods of the improvement of the art have thus been carefully and critically fixed, a proper place is more easily assigned to some special, though anomalous works.

With regard to the names of the several styles of architecture which appeared in Europe after the decay of Roman architecture, and continued till the sixteenth century, when they were superseded by the modern Greco-Roman art, they were all for a long time comprised under the general name of Gothic architecture. This epithet was afterwards applied to the pointed arch style, which predominated in the thirteenth century. At present it is well known

Georg Moller (1784–1852), from *Denkmähler der deutschen Baukunst* [Monuments of German architecture] (1815–21), trans. W. H. Leeds, in *Moller's Memorials of German-Gothic Architecture*. London: John Weale, 1836, pp. 5–7.

that the appellation of Gothic architecture is not a suitable one: but as those of Byzantine, Saxon, and German architecture, by which it has been attempted to supersede it, are neither generally received, nor sufficiently distinct, I shall content myself with designating the different styles of architecture by the century and the country in which they flourished. In respect, however, of the question, to whom the merit of the invention and of the improvement of the art is to be ascribed, the following more architectural than historical observations may perhaps be of some importance in the inquiry.

The forms of buildings are far from being arbitrary and accidental in their origin. The climate, the building materials, and the character of the nation, exercise a very essential influence on them, and cause those diversified appearances which vary as much as the physiognomy of countries and the situation of nations. Whatever is produced by these causes is singular in its kind, and in harmony with itself. Every species of architecture, on the contrary, which, owing its origin to foreign nations, to a different climate and different circumstances, is transferred to other people and other countries, retains the character of unsuitableness and unconnectedness, until some artist of eminent talents successfully appropriates it to his own use, and forms out of it a new, national, and consistent style of building. If this be admitted, that nation undoubtedly has the merit of a particular style of architecture, whose edifices –

1. *Correspond with the climate, with the style of construction adapted to the materials, and with the sentiments and manners of the nation and of the times*; and

2. *Constitute in their principal forms, and in their several parts and ornaments, a whole in harmony with itself, which excludes or rejects every thing foreign and unsuitable.*

These principles, which, without a view to any particular school, may be applied alike in forming a judgment of the works of all ages and all nations, are a sure guard against any partial over or under-rating, and will hereafter serve to regulate our examination of the several hypotheses concerning the architecture of the middle age.

147   THOMAS RICKMAN
from *An Attempt to Discriminate the Styles of English Architecture* (1817)

Almost simultaneous with the historical efforts of Moller was the work of the British architect Thomas Rickman. A man of many professional starts and fits, Rickman first worked as a chemist, physician, businessman, and insurance broker before turning his attention to architecture in 1812. Following the creation of the Church Building Commission in 1818, his talents as a designer of Gothic churches would be much in demand, but his essential historical contribution to the Gothic Revival lies elsewhere. It first takes the form of a

Thomas Rickman (1776–1841) from *An Attempt to Discriminate the Styles of English Architecture from the Conquest to the Reformation.* London: Longman, Hurst, Rees, Orme, and Brown, 1817, pp. 37–9.

paper he published in 1815, in which he defined three stylistic phases for English (Romanesque and Gothic) architecture: Early English (until 1189), Decorated (until 1377), and Perpendicular (until 1640). Two years later he expanded the paper into a small textbook (now naming the Norman style as the Romanesque phase of English architecture); the textbook would go through various editions and promulgate his stylistic distinctions as the accepted nomenclature in Britain. As the following excerpt shows, Rickman accepts the Gothic style as largely (but not solely) a national creation of the English; at the same time he, like his German counterpart, was also careful to point out the national variations of this style in each country and therefore the unique aspects of "English Architecture" over the Gothic style in other lands.

English Architecture

In a work like the present, there will be little propriety in a lengthened disquisition on the origin of this mode of building; we shall therefore proceed to the detail of those distinctions, which, being once laid down with precision, will enable persons of common observation to distinguish the difference of age and style in these buildings, as easily as the distinctions of the Grecian and Roman orders.

It may, however, be proper here to offer a few remarks on the use of the term English, as applied to that mode of building usually called the Gothic, and by some the pointed architecture. Although, perhaps, it might not be so difficult as it has been supposed to be, to show that the English architects were, in many instances, prior to their continental neighbours, in those advances of the styles about which so much has been written, and so little concluded; it is not on that ground the term is now used, but because, as far as the author has been able to collect from plates, and many friends who have visited the Continent, in the edifices there, (more especially in those parts which have not been at any time under the power of England,) the architecture is of a very different character from that pure simplicity and boldness of composition which marks the English buildings. In every instance which has come under the author's notice, a mixture, more or less exact or remote, according to circumstances, of Italian composition, in some parts or other, is present; and he has little doubt that a *very* attentive observation of the continental buildings called Gothic, would enable an architect to lay down the regulations of French, Flemish, Spanish, German, and Italian styles, which were in use at the time when the English flourished in England.

On the origin of the pointed arch, about which, perhaps, there may be now more curiosity than ever, from the numerous accounts given by travellers of apparently very ancient pointed arches in Asia, Africa, and various parts of the Continent; it will, doubtless, be expected that something should be said; and what is necessary may be said in a few lines. To say nothing on the impossibility, as far as at present appears, of fixing an *authentic* date to those, which if dated, might be of the most importance, there appears little difficulty in solving the problem, if the practical part of building is considered at the same time with the theoretical. Intersecting arches were most likely an early, and certainly a very widely-spread mode of embellishing Norman buildings, and some of them were constructed in places, and with stones, requiring centres to turn them on, and the construction of these centres must have been by something equivalent to compasses: thus, even supposing (which could hardly have been the case) that the arches were constructed without a previous delineation, the centres would have led to the construction of the pointed arch; and when once formed, its superior lightness and applicability would be easily observed. To this remark it may be added, that the arches necessarily arising in some parts from Norman groining would be pointed. – A careful examination of a great number of Norman buildings will also lead to this conclusion – that the style was constantly assuming a lighter character, and that the gradation is so gentle into Early English, that it is difficult, in some buildings, to class them, so much have they of both styles: the same may be said of every advance; and this seems to be a convincing proof that the styles were the product of the gradual operations of a general improvement, guided by the hand of genius, and not a foreign importation.

During the eighteenth century, various attempts, under the name of Gothic, have arisen in repairs and rebuilding ecclesiastical edifices, but these have been little more than making clustered columns and pointed windows, every real principle of English architecture being, by the builders, either unknown or totally neglected.

English architecture, may be divided into four distinct periods, or styles, which may be named,

1st, the Norman style,

2nd, the Early English style,

3rd, the Decorated English style, and

4th, the Perpendicular English style.

The dates of these styles we shall state hereafter, and it may be proper to notice, that the clear distinctions are now almost entirely confined to churches; for the destruction and alteration of castellated buildings have been so great, from the changes in the modes of warfare, &c. that, in them, we can scarcely determine what is original and what addition.

148   WILLIAM WHEWELL
from *Architectural Notes on German Churches* (1830)

I f Rickman set an early standard for Gothic scholarship in Britain, the critical expectation was considerably raised and refined by this impressive study of William Whewell – a mathematician and minister, professor of mineralogy and moral philosophy, and in 1841 Master of Trinity College in Cambridge. A friend of Rickman, Whewell had traveled with him to France and Germany in 1829, the trip from which much of this scholarship derives. But Whewell's outlook is at the same time fresh and innovative. For one thing, the fact that a historian of one country is studying in depth the architecture of another lends an air of critical detachment, apart from the nationalist sentiments so evident in earlier studies. For another thing, Whewell – although examining close to 100 churches – focused his analytical energies on the late-Romanesque and early-Gothic styles in Germany, specifically on what took place in the pivotal transition between the two styles. In addition, the historian Nikolaus Pevsner has

William Whewell (1794–1866), from *Architectural Notes on German Churches; with Notes Written during an Architectural Tour in Picardy and Normandy* (1830). Cambridge: J. and J. J. Deighton and London: John W. Parker, 1842 (third edition), pp. 47–52.

credited Whewell with being "the first ever to establish the autonomy of criteria of style for the dating of architecture — *Stilkritik*, as German art historians were to call it much later."

Whewell — as his distinction between the Romanesque and Gothic styles makes clear — was a man capable of both generalist and specialist reasoning. If he was not the first historian to note that the principal distinction between the two styles lay in the "mode of VAULTING," he was indeed the first to recognize that this distinction was not a chance discovery or imported device but the logical solution to a spatial and mathematical problem that brought with it a whole range of formal changes: from Gothic verticality to the angling of the moldings and the use of pinnacles at the top. Hence the transition represented a profound stylistic change.

Of the Romanesque and Gothic Styles

The ancient churches of Europe offer to us two styles of architecture, between which, when we consider them in their complete development, the difference is very strongly marked.

During the first thousand years of the Christian period, religious edifices were built in the *former* of these two styles. Its characters are a more or less close imitation of the features of Roman architecture. The arches are round; are supported on pillars retaining traces of the classical proportions; the pilasters, cornices and entablatures have a correspondence and similarity with those of classical architecture; there is a prevalence of rectangular faces and square-edged projections; the openings in walls are small, and subordinate to the surfaces in which they occur; the members of the architecture are massive and heavy; very limited in kind and repetition; the enrichments being introduced rather by sculpturing surfaces, than by multiplying and extending the component parts. There is in this style a predominance of *horizontal* lines, or at least no predominance and prolongation of vertical ones. For instance, the pillars are not prolonged in corresponding mouldings along the arches; the walls have no prominent buttresses, and are generally terminated by a strong horizontal tablet or cornice. This style may conveniently be designated by the term ROMANESQUE. The appellation has been proposed by Mr Gunn, as implying a corrupted imitation of the Roman architecture: and though the etymological analogy according to which the word is formed, is perhaps not one of extensive prevalence, the expression seems less liable to objection than any other which has been used, and has the advantage of a close correspondence with the word *Romane*, which has of late been commonly employed by the French antiquarians to express the same style. This same kind of architecture, or perhaps particular modifications of it, have been by various persons termed Saxon, Norman, Lombard, Byzantine, &c. All these names imply suppositions with regard to the history of this architecture which it might be difficult to substantiate; and would, moreover, in most cases not be understood to describe the style in that generality which we learn to attribute to it, by finding it, with some variations according to time and place, diffused over the whole face of Europe.

The *second* style of which we have spoken, made its appearance in the early centuries of the second thousand years of the Christian world. It is characterized by the pointed arch; by pillars which are extended so as to lose all trace of classical proportions; by shafts which are placed side by side, often with different thicknesses, and are variously clustered and combined. Its mouldings, cornices and capitals, have no longer the classical shapes and members; square edges, rectangular surfaces, pilasters, and entablatures disappear; the elements of building become slender, detached, repeated and multiplied; they assume forms implying flexure and ramification. The openings become the principal part of the wall, and the other portions are subordinate to these. The universal tendency is to the predominance and prolongation of *vertical* lines; for instance, in the interior, by continuing the shafts in the arch-mouldings; on the exterior, by employing buttresses of strong projection, which shoot upwards through the line of parapet, and terminate in pinnacles.

All over Europe this style is commonly termed GOTHIC; and though the name has often been objected to, it seems to be not only convenient from being so well understood, but also by no means inappropriate with regard to the associations which it implies. That the Goths as a particular people had nothing to do with the establishment of the style in question, is so generally notorious, that there can be no fear of any one being, in that respect, misled by the term. The notion which suggested the use of the word was manifestly the perception, that the style under consideration was a complete deviation from, and contrast to, the whole principle and spirit of Roman architecture; and that this innovation and antithesis were connected with the course which taste and art took among the nations who overthrew the Roman empire, and established themselves on its ruins. And this is so far a true feeling of the origin and character of the new architecture, that we may consent to accept the word by which it has been thus designated, without being disturbed by the reflexion that those who first imposed this name, considered it as conveying the reproach of barbarism. We, indeed, should take a very different view from theirs of the merit and beauty of the new style. We should maintain, that in adopting forms and laws which are the reverse of the ancient ones, it introduced new principles as fixed and true, as full of unity and harmony, as those of the previous system; that these principles were applied with as extensive a command of science and skill, as great a power of overcoming the difficulties and effecting the ends of the art, as had ever been attained by Greek or Roman artists; and that they gave birth to monuments as striking, of as august and elevated a character, as any of which we can trace the existence in the ancient world. Our present business however is not with the merits, but the history, of the art.

The question of the causes of the transition from one of these styles to the other has been much agitated during the last half century. In the course of these discussions "the origin of the pointed arch" has generally been put forwards as the most important branch of the enquiry; a natural result of the common disposition to reduce a problem to the most definite and simple form. This is however an imperfect statement of the real question; for the pointed arch, far from being the single novelty in that change in architecture to which reference is made, is but one among a vast number of peculiarities which, taken altogether, make up the newer style: and this style would continue to exhibit a contrast with the one which preceded it, even if the round arch were used instead of the pointed one, as in some instances is actually the case.

Still, however, if we could shew with probability the reason which produced the prevalence of the pointed arch, this would be an important step in the history of the architectural revolution, and might throw much light on other parts of this history. Now we can point out a cause, which not only might possibly, but which must almost necessarily, have given rise to the general use of such arches; and it is one object of this Essay to illustrate this necessity, and the manner in which it affected ecclesiastical buildings.

The cause to which I refer, is the mode of VAULTING churches; and the instances in which I have been enabled to trace its operation, are the churches in the neighbourhood of the Rhine principally, and also in some other parts of the Continent.

149   ROBERT WILLIS
from *Remarks on the Architecture of the Middle Ages* (1835)

I n 1831 the German art historian Karl Friedrich Rumohr (1785–1843) published a little-known but remarkable essay "Über den gemeinschaftlichen Ursprung der Bauschulen des Mittelalters" (On the common origin of the building schools of the Middle Ages). Its leading thesis was that the Gothic style had developed organically out of Greco-Roman techniques of vaulting, as practiced by the early Christian and Byzantine schools of the western (northern Italian) and eastern Roman empires. The novelty of Rumohr's contention can be measured by this book of Robert Willis, which, while accepting a degree of historical continuity, takes a somewhat different view regarding the formal innovations of the northern Gothic style.

Willis was a friend and younger colleague of Whewell at Cambridge University. His tour of Gothic works in Germany, France, and Italy was undertaken in 1832–3. Like his mentor, he too viewed the Gothic style largely through its vaulting techniques, and in fact Gothic's structural innovations were the subject of several of his essays of the 1840s. But this book of 1835 underscores an interesting dilemma taking shape within the Gothic Revival movement. On the one hand Willis presumes the vast superiority of the northern Gothic style over that of the Italian south (and thus is apologetic about his choice of subject); on the other hand his expansion of historical interest into medieval Italy raises the interesting issue of just what were the connections of Gothic vaulting techniques with the Romanesque and pre-Romanesque building traditions of the south. Willis here tends to minimize the connections, while other historians will shortly study the matter more closely and underscore the continuity of structural development.

What style however would have eventually resulted from this conflict, had the empire retained its flourishing condition and the arts their perfection, it is impossible to say. The Romans were making rapid strides in the art of vaulting when the removal of the seat of empire to Constantinople, and with it of the best artists of all classes, appears to have also transplanted this growing art to the soil of the East. The latest vaulted hall in Rome is the so called Temple of Peace, now held by the Italian antiquaries to be a Basilica erected by Constantine. In the East, vaulting on a large scale continued to be practised, and received the improvement of suspending a dome over a square by means of pendentives, of which St Sophia at Constantinople is the great specimen. This *Byzantine* style, so regularly derived from the Roman, was brought back to the West, first to Ravenna by the exarchs, and afterwards by the Venetians in the eleventh century, as exemplified in St Marc and other buildings of their district.

Robert Willis (1792–1874), from *Remarks on the Architecture of the Middle Ages, Especially of Italy* (1835). Cambridge: Pitt Press, 1835, pp. 18–21.

In the meantime the great Christian churches erected at Rome, under the patronage of Constantine and his successors, shew but too plainly the deplorable state of architecture in the West. They are to be sure large and lofty, but consist of parallel ranges of columns, of different orders, adapted without skill from the destroyed temples, and sustaining upon arches, walls of disproportionate height, covered with open wooden roofs; the whole bearing every mark of ignorance and neglect of rules.

In the districts remote from Rome another process of architectural change was going on. Here the ravages of the Barbarians swept away the ancient rules altogether, and left only the shattered examples; and here we find that after they had settled themselves in their conquests, their builders, working as unschooled imitators, copied the construction of these ruins, and employed their materials, using the fragments of decoration, but naturally placing them so as to be entirely subservient to the actual construction of the building. Where new ornaments were required they imitated the old ones or invented others.

In this way were formed the various styles of the ages preceding the eleventh century, the German and French Romanesque, the Lombard, Saxon, Norman, Saracen and others, all of which have features differing entirely from those by which the Byzantine and Christian Roman are separated from their common origin, and all exhibit more or less of a barbarous and rude character.

They constitute however so many different and independent sources from which may be traced the formation of the Gothic, some supplying one feature and some another, while others, after enduring many transitions, were entirely superseded by the introduction of some descendant of the first.

It will be seen that I have supposed two ways in which these architectural sources were produced; one by regular transition from the antique, as the Byzantine and Christian Roman, to which may be added the Pisan; the other by imitation, as in the Barbarian inventions. But although each style has many distinct features, they have others in common which may easily be accounted for by the universality of the church, in which it was not unusual for her ministers to be also her architects. It is probable that most of the cases in which new styles or decorations are brought into a country, may be traced either to the introduction of foreign priests, or to the pilgrimages of the native ones.

In tracing architecture from these sources, we soon find it throwing off its barbarous characters; the arch and vault no longer trammelled by an incompatible system of decoration, but favoured by more tractable forms, are only limited by the skill of the builders, and at length a new decorative construction is matured; again, with admirable ingenuity separating itself from the mechanical construction, but not, as at first, thwarting and controlling it, but assisting and harmonizing with it; this is in the complete Gothic style.

This style is remarkable for the skill with which all the ornamental parts are made to enter into the apparent construction. Every member, may, almost every moulding is a sustainer of weight, and it is by this multiplicity of props assisting each other, and the consequent subdivision of weight, that the eye becomes satisfied of the stability of the building, notwithstanding their slender proportions. Add to this, that the greatest pains are bestowed in giving apparent lightness to the weight sustained, while in the mechanical construction, no less practical knowledge is displayed in proportioning props to pressures. To appreciate this, it is only necessary to compare the Roman vaulted halls with the Gothic cathedrals.

Whilst, however, this style was maturing itself on the north of the Alps, the great and increasing influence of the schools of art at Pisa appears to have prevented its adoption in Italy in its genuine form. They borrowed its ornamental characteristics, but gave it a fashion and proportions of their own, more nearly agreeing with those Greek notions of art which they seem never to have forgotten.

They succeeded, however, in forming a style which I shall call Italian Gothic, of which the best specimens are those of Tuscany, especially of Florence; this arose at the end of the thirteenth century, about the same period at which the Decorated style was introduced into our own country.

150   A. W. N. PUGIN
from *Contrasts* (1836)

Within the Gothic Revival movement in Britain, we have thus far seen two distinct phases. The first was a growing fascination with Gothic forms primarily as a novelty, an interest initially connected with the development of picturesque aesthetics. Second there was a focus on Gothic architecture as a historical phenomenon, as a resurrection of some important part of the European heritage. By the middle of the 1830s the Gothic Revival in Britain enters a third and well-defined phase, in which the style now becomes openly embraced for its relevance to contemporary practice. Two milestones of 1836 define the start of this phase. One is Charles Barry's competition-winning Gothic design for the Palace of Westminster and the Houses of Parliament – emphasizing the medieval roots of the British government. The second is this short polemical book by Augustus Welby Pugin, whose name will shortly become synonymous with the Gothic Revival in Britain.

A. W. N. Pugin was the son of Augustus Charles Pugin, a French émigré of 1792 and the respected author of *Specimens of Gothic Architecture* (1821–3), consisting of carefully drawn details of Gothic buildings. The elder Pugin had worked with the publisher and illustrator John Britton (himself an author of many visual studies of British antiquities) and also with the architect John Nash. The younger Pugin was thus initiated early both into architecture and into the nuances of the Gothic style; he also combined this architectural training and historical interest with a brilliant but fragile mind, and with an extreme penchant for work that no doubt contributed to his early death. In his teens the younger Pugin designed furniture and composed stage scenery. At 17 he began an apprenticeship with the architect Gillespie Graham, and at the age of 22 he published his first book on Gothic ecclesiastical designs. With the death of his father in 1832, he also took over the production of the second volume of *Examples of Gothic Architecture* (1836). In that year he was asked by Barry to serve as a design consultant on the design of the Houses of Parliament. Also in the same year Pugin published the first of his polemical works, *Contrasts: or, A Parallel between the Noble Edifices of the Middle Ages, and Corresponding Buildings of the Present Day; Shewing the Present Decay of Taste.*

Crucial to Pugin's outlook was his conversion to Catholicism in 1835. The theme of this study is thus exceedingly simple. Britain should return to the use of the Gothic style for reasons of climate and customs, but most especially for its association with the principles of Catholic Christianity. The theme is articulated in words, but even more

Augustus Welby Northmore Pugin (1812–52), from *Contrasts: or, A Parallel between the Noble Edifices of the Middle Ages, and Corresponding Buildings of the Present Day; Shewing the Present Decay of Taste* (1836). Leicester: Leicester University Press, 1973 (facsimile edition), pp. 1–3.

effectively in the book's plates, where fancied and pious images of Gothic medieval works are contrasted with the "pagan" inferior styles of modern times – thus equating the perceived decline in Christian morality in Pugin's day with the secular pulse of the industrial age. The book is not polite toward the leading architects of the day, in that such classical architects as William Wilkins, John Smirke, John Nash, and John Soane are irreverently satirized. It is however a polemical masterpiece – not just for its exaggeration but also for Pugin's desire to frame the return to Gothic style strictly for its presumed morality.

On the Feelings which Produced the Great Edifices of the Middle Ages

On comparing the Architectural Works of the last three Centuries with those of the Middle Ages, the wonderful superiority of the latter must strike every attentive observer; and the mind is naturally led to reflect on the causes which have wrought this mighty change, and to endeavour to trace the fall of Architectural taste, from the period of its first decline to the present day; and this will form the subject of the following pages.

It will be readily admitted, that the great test of Architectural beauty is the fitness of the design to the purpose for which it is intended, and that the style of a building should so correspond with its use that the spectator may at once perceive the purpose for which it was erected.

Acting on this principle, different nations have given birth to so many various styles of Architecture, each suited to their climate, customs, and religion; and as it is among edifices of this latter class that we look for the most splendid and lasting monuments, there can be little doubt that the religious ideas and ceremonies of these different people had by far the greatest influence in the formation of their various styles of Architecture.

The more closely we compare the temples of the Pagan nations with their religious rites and mythologies, the more shall we be satisfied with the truth of this assertion.

In them every ornament, every detail had a mystical import. The pyramid and obelisk of Egyptian Architecture, its Lotus capitals, its gigantic sphynxes and multiplied hieroglyphics, were not mere fanciful Architectural combinations and ornaments, but emblems of the philosophy and mythology of that nation.

In classic Architecture again, not only were the forms of the temples dedicated to different deities varied, but certain capitals and orders of Architecture were peculiar to each; and the very foliage ornaments of the friezes were symbolic. The same principle, of Architecture resulting from religious belief, may be traced from the caverns of Elora, to the Druidical remains of Stonehenge and Avebury; and in all these works of Pagan antiquity, we shall invariably find that both the plan and decoration of the building is mystical and emblematic.

And is it to be supposed that Christianity alone, with its sublime truths, with its stupendous mysteries, should be deficient in this respect, and not possess a symbolical architecture for her temples which would embody her doctrines and instruct her children? surely not, – nor is it so: from Christianity has arisen an architecture so glorious, so sublime, so perfect, that all the productions of ancient paganism sink, when compared before it, to a level with the false and corrupt systems from which they originated.

Pointed or Christian Architecture has far higher claims on our admiration than mere beauty or antiquity; the former may be regarded as a matter of opinion, – the latter, in the abstract, is no proof of excellence, but in it alone we find *the faith of Christianity embodied, and its practices illustrated.*

151 A. W. N. PUGIN
from *The True Principles of Pointed or Christian Architecture* (1841)

Five years after the appearance of *Contrasts*, Pugin published a book that expanded his campaign in favor of Gothic architecture on functional grounds. As with his earlier book, his principal argument is expressly and succinctly stated in the opening paragraphs of the book, but these "two great rules for design" should now be seen in a broader context. In their phrasing they do not particularly apply to Gothic architecture; in fact, it has long been noted that they come out of the French academic tradition, which Pugin knew well through readings from his French father's library. But within the context of the 1840s in Britain, they constitute what might be viewed as the first volley for reform within the British decorative arts. Pugin, in fact, pursues these rules over many pages by cautioning the designer, for instance, against employing three-dimensional patterns on wallpapers or carpets, or against emulating Gothic forms for products "produced from those inexhaustible mines of bad taste, Birmingham and Sheffield." In these principles, therefore, lies Pugin's great contribution to British theory – a contribution that would become more evident a decade later with the writings of John Ruskin and the criticisms surrounding the Great London Exhibition of 1851 (see part VI).

The object of the present Lecture is to set forth and explain the true principles of Pointed or Christian Architecture, by the knowledge of which you may be enabled to test architectural excellence. The two great rules for design are these: 1*st, that there should be no features about a building which are not necessary for convenience, construction, or propriety; 2nd, that all ornament should consist of enrichment of the essential construction of the building.* The neglect of these two rules is the cause of all the bad architecture of the present time. Architectural features are continually tacked on buildings with which they have no connexion, merely for the sake of what is termed effect; and ornaments are *actually constructed*, instead of forming the decoration of *construction*, to which in good taste they should be always subservient.

In pure architecture the smallest detail should *have a meaning or serve a purpose;* and even the construction itself *should vary with the material employed*, and the designs should be adapted to the material in which they are executed.

Strange as it may appear at first sight, it is in *pointed architecture alone that these great principles have been carried out*; and I shall be able to illustrate them from the vast cathedral to

Augustus Welby Northmore Pugin, from *The True Principles of Pointed or Christian Architecture* (1841). London: Academy Edition, 1973 (facsimile edition), pp. 1–2.

the simplest erection. Moreover, the architects of the middle ages were the first who *turned the natural properties of the various materials to their full account*, and made *their mechanism a vehicle for their art.*

152   JOHN MASON NEALE AND BENJAMIN WEBB

from *The Ecclesiologist* (1841)

Following in the moralistic footpath of Pugin's religious and architectural crusade, although within the bounds of the Anglican church, were the efforts of the Cambridge Camden Society, a church society founded in 1839 by John Mason Neale and Benjamin Webb. Nikolaus Pevsner has summarized the aims of the society as three-fold: (1) to reintroduce Catholic ritual into the Anglican Church, (2) to promote the knowledgeable restoration of older churches, and (3) to serve as a stylistic watchdog for new church construction. The society strove for an "approved" authenticity in all things, which architecturally meant a faithful return to the English Gothic architecture of the mid-twelfth to mid-thirteenth centuries. If the first of the society's aims was highly controversial and created a defiant backlash across Anglican Britain, the society was far more successful on the last two counts. By 1841 its membership roll had grown into the hundreds, and Neale and Webb channeled the enthusiasm into the journal *The Ecclesiologist*, which became a prominent voice in current debates; it too was not shy in condemning all styles for church design other than the English Decorated Gothic.

The principal design of the present periodical, is to furnish such members of the Cambridge Camden Society as may reside at a distance from the University, with the information which they have a right to expect, but at present cannot easily obtain, unless at long intervals and from uncertain sources, respecting its proceedings, researches, publications, meetings, grants of money, and election of members. The want of such information, which virtually excludes many zealous members of the Society from co-operating as effectively as they are desirous to do, and the manifest impossibility of regularly supplying it by means of written correspondence to nearly five hundred individuals dispersed over all parts of the kingdom, has rendered the publication of such a periodical as the present an advisable, if not a necessary, expedient. THE ECCLESIOLOGIST is therefore, strictly speaking, a periodical report of the Society, primarily addressed to, and intended for the use of, the members of that body. But it is contemplated at the same time to conduct the publication in such a manner that its pages may convey both interesting and useful information to all connected with or in any way engaged in church building, or the study of ecclesiastical architecture and antiquities. It is intended to give with each number, among other matters pertaining to Ecclesiology in general, critical notices of churches recently completed, or in the progress of building: to give publicity to projects of church building or church enlargement, and thereby, it is hoped, to aid the erection or the endowment of the edifices in contemplation: to suggest, where it

John Mason Neale and Benjamin Webb, from *The Ecclesiologist* (first issue), published in 1841, and later bound in Cambridge by Stevenson, 1842, pp. 1–4.

can be done without unwarrantable interference or presumption, alterations or improvements in the arrangements and decorations of new designs: to describe accurately and impartially the restorations of ancient churches: to point out those which, from their dilapidated condition, antiquity, or architectural interest, are peculiarly deserving of repair, and to suggest the means of effecting it: and to supply notices and reviews of any antiquarian researches, books, or essays, connected with the subject of Ecclesiology. At the same time it is intended to afford, by means of this periodical, a convenient medium of communication between architects and ecclesiologists, who may or may not belong to the Society, and the Society itself; and to afford facilities for proposing and obtaining answers to questions on any points of taste or architectural propriety upon which the clergy may wish to consult the Society – a practice which has, since the institution of the Society, been resorted to by them to a very considerable extent, and from which, it is hoped, satisfactory and useful assistance has been in many instances obtained. Papers read before the Society at their general meetings; extracts from their correspondence, if of peculiar interest or importance; notices of presents received or made by them; and accounts of churches visited and deposited in the Society's records, with various other matters of a like nature, will be occasionally inserted as circumstances may permit. It is anticipated, moreover, that THE ECCLESIOLOGIST may be made an important means of strengthening the connexion and increasing the co-operation between the Cambridge Camden, the Oxford Architectural, and other Societies of kindred character and pursuits now beginning to be established in several parts of the kingdom, and already flourishing under happy auspices in two of our principal cities.

With respect to the non-resident members of the Cambridge Camden Society, for whom we have stated that THE ECOLESIOLOGIST is mainly intended, it is presumed that no better means can be devised for supplying the want, which is generally felt and complained of by them, of regular and authentick information about the proceedings, publications, and expenditure of the Society, in which they are, themselves so intimately concerned. Every member will naturally feel an interest in hearing of the prosperity, and taking part in the operations, of a band of zealous Churchmen, to which he attached himself, not from curiosity, or fancy, or caprice, or mere personal gratification, but from a hearty wish to join them in the good work of restoring GOD's temples to their ancient honours, and of raising from the dust the mighty works of an age long since past away. The good of the Church is the one great end to which all the Society's resources and all its energies have hitherto been and will continue to be devoted. And in carrying this object into effect, they have issued a considerable number of publications, the circulation of which, although in some instances already very large, may in all probability be materially promoted by the periodical issue of a paper such as THE ECCLESIOLOGIST; and the benefit which they were designed to confer may be in consequence proportionably increased.

It is earnestly hoped that the motive of this little publication, liable as it undoubtedly is to misconstruction, will not be mistaken. The Society have not the slightest wish to make it the instrument of proclaiming throughout the land a fame which they neither possess nor are desirous to acquire by, any such means. They do not wish to obtrude themselves upon the notice of any. Their object is altogether different. To render it subservient to the good of the Church, to which the Society deems it no small privilege to be the humblest handmaid; to convey practical suggestions upon points of church architecture at present too much forgotten or neglected; to supply, from their already large and constantly increasing stores of drawings, engravings, and surveys of English and foreign churches, examples and precedents upon doubtful points or disputed usages; and to assist by advice the clergy or churchwardens in carrying into effect, with propriety and correct taste, proposed alterations and improvements; – these and similar aidances are their highest ambition and their sole desire. And the Society trusts that this distinct avowal of the motives which have induced them to undertake the publication of The Ecclesiologist, while it releases them from the charge of forwardness or presumption, will at the same time serve to apprise the clergy in general where they may at all times find advice in practical difficulties, co-operation in their designs, and sympathy in their labours.

153 VICTOR HUGO
from *The Hunchback of Notre-Dame* (1832)

The Gothic Revival appeared somewhat later in France than in Germany and Britain, but by the start of the 1840s it had become an architectural cause with a spirited cadre of followers. It was also differently formed than elsewhere in Europe, in that the religious premise for its revival was almost entirely lacking. The structural admiration of architects such as Perrault and Soufflot, the aesthetic appreciation of Chateaubriand (only a few years after many medieval works had been destroyed by the excesses of the Revolution), and the historical investigations of the 1820s of Arcisse de Caumont (suggesting that Gothic architecture had indeed first developed as a mature style in France) – had all laid the basis for a Gothic movement. But several events of the 1830s carried forward these impulses in a much more systematic way. At the start of this decade the distinguished historian François-Pierre-Guillaume Guizot was named the Interior Minister of the new government, and one of his first acts was to create the post of Inspecteur Général des Monuments Historiques. This established a governmental bureaucracy to protect historic monuments, and another commission was formed in 1837 to initiate and oversee the restoration of medieval works. Highly able administrators like Ludovic Vitet, Jean Vataut, and above all Prosper Mérimée rallied in the 1830s to the Gothic cause, but perhaps the most influential voice in this regard remained that of Victor Hugo. As we saw earlier (chapter 137 above), his Romantic message was on the one hand a pessimistic reply to the Saint-Simonian movement regarding the presumed death of architecture; on the other hand, it was a strong appeal to restore such Gothic works as the Paris church of Notre Dame as a monument to French culture. This reaffirmation of Gothic architecture as something uniquely revelatory of a national French spirit convinced a generation of students to pursue historical investigations of medieval architecture.

Without a doubt the Cathedral of Notre-Dame is, even today, a majestic and sublime edifice. Though it has preserved a noble mien in aging, it is difficult to suppress feelings of sorrow and indignation at the countless injuries and mutilations which time and man have wrought

Victor Hugo, from *Notre-Dame de Paris* (1832), trans. Walter J. Cobb as *The Hunchback of Notre-Dame*. Signet, 1964, pp. 106–7 (excerpt). © 1965 by Walter J. Cobb. Used by permission of Dutton Signet, a division of Penguin Group (USA) Inc.

upon this venerable monument between the time of Charlemagne, who laid its first stone, and that of Philip-Augustus, who laid its last.

On the face of this old queen of French cathedrals, beside each wrinkle you always find a scar. *Tempus edox, homo edacior*,[1] which I would translate: Time is blind, but man is stupid.

If we had time to examine with the reader, one by one, the many traces of destruction stamped on this ancient church, the ravages of time would be found to have done the least; the worst destruction has been perpetrated by men, especially by men of art. We must say "men of art," because there have been men in France who, in the last two centuries, have assumed the character of architects.

First of all, to cite only a few outstanding examples, there are without any question few finer architectural examples than that facade of the Parisian cathedral, in which, successively and at once, you see three deep Gothic doors; the decorated and indented band of twenty-eight royal niches; the immense central rose-window, flanked by two lateral ones, like the priest flanked by the deacon and subdeacon; the lofty and fragile gallery of trifoliated arcades, supporting a heavy platform upon its delicate columns; finally the two dark and massive towers, with their eaves of slate, harmonious parts of one magnificent whole, rising one above the other in five gigantic stories, unfold themselves to the eye. These towers are grouped, yet unconfused, even with their innumerable details of statuary, sculpture, and carving; they are more powerfully wedded to the tranquil grandeur of the whole. The cathedral is a vast symphony in stone, so to speak, the colossal work of a man and of a nation, a unified complex ensemble, like the Iliads and the Romanceros, to which it is a sister production. Notre-Dame's facade is the prodigious result of the combination of all the resources of an age, in which, upon every stone, is seen displayed in a hundred forms the imagination of the craftsman disciplined by the genius of the artist. Here is a sort of human creation; in short, mighty and fertile like the divine creation, from which this cathedral seems to have borrowed the double character of variety and eternity.

And what we have here said of the facade must be said of the church as a whole; and what we say of the cathedral of Paris must be said of all the churches in Christendom during the Middle Ages. Everything has its place in that self-created, logical, well-proportioned art. By measuring the toe, we estimate the giant.

NOTE

1   "Time gnaws, man gnaws more."

154 LÉONCE REYNAUD
from "Architecture" in the *New Encyclopedia* (1834)

For a new appreciation of Gothic architecture to emerge, there was also the need for a new historical perspective on its appearance and development. It was supplied by the notion of "continuous progress" that emerged around 1830 – and as seen in the earlier excerpt of Reynaud's article (chapter 139 above). In advancing Saint-Simonian theory, he saw architecture pursuing a course of progressive artistic and scientific development, in which slenderer proportions or the quest for more efficient structural systems was one of the driving forces. In his analysis Christianity – with its exploitation of the "arcade on columns" – constituted a new page in architectural development in that the Christians adapted the basilica form of the Romans to the expressive demands of the new faith. In such a view, Gothic architecture appears not as a dark anomaly against the backdrop of classicism, but as a glorious and innovative system of structural perfection at the culmination of 14 centuries of architectural development. The following passage speaks to the development of Christian architecture in medieval times.

But art developed with religion, and the resources placed at its disposal increased alongside the forces of the faithful. Christian architecture made rapid progress, and in modifying itself continually it came to vary its expression with the tastes and ideas of the people who adopted the new faith. The principle of construction remained the same in the sense that it always used the arcade on columns. We find them everywhere in Byzantine architecture, Lombard architecture, and in that of the Normans. And these architectures differ only by the manner in which these arcades were disposed, and by the forms, proportions, and ornaments they received. All constructional progress had the goal of giving monuments greater solidity, of substituting vaults for carpentry, of making everything more slender, and of elevating everything to the greatest possible height. And when, in the eleventh century (in German architecture in the North and in Arabian architecture in the South), these architectures came to display new forms and to produce effects unknown until then; they advanced art not a step more than that taken by science. All these bizarre forms, all these slender spires, all this evidence (which at first glance appears to be simply the product of the imagination or the capricious whim of an artist, and has no other goal than to satisfy some aesthetic considerations) must be attributed – when one studies the reciprocal relationships – to the thoughtful reflection and laborious investigations of a knowledgeable builder. These architectural vaults were designed and combined so that they were able to be as slender as possible, to counterbalance their loads, or to lead them over to places where the light flying buttresses transmitted them outside. The piers were loaded on their upper part and thus acquired, with the same thickness, more stability. Finally, the galleries and the openings were disposed in such a way that they contributed to the solidity of the edifice by diminishing the loads carried by the interior arcades. Christian art was thus constituted and a number of

Léonce Reynaud, from entry on "Architecture," in *Encyclopédie nouvelle* (1834), trans. Harry Francis Mallgrave from facsimile edition. Geneva: Slatkine Reprints, 1991, pp. 776–7.

impressive structures were built. In the fourteenth century it arrived at a degree of perfection that it has not since shown, and from which it was soon destined to decline. Never have religious monuments received a character more complete and more suitable, never have they better identified with the sentiments to which they bore witness, never have they better summarized and better understood all the poetry of their epoch. Never, as well, had interior spaces been executed in a grander or more sublime manner, with such sparse and light points of support. Art and science had marched together and mutually assisted one another; the savant and the artist were equally content in viewing these admirable creations.

155   EUGÈNE-EMMANUEL VIOLLET-LE-DUC
from "On the Construction of Religious Buildings in France" (1844)

The most prominent leader of the Gothic movement to emerge in the 1840s was Viollet-le-Duc. He was born into a respected family in Paris, trained in his early years in drawing by Jean Délecluze, and had every possible benefit of circumstance and education. Henri Stendhal, Ludovic Vitet, and Prosper Mérimée, among many others, were all regular visitors at the Viollet-le-Duc household, and Mérimée in particular was of great assistance in furthering the young architect's career. Viollet-le-Duc traveled extensively and trained with several architects, and in 1840 he was offered the governmental post of restoring the Romanesque church of the Madeleine at Vézelay. The architect would literally leap to the forefront of the restoration movement in 1844 when he, together with Jean-Baptiste Lassus, won the national competition for the restoration of Notre Dame of Paris. The building had fallen into considerable disrepair over the years and in addition had been much damaged during the Revolution.

Around he same time, Viollet-le-Duc also befriended Adolphe-Napoléon Didron, who in May 1844 founded the journal *Annales archéologiques*. Didron championed not only the funding of medieval restoration projects by the government but also the need to put them into the hands of qualified architects who possessed a proper historical understanding. To this end he commissioned Viollet-le-Duc, beginning with the first issues, to write a series of historical essays under the above title. This was Viollet-le-Duc's first serious foray into theory and he used the occasion (over the next 3 years and 9 articles in all) to write what was in effect a lengthy homily of faith to the Gothic movement and its rational principles of construction. The excerpt here is the full preface to the first article and is notable in two respects. First, there is his rejection of all architecture development since the sixteenth century, that is, the rejection of both the Renaissance and classical styles for their lack of logic and originality. Second, although here only vaguely implied, is the suggestion that architects return to the true path of Gothic architecture to find their principles and forms for contemporary design. In a few years hence Viollet-le-Duc would come to reject the imitation of Gothic works, but he would always retain his fervor for its founding rational principles and nationalist spirit.

Eugène-Emmanuel Viollet-le-Duc (1814–79), from "De la construction des édifices religieux en France" [On the construction of religious buildings in France], trans. Harry Francis Mallgrave from *Annales Archéologiques* (1844), pp. 179–81.

It should not be thought that archaeological studies are an innovation. They are found among all people at times when they feel the need to review the past, to gather and catalogue all the artistic works left behind by previous generations, and submit them to a new examination in order to critique, reform, and select.

We can scarcely explain how and why the human mind suddenly stops marching forward in order to revisit a past that it hardly knows. Perhaps it is an instinctive feeling of its present error and the desire to depart from a false path. Whatever it may be, this return to the past is almost always a sign of distress, an extreme resort to which the mind turns when it despairs of the present. This expedient occasionally succeeds; history has left us a few examples. Egypt under the Ptolemies, Rome under Hadrian, Italy and France in the Renaissance period – they found a method of production by re-immersing themselves in the past. These second growths, to use an expression, never have the vigor or the sap of the first; they are often pale and emaciated. But in the end they are offshoots of a good stock, and it is well to reserve judgment on them.

We are today in one of these periods when, as I noted, some minds – bewildered and lost in the chaos of the system that is contradictory, bruised by an extended burst of often-justified criticisms, exhausted by ill-starred efforts – have searched the past for a new form. Germany and England have preceded us in this endeavor. For some 20 years now intellectuals and artists in our country have made great and laudable efforts to bring to light a multitude of forgotten facts about these works long disdained. Without allowing themselves to be put off by the difficulties of each genre, they gave to an astonished public the first glimpse of the material lost in our libraries, archives, museums, and monuments. With this first step taken, societies were formed, all those instructed were moved, and the government offered assistance. Despite the devastations of our religious wars and political revolutions, despite the negligence of our entire century, we found ourselves as rich as Italy, Germany, and England. Each day archaeology has seen the expansion of its domain; each day has led to a new discovery, and the studies must no longer be limited in order for so much material to be ordered. Monuments long abandoned had fallen into ruin; we had to conserve them like works of art, like religious or civil monuments. This is where the work of archaeology became really useful, because a false direction, an ignorance of the arts and the ancient techniques, could have led the artists charged with restoration into deplorable errors, more fatal to our monuments than indifference or forgetting them altogether. The peril was imminent; enlightened minds understood it, and the ministers of the interior and of public instruction formed commissions charged with reviewing these works and stopping the devastation. Wise principles were issue and instruction became widespread. Archaeology was no longer a vain science; it was organized administratively and became the center of an immense project. If science must be proud, here is one of the greatest triumphs that it has ever achieved.

We therefore sat down to the work; the principle was good but the application difficult. In effect, or order to understand archaeologists, it is necessary that artists themselves become archaeologists. Moreover, these governmental commissions were not able to inquire into all of the minute details of a building; they could not examine all of the profiles created by artists, even less their means of execution. They could not ensure that in rebuilding an edifice, none of the ancient parts were modified. But for their part, some architects studied these monuments so long forgotten; they discovered there some great qualities, an art profoundly rational and with endless beauty. At first seduced by the charm and the richness of the edifices of the fifteenth and sixteenth centuries, they were led little by little to penetrate further back in time. That is the nature of the human spirit: in historical studies it always goes back to the point in time that is closest to it, searching for the cause of the effects that strike it, and tending so to speak, despite itself, toward sources at which it will never be possible to arrive. It therefore happened that artists studied archaeology, came to appreciate the value of our ancient monuments and were eager to conserve them. In everything it was a revolution.

Architecture has lost all originality since the period of Louis XIV; up to then it had been so national in France. The reign of the great king had the last word for this art, as he had for literature and painting. The principle – "The state, it is I" [L'Etat, c'est moi] – summarizes everything that we can say on this subject. After the great king there was nothing more; he carried away everything to his grave.

Let us therefore work or even assist, as much as possible, this small troop of scholars and artists who seek to recover the splendid arts of our forefathers, to pick up that thread severed by the seventeenth and eighteenth centuries. Do not say that they want us to become retrograde, but rather that they want to take up again the true path that some have never abandoned.

These studies of the past have already been very productive. Artists who have devoted themselves to the work, first preoccupied with the exterior form and envelope of the monuments they have studied, were soon led to examine the methods that the ancient masons employed. The numerous restorations that have been undertaken, as well as investigations throughout Europe, have already shed some light on the practical arts of these centuries. Faith pledged to this course, so long neglected, has made rapid progress. The discoveries made each day seem to us to be very serious, and should even influence in part the architectural studies that we have thought would be useful for ordering all this information and supporting it with particular observations. The initial work on material so extensive and complicated cannot be complete; but if it only had the advantage of opening the eyes of architects to the techniques that their predecessors employed in construction, and of calling their attention to a practical art, the goal will be served. We should be happy when others, struck as we have been by the profound experience, by good sense, and by the science that presided over the work bequeathed to us by the past centuries, might be able to fill the lacunas left for us or to rectify the errors that we may commit.

This survey will perhaps also be able in some cases to focus on the architects charged with restoring ancient monuments. When it is a question of restoring destroyed parts, it will stress to them that in restorations it is as important to conserve the manner of construction adopted by each epoch, as it is to conserve the form of the profiles and ornaments.

For a long time we have wanted to believe that the monuments raised since the origins of Christianity, and especially since the fall of the Roman Empire, were owed to caprice – sometimes happy, often barbaric, and always ignorant. Trapped by this principle, we did not take the time to study the works judged in such a severe manner; they were, moreover, rather simple. Content with an admiration, exclusive and without choice, for an antiquity of convention, which had only a very distant connection with true antiquity, we should then have to accuse someone of being paradoxical who would come to say: "These disdained monuments of our forefathers are the masterpieces of reason, wisdom, unity, and grandeur. They were raised by men who knew thoroughly the art that they practiced. You will not find a single useless stone in all of these grand constructions built to house entire populations; as in a divine work, everything has its place and role. Remove a part and you will destroy the whole."

Today people happily do not profess that exclusive rigor that wishes not to see the good and the beautiful in the works that we have under our hand. No one is a prophet in his own country! Human productions in this regard are like the men, and we have been the last in Europe to realize that our monuments have some value.

Now so that one does not accuse us of being exclusive, let us also applaud and admire antiquity and regard it as endowed with rare good sense. We are convinced that if by chance Ictinus or Vitruvius would return to the world, they would greatly admire some of our cathedrals; they would know perfectly well how to recognize their merit.

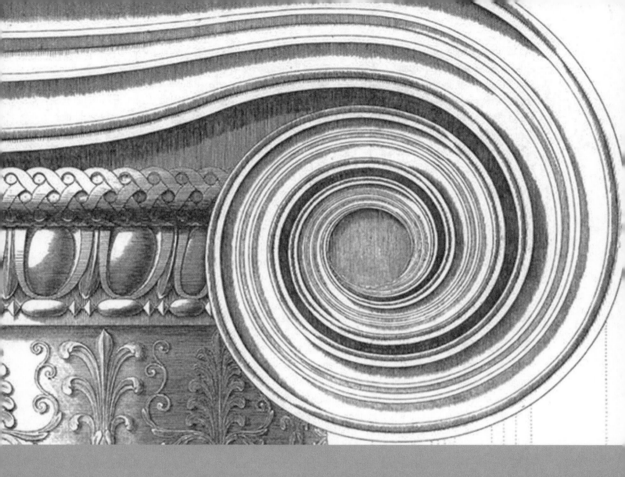

C.   THE GERMAN STYLE DEBATE

Introduction

The appearance of Germany as a cultural force throughout Europe was in part delayed by the fact that the country was never politically unified and existed as a confederation of states, in Renaissance times under the protection of the Habsburg Empire. This situation began to change in the second half of the eighteenth century with the ascendancy of Prussia under Frederick the Great. The latter defined Prussia as a military power, and with a state policy of religious and intellectual toleration it also became a haven for both persecuted religious groups and other exiles such as Voltaire. A "German" consciousness also first becomes evident during these years, and in quick succession a number of great writers and philosophers — among them Johann Gottfried Herder, Johann Wolfgang Goethe, Immanuel Kant, and Friedrich Schiller — laid the basis for Germanic cultural unity. Germany's first state-recognized architectural school — the Berlin Bauakademie — was founded in that city in 1799. The curriculum was for the most part technically oriented (its curriculum was based on the Ecole Polytechnique in Paris and not that of the now-defunct Royal Academy of Architecture), and the prevailing stylistic current of the day was neoclassicism. With Germany's progressive industrialization in the nineteenth century, other cultural centers and schools (both official and private) began to appear in such cities as Karlsruhe, Dresden, Stuttgart, and Munich. Thus within the course of a single generation — and beginning in the 1820s — German theory seemingly materializes overnight and German architects initiate the first round of what becomes a very lively architectural debate. By the 1840s, in fact, nowhere in Europe was the discussion regarding the choice of a style more intense or widespread. A still divided Germany was now challenging Italy, France, and Britain for preeminence in theory.

156 IMMANUEL KANT
from *Critique of Judgment* (1790)

From the very beginning German architectural theory was very much driven by the notion of "purpose." Whereas part of the explanation for this may lie with the absence in Germany of the strong painterly tradition of southern Europe, or with a greater (rural) emphasis on practicality, part also has to do with the philosophical traditions underlying German thought. For architecture these traditions begin with Immanuel Kant's *Critique of Judgment*. While the book is very much influenced by the British tradition of Shaftesbury, Hume, and Burke, it is also specifically Germanic in its abstract analysis of ideas. Kant's theory of beauty rests on four "moments" — of which the third is of particular importance for architecture. It is of interest because Kant must now distinguish between two kinds of beauty: "free beauty" or beauty intuited without an end or purpose in mind, and "dependent beauty" or beauty (such as a building) for which we bring a particular purpose into the judgment. He really wants to take this "dependent beauty" out of the equation, and thus he summarizes this third moment as "the form of the *purposiveness* [*Zweckmässigkeit*] of an object, so far as this is perceived in it *without any representation of a purpose.*"

But here is also where the problem arises for architectural theory. *Zweckmässigkeit* in German can signify "suitability," "appropriateness," and even "functionality," but Kant, from his eighteenth-century perspective, seems to have endowed it with a more subtle meaning. Ernst Cassirer, for instance, has defined Kant's idea of *Zweckmässigkeit* or purposiveness as "the general expression for every harmonious unification of the parts of a manifold" — an idea that seems to be closely related to the Renaissance idea of concinnity or harmony. It would be left for others to work out the precise relationship between purposiveness and purpose.

There are two kinds of beauty: free beauty (*pulchritudo vaga*), or merely dependent beauty (*pulchritudo adhaerens*). The first presupposes no concept of what the object ought to be; the second does presuppose such a concept and the perfection of the object in accordance therewith. The first is called the (self-subsistent) beauty of this or that thing; the second, as dependent upon a concept (conditioned beauty), is ascribed to objects which come under the concept of a particular purpose.

Immanuel Kant (1724–1804), from *Kritik der Urtheilskraft* [Critique of judgment] (1790), trans. J. H. Bernand as *Critique of Judgment*. New York: Hafner Press, 1951, pp. 65–7, 73. © 1951 by Hafner Press. Reprinted with permission of The Free Press, a division of Simon & Schuster Adult Publishing Group.

Flowers are free natural beauties. Hardly anyone but a botanist knows what sort of a thing a flower ought to be; and even he, though recognizing in the flower the reproductive organ of the plant, pays no regard to this natural purpose if he is passing judgment on the flower by taste. There is, then, at the basis of this judgment no perfection of any kind, no internal purposiveness, to which the collection of the manifold is referred. Many birds (such as the parrot, the humming bird, the bird of paradise) and many sea shells are beauties in themselves, which do not belong to any object determined in respect of its purpose by concepts, but please freely and in themselves. So also delineations *à la grecque*, foliage for borders or wall papers, mean nothing in themselves; they represent nothing – no object under a definite concept – and are free beauties. We can refer to the same class what are called in music phantasies (i.e. pieces without any theme), and in fact all music without words.

In the judging of a free beauty (according to the mere form), the judgment of taste is pure. There is presupposed no concept of any purpose which the manifold of the given object is to serve, and which therefore is to be represented in it. By such a concept the freedom of the imagination which disports itself in the contemplation of the figure would be only limited.

But human beauty (i.e. of a man, a woman, or a child), the beauty of a horse, or a building (be it church, palace, arsenal, or summer house), presupposes a concept of the purpose which determines what the thing is to be, and consequently a concept of its perfection; it is therefore adherent beauty. Now as the combination of the pleasant (in sensation) with beauty, which properly is only concerned with form, is a hindrance to the purity of the judgment of taste, so also is its purity injured by the combination with beauty of the good (viz. that manifold which is good for the thing itself in accordance with its purpose). [. . .]

A judgment of taste, then, in respect of an object with a definite internal purpose, can only be pure if either the person judging has no concept of this purpose or else abstracts from it in his judgment. Such a person, although forming an accurate judgment of taste in judging of the object as free beauty, would yet by another who considers the beauty in it only as a dependent attribute (who looks to the purpose of the object) be blamed and accused of false taste, although both are right in their own way – the one in reference to what he has before his eyes, the other in reference to what he has in his thought. By means of this distinction we can settle many disputes about beauty between judges of taste, by showing that the one is speaking of free, the other of dependent, beauty – that the first is making a pure, the second an applied, judgment of taste. [. . .]

Beauty is the form of the *purposiveness* of an object, so far as this is perceived in it *without any representation of a purpose.*

157 AUGUST SCHLEGEL
from *Lectures on Literature and the Fine Arts* (1801–2)

Kant's notion of *Zweckmässigkeit* underwent further elaboration after 1800 in the aesthetic theory of August Schlegel, whose lectures on the fine arts were first given in Berlin in 1801–2. Schlegel first wants to acknowledge architecture's primary foundation in purpose, but if architecture remains tied to this it would no longer be an art. To rescue architecture, as it were, he returns to Kantian purposiveness, but now with a slightly different twist. It is not the concinnity of purposiveness that saves architecture, but rather the "appearance of purposiveness." His thesis in the end is that architecture does not imitate nature but rather her idealized "methods," that is to say, such higher concepts as regularity, symmetry, proportion, and the physical and psychological laws of form (against gravity).

We define architecture as the art of designing and constructing beautiful forms in things without a definite model in nature, but freely after a suitably original idea of the human mind. Because its works, however, make visible none of the great eternal ideas that nature impresses on its creations, it must define a human idea, that is, it must be directed toward a purpose. From this at the same time comes the demand for utility that is made upon architecture, and to be sure in such a way, as we will see, that it can never yield to that of beauty. Beauty can exist here only on the condition of purposiveness [*Zweckmässigkeit*]. [. . .]

Because beauty is always a meaningful appearance, beautiful form in construction, for which the determination of a certain purpose is the essential thing, must reside first and foremost in the appearance of this purposiveness; then can something more be added that exceeds it, although it may never contradict it. We will soon see more clearly what this is. [. . .]

* * *

Thus the architect must take into account a number of relationships. It is not enough that he assemble the parts following some mechanical rules in themselves and proportioned in relation to others, but he must view them in their living relationships. His work must be designed from a single unifying idea, such that every part determines all others, and is conversely determined by them. It follows from this that architecture, although the most rigorous science, is however an art that cannot be completely learned, but one that must be practiced in a truly inspired way. In building the first requirement is the need, the second is the appearance of purposiveness (in which essential beauty consists), the third is adornment.

August Schlegel (1767–1845), from *Vorlesungen über schöne Litteratur und Kunst* [Lectures on literature and the fine arts] (1801–2) in *A. W. Schlegels Vorlesungen über schöne Litteratur und Kunst*. Heilbronn, 1884 and Kraus, 1968 (facsimile edition), pp. 160–2, 178–9, trans. Harry Francis Mallgrave.

158 FRIEDRICH GILLY

from "Some Thoughts on the Necessity of Endeavoring to Unify the Various Departments of Architecture . . ." (1799)

Architectural theory in Germany takes its start in the creation of the Berlin Architectural Academy or Bauakademie. The school was largely the creation of David Gilly (1748–1808), a Pomeranian architect who had been summoned to Berlin in the late 1780s by Friedrich II. Earlier David Gilly had operated a small private school for architectural instruction, and in Berlin in 1793 he reopened his school as an institute. In 1799 it was officially sanctioned by the crown, and by this date the school's intellectual direction had been assumed by David Gilly's son, Friedrich. The younger Gilly had been instructed in drawing at an early age, and largely on the basis of his exceptional talent he won the competition for a monument to Frederick the Great in 1796 with a classical design. Friedrich was also drawn to theoretical matters, and, spurred on by a visit to France in 1797, he joined with his friend Johann Heinrich Gentz in 1799 in creating a "Private Society of Young Architects" — a forum for theoretical discussions through readings and mutual criticism. In the same year he joined his father's school as a professor.

The essay from which the following excerpt is taken speaks to the younger Gilly's pedagogical and theoretical concerns. In some respects it is critical of the curriculum of the school, which was based in engineering or technical courses. Gilly counters with the insistence, similar to Kant and Schlegel, that architecture is both a science and an art, and in the last regard it has higher poetic values to satisfy. The philosopher to whom he refers in this passage is Karl Heinrich Heydenreich, but the emphasis on architecture as a fine art, not one bound to simple purpose, defines this early stage of German theory. Gilly personifies the romantic artist, and one year after writing this essay he died tragically at the age of 28 of a pulmonary disorder.

At this juncture a few remarks would seem to be in order concerning the changes in the *status of architecture itself, especially of late:* the way in which it has been regarded and treated has necessarily affected its status, leading to differences on matters of substance and opinion, both in general and in particular, that have often been mutually damaging. A glance at this issue is therefore very much in the general interest.

The status of architecture in antiquity – quite apart from the many difficulties attendant on any attempt to describe it – is too remote for comparison with the present situation. Whatever may have been its status or its connection with the sciences, it was then, more than at any other time, that architecture naturally enjoyed a close alliance with the *arts.* Yet only an unequaled combination of knowledge and talent could have produced the perfection of the works of that age.

Friedrich Gilly (1772–1800), from "Einige Gedanken über die Notwendigkeit, die verschiedenen Theile der Baukunst . . . zu vereinen" [Some thoughts on the necessity of endeavoring to unify the various departments of architecture in both theory and practice] (1799), trans. David Britt, in *Friedrich Gilly: Essays on Architecture 1796–1799.* Santa Monica: Getty Publication Programs, 1994, pp. 169–71. Reprinted with permission of Getty Publications.

As architecture declined, it sank to the level of mere craftsmanship, a state from which it then had to be rescued. At length, the country that is the cradle of all the arts fortunately produced architects of force and vigor, to whom we owe a rebirth of architecture in its capacity as an art. In that connection, however, the teaching and dissemination of architecture thenceforward took a noteworthy course. With the spread of learning, architecture came to be treated as a largely scholarly pursuit. The age of the manuals now dawned. Mathematics, in particular, took architecture in hand and even presumed – if only in an appendix – to solve the problem of taste. This did not, of course, put an end to the existence of craftsmanship; and for the first time architects emerged who were master builders in the true sense and who were capable of combining the two.

It cannot be denied that, as a result of these developments, first one aspect of the subject and then another suffered and was suppressed; that a pernicious *one-sidedness*, not to say *division*, prevailed within a combined art and science that always has to function *in unison* and as an *entity*. As a result, the practice of architecture came to be governed by the character and methods of each individual nation, or by mere force of opinion, or even by fashion; and so it remains to this day, divided into national variants that seldom work to its advantage.

The want of that precious balance that leads to a higher and shared perfection has undoubtedly been due, first and foremost, to this one-sidedness; to this individual caprice; and, worst of all, to this division. This has been so in a number of otherwise excellent schools of architecture; and what reader will not recall, in this connection, the futile feuds and controversies between the academic architects and their various adversaries in France and England, with all the dire consequences that ensued?

Along with the schools of art, there arose critiques of art and theoretical formulas; and these, whatever their intrinsic value, served to exacerbate the prevailing feuds. In the course of imposing a general classification, criticism was compelled to include architecture; but the systems that emerged were naturally as controversial as they were diverse. Architecture had long since been admitted as a true companion of the fine arts; but few now came forward to defend this right or even its right to the name of art. Some conceded it half a vote in the congress of the arts, but others struck it entirely from the list, citing its ignominious subservience to necessity and utility. And so architecture came to be considered merely a mechanical pursuit, and it was subordinated first to one superior authority and then to another: its task was to serve and be useful.

So harsh a verdict has compelled more recent critics to review the case and to pass a more temperate judgment; and one philosopher, by advancing an *entirely new conception*, has shown that – on certain conditions – architecture can still be recalled from exile and restored to its ancient rights. In the schools and among the architects themselves, the old, one-sided categorization of architecture was not without its practical effect. One-sidedness frequently brought division and disaster in its train; for many it was an incitement to division – and even, be it said, to mutual contempt.

At a time when art and science are everywhere so closely allied, a general community of interest must necessarily prevail, the more so as their interdependence increases; and all who are conscious and desirous of the general good must surely strive toward this end. And so, first of all, there must surely be no more talk of division, utterly opposed as it is to all secure achievement, to the true and reciprocal advantages of education, and to progress.

Those advantages can be secured for architecture only when every individual – while advancing his own abilities and his own talent, wherever these may lie – simultaneously seeks to improve himself in other directions: the more so, the closer they lie to his own concerns. He will add to his store of always profitable knowledge by following others in studies more or less closely related to his own. At the very least, we may surely expect that he will not be a total stranger to all that lies outside his own field, and that he will welcome the interest of others in that field; and no one, I trust, will seek to assert that such an enhanced breadth of concern would threaten the talents or the interests of anyone.

In this way alone can the preeminent abilities and particular studies of one individual bear fruit for others, exert an influence on them, and elicit from them a respect that must become mutual. For everywhere the architect must learn to *value* the scientist, and the scientist to value the architect; architects, each with particular talents and native gifts, must *work together in mutual respect*; and no vain pride must mark out the supposed "artist" [*Baukünstler*] among them. Each must extend a hand to all in the interest of mutual aid – all the more so as the goal to which all aspire grows ever more distant and more manifold.

Only from such an association and from such reciprocal influence can we expect any general advance toward perfection, especially as things are at present; and for this the ground cannot be laid too soon. Above all, if a school duly combines all the important and related parts of so extensive a discipline, it can have the most beneficial effects and spread the true advantages of learning.

159   KARL FRIEDRICH SCHINKEL
Literary fragments (c.1805)

The artistic mantle of leadership that Gilly wore at his death was soon passed to the student Karl Friedrich Schinkel, who would become the most important architect of nineteenth-century Germany. Schinkel was an architect of enormous intellect and erudition. The 16-year-old student presented himself to the elder Gilly for entry into the school in 1797 – reportedly after viewing the competition-winning drawings of the younger Gilly for the monument to Frederick the Great. He was the youngest member of the Private Society for Young Architects, and after Gilly's death he inherited many of his mentor's drawings and personal papers. Schinkel traveled to Italy, Sicily, and France between 1803 and 1805, but his return was ill-timed for beginning his career, as Napoleon's defeat of the Prussian army at Auerstedt and Jena in the fall of 1806, followed by the humiliating occupation of Berlin, would soon plunge Prussia into a decade of economic ruin. The young architect was thus forced to support himself for many years by painting and designing panoramas, dioramas, and stage sets.

Schinkel's diaries and notes, scrupulously maintained over his career, document both his great concern with philosophy and with defining the meaning of architecture apart from French academic theory. Shortly after Gilly's death he befriended the philosopher Wilhelm Ferdinand Solger (1780–1819), who was a lecturer on aesthetics at the University of Berlin. Through him he also became acquainted with the idealism of Johann Gottbieb Fichte,

Karl Friedrich Schinkel (1781–1841), literary fragments (c.1805), trans. Harry Francis Mallgrave from Schinkel's papers as assembled by Goerd Peschken, *Das architecktonische Lehrbuch*. Berlin: Deutscher Kunstverlag, 1979, pp. 21–2.

Friedrich von Schelling, and may very well have attended the lectures of August Schlegel. Thus the idea of "purposiveness" voiced here seems to reflect the double sense of Kantian harmony and simple purpose.

The Principle of Art in Architecture

1. To build means to join different materials into a whole, corresponding to a defined purpose.
2. This definition, encompassing building in both its spiritual and material aspects, demonstrates clearly that *purposiveness [Zweckmässigkeit]* is the basic principle of all building.
3. The material building, which now presumes a spiritual aspect, is here the subject of my consideration.
4. The purposiveness of any building can be considered from three principal perspectives, which are:
   A. *Purposiveness* of *spatial distribution* or *of the plan*;
   B. *Purposiveness* of *construction* or the *joining of materials* appropriate to the plan;
   C. *Purposiveness* of *ornament* or *decoration*.
5. These three points determine the form, proportion, and character of the building.
6. *Purposiveness of spatial distribution* or of the plan contains the following three principal attributes:
   a) greatest economy of the *space*;
   b) greatest *order* in the *layout*;
   c) greatest *comfort* in the space.
7. *Purposiveness of Construction* contains the following three main attributes:
   a) *best material*;
   b) *best preparation and assembly* of the materials;
   c) *most visible* indication of the best *materials*, of the best *preparation and assembly* of the materials.
8. *Purposiveness of ornament* or *decoration* contains the following three main attributes:
   a) best selection of the *place* of the decoration;
   b) best selection of the *decoration*;
   c) best preparation of the *decoration*.

The Place of Architecture in Relation to the Other Arts

It is often disputed (1) what place architecture occupies among the other arts, and (2) whether it can be counted in general among the other arts, or whether it is a handicraft or science, or both at the same time. The first question is more difficult to decide than the second.

The question "What is a work of art?" can be answered most succinctly as *presentation of the Ideal.*

The *Ideal* is that which bears the highest character of its species, therefore the most intelligible, the best, and the most perfect of its species.

The more the work of art bears these attributes, the closer it is to the Ideal, the more character it has, and the greater its value.

The various categories of things, from whose basic principle the Ideal is constituted, are for us more or less valuable, *more or less important*, closer or more distant. In this regard these categories determine the relative higher or lower stages of a work of art.

It is therefore possible that two works of art, which are on the same level in the presentation of the Ideal, might have different relative levels particular to the category of each. This would be the case, for instance, between a scene of gods of the best Italian school and a rustic bacchanal of the best Dutch school.

Therefore the question arises of whether this concept can be applied to architecture, and it must certainly be answered in the affirmative. Therefore the question arises of what defines artistic merit in architecture. Because purposiveness is the basic principle of all building, purposiveness determines the greatest possible presentation of the Ideal; it is the character or the physiognomy of building, its artistic value.

How does the work of architecture stand with respect to the other arts? It has the advantage that in its presentation it combines the real and actual content of its presentation, while in the other arts only absolute presentation takes place . . .

160 GEORG WILHELM FRIEDRICH HEGEL
from *The Philosophy of Fine Art* (1820s)

One of the most important early German writers on architecture was the philosopher G. W. F. Hegel. *The Philosophy of Fine Art* is based on lectures he gave at the University of Berlin in the 1820s (especially between 1823 and 1827); they were not published in his lifetime, but later assembled from student notes of his lectures. His broader ideas on metaphysics and history are based on the premise that the human race is progressively advancing toward more self-conscious stages of awareness, always toward a higher understanding of the Absolute or Spirit. Art and architecture also strive toward this Absolute in three identifiable stages: the Symbolic, the Classical, and the Romantic. In symbolic architecture, which Hegel identifies with preclassical times, the Ideal is still trapped, as it were, in inorganic matter and is thus unable to manifest itself fully because of its material limitations. With classical architecture, by contrast, buildings acquire a spiritual import independent of form; classical architecture achieves a certain ideal perfection, but it is still not the highest perfection. This stage is attained in the Romanic period of Gothic times, when "infinite significance" now supersedes all material restraints, including the idea of purpose. The problem with such a scenario, as many architects understood, was that it left this art essentially with nowhere to go. But what was extremely influential here was the underlying Hegelian dialectic, that is, the

Georg Wilhelm Friedrich Hegel (1770–1831), from *The Philosophy of Fine Art* (1820s), trans. F. P. B. Osmaston, in *The Philosophy of Fine Art*, Vol. III. London: G. Bell and Sons, 1920, pp. 89–91.

metaphysical notion that architecture (or style) begins at a lower stage (thesis), is contested by an opposing ideal (antithesis), and ultimately moves into a higher stage of development (synthesis).

Romantic Architecture

The Gothic architecture of the Middle Ages, which constitutes here the characteristic centre of the truly romantic type, has for a long time, more especially since the popularization and predominance of the French taste, been regarded as something rude and barbarous. In recent times it was Goethe who mainly, in the first instance, and in the youthful freshness of his own nature and artistic outlook, brought once more the Gothic type to its place of honour. Critical taste has been more and more concerned to appreciate and respect these imposing works as giving effective expression both to the distinctive purpose of Christian culture, and the harmonious unity thereby created between architectonic form and the ideal spirit of Christendom.

1. *General character*

In so far as the general character of these buildings is concerned, in which religious architecture is that which is most prominent, we discovered already in our introduction to this part of our inquiry that in this type both those of *independent* and *serviceable* architecture are *united*. This unity, however, does not in any way consist in a fusion of the architectural forms of the Oriental and the Greek, but we must look for it in the fact that, on the one hand, the house or *dwelling-enclosure* furnishes yet more the fundamental type than in the Greek temple construction, and, on the other, mere *serviceableness* and purpose is to that extent *eliminated*, and the house is emphasized apart from it in its *free independence*. No doubt these houses of God and other buildings of this type appear to the fullest extent as constructed for definite objects, as already stated, but their true character is precisely this, that it reaches over and beyond the determinate aim and presents itself in a form of self-seclusion and positive local independence. The creation stands up in its place independent, secure, and eternal. For this reason the character of the entirety is no longer to be deduced from any purely scientific or theoretical relation. Within the interior the box-like envelope of our Protestant churches falls away which are built simply that they may be filled with men and women, and do not possess church pews as stalls; in their exterior, the building soars in its roofing and pinnacles freely upwards, so that the relation of purpose, however much it be also present, tends again to disappear, leaving the impression of the whole that of a self-subsistent existence. Such a building is entirely filled up by nothing expressly; everything is absorbed in the grandeur of the whole: it possesses and declares a definite object, but in its grandiose proportions and sublime repose it is essentially and with an infinite significance exalted above all mere intentional serviceableness. This exaltation over finitude and simple security is that which constitutes the *unique* characteristic aspect of it. From another point of view it is precisely in this type that architecture finds the greatest opportunity for *particularisation*, diversion of effect and variety, without permitting, however, the whole to fall into mere details and accidental particulars. The imposing character of the art we are considering restores, on the contrary, this aspect of division and dismemberment in the original impression of simplicity. It is the substantive being of the whole which is set in division and dismemberment in an infinite multiplicity throughout the entire complexus of individual and varied distinctions; but this unbounded complexity is subdivided in a simple way, is articulated according to rule, broken into parts symmetrically by the same substance, which is the motive and constitutive principle throughout in a harmonious co-ordination which entirely satisfies, and which combines without let or hindrance the mass of detail in all their length and breadth in securest unity and most perspicuous independence.

2. *Particular architectural modes of conformation*

If we pass now to a consideration of the particular forms in which romantic architecture receives its specific character we shall find, as we have already above noticed, that our entire discussion will be confined to what is genuine Gothic architecture, and mainly that of the church buildings of Christendom, in their contrast to the Greek temple.

(*a*) As fundamental form underlying all the rest, we have here the *wholly shut off dwelling-house*.

(α) In other words, just as the Christian spirit withdraws itself within an ideal realm, the building is the place essentially delimited on all sides for the congregation of the Christian community and the gathering together of spiritual life. It is the concentration of essential soul-life which thus encloses itself in spatial relations. The devotion of the Christian heart, however, is at the same time and in the same degree an exaltation over finitude, so that this exaltation, moreover, determines the character of God's house. Architecture secures thereby as its significance, independently of the object which renders it necessary as a building, this exaltation to the Infinite, a significance which it is forced to express through the spatial relations of architectual forms. The impression, therefore, which art is now called upon to emphasize is, in one aspect of it, and in contrast to the open gaiety of the Greek temple, that of the tranquillity of the soul which, released from external nature and worldly conditions, retires wholly into self-seclusion; in the other aspect of it it is that impress of a solemn sublimity, which strains and soars over and beyond all rational limits. If, therefore, the buildings of classical architecture as a rule offer the expansion of breadth, we find in contrast to this that the romantic character of Christian churches asserts itself in the growth upwards from the soil and a soaring to the skies. [. . .]

(γ) We may fix as the pervading type by which the house of God is generally and with particular reference to its sections characterized that of the free rise and running up into *pinnacles*, whether they be built up by means of the arch or straight lines. In classical architecture, where we find columns and piers with superimposed beams is the fundamental form, rectangularity and the office of support is the feature of importance. For the construction superimposed at right angles marks in a definite way that it is supported. And even though the beams do in their turn carry the roofing, the surfaces of this latter portion incline to one another in an obtuse angle. In such a construction we find no trace of a genuine tendency to points and a soaring up: we find simply repose and support. In the same way, too, a circular arch, which extends in a continuous and equally gradated incline from one column to another, and is referable to one and the same centre, rests on its substructure of support. In romantic architecture, however, we no longer find the relation of support simply and rectangularly the fundamental form, but rather we have before us the fact that all that is enclosed either on its interior or exterior side independently springs upward, and, without the secure and express distinction between the relationship of weight and support, concentrates in a point. This pre-eminently free striving upwards and tendency to inclines that run to culminating points is what constitutes here the essential determinant, by virtue of which either acute-angled triangles with a more slender or broader base or pointed arches appear, both of which aspects stand out most obviously in the characterization of Gothic architecture.

161 FRIEDRICH VON GÄRTNER
from Letter to Johann Martin von Wagner (1828)

Hegel's dialectic synthesis can actually be traced back to the start of the century and be found in the thought of Johann Fichte and Friedrich Schelling. As early as 1811, Schinkel, in his design for Berlin's Petrikirche, specifically set out to synthesize the principles of the Greek and Gothic styles. As the medieval movement manifested itself in Germany in the 1820s, historical interest was not limited to the Gothic style. Works from the Romanesque period were also appreciated by some architects, among them Friedrich von Gärtner, a professor at the Munich Academy of Fine Arts. Gärtner's fortunes as an architect were owed to the favor of Ludwig I, who ascended to the Bavarian throne in 1825 with the ambition to have his city of residence – Munich – match Berlin in cultural importance. For several years prior to his ascension Ludwig had employed Leo von Klenze as his architect, and the latter had responded with several designs in both classical and Renaissance styles. For the new church of his namesake, St. Ludwig, however, Ludwig turned in 1827 to Gärtner and asked for a church in "a purified Byzantine style" – actually in a Romanesque style not dissimilar to Klenze's near contemporary royal chapel, the Allerheiligenhofkirche (1826–37).

In this short excerpt from a letter to a friend, Gärtner discloses his ideas for this novel design, one that would attempt to be a synthetic mean between the strict austerity of classicism and the presumed fantasy of the Gothic style. This German reference to the "Byzantine style" precedes by several years the use of this term by French historians and architects; the style of this church would also be come to be known in Munich as the *Gärtnerstil* or "Gärtner Style." Gärtner is first speaking of recent churches in Germany.

These churches were entirely in the Greek style or very ordinary, as in the case with Pertsch, or so modern that only the one from Klenze could be spoken of; – the trip last summer to Italy has in some respects awakened ideas in me, and changed or emphasized views; particularly in regard to church building, I take delight in those [churches] from the Middle Ages and those from the earliest times of Christianity, erected near the ancient basilicas; and I cannot develop a taste for those Greek forms translated into Christian ones; and I am of the

Friedrich von Gärtner (1792–1837), from Letter to Johann Martin von Wagner (Jan. 13, 1828) in Kathleen Curran, *The Romanesque Revival: Religion, Politics, and Transnational Exchange*. University Park: Pennsylvania State University Press, 2003, p. 51. © 2003 by Pennsylvania State University Press.

opinion that something must lie between these austere Greek or, more generally, these strictly *formulated* architectural *rules* and the purely feeling-inspired, fantastic [ones] of the Middle Ages, so that if they could be combined, [this] would prove the best [solution] for Christian, and particularly Catholic, churches.

162 HEINRICH HÜBSCH
from *In What Style Should We Build?* (1828)

I f both Schinkel and Gärtner struggled privately with the creation of a new style for church building, the idea of a new style for German architecture was broached publicly in 1828 with the appearance of this very important pamphlet by Heinrich Hübsch. The young architect was well suited to take up the matter. Initially trained in philosophy and mathematics at the University of Heidelberg, he moved to Karlsruhe in 1815 to study architecture under Friedrich Weinbrenner at his private school. On a 4-year tour, he next traveled to Italy (where he studied Italian medieval architecture), Greece, and Constantinople. During this time he also became a close acquaintance of the historian Friedrich von Rumohr, who was a specialist of late-Roman (Eastern and Western empires) and medieval Italian architecture. In 1826 Hübsch succeeded Weinbrenner as the municipal architect of Karlsruhe. One year earlier he had published his first book *Über griechische Architecture* (On Greek architecture), in which he first promised to liberate modern architecture "from the chains of antiquity." *In What Style Should We Build?* again makes good on this promise.

The pamphlet simply resounded within German architectural circles. It is a highly logical exposition that begins with the premise that the decorative side of architecture can provide no reliable principles of design, and one should therefore start with the twin criteria of purposiveness (*Zweckmässigkeit*) — fitness for purpose and solidity — to ground a new style. For Hübsch the roof and its supports were the essential features defining a style, and on this basis of this premise he embarks on a historical review of the existing styles to find the conceptual seed from which to launch a new one. He eventually reduces the matter to a choice between a "pointed-arch" or "rounded-arch" system of walling (hence his term *Rundbogenstil*), and — strictly on the basis of modern needs or practicality — he opts for the latter. The two selections emphasize two aspects of his analysis. The first characterizes the spirited logic of his argument, and what he terms "technostatic" progress we might call technology or structural progress. The second selection underscores both his practicality and the fact that the proposed *Rundbogen* style was not to be a direct imitation of Romanesque forms, but rather an abstracted version "unimpeded by all harmful reminiscences of the ancient style." Hübsch's interpretation of the term *Zweckmässigkeit* may be more limited than that of Schinkel, but his attempt to rationalize the elements of a new style is remarkably progressive for this early date and his early buildings display this same desire.

Heinrich Hübsch (1795–1863), from *Im welchem Style sollen wir bauen?* (1828), in *In What Style Should We Build? The German Debate on Architectural Style*, ed. and trans. Wolfgang Herrmann. Santa Monica: Getty Publication Programs, 1992, pp. 67–9, 99. © 1992 by Getty Publications. Reprinted with permission of Getty Publications.

Having now established what is meant by style, we must examine its manifestations in the various original forms of architecture.

The principal formative factors, as can be deduced a priori as well as confirmed historically, are climate and building material. In the first place the climate, as already mentioned, gives a uniform character to the needs of one country as compared with another. Thus, a mild southern climate makes less exacting demands than the rough climate of the north; all eastern buildings appear to be somewhat open in contrast to the anxiously closed-in buildings of the north.

Secondly, the exterior will be given greater or lesser protection, depending on the rigor or mildness of the climate; this becomes apparent in the form of the roof and of other elements. Egypt, with no rainfall at all, has buildings without any roof; the medieval buildings of the north have tall roofs, and all their projecting parts are formed in such a way that the water can easily run off.

The materials that chiefly affect the form of the architectural elements are wood and stone. Even in countries where stone is scarce, the more important buildings use stone not only for walls and piers but also for the members that connect the piers or span the openings, wherever these are exposed to weathering. Often, even large interior ceilings are made of stone so as to last.

The basic form of walls and piers is not much affected by the nature of the material, since they have to stand vertically, whether made of wood or stone, and have the same thickness from top to bottom. The material has a greater effect on the ratio of thickness to height; this is determined by the resistance of the material to compression and buckling (reactive strength). Therefore, height, load, and all other circumstances being equal, a pier of hard marble is made thinner than one made of soft tuff. The material has its greatest effect on the main form and on the proportions of spans and ceilings. Wood grows straight to a considerable length and offers strong resistance to fracture. Therefore, it is in the nature of a wooden ceiling always to be rectilinear and to have a low ratio of thickness or height to unsupported span. Stone usually breaks into cube-shaped or slablike pieces and is rarely – in many places never – found in long beamlike pieces. Stone also has little resistance to breaking (relative strength), to which must be added its considerable specific weight. It, therefore, cannot sustain its own weight over a wide horizontal span and must be thicker than a wooden beam of equal length. Yet there are great differences among the different kinds of stone. In Greek monuments, mostly built of marble (the stone with the highest elasticity and relative strength), all column lintels (architraves) and soffits consisted of stone beams and plates, so that there were continuous horizontal spans in stone like those in timber, sometimes of very light proportions. It should be noted that the architectural proportions so far dealt with should more correctly be called *technostatic* proportions, as distinct from the main proportions that derive from the purpose of the building. These latter proportions include the ratio of length to height, both in the building as a whole and in its individual rooms and sections: for instance, the relation of the width (depth) of a portico to its height.

In countries where the available varieties of stone are brittle and not found in great lengths, attempts were soon made to span the opening with more than one piece of stone. The crowning result of these attempts was the vault. With vaulting, aided by mortar, the widest openings could be spanned with pieces of almost any size, however small. The vault not only greatly influenced the form of covering, since its construction naturally followed a curve rather than the straight line of a single lintel, but also changed the form of the piers and walls on which, by resting on them, it exerted a lateral pressure. Thus almost every architectural element changed – in other words the whole style – so that it may be said that essentially there are only two original styles: one with straight, horizontal stone architraves; the other with curved vaults and arches.

4

Building, being a skilled craft, is of course bound to improve with time. With the advance of civilization, the needs and demands for comfort expand, as do the tasks of architecture; and so people try to carry them out more efficiently and with less mechanical work. Apart from making improvements in the treatment of the material as such, they seek in the first place to obtain the necessary solidity through ingenious construction rather than through a mere accumulation of heavy masses. In the second place, even with unchanged methods of construction, they seek to reduce the mass of material, which with the growing need for comfort becomes more and more of an impediment: successive new buildings become lighter while remaining safe. In other words, lighter technostatic proportions are applied than in those older buildings that by their continued existence have proved to be of sufficient strength. This empirical progress in technostatics – or, if I may thus express it, in technostatic judgment by eye – must happen all the more regularly because a nation's previous experience is never lost but is constantly available to succeeding generations through the buildings that survive.

That this progress regularly occurs is shown by the monuments of nations known to us. It is even transmitted through a succession of nations in contact with each other. Of course the pace of progress, impeded in any case by the need for stability and by the force of custom, differs considerably among nations. It depends, in general, on how flexible and unimpeded their evolution has been and on the effect of political events. In Egypt where the priests had many workmen at their disposal, progress was very slow: all buildings were massive, and no real difference is apparent even over many centuries. The freer Greeks advanced more quickly; thus, the monuments built one to two hundred years after Pericles used considerably less material than those built before Pericles. With the Romans – who took over the architecture of the Greeks and who, having far more diverse needs, were necessarily more concerned with spaciousness and economy of material – lightness steadily increased to reach its peak in the medieval style.

Although reduction of mass and bolder construction (that is, lighter technostatic proportions) apply equally to lintels, ceilings, walls, and piers, this is less obvious in ceilings and walls, whose thickness can hardly be seen, than it is in freestanding piers with longer unsupported spans that lead to wider and bolder spacing. This is, of course, especially apparent in porticoes, where the distance between piers is least conditioned by the particular purpose of the structure.

To summarize this section: while it is true that the technostatic proportions of the architectural elements mainly derive from the material, they constantly evolve with advancing architectural experience and, in fact, are subject to permanent change. The basic forms of the architectural elements were set out in section 3, above. In what follows we shall explain how the progress of architecture as a fine art affects the specific shape of these elements.

★ ★ ★

Everyone will realize at once that the new style must come closest to the *Rundbogenstil* – that it is, in fact, essentially the *Rundbogenstil* as it would have evolved had it developed freely and spontaneously, unimpeded by all harmful reminiscences of the ancient style. This resemblance arises from the nature of things and was not brought about by authoritarian influence or individual preference. All the qualities of the new style described in this last section have either been substantiated by what has been said in the earlier sections or are based on structural laws that for the sake of brevity have been assumed to be known. Where the same task allowed several solutions, all have been accepted. The influence of reality in all its complexity has consistently been upheld. No rule that had proved correct in only a few cases or that in itself could not possibly be generally valid has been heedlessly proclaimed as a far-reaching principle applicable to all cases. The theory of art developed here is not, therefore, like those scholarly theories that relate to reality in only a few issues and in which rules abstracted from such theories are unhesitatingly made into general laws. This theory is thoroughly practical.

163   RUDOLF WIEGMANN
from "Remarks on the Book: In What Style Should We Build?" *(1829)*

Hübsch's pamphlet quickly ignited a controversy across Germany, as his suggestion to embrace the *Rundbogen* style would be countered by proponents for the Gothic style, the Renaissance style, the classical style, and by those architects insisting on emulating no historical styles. This excerpt of a review of Hübsch's book by Rudolf Wiegmann, however, also underscores the difficulty of imagining a new style *ex novo*. Wiegman had studied architecture under Georg Moller in Darmstadt and undertook studies in Italy between 1828 and 1832. He was thus still a student when he reviewed the book, as his youthful idealism and rejection of the past

Rudolf Wiegmann (1804–65), from "Bemerkungen über die Schrift [Remarks on the book]: *Im welchem Style sollen wir bauen?*" (1829) in *In What Style Should We Build? The German Debate on Architectural Style*, ed. and trans. Wolfgang Herrmann. Santa Monica: Getty Publication Programs, 1992, pp. 105–6, 111. © 1992 by Getty Publications. Reprinted with permission of Getty Publications.

make clear. What is less clear is what form a new style devoid of past reminiscences should take. While the Romantic plea for a harmony with the artist's spirit and the spirit of the age sounds right, it offers no guidelines for the real business of architectural form-making. Incidentally, Wiegmann later became a professor and by the early 1840s would come over to Hübsch's side to embrace the *Rundbogen* approach.

Before entering into details, we wish to make a few remarks about the term "style," which are absolutely necessary in order to arrive at an understanding with H. H. Throughout, he attaches to the term "style" a meaning that relates to material and construction, whereas in everyday language it is used in a spiritual sense only. Style is not a definite and unalterable system of construction and decoration; even less does it exclusively signify two different approaches to spanning – the arch and the straight architrave. In aesthetics, style has only two possible meanings: first, the signal character of a nation and an epoch, which is always reflected in any work of art (one speaks, for instance, of the Greek style, the Old-German style, or the Raphaelite style); second, a distinctive mode of expression or specific quality (in this sense, one speaks of a light, a sublime, or a grave style). In the latter meaning, it has nothing at all to do with construction, since the light, the sublime, and the grave style can appear in an arch just as well as in a straight architrave.

Consequently, a period cannot strive for a single style. In the first sense of the word, each period will automatically have a style of its own; in the second sense, it will include them all. The art of the Middle Ages, of the age of Pericles, and even that of the periwig age left an unmistakable impression of the time and its point of view – that is, of what we call style – although at those periods no conscious effort was made to strive for a particular style. Instead, style crystallized organically out of the time and the circumstances. Yet in every style in the first sense, there are various specific qualities that signify style in the second sense.

This being granted, the author cannot have meant anything by the new style that he wishes to establish but a matter of material and construction. Precepts of this kind nip artistic creation in the bud, clip the wings of genius, and lead it down a false and narrow path when, left to itself, it would create works that would be admired. Only what is already known can be prescribed; an original work is born unassisted. If the works of the most inspired masters of any art had been obliged to follow a pattern devised by others, what would they then have been like? The artist must create as a free man; he must obey only the spirit of his time and be the master of his material. He should master it but not tyrannize it. He should be obedient to the spirit of the time; but this spirit also lives in him. These are the conditions that will always bring forth true works of art. If the construction, which is a rational matter, is prescribed, the resulting works will of course be rational. But will that make them beautiful? With beautiful works, on the other hand, rationality may be taken for granted. The history of art shows that construction is not the cause but the result of the formal idea. If the ancient Greeks had wanted to create a building according to the idea of a medieval cathedral, they would have been just as unable to manage it with their system of construction as the Old-German masters would have been if they had planned a work according to the idea of the Parthenon. In both periods the construction was attuned to the total character of the architecture; and although both manners of construction were rational, they were poles apart. If a system of construction were to be laid down dogmatically, this would act as a barrier against ideas and ideals. Therefore, construction follows the idea. This is a universally valid law. If a person believes that one particular system of construction is adequate for the present time, this is only his personal belief, and he should therefore allow others the same right that he has arrogated to himself. There may be only one path to an ideal, but who wants to subscribe to one particular ideal and not acknowledge another equally sublime? [. . .]

Although many of the points raised here are not contested by H. H. in his essay, and although he no doubt largely shares our point of view, nevertheless this seems to be the right place to make some suggestions that might serve to prevent the revival of past artistic systems (which is spreading more and more) and clear the way for true art. All systems are based on the records and facts of past ages. For that reason, a living art has no system as such. We should thus strive to attain a living art that faithfully reflects and is nourished by the character of our own time. Admittedly, architecture is also better fitted than any other art to express the character of the present time, which might be described as lacking in independence. To attain this independence and to transform and shape the age is now the supreme duty of an artist, nay of a man. Success depends on circumstances, and it would be futile to imagine that a few individuals could bring about a salutary reform. Not until the artist encounters true artistic sense, pure taste among the people, and a warm and encouraging response to what he has to offer can a single person – however right and however sincere he might be – achieve anything of importance. Nevertheless, while the time of fulfillment has not arrived, he ought to give his loyal support to preparatory work. He must, however, look upon history as history and not as a source for precepts! The idea thus embodied may find some fortuitous historical counterpart; but it still belongs to its own time, whose freeborn child it is. It makes no difference whether columns, arches, or architraves carry the load. Every means of spanning space can, in its proper place, be the best and the most beautiful. When art is no longer directed solely by arbitrary human laws, when its principles and its essence are in harmony with the artist's spirit and with that of his age, then art will have found not only a solid basis but also a freedom that ensures its fullest blossoming.

164   KARL FRIEDRICH SCHINKEL
from Notes for a textbook on architecture (c.1830)

After peace was reestablished in Europe following the exile of Napoleon, Schinkel returned to architectural practice with a high position in Prussian state service and began his illustrious career. His principal theoretical concern remained always style, or more specifically, how to create a new style in keeping with the ambitious ideals of an expanding Prussian statehood. The Romanticism of his early period, which initially inclined toward the Gothic style, gave way in the late 1810s to a stripped-down classicism, as seen in his Berlin Guardhouse

Karl Friedrich Schinkel, from Notes for a textbook on architecture (c.1830), trans. Harry Francis Mallgrave from *Das architekonische Lehrbuch*, ed. Goerd Peschken. Berlin: Deutscher Kunstverlag, 1979, pp. 114–15.

(1816–18) and Berlin Playhouse (1818–21). The 1820s also saw further experimentation with elements of the Italian vernacular and most importantly with his efforts to design buildings with no stylistic reminiscences whatsoever. At the same time Schinkel was much concerned with composing a textbook for architectural students, and throughout the 1820s it took the form of a comparative morphology of structural solutions and building forms. The following passage, probably penned around 1830, gives voice to this concern with construction during this phase of his development, but also in his desire to expand his conception of architecture beyond it.

Every work of art, of whatever kind, must always bring a new and living element into the world of art. Without this genuine element, the artist cannot have true and necessary tension, nor does the work of art offer the public an advantage, to the world in general a gift. This is the moral value of a work of art from which the individual soul of the artist speaks, and to be sure in such a distinctly characteristic manner that no other kind of expression can display it. [...]

In architecture the artist needs above all a general education. It is not that he should carry around in his head an excess of idle knowledge and on its basis take every occasion to instruct with a professorial language, or excel with a positive knowledge of the existing, or discuss what exists in terms of philosophical concepts, abstractions, and syntheses. But rather, his spirit must be so imbued with the essence of the classical period that his activity, which can only be directed to the new conditions within the new circumstances, may freely proceed in the spirit of those classical times and, with an unimpeded cadence, bring forth the correct, the beautiful, and the characteristic from among the new and transformed conditions.

In order to catch a foothold in the broad field of architecture of our time – where the confusion or the total lack of principles had increased with regard to style, as useful criticism becomes very difficult because of the endless number of buildings that have arisen in the various epochs of the world – I will speak the following basic principle:

Architecture is construction.

In architecture everything must be true, and any masking or concealing of the construction is an error. The real task here is to make every part of the construction beautiful within its character.

In the word "beautiful" resides the whole story, the whole nature, and the whole feeling for conditions. In itself it expresses, in short, everything of trivial purposiveness [*Zweckmässigkeit*], which at the same time it may never lack, even when it can be invested with greater or lesser insight.

The second basic principle for architecture with style leads me to the following consideration:

Every perfect construction in a specific material has its own very distinct character, and cannot be rationally carried out in the same way in another material. This individual separation of one material from the other forbids any complete mixing of different materials during construction, wherever one material, the internally complete and perfect, shames the other. Even the simplicity of the viewer's conception would get lost.

In architecture with style, therefore, every construction produced in a specific material must be complete in itself and whole. It may exist beside or above something else, but may not mix with it; it remains self-sufficient in itself and displays its full character.

165   KARL FRIEDRICH SCHINKEL
from Notes for a textbook on architecture (c.1835)

One of the more interesting phases of Schinkel's architectural experimentation of the 1820s and early 1830s were several designs for buildings and residences with no allusions to a historical style. Projects such as his design for a market for Unter den Linden (1827) are entirely utilitarian in character. Certainly the most significant of his experiments in this regard was his design for the new building of the Berlin Bauakademie (1831–6), which in its supreme constructional logic defies any stylistic designation. But Schinkel was at the same time always rethinking his position, and sometime toward the middle of the 1830s he had come to reject what he termed his "error of pure radical abstraction." This passage is really one of the most remarkable in all architectural literature because of its insights and candidness. It vividly underscores the difficulty of inventing a new style and how essential Schinkel felt art was to the creative process.

After I began my architectural studies and had made some progress in the different branches, I soon felt a stirring within my soul, which became all the more important the more I sought to clarify it.

I noticed that all architectural forms were based on three basic ideas: (1) on forms of construction; (2) on forms possessing traditional or historical importance; (3) on forms meaningful in themselves and taking their model from nature. I noticed further that an enormous treasury of forms had already been invented or deposited in the world over many centuries of development and through the executed works of very different peoples. But I saw at the same time that our use of this accumulated treasury of often very heterogeneous objects was arbitrary, because each individual form carries its own particular charm through a dark presentiment of a necessary motif – be it historical or constructive – that intensifies and continues to seduce us as we employ it. We believe that by invoking such a motif we invest our work with a special charm, even though the most pleasing effect produced by its primitive appearance in old works is often completely contradicted by its use in our present works. It became especially clear to me that this willfulness of use is the reason for the lack of character and style that seems to plague so many of our new buildings.

It became my life's goal to clarify this matter. But the more I considered the problem, the more I saw the difficulties opposing my efforts. Very soon I fell into the error of pure radical abstraction, by which I conceived a specific architectural work entirely from utilitarian purpose and construction. In these cases there emerged something dry and rigid, something that lacked freedom and altogether excluded two essential elements: the historic and the poetic.

I investigated further but soon found myself trapped in a great labyrinth where I had to ponder how far the rational principle should be applied in defining the trivial concept of the object, and how far, on the other hand, those higher influences of the historical and artistic-poetic purposes should be allowed in order to raise it to a work of art. In this regard it was

Karl Friedrich Schinkel, from Notes for a textbook on architecture (c.1835), trans. Harry Francis Mallgrave from *Das architekonische Lehrbuch*, ed. Goerd Peschken. Berlin: Deutscher Kunstverlag, 1979, pp. 149–50.

not difficult to recognize that the governing relation of such different principles had to be different in each concrete case, and it was equally clear to me that in this regard we can speak of architecture only where the true artistic element assumes its place in this art, and that in all other cases it is and remains an objective handiwork. Therefore here, as everywhere else in the fine arts, an effective theory is difficult and reduces itself in the end to the cultivation of feeling. From what was said above it should also be evident that feeling in architecture certainly embraces a very wide circle, and, if from its productions a favorable result should be expected, it should be cultivated from the most varied and different sources. It seems to me therefore important to set down beside one another the different realms in which the feeling of the architect should be cultivated in order to understand the extent of art.

First of all, we should consider what our age demands in its architectural undertakings. This task entails simultaneously a critique of what is clear or unclear with regard to the spirit of the time; how these undertakings are impeded by false views and judgments, ignorance, lack of imagination, and a distrust of the contemporary technical possibilities in possible new inventions and for the removal of hindrances; how freedom in these undertakings is curtailed, in conventional arrangements again and again driven off until the creative urge is completely extinguished. Second, it is necessary to review the past in order to see what has already been discovered for similar purposes, and which of those things already perfected might be of use and welcome to us. Third, what modifications need to be made to those things found useful. Fourth, how and in what way we must employ the imagination in these modifications to produce something totally new; and how we must treat these new inventions in order to bring them into a harmonious accord with the old, and raise not only the expression of style in works but also allow the feeling for something totally new to emerge with the style feelings of the viewer. Here will arise a happy creation of our age in which there is both the recognition of stylistic suitability and the primitive effect. In some cases we can even create the sense of the naive and endow the work with a double charm.

166 RUDOLF WIEGMANN
from "Thoughts on the Development of a National Architectural Style for the Present" (1841)

The question of a style for the present, which both Schinkel and Hübsch had posed in the 1820s, mushroomed into a full-scale debate in the 1840s. The profession, in fact, in itself was in the midst of sweeping changes across the German-speaking lands. Professional education for architects had become a reality in Germany and Austria, and schools were now operating with a high degree of competence and efficiency. In 1837 in Vienna, Ludwig Förster founded the first German-speaking professional journal for architecture, the *Allgemeine Bauzeitung*,

Rudolf Wiegmann, from "Gedanken über Entwickelung eines zeitgemässen nationalen Baustyls" [Thoughts on the development of a national architectural style for the present], trans. Harry Francis Mallgrave from *Allgemeine Bauzeitung*, Vol. 6 (1841), pp. 208, 213.

which quickly became a forum for debate. And in 1843 the first national union or association of German architects met in Bamberg; these annual congresses of the brightest architects also brought much discussion to the issue of founding a new style. This essay by Rudolf Wiegmann, now a professor of architecture in Düsseldorf, underscores the high level of the debate. Wiegmann had earlier been critical of Hübsch's book, but now sides with him in proposing that the rounded-arch or *Rundbogen* style should form the basis of a national style — mainly to counter the proliferation of eclectic tendencies. Germany, incidentally, was not yet unified, and the push toward national unity later in the 1840s would lead to a political disaster.

This truth is so simple and evident that it might appear to be superfluous to utter it one more time. And yet, how stridently architecture in its present practice stands in contradiction to its era! If it is correct that art is the truest mirror of the epoch and national conditions with the unadulterated reflection of its culture, morals, intellectual pursuits, and feelings – and as such we must necessarily consider the older art – what do we find then as the basic character of our architecture? Apparently it is nothing other than abominable, inconsistent vacillation without a goal, sense, or depth. How motley and confusedly are our present building efforts: Greek, Roman, Byzantine, Gothic, and Italian, basilicas and Gothic cathedrals, Roman triumphal arches, Antonius columns, Parthenons, obelisks, and much more!

On the purposiveness of a specific style, or a particular architectural form for reuse, much indeed has been very plausibly reasoned. For instance, because the old-German cathedral was so deeply moving to the heart and therefore was so uncommonly suited to its purpose, we should also continue to use this style for all churches. But in other buildings, in residences for instance, which have to fulfill completely different functions, the Greek or Roman style is more suitable. For palaces, moreover, the Pitti Palace should serve as a model; for theaters or museums the Greek temple, etc. Thus it has happened that when we divide art history into certain epochs and peoples always with one style, even if details are often modified – demonstrating in general a logically continuous style as the expression of a harmonious union of the materials with the spiritual and moral conditions of its time – today we introduce any style with equal justification. This eclecticism has brought confusion to this art, whose end is scarcely imaginable; and the criteria for it is so crazy that even educated minds are moved to judge our modern buildings more from the viewpoint of fashion than from the viewpoint of genuine art. For while we always place upon painting and especially upon poetry the demands that they should create works out of the innermost kernel of our spiritual life, that these works should be conceived as the organic blossoms on the trunk of our present culture and current spiritual and moral interests in all its interrelations, down to their deepest roots – almost no one thinks that this demand, with the same right, should also be applied to architecture. What has happened that this elevated art at present should no longer be able, as it once was, of being the particular impression of such an industrious and multifaceted, stimulating time and of its driving spirit!

★ ★ ★

The German pointed-arch style, however, cannot be that which our present architecture should follow. There remains for us, however, only the Romanesque *Rundbogen* style. Certainly this style, in that it developed earlier, belongs to a time that has little in common with the present, but we should consider one thing. It did not grow to completion and it does not lie behind us as a whole: finished and complete in all its parts. The style was rather suddenly interrupted in the thirteenth century by an eccentric fanaticism, in which feeling abandoned the expense of reason and suddenly interrupted its logical development, as its simple forms – articulated and endlessly decorated – were stretched out by a holy mysticism toward heaven. From this arose the wonderful style that we met in its greatest purity in the Cologne Cathedral. Whereas before an excess of mass assured a static balance, now there was the artistic daring of thrust and counterthrust, above all the boldness and security that today still astonish us. From such a school naturally an uncommonly refined technology had to emerge, which in and for itself was very respectable. But in its high self-consciousness it soon led to the complete corruption of the sacred art, until in the end a work as degenerate as the Munster at Ulm could be conceived as the last boundary-stone of the blossoming of this style. One had gradually learned to despise what was possible with the *simple, purposeful, true*, and unaffected; in the thirteenth century we left behind the promising beginnings of the *Rundbogen* style. The elements of that arch-style, however, are more rationally suited to our materials, climate, and needs than any other style, and they have not fully developed. Works of high artistic value were raised for that time, and as a consequence when it is further developed under the control of a taste refined by antiquity something far more perfect will blossom from it.

167 JOHANN HEINRICH WOLFF
from "Remarks on the Architectural Questions Broached by Professor Stier..." (1845)

At the first congress of the Association of German Architects in 1843, the Berlin architect Friedrich Wilhelm Ludwig Stier delivered the keynote address, entitled "Review of Noteworthy Efforts and Questions for Understanding the Architecture of the Present and Recent Past." In it he posed three questions – the first two dealing with general principles of architecture. The third question dealt with the issue of originality in design, or what constitutes architectural originality and in what way is it manifested in present-day practice. The three questions drew a lengthy response from J. H. Wolff, a former student of Leo von Klenze and Charles Percier as well as a professor at the Fine Arts Academy in Kassel. Wolff had long been an active voice in the contemporary debate, and in his *Beiträge zur Aesthetik der Baukunst* (Contribution to the aesthetics of architecture, 1834) he skillfully and at length defended the principles of classicism. Wolff brings the same classical perspective to this analysis, which begins with a historical overview of all the styles down to the Renaissance.

Johann Heinrich Wolff (1792–1869), from "Einige Worte über die von Herrn Professor Stier bei der Architektenversammlung zu Bamberg zur Sprache gebrachten... architektonischen Fragen" [Remarks on the architectural questions broached by Professor Stier at the meeting of architects at Bamberg, 1845] (1845), trans. Wolfgang Herrmann, in *In What Style Should We Build? The German Debate on Architectural Style*. Santa Monica: Getty Publication Programs, 1992, pp. 143–5. © 1992 by Getty Publications. Reprinted with permission of Getty Publications.

What can I say now about our latest period? We are the heirs to all the acquisitions and accomplishments, to all the attempts and efforts on which I have cast a fleeting light. Yet instead of profiting from these experiences and adopting only what is true and everlasting, we take pleasure in admitting into our art all the mistakes committed by our predecessors; and, moreover, we still cling to the misguided idea that we can succeed in inventing a new style that has never existed before. It is just this confusion of ideas that has prompted me to make this historical review. I have sought to show that real benefit cannot be expected to accrue from further attempts to create new styles but rather from the recognition that the great periods of architecture, those that brought real advances and added new architectural elements, ended with the climax of Greek (Ionic and late Doric) architecture. Furthermore, I have sought to show that the addition of the arch by the Romans represented a significant gain, though more of a material nature: an element that in appropriate places and in an appropriate manner we may have to introduce into our architecture. Since we have become acquainted with the original buildings, a privilege not granted to our medieval predecessors, and can make use of the advances achieved in aesthetics and the history of art – and, indeed, of all the groundwork done by so many experts and scholars – we would be unworthy of so many treasures if we were not to return to what alone is true and what fulfills all our requirements.

After what has been said, Professor Stier's question "What kind of originality can we expect to find in present day architecture?" finds its own answer. We are called upon to be new only in the sense of modifying and rearranging the architectural elements that naturally evolved in antiquity. This leaves for invention an admittedly finite but still extremely wide field, a terrain whose fertility will never be exhausted. Invention is restricted to demonstrating that the eternal laws and forms discovered by the ancients can be applied in many new ways that conform to the idea of each particular building, to the material conditions, and therefore also to the particular requirements of our age and our nation. In this, our guide can again be the careful observation and contemplation of the ancient models with their fine sense of what is appropriate.[1] However, we lack the vocation and the ability to create new forms and therefore must forgo the fame of having a national and truly original style. The character and – I am convinced – the merit of our period resides in the fact that art has relinquished the claim to be particular and national in order to become universally valid. Even on this higher level, those differences between nations and countries that are rooted in nature will assert themselves, albeit in a subordinate way and only if they are not consciously sought. If every artist strives after what is true and right, then his work will in itself carry the imprint of his mind.

I will conclude by expressing the hope that no preconceived opinion will stand in the way of a general acceptance and propagation of this basic truth, upon which alone, in my opinion, our art can thrive. Of course, I can foresee that many dissenting opinions will first be raised: one might quote in this connection what Goethe once remarked in a letter to Schiller, "Many who resist truth do so simply because they would perish if they were to acknowledge it." All who share this belief (however few in number) must therefore close ranks and with unwavering courage wrest the ground from the adversary, inch by inch. Art is of a rank equal to religion and philosophy; joined to these, it must extend and establish the realm of the spirit, as far as it is humanly possible. Let us start to sow the seeds from which will rise mighty trees that will afford no room for rampant weeds and spread their magnificent branches wide to choke the thistles and thorns. Then we shall fulfill the vocation that the age has imposed upon us as recognized at first by a few but later unfailingly by all.

NOTE

1   In my reviews, I have frequently declared this to be the aim of present-day architecture. Therefore, I will never acknowledge – as some architects do, who generally pursue a more correct course – that it is pleasant and interesting here and there to encounter a little building recently erected in the Byzantine or Moorish style. All these various manners of building should nowadays appear only in historical paintings, vignettes, stage sets, etc., where their presence is historically justified as a kind of costume that helps us to imagine ourselves transported to the times to which these buildings belong.

168   EDUARD METZGER
from ''Contribution to the Contemporary Question: In What Style Should One Build!'' (1845)

Still another direction was opened in the German architectural debate of the 1840s by a few architects who continued to argue that the present age was on the verge of inventing an entirely new style. Eduard Metzger upheld such a position. He had studied architecture in the late 1820s in Munich under Leo von Klenze and Friedrich Gärtner, and after a tour of the south that included Greece, he returned to Munich and was appointed a professor of architecture at the newly founded polytechnical school. In early writings he stressed that architectural development follows a rational process: consisting of utilitarian, climatic, and structural principles of development. However, in this particular essay – responding to Hübsch's book some 17 years later – Metzger carries his thinking one step further. Pointing to the recent use of iron trusses in European architecture, Metzger now sees his age as fulfilling the promise of an entirely new style. In his dialectical view of history, architecture had passed from the compressive logic of the pyramids to the trabeated system of the column to the perfection of the pointed arch in Gothic times. This last perfect style, with its complex network of ribs, shares a special affinity with the linear forms of iron construction, hence iron – with its ''finely felt linear configurations, soaring upward'' – will create for architecture a new style once the material begins to be treated artistically. Metzger is still sketchy as to just what this new style would look like, but this essay stands near the beginning of a long line of German speculations on the creation of a new style, which would continue down through the century.

Eduard Metzger, from ''Beitrag zur Zeitfrage: In welchem Stil man bauen soll!'' [Contribution to the contemporary question: in what style should one build!], trans. Harry Francis Mallgrave from *Allgemeine Bauzeitung*, Vol. 10 (1845), pp. 177–8.

The *pointed-arch style* is the German national system of building. The *pointed arch* is the technically most advanced form of the vault. The *pointed-arch system of building* is the most closely related to collective German sensitivities and manners of perception, and it responded to the heart; thus it became the most useful instrument for the Christian religion. The *pointed arch* is artistically capable of the greatest possible flexibility; it is for the artist a happy dissonance that struggles for resolution, which it finds in other architectural bodies, while other useful arch forms in themselves remain quiet. Finally, the *pointed-arch formal element* is that by which the building trade awoke to higher artistic activity and spontaneously elevated itself.

But since the golden age of the pointed-arch system we have become richer in insight and practical experience, if poorer in means (if also only relatively). Civic spirit has taken another turn. The *picture* demands another body; which is why practical experience has also pursued other paths. The *vegetablization* and fine distortions of that building system made it less durable and climatically inadmissible. Instead of vaulted arches, *iron construction* has come along.

For this I return to the path of development where I had left off above! The network of the pointed-arch system of building in its complex of ribs is closely related to the nature of iron when suitably developed. Circles and triangles are also here the basic forms needed for bracing. Therefore in recent structural developments we return to the beginning and to the old basic elements that were gradually raised to independent artistic organisms. Iron construction will have the greatest influence on roofing if we let this material develop freely and without force. One should not be put off by the expression "iron"; where it does not suffice there is bronze. Both are similar organisms with regard to formal development. What advantage does iron offer in the roofing of a large space? What techniques, for instance, might one imagine today for constructing a domed vault, such as replacing the masonry used in St. Peters church in Rome?! Today England, France, Belgium, Russia have numerous examples of iron roofs over moderate spaces. In essence, iron only lacks artistic development, which has to be raised in line with the organizing principles of this building material. Indeed this must not be brought about by employing thick iron beams, which is striking in itself; we would also seriously err if we were to consider only a *straight-line* roof. These are simply directions contrary to the nature of the material. For *commanding* spaces, it is probably closer in an organic sense to the vault, to which, as noted above, it remains related. To give as the most general starting point, I am reminded here of Norman timber roofs.

The above suffices only to throw open to the specialist the rich field of future architecture. He sees here other architectural forms needed to raise a new and rejuvenated body. I have studied the matter well before writing; for many years I have made a conscious effort to complete a number of drawings of churches, monuments, and profane buildings of every conceivable kind, and I believe in the victory of the time. It should therefore not be said that the present does not already have sufficient forces to take a major step forward, if it would only bring itself to let the imagined material develop according to its nature, if it does not force iron to assume forms contrary to its nature. Those characteristic rib-like forms in the German architectural style may stand, accordingly, in the closest immediacy to the newly developed forms in question by means of iron struts. Therefore we should add that this active artistic element in the German architectural style not only artistically yields nothing foreign to the traditional ways of thinking and feeling, but in many cases it would even affirm them.

If with the introduction of iron into the architectural body the possible changes can be assumed to be lighter, so is it all the more difficult to express how it will affect a more massive, total building body with respect to the well-known German style. It seems almost as if iron trusses and massive building fabrics are express opposites, and yet I add, they will both react to one another in such a way that a total organism will be the result, and the body will raise itself purely as from cast iron! The architect knows well the artistic means he has at his disposal in order to neutralize the apparent contradictions, and even in this overcoming will be seen the power of art, that of the artist. The fear that has been voiced that from this material later would emerge a new and more boring architectural body... will likewise be found ungrounded, as the notion of mass in no way means a piling up of stone, which we all know is still not called art! On the contrary I imagine slender, finely felt linear configurations, soaring upward, strong or delicate according to circumstances, for the most part intersecting the horizontal lines. For the nature of iron itself demands this, as did the pointed arch, which accordingly was organic to the extent that an artistic form of vault became a component of the transformed building body.

169 CARL BÖTTICHER
from "The Principles of Hellinic and Germanic Ways of Building" (1846)

Metzger's essay of the previous year was probably the stimulus for what was arguably the most important writing in German theory in the first half of the nineteenth century – a commemorative address delivered in Berlin in 1846. Its speaker was long associated with Schinkel and the Berlin educational system. In the 1820s he had studied at an industrial-arts school and his early interests lay with ornamentation and textiles. After teaching at various of these schools, Bötticher was appointed by Schinkel in 1839 to teach at the Bauakademie, and he subsequently turned his attention full-time to architecture. Schinkel died in 1841 and three years later Bötticher passed his state examinations and became a professor. By this date Bötticher had already published the first volume of his influential book *Die Tektonik der Hellenen* (The tectonics of the Hellenes; see chapter 218 below). The address of 1846 was an annual affair, in which all members of the Berlin architectural community gathered to pay homage to the memory of Schinkel.

Bötticher's argument is exceptionally lucid. Employing the Hegelian dialectic, he reasons that a style is first defined by its space-covering or structural principle, and there had been two perfect styles in architectural history:

Carl Gottlieb Wilhelm Bötticher (1806–99), from "Das Prinzip der hellenischen und germanischen Bauweise hinsichtlich der Übertragung in de Bauweise unserer Tage" [The principles of the Hellenic and Germanic ways of building with regard to their application to our present way of building] (1846), trans. Wolfgang Herrmann, in *In What Style Should We Build? The German Debate on Architectural Style*. Santa Monica: Getty Publication Programs, 1992, pp. 156–9. © 1992 by Getty Publications. Reprinted with permission of Getty Publications.

first the trabeated system developed by the Greeks, second the arcuated system that achieved its pinnacle in Gothic times (the *Spitzbogen* or pointed-arch style). Each had employed different structural principles, and both had exhausted any possibility for further development. Hence for a new style to emerge, a new spatial system must develop, one that would employ a new material and new logical principle. The new material was in fact iron; its new principle would be a mediation of the spatial possibilities of the Gothic style with the symbolic or highly refined artistic sensibilities of the Greek style. The day of this new style was now dawning; eclecticism would be destroyed and the source of new artistic invention would be opened.

Bötticher's optimism, incidentally, would soon prove elusive to realize. The political turmoil in the German-speaking lands in 1848–9 (a failed attempt at unification) shattered all such optimism, and the full structural possibilities of iron still had to await the technical development of steel, which would not become evident until toward the end of the century. Nevertheless, here is an instance where theory precedes practice.

The Hellenic art-forms gradually disappeared; they were finally eliminated from the system when structural explicitness came to be the aim. Only faint traces of the Hellenic element remained in certain parts of the Germanic style. Yet whether this style with its emancipation from the material – leading to a withdrawal from nature and the sensory world – replaced the Hellenic art-forms with others of equal value is a question to which we can only respond with a definite "no." With regard to our perception of style, the Middle Ages differ from antiquity. The works of the Christian style are still before us; they still serve the same purpose as when they were built. Their ethical and functional significance hold no mystery for us, and the structural system in all its evolutionary stages is clearly displayed: all it needs for a full perception is our willingness to see. It is quite different with antiquity. Not only have very few of its buildings survived – and these only in scarcely recognizable remains – but the arrangement and particular function of the interior is still hidden from us behind an impenetrable veil. We have neither the ability nor the desire to return to Hellenic art, because this would mean regressing by more than two thousand years at least. But it would be equally impossible to breathe new life into Germanic art. To seek to continue with either style would mean trying to perfect perfection. Both styles have had their existence and will never exist again. And yet another art will emerge from the womb of time and will take on a life of its own: an art in which a different structural principle will sound a more ringing keynote than the other two. Another style will be born but only after the other two have made their contributions. Because this style will have its origin and its basis in the principles of the two other styles, it cannot exclude either of them; but it will embrace both and allow them to serve it jointly.

Is it possible for yet another new style to be developed in addition to these two traditional styles, one specific to our generation, in which a structural force different from that of the other two styles acts as the principle of its system of covering? And what force would be its active principle? In view of what has just been said, it is possible without needing the gift of clairvoyance to answer this question. As always with things that are still coming into existence, no more than hints can be given, although there are clear indications that the beginning has already become a reality.

Aside from the fact that a single person cannot promulgate a style and that only a whole nation can cause its inception and a whole epoch suffice for its development, the truth of the matter can only be as follows.

Our contention that the manner of covering determines every style and its ultimate development is confirmed by the monuments of all styles. Equally evident is the truth that from the earliest and roughest attempts to cover spaces by using stone, to the culmination represented by the *Spitzbogen* vault, and down to the present time, all the ways in which stone could possibly be used to span a space have been exploited, and they have completely exhausted the possible structural applications of this material. No longer can stone alone form a new structural system of a higher stage of development. The reactive, as well as relative, strength of stone has been completely exhausted. A new and so far unknown system of covering (which will of course bring in its train a new world of art-forms) can appear only with the adoption of an unknown material, or rather a material that so far has not been used as a guiding principle. It will have to be a material with physical properties that will permit wider spans, with less weight and greater reliability, than are possible when using stone alone. With regard to spatial design and construction, it must be such as will meet any conceivable spatial or planning need. A minimal quantity of material should be needed for the walls, thus rendering the bulky and ponderous buttresses of the *Spitzbogenstil* completely superfluous. The whole weight of the covering system would be confined to vertical pressure, that is, to the reactive strength of walls and supports. Of course, this does not mean that the indirect use of stone vaulting, especially the system of ribbed and stellar vaulting, will be excluded; on the contrary, the latter will be widely used. But it does mean that, for those parts on which the whole system rests, another material will be used, one that makes it possible to transfer their structural function to other parts in which a different principle operates. It makes no difference whether the members to be replaced are buttresses or members that support the ceiling, such as ribs, bands, etc.

Such a material is iron, which has already been used for this purpose in our century. Further testing and greater knowledge of its structural properties will ensure that iron will become the basis for the covering system of the future and that structurally it will in times to come be as superior to the Hellenic and medieval systems as the arcuated medieval system was to the monolithic trabeated system of antiquity. Disregarding the fragile wooden ceiling (which in any case cannot serve as a comparison) and using mathematical terms, one can say that iron is indeed the material whose principle, yet unutilized, will introduce into architecture the last of the three forces, namely, absolute strength. In particular it will be active in those anchor bands that will replace buttresses and flying buttresses. In this way, absolute force will be established as the guiding principle of the system of covering. Therefore, if relative strength is the principle of the classical trabeated system and reactive strength that of the arcuated system, then the system of a vaulted stone covering with iron ribs can adopt from the arcuated system only its relative strength, to which – as its defining feature – it must add the absolute strength of the anchor bands. The relative strength of iron beams, replacing those made of stone in the trabeated system, can play only an indirect and minor role; to replace the Hellenic trabeated stone system with a trabeated iron system would represent only a change of material, not a change of principle. It would lead to one-sided and very limited progress and would prove as inadequate as stone beams for spanning wide spaces.

The structural principle is thus to be adopted from the arcuated system and transformed into a new and hitherto unknown system; for the art-forms of the new system, on the other hand, the formative principle of the Hellenic style must be adopted in order to give artistic expression to the structural forces within the parts, their correlation, and the spatial concept. This alone will create the true mediation, the right synthesis of the two preceding styles. In what manner and by what art-forms the structural and spatial character might be expressed within this newly formed system is a question that the thoughtful person will not find too difficult to answer. Nor is it necessary to say that it is technically possible to protect the forms of the iron parts against rusting with a tin or copper-plating process or that this coating should be sufficiently thick to outline the forms clearly in a way appropriate to each part of the vault.

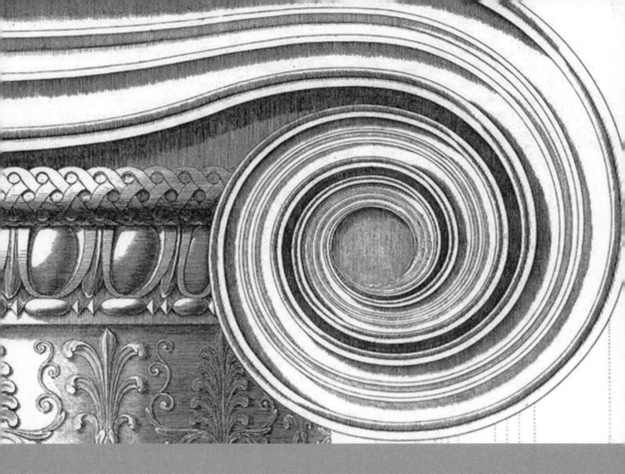

D. THE RISE OF AMERICAN THEORY

Introduction

The United States also emerged as a new cultural entity in the nineteenth century. Its early competing courses of architectural practice were largely defined by the Puritanical tradition of New England and the Jeffersonian tradition of the South. The former was derivative of British practice, although with material variations made necessary by the new landscape and climate. Jefferson was enamored with classicism as a way to represent America's democratic political values. Through the efforts of America's first great architect – Benjamin Latrobe – this style became in effect the national style in the first three decades of the century. By the 1840s, however, classicists were increasingly opposed on the one hand by a growing number of enthusiasts of the Gothic Revival emanating from Britain, and on the other hand by practitioners of the *Rundbogen* style emigrating from Germany. Thus there was a pluralism in mid-century in North America as well, a tendency that continued with the popularity of the Second

Empire style in the 1860s coming out of France. But in the middle of the century something else happened to America as well. The essayist Ralph Waldo Emerson and the sculptor Horatio Greenough began to lay the case for a uniquely American artistic culture and therefore for an uniquely American architecture and its functional basis. It was, in a more exalted way, to be founded not on the values of the Old World but on a transcendental vision of the New World and its growing importance in the world. This idealistic vision, individualistic and pioneering at its roots, would prepare the cultural way for a flourishing of American practice later in the century.

170   THOMAS JEFFERSON
Letters (1787, 1791, 1805, 1810)

A merican theory, like its culture and population, was almost entirely dependent on European ideas throughout the late eighteenth and early nineteenth centuries. British colonial settlers revolted against the British crown in 1776 and defined the principles of a nonroyalist form of government – all the while retaining a close dependence on British civic and religious values. French influence on American thought was also strong in the early years of the country, in part because of France's (anti-British) support during the American revolutionary years. During the nineteenth century, waves of immigrants from Germany, Ireland, and Italy, among many other European states, settled into the new land and further contributed to the cultural mosaic that became America.

Notwithstanding these close European dependencies, it is still possible to speak of a developing American body of architectural theory. Its roots in part lie with Thomas Jefferson, who remained throughout his life almost as avid a devotee to architecture as he was to politics. His interest in this field stemmed from his student days at the College of William and Mary, and shortly thereafter, in 1767, he began construction of his country seat Monticello, basing his design on plates from Palladio's *Four Books of Architecture* and Robert Morris's *Select Architecture* (1755). The political revolution of course intervened and interrupted his efforts. After writing the Declaration of Independence in 1776 he was elected governor of Virginia and almost immediately had to cope with the invasion of British forces into Virginia. In 1784 he was asked by Congress to join John Adams and Benjamin Franklin in Europe in negotiating treaties of peace and commerce, and in the following year he succeeded Franklin as the minister or ambassador to France, where he lived until 1789. After returning home, he served as George Washington's first Secretary of State, and in 1800 became the third president of the United States. After his retirement from politics he devoted himself to Monticello and to various other activities, chief of which was the founding of the University of Virginia.

The following four letters plot Jefferson's architectural development over the course of his career. In the first letter of 1787, he displays his early enthrallment with the architecture of France, both modern and ancient. For the American Embassy in Paris, he leased the somewhat luxurious Hôtel de Langeac, a neoclassical work of Jean-François-Thérèse Chalgrin on the Champs Elysée, across the street from one of Claude-Nicolas Ledoux's toll houses. Jefferson was also "violently smitten" with Pierre Rousseau's Hôtel de Salm (1782–5), and he admired Soufflot's church of Sainte Geneviève (1756–90) and the laminated timber dome of the Halle au Blé (1782–3). He also traveled the countryside of England with John Adams in 1786 to study country estates and that new phenomenon of

Thomas Jefferson (1743–1826), from Letter to Madame de Tessé, March 20, 1787; Letter to Major L'Enfant, March 10, 1791; Letter to Littleton Waller Tazewell, Jan. 5, 1805; Letter to Messrs. Hugh L. White and Others, May 6, 1810, in *Thomas Jefferson: Writings*. New York: The Library of America, 1984, pp. 891–2, 975–6, 1149–50, 1222–3.

"picturesque" gardens. His favorite architectural monument, however, was the Roman Maison Carrée in Nîmes (first century BC), the temple that had earlier enthralled Laugier. In the collaboration of the French architect Charles-Louis Clérisseau, Jefferson used it as a model for the design of the Virginia State Capitol (1785–99). Here he records his impressions of this temple and other classical works, in a letter written to his female friend, the Countess de Tessé.

The second letter stems from his tenure as the first Secretary of State. In that capacity he became keenly interested in the planning of the new capital city along the Potomac and its principal monuments. In 1791 George Washington commissioned Pierre-Charles L'Enfant, a French painter and architect, to prepare a plan for the new city, and Washington – knowing Jefferson's interest – requested that L'Enfant contact the Secretary of State. Jefferson responded to the Frenchman with maps of several European cities from his own library. His comments in this letter on the design of the Capitol also demonstrate his concern for this project. A competition was held in 1792 for its design, and was won by William Thornton. Construction, however, was plagued with difficulties, and Jefferson, as President, was later able to exert considerable influence over its redesign when he named Benjamin Latrobe as the new architect of the Capitol in 1803.

The third and fourth letters deal with Jefferson's efforts to create the University of Virginia. Aside from the importance of the school itself in furthering democratic values, Jefferson always had a very specific vision of the university. In the letter of 1805 he not only distinguishes how a modern university should differ from the examples at Oxford and Cambridge, but he also makes the architectural stipulation that it should be not housed in a single large building, but in a "village" of smaller units. This proposal may have emanated from an encyclopedia entry on "colleges," written by A. C. Quatremère de Quincy in 1788.

In the fourth letter of 1810 Jefferson further refines his concept of an "academical village." Here in fact he describes the plan that he would draw up around 1817 – minus the headpiece of the library at the top of the scheme. The cornerstone to the university was also laid in that year, after Latrobe suggested to Jefferson the desirability of a campus focal point. Jefferson closely attended to the details of construction, and when the campus was completed in 1826 the Founding Father had achieved his greatest architectural work, one that is still regarded today as an architectural masterpiece. The design is quintessentially American in its anti-urban and individualist yearnings.

The Maison Carrée: *To Madame de Tessé*

Nismes, March 20, 1787

Here I am, Madam, gazing whole hours at the Maison quarrée, like a lover at his mistress. The stocking weavers and silk spinners around it, consider me as a hypochondriac Englishman, about to write with a pistol, the last chapter of his history. This is the second time I have been in love since I left Paris. The first was with a Diana at the Chateau de Laye-Epinaye in Beaujolois, a delicious morsel of sculpture, by M. A. Slodtz. This, you will say, was a rule, to fall in love with a female beauty: but with a house! It is out of all precedent. No, Madam, it is not without a precedent, in my own history. While in Paris, I was violently smitten with the Hotel de Salm, and used to go to the Thuileries almost daily, to look at it. The *loueuse des chaises*, inattentive to my passion, never had the complaisance to place a chair there, so that sitting on the parapet, and twisting my neck round to see the object of my admiration, I generally left it with a *torti-colli*.

From Lyons to Nismes I have been nourished with the remains of Roman grandeur. They have always brought you to my mind, because I know your affection for whatever is Roman and noble. At Vienne I thought of you. But I am glad you were not there; for you would have seen me more angry than, I hope, you will ever see me. The Prætorian palace, as it is called, comparable, for its fine proportions, to the Maison quarrée, defaced by the barbarians who have converted it to its present purpose, its beautiful fluted Corinthian columns cut out, in part, to make space for Gothic windows, and hewed down, in the residue, to the plane of the building, was enough, you must admit, to disturb my composure. At Orange too, I thought of you. I was sure you had seen with pleasure, the sublime triumphal arch of Marius at the entrance of the city. I went then to the Arenæ. Would you believe, Madam, that in this eighteenth century, in France, under the reign of Louis XVI. they are at this moment pulling down the circular wall of this superb remain, to pave a road? And that too from a hill which is itself an entire mass of stone, just as fit, and more accessible? A former intendant, a M. de Basville has rendered his memory dear to the traveller and amateur, by the pains he took to preserve and restore these monuments of antiquity. The present one (I do not know who he is) is demolishing the object, to make a good road to it. I thought of you again, and I was then in great good humor, at the Pont du Gard, a sublime antiquity, and well preserved. But most of all here, where Roman taste, genius and magnificence, excite ideas analogous to yours at every step. I could no longer oppose the inclination to avail myself of your permission to write to you, a permission given with too much complaisance by you, and used by me, with too much indiscretion. Madame de Tott did me the same honor. But she, being only the descendant of some of those puny heroes who boiled their own kettles before the walls of Troy, I shall write to her from a Grecian, rather than a Roman canton: when I shall find myself, for example among her Phocæan relations at Marseilles. . . .

Capitol on the Potomac: *To Major L'Enfant*

Philadelphia, April 10, 1791

Sir, – I am favored with your letter of the 4th instant, and in compliance with your request, I have examined my papers, and found the plans of Frankfort-on-the-Mayne, Carlsruhe, Amsterdam, Strasburg, Paris, Orleans, Bordeaux, Lyons, Montpelier, Marseilles, Turin, and Milan, which I send in a roll by the post. They are on large and accurate scales, having been procured by me while in those respective cities myself. As they are connected with the notes I made in my travels, and often necessary to explain them to myself, I will beg your care of them, and to return them when no longer useful to you, leaving you absolutely free to keep them as long as useful. I am happy that the President has left the planning of the town in such good hands, and have no doubt it will be done to general satisfaction. Considering that the grounds to be reserved for the public are to be paid for by the acre, I think very liberal reservations should be made for them; and if this be about the Tyber and on the back of the town, it will be of no injury to the commerce of the place, which will undoubtedly establish itself on the deep waters towards the eastern branch and mouth of Rock Creek; the water about the mouth of the Tyber not being of any depth. Those connected with the government will prefer fixing themselves near the public grounds in the centre, which will also be convenient to be resorted to as walks from the lower and upper town. Having communicated to the President, before he went away, such general ideas on the subject of the town as occurred to me, I make no doubt that, in explaining himself to you on the subject, he has interwoven with his own ideas, such of mine as he approved. For fear of repeating therefore what he did not approve, and having more confidence in the unbiassed state of his mind, than in my own, I avoided interfering with what he may have expressed to you. Whenever it is proposed to prepare plans for the Capitol, I should prefer the adoption of some one of the models of antiquity, which have had the approbation of thousands of years; and for the President's house, I should prefer the celebrated fronts of modern buildings, which have already received the approbation of all good judges. Such are the Galerie du Louire, the Gardes meubles, and two fronts of the Hotel de Salm. But of this it is yet time enough to consider. In the meantime I am, with great esteem, Sir, your most obedient humble servant.

Blueprint of the University: *To Littleton Waller Tazewell*

Washington, Jan. 5, 1805

Dear Sir, – Your favor of December 24 never came to my hands till last night. It's importance induces me to hasten the answer. No one can be more rejoiced at the information that the legislature of Virginia are likely at length to institute an University on a liberal plan. Convinced that the people are the only safe depositories of their own liberty, & that they are not safe unless enlightened to a certain degree, I have looked on our present state of liberty as a short-lived possession unless the mass of the people could be informed to a certain degree. This requires two grades of education. First some institution where science in all it's branches is taught, and in the highest degree to which the human mind has carried it. This would prepare a few subjects in every State, to whom nature has given minds of the first order. Secondly such a degree of learning given to every member of the society as will enable him to read, to judge & to vote understandingly on what is passing. This would be the object of the township schools. I understand from your letter that the first of these only is under present contemplation. Let us receive with contentment what the legislature is now ready to give. The other branch will be incorporated into the system at some more favorable moment.

The first step in this business will be for the legislature to pass an act of establishment equivalent to a charter. This should deal in generals only. It's provisions should go 1. to the object of the institution. 2. it's location. 3. it's endowment. 4. it's Direction. On each of these heads I will hazard a first thought or two. 1. It's object should be defined only generally for teaching the useful branches of science, leaving the particulars to the direction of the day. Science is progressive. What was useful two centuries ago is now become useless, e.g. one half the professorships of Wm & Mary. What is now deemed useful will in some of it's parts become useless in another century. The visitors will be the best qualified to keep their institution up in even pace with the science of the times. Every one knows that Oxford, Cambridge, the Sorbonne, etc. are now a century or two behind the science of the age. 2. The location. The legislature is the proper judges of a general position, within certain limits, as for instance the county in which it shall be. To fix on the spot identically they would not be so competent as persons particularly appointed to examine the grounds. This small degree of liberty in location would place the landholders in the power of the purchasers: to fix the spot would place the purchaser in the power of the landholder. 3. It's endowment. Bank stock, or public stock of any kind should be immediately converted into real estate. In the form of stock it is a dead fund, it's depreciation being equal to it's interest. Every one must see that money put into our funds when first established (in 1791) with all its interest from that day would not buy more now than the principal would then have done. Mr. Pitt states to parliament that the expenses of living in England have, in the last 20 years, increased 50. percent: that is that money has depreciated that much. Even the precious metals depreciate slowly so that in perpetual institutions, as colleges, that ought to be guarded against. But in countries admitting paper, the abusive emissions of that produces two, three or four courses of depreciation & annihilation in a century. Lands will keep *advancing* nominally so as to keep *even* really. Canal shares are as good as lands, perhaps better: but the whole funds should not be risked in any one form. They should be vested in the visitors, without any power given them to lessen their capital, or even to *change* what is real. 4. The Direction. This would of course be in the hands of Visitors. The legislature would name the first set, & lay down the laws of their succession. On death or resignation the legislature or the Chancellor might name three persons of whom the visitors should chuse one. The visitors should be few. If many, those half qualified would by their numbers bring every thing down to the level of their own capacities, by out-voting the few of real science. I doubt if they should exceed five. For this is an office for which good sense alone does not qualify a man. To analyse science into it's different branches, to distribute these into professorships, to superintend the course practiced by each professor, he must know what these sciences are and possess their outlines at least. Can any state in the union furnish more than 5. men so qualified as to the whole field of the sciences. The Visitors should receive no pay. Such qualifications are properly rewarded by honor, not by money.

The charter being granted & the Visitors named, these become then the agents as to every thing else. Their first objects will be 1. the special location. 2. the institution of professorships. 3. the employment of their capital. 4. the necessary buildings. A word on each. 1. Special location needs no explanation. 2. Professorships. They would have to select all the branches of science deemed useful at this day, & in this country: to groupe as many of these together as could be taught by one professor and thus reduce the number of professors to the minimum consistent with the essential object. Having for some years entertained the hope that our country would some day establish an institution on a liberal scale, I have been taking measures to have in readiness such materials as would require time to collect. I have from Dr. Priestley a designation of the branches of science grouped into professorships which he furnished at my request. He was an excellent judge of what may be called the old studies, of those useful and those useless. I have the same thing from Mr. Dupont, a good judge of the new branches. His letter to me is quite a treatise. I have the plan of the institutions of Edinburgh, & those of the National institute of France; and I expect from Mr. Pictet, one of the most celebrated professors of Geneva, their plan, in answer to a letter written some time ago. From these the Visitors could select the branches useful for the country & how to groupe them. A hasty view of the subject on a former occasion led me to believe 10. professorships would be necessary, but not all immediately. Half a dozen of the most urgent would make a good beginning. The salaries of the first professors should be very liberal, that we might draw the first names of Europe to our institution in order to give it a celebrity in the outset, which will draw to it the youth of all the states, and make Virginia their cherished & beloved Alma mater. I have good reasons to believe we can command the services of some of the first men of Europe. 3. The emploiment of their capital. On this subject others are so much better judges than myself that I shall say nothing. 4. Buildings. The greatest danger will be their over-building themselves, by attempting a large house in the beginning, sufficient to contain the whole institution. Large houses are always ugly, inconvenient, exposed to the accident of fire, and bad in cases of infection. A plain small house for the school & lodging of each professor is best. These connected by covered ways out of which the rooms of the students should open would be best. These may then be built only as they shall be wanting. In fact an University should not be an house but a village. This will much lessen their first expenses.

Not having written any three lines of this without interruption it has been impossible to keep my ideas rallied to the subject. I must let these hasty outlines go therefore as they are. Some are premature, some probably immature: but make what use you please of them except letting them get into print. Should this establishment take place on a plan worthy of approbation, I shall have a valuable legacy to leave it, to wit, my library, which certainly has not cost less than 15,000 Dollars. But it's value is more in the selection, a part of which, that which respects America, is the result of my own personal searches in Paris for 6. or 7. years, & of persons employed by me in England, Holland, Germany and Spain to make similar searches. Such a collection on that subject can never again be made. With my sincere wishes for the success of this measure accept my salutations & assurances of great esteem & respect.

"An Academical Village": *To Messrs. Hugh L. White and Others*

Monticello, May 6, 1810

Gentlemen, – I received, some time ago, your letter of February 28th, covering a printed scheme of a lottery for the benefit of the East Tennessee College, and proposing to send tickets to me to be disposed of. It would be impossible for them to come to a more inefficient hand. I rarely go from home, and consequently see but a few neighbors and friends, who occasionally call on me. And having myself made it a rule never to engage in a lottery or any other adventure of mere chance, I can, with the less candor or effect, urge it on others, however laudable or desirable its object may be. No one more sincerely wishes the spread of information among mankind than I do, and none has greater confidence in its effect towards supporting free and good government. I am sincerely rejoiced, therefore, to find that so excellent a fund has been provided for this noble purpose in Tennessee. Fifty-thousand dollars placed in a safe bank, will give four thousand dollars a year, and even without other aid, must soon accomplish buildings sufficient for the object in its early stage. I consider the common plan followed in this country, but not in others, of making one large and expensive building, as unfortunately erroneous. It is infinitely better to erect a small and separate lodge for each separate professorship, with only a hall below for his class, and two chambers above for himself; joining these lodges by barracks for a certain portion of the students, opening into a covered way to give a dry communication between all the schools. The whole of these arranged around an open square of grass and trees, would make it, what it should be in fact, an academical village, instead of a large and common den of noise, of filth and of fetid air. It would afford that quiet retirement so friendly to study, and lessen the dangers of fire, infection and tumult. Every professor would be the police officer of the students adjacent to his own lodge, which should include those of his own class of preference, and might be at the head of their table, if, as I suppose, it can be reconciled with the necessary economy to dine them in smaller and separate parties, rather than in a large and common mess. These separate buildings, too, might be erected successively and occasionally, as the number of professorships and students should be increased, or the funds become competent.

I pray you to pardon me if I have stepped aside into the province of counsel; but much observation and reflection on these institutions have long convinced me that the large and crowded buildings in which youths are pent up, are equally unfriendly to health, to study, to manners, morals and order; and, believing the plan I suggest to be more promotive of these, and peculiarly adapted to the slender beginnings and progressive growth of our institutions, I hoped you would pardon the presumption, in consideration of the motive which was suggested by the difficulty expressed in your letter, of procuring funds for erecting the building. But, on whatever plan you proceed, I wish it every possible success, and to yourselves the reward of esteem, respect and gratitude due to those who devote their time and efforts to render the youths of every successive age fit governors for the next. To these accept, in addition, the assurances of mine.

171   BENJAMIN LATROBE
from Letter to Thomas Jefferson (1807)

Much can be gleaned about the architectural situation in the young United States from this single letter of Benjamin Latrobe. He was born in England, schooled and trained as an engineer in Germany, practiced architecture in Britain, and immigrated to Virginia in 1796. When he landed he was the only architect in the country who had been trained in structural engineering, and he soon sought out the support of George Washington and Thomas Jefferson to further his career. Initial attempts to find substantial work failed, however, and in 1799 Latrobe moved from Richmond, where he had just designed the state's new penitentiary (1797), to Philadelphia, the country's wealthiest and largest city at the time. Here he designed the Philadelphia Water Works (1799) and the Bank of Pennsylvania (1799–1801) – the last the country's first masonry-domed classical building.

President Jefferson was now taking notice of Latrobe from afar, and in 1803 – after tiring of the feuds over the design of the Washington Capitol – he named Latrobe to the supervisory post of Surveyor of Public Buildings for Washington DC. The Democrat Latrobe moved to the capital and soon fought with the Federalist Thornton (who was still a building commissioner) over his proposed changes for the Capitol. Latrobe would gain the upper hand, but he eventually resigned his post in 1811 and moved to Pittsburgh. Two years later warring British troops arrived in the

Benjamin Latrobe (1764–1820), Letter to Thomas Jefferson, May 21, 1807, from *Thomas Jefferson and the National Capital*, ed. Saul K. Padover. Washington: United States Government Printing Office, 1946, pp. 389–92.

nation's capitol and proceeded to burn the Capitol to the ground. Latrobe thus returned to Washington in 1815 to start the work of rebuilding the Capitol from a plan more to his own liking. This nation's most symbolic building was later enlarged and completed by Charles Bullfinch and Thomas U. Walter.

Latrobe's letter to Jefferson has an interesting context. Latrobe was frequently at odds with Jefferson over matters of design, and his reference to himself as a "bigotted Greek" was his attempt to distinguish what he saw as his own Greek classicism from Jefferson's reliance on Roman-inspired examples. In effect it was a late round in the Greco-Roman debate. Jefferson in an earlier letter had complained that Latrobe's design for the cupola over the House of Representatives lacked classical precedent and was simply "an Italian invention" (that is, of the little respected Renaissance). Latrobe defended his design with a rebuke of Jefferson's bookishness and his unwillingness to allow for artistic invention. Jefferson, however, would wear Latrobe down in the dispute, but the President's own design for skylights, which were built under protest by Latrobe, had severe leakage and condensation problems. Latrobe eventually rectified the problem in his redesign of the Capitol of 1815.

Philadelphia, May 21, 1807

THE PRESIDENT OF THE UNITED STATES

Sir: In arranging the papers which I brought with me from Washington I have had the mortification of finding the inclosed letter, written immediately before my departure from the city and intended to have been forwarded by the post of the evening, but which, it appears, in the hurry of packing up, had slipped into my paper case. I still beg the favor of you to read it, as it contains my reason for the measures I took previous to my departure, and will explain the manner in which I hope to accomplish your objects as respects the arrangement of the ground around the President's house.

On the 16th inst. your letter, Monticello, April 22, reached me here, being forwarded by Mrs. Lenthall. Hoping to be at Washington as soon at least as you return I did not immediately answer it. But I am waiting from day to day for the arrival of one of the Georgetown packets in order to put my things on board previous to my removal.

I am very sensible of the honor you do me in discussing with me the merits of the detail of the public building. I know well that *to you* it is my duty to obey implicitly or to resign my office: to myself it is my duty to maintain myself in a situation in which I can provide for my family by all honorable means. If in any instance my duty to you obliged me to act contrary to my judgment, I might fairly and honorably say with Shakespeare's apothecary: "My poverty, not my will consents." Such excuse, however, I have never wanted, for although in respect to the panel lights I am acting diametrically contrary to my judgment, no mercenary motive whatever has kept me at my post, but considerations very superior to money – the attachment arising from gratitude and the highest esteem. At the same time I candidly confess that the question has suggested itself to my mind: What shall I do when the condensed vapor of the hall showers down upon the heads of the members from one hundred skylights, as it now does from the skylights of our anatomical hall, as it did from the six skylights of the Round House, as it does from the lantern of the Pennsylvania Bank, and as it does from that of our university – an event I believe to be as certain as that cold air and cold glass will condense warm vapor? This question I have asked myself for many months past. I shall certainly not cut my throat as the engineer of Staines Bridge did when the battlement failed, and his beautiful bridge fell because the commissioners had ordered him to proceed contrary to his judgment. But I dare not think long enough on the subject to frame an answer to my own mind, but go blindly on, hoping that *"fata viano invenient."*

In respect to the general subject of cupolas, I do not think that they are *always*, nor even *often*, ornamental. My *principles* of good taste are rigid in Grecian architecture. I am a bigoted Greek in the condemnation of the Roman architecture of Baalbec, Palmyra, Spaletro, and of all the buildings erected subsequent to Hadrian's reign. The immense size, the bold plan and arrangements of the buildings of the Romans down almost to Constantine's arch, plundered from the triumphal arches of former emperors, I admire, however, with enthusiasm, but think their decorations and details absurd beyond tolerance from the reign of Severus downward. Wherever, therefore, the Grecian style can be copied without impropriety, I love to be a mere, I would say a *slavish*, copyist, but the forms and the distribution of the Roman and Greek buildings which remain are in general inapplicable to the objects and uses of our public buildings. Our religion requires churches wholly different from the temples, our Government, our legislative assemblies, and our courts of justice, buildings of entirely different principles from their basilicas; and our amusements could not possibly be performed in their theaters or amphitheaters. But that which principally demands a variation in our buildings from those of the ancients is the difference of our climate. To adhere to the subject of cupolas, although the want of a belfry, which is an Eastern accession to our religious buildings, rendered them necessary appendages to the church, yet I cannot admit that because the Greeks and Romans did not place elevated cupolas upon their temples, they may not when necessary be rendered also beautiful. The Lanthorne of Demosthenes, than which nothing of the kind can be more beautiful, is mounted upon a magnificent mass of architecture harmonizing with it in character and style. The question would be as to its real or apparent utility in the place in which it appeared, for nothing in the field of good taste, which ought never to be at warfare with good sense, can be beautiful which appears useless or unmeaning.

If our climate were such as to admit of doing legislative business in open air, that is under the light of an open orifice in the crown of a dome, as at the Parthenon, I would never put a cupola on any spherical dome. It is not the *ornament*, it is the *use* that I want.

If you will be pleased to refer to Degodetz, you will see that there is a rim projecting above the arch of the Parthenon at the opening. This rim, in the dome projected for the centerpiece of the Capitol, is raised by me into a low pedestal for the purpose of covering a skylight, which could then be admitted, although I think it inadmissible in a room of business. But I should prefer the hemisphere, I confess. As to the members of Congress, with the utmost respect for the Legislature, I should scarcely *consult*, but rather *dictate* in matters of taste.

I beg pardon for this trespass on your time. You have spoiled me by your former indulgence in hearing my opinions expressed with candor. A few days will give me the pleasure of personally assuring you of the profound respect of yours faithfully.

B. H. LATROBE

172   GEORGE TUCKER
from "On Architecture" (1814)

T he dispute between Jefferson and Latrobe over whether American classicism should have a Greek or Roman cast was really a dispute of nuance rather than substance. Through their combined efforts classicism became the governmental style for federal buildings throughout much of the nineteenth century, and some classical works, such as the Lincoln Memorial, were even designed and constructed well into the twentieth century.

This stylistic trend in its earlier stages is also historically identified as the American "Greek Revival," and the following remarks excerpted from an article written in 1814 by George Tucker, could serve as a paean to the movement. The Philadelphian Tucker was an early biographer of Jefferson, but he also knew something of architecture. Drawing upon arguments of the Earl of Shaftesbury and Edmund Burke, Tucker considers the question of whether American architects should continue to adhere to the Greek model, which he strongly supports, even though his conclusion belies some aspects of his argument. Although he is critical of Latrobe for the capitals of his columns for the United States Capitol as well as of Jefferson for his deviation from classical precedent at the Virginia State Capitol, he acknowledges as well the human pleasure in perceiving variety and contrast. Tucker defines the Greek Revival near the moment it was achieving its greatest popularity, and architects of the next generation were not willing to be so "slavish" and forgo invention and innovation – as Tucker here argues.

All the most civilized nations of the earth unite in considering the Grecian architecture as the standard of excellence; and its forms and proportions, even to the minutest particular, are copied with an exactness that precludes all invention. Nor is this absolute dominion over human taste the temporary fashion of the day. It has existed with a single intermission, for more than two thousand years, throughout the improved parts of Europe, and has partially extended itself to the other quarters of the world. When we see that it has invariably maintained its foothold wherever it has been once introduced, we may infer that it is not universally preferred only because it is not universally known.

How then! it has been indignantly said, is the whole civilized part of mankind always thus tamely to copy the Greeks? whilst every human invention advances and improves, is this noble and useful art alone to remain stationary?

★ ★ ★

We have yet to notice the last remaining cause of the scrupulous adherence to the forms of Grecian architecture. Accustomed, as we are, to regard the ancients as standards of perfection, in all works of taste, we feel a prejudice against every deviation from the rules they have prescribed to themselves, and are prepared to believe, that every change would be for the worse, even in things that are indifferent. Finding that their productions stand the test of every rule of beauty, where rules can be applied, we naturally attribute to them the same excellence, in cases not susceptible of such a test. We perceive much real merit; we imagine a great deal more. We examine minutely every part of their works in architecture, and having ascertained the principles of their formation, and the relative proportions of the several

George Tucker, from "Thoughts of a Hermit – For the Port Folio: On Architecture" in the journal *Port Folio*, IV (1814), pp. 559, 566–9.

parts, we implicitly adopt them; and feel somewhat of the same reverence for men, who were able to produce such noble specimens of art, as succeeding epic poets have felt for the authority of Homer. Hence it is, that the orders of architecture are not multiplied, and that the decorations and proportions of the different orders are never blended. It is therefore too, that the new ornament which has been placed on the Corinthian columns of the capitol in Washington,[1] though of an agreeable form in itself, perhaps offends the eye of a connoisseur as a licentious innovation, more than it pleases as a novelty. The capitol or state-house of Virginia, furnishes a striking example of our profound respect for the authority of the ancients in architecture. This building was modelled after an ancient edifice at Nismes in France, supposed to have been originally a temple, and has, like its prototype, a hexastyle portico, surmounted with a pediment at one end. As the model, in common with other ancient temples, consisted of a single room, it had a single entrance; this was designated by a portico, which afforded shelter to its numerous religious votaries, and to which they were conducted by a spacious flight of steps. But in the copy at Richmond, the various purposes for which it was intended, requiring it to be divided into several different apartments, it became necessary to enter, and approach it at the sides. The door, therefore, is at one place, and the sign of the door at another – the real entrance is without a shelter, and the apparent, without the means of approach. A blind admiration of what is as well adapted to its purpose, as it is really beautiful, has made the modern architect disregard all ideas of congruity and convenience.

Whilst the causes which have been mentioned, operate so strongly to establish and maintain an exclusive preference for the ancient architecture, there are also some minor considerations, why the modern architect should be no more disposed to attempt innovation, than the beholder is to tolerate it. Besides the high relish for the models of antiquity, which, from the natural effect of cultivation, he is likely to feel in a somewhat greater degree than others, he is cautious of hazarding new ornaments where little can be gained, and much may be lost. If the alteration be inconsiderable, it will be either unnoticed, or regarded as frivolous, and if important, the architect must hazard the imputation of unsuccessful temerity, in a subject too, in which his failure is neither easily repaired nor soon forgotten. And while a well grounded diffidence may check innovation in some, vanity itself has a similar tendency in others. Ever since the rules and proportions of Grecian architecture, have been digested into a system, it has been held a valuable accomplishment to relish and understand them. The art which it has cost much labour to acquire, and which distinguishes its possessor from the common mass of mankind, he will seek to display by a rigid observance of its precepts. It is this technical pride, which cherishes and perpetuates much of the pedantry of all professional men, who are content to be thought ostentatious of their learning, rather than be supposed not to have acquired it: and in like manner, architects implicitly copy the rules of Vitruvius or Palladio, as much to show their acquaintance with those rules, as from a sense of their superior merit.

Thus it appears, that the Grecian architecture owes its proud ascendency, partly to the natural advantages of intrinsic *utility* and *beauty,* and partly to its adventitious influence from *habit* and *authority:* and the same causes, which make it the model of imitation among moderns, first produced uniformity among the Greeks themselves – afterwards transmitted it to the Romans – and from them handed it down, without addition or diminution, from the age of Pericles to the present day.

But whether the rules of the art, must ever remain stationary, or whether an uncontrollable thirst for novelty, may not hereafter incorporate some of the infinite diversity of untried forms, and having once overleapt the bounds, which have hitherto checked the luxuriant wanderings of taste, at length incessantly affect capricious novelties, it is for time only to show. Although there does, indeed, seem to be no absolute necessity, why we should not decorate the exterior of our buildings, with those agreeable objects of nature or forms of fancy, which are so pleasing to us in their internal ornaments, and use the same variety in this species of embellishment, which we solicit in every other, yet, when we reflect on the long duration and steady advancement of the Grecian architecture, it seems probable, that it will continue to rule our tastes until some moral convulsion shall sweep away in one common ruin, civilized man and the works he has created. If this be the case, the moderns, though they may have as pure a taste for the beautiful and the grand, as their Grecian preceptors, as happy an invention, and as fair a field for its exertion in the erection of as magnificent fabrics as ever existed before, must be content to rank with the *servum pecus*, and however original they may aspire to be in other arts, to remain slavish imitators in architecture.

NOTE

1 This costly edifice, which lately proclaimed our early relish for the arts, is now in ruins; and is equally a monument of mortification to us for our inadequate defence of the Metropolis, and of disgrace to the enemy for his barbarous mode of warfare.

173 WILLIAM STRICKLAND
from Introductory lecture on architecture (1824)

Another prominent classical architect from the first half of the century was the Philadelphian William Strickland. He had trained under Latrobe on the Bank of Pennsylvania and built a Gothic Masonic Hall in 1808–11, before the War of 1812 intervened. In 1818 he returned to practice in an impressive way by winning the national competition for the Second Bank of the United States in Philadelphia (1819–24), which he modeled on the Athenian Parthenon.

This lecture of 1824 is important for several reasons. In 1824 a group of civic-minded Philadelphians created "The Franklin Institute of the State of Pennsylvania, for the Promotion of the Mechanic Arts." Among the "mechanic arts" was construction, and Strickland in 1824 was appointed the first professor in what might be considered the first school of architecture in the United States. In 1824–5 – the only year of his teaching – he delivered at least eight lectures, of which six dealt with Greek architecture and the orders. This "introductory" lecture was meant to provide his audience, which was composed largely of craftsmen or carpenters, with the rudiments of architectural history.

William Strickland (1788–1854), from an introductory lecture on architecture, delivered at the Franklin Institute, Nov. 13, 1824. The manuscript is part of the "Wyck Papers" at the American Philosophical Society in Philadelphia.

Strickland pursues historically the "Hindoo," Persian, and Egyptian styles before coming to that of the Greeks, which he knows largely through the volumes of Stuart and Revett. He is also appreciative of the Gothic style, but in the end he returns once again to the classical ideal, which he squarely aligns with the artistic fortunes of the new country. The lecture, another tribute to the Greek Revival, is preserved through a handwritten copy of the remarks made by Rueben Hains.

Buildings of a public nature ought to express in their design the uses and purposes for which they are erected; so that when we behold a *Church, Bank, Courthouse, Prison* etc. we may understand them to be such from some external characters in the design without the aid of a painted sign or inscribed tablet.

Allegorical decoration when applied to Architecture is a source through which we always derive pleasure and information, as it calls on our *taste, judgment*, and literary acquirements for the solution of objects in the Fine and dignified arts.

In a young country like ours where its inhabitants are scattered over an immense tract of Territory, a great portion of which is unsettled and uncultivated and where its only resources are drawn from agriculture and commerce, distributing and equalizing wealth, it cannot be reasonably expected that architectural works of great magnificence and duration should be constructed on so great a scale as the buildings of Europe where labour and funds are directed by sovereignty and independent priesthood. The associations of men of wealth and taste for the construction of Buildings of a public nature, and for the establishment of institutions for the promotion of the Fine and liberal arts are highly honourable to the genius and liberality of the American character. And it is entirely owing to such associations and exertions that we can trace the perfection which now exists in every department of the arts.

The native enterprise and perseverance of the country at large in the advancement of the science of architecture has fully evinced itself in the many flourishing and populous cities spread over an immense *continent* which two centuries ago was the abode of man in a state of nature.

The splendid and extensive buildings at Washington, Baltimore, Philad^a and New York exhibit great skill in the Science. The Capitol at Washington is perhaps the greatest effort of our Republic in point of extent and workmanship. The next is the City Hall in New York, and a number of beautiful churches built of stone.

The Pennsylvania and United States banks in this city are faithful copies of Greek originals and as such they may truly be said to be the most beautiful buildings on the continent. They have never yet failed to be admired for their simplicity and true proportions.

The value attached to works of this nature may be judged of from the city of Ephesus refusing to suffer the Temple of Diana to be inscribed with the name of Alexander, although this prince offered to purchase that honour by defraying the whole expense attending its erection. From the Athenians rejecting a like offer from *Pericles* with regard to the splendid and extensive Edifices with which *he* had ornamented Athens. And from the city of Cnidia refusing to part with *one statue*, the *Venus* of Praxiteles, although King *Nicomedes* proposed to free them from Tribute if they complied with the request.

Philadelphia undoubtedly possesses great advantages for building; its neighbourhood abounds with every kind of material, with every requisite for bringing it into operation through the means and possession of the best practical artificers. All that appears to be necessary is the cultivation of a correct taste, which must inevitably lead to the amusement and accomplishment of the enlightened traveler, whether in Athens or at Philadelphia. It is by Philadelphia then that should be claimed the proud title of the Classical City.

174   THOMAS U. WALTER
from "Of Modern Architecture"
(1841)

T he last of the major Greek Revivalists in the United States was Thomas U. Walter, whose fame today derives from the cast-iron dome he placed atop the Washington Capitol (1855–65). He began his apprenticeship in Strickland's office, and seems also to have attended his lectures in 1824–5. He opened his own office in the early 1830s, and in 1833 won the competition for Girard College, a grand complex of classical buildings that has been called "the last word in American Greek Revivalism." In 1840 Walter accepted the architectural professorship from the Franklin Institute, which had been dormant since Strickland's lectures. The fifth lecture of his series, entitled "On Modern Architecture," stands out as a superb summary of contemporary ideas and competing tendencies. Walter opines on many of the major European and American architects since the Renaissance, crediting Stuart and Revett with establishing "Grecian chasteness and elegance in architecture throughout the civilized world" and lauding Latrobe "for the high degree of intellectual pleasure" of his Bank of Pennsylvania. But Walter was also aware that the popularity of the classical style was in decline: challenged by eclectic tendencies on the one hand, and by the public demand for simpler and less expensive monuments on the other hand.

It must therefore be obvious, that in the present state of society it would be wholly impossible for any civilized people to resist the influences of the great mass of architectural ideas with which all are now surrounded, so as to admit of their originating any new mode of building superior to, and at the same time independent of, all existing styles and fashions.

It should however be remarked that although the architecture of all the world is now the property of every civilized people, and that the materials for thought in architecture are the same in all countries; still there are peculiarities of climate, – in manners and customs, – and of government which influence the taste of every nation, and which impart a peculiar character to the architecture of each, even in the adaptation of similar principles.

Hence the general diffusion of knowledge, and the subdivision of wealth which characterize our own free institutions must eventually make as great a difference between American and European Architecture in point of taste, as that which now exists in the character of their governments: – instead of the magnificence, grandeur, and showy gorgeousness always affected under hereditary monarchies, we shall gradually settle down into a simpler, chaster, more decided taste – a taste like that which marked the triumphant career of Republican Greece, and to which even the severe and equalizing laws of Lycurgus

Thomas U. Walter (1804–87), from "Of Modern Architecture," a lecture delivered at the Franklin Institute, Dec. 9, 1841. The manuscript is part of the "Walter Papers" held by the Athenaeum of Philadelphia.

opposed no obstacle; in the language of a celebrated English writer, "the purest system of civil freedom, is creative of the noblest powers of intellectual excellence."

In this country therefore more than any other, the progress and influence of architecture depend on the estimation in which it is held by the people. – Here we have no nobles rolling in unbounded wealth – no Despot to wield the public treasure at his will; – the people are the nobility – the people are the Sovereign; – the wealth is theirs, – the power is theirs, – and on their intelligence and taste rests the character of the nation. – Hence a general knowledge of Architecture should be diffused in all classes of society; – its *history* and its *elementary principles* ought to form part of every system of popular education, while its *poetry* and *philosophy* should constitute an indispensable branch of Collegiate Studies.

Such a Cultivation of the Public taste would tend to irradiate the social firmament, – to purify, expand, and ennoble the public minds, – to soften and humanize the sensibilities, – to elevate the standard of civilization, – to adorn and dignify the national character; and to perpetuate the memory of noble and patriotic deeds.

175 ARTHUR DELAVAN GILMAN
from "Architecture in the United States" (1844)

The Greek Revival in America began to experience a rather precipitous decline in the 1840s, as opposition formed along three main fronts: (1) the Gothic revivalists influenced in particular by developments in England; (2) the *Rundbogen* or "rounded-arch" architects who were emigrating from Germany; and (3) those who simply insisted that America should develop its own style, suited to the uniquely American climate, culture, and democratic form of government. The New Englander Arthur Gilman, later an architect of stature in the Boston area, represents here the first of these tendencies. Barely 22 years of age, he came upon the American architectural scene in 1843–4 with a series of book reviews in the *North American Review*. Gilman is a complex figure to categorize. He took note of the third tendency itemized above, and was quite sympathetic to Andrew Jackson Downing's plea to adopt a less formal taste and greater functionality in residential design. Later in his career he was also comfortable with the English baroque and the Second Empire style coming out of France. But in this particular review of Edward Shaw's *Rural Architecture* (1843), Gilman is particularly smitten with the theory of Pugin as well as the Gothic style of Richard Upjohn and the Renaissance style of Charles Barry. He employs British theory primarily as a means to attack the Greek Revival and pleads for a more convenient and less monumental style.

Architecture is, beyond question, the oldest and most impressive of the fine arts. In several important points of view, it demands precedence over its more popular accessories, sculpture and painting. Without claiming for it a higher station than will be readily conceded by persons of taste, it may be observed, that these two arts are merely its subsidiary embel-

Arthur Delavan Gilman (1821–82), from "Architecture in the United States," a book review published in the *North American Review*, April 1843, pp. 436–9.

lishments, and that, in some degree, it is the union and embodiment of both. It ought not, then, to be viewed as less interesting than either. Its various stages of progress furnish abundant opportunity for reflection, and a wide theme for profitable remark. It has been regarded as so direct a means of inspiring the imagination, and creating sublime ideas in the mind, as to be assigned, by ingenious writers, to a high place among those causes which affect the character of an age, and exert a prominent influence over the moral and intellectual habits of a people. It is not, then, from any want of untouched matter, or of fresh subjects for the use of the pen, that so little notice of its present condition among us, has lately appeared in this Journal. On the contrary, there is quite enough in the recent works of our builders to engage the attention of the *amateur*, and demand the animadversions of the critic. We will readily admit, indeed, that the maxim, *nil dictum quod non dictum prius*, should be carefully kept in view while speaking of this polite and liberal art. But this maxim, in architecture as in law, should be applied to general principles, and not to new circumstances, or to novel combinations of facts. Whenever these arise, it is certainly well to improve upon them. We would not attempt to advance new doctrines, or to advocate any startling novelties of opinion; we would only bring some of those true principles again before the public, which were long since settled and acknowledged by high authority, but which seem in frequent danger, among us, of being overlooked, slighted, or forgotten. We enter upon this course with the full conviction, that the pursuit of it has always proved beneficial to the art. For the common consent of cultivated minds has fully established this truth, that the system of the ancient architects does not admit of any wide departure from precedent and usage, and if its fundamental principles are in any degree contravened, the certain and speedy consequence will be the degradation and debasement of all its real beauties.

With pleasure, therefore, should we hail even the faint indication of a desire to study the spirit and meaning, instead of reproducing the mere forms and details, of the works of our predecessors. So long as this energy, this sensibility of taste, is wanting, there remains one, at least, of the highest marks of civilization, to which we can have no valid claim. The great test of excellence in design has been repeatedly declared to be this, – that there should be no parts about a building which are not necessary for *convenience, construction*, and *propriety,* while the neglect of this rule is undoubtedly the immediate cause of all the bad architecture of the present time. Mr. Jefferson is said to have remarked, in reference to the style of building which prevailed in his day, that "the genius of architecture seemed to have shed a peculiar malediction over America." Little is it to be wondered at, that such should have been the honest conviction of an acute observer, and a man of tolerable taste, at a time when the weak puerilities of Latrobe and his rivals formed the most elevated standard of our architectural excellence. Those flaunting and meretricious edifices, the Capitol at Washington, and the State-house at Boston, stand forth to us as the highest efforts of their composition and invention, while all below them was left to the indiscriminate mercies of the house-joiner and the mason. But if this was the opinion of Mr. Jefferson forty years ago, it cannot be said that, at the present day, there is any reason to reverse the desponding verdict. The architectural faults and follies of his times have indeed passed away; but we do not hesitate to affirm, that they have been succeeded by others of a different and more deplorable kind. If baldness and want of fancy were the bane of that period, the ostentatious meanness and stilted pretension of our contemporaries are not a whit better. An expression of character and appropriateness might have been wanting in the works of the former builders; still it was, at least, aimed at and attempted; the church was erected in one style, the senate-house in another, the private mansion in another. But with us, such discrimination is rarely shown; the elevation of the Parthenon, Erectheum, or the Ilissus is the Procustes bed, on which the relentless measure of all our public and private wants and uses is taken, and we are seldom allowed any alternative. Because a *façade* is beautiful in one situation, it is without hesitation adopted in all. A leaf cut out of Stuart's "Athens," that inexhaustible quarry of bad taste, supplies our *architect* with his design and his detail; he duplicates the columns of the Choragic monument under the crowded portico of the suburban citizen's *box*; and sacrifices, in every situation, all discrimination and all distinctive character to his imaginary Moloch of classical chasteness. We are almost tempted to suppose, that whenever he sits down to his drawing-board, an attendant stands close at his elbow, to whisper in his ear the dismal motto which, as Montaigne relates, was every day repeated by the pages of Darius; "Sir, remember the Athenians." So effectually does he remember them, that he finds room in his memory for nothing else. Without columns, he cannot compose any thing; and with them, he seems to think he cannot fail of being fine. Thus, market-house, cottage, bank, town-hall, law-school, church, brewery, and theatre, with him are all the same. It matters not how widely different their character, how exactly opposite their purpose. His blind admiration for the Grecian colonnade seems to obtrude the object of its bigotry into every situation where its inappropriateness becomes most evident and most ridiculous. Yet we grieve to record, that this servile manner of repetition has established itself in general practice, and finds plenty of advocates among those

> "Who talk of principles, but nothing prize,
> And all to one loved folly sacrifice."

Thus the hexastyle portico of Athens is, indeed, reproduced in every locality, and with every variety of material that ingenuity can devise; but the *fitness of the design to the purpose* for which it is intended, if recognized at all in theory, is much oftener honored in the breach than the observance, in practice.

While, then, these objects of tasteless and ignorant imitation are looking us in the face at every turn, it is scarcely possible for any one to believe, that our architects possess a particle of that first of all requisites – invention. Is there any proof of its existence among them, when we see the same idea repeated by all, – flimsily disguised, perhaps, but still the same, hashed up and set before us again and again? It does not even appear, that they have often cultivated that lower excellence, which Reynolds allows the young painter sometimes to aim at, – the ability to borrow *with judgment* from the ideas of others, and to use them with grace and fancy. But how could any other result than this be expected? Like those self-satisfied Platonists, who, instead of following out their great master in his search for all truth, are content to stop short exactly where Plato left them, – they seem to have proposed to themselves a definite mark in their art, a limited boundary, beyond which they do not care to go. They are satisfied to overlook the fundamental rules of their profession, because they can earn a cheap and vulgar distinction by disregarding them; by reërecting the eternal temples of the tropics, in timber and plaster imitations on the bleak shores of New England.

176 THOMAS ALEXANDER TEFFT
from "The Cultivation of True Taste" (1851)

An equally critical review of present-day efforts was presented a few years later by Thomas Alexander Tefft. While still a student at Brown University, Tefft came into prominence by winning the design commission for the Providence Union Depot (1848–53), one of the earliest and most successful examples of the *Rundbogen* style in the United States. He continued in the 1850s with a very productive practice, although it was abruptly cut off by his early death in 1859. This lecture is instructive – if only for what it reveals of the increasing impatience of American architects for better design. He is not opposed in principle to the classical style, and he too was impressed with the Gothic designs of Richard Upjohn. But his favorite style seems to have been the *Rundbogen*, with its "real beauty of design" and "pure and appropriate decorations." The latter style reached its apogee of influence in American practice in the mid-1850s, in part because many German architects had fled to America to escape the political repression of their homeland.

Of the architecture of the present day, we must confess there is far more to condemn than to admire. [. . .] There are revivals of the medieval schools of art – and possess real beauty of design – pure and appropriate decorations. The round arch school of Germany is employing much invention and originality in their designs and we hasard but little in predicting a favorable result.

The great work of the age, the Westminster Palace, is regarded by every connoisseur as a prodigious failure. Its exterior is anything but prepossessing in its distant views, while a closer inspection reveals a repetition and replication of ornament that is repulsive in the extreme. Its interior is most ill-adapted to the purpose for which it was designed, while many of its richly ground ceilings are the paltry daubs of the plasterers instead of the enduring marks of chisel work. The great principles of design have been lost sight of, such as adaptation, purely decorated construction, and the general effect of the whole.

In our own country we have as yet but five public monuments of sterling worth. Our national Capitol is a very effective building in its exterior, remarkable for its purity of style and its miserably arranged interior. How far its accommodation will be improved or its external effect destroyed in the present improvements remains to be seen. Trinity Church tower is the most imposing, best architectural monument yet seated in the Western world. Would that the church attached was worthy of so proud a place, but [its] richly ground ceiling made of lath and plaster in such a place is too indecently shabby for toleration.

Bedford Street Church in Boston is a perfect gem, and Kings Chapel is famous for its good taste and truthful honesty. The purity of style in Grace Church, Providence, is in our estimation without a parallel. But like many others of Upjohn's churches, its interior is disfigured with a detestable sham clerestory. [. . .]

Thomas Alexander Tefft (1826–59), from the lecture "The Cultivation of True Taste" (1851), pp. 13–16. The manuscript is part of papers held by the Rhode Island Historical Society.

177 RALPH WALDO EMERSON
from "Self-Reliance" (1841)

Ralph Waldo Emerson was almost certainly the most influential American thinker of the nineteenth century – architecture included. The son of a Unitarian minister, he too prepared for the ministry by attending Harvard University and Harvard Divinity School. In 1829 he obtained a post of assistant pastor at Boston's Second Church, but he resigned this position in 1832 to embark on a trip to Europe. There he met Samuel Taylor Coleridge, Thomas Carlyle, and William Wordsworth, and when he returned home to his ancestral house in Concord, Massachusetts, he began to work out the elements of his "Transcendental" philosophy. The gist of his thought is the quasi-pantheistic idea of an "Over-Soul," that is, of a divine spirit that pervades the universe, of which humanity is but an extension or projection. Nature provides the foundation to Emerson's idealistic metaphysics, and it was the title of his first book of 1836.

Another dimension of Emerson's thought comes forward in his classic essay "Self-Reliance," which was published in 1841 in the first selection of *Essays*. The idea of self-reliance refers not to one's material or economic self-reliance, but rather to the intellectual self-reliance of this new Western nation and its people. Emerson's vision for America is essentially eschatological; it is the responsibility, even destiny, of the new nation to advance human civilization to a higher stage within the redemptive story of humanity. Americans therefore cannot complacently wrap themselves in the comfortable mantle of European culture; they must tackle the hard work of manufacturing a new fabric and pattern suited to the promise and ideals of a new democratic society. The architectural transposition of this manifesto is self-evident, and its influence on such later architects as Louis Sullivan and Frank Lloyd Wright would be profound.

There is a time in every man's education when he arrives at the conviction that envy is ignorance; that imitation is suicide; that he must take himself for better, for worse, as his portion; that though the wide universe is full of good, no kernel of nourishing corn can come to him but through his toil bestowed on that plot of ground which is given to him to till. The power which resides in him is new in nature, and none but he knows what that is which he can do, nor does he know until he has tried. Not for nothing one face, one character, one fact, makes much impression on him, and another none. This sculpture in the memory is not without preëstablished harmony. The eye was placed where one ray should fall, that it might testify of that particular ray. We but half express ourselves, and are ashamed of that divine idea which each of us represents. It may be safely trusted as proportionate and of good issues, so it be faithfully imparted, but God will not have his work made manifest by cowards. A man is relieved and gay when he has put his heart into his work and done his best; but what he has said or done otherwise, shall give him no peace. It is a deliverance which does not deliver. In the attempt his genius deserts him; no muse befriends; no invention, no hope.

Trust thyself: every heart vibrates to that iron string. Accept the place the divine providence has found for you, the society of your contemporaries, the connection of events. Great men have always done so, and confided themselves childlike to the genius of their age, betraying their perception that the absolutely trustworthy was seated at their heart, working

Ralph Waldo Emerson (1803–82), from the essay "Self-Reliance" (1841), in the Library of America edition of *Ralph Waldo Emerson: Essays & Lectures*, New York, 1983, pp. 259–60, 277–9.

through their hands, predominating in all their being. And we are now men, and must accept in the highest mind the same transcendent destiny; and not minors and invalids in a protected corner, not cowards fleeing before a revolution, but guides, redeemers, and benefactors, obeying the Almighty effort, and advancing on Chaos and the Dark.

★ ★ ★

It is for want of self-culture that the superstition of Travelling, whose idols are Italy, England, Egypt, retains its fascination for all educated Americans. They who made England, Italy, or Greece venerable in the imagination did so by sticking fast where they were, like an axis of the earth. In manly hours, we feel that duty is our place. The soul is no traveller; the wise man stays at home, and when his necessities, his duties, on any occasion call him from his house, or into foreign lands, he is at home still, and shall make men sensible by the expression of his countenance, that he goes the missionary of wisdom and virtue, and visits cities and men like a sovereign, and not like an interloper or a valet.

I have no churlish objection to the circumnavigation of the globe, for the purposes of art, of study, and benevolence, so that the man is first domesticated, or does not go abroad with the hope of finding somewhat greater than he knows. He who travels to be amused, or to get somewhat which he does not carry, travels away from himself, and grows old even in youth among old things. In Thebes, in Palmyra, his will and mind have become old and dilapidated as they. He carries ruins to ruins.

Travelling is a fool's paradise. Our first journeys discover to us the indifference of places. At home I dream that at Naples, at Rome, I can be intoxicated with beauty, and lose my sadness. I pack my trunk, embrace my friends, embark on the sea, and at last wake up in Naples, and there beside me is the stern fact, the sad self, unrelenting, identical, that I fled from. I seek the Vatican, and the palaces. I affect to be intoxicated with sights and suggestions, but I am not intoxicated. My giant goes with me wherever I go.

But the rage of travelling is a symptom of a deeper unsoundness affecting the whole intellectual action. The intellect is vagabond, and our system of education fosters restlessness. Our minds travel when our bodies are forced to stay at home. We imitate; and what is imitation but the travelling of the mind? Our houses are built with foreign taste; our shelves are garnished with foreign ornaments; our opinions, our tastes, our faculties, lean, and follow the Past and the Distant. The soul created the arts wherever they have flourished. It was in his own mind that the artist sought his model. It was an application of his own thought to the thing to be done and the conditions to be observed. And why need we copy the Doric or the Gothic model? Beauty, convenience, grandeur of thought, and quaint expression are as near to us as to any, and if the American artist will study with hope and love the precise thing to be done by him, considering the climate, the soil, the length of the day, the wants of the people, the habit and form of the government, he will create a house in which all these will find themselves fitted, and taste and sentiment will be satisfied also.

Insist on yourself; never imitate. Your own gift you can present every moment with the cumulative force of a whole life's cultivation; but of the adopted talent of another, you have only an extemporaneous, half possession. That which each can do best, none but his Maker can teach him. No man yet knows what it is, nor can, till that person has exhibited it. Where is the master who could have taught Shakspeare? Where is the master who could have instructed Franklin, or Washington, or Bacon, or Newton? Every great man is a unique.

The Scipionism of Scipio is precisely that part he could not borrow. Shakspeare will never be made by the study of Shakspeare. Do that which is assigned you, and you cannot hope too much or dare too much. There is at this moment for you an utterance brave and grand as that of the colossal chisel of Phidias, or trowel of the Egyptians, or the pen of Moses, or Dante, but different from all these. Not possibly will the soul all rich, all eloquent, with thousand-cloven tongue, deign to repeat itself; but if you can hear what these patriarchs say, surely you can reply to them in the same pitch of voice; for the ear and the tongue are two organs of one nature. Abide in the simple and noble regions of thy life, obey thy heart, and thou shalt reproduce the Foreworld again.

178   RALPH WALDO EMERSON
from "Thoughts on Art" (1841)

Underlying Emerson's aesthetics is the belief that just as we are a part of nature's divine plan, so should we in our artistic endeavors emulate nature's way of creating. Nature contains a universal and spiritually creative element, and in nature everything works for the greater whole. Saying this another way, everything has fitness to purpose. Thus art and architecture should not strive to exhibit a shallow beauty but must display purpose and at the same time speak to the higher aspirations of the human soul. Emerson refers to this functional underpinning as being "organically reproductive" – or simply organic – a notion that he will define a few years later as the "perfect economy" of the material with its means. On the one hand, this notion of the organic with its corollary "fitness" sets down the future path of American pragmatism – as well as a scorn for all ornamental trappings. On the other hand, architecture in this scheme must also retain something of the ideal, even if it must be economically expressed. Thus there was no room for pomp and circumstance in Emerson's thought; neither should such attributes be found in architecture.

Herein is the explanation of the analogies which exist in all the arts. They are the reappearance of one mind, working in many materials to many temporary ends. Raphael paints wisdom; Handel sings it, Phidias carves it, Shakspeare writes it, Wren builds it, Columbus sails it, Luther preaches it, Washington arms it, Watt mechanizes it. Painting was called "silent poetry"; and poetry "speaking painting." The laws of each art are convertible into the laws of every other.

Herein we have an explanation of the necessity that reigns in all the kingdom of art.

Arising out of eternal reason, one and perfect, whatever is beautiful rests on the foundation of the necessary. Nothing is arbitrary, nothing is insulated in beauty. It depends forever on the necessary and the useful. The plumage of the bird, the mimic plumage of the insect, has a reason for its rich colors in the constitution of the animal. Fitness is so inseparable an accompaniment of beauty, that it has been taken for it. The most perfect form to answer an end, is so far beautiful. In the mind of the artist, could we enter there, we should see the sufficient reason for the last flourish and tendril of his work, just as every tint

Ralph Waldo Emerson, from "Thoughts on Art" (1841) in *The Works of Ralph Waldo Emerson*. New York: Tudor Publishing, 1900, Vol. IV, pp. 66–71.

and spine in the sea-shell preëxists in the secreting organs of the fish. We feel, in seeing a noble building, which rhymes well, as we do in hearing a perfect song, that it is spiritually organic, that is, had a necessity in nature, for being, was one of the possible forms in the Divine mind, and is now only discovered and executed by the artist, not arbitrarily composed by him.

And so every genuine work of art has as much reason for being as the earth and the sun. The gayest charm of beauty has a root in the constitution of things. The Iliad of Homer, the songs of David, the odes of Pindar, the tragedies of Æschylus, the Doric temples, the Gothic cathedrals, the plays of Shakspeare, were all made not for sport, but in grave earnest, in tears, and smiles of suffering and loving men.

Viewed from this point, the history of Art becomes intelligible, and, moreover, one of the most agreeable studies in the world. We see how each work of art sprang irresistibly from necessity, and, moreover, took its form from the broad hint of Nature. Beautiful in this wise is the obvious origin of all the known orders of architecture, namely, that they were the idealizing of the primitive abodes of each people. Thus the Doric temple still presents the semblance of the wooden cabin, in which the Dorians dwelt. The Chinese pagoda is plainly a Tartar tent. The Indian and Egyptian temples still betray the mounds and subterranean houses of their forefathers. The Gothic church plainly originated in a rude adaptation of forest trees, with their boughs on, to a festal or solemn edifice, as the bands around the cleft pillars still indicate the green withs that tied them. No one can walk in a pine barren, in one of the paths which the woodcutters make for their teams, without being struck with the architectural appearance of the grove, especially in winter, when the bareness of all other trees shows the low arch of the Saxons. In the woods, in a winter afternoon, one will see as readily the origin of the stained glass window with which the Gothic cathedrals are adorned, in the colors of the western sky, seen through the bare and crossing branches of the forest. Nor, I think, can any lover of nature enter the old piles of Oxford and the English cathedrals, without feeling that the forest overpowered the mind of the builder, with its ferns, its spikes of flowers, its locust, its oak, its pine, its fir, its spruce. The cathedral is a blossoming in stone, subdued by the insatiable demand of harmony in man. The mountain of granite blooms into an eternal flower, with the lightness and delicate finish, as well as aerial proportions and perspective of vegetable beauty.

There was no wilfulness in the savages in this perpetuating of their first rude abodes. The first form in which they built a house would be the first form of their public and religious edifice also. This form becomes immediately sacred in the eyes of their children, and the more so, as more traditions cluster round it, and is, therefore, imitated with more splendor in each succeeding generation.

In like manner, it has been remarked by Goethe, that the granite breaks into parallelo-pipeds, which, broken in two, one part would be an obelisk; that in Upper Egypt the inhabitants would naturally mark a memorable spot by setting up so conspicuous a stone. Again, he suggested we may see in any stone wall, on a fragment of rock, the projecting veins of harder stone, which have resisted the action of frost and water, which has decomposed the rest. This appearance certainly gave the hint of the hieroglyphics inscribed on their obelisk. The amphitheatre of the old Romans, – any one may see its origin, who looks at the crowd running together to see any fight, sickness, or odd appearance in the street. The first comers gather round in a circle; those behind stand on tiptoe; and further back they climb on fences or window sills, and so make a cup of which the object of attention occupies the hollow area. The architect put benches in this order, and enclosed the cup with a wall, and behold a coliseum.

It would be easy to show of very many fine things in the world, in the customs of nations, the etiquette of courts, the constitution of governments, the origin in very simple local necessities. Heraldry, for example, and the ceremonies of a coronation, are a splendid burlesque of the occurrences that might befal a dragoon and his footboy. The College of Cardinals were originally the parish priests of Rome. The leaning towers originated from the civil discords which induced every lord to build a tower. Then it became a point of family pride, – and for pride a leaning tower was built.

This strict dependence of art upon material and ideal nature, this adamantine necessity, which it underlies, has made all its past, and may foreshow its future history. It never was in the power of any man, or any community, to call the arts into being. They come to serve his actual wants, never to please his fancy. These arts have their origin always in some enthusiasm, as love, patriotism, or religion. Who carved marble? The believing man, who wished to symbolize their gods to the waiting Greeks.

The Gothic cathedrals were built, when the builder and the priest and the people were overpowered by their faith. Love and fear laid every stone. The Madonnas of Raphael and Titian were made to be worshipped. Tragedy was instituted for the like purpose, and the miracles of music; – all sprang out of some genuine enthusiasm, and never out of dilettantism and holidays. But now they languish, because their purpose is merely exhibition. Who cares, who knows what works of art our government have ordered to be made for the capitol? They are a mere flourish to please the eye of persons who have associations with books and galleries. But in Greece, the Demos of Athens divided into political factions upon the merits of Phidias.

In this country, at this time, other interests than religion and patriotism are predominant, and the arts, the daughters of enthusiasm, do not flourish. The genuine offspring of our ruling passions we behold. Popular institutions, the school, the reading room, the post office, the exchange, the insurance company, and an immense harvest of economical inventions, are the fruit of the equality and the boundless liberty of lucrative callings. These are superficial wants; and their fruits are these superficial institutions. But as far as they accelerate the end of political freedom and national education, they are preparing the soil of man for fairer flowers and fruits in another age. For beauty, truth, and goodness are not obsolete; they spring eternal in the breast of man; they are as indigenous in Massachusetts as in Tuscany, or the Isles of Greece. And that Eternal Spirit, whose triple face they are, moulds from them forever, for his mortal child, images to remind him of the Infinite and Fair.

179 HORATIO GREENOUGH
from Letter to Washington Allston (1831)

In his occasional remarks on architecture, Emerson once acknowledged that he was much indebted in these matters to Horatio Greenough, the American neoclassical sculptor. Greenough too had attended Harvard, but by the time of graduation in the mid-1820s he had decided on a career as a sculptor. In 1829 he set up a studio in Florence and in 1832 he received his first major commission: a half-draped statue of George Washington in a Roman toga, which was intended to be placed in the rotunda of the Capitol. Emerson first met Greenough in the sculptor's studio in Florence in 1833.

Although Greenough's artistic talent has often been contested, he was nevertheless an extremely shrewd critic of contemporary events and he had an astute and particular interest in architecture. Shortly after arriving in Rome he is said to have met Henri Labrouste, who was then completing his studies at the French Academy. Greenough was at the same time curious about the work of Schinkel in Berlin, which he apparently only knew from drawings. And it is highly likely that Greenough read Andrea Memmo's edition of Lodoli's quasi-functionalist theory, which had appeared in Italy in two volumes in 1833–4. Despite his classical training in sculpture, Greenough (as this excerpt makes clear) was adamantly opposed to the formalism of classical architecture. He is equally antipathetic to a return to the Gothic style, and in hypothesizing an alternative he proved himself to be a most original thinker. In this early expression of his ideas, Greenough settles on "Nature" as the "only true school of art," but this formula will soon translate – as his vitally important naval metaphor suggests – into a precocious functionalism.

In the many conversations we had on Art when I was last in America though you expressed much pleasure at the efforts that were making in Architecture among us, yet I remember you fully agreed with me that broader principles of art and a more intelligent imitation were necessary to the formation of a pure and masculine style of building – This remembrance of your sympathy induces me to communicate to you a few thoughts of this art, as I have had opportunity to observe it, my impressions with regard to its present state among us and what it strikes me may be done to improve it – I will give you briefly my opinion of what I have seen and in suggesting any thing I beg to have it understood that I do it with my hat in my hand, – with a deep sense of the merit of those who have modelled our later buildings and a wish that it may be reciprocated by a frank expression of the views taken of my art of its capabilities among us and the hopes of its advancement.

Architecture seems to me to have been enthralled ever since a claim to *universal* and *indiscriminate* admiration has been established for the Greek school – I shall join you of course in excepting the Gothic which by throwing out the greek canons and recurring to nature to express a new sentiment got a new style, at once grand and pathetic as a whole and harmoniously rich in detail – The Gothic embodied the poetry of religion and triumphed over matter to deify spirit – The Greek adored matter and instead of sending towers high

Horatio Greenough (1805–52), from Letter to Washington Allston (Oct. 1831) in *Letters of Horatio Greenough: American Sculptor*, ed. Nathalia Wright. Madison: University of Wisconsin Press, 1972, pp. 88–91.

into the blue as twere to seek a heaven or to shew it when found it kept every member of its temples where the eye might taste their beauty and so proportioned and posed that it should be not only safe but strong – The Gothic by a mysterious combination of lines seems to lift the spirit from earth and shew her her home – The Greek woos the eye and lulls us into content below while its horizontal lines seem to measure the steps the mind may take beyond which all is dark. The uses for which the Greek temple were made were one – the form was unity itself – its parts harmonized with the whole –

The attempts in Italy to graft the christian sentiment on the greek stock – to expand the Pantheon to hold the Hebrew God, to recombine the greek elements into a new form for a new worship seem to me to have produced but a bastard result – No one is readier than myself to admit how much there is for the heart as well as for the imagination and the eye in the Italian church – I love their vast hushed interiour, their mild air and their mellow light – Their historic and poetic shadowings of art which seem as the incense rises and the chant peals, to take life and join in the worship – But these churches – this worship are the product of times in which a corrupt priesthood had engrossed government religion arts, sciences and even society and each of these institutions was promoted or sacrificed as the interests of that priesthood required – Our religion not only does not ask these sacrifices but forbids them – Our church is but an oratory a lecture room – We do not make it too large to be filled by one human voice – it possesses but two important features – the pulpit whence issues the word of God to man – The organ loft whence earth answers to heaven – Here is great simplicity of worship yet do I think these elements capable of very grand combinations –

In America we have since we began to look for art in buildings, made several attempts more or less successful, to place our Architecture on a footing with that of other nations – We have built combinations, Italian in intention at least if not in feeling – but they seem not to have satisfied any one – We have made pointed windows and clustered columns, but the small proportion of our means devoted to this end, have not allowed us either the vastness or the rich detail of the gothic – so that our happiest efforts in this way are as far from their models as is a horseshed from the temple of Venus – In our despair we have recurred to ancient Greece the mother of art – We have warmed at the praises bestowed on her buildings and have resolved to take to ourselves by a *coup de main* both the style and the praise – We have done with her temples what modern Europe has so often tried with every department of her literature and with no better success. The Dram's Personae may indeed be reduced to the classic 3 or 4, the chorus may be introduced and the lyric entre actes divided into strophe and antistrophe but a pale and insipid imitation is the only fruit – These spirits in the vasty deep of past epochs *will not come when we do call for them*[1] – The parthenon in Philadelphia,[2] shoved in between the common buildings of a street – shorn of its lateral colonnades and pierced every where for light reminds us of a noble captive stripped alike of arms and ornaments and set at work with the other drudges of his conqueror. If his grand air be not quite gone, if some vestige of his former comeliness or some badge of office be still visible about him they only serve to render his present degradation more apparent –

In a letter which I wrote to the committee of the Bunker Hill monument, I endeavoured to shew that by taking a member – a dependent part and making of it a monument, an inconsequent and unmeaning whole would result – for if that member be fitted for its situation all those features which connect it with the surrounding parts become absurd when it stands alone – T'is a limb without a body, a sentence without a verb, a tune broken off in the middle – As a column was in Greece organized to pose upon the earth and to support an entablature; so was the whole fabric constructed with an eye to its exposure and the worship for which it was intended – if well adapted to that exposure and that worship how shall it be fitted for a climate and a service so different?

Let us turn now to Nature the only true school of art – Has she ever been the slave of any one idea of beauty or of grandeur? Her sublimity is manifest alike in the sailing eagle, the bounding lion and the rolling whale – Her beauty asks no sacrifice of the existence or even of the comfort of its wearer – There's scarce a member which may not be found enlarged or annihilated by turns in the animal creation, as the wants of the creature demand. She always organizes the frame for its exposure and its work yet always leaves it beautiful – We propose then that she be imitated in this important respect more compleatly than has been done, we would recommend the use of the combinations we have inherited from preceding schools whenever they will serve our turn and harmonize with the plan of our work – Nor do we mean merely that the object for which a building is constructed shall be nowise sacrificed to an abstract idea of form – we would that the shell of each fabric be as it were, moulded on the wants and conveniences desired – Such has been the case with naval architecture – and he who has seen a ship at sea will confess that in that work man has approached nearest his maker – Our fleets alone can shew that the world is not retrograde –

In a bank for instance where the business transacted requires light we propose to get it not by stealth as if we were ashamed of it, but as openly as tis given by the creator to our own brain and that without fear of consequences – Where the business done within is so much connected with what is abroad as in a Bank we propose to render ingress and egress as convenient as possible to numbers, and so on with every want that those employed in such buildings may have experienc'd – And we shall receive all condemnation of such art as we would the complaint that the greyhound is too light for beauty, the horse too heavy – that horns are monstrous, or the necks of grazing cattle too long for proportion – We can at least shew that he who condemns us condemns with us the principles of creation – nor shall we be mortified at not having pleased men whom God himself has not been fastidious to satisfy – It is true that this style of art asks for much in feeling of which we have but the germ but why should we be discouraged – In our political institutions we have dared to be new – Can we not shew that art too has a reason as well as government? and that no model of past times when science was less and superstition reigned has a prescriptive right to cramp our convenience or to repress our invention?

That no one individual can accomplish the task we have thus planned is clear at a glance – It requires all the knowledge among us – all the light which can be thrown on the requisites of a building by those who are to occupy it, all the science of our engineers and mathematicians to find the most direct rout to their attainment, all the feeling and the imitation of our architects and painters to give a harmonious connection to the parts thus assembled – that these different bodies of men are equal to it is shewn by what they have already achieved in their various departments, for as we are [we] have no reason to decline a comparison with the present nations of Europe as far as *taste* in Architecture is concerned –

NOTES

1 See *Henry IV,* III, i, 53–5.
2 The Second Bank of the United States in Philadelphia, erected between 1818 and 1824, was designed by William Strickland to resemble the Parthenon. Presumably Greenough saw it in 1828.

180 HORATIO GREENOUGH
from "American Architecture"
(1843)

I n the early 1840s Greenough returned to the United States for a visit, and in the process was asked to write several essays for the *United States Magazine and Democratic Review.* The result is one of the most important, and surely one of the least unexpected, essays in the literature of modern architectural theory. Echoing Emerson's recently published essay "Self-Reliance," Greenough now seconds the theme that it is time for America to sever its cultural dependence on European ways and "form a new style of architecture" suited to the climate, needs, and institutions of the new country. Greenough's earlier insistence on emulating nature now takes more concrete form with his "law of adaptation," whereby form should be determined simply and economically by the function it has to fulfill. His earlier regard for the functional lines of a naval vessel is reiterated here in an expanded version of the same ideas.

The mind of this country has never been seriously applied to the subject of building. Intently engaged in matters of more pressing importance, we have been content to receive our notions of architecture as we have received the fashion of our garments and the form of our entertainments, from Europe. In our eagerness to appropriate, we have neglected to adapt, to distinguish, – nay, to understand. We have built small Gothic temples of wood and have omitted all ornaments for economy, unmindful that size, material, and ornament are the elements of effect in that style of building. Captivated by the classic symmetry of the Athenian models, we have sought to bring the Parthenon into our streets, to make the temple of Theseus work in our towns. We have shorn them of their lateral colonnades, let them down from their dignified platform, pierced their walls for light, and, instead of the storied relief and the eloquent statue which enriched the frieze and graced the pediment, we have made our chimneytops to peer over the broken profile and tell, by their rising smoke, of the traffic and desecration of the interior. Still the model may be recognized, some of the architectural features are entire; like the captive king, stripped alike of arms and purple and drudging amid the Helots of a capital, the Greek temple, as seen among us, claims pity for its degraded majesty, and attests the barbarian force which has abused its nature and been blind to its qualities.

Horatio Greenough, from "American Architecture" (1843) in Horatio Greenough, *Form and Function: Remarks on Art, Design, and Architecture,* ed. Harold A. Small, Berkeley: University of California Press, 1947, pp. 53–5, 57–9, 60–2.

If we trace architecture from its perfection in the days of Pericles to its manifest decay in the reign of Constantine, we shall find that one of the surest symptoms of decline was the adoption of admired forms and models for purposes not contemplated in their invention. The forum became a temple; the tribunal became a temple; the theater was turned into a church; nay, the column, that organized member, that subordinate part, set up for itself, usurped unity, and was a monument! The great principles of architecture being once abandoned, correctness gave way to novelty, economy and vainglory associated produced meanness and pretension. Sculpture, too, had waned. The degenerate workmen could no longer match the fragments they sought to mingle, nor copy the originals they only hoped to repeat. The moldering remains of better days frowned contempt upon such impotent efforts, till, in the gradual coming of darkness, ignorance became contempt, and insensibility ceased to compare. [. . .]

If, as the first step in our search after the great principles of construction, we but observe the skeletons and skins of animals, through all the varieties of beast and bird, of fish and insect, are we not as forcibly struck by their variety as by their beauty? There is no arbitrary law of proportion, no unbending model of form. There is scarce a part of the animal organization which we do not find elongated or shortened, increased, diminished, or suppressed, as the wants of the genus or species dictate, as their exposure or their work may require. The neck of the swan and that of the eagle, however different in character and proportion, equally charm the eye and satisfy the reason. We approve the length of the same member in grazing animals, its shortness in beasts of prey. The horse's shanks are thin, and we admire them; the greyhound's chest is deep, and we cry, beautiful! It is neither the presence nor the absence of this or that part, or shape, or color, that wins our eye in natural objects; it is the consistency and harmony of the parts juxtaposed, the subordination of details to masses, and of masses to the whole.

The law of adaptation is the fundamental law of nature in all structure. So unflinchingly does she modify a type in accordance with a new position, that some philosophers have declared a variety of appearance to be the object aimed at; so entirely does she limit the modification to the demands of necessity, that adherence to one original plan seems, to limited intelligence, to be carried to the very verge of caprice. The domination of arbitrary rules of taste has produced the very counterpart of the wisdom thus displayed in every object around us; we tie up the camelopard to the rack; we shave the lion, and call him a dog; we strive to bind the unicorn with his band in the furrow, and make him harrow the valleys after us! [. . .]

Let us now turn to a structure of our own, one which, from its nature and uses, commands us to reject authority, and we shall find the result of the manly use of plain good sense, so like that of taste, and genius too, as scarce to require a distinctive title. Observe a ship at sea! Mark the majestic form of her hull as she rushes through the water, observe the graceful bend of her body, the gentle transition from round to flat, the grasp of her keel, the leap of her bows, the symmetry and rich tracery of her spars and rigging, and those grand wind muscles, her sails. Behold an organization second only to that of an animal, obedient as the horse, swift as the stag, and bearing the burden of a thousand camels from pole to pole! What academy of design, what research of connoisseurship, what imitation of the Greeks produced this marvel of construction? Here is the result of the study of man upon the great deep, where Nature spake of the laws of building, not in the feather and in the flower, but in winds and waves, and he bent all his mind to hear and to obey. Could we carry into our civil architecture the responsibilities that weigh upon our shipbuilding, we should ere long have edifices as superior to the Parthenon, for the purposes that we require, as the *Constitution* or the *Pennsylvania* is to the galley of the Argonauts. Could our blunders on terra firma be put to the same dread test that those of shipbuilders are, little would be now left to say on this subject.

Instead of forcing the functions of every sort of building into one general form, adopting an outward shape for the sake of the eye or of association, without reference to the inner distribution, let us begin from the heart as the nucleus, and work outward. The most convenient size and arrangement of the rooms that are to constitute the building being fixed, the access of the light that may, of the air that must be wanted, being provided for, we have the skeleton of our building. Nay, we have all excepting the dress. The connection and order of parts, juxtaposed for convenience, cannot fail to speak of their relation and uses. As a group of idlers on the quay, if they grasp a rope to haul a vessel to the pier, are united in harmonious action by the cord they seize, as the slowly yielding mass forms a thorough-bass to their livelier movement, so the unflinching adaptation of a building to its position and use gives, as a sure product of that adaptation, character and expression.

181   HORATIO GREENOUGH
from "Structure and Organization" (1852)

B y 1851 Greenough had resettled in the United States, although only for a brief period before his early death. In a letter written to Emerson in late December of that year, he now summarized his "theory of structure" as "a scientific arrangement of spaces and forms to functions and to site — An emphasis of features proportioned to their graduated importance in function — Colour and ornament to be decided and arranged and varied by strictly organic laws — having a distinct reason for each decision — The entire and immediate banishment of all make-shift and make believe." The essay "Structure and Organization," published posthumously in 1853, seems to have been written around the same time for it contains a similar theme.

Here is perhaps the clearest articulation of his "organic" theory of functionalism, which would later have such a strong impact on such American architects as Louis Sullivan.

In all structure that from its nature is purely scientific – in fortifications, in bridges, in shipbuilding – we have been emancipated from authority by the stern organic requirements of the works. The modern wants spurned the traditional formula in these structures, as the modern life outgrew the literary molds of Athens. In all these structures character has taken the place of dilettantism, and if we have yet to fight for sound doctrine in all structure, it is

Horatio Greenough, from "Structure and Organization" (1852) in Horatio Greenough, *Form and Function: Remarks on Art, Design, and Architecture*, ed. Harold A. Small, Berkeley: University of California Press, 1947, pp. 116–18, 120–2, 127–8.

only because a doctrine which has possession must be expelled, inch by inch, however unsound its foundation.

The developments of structure in the animal kingdom are worthy of all our attention if we would arrive at sound principles in building. The most striking feature in the higher animal organizations is the adherence to one abstract type. The forms of the fish and the lizard, the shape of the horse, and the lion, and the camelopard, are so nearly framed after one type that the adherence thereto seems carried to the verge of risk. The next most striking feature is the modification of the parts, which, if contemplated independently of the exposure and functions whose demands are thus met, seems carried to the verge of caprice. I believe few persons not conversant with natural history ever looked through a collection of birds, or fish, or insects, without feeling that they were the result of Omnipotence at play for mere variety's sake.

If there be any principle of structure more plainly inculcated in the works of the Creator than all others, it is the principle of unflinching adaptation of forms to functions. I believe that colors also, so far as we have discovered their chemical causes and affinities, are not less organic in relation to the forms they invest than are those forms themselves. [. . .]

Let us now turn to the human frame, the most beautiful organization of earth, the exponent and minister of the highest being we immediately know. This stupendous form, towering as a lighthouse, commanding by its posture a wide horizon, standing in relation to the brutes where the spire stands in relation to the lowly colonnades of Greece and Egypt, touching earth with only one-half the soles of its feet – it tells of majesty and dominion by that upreared spine, of duty by those unencumbered hands. Where is the ornament of this frame? It is all beauty, its motion is grace, no combination of harmony ever equaled, for expression and variety, its poised and stately gait; its voice is music, no cunning mixture of wood and metal ever did more than feebly imitate its tone of command or its warble of love. The savage who envies or admires the special attributes of beasts maims unconsciously his own perfection to assume their tints, their feathers, or their claws; we turn from him with horror, and gaze with joy on the naked Apollo.

I have dwelt a moment on these examples of expression and of beauty that I may draw from them a principle in art, a principle which, if it has been often illustrated by brilliant results, we constantly see neglected, overlooked, forgotten – a principle which I hope the examples I have given have prepared you to accept at once and unhesitatingly. It is this: in art, as in nature, the soul, the purpose of a work will never fail to be proclaimed in that work in proportion to the subordination of the parts to the whole, of the whole to the function. If you will trace the ship through its various stages of improvement, from the dugout canoe and the old galley to the latest type of the sloop-of-war, you will remark that every advance in performance has been an advance in expression, in grace, in beauty, or grandeur, according to the functions of the craft. This artistic gain, effected by pure science in some respects, in others by mere empirical watching of functions where the elements of the structure were put to severe tests, calls loudly upon the artist to keenly watch traditional dogmas and to see how far analogous rules may guide his own operations. You will remark, also, that after mechanical power had triumphed over the earlier obstacles, embellishment began to encumber and hamper ships, and that their actual approximation to beauty has been effected, first, by strict adaptation of forms to functions, second, by the gradual elimination of all that is irrelevant and impertinent. The old chairs were formidable by their weight, puzzled you by their carving, and often contained too much else to contain convenience and comfort. The most beautiful chairs invite you by a promise of ease, and they keep that promise; they bear neither flowers nor dragons, nor idle displays of the turner's caprice. By keeping within their province they are able to fill it well.

★ ★ ★

I would fain beg any architect who allows fashion to invade the domain of principles to compare the American vehicles and ships with those of England, and he will see that the mechanics of the United States have already outstripped the artists, and have, by the results of their bold and unflinching adaptation, entered the true track, and hold up the light for all who operate for American wants, be they what they will.

In the American trotting wagon I see the old-fashioned and pompous coach dealt with as the old-fashioned palatial display must yet be dealt with in this land. In vain shall we endeavor to hug the associations connected with the old form. The redundant must be pared down, the superfluous dropped, the necessary itself reduced to its simplest expression, and then we shall find, whatever the organization may be, that beauty was waiting for us, though perhaps veiled, until our task was fully accomplished.

182   HENRY DAVID THOREAU
from his journal (1852)

Sometime early in 1852, Emerson showed to Henry David Thoreau a letter he had received from Greenough. Thoreau noted in his journal on January 11 how much Emerson liked its contents, but Thoreau himself was not convinced of its argument and in fact in his diary accused Greenough of being a dilettante. Notwithstanding this, Thoreau's views on architecture were not nearly as refined as those of Emerson or Greenough. He had apparently given architecture little thought up to this point within his personal philosophy, and only now begins to consider its meaning. What is striking in Thoreau's remarks is his puritanical rejection of all pretense and ornament. Architecture for him is entirely utilitarian, and ideally one's house should be constructed by the owner himself rather than by someone trained in the arts. In another passage in his journal, written a few months later, he goes so far as to argue that a 3-foot by 6-foot box with a few holes bored for air and light "might provide someone with adequate shelter." This extreme pragmatism, anti-aesthetic at heart, captures one aspect of American consciousness in the mid-nineteenth century.

R. W. E. [Emerson] showed me yesterday a letter from H. Greenough, the sculptor, on architecture, which he liked very much. Greenough's idea was to make architectural ornaments have a core of truth, a necessity and hence a beauty. All very well, as I told R. W. E., from Greenough's point of view, but only a little better than the common dilettant-ism. I was afraid I should say hard things if I said more.

Henry David Thoreau (1817–62), comments from his journal (Jan. 11, 1852) from *The Writings of Henry David Thoreau*, Vol. III: Journal, ed. by Bradford Torrey, Boston: Houghton Mifflin Co., 1906, pp. 181–3.

We sometimes find ourselves living fast, – unprofitably and coarsely even, – as we catch ourselves eating our meals in unaccountable haste. But in one sense we cannot live too leisurely. Let me not live as if time was short. Catch the pace of the seasons; have leisure to attend to every phenomenon of nature, and to entertain every thought that comes to you. Let your life be a leisurely progress through the realms of nature, even in guest-quarters.

This reminds me that the old Northman kings did in fact board round a good part of the time, as school-masters sometimes with us.

But as for Greenough, I felt as if it was dilettantism, and he was such a reformer in architecture as Channing in social matters. He began at the cornice. It was only how to put a core of truth within the ornaments, that every sugar-plum might in fact have an almond or carroway seed in it, and not how the inhabitant, the indweller, might be true and let the ornaments take care of themselves. He seemed to me to lean over the cornice and timidly whisper this half truth to the rude indwellers, who really knew it more interiorly than he. What of architectural beauty I now see, I know has gradually grown from within outward, out of the character and necessities of the indweller and builder, without even a thought for mere ornament, but an unconscious nobleness and truthfulness of character and life; and whatever additional beauty of this kind is destined to be produced will be preceded and accompanied, aye, created, by a like unconscious beauty of life. One of the most beautiful buildings in this country is a logger's hut in the woods, and equally beautiful will be the citizen's suburban box, when the life of the indweller shall be as simple and as agreeable to the imagination, and there is as little straining after effect in the style of his dwelling. Much it concerns a man, forsooth, how a few sticks are slanted under him or over him, what colors are daubed upon his box! One man says, in his despair, "Take up a handful of the earth at your feet, and paint your house that color!" What an abundance of leisure he must have on his hands! An enterprise to improve the style of cottage architecture! Grow your own house, I say. Build it after an Orphean fashion.

183 ANDREW JACKSON DOWNING
from *A Treatise on the Theory and Practice of Landscape Gardening* (1841)

Concomitant with the architectural discussions taking place within Emerson's Concord Circle were the not-unrelated ideas of Andrew Jackson Downing. Although his life was precipitously cut short by a drowning accident, Downing's influence on the American architectural profession was nothing less than momentous. Born to a niece of John Quincy Adams, the sixth President of the United States, Downing left school at the age of 16 to join the family nursery in the town of Newburgh, New York. In 1837 he began construction of his own "Elizabethan" residence, basing its design on plates from books by the British writers John Loudon and Francis

Andrew Jackson Downing (1815–52), from *A Treatise on the Theory and Practice of Landscape Gardening, Adapted to North America; with a View to the Improvement of Country Residences*. New York: Wiley and Putnam, 1841, pp. 296–300.

Goodwin. This English influence is also evident in Downing's first book of 1841, *A Treatise on the Theory and Practice of Landscape Gardening*, which owes a heavy debt in particular to Humphry Repton's picturesque theory. Such British precedents, however, merely served as a ground for the subsequent evolution of Downing's ideas. Already his aim in the *Treatise* is not so much to transplant British ideas as to interpret them in light of the peculiarities of the American soil, climate, landscape, and culture. Also underlying Downing's overall philosophy, which he shares with the Concord circle, is the belief that rural life is superior to urban life, that the countryside imbues its inhabitants with moral certitude, strength, character, and a spirit of patriotism.

Near the end of his largely technical study, Downing adds a chapter on architecture, to which up to this point he had devoted almost no attention. These passages thus form an interesting starting point for his interests. First and foremost among his points is his insistence that the formal styles inherited from Europe, such as classicism, are — because of their adherence to such principles as symmetry — incongruous with the nature of the rural residence, which should be less formal and far more functional in its design. He summarizes his beliefs under the three principles of fitness, expression of purpose, and expression of architectural style — another early functionalist theory.

Architecture, either practically considered, or viewed as an art of taste, is a subject so important and comprehensive in itself, that volumes would be requisite to do it justice. Buildings of every description, from the humble cottage to the lofty temple, are objects of such constant recurrence in every habitable part of the globe, and are so strikingly indicative of the intelligence, character, and taste of the inhabitants, that they possess in themselves a great and peculiar interest for the mind. To have a "local habitation," – a permanent dwelling, that we can give the impress of our own mind, and identify with our own existence, – appears to be the ardent wish, sooner or later felt, of every man: excepting only those wandering sons of Ishmael, who pitch their tents with the same indifference, and as little desire to remain fixed, in the flowery plains of Persia, as in the sandy deserts of Zahara or Arabia.

In a city or town, or its immediate vicinity, where space is limited, where buildings stand crowded together, and depend for their attractions entirely upon the style and manner of their construction, mere architectural effect, after convenience and fitness are consulted, is of course the only point to be kept in view. There the façade which meets the eye of the spectator from the public street, is enriched and made attractive by the display of architectural style and decoration; commensurate to the magnitude or importance of the edifice, and the whole, so far as the effect of the building is concerned, comes directly within the province of the architect alone.

With respect to this class of dwellings, we have little complaint to make, for many of our town residences are highly elegant and beautiful. But how shall we designate that singular perversity of taste, or rather that total want of it, which prompts the man, who, under the name of a villa residence, piles up in the free open country, amid the green fields, and beside the wanton gracefulness of luxuriant nature, a stiff modern 'three story brick,' which, like a well bred cockney with a true horror of the country, doggedly seems to refuse to enter into harmonious combination with any other object in the scene, but only serves to call up the exclamation,

Avaunt stiff pile! why did'st thou stray
From blocks congenial in Broadway!

Yet almost daily we see built up in the country huge combinations of boards and shingles, without the least attempts at adaptation to situation; and square masses of brick start up here and there, in the verdant slopes of our village suburbs, appearing as if they had been transplanted, by some unlucky incantation, from the close-packed neighbourhood of city residence, and left accidentally in the country.

What then are the proper characteristics of a rural residence? The answer to this in a few words is, such a dwelling, as from its various accommodations, not only gives ample space for all the comforts and conveniences of a country life, but by its varied and picturesque form and outline, its porches, verandas, etc., also appears to have some reasonable connection, or be in perfect keeping, with surrounding nature. *Architectural beauty* must be considered conjointly with the *beauty of the landscape* or situation. Buildings of almost every description, and particularly those for the habitation of man, will be considered by the mind of taste, not only as architectural objects of greater or less merit, but as component parts of the general scene; united with the surrounding lawn, embosomed in tufts of trees and shrubs, if properly designed and constructed, they will even serve to impress a character upon the surrounding landscape. Their effect will frequently be good or bad, not merely as they are excellent or indifferent examples of a certain style of building, but as they are happily or unhappily combined with the adjacent scenery. The intelligent observer will readily appreciate the truth of this, and acknowledge the value as well as necessity of something besides architectural knowledge. And he will perceive how much more likely to be successful, are the efforts of him, who in composing and constructing a rural residence, calls in to the aid of architecture, the genius of the landscape; – whose mind is imbued with a taste for beautiful scenery, and who so elegantly and ingeniously engrafts art upon nature, as to heighten her beauties; while by the harmonious union he throws a borrowed charm around his own creation.

The English, above all other people, are celebrated for their skill in what we consider *rural adaptation*. Their residences seem to be a part of the scenes where they are situated; for their exquisite taste and nice perception of the beauties of Landscape Gardening and rural scenery, lead them to erect those picturesque edifices, which, by their varied outlines, seem in exquisite keeping with nature; while by the numberless climbing plants, shrubs, and fine ornamental trees with which they surround them, they form beautiful pictures of rural beauty. Even the various offices connected with the dwelling, partially concealed by groups of foliage, and contributing to the expression of domestic comfort, while they extend out, and give importance to the main edifice, also serve to connect it, in a less abrupt manner, with the grounds.

So different indeed is the general character of the cottage and villa architecture of England, that many an American, on looking over the illustrated works of their writers on domestic architecture, while he acknowledges their high scenic beauty, generally regards them in much the same light as he does Moore's description of the vale of Cashmere, in Lalla Rookh – beautiful imaginative creations of the artist, but which can never be realized in every day life, and a comfortable dwelling. The fact however is, it is well known, quite the contrary; for many of the English country residences are really far more beautiful than the pictorial representations; and no people gather around themselves more of those little comforts and elegancies, which make up the sum total of *home*, than the inhabitants of that highly cultivated and gardenesque [nation].

The leading principles which should be our guide in Landscape or Rural Architecture, have been condensed by an able writer in the following heads. "1st, As a useful art, in FITNESS FOR THE END IN VIEW: 2d, as an art of design, in EXPRESSION OF PURPOSE: 3d, as an art of taste, in EXPRESSION OF SOME PARTICULAR ARCHITECTURAL STYLE."

184 ANDREW JACKSON DOWNING
from *Cottage Residences* (1842)

I n 1842 Downing followed his landscape study with *Cottage Residences*, a book devoted to architectural design and one that began his famous collaboration with the architect Alexander Jackson Davis (1803–92). It was a marriage of talents made in heaven. Davis had honed his architectural skills in New York City in the 1820s and in 1829 he formed a partnership with Ithiel Town, which would soon become one of the most prominent architectural offices in the country specializing in the classical style. Despite its success, Davis broke up the partnership in 1835, in part because his interests had veered away from classicism through his own deepening appreciation for the undisturbed American landscape. He now became a residential designer in search of an American style, and in 1836 (in renovating a country estate for Robert Donaldson) he wrapped a veranda around three sides of an existing house to frame and feature the view out toward the Hudson River. When Downing visited the residence a few years later in search of new ideas, he was impressed with the informal sensitivity of the architect and traveled into New York City to meet him personally.

The result of their first collaboration – *Cottage Residences* – was an extremely popular "how to" manual for residential design for which Davis prepared the drawings (and two very important designs) and Downing supplied sketches for designs and provided the text. The book opens with the chapter "Architectural Suggestions," in which Downing now elaborates upon his three principles of good residential design and offers a wealth of ideas on how best to make a home both functional and expressive of the sentiments of the occupants. The preface, which is reprinted here, offers an overview of his broader intentions. The great American love affair with a single-family house set within a suburban landscape begins here, and the formula would prove congruous with the geographic conditions of the United States.

A hearty desire to contribute something to the improvement of the domestic architecture and the rural taste of our country, has been the motive which has influenced me in preparing this little volume. With us, almost every man either builds, or looks forward to building, a home for himself, at some period of his life; it may be only a log-hut, or a most rustic cottage, but perhaps also a villa, or a mansion. As yet, however, our houses are mostly either of the plainest and most meagre description, or, if of a more ambitious, they are frequently of a more objectionable character – shingle palaces, of very questionable convenience, and not in the least adapted by their domestic and rural beauty to harmonize with our lovely natural landscapes.

Now I am desirous that every one who lives in the country, and in a country-house, should be in some degree conversant with domestic architecture, not only because it will be

Andrew Jackson Downing, from *Cottage Residences* (1842), reprinted in *Victorian Cottage Residences*. New York: Dover, 1981, pp. vi–x.

likely to improve the comfort of his own house, and hence all the houses in the country, but that it will enlarge his mind, and give him new sources of enjoyment.

It is not my especial object at this moment to dwell upon the superior convenience which may be realized in our houses, by a more familiar acquaintance with architecture. The advantages of an ingeniously arranged and nicely adapted plan, over one carelessly and ill-contrived, are so obvious to every one, that they are self-evident. This is the ground-work of domestic architecture, the great importance of which is recognized by all mankind, and some ingenuity and familiarity with practical details are only necessary to give us compact, convenient, and comfortable houses, with the same means and in the same space as the most awkward and unpleasing forms.

But I am still more anxious to inspire in the minds of my readers and countrymen livelier perceptions of the BEAUTIFUL, in everything that relates to our houses and grounds. I wish to awaken a quicker sense of the grace, the elegance, or the picturesqueness of fine forms that are capable of being produced in these by Rural Architecture and Landscape Gardening – a sense which will not only refine and elevate the mind, but open to it new and infinite resources of delight. There are perhaps a few upon whose souls nearly all emanations of beauty fall impressionless; but there are also many who see the Beautiful, in nature and art, only feebly and dimly, either from the want of proper media through which to view her, or a little direction as to where she is to be found. How many, too, are there, who even discover the Beautiful in a picture or a statue, who yet fail to admire her, rounding with lines of grace, and touching with shades of harmony all common nature, and pervading silently all material forms! "Men," says Goethe, "are so inclined to content themselves with what is commonest, so easily do the spirit and the sense grow dead to the impression of the Beautiful and the Perfect, that every person should strive to nourish in his mind the faculty of feeling these things, by everything in his power, for no man can bear to be wholly deprived of such enjoyment; it is only because they are not used to taste of what is excellent, that the generality of people take delight in silly and insipid things, provided they be new. For this reason, every day one ought to see a fine picture, read a good poem, hear a little song, and, if it were possible, to speak a few reasonable words."

It is in this regard that I wish to inspire all persons with a love of beautiful forms, and a desire to assemble them around their daily walks of life. I wish them to appreciate how superior is the charm of that home where we discover the tasteful cottage or villa, and the well designed and neatly kept garden or grounds, full of beauty and harmony, – not the less beautiful and harmonious, because simple and limited; and to become aware that these superior forms, and the higher and more refined enjoyment derived from them, may be had at the same cost and with the same labor as a clumsy dwelling, and its uncouth and ill-designed accessories.

More than all, I desire to see these sentiments cherished for their pure moral tendency. "All BEAUTY is an outward expression of inward good," and so closely are the Beautiful and the True allied, that we shall find, if we become sincere lovers of the grace, the harmony, and the loveliness with which rural homes and rural life are capable of being invested, that we are silently opening our hearts to an influence which is higher and deeper than the mere *symbol*; and that if we thus worship in the true spirit, we shall attain a nearer view of the Great Master, whose words, in all his material universe, are written in lines of Beauty.

And how much happiness, how much pure pleasure, that strengthens and invigorates our best and holiest affections, is there not experienced in bestowing upon our homes something of grace and loveliness – in making the place dearest to our hearts a sunny spot, where the social sympathies take shelter securely under the shadowy eaves, or grow and entwine trustfully with the tall trees or wreathed vines that cluster around, as if striving to shut out whatever of bitterness or strife may be found in the open highways of the world. What an unfailing barrier against vice, immorality, and bad habits, are those tastes which lead us to embellish a home, to which at all times and in all places we turn with delight, as being the object and the scene of our fondest cares, labors, and enjoyments; whose humble roof, whose shady porch, whose verdant lawn and smiling flowers, all breathe forth to us, in true, earnest tones, a domestic feeling that at once purifies the heart, and binds us more closely to our fellow-beings!

In this volume, the first yet published in this country devoted to Rural Architecture, I am conscious of offering but a slight and imperfect contribution to this important subject, which I trust will be the precursor of more varied and complete works from others, adapted to our peculiar wants and climate. The very great interest now beginning to manifest itself in rural improvements of every kind, leads us to believe and to hope, that at no distant day our country residences may rival the "cottage homes of England," so universally and so justly admired.

The relation between a country house and its "surroundings" has led me to consider, under the term residences, both the architectural and the gardening designs. To constitute an agreeable whole, these should indeed have a harmonious correspondence, one with the other; and although most of the following designs have not actually been carried into execution, yet it is believed that they will, either entirely or in part, be found adapted to many cases of every-day occurrence, or at least furnish hints for variations suitable for peculiar circumstances and situations.

185   ANDREW JACKSON DOWNING
from *Hints to Persons about Building in the Country* (1847)

During the 1840s both Davis and Downing had become successful in their own ways. Davis would emerge as one of the most sought-after residential architects in the country, and he was transforming the face of American practice with his original designs. Downing was intensifying the pace of writing, and in 1846 he sold his nursery to take over the editorship of the journal *The Horticulturist*. The next year he teamed up with the architect George Wightwick to co-publish two small books (Wightwick's contribution was *Hints to Young Architects*), in which Downing once again reiterated his three principles of good design. The following excerpt from his third principle – the expression of style – best reveals what he meant by style and reiterates his aversion to the high or formal styles of the past in favor of the less pretentious vernacular manners of England, Switzerland, and Italy.

Andrew Jackson Downing, from *Hints to Persons about Building in the Country*. New York: Wiley and Putnam, 1847, pp. xiv–xvii.

We conceive it to be true that the same principle should govern us in the choice of a style for a dwelling-house. Although we would reject no foreign style because it is foreign, we would adopt nothing in our domestic architecture which has not some obvious beauty of purpose, or some significance for our country and climate – which has not, in short, that fitness and propriety which a refined and just taste can fully approve.

This would lead us to reject at once all styles of building belonging to barbarous and semi-civilized people, as too grotesque in effect, and too much at variance with our habits of life, to be a significant and true expression of our age and social life. It would confine our choice to what may properly be called European styles – such as Gothic, Grecian, Roman, Italian, Swiss; or to new and more suitable modifications of these styles. A country of the variety of climate and geographical breadth of ours, indeed demands a like variety of style in its domestic architecture. In the houses of the north, warmth and shelter are the first requisites, and the comfortable dwellings of England and the north of Europe may be studied to advantage. In those of the south the cool verandas and the spacious colonnades of Italian architecture will be most appropriate and significant. One of the leading rules in selecting plans for a dwelling, which we deduce from the principles of fitness and propriety, is that of abjuring all styles or modifications of styles not warranted by our social and domestic habits.

It is one of the most common errors into which persons fall, whose architectural taste is just awakening, to rush to the very verge and extreme limits of architectural style. Not content with simplicity, or a moderate degree of ornament, everything they do must have a "strong relish" about it. If they are about to build Gothic, it must be an imitation of a castle of the middle ages at least; if Grecian, nothing short of a copy of the Parthenon will satisfy them. Now there is little meaning, to our eyes, in the mock heroic air of a puny Gothic castle built in a style which was warranted by feudal times and feudal robberies, for the habitation by a meek and quiet merchant, who has not the remotest idea of manifesting anything offensive or defensive to any of his peace-loving neighborhood. And we cannot greatly admire the effect of a huge Greek colonnade round four sides of the house, supported on columns two stories high, affording little shade or shelter, and costing half the entire sum that ought to have been expended in the dwelling itself.

It is the *later* modifications of European architecture which ought to be studied and adopted by our architects, and persons about building, at the present time. These are based upon modern comforts, and modern wants, and their beauty is the more beautiful that it grows out of, and is in keeping with, the spirit of utility. Hence the Tudor or Elizabethan villa, and the Rural English cottage, are the varieties of the Gothic style which may be copied with more propriety in this country. For the same reason the Roman style is preferable to the Greek, and the modern Italian, in its many variations, to the Roman itself. Significance, fitness, propriety, immediately lead us to ask for verandas, piazzas, porches, balconies, clustered chimneys, window-blinds, and all the numerous architectural features that denote refined comforts and the enjoyments of our social life. Since these do not belong, and cannot with propriety be attached to the old Gothic castle and Greek temple, let us eschew these latter, and take some more pliant and appropriate style of which they properly form a part.

186 ANDREW JACKSON DOWNING
from *The Architecture of Country Houses* (1850)

By 1849 Downing was determined to become an architect, and in this capacity he approached Davis and proposed a partnership. The latter declined, and in July 1850 Downing — still the Anglophile — sailed to England specifically to find an architectural partner who would also immigrate to the United States. He found such a person in the young architect Calvert Vaux. Just before leaving for England, Downing completed the manuscript of *The Architecture of Country Houses*, his last and most significant venture with Davis.

The book was more ambitious than earlier ones in that Downing and Davis devoted more attention to less expensive dwellings, and more to simple cottages intended for laborers. Downing now advocates less expensive timber construction for housing and champions Davis's board-and-batten construction. On a theoretical front, Downing had just read Ruskin's *Seven Lamps of Architecture*, and he is inspired to compose an introductory essay "On the Real Meaning of Architecture," in which he praises at length the meaning of utility, beauty, variety, character, picturesqueness, and truth in architecture. The short Preface is also a masterpiece of content, as the moral connection of a home with civilization and social values neatly transposes the Anglo-Saxon notion of a "home" into the American psyche.

There are three excellent reasons why my countrymen should have good houses.

The first is, because a good house (and by this I mean a fitting, tasteful, and significant dwelling) is a powerful means of civilization. A nation, whose rural population is content to live in mean huts and miserable hovels, is certain to be behind its neighbors in education, the arts, and all that makes up the external signs of progress. With the perception of proportion, symmetry, order, and beauty, awakens the desire for possession, and with them comes that refinement of manners which distinguishes a civilized from a coarse and brutal people. So long as men are forced to dwell in log huts and follow a hunter's life, we must not be surprised at lynch law and the use of the bowie knife. But, when smiling lawns and tasteful cottages begin to embellish a country, we know that order and culture are established. And, as the first incentive towards this change is awakened in the minds of most men by the perception of beauty and superiority in external objects, it must follow that the interest manifested in the Rural Architecture of a country like this, has much to do with the progress of its civilization.

The second reason is, because the *individual home* has a great social value for a people. Whatever new systems may be needed for the regeneration of an old and enfeebled nation, we are persuaded that, in America, not only is the distinct family the best social form, but those elementary forces which give rise to the highest genius and the finest character may, for the most part, be traced back to the farm-house and the rural cottage. It is the solitude and freedom of the family home in the country which constantly preserves the purity of the nation, and invigorates its intellectual powers. The battle of life, carried on in cities, gives a sharper edge to the weapon of character, but its temper is, for the most part, fixed amid those communings with nature and the family, where individuality takes its most natural and strongest development.

Andrew Jackson Downing, from *The Architecture of Country Houses* (1850). New York: Dover Publications, 1969 (facsimile edition), pp. xix–xx.

The third reason is, because there is a moral influence in a country home – when, among an educated, truthful, and refined people, it is an echo of their character – which is more powerful than any mere oral teachings of virtue and morality. That family, whose religion lies away from its threshold, will show but slender results from the best teachings, compared with another where the family hearth is made a central point of the Beautiful and the Good. And much of that feverish unrest and want of balance between the desire and the fulfilment of life, is calmed and adjusted by the pursuit of tastes which result in making a little world of the family home, where truthfulness, beauty, and order have the largest dominion.

The mere sentiment of home, with its thousand associations, has, like a strong anchor, saved many a man from shipwreck in the storms of life. How much the moral influence of that sentiment may be increased, by making the home all that it should be, and how much an attachment is strengthened by every external sign of beauty that awakens love in the young, are so well understood, that they need no demonstration here. All to which the heart can attach itself in youth, and the memory linger fondly over in riper years, contributes largely to our stock of happiness, and to the elevation of the moral character. For this reason, the condition of the family home – in this country where every man may have a home – should be raised, till it shall symbolize the best character and pursuits, and the dearest affections and enjoyments of social life.

After the volumes I have previously written on this subject, it is needless for me to add more on the purpose of this work. But it is, perhaps, proper that I should say, that it is rather intended to develop the growing taste of the people, than as a scientific work on art. Rural Architecture is, indeed, so much more a sentiment, and so much less a science, than Civil Architecture, that the majority of persons will always build for themselves, and, unconsciously, throw something of their own character into their dwellings. To do this well and gracefully, and not awkwardly and clumsily, is always found more difficult than is supposed. I have, therefore, written this volume, in the hope that it may be of some little assistance to the popular taste. For the same reason, I have endeavored to explain the whole subject in so familiar a manner, as to interest all classes of readers who can find any thing interesting in the beauty, convenience, or fitness of a house in the country.

187   CALVERT VAUX
from *Villas and Cottages* (1857)

The Englishman Vaux immigrated to the United States in 1850 and formed a partnership with Downing, a venture that soon resulted in their picturesque, prize-winning design for the Mall in Washington DC. Downing's accidental death came at the time when political opposition was forming against the scheme, and their competition design was never implemented. Vaux continued with residential practice in New York throughout most of the 1850s, but in 1857 he teamed up with Frederick Law Olmstead to win the competition for

Calvert Vaux (1825–95), from *Villas and Cottages: A Series of Designs Prepared for Execution in the United States* (1857). New York: Harper and Brothers, 1864 (second edition) and New York: Dover, 1970 (facsimile edition), pp. 28–32.

the design of New York City's Central Park. This was the first of several collaborative and individual designs that transformed the face of urban America and brought Vaux to the forefront of his profession.

Vaux's first book *Villages and Cottages* is to a large extent a continuation of Downing's theory, taken one stage further. Combining the social consciousness of Downing with the transcendental spirit of Emerson, the transplanted Englishman sees good residential architecture in the United States as the "rock" upon which an ethical and populist American democracy is to be based. Even more so than Downing, he pleads for a genuinely American architecture to arise of the climate, habits, and democratic aspirations of the young country. The spirit of these remarks also neatly summarizes the attitudes of American residential design on the eve of its great expansion or proliferation after the Civil War.

Till within a comparatively recent period the fine arts in America have been considered by the great bulk of the population as pomps and vanities so closely connected with superstition, popery, or aristocracy, that they must be eschewed accordingly, and the result is not *altogether* undesirable, though it has appeared to retard the advance of refinement and civilization. The awakening spirit of republicanism refused to acknowledge the value of art as it then existed, a tender hot-house plant ministering to the delights of a select few. The democratic element rebelled against this idea *in toto*, and tacitly, but none the less practically, demanded of art to thrive in the open air, in all weathers, for the benefit of all, if it was worth any thing, and if not, to perish as a troublesome and useless encumbrance. This was a severe course to take, and the effects are every where felt. But, after all, it had truth on its side; and candor must allow that no local, partial, class-recognizing advance in art, however individually valuable its examples might have been, could, in reality, have compensated for the disadvantage that would have attended it. Now, every step in advance, slow though it be, is a real step taken by the whole country. When we look at the ruins of old Rome, we say, What a great people! what temples! what mighty works! and undoubtedly Rome was really great *in individuals;* very great in a strong and clever minority, who spent with marked ability the labor of the weak and ignorant majority; but the *plebs*, the unlettered, unthought-of common people, the million, were not great, nor were they taught to be so, and therefore Rome fell.

During the last hundred years there has been a continuous effort to give to the American million the rudiments of self-reliant greatness, to abolish class legislation, and to sink the importance of individuals. *"Aut America aut nullus"* – "America or no *one*," has been, is, and will probably ever be the practical motto. It is not surprising, then, that the advancement in the arts has been somewhat less rapid than the progress in commercial prosperity and political importance. The conditions were new, and, it must be confessed, rather hard. Continuous ease and leisure readily welcome art, while constant action and industry require time to become acquainted with its merits. To the former, it may be a parasite and yet be supported; to the latter, it must be a friend or nothing. The great bulk of money that is laid out on building in the United States belongs to the active workers, and is spent by them and for them. The industrious classes, therefore, decide the national standard of architectural taste.

The question then occurs, How is this universal taste to be improved? There is the sound, healthy material, unprejudiced, open to conviction, with a real though not thoroughly understood desire for what is good and true – there is plenty of prosperity and opportunity, plenty of money and industry, plenty of every thing but education and the diffusion of knowledge. This language may seem inapplicable to America, to whom humanity is indebted for the successful introduction of the common school system, which lies at the root of every healthy idea of reform now at work in the world, but is, nevertheless, true. The genius of American art may, with justice, say of the genius of American education:

> "If she be not so to me,
> What care I how fair she be!"

Education must be liberal and comprehensive as well as universal and cheap, or the result will remain incomplete. To secure any thing permanently satisfactory in the matter of architecture, professors of ability, workmen of ability, and an appreciative, able public are necessary. It would seem that the architects practicing in America are not at present, in the majority of cases, born or bred in the United States. They have, therefore, to learn and unlearn much before the spirit instilled into their designs can be truly and genuinely American. There is no good reason now why this state of affairs should continue. Architecture is a profession likely to be in considerable request here for several hundred years at least, and the demand is steadily increasing. Why, then, should not parents speculate for their sons in this line? Why should not the article, as it is for home consumption, be raised at home? It is an honorable calling; not certainly offering such splendid fortunes as the merchant *may* realize, but it is a fair opening, and the only capital that it requires, beyond brains and industry, is the expense for books and an education. When a fair share of Young America enters upon this study heart and soul, as a means of earning an independent position, we may expect a rapid, natural development of the architectural resources of the country, and that the present meagre facilities for artistic education will be gradually increased; the schools and colleges, also, will probably be induced, after a time, to include in their course of study subjects calculated to discover and foster, in the rising generation, such natural gifts as have a bearing on these and similar matters.

To insure workmen of ability, a reasonable chance to improve is the chief thing wanted. So long as the general demand is for monotonous, commonplace, stereotyped work, the average of ability will necessarily be low; but with opportunity, good, cheap, illustrated works, and a spirited weekly paper devoted to the special discussion of the subjects interesting to architects, engineers, carpenters, masons, and all the other trades connected with building – a paper that would diffuse sound theoretical and practical information on the art in general and in detail throughout the whole country, the advance would be rapidly felt; for wherever there is an American, there at least, be he rich or poor, is a reader, a thinker, and an actor. Self-supporting schools of design for painters, decorators, modelers, carvers, paper-stainers, etc., must follow in due course, for the positiveness of the need would soon become evident, and the object would then be almost gained. With reference to the appreciative and able public, the press is the improving power that is to be mainly looked to. Cheap popular works on architecture in all its bearings, popular lectures, popular engravings – and hundreds of them, and yet all good – these are the simple, truthful, and effective means that are to influence the public, by supplying a medium through which it may see clearly, and thus be led to criticise freely, prefer wisely, and act judiciously. Every year offers proofs of an advancing interest in this subject, and shows an increasing desire to respond to it in newspapers, magazines, books, etc., while the public is certainly not slow to buy and read.

The truth is, not that America is a dollar-worshiping country, with a natural incapacity to enjoy the arts, but a dollar-making country, with restricted opportunities for popular, artistic education, *as yet;* but when this want is freely ministered to, in the spirit that it may be, and it is hoped will be, ere long, there is every reason to conjecture that correct architectural taste may be as generally diffused throughout the United States as we at present find the idea of a republican form of government. We shall *then* hope for genuine *originality* as well as intrinsic beauty in American buildings; and this interesting subject of originality is, perhaps, worthy of a separate analysis and consideration.

188   JAMES JACKSON JARVES
from *The Art-Idea* (1864)

J ames Jackson Jarves is one of the fascinating intellectual figures of nineteenth-century America. A native of Boston, he traveled widely in his youth, including Central America and the Hawaiian Islands, for which he wrote a historical study. In the 1850s he traveled throughout Europe, where he maintained his home base in Florence. He painted, wrote (often books on art for the public), and collected works of art, including Venetian glass. In 1876 he published the first book by an American on Japanese art and thus was influential with the artistic generation of Louis Tiffany and John LaFarge. Lewis Mumford once referred to him as the "American Ruskin," who in his critical role stood "midway between Greenough and Montgomery Schuyler." This particular selection of remarks on architecture aligns him squarely with the viewpoint of Greenough, only with a later sense of impatience, if not despair.

Our synopsis of the Art-Idea would be incomplete without referring to the condition of architecture in America. Strictly speaking, we have no architecture. If, as has happened to the Egyptians, Ninevites, Etruscans, Pelasgians, Aztecs, and Central American races, our buildings alone should be left, by some cataclysm of nations, to tell of our existence, what would they directly express of us? Absolutely nothing! Each civilized race, ancient or modern, has incarnated its own æsthetic life and character in definite forms of architecture, which show with great clearness their indigenous ideas and general conditions. A similar result will doubtless in time occur here. Meanwhile we must look at facts as they now exist. And the one intense, barren fact which stares us fixedly in the face is, that, were we annihilated to-morrow, nothing could be learned of us, as a distinctive race, from our architecture. It is simply substantial building, with ornamentation, orders, styles, or forms, borrowed or stolen from European races, an incongruous medley as a whole, developing no system or harmonious principle of adaptation, but chaotic, incomplete, and arbitrary,

James Jackson Jarves (1818–88), from *The Art-Idea* (1864). Cambridge, MA: The Belknap Press of Harvard University Press, 1960 (facsimile edition), pp. 286–90.

declaring plagiarism and superficiality, and proving beyond all question the absolute poverty of our imaginative faculties, and general absence of right feeling and correct taste. Whether we like it or not, this is the undeniable fact of 1864. And not merely this: an explorer of our ruins would often be at a loss to guess the uses or purposes of many of our public edifices. He could detect bastard Grecian temples in scores, but would never dream they were built for banks, colleges, or custom-houses. How could he account for ignoble and impoverished Gothic chapels, converted into libraries, of which there is so bad an example at Cambridge, Massachusetts, or indeed for any of the architectural anomalies which disfigure our soil and impeach our common sense, intensified as they frequently are by a total disregard of that fundamental law of art which demands the harmonious relation of things, condemning the use of stern granite or adamantine rock in styles where only beautiful marbles can be employed with æsthetic propriety, or of cold stones in lieu of brick, or the warmer and yet more plastic materials belonging of right to the variety and freedom of Gothic forms? If the mechanical features of our civilization were left to tell the national story, our ocean-clippers, river-steamers, and industrial machines would show a different aspect. They bespeak an enterprise, invention, and development of the practical arts that proclaim the Americans to be a remarkable people. If, therefore, success attend them in whatever they give their hearts and hands to, it is but reasonable to infer that cultivation need but be stimulated in the direction of architecture to produce results commensurate with the advance in mechanical and industrial arts. If one doubt this, let him investigate the progress in shipbuilding from the point of view of beauty alone, and he will discover a success as complete in its way as was that of the builders of Gothic cathedrals and Grecian temples. And why? Simply, that American merchants took pride in naval architecture. Their hearts were in their work; their purses opened without stint; and they built the fastest and handsomest ships.

To excel in architecture we must warm up the blood to the work. The owner, officer, and sailor of a gallant ship love her with sympathy as of a human affinity. A ship is not *it*, but *she* and *her*, one of the family; the marvel of strength and beauty; a thing of life, to be tenderly and lovingly cared for and proudly spoken of. All the romance of the trader's heart – in the West, the steamboat holds a corresponding position in the taste and affections of the public – goes out bountifully towards the symmetrical, stately, graceful object of his adventurous skill and toil. Ocean-clippers and river-steamers are fast making way for locomotive and propeller, about which human affections scarce can cluster, and which art has yet to learn how to dignify and adorn. But the vital principle, *love of the work*, still lives, that gave to the sailing-vessel new grace and beauty, combining them with the highest qualities of utility and strength into a happy unity of form. As soon as an equal love is turned towards architecture, we may expect as rapid a development of beauty of material form on land as on the ocean.

PART VI   HISTORICISM IN THE INDUSTRIAL AGE

A.   THE BATTLE OF THE STYLES IN BRITAIN

Introduction

The European stylistic skirmishes of the 1830s and early 1840s escalated into a full-blown war in the middle decades of the century. It was again a time of vibrant intellectual activity and massive social change, as many factors were coming together to alter, and in many instances to complicate, the course of European development. The Industrial Revolution, which had begun in the last half of the eighteenth century in Britain and France, now shifted into high gear across a greater Europe. The coeval migrations of people from the countryside to expanding urban centers had a leveling affect on earlier class relations, and at the same time produced an enormous strain on social conditions. Railways for the first time allowed individuals to travel easily across the Continent while also contributing to industrial expansion. Institutions such as public museums and public theaters were created in every town and initiated the new middle classes into the nuances of what was formerly regarded as high culture. Education in many countries became mandatory, and the mid-nineteenth century witnessed an unprecedented growth of those participating in higher education. New disciplines, both scientific and otherwise, appeared along every front, and many had an affect on architectural thinking. Historians, with increasing knowledge at their disposal, began to view the world in broader evolutionary and cosmopolitan terms, reinforcing architectural concerns with historicism. New fields such as psychology and ethnology defined themselves almost overnight into influential forces for interpreting the world. Darwin's theory of natural selection, which took shape in the 1840s, forever transformed the privileged perspective of the human race, while Karl Marx put forth his materialist theory of economic and political revolution. Everywhere there was activity, as well as increasing resistance to the profound nature of the changes taking place.

The upheaval in the arts was no less compelling. With the stylistic debate now achieving a crescendo, the hope that many architects held out in the early 1840s for a unified "nineteenth-century style" gave way, out of necessity, to an acceptance of stylistic pluralism. The simple growth of historical knowledge and its stylistic options was one factor forcing this position. Another was the pace of building activity, as such medium-size towns as Berlin and Vienna transformed themselves in just a few decades into major urban centers. Still another factor was that new materials, such as iron, were beginning to find their way into practice, and their use became a topic of continuing debate. A forum for such was provided by the rise of professional organizations and professional journals. Almost everyone bemoaned the absence of a unified formal language in practice, but then again nearly everyone had his own particular solution to the problem.

Political fortunes and national characteristics also weighed heavily on these artistic transformations, as the former dominance of French theory within Europe began to give way. Great Britain, which enjoyed a period of political stability and steady economic expansion throughout the middle years of the century, continued to pursue a relatively independent course. The great symbol of its success was the Great London Exhibition of 1851, which brought to light both the abundant material benefits and evident shortcomings of industry in terms of artistic development. The energetic force behind the event was Henry Cole, who in 1852 also assumed control of the national schools of design. During the next two decades he created the complex of the Victoria and Albert Museum and dedicated himself to the reform of the industrial arts through education — all in the name of furthering British exports. Cole was opposed in his endeavors by John Ruskin, who had inherited Pugin's puritanical morality and love of Gothic architecture. Ruskin, also with his intense dislike of industrialization and the social ills associated with it, advocated a picturesque aesthetics and a vision of medieval socialism founded on the idea of a guild. His protégé and colleague, William Morris, transformed such a vision into the Arts and Crafts movement.

189 THOMAS HOPE
from *Observations on the Plans and Elevations Designed by James Wyatt* (1804)

Although picturesque thought had gained ascendancy in Britain in the last part of the eighteenth century, classicism itself did not disappear. In fact the classical spirit was a phenomenon of longer duration in Britain in the nineteenth century than in any other country except the United States. British archaeological pursuits were largely driving these interests. The success of Stuart and Revett spawned numerous other British expeditions to the Eastern Mediterranean in the second half of the eighteenth century. Around 1800 another wave of British

Thomas Hope (1769–1831), from the pamphlet *Observations on the Plans and Elevations Designed by James Wyatt, Architect, for Downing College, Cambridge*, printed by D. N. Shury, London, 1804, pp. 15–17.

travelers descended upon Greece, the most notable of whom was the Scot, Thomas Bruce, the seventh Earl of Elgin, who would purchase the decorative sculptures of the Parthenon from the Ottoman government and ship them back to England. After Napoleon's defeat, still a third contingent of British architects visited the East, among them William Kinnard, George Basevi, Thomas Leverton Donaldson, and Charles Robert Cockerell. All would remain sympathetic toward classicism throughout their careers, and all would occupy influential positions within the British architectural profession.

This interest in Greece, more so than in Rome, also created a British counterpart to the American Greek Revival – adding to the context of the dispute between Jefferson and Latrobe. The outlines of such a debate were clearly drawn in a controversy surrounding recently endowed Downing College, Cambridge, at the beginning of the century. The design for the new building had been prepared by the prominent neoclassicist James Wyatt, and the Master of the college sought the advice of Thomas Hope on the proposed design. The latter was a son of a wealthy English merchant who between 1787 and 1795 had undertaken his grand tour of Sicily, Egypt, Turkey, Syria, and Greece. Hope responded to the request by publishing a 35-page pamphlet, in which he expressed his keen disappointment with the design because it was in "the Roman style of building" and not in a genuine "Grecian style." In the end Hope dissuaded Downing College from accepting Wyatt's design, and the commission eventually went to the young architect William Wilkins, who had just returned from his tour of Greece.

I have often regretted that in the new building at Fonthill, where, had the Grecian orders been employed, a mansion might have arisen, unrivalled in the most distant parts of the island, a style had on the contrary been adopted, which subjected every one of its details to disadvantageous comparisons with the cathedral at Salisbury, whose proud spire rises in its very sight. Nothing of this kind, at least, is to be apprehended here; and King's College, Cambridge, will never subject Downing College, of the same city, to the danger of an hourly parallel, and consequently to the stigma of an humble imitation.

I cannot however, my dear Sir, help wishing for something more still. In a building which, from the immensity of the sum allotted to its construction, is enabled, as well as intended, to become one of the first ornaments to the country, I could wish that, instead of the degraded architecture of the Romans, the purest style of the Greeks had been exclusively adhibited.

I could wish, instead of that spurious order which a nation, more versed in the arts of war and politics than in those of beauty, chose to call Doric, notwithstanding no example of the same be discoverable among the Greeks, that legitimate order had been introduced, which alone was acknowledged as theirs, by all the nations of Doric race.

As most architects, whose good fortune permitted them to design grand buildings in England, never travelled, and thus never looked for models, beyond Italy; and as those who did extend their travels to Greece, had not the advantage of being entrusted with constructions, on which to display their more improved ideas, the Roman style of building has been the only one, in vogue among the ancients, hitherto seen in monuments of importance among this nation; and a noble edifice in the true Grecian style would thus be really unique.

190 THOMAS HOPE
from *An Historical Essay on Architecture* (1835)

Thomas Hope, over the long course of his architectural development, could serve as a symbol for the emergence of nineteenth-century eclecticism. While supporting Wilkins on the Greek ideal in 1804, he was renovating his London townhouse (originally designed by Robert Adam) in the French Empire style of Napoleon. In other building activities he later flirted with the picturesque, the German *Rundbogen*, and with the Italian Renaissance (which he calls the *Cinque-centro* style). Eventually he came to define the meaning of eclecticism within British theory. This was the position he espoused, at least, in the concluding pages of his posthumous *An Historical Essay on Architecture* (1835) – really the first world history of architecture written in English.

Eclecticism, as we have seen, was a position tentatively put forth by Piranesi in the 1760s. It was also a view advocated by Payne Knight at the beginning of the nineteenth century, and it was to some extent an idea exemplified in the architecture of John Soane. It is also a term and a position that unfortunately was much maligned in later histories of this period. In its philosophical sense, it is simply composing an intellectual system by judiciously selecting parts or viewpoints from other systems. In architectural theory it might signify the creative selection of elements from the past in the effort to construct a contemporary style. Hope's final pages of the lengthy *An Historical Essay on Architecture* speak to this view and interpretation, and this perspective would indeed find many advocates.

This taste, like all the former born in Italy, soon passed into France. It graced the dotage of the fourteenth Louis, whose youth had seen better things. It gained strength under the Regent, and it adorned the pedestal of the statue which represented Louis XV, on his accession, in a large powdered periwig, with flowing curls, a square-skirted coat, high-heeled shoes, a tear in his eye, his nose inclined upwards into the air, and his hand thrust into his side. From France it spread like wildfire all over the Continent, and was wafted across the Channel to the British shores, where, as it is well shown in Italy, in the modern part of Piranesi's prints, and in France in the pictures of Watteau, it is happily exemplified in the furniture of Hogarth's compositions, and known by the name of the old French taste, though Italy has the credit of the invention. Its proper name should be the inane or frippery style.

In fact, such was the *ennui* which its unmeaningness and inspidity caused, that already, before the Revolution, the French had begun to shake it off, as may be seen at Paris in the church of Sainte Géneviève, the new additions to the Palais Bourbon, and other edifices; and that, since that period, they have greatly improved their architecture, and all the arts connected with it.

In England, government, by taxing alike heavily, brick and stone, which form the solid walls; and the apertures from which they are absent for the admission of light; discourages in architecture both solidity of construction and variety of form; copyhold tenures, short leases,

Thomas Hope, from *An Historical Essay on Architecture* (1835). London: John Murray, 1840 (third edition), pp. 489–92.

and the custom of building whole streets by contract, still increase the slightness, the uniformity, the poverty of the general architecture. Here the exterior shell of most edifices is designed by a surveyor who has little science, and no knowledge of the fine arts; and the internal finishing – regarded as distinct from the province of the architect – is left to a mere upholder, still more ignorant, who most frequently succeeds in the apparent object of marring the intentions of the builder. Thus has arisen at least that species of variety in building which proceeds from an entire and general ignorance of what is suitable and appropriate to the age, nation, and localities.

Some, still reviving the name of the antique – the classic style; but only acquainted with its nature in public edifices, those which alone have, in some degree, survived the wreck of ages, by building houses in the shape of temples, have contrived for themselves most inappropriate and uncomfortable dwellings.

Some, reverting to the pointed style, as more indigenous, more national; but in England, where there are few private buildings to serve as models for it, taking all their ideas from religious edifices, instead of a temple, have lodged themselves in a church.

Others have, in times of profound peace, or at least of internal security and refinement, affected to raise rude and embattled castles, as if they expected a siege.

Others, again, wishing for more striking novelty, have sought their models among the ancient Egyptians, the Chinese, or the Moors; or, by way of leaving no kind of beauty unattempted, have occasionally collected and knit together, as if they were the fragments of an universal chaos, portions of all these styles, without consideration of their original use and destination.

Finally, as if in utter despair, some have relapsed into an admiration of the old scroll-work – the old French style – of which the French had become ashamed, and which they had rejected, and greedily bought it up. Not content with ransacking every pawnbroker's shop in London and in Paris, for old buhl, old porcelain, old plate, old tapestry, and old frames, they even set every manufacture at work, and corrupted the taste of every modern artist, by the renovation of this wretched style.

No one seems yet to have conceived the smallest wish or idea of only borrowing of every former style of architecture, whatever it might present of useful or ornamental, of scientific or tasteful; of adding thereto whatever other new dispositions or forms might afford conveniences or elegancies not yet possessed; of making the new discoveries, the new conquests, of natural productions unknown to former ages, the models of new imitations more beautiful and more varied; and thus of composing an architecture which, born in our country, grown on our soil, and in harmony with our climate, institutions, and habits, at once elegant, appropriate, and original, should truly deserve the appellation of *"Our Own."*

191 THOMAS LEVERTON DONALDSON
from "Preliminary Discourse before the University College of London" (1842)

T. L. Donaldson was among the third contingent of British architects to visit Italy and Greece between 1818 and 1823, and he became a brilliant draftsman in recording his visions of the classical past. In 1834 he was the motivating force in the creation of the Institute of British Architects (later Royal Institute of British Architects), which was committed to upgrading the profession of architecture. In his architectural practice – if we may judge from his competition design for the Royal Exchange (1839) – Donaldson inclined more toward a Roman vision of classicism. But Donaldson at the same time was quite influential as a teacher. In 1842 he became the first professor of construction and architecture at University College, London, where he taught for 23 years. This brief excerpt from his inaugural lecture of 1842 reveals him to be an eclectic in the spirit of Hope, acknowledging that his age demanded experimentation and an amalgamation of styles.

Styles in Architecture may be compared to languages in literature. There is no style, as there is no language, which has not its peculiar beauties, its individual fitness and power – there is not one that can be safely rejected. A principle reins in each, which the Architect may hap[pi]ly apply with peculiar propriety on some emergency. And as the traveller, who is master of several languages, finds himself at home and at ease among the people with whose language he is familiar, so the Architect is more fitted for the emergencies of his difficult career, who can command the majesty of the classic styles, the sublimity of the Gothic, the grace of the revival or the brilliant fancies of the Arabic. And to pursue the analogy still further, as no scholar can fully master a language, who is not familiar with the literature and manners and religion of the people, so no Architect can fully appreciate any style, who knows not the history of the country, and the habits of thought, the intelligence, and customs of the nation.

Thomas Leverton Donaldson (1795–1885), from "Preliminary Discourse Pronounced before the University College of London, upon the Commencement of a Series of Lectures on Architecture" (1842).

192 JOHN RUSKIN
from *The Seven Lamps of Architecture* (1849)

T
he British architectural debate of the early 1840s began to take on an entirely different character by the end of the decade, as the forces supporting classicism, the Gothic, the Renaissance, eclecticism, and the creation of an entirely new style now clashed in a highly spirited and for the most part quite sophisticated debate. Perhaps the most prominent figure to emerge during this decade was John Ruskin, a writer who would influence architectural theory in Britain and the United States like no author before him. Although he too had no formal architectural training, he was a man of high intellect and moral pretension, a complex, even fragile, personality, whose mind eventually cut itself off from commerce with the real world. While still a student at Oxford in the 1830s, he wrote several articles entitled "The Poetry of Architecture" for J. C. Loudon's *Architectural Magazine*, but he established his reputation as a critic with the first volume of *Modern Painters*, which appeared in 1843. In the same decade he made several trips to the Continent, during which he studied medieval architecture, in particular that of France and Italy. As a result Ruskin came to despise every other style – the classical and the Renaissance in particular – and he shared with Pugin the belief that humanity can only be saved by returning to a medieval culture of piety and humility. He was firm in his rejection of industrialization and an undying foe of the ugliness that he ascribed to modern civilization; politically, he was socialist who later tried, but failed, to establish a rural guild based on communal principles of ownership and labor.

The Seven Lamps of Architecture is a book written by someone who was still little more than an amateur in the field. The seven lamps – sacrifice, truth, power, beauty, life, memory, obedience – are beacons to serve the aspiring architect. They are eternal principles for Ruskin that transcend the everyday world and that provide the designer with a larger mission than of simply providing shelter. Ruskin's definition of architecture as the art that "impresses on its forms certain characters venerable or beautiful, but otherwise unnecessary" is at heart an ornamental conception of architecture, and one that is sensuous in its exaltation of materiality. The three passages chosen here, which by themselves can scarcely circumscribe his larger theory, reveal three aspects of his conception. Truth is for Ruskin inextricable from human virtue, but in architecture it also has specific meaning under three general categories – the last of which will ultimately reject the use of iron in all but exceptional cases. The second passage is taken from the Lamp of Life and exposes his animate conception of architecture. The third passage, from his Lamp of Obedience, reveals his somewhat naive reasoning in commending the "English early decorated" as the "safest choice" of a style for the present.

V. The violations of truth, which dishonour poetry and painting, are thus for the most part confined to the treatment of their subjects. But in architecture another and a less subtle, more contemptible, violation of truth is possible; a direct falsity of assertion respecting the nature of material, or the quantity of labour. And this is, in the full sense of the word, wrong; it is as truly deserving of reprobation as any other moral delinquency; it is unworthy alike of architects and of nations; and it has been a sign, wherever it has widely and with toleration existed, of a singular debasement of the arts; that it is not a sign of worse than this, of a

John Ruskin (1819–1900), from *The Seven Lamps of Architecture*. London: Smith, Elder, and Co., 1849, pp. 31–2, 136–7, 190–2.

general want of severe probity, can be accounted for only by our knowledge of the strange separation which has for some centuries existed between the arts and all other subjects of human intellect, as matters of conscience. This withdrawal of conscientiousness from among the faculties concerned with art, while it has destroyed the arts themselves, has also rendered in a measure nugatory the evidence which otherwise they might have presented respecting the character of the respective nations among whom they have been cultivated; otherwise, it might appear more than strange that a nation so distinguished for its general uprightness and faith as the English, should admit in their architecture more of pretence, concealment, and deceit, than any other of this or of past time.

They are admitted in thoughtlessness, but with fatal effect upon the art in which they are practised. If there were no other causes for the failures which of late have marked every great occasion for architectural exertion, these petty dishonesties would be enough to account for all. It is the first step and not the least, towards greatness to do away with these; the first, because so evidently and easily in our power. We may not be able to command good, or beautiful, or inventive architecture; but we *can* command an honest architecture: the meagreness of poverty may be pardoned, the sternness of utility respected; but what is there but scorn for the meanness of deception?

VI. Architectural Deceits are broadly to be considered under three heads: –

1st. The suggestion of a mode of structure or support, other than the true one; as in pendants of late Gothic roofs.

2nd. The painting of surfaces to represent some other material than that of which they actually consist (as in the marbling of wood), or the deceptive representation of sculptured ornament upon them.

3rd. The use of cast or machine-made ornaments of any kind. [...]

The Lamp of Life

I. Among the countless analogies by which the nature and relations of the human soul are illustrated in the material creation, none are more striking than the impressions inseparably connected with the active and dormant states of matter. I have elsewhere endeavoured to show, that no inconsiderable part of the essential characters of Beauty depended on the expression of vital energy in organic things, or on the subjection to such energy, of things naturally passive and powerless. I need not here repeat, of what was then advanced, more than the statement which I believe will meet with general acceptance, that things in other respects alike, as in their substance, or uses, or outward forms, are noble or ignoble in proportion to the fulness of the life which either they themselves enjoy, or of whose action they bear the evidence, as sea sands are made beautiful by their bearing the seal of the motion of the waters. And this is especially true of all objects which bear upon them the impress of the highest order of creative life, that is to say, of the mind of man: they become noble or ignoble in proportion to the amount of the energy of that mind which has visibly been employed upon them. But most peculiarly and imperatively does the rule hold with respect to the creations of Architecture, which being properly capable of no other life than this, and being not essentially composed of things pleasant in themselves, – as music of sweet sounds, or painting of fair colours, but of inert substance, – depend, for their dignity and pleasurableness in the utmost degree, upon the vivid expression of the intellectual life which has been concerned in their production.

II. Now in all other kind of energies except that of man's mind, there is no question as to what is life, and what is not. Vital sensibility, whether vegetable or animal, may, indeed, be reduced to so great feebleness, as to render its existence a matter of question, but when it is evident at all, it is evident as such: there is no mistaking any imitation or pretence of it for the life itself; no mechanism nor galvanism can take its place; nor is any resemblance of it so striking as to involve even hesitation in the judgment; although many occur which the human imagination takes pleasure in exalting, without for an instant losing sight of the real nature of the dead things it animates; but rejoicing rather in its own excessive life, which puts gesture into clouds, and joy into waves, and voices into rocks.

The Lamp of Obedience

VII. How surely its principles ought at first to be limited, we may easily determine by the consideration of the necessary modes of teaching any other branch of general knowledge. When we begin to teach children writing, we force them to absolute copyism, and require absolute accuracy in the formation of the letters; as they obtain command of the received modes of literal expression, we cannot prevent their falling into such variations as are consistent with their feeling, their circumstances, or their characters. So, when a boy is first taught to write Latin, an authority is required of him for every expression he uses: as he becomes master of the language he may take a license, and feel his right to do so without any authority, and yet write better Latin than when he borrowed every separate expression. In the same way our architects would have to be taught to write the accepted style. We must first determine what buildings are to be considered Augustan in their authority; their modes of construction and laws of proportion are to be studied with the most penetrating care; then the different forms and uses of their decorations are to be classed and catalogued, as a German grammarian classes the powers of prepositions; and under this absolute, irrefragable authority, we are to begin to work; admitting not so much as an alteration in the depth of a cavetto, or the breadth of a fillet. Then, when our sight is once accustomed to the grammatical forms and arrangements, and our thoughts familiar with the expression of them all; when we can speak this dead language naturally, and apply it to whatever ideas we have to render, that it is to say, to every practical purpose of life; then, and not till then, a license might be permitted; and individual authority allowed to change or to add to the received forms, always within certain limits; the decorations, especially, might be made subjects of variable fancy, and enriched with ideas either original or taken from other schools. And thus, in process of time and by a great national movement, it might come to pass that a new style should arise, as language itself changes; we might perhaps come to speak Italian instead of Latin, or to speak modern instead of old English; but this would be a matter of entire indifference, and a matter, besides, which no determination or desire could either hasten or prevent. That alone which it is in our power to obtain, and which it is our duty to desire, is an unanimous style of some kind, and such comprehension and practice of it as would enable us to adapt its features to the peculiar character of every several building, large or small, domestic, civil, or ecclesiastical. I have said that it was immaterial what style was adopted, so far as regards the room for originality which its development would admit: it is not so, however, when we take into consideration the far more important questions of the facility of adaptation to general purposes, and of the sympathy with which this or that style would be popularly regarded. The choice of Classical or Gothic, again using the latter term in its broadest sense, may be questionable when it regards some single and consider-able public building; but I cannot conceive it questionable, for an instant, when it regards modern uses in general: I cannot conceive any architect insane enough to project the vulgarization of Greek architecture. Neither can it be rationally questionable whether we should adopt early or late, original or derivative Gothic; if the latter were chosen, it must be either some impotent and ugly degradation, like our own Tudor, or else a style whose grammatical laws it would be nearly impossible to limit or arrange, like the French Flamboyant. We are equally precluded from adopting styles essentially infantine or barbar-ous, however Herculean their infancy, or majestic their outlawry, such as our own Norman, or the Lombard Romanesque. The choice would lie I think between four styles: – 1. The Pisan Romanesque; 2. The early Gothic of the Western Italian Republics, advanced as far and as fast as our art would enable us to the Gothic of Giotto; 3. The Venetian Gothic in its purest developement; 4. The English earliest decorated. The most natural, perhaps the safest choice, would be of the last, well fenced from chance of again stiffening into the perpen-dicular; and perhaps enriched by some mingling of decorative elements from the exquisite decorated Gothic of France, of which, in such cases, it would be needful to accept some well known examples, as the North door of Rouen and the church of St. Urbain at Troyes, for final and limiting authorities on the side of decoration.

193   JAMES FERGUSSON
A. W. N. Pugin, Edward Lacy Garbett, and Robert Kerr, from *The Builder* (1850)

Only a few months after Ruskin threw his hat into the ring on the matter of style, a lively controversy erupted over the issue in the pages of Britain's weekly architectural journal, *The Builder*. This latter had been founded in 1842 by George Godwin (1815–88), an architect with keen social interests who seemed to enjoy fanning debate on a variety of issues. Here it is both the eloquence of the various writers and the intensity of the debate that make these articles so lively and rewarding. The prompt to the debate was a complaint that Pugin had sent to another journal, *The Rambler* – that the lack of money for church building was forcing builders to skimp on materials and thus compromise the truth of design. Pugin, of course, was Britain's leading crusader for the Gothic

James Fergusson (1808–86), A. W. N. Pugin, Edward Lacy Garbett (d. 1898), and Robert Kerr (1823–1904), from the debate in *The Builder* (1850), pp. 122, 134–5, 209, 219, 541–3.

Revival, and he demanded authenticity in all matters of detailing and design. James Fergusson countered in *The Builder* on March 16 with an article entitled "Effect of the Want of Reality on the Works of Modern Architects." The historian Fergusson had just appeared on the scene with his book *An Historical Inquiry into the True Principles of Beauty in Art* (1849). In it, he took aim at the "monkey styles of modern Europe," that is, the period of "copyism" that began in the sixteenth century with the various revivals and that continued down to the present day. Fergusson countered with his "common-sense" style, which he had yet to define fully. Pugin defended his position on March 23 with an article "How Shall We Build our Churches?" The Gothic designer G. G. Scott supported Pugin's stance a few issues later. Fergusson continued the widening debate on May 4 with his article "The Question of Copyism." The following week, May 11, a new and forceful protagonist entered the fray, Edward Lacy Garbett. He had just published his book *Rudimentary Treatise on the Principles of Design in Architecture* (1850), in which he would propose a very original position regarding the creation of a new style (see chapter 194 below). In his article for *The Builder* he advances the argument that the Gothic Revival had failed because architects were imitating the forms and not the structural principles of the style.

The debate continued over the summer and simmered down, but its main points were recapitulated in a lecture given in November at the *Architectural Association* by Robert Kerr – also published in *The Builder* on November 16. It was entitled "Copyism in Architecture" and it stands as one of the most astute writings of this period. Kerr was born in Scotland and trained for a few years in New York City, before he returned to London to found the Architectural Association in 1847. He was a vocal critic of the profession, of antiquarianism, and of those who view architecture as a "style." This lecture also refines his position first voiced in *The Newleafe Discoures on the Fine Art Architecture* (1846), a series of papers that earlier had been published in *The Builder*.

Effect of the Want of Reality on the Works of Modern Architects

Before descending to particulars I must first try and state the question generally. Anterior to the Reformation in the sixteenth century, architecture in Europe, and in all other countries down to the present day, was a progressive art, in which copying and retrocession were unknown, and decorated construction the elemental formula.

Subsequent to the Reformation a new element was introduced in Europe – that of copying antecedent and dead styles; progress was unknown, retrocession the fashion, and construction generally concealed. Prior to the Reformation, all buildings in Europe – and down to this day in all other countries – are satisfactory, more or less beautiful, and worthy of study. Subsequently to that period none are quite satisfactory in Europe, and all contain falsehoods and deformities, of which we become ashamed as soon as the fluctuating fashion that produced them has passed away.

Lastly, no buildings in the first period show the defects of which Mr. Pugin complains; and neither in the lives of the architects, nor in their works, do we find any evidence of that struggle between the architect and his employer, which he so pathetically deplores. Few buildings since the Reformation do not bear marks of the struggle on their face, and every architect has repeated his complaint. [. . .]

The above is as true if applied to Grecian as to Gothic architecture. If an architect gets a commission for a Grecian Doric church, his first idea is a Parthenon: glorious dream! The side colonnades, however, soon vanish; but he may venture to propose a portico in rear as well as in front; but even that is not tolerated: perhaps two or four three-quarter columns?

No. Then the inner range of the front portico? No: that too must disappear; so must also the more extensive adjuncts and ornaments; and he is left with a skeleton, of which both he and the public are ashamed. The truth is, the architect wants as many columns as he can get; the public as few as possible, because they are useless, expensive, and inconvenient. Every argument of common sense is against them – *"hinc illæ lachrymæ"* – the struggle between archæology and common sense commences. In nine cases out of ten the former is beaten.

It is not, however, that the public are more niggardly than they were. They never, so far as I can observe, object to pay for what they want, when they are satisfied they are getting full value for their money: but they do object to pay for what they do not want, and will not spend their money in what is not only useless but inconvenient.

Mr. Pugin seems to think that when the public are better informed in matters of art, this state of things will end. The conclusion I have arrived at is diametrically opposed to this; my belief being that as soon as the public are informed as to the processes by which these ancient buildings were erected, they will insist on architects repeating them, if only for an experiment, to try if what is true in everything else may not be true in architecture, that like causes produce like effects. Up to this time no information on the subject has been published, but once the public are as familiar with the modes in which Gothic buildings were produced as they are with the forms, I am very much mistaken if they do not adopt the spirit, and reject the form; and the moment they do, there is an end of all Gothic or pagan reproduction. Architecture will resume her progressive and creative course, and servile copying and retrocession become impossible.

J. F.

How Shall We Build our Churches?

I beg to offer a few remarks on a letter which appeared in your last number relative to a recent pamphlet of mine. I may premise that I am totally unacquainted with the writer, and therefore my observations must not be considered in the slightest degree personal, as I merely judge of his principles from his argument. I must say it was with no little surprise that I found myself attacked as the advocate of an artificial system of architecture, when not only by my writings but in my works I have always endeavoured to set forth that most important principle of *reality, both in design, material, and construction*, and of scrupulously avoiding all shams, or dressing-up of buildings with unreal features. But on a further perusal of the article, I felt satisfied that the writer belonged to a class of persons who are not in a position to comprehend the basis of my arguments, or the principles on which I, in common with so many persons usually termed ecclesiologists, advocate the restoration of ancient ecclesiastical architecture. It is evident that the writer's idea of a place of worship is nothing more than a preaching-room. What he calls a *common-sense church* is, in reality, no church at all, but a most decided *conventicle*. He would abolish pillars, as hindering a view of the preacher; he advocates galleries, as affording cheap accommodation to a large auditory; he objects to a deep chancel, as *diminishing* the *voice* of the clergyman (he evidently imagines a chancel is a preaching place); with him it is all *vox*, and, I may add, *præterea nihil*. I am willing to admit that his common-sense church is perfectly adapted for persons of his class, who are unable to enter either into the solemnities of religious worship, or the symbolism of ecclesiastical architecture; his great galleried room, with its flat roof and open space, is a very natural expression of a huge dissenting preaching-house; moreover, it possesses the advantage of being what is technically termed a convertible building; should the orator fail in collecting a sufficient auditory to pay the proprietors, by removing the pews and erecting an orchestra, it would make an excellent casino, with reserved seats in the galleries; or if that might be considered objectionable on moral grounds, or the neighbourhood too retired, by flooring it over in stages a most eligible set of coachmaker's premises are produced at a comparatively small additional outlay. [. . .]

I hate the modern boastful spirit which would exalt the mechanical superiority of our age at the expense of all that is admirable in the past. For my own part I never return from the examination of one of these glorious old churches, without feelings of the deepest humility: when I consider the amount of thought, practice, and labour it requires to reproduce one out of the multitude of their magnificent details. I can duly appreciate the talent that originally formed them; and if with all our increased facilities we find it so difficult to restore, what veneration ought we not to feel for the *creators* of this divine style! When, therefore, I find a man who, having attained some mechanical skill and experience in the tension of timber, attempts to laugh down as clumsy contrivances the great roof at Westminster or the stupendous vaults of Cologne, I cannot refrain from exposing the fallacy of his positions. I have no doubt that he is a very good and useful man in his way, and if I had to construct a viaduct over a canal at the least elevation, I should gladly avail myself of his trussing experience; but do not let him interfere with the masons of the church. We pointed men have pointed tools, and can contrive occasionally to cut other things besides crockets.

A. Welby Pugin.

The Question of Copyism

But to come to the point: if we abandon Greek and Gothic copying, what is to be substituted? The three following rules may perhaps make this clearer: – 1st. *Design* a building wholly and solely for the purposes for which it is to be used, without the least reference to any bygone age or style; 2nd. *Construct* it with reference to the best material available; using each material – whether it be brick, stone, marble, or wood, or metal – according to its own properties, and these only, never allowing one to take the form or interfere with the province of the other; and, lastly, *Ornament* the building so designed and constructed in whatever manner you can conceive as most appropriate and most elegant, never concealing or even disguising construction or material, – only dressing them, to use a familiar phrase, – and likewise without any reference to any style, or ever looking back, but always forward, – trying to surpass whatever has been done before.

A strict adherence to these three rules, which sound almost like truisms, when so stated, has enabled every nation, in every age, except the present, to elaborate a beautiful and appropriate style of their own. It remains for some one to show why it should not do so in modern Europe.

J. F.

A Principle or a Principal, – Which?

It is with much regret I learn from your paper last week, the retirement of "J. F." from a conflict which I have watched with great interest, and in which, were my humble services likely to be of any use, I should give in my cordial adherence to "J. F." in all essential points, except one in his last letter, which was very possibly a slip of the pen. When, in his first rule, he says we are to plan a building with reference solely to its actual purposes, and to no past style, I perfectly agree with him; but when, in rule 3, relating to ornament, he repeats the same clause, I must humbly differ. For the word *no*, I take the liberty of reading *every*, – with reference to *every* style known to the designer, and to *every* accessible source of artistic precedent, copying nothing, but digesting and assimilating everything containing nutriment, be it from old Egypt or young America, – from polished Greece or the savage isles of the south; but swallowing nothing unchewed, adopting nothing without a distinctly understood reason, and insisting that neither antiquity nor novelty are any reasons at all.

As the grand question, however, of mimicry or reality is for the present stopped in your columns, my object now is to ask whether you will admit the discussion of another, which, though it may seem trivial compared with the above, has yet no small bearing on the architecture of the day, even if not involving (as I think it does) the fate of a principle very generally followed in ancient and mediæval practice, and held up by all modern theorists (though with small effect on our practice), viz., the principle of constructive and decorative truth or consistency, – the second (if I remember right) of Mr. Ruskin's lamps, and which should have been the first. The fact is this, – having very early in my studies encountered this principle, and become strongly biassed in its favour, I soon found that it applied to all the admired productions of the past, with one notable exception, the Gothicized timber roof, of which Westminster Hall is the great generic type. To my admission of this principle they offered a stumbling block, nor have all my efforts sufficed to reconcile them. Years ago I was forced to conclude, that if this be really a principle, the admiration bestowed on these roofs must have been all along misplaced; and that if they be right, this supposed principle is moonshine, and architecture is (reversing Mr. Pugin's definition) *constructed decoration*, and nothing more.

E. L. G.

Copyism in Architecture

I am always proud to answer your call for a contribution to your miscellany of architectural discussion, but in the present instance you give me too short notice for any attempt more formidable than a general gossip on some subject which comes prominently to hand.

And the first subject which occurs to me is our old theme of Copyism, as lately discussed by Messrs. Pugin, Scott, and Fergusson in the columns of THE BUILDER. It was only a little time ago that I first heard of this famous tournament; for, however strange the confession may appear, I had positively not seen my old friend THE BUILDER for months, till one afternoon lately I got hold of the file for a year, and plunged over head and ears into it for the rest of the day. I could not but feel surprised at the altered tone of the defenders of

Copyism in this case – indeed, the entirely altered ground which is assumed. The question is one of Gothic architecture alone, in the first place. For the once universal "authority" of the classic standards there seems to be no one to advance a word! There was an opening, as I think, for the Orders, every one of them, to edge themselves into the dispute, but not an order was ever mentioned – the fight was altogether for revived Mediævalism. Secondly, the argument showed an abandonment of even the ordinary ground of the authority of the pure "examples" – the excellence of authenticity: the plea is an entirely new one, and is, moreover, accompanied with so clear and straightforward a statement of principles, premises, and conclusions, that nothing could be more fair or satisfactory. Mr. Pugin evinces a slight acidity, certainly, but otherwise speaks plainly out; and Mr. Fergusson and Mr. Scott (particularly the latter) expound their views with admirable manliness. [. . .]

But further than this, I would now assert, first, that a natural style of architecture is such as can accomplish the wants of the circumstances in the way of building in the most suitable and economical manner with the full advantage of all the materials and other appliances at command; secondly, that a natural style for us now-a-days must of necessity be much varied for the variety of subjects; thirdly, that, taking many circumstances into account, the present age is one which is eminently calculated for the development of natural style, and the overthrow of whatever is upheld by nothing better than tradition and association.

In walking along the new streets of any town, where houses are built without the expense of any vestige of "the styles of architecture," do you see no *style* appearing? Are they not all similar? This is one part of the natural style in its elements, at the least, its principles, based on pure construction. The glass palace is another instance. The "conventicles" of the very poor Dissenters, where they cannot afford conventional decoration, are another instance. And between classical Italy and mediæval England I certainly think that the sympathies of our age, as thus evidenced in their elements, cannot be denied to be assuredly more in unison with those of the former than those of the latter: this, generally speaking, of course, and so far as an indication may be had of the tendency of the age.

My advice, if you would have me speak with candour, to all young students, certainly is this: study classical antiquities for their excellence; mediæval antiquities (in proper selection) for their excellence too; and the principles evinced in common English 19th century housebuilding, for the development of their tendency in natural style. To begin where we left off is to my mind absurd, for not only do I deny the one of Mr. Scott's premises to which I have directed attention, but I am equally unable to admit the Gothic style to be the offspring either of our race – although of Englishmen – or *our* religion in any way at all. I have long viewed Gothic architecture as having really no firmer hold on the present mind than mere fashion – the same fashion which produced St. Paul's from the mind of Wren, and St. Pancras from that of our own Inwood. Many are the beauties of the works of the middle ages, but let beauty be the test, and not mere authenticity, for very many are their deformities likewise. Their beauties are a valuable study, but assuredly not more so than those of the classical times and the pure revival: if the clergy *will* have Gothic, give them what they wish, for they have a right to choose; but I for one cannot help seeing that the Gothic churches, one and all, and the Houses of Parliament, with all their grandeur, both sink equally into dispute with the common-sense practical judgment of plain men, beside the comfortable "preaching-house" of Mr. Pugin's wrath, and the comfortable walls and ceiling, windows and doors, of an ordinary dwelling-house. And herein is evinced the tendency of the *natural* style of our period; and whether to study that fact, or "begin where we left off," I must leave you to determine for yourselves.

R. K.

194   EDWARD LACY GARBETT

from *Rudimentary Treatise on the Principles of Design in Architecture* (1850)

O f Garbett we know very little, other than that he obviously had some architectural training, perhaps through a father or relative, and that in later life he focused on non-architectural matters. His book of 1850, however, is a work of startling originality. The first part of the book owes something to the themes of Ruskin's *The Seven Lamps* and Garbett did not shy away from attacking Ruskin for the "error of mistaking ornament for beauty" and for advocating the use of a style from the past. In the latter part of his study, Garbett proceeds more methodically with a structural argument that perhaps owes something to the German debate of the mid-1840s. Accepting the reasoning that both the classical and Gothic styles were "pure systems" founded on the structural principles of trabeated and arcuated design — Garbett now proposes a third structural alternative, the "tensile" system, that will lead to a new style. This system for Garbett is best represented in the structural possibilities of the iron truss. The question of whether Garbett knew of Bötticher's address of four years earlier is one for which we shall probably never know the answer, but his argument is identical. That this point should be made on the eve of the Great London Exhibition of 1851 only underscores its relevance.

But the two pure systems, perhaps it will be said, are things too good ever to be entirely given up. If so, far more are they too good to be abused and caricatured. If they are worth copying at all, they are worth copying completely; and this can never be done but by copying their *construction* as well as their decoration. If modern habits or means will not permit this, they will not permit the old style. Count the cost, therefore. If you want to imitate the archless style, your building must be archless, or a huge lie. If you imitate the beamless style, it must be beamless; and every unvaulted building, ancient or modern, that apes this style, is a motiveless and unmeaning sham.

Not less preposterous than the attempt to revive *dead styles*, is the requirement to invent, for ordinary buildings, a *new* one. As long as we have no new style in construction, we *can* have none in architecture; but if we call the mixed construction a new kind, we *have* a new style adapted to it, – a modern, a living style; the growth of modern circumstances and of the existing modes of construction: – *new*, moreover, inasmuch as we are only on the threshold of its possible combinations and varieties, far more inexhaustible than those of either of the pure systems. In this country particularly, the beauties of the modern archi-

Edward Lacy Garbett, from *Rudimentary Treatise on the Principles of Design in Architecture, as Deducible from Nature and Exemplified in the Works of the Greek and Gothic Architects.* London: J. Weale, 1850, pp. 260–4.

tecture are hardly known, nor can it be said to have ever had a fair trial, or indeed any trial in more than one or two classes of buildings.[1] It would be ridiculous self-conceit in an architect, to pretend wilfully to go back and try to solve anew that which has been already solved, and only by the succession of a long line of great artists. He can never hope to overtake them with such a start in their favour; while by commencing from the point they reached, the poorest talents may advance beyond them.

But while no inventive architect would *wish* for a new style, convinced that there is far more scope for variety and new combination in one already enriched with the accumulated genius of three centuries; it is certain that, in another point of view, a new style is indispensable. There *is* a class of buildings tending towards a new style of construction, – becoming less mixed in this respect, – and approaching a consistent use of *tensile* covering to the exclusion of every other. To this third system of constructive unity, there is NO old style adapted. None was invented for it. It is a new thing, and its treatment must be NEW, – new, because subject to old principles; and to be effected only by a patient search into those old principles. Let us not mistake what we have to do. It is that which has been done only twice before; in the time of Dorus, and in the thirteenth century. [. . .]

There is, among other art-destroying fallacies, a notion now prevalent, that architectural styles spring up of themselves, and that if we wait long enough, in process of time a new one may grow up, we know not how. A new railway is more likely to grow up. Decorative *manners, fashions*, are not to be confounded with a new style, still less with a new system, such as THE TWO, the only two, that possess constructive and decorative unity. Yet even a new fashion does not come unsought, – without search after *novelty*. Far less can an architectural system arise but by an earnest and rightly directed search after TRUTH. For five thousand years have all the nations beyond the radius of Greek influence sought a true system of beam architecture, and *never* found it. For fifteen centuries did Europeans use the arch, and seek a system of arch architecture, before they found it. For a much longer time have Arabs, Turks, Chinese, sought the same, and *never* attained it. For twenty centuries did the Italians practise mixed construction, and seek a system thereof, before they attained it. Let us not deceive ourselves: a style never grew of itself; it never will. It *must* be sought, and sought the right way. We may blunder on in a wrong path for ever, and get no nearer the goal.

A new style requires the generalized imitation of nature and of *many* previous styles; and a new system requires, in addition to this (as Professor Whewell has remarked), the binding of all together by a new *principle of unity*, clearly understood, agreed upon, and kept constantly in view. Constructive statics affords three such principles, – the DEPRESSILE, the COMPRESSILE, and the TENSILE methods, – the *beam* – the *arch* – the *truss*; of which the two former have been made the bases of past systems: the third is ours, to be used in the same manner.

Such I believe to be the problem Truth propounds to the architects of the present time; but its solution will be found utterly hopeless, as long as we indulge any hankering after *novelty for its own sake*; any mean disposition to follow instead of correcting *popular taste*; and above all, let none dare attempt it till we have engraved on our compasses a hacknied sentence, but one which I suspect to contain nearly the whole theory of art, – SEEK NOT TO SEEM WHAT YOU WOULD BE, BUT TO BE WHAT YOU WOULD SEEM.

1.   What are called classic churches, for instance, are, for the most part, mere anti-art, no more Classic than they are Chinese. Wren had no opportunity of erecting a handsome parish church. His pupils fell either into littleness or Borominian corruption; and since their time, there have only been hole-in-the-wall preaching rooms, – sham temples, – and now pseudo-Gothicesque barns, copies of copies by mediæval village masons. England does not possess a modern church in the modern style.

195   JOHN RUSKIN
from "The Nature of Gothic" (1851–3)

The Stones of Venice – whatever one's view of Ruskin's ideas – is without question one of the few great books in all of architectural literature. After completing the *Seven Lamps* in 1849, Ruskin traveled to Venice, a city that had just experienced a 16-month siege by Austrian forces. Martial law was in effect, cholera and starvation were prevalent. Ruskin arrived oblivious to the dangers and on a mission to record every detail of every Byzantine and Gothic building of the threatened city. Here he would pass from being an architectural amateur to becoming an authority on Venetian architecture.

The book consists of several relatively independent essays, the most important of which is his literary masterpiece "The Nature of Gothic." Its arguments derive from his earlier book, but Ruskin now vividly spotlights the gist of his reasoning. Gothic architecture for him is not an arbitrary stylistic choice but rather an ethical way of life: a humble recognition of human imperfection and of human striving for salvation. Other styles, such as the classical, enslave human nature by demanding strict geometric ("servile") perfection in their ornamental details. The Gothic style acknowledges human limitations and respects them by allowing free inventions in design and execution; it demands not formal perfection but only the evidence of the workers' happiness. Hence Gothic architecture is more moral than any other style; it espouses such "picturesque" attributes as savageness, changefulness, naturalism, grotesqueness. Once again Ruskin's conception of architecture is essentially ornamental.

In the 13th and 14th paragraphs of Chapter XXI. of the first volume of this work, it was noticed that the systems of architectural ornament, properly so called, might be divided into three: – 1. Servile ornament, in which the execution or power of the inferior workman is entirely subjected to the intellect of the higher: – 2. Constitutional ornament, in which the executive inferior power is, to a certain point, emancipated and independent, having a will of its own, yet confessing its inferiority and rendering obedience to higher powers;–and 3. Revolutionary ornament, in which no executive inferiority is admitted at all. I must here explain the nature of these divisions at somewhat greater length.

John Ruskin, from "The Nature of Gothic," in *The Stones of Venice*, Vol. 2 (1851–3). The text is taken from an undated nineteenth-century American edition of the book, published in New York by John W. Lovell, pp. 159–62.

Of Servile ornament, the principal schools are the Greek, Ninevite, and Egyptian; but their servility is of different kinds. The Greek master-workman was far advanced in knowledge and power above the Assyrian or Egyptian. Neither he nor those for whom he worked could endure the appearance of imperfection in anything; and, therefore, what ornament he appointed to be done by those beneath him was composed of mere geometrical forms, – balls, ridges, and perfectly symmetrical foliage, – which could be executed with absolute precision by line and rule, and were as perfect in their way when completed, as his own figure sculpture. The Assyrian and Egyptian, on the contrary, less cognizant of accurate form in anything, were content to allow their figure sculpture to be executed by inferior workmen, but lowered the method of its treatment to a standard which every workman could reach, and then trained him by discipline so rigid, that there was no chance of his falling beneath the standard appointed. The Greek gave to the lower workman no subject which he could not perfectly execute. The Assyrian gave him subjects which he could only execute imperfectly, but fixed a legal standard for his imperfection. The workman was, in both systems, a slave.[1]

§ x. But in the mediæval, or especially Christian, system of ornament, this slavery is done away with altogether; Christianity having recognized, in small things as well as great, the individual value of every soul. But it not only recognizes its value; it confesses its imperfection, in only bestowing dignity upon the acknowledgment of unworthiness. That admission of lost power and fallen nature, which the Greek or Ninevite felt to be intensely painful, and, as far as might be, altogether refused, the Christian makes daily and hourly, contemplating the fact of it without fear, as tending, in the end, to God's greater glory. Therefore, to every spirit which Christianity summons to her service, her exhortation is: Do what you can, and confess frankly what you are unable to do; neither let your effort be shortened for fear of failure, nor your confession silenced for fear of shame. And it is, perhaps, the principal admirableness of the Gothic schools of architecture, that they thus receive the results of the labor of inferior minds; and out of fragments full of imperfection, and betraying that imperfection in every touch, indulgently raise up a stately and unaccusable whole.

§ xi. But the modern English mind has this much in common with that of the Greek, that it intensely desires, in all things, the utmost completion or perfection compatible with their nature. This is a noble character in the abstract, but becomes ignoble when it causes us to forget the relative dignities of the nature itself, and to prefer the perfectness of the lower nature to the imperfection of the higher; not considering that as, judged by such a rule, all the brute animals would be preferable to man, because more perfect in their functions and kind, and yet are always held inferior to him, so also in the works of man, those which are more perfect in their kind are always inferior to those which are, in their nature, liable to more faults and shortcomings. For the finer the nature, the more flaws it will show through the clearness of it; and it is a law of this universe, that the best things shall be seldomest seen in their best form. The wild grass grows well and strongly, one year with another; but the wheat is, according to the greater nobleness of its nature, liable to the bitterer blight. And therefore, while in all things that we see, or do, we are to desire perfection, and strive for it, we are nevertheless not to set the meaner thing, in its narrow accomplishment, above the nobler thing, in its mighty progress; not to esteem smooth minuteness above shattered majesty; not to prefer mean victory to honorable defeat; not to lower the level of our aim, that we may the more surely enjoy the complacency of success. But, above all, in our dealings with the souls of other men, we are to take care how we check, by severe requirement or narrow caution, efforts which might otherwise lead to a noble issue; and, still more, how we withhold our admiration from great excellences, because they are mingled with rough faults. Now, in the make and nature of every man, however rude or simple, whom we employ in manual labor, there are some powers for better things: some tardy imagination, torpid capacity of emotion, tottering steps of thought, there are, even at the worst; and in most cases it is all our own fault that they *are* tardy or torpid. But they cannot be strengthened, unless we are content to take them in their feebleness, and unless we prize and honor them in their imperfection above the best and most perfect manual skill. And this is what we have to do with all our laborers; to look for the *thoughtful* part of them, and get that out of them, whatever we lose for it, whatever faults and errors we are obliged to take with it. For the best that is in them cannot manifest itself, but in company with much error. Understand this clearly: You can teach a man to draw a straight line, and to cut one; to strike a curved line, and to carve it; and to copy and carve any number of given lines or forms, with admirable speed and perfect precision; and you find his work perfect of its kind: but if you ask him to think about any of those forms, to consider if he cannot find any better in his own head, he stops; his execution becomes hesitating; he thinks, and ten to one he thinks wrong; ten to one he makes a mistake in the first touch he gives to his work as a thinking being. But you have made a man of him for all that. He was only a machine before, an animated tool.

§ XII. And observe, you are put to stern choice in this matter. You must either make a tool of the creature, or a man of him. You cannot make both. Men were not intended to work with the accuracy of tools, to be precise and perfect in all their actions. If you will have that precision out of them, and make their fingers measure degrees like cog-wheels, and their arms strike curves like compasses, you must unhumanize them.

NOTE

1   The third kind of ornament, the Renaissance, is that in which the inferior detail becomes principal, the executor of every minor portion being required to exhibit skill and possess knowledge as great as that which is possessed by the master of the design; and in the endeavor to endow him with this skill and knowledge, his own original power is overwhelmed, and the whole building becomes a wearisome exhibition of well-educated imbecility. We must fully inquire into the nature of this form of error, when we arrive at the examination of the Renaissance schools.

196 MATTHEW DIGBY WYATT
from *The Industrial Arts of the Nineteenth Century* (1851)

A s the style debate was unfolding along the professional front, another major venue for spirited discussion was prompted by the Great London Exhibition of 1851. The event was the brainchild of Henry Cole, who in the 1840s had authored a series of children's books called the Summerly Home Treasury series. The books were notable in that Cole commissioned a number of respected artists — among them Richard Redgrave — to do the illustrations. Out of this venture, Cole created Summerly Art Manufactures, an alliance of artists whose talents and designs Cole attempted to sell to manufacturing firms. On their joint behalf, Cole put together annual exhibitions that were intended to display the fruits of British industrial art; the increasing success of these exhibitions between 1846 and 1849 led to the decision by Prince Albert to host an international exhibition in 1851. Cole by this date was working closely with three other talented people — Matthew Digby Wyatt, Richard Redgrave, and Owen Jones — who collectively controlled the decisions regarding the Great Exhibition. Cole was the superintendent in charge of the affair, while the architect Wyatt was secretary to the Executive Committee and supervised the construction of Joseph Paxton's building. Redgrave was in charge of laying out the goods on display and he chaired the head jury on design, while Jones wrote extensively on the event and devised the decorative paint scheme for the iron structure. All also worked with Cole in 1849 in starting the *Journal of Design and Manufactures* — a strident voice in demanding reform in the industrial arts and education.

Wyatt was descended from a long line of distinguished architects, going back to the neoclassicist James Wyatt — whom Hope had dethroned. On his grand tour in the mid-1840s he focused on mosaics in Germany, France, Italy, and Sicily, and in 1848 he produced a respectable folio study on the topic. He was a regular contributor to the *Journal of Design* and it was probably he who, in an anonymous review of Ruskin's *Seven Lamps* in 1849, roundly condemned Ruskin's backward leanings and "lopsided view of railway architecture" — leading Ruskin forever to hold Cole personally in contempt. Wyatt and Ruskin also differed in one other important respect: the former warmly embraced industrial progress and advancing technology. In the Preface to his illustrated survey of the Great Exhibition, Wyatt characterized the pace of industrial change as "double speed" and the Great Exhibition itself as a beacon to the industrial age, just as the Olympic Games had been to Greece. This excerpt stresses the influence of industrialization on art.

The almost incessant wars which so long devastated Europe, and which only terminated in 1815, impeded the culture of those arts which have been emphatically designated the "Arts of Peace." Those wars, however, had no sooner terminated than an extraordinary activity was manifested, more especially in this country; and on looking back over the last six-and-thirty years, elements of change must be found to have been introduced, calculated to derange the whole previous system of fabrication and demand. The extension of the application of steam, gas, &c. to the thousand purposes upon which they are now brought to bear, have scarcely less affected National Industry by changing the conditions of supply, than has the spread of popular education by entirely altering the nature and peculiarities of demand. The

Matthew Digby Wyatt (1820–77), from *The Industrial Arts of the Nineteenth Century: A Series of Illustrations*. London: Day and Son, 1851, pp. vii–viii.

most remarkable feature of the movement to which we are alluding – that, namely, which has taken place in this country during the last six-and-thirty years – is the universality of development attained by combining the division of labour in manufacture with the aggregation of its results in commerce. Sympathising, on the one hand, with the highest excellence both of art and manufacture, modern English production has, on the other, effected a concurrent and unprecedented reduction in price. An amount of thought and ingenuity equal to the origination of many of the monster engineering works which form the pride, the boast, and the glory of the present day, has been bestowed upon an attempt to reduce the cost of a common cotton print the fraction of a farthing per yard. Other nations have not been idle while England has worked, and it is, therefore, little wonderful that, under the action of a progress worthy to have enlisted the pens of men such as Babbage, Brougham, Macculloch, Porter, &c. to record, the great festival, in which that progress finds its tangible embodiment, should speak eloquently, chronicling the race which has been run by all nations for pre-eminence in a glorious, though peaceful, competition.

Were it but possible now to procure some pictures vivid enough to recall a series of the principal elements and objects which adorned those triumphs of industry of past ages to which allusion has been made, how interesting and improving would the examination of such collections be: as it is, years of study must now be given to realise in any degree the tangibilities of history, of which, unfortunately, too few indications have survived to our day. That it is incumbent on every age to leave to its successor the best possible data as to the fruits of its labours and experiences, few will feel disposed to deny; nor will they, probably, be less likely to admit, that if ever an occasion existed, worthy of the best record the art of the nineteenth century could create, that occasion most assuredly is to be met with in the Great Exhibition of Works of Industry of 1851.

In the choice of the subjects for illustration the Author will not, it is hoped, expose himself to the charge of having made in any way an invidious selection, or be supposed to pledge himself to an expression of opinion on relative merits. His aim has been to engrave such specimens as he believed would be likely to be practically useful in naturalising among us improvements in purity of form or colour; in placing in juxtaposition the excellencies of various nations; in furnishing models for manufacturers to study and surpass; and by means of which the Public may be enabled hereafter to test the future progress of Industrial Art in this and other countries.

197 RICHARD REDGRAVE
from "Supplementary Report on Design" (1852)

Richard Redgrave was not an architect, but a painter and royal academician, who for several years had been allied with Cole in the matter of reforming industrial-art education. His particular expertise was design, however, and in his official capacity as head juror for the Great Exhibition he distributed prizes and published the formal exhibition report, which was quite critical of many of the artistic wares displayed. Influential in Redgrave's thinking were the design principles of Pugin, who was not at all inimical to the efforts of the Cole Circle. But, as with Ruskin, there was also a crucial difference in their thinking. Pugin was a gothicist, while those within the Cole circle firmly rejected the use of any past style in the present, the Gothic style in particular.

We have spoken of design and of ornamental decoration. These are two essentially different things, and it is highly necessary that they should, from the first, be considered as separate and distinct. "Design" has reference to the construction of any work both for use and beauty, and therefore includes its ornamentation also. "Ornament" is merely the decoration of a thing constructed.

Ornament is thus necessarily limited, for, so defined, it cannot be other than secondary, and must not usurp a principal place; if it do so, the object is no longer a work ornamented, but is degraded into a mere *ornament*. Now the great tendency of the present time is to reverse this rule; indeed it is impossible to examine the works of the Great Exhibition, without seeing how often utility and construction are made secondary to decoration. In fact, when commencing a design, designers are too apt to think of ornament before construction, and, as has been said in connexion with the nobler art of architecture, rather to construct ornament than to ornament construction. This, on the slightest examination, will be found to be the leading error in the Exhibition, an error more or less apparent in every department of manufacture connected with ornament, which is apt to sicken us of decoration, and leads us to admire those objects of absolute utility (the machines and utensils of various kinds), where use is so paramount that ornament is repudiated, and, fitness of purpose being the end sought, a noble simplicity is the result.

The primary consideration of construction is so necessary to pure design, that it almost follows that, whenever style and ornament are debased, construction will be found to have been first disregarded; and that those styles which are considered the purest, and the best periods of those styles, are just those wherein constructive utility has been rightly understood and most thoroughly attended to. A dissertation upon difference of styles would be out of place in this Report, as well as an expressed preference for any particular one, since each, doubtless, contains some qualities of beauty or excellence which will justify its use when restrained and regulated by fixed principles. It may not, however, be improper to illustrate by a few remarks the opinion expressed above, since it involves important

Richard Redgrave (1804–88), from "Supplementary Report on Design" in *Reports by the Juries*. London: William Clowes & Sons, 1852, pp. 708, 712–13.

principles connected with a proper consideration of works coming within the scope of the Report.

★ ★ ★

The objects in the Great Exhibition which range under the two first heads of this section belong to almost every known style of ornament, and are so various in their character and uses that it is hardly possible so to arrange them as to bring them under general criticism, or to define any principles which would be universally applicable to their design. They consist, 1st, Of decorative treatments exhibited as efforts of skill. 2ndly, Of restorations of parts of buildings, and of ornamental constructive parts. And, 3rdly, Of works intended to form integral parts of a building, but which are *manufactured* so as to be adventitiously applied. Properly speaking, the design for the decoration of any building, both externally and internally, is the province of its architect, since in this case decoration is essentially a part of architecture. If the principle insisted upon in the prefatory remarks to this Report, that ornament is the decoration of construction, be just, it will be apparent that it is hardly possible to judge of the one without the other. In works wherein the decorator makes his own sham construction in order to ornament it, as well as in those multiplied manufactured "parts" which form the staple *ornament* of a large class of *workmen* in this line, we may admire the skill of the execution the cleverness of the details, the excellence of the manufacture, or the imitation of early works of acknowledged merit; but to appreciate "decoration" we must view it as a whole in the place for which it was specially designed, and in harmony with the building whose construction it ornaments. Moreover, it must mainly originate in local circumstances, and ought to have an individual significance. Here, however, the moment we enter upon the varied inspection we become sensible how impracticable it is to lay down any general canon for works which differ almost as widely as the beginning and end of time. In other ages of the world, nations have been fortunate in so adapting design to prevailing wants, and in sympathy with existing feelings, as to produce a national style. But in the present day men no longer attend to such considerations; they are wholly without such guiding principles, and consequently are totally without a characteristic style. They are satisfied with the indiscriminate reproduction of the architecture of Egypt, Greece, and Rome, or of Christendom in any, or all, its marked periods. Originality they have none. One man delights in a Gothic villa; another prefers the style of Italy: even India and China have their advocates, who never consider that climate and use should rule the choice, rather than fantasy and whim, and that there *must* be conditions arising from the present state of society, from fiscal regulations, modern habits, &c., which, duly attended to, would, in addition to utility, be likely to result in novelty and beauty.

It is this merely imitative character of architecture which has so largely contributed to decorative *shams*, to the age of putty, papier maché, and gutta percha. These react upon architecture; and, from the cheapness with which such ornament can be applied and its apparent excellence, the florid and the gaudy take the place of the simple and the true. A popular writer describes the wearer of cheap finery as having his jewellery "a size larger than anybody else;" and so it is with the cheap finery of imitative ornament: it is always "a size larger" than it should be – bolder, coarser, and more impudent than the true thing; it excites our contempt by its flashy tawdriness, so incongruous with the meanness and vulgarity it is intended to adorn.

From this *manufacture of ornament* arises all that mixture of styles, and that incongruity of parts, which, perhaps, is itself "the style" of this characterless age. Through it, also, the plasterer and the paper-hanger too often usurp the place of the architect, to the certain dismissal of the mason and the wood-carver; and ornament, perchance in itself unobjectionable, is sure in such hands to be grossly misapplied.

198   OWEN JONES
from *The Grammar of Ornament* (1856)

The fourth member of the Cole Circle was the Welshman Owen Jones. On his extensive tour of southern Europe in the early 1830s, he had been attracted to the polychromy of the Alhambra in Spain, for which he prepared a lavish chromolithographic folio between 1836 and 1845. By the latter date he was also practicing architecture in London, experimenting with a "Saracenic" or "Moorish" style, although this enthusiasm would not be lasting. For the *Journal of Design* in 1851, Jones wrote a regular column, "Gleanings from the Exhibition of 1851," in which he repeatedly applauded the high quality (especially with regard to design and color) of the artistic goods on display from India, Tunis, Egypt, and Turkey. This praise came with the condemnation of almost everything produced in Europe. In these "Gleanings" Jones also began to enunciate a series of principles or design propositions (later used by Cole as a catechism at the School of Design), which would ultimately number 37 and stand at the head of his *Grammar of Ornament*. His most important comments on the creation of a new architectural style, however, appear in the final chapter of the book, in which he discusses the ornamental design of "Leaves and Flowers from Nature." His thesis that a new style would arise in architecture out of a naturalistic ornamental grammar — and conversely his rejection of the materialist premise of Garbett — was quite unique at this time.

Although ornament is most properly only an accessory to architecture, and should never be allowed to usurp the place of structural features, or to overload or to disguise them, it is in all cases the very soul of an architectural monument.

By the ornament of a building we can judge more truly of the creative power which the artist has brought to bear upon the work. The general proportions of the building may be good, the mouldings may be more or less accurately copied from the most approved models; but the very instant that ornament is attempted, we see how far the architect is at the same time the artist. It is the best measure of the care and refinement bestowed upon the work. To put ornament in the right place is not easy; to render that ornament at the same time a superadded beauty and an expression of the intention of the whole work, is still more difficult.

Unfortunately, it has been too much the practice in our time to abandon to hands most unfitted for the task the adornment of the structural features of buildings, and more especially their interior decorations.

Owen Jones (1807–88), from *The Grammar of Ornament* (1856). New York: Van Nostrand Reinhold Company, 1982 (facsimile edition), pp. 154–6.

The fatal facility of manufacturing ornament which the revived use of the acanthus leaf has given, has tended very much to this result, and deadened the creative instinct in artists' minds. What could so readily be done by another, they have left that other to do; and so far have abdicated their high position of the architect, the head and chief.

How, then, is this universal desire for progress to be satisfied – how is any new style of ornament to be invented or developed? Some will probably say, A new style of architecture must first be found, and we should be beginning at the wrong end to commence with ornament.

We do not think so. We have already shown that the desire for works of ornament is co-existent with the earliest attempts of civilisation of every people; and that architecture adopts ornament, does not create it.

The Corinthian order of architecture is said to have been suggested by an acanthus leaf found growing round an earthen pot; but the acanthus leaf existed as an ornament long before, or, at all events, the principle of its growth was observed in the conventional ornaments. It was the peculiar application of this leaf to the formation of the capital of a column which was the sudden invention that created the Corinthian order.

The principle of the foliation, and even the general form of the leaves, which predominate in the architecture of the thirteenth century, existed long before in the illuminated MSS.; and derived as they were, most probably, from the East, have given an almost Eastern character to early English ornament. The architects of the thirteenth century were, therefore, very familiar with this system of ornamentation; and we cannot doubt, that one cause of the adoption so universally of this style during the thirteenth century arose from the great familiarity with its leading forms which already existed.

The floral style, in direct imitation of nature, which succeeded, was also preceded by the same style in works of ornament. The facility of painting flowers in direct imitation of nature in the pages of a missal, induced an attempt to rival them in stone in the buildings of the time.

The architectural ornament of the Elizabethan period is mostly a reproduction of the works of the loom, the painter, and the engraver. In any borrowed style, more especially, this would be so. The artists in the Elizabethan period were necessarily much more familiar with the paintings, hangings, furniture, metal-work, and other articles of luxury, which England received from the Continent, than they would be with the architectural monuments; and it is this familiarity with the ornamentation of the period, but imperfect knowledge of the architecture, which led to the development of those peculiarities which distinguish Eliza-bethan architecture from the purer architecture of the Revival.

We therefore think we are justified in the belief, that a new style of ornament may be produced independently of a new style of architecture; and, moreover, that it would be one of the readiest means of arriving at a new style: for instance, if we could only arrive at the invention of a new termination to a means of support, one of the most difficult points would be accomplished.

199 JOHN RUSKIN
from "The Deteriorative Power of Conventional Art over Nations" (1859)

I f the Gothic Revival can be said to have had its last word in the nineteenth century, it would be this single paragraph from the pen of Ruskin. Whereas "The Nature of Gothic" has long been regarded as the definitive statement of Ruskin's ornamental theory of architecture, the following remark (curiously, given in a lecture at Cole's Kensington Museum in January 1858) reaches to the heart of Ruskin's picturesque conception. The much-in-demand speaker is here discussing the unusually thin statuary on the west front of Chartres, which he was displaying for his audience with a large drawing. Little needs to be added to this statement, except to say that for Ruskin all great architecture was, or should be, a transcendental experience. In Ruskin's view the purpose of architecture is to draw the imperfect human spirit into the sublime reaches of the divine.

These statues have been long, and justly, considered as representative of the highest skill of the twelfth or earliest part of the thirteenth century in France; and they indeed possess a dignity and delicate charm, which are for the most part wanting in later works. It is owing partly to real nobleness of feature, but chiefly to the grace, mingled with severity, of the falling lines of excessively *thin* drapery; as well as to a most studied finish in composition, every part of the ornamentation tenderly harmonizing with the rest. So far as their power over certain tones of religious mind is owing to a palpable degree of non-naturalism in them, I do not praise it – the exaggerated thinness of body and stiffness of attitude are faults; but they are noble faults, and give the statues a strange look of forming part of the very building itself, and sustaining it – not like the Greek caryatid, without effort – nor like the Renaissance caryatid, by painful or impossible effort – but as if all that was silent, and stern, and withdrawn apart, and stiffened in chill of heart against the terror of earth, had passed into a shape of eternal marble; and thus the Ghost had given, to bear up the pillars of the church on earth, all the patient and expectant nature that it needed no more in heaven. This is the transcendental view of the meaning of those sculptures.

John Ruskin, from "The Deteriorative Power of Conventional Art over Nations," in *The Two Paths: Being Lectures on Art, and Its Application to Decoration and Manufacture, Delivered in 1858–9.* London: Smith, Elder and Co., 1859, pp. 34–5.

200 ROBERT KERR
"The Battle of the Styles," from *The Builder* (1860)

By the end of the 1850s architects in Britain seem to have grown weary of the style debate. At least this can be inferred from this lecture given in London by Robert Kerr at an architectural exhibition of 1860, fittingly entitled "The Battle of the Styles." The lecture itself was not published, but summary notes of the talk by one listener did appear in *The Builder*. Kerr was apparently very entertaining. He recounted, somewhat humorously, the stylistic revivals in Britain since "English Palladianism" and "Eighteenth Century Gothicism," and concluded with remarks on the "New Italian School," "Ecclesiology," "Latitudinarianism" (Ruskin), and "Eclecticism." His concluding remarks, now suggesting a stylistic compromise, are presented here.

Present Position and Prospects. – In *Classicism*, of late years, the Royal Exchange (1839), St. George's Hall of Liverpool, and the Town Hall at Leeds were the chief works of the grand monumental class, and, with various others of less magnitude, very successful; while, for more ordinary civil and domestic buildings, the Palatial Italian style had been almost universal, and exhibited in great merit. The present tendency, however, was towards the early Italian manner, – the Gothic germ. The picturesque also was much sought, – a step in the same direction.

In *Gothicism* it might be said that, in the course of a rapid and brilliant career of revivalism, the native English styles had successively gone out of fashion in favour of Continentalism: even Mr. Scott rested upon thirteenth-century French as the great central point of excellence. The tendency, however, was now very strong towards Mediæval Italian, – the beforementioned germ of the Palatial. The use of colour was a step in the same course. The endeavour to adapt the style to common domestic forms was the same. The merit of our Gothic domestic designers could not possibly be overrated. Carpenter, Butterfield, and numerous others might be alluded to; but the remarkable felicity of design and draughtsmanship in Mr. Burges and Mr. Street, as displayed in the competitions for Lille Cathedral and the church at Constantinople, took us by surprise, and led us to look for universal merit in the works of rising men of such great power. In the Government Offices competition, also, the drawings of Mr. Scott and Mr. Street, and, perhaps, more than all, that of Mr. Woodward, were strikingly fine. But Mr. Scott had lately drawn attention to a point which young Gothicists would do well to consider. They were deficient, said Mr. Scott, in grace and proportion. This was undeniably true, and it was really the most important of all present questions affecting the style, whether a spirit of more elegance and refinement of form could not be cultivated. Whether the Gothic style was likely ever to prevail in England for everyday purposes was a point much argued; but, however unsuitable, as at present practised, time and much modification might do a great deal for the style with this view, provided Mr. Scott's complaints were not neglected.

Robert Kerr, "The Battle of the Styles," from the summary in *The Builder*, May 12, 1860, p. 294.

In *Eclecticism* the latest remarkable occurrence was the Government Offices competition in 1857. In that transaction the question of style had been left open as if to promote a settlement of the point; but the result had been most unsatisfactory. The excellence of the Gothic designs had been just alluded to. The design of Mr. Garling might be safely pointed out as one of several equally excellent on the other side.

In *Ecclesiology*, of late years, theory had become more subdued; but the practice of Continental style and arrangements, if not kept in check, might rouse the susceptibilities of Protestantism, and it was time that some of the Gothic school should take up Protestantism as fundamental ground.

Latitudinarianism had served its purpose, so far as theory went: copyism was almost extinct, and precedent a dead letter: clever novelties were the rule, and the drawings then in the Architectural Exhibition would have been considered, some twenty years ago, not merely as extravagances, but as the outlandish products of some other sphere. The picturesque, however, was much overvalued, and fantastic design was the bane of both Gothic and Classic efforts. Dashing drawing, also, was much to be condemned, as the most treacherous of all things to the student, causing him to overlook all those delicate questions which constituted the very life of architecture in the solid, but which, in the midst of masterly picturesque sketching, red, blue, and yellow colouring, and artificial *chiaroscuro*, were utterly lost sight of.

In conclusion, *the battle of the styles* seemed thus to be approaching near the end of all honourable and creditable conflict, namely, alliance. If Classicism was tending towards the early Italian, the Gothic germ of the later style, and becoming also more and more picturesque, and, therefore, more and more Gothic (the picturesque being the essence of Gothic taste); and if Gothicism was similarly tending towards the examples of Italy, and becoming more and more graceful and refined, and therefore more Classic (grace and proportion being the Classic essence); then it might surely be said that the rival styles, mutually modified, were approaching one common centre. The result might not be any new style, – for it was questionable whether the phraseology of architecture, except in respect of new materials, was not exhausted long ago (like that of music, and perhaps that of painting and sculpture); but there would be a federation and unison of purpose; the *quasi* Classic on one side of the way, and the *quasi* Gothic on the other, although clearly distinguishable in criticism, would display accordance and sympathy, and look each other fairly in the face. If the impression created by the present argument had been to this effect, exhibiting the battle of the styles as not a party squabble, but an intellectual process, honourable to all engaged in it (and honourable, by the bye, to England as having had little or no help from abroad throughout its whole course), then the lecture had at any rate left the world a little better than an hour ago it had found it.

To show that the lecturer's *personal* remarks were not made in an arrogant or unpleasant spirit, we may mention the fact that his allusions to the distinguished architects of past and present time, and also the references to the current questions of the day, were received by the audience with approbation throughout.

201 JAMES FERGUSSON
History of the Modern Styles of Architecture (1862)

In 1855 James Fergusson published two volumes of a projected three-volume *Handbook of Architecture*, which was intended – following Hope – to be a comprehensive history of architecture of all countries, from the earliest times until the present day. In 1862 this third volume appeared, although under a different title. Now Fergusson, in his concluding pages, proposes his own stylistic compromise of sorts – the "*tertium quid*" or "common-sense style" that draws its inspiration from the Italian Renaissance. Throughout much of the nineteenth century the Italian Renaissance had been little regarded by architects and historians; it was seen as a second-rate imitation of the classical style and thus as stylistically inferior. This view began to change around mid-century – in light of the efforts of Charles Barry, Henri Labrouste, and Gottfried Semper – and the style had now come to be seen not only as rich in its artistic motifs but also as a less expensive alternative to either classicism or Gothic buildings. The final pages of Fergusson's argument are cited here.

The great lesson we have yet to learn before progress is again possible is, that *Archæology is not Architecture*. It is not even Art in any form, but a Science, as interesting and as instructive as any other; but from the very nature of things it can neither become an art, nor in any way take the place of one. Our present mistake is, first, in insisting that our architects must be archæologists; and fancying, in the second place, that a man who has mastered the science is necessarily a proficient in the art. Till this error is thoroughly exploded, and till Architecture is practised only for the sake of supplying the greatest amount of convenience attainable, combined with the most appropriate elegance, there is no hope of improvement in any direction in which Architecture has hitherto progressed.

As the case at present stands, the Gothic style has obtained entire possession of the Church; and any architect who would propose to erect an ecclesiastical edifice in any other style would simply be laughed at. It is employed also, exclusively or nearly so, for schools and parsonage-houses – generally, wherever the clergy have influence this style is adopted. If it is true that the Gothic period was the best and purest of the Christian Church, and that we are now in this respect exactly where we were between the thirteenth and fifteenth centuries, this is perfectly logical and correct; but if we have progressed, or been refined, or take a different view of these matters from the one then taken, the logic will not hold good; but this the architect is not called upon to decide.

On the other hand, the Classical styles still retain a strong hold on town-halls and municipal buildings. Palaces are generally in this style, and club-houses have hitherto successfully resisted the encroachments of the enemy; and but very recently all the domestic and business buildings of our cities were in the non-Gothic styles. In this country, mansions and villas are pretty equally divided between the two, and it is difficult to estimate which is

James Fergusson, from *History of the Modern Styles of Architecture: Being a Sequel to the Handbook of Architecture*. London: John Murray, 1862, pp. 328–9.

gaining ground at this moment. Generally it may be said that the Gothic is the style of the clergy, the Classical that of the laity; and though the buildings of the latter are the most numerous, those of the former are the most generally architectural.

For the philosophical student of Art it is of the least possible consequence which may now be most successful in encroaching on the domains of its antagonist. He knows that both are wrong, and that neither can consequently advance the cause of true Art. His one hope lies in the knowledge that there is a *"tertium quid,"* a style which, for want of a better name, is sometimes called the Italian, but should be called the common-sense style. This, never having attained the completeness which debars all further progress, as was the case in the purely Classical or in the perfected Gothic styles, not only admits of, but insists on, progress. It courts borrowing principles and forms from either. It can use either pillars or pinnacles as may be required. It admits of towers, and spires, or domes. It can either indulge in plain walls, or pierce them with innumerable windows. It knows no guide but common sense; it owns no master but true taste. It may hardly be possible, however, because it requires the exercise of these qualities; and more than this, it demands thought, where copying has hitherto sufficed; and it courts originality, which the present system repudiates. Its greatest merit is that it admits of that progress by which alone man has hitherto accomplished anything great or good, either in Literature, in Science, or in Art.

202 WILLIAM MORRIS
Prospectus for Morris, Marshall, Faulkner and Company (1861)

I f the style debate by 1860 had exhausted its possibilities, a new path of development was soon to open. In 1861 William Morris published his business Prospectus for "Morris, Marshall, Faulkner & Company, Fine Workmen in Painting, Carving, Furniture and the Metals." The Arts and Crafts movement was unofficially born. Morris was a charismatic figure. He was educated at Oxford in the first half of the 1850s and – inspired by Ruskin – contemplated a feudal brotherhood devoted to the arts. In 1855 he articled himself to the architect George Street, in whose office he met his life-long friend Philip Webb (1831–1915). Morris would soon give up his interest in architecture and move to London to study painting and the decorative arts under Dante Gabriel Rossetti (1828–82). Morris's "bohemian" years ended in 1859 when he married Jane Burden, and the artist next collaborated with Webb in designing the "Red House" in Bexleyheath. It was in this monument to English modernism that Morris launched his first arts-and-crafts studio. His success inspired both imitators and an entire artistic movement, one always paying spiritual homage to Ruskin.

William Morris (1834–96), Prospectus for Morris, Marshall, Faulkner and Company (1861) from Ray Watkinson, *William Morris as Designer*. New York: Reinhold Publishing Corporation, 1990, pp. 16–17.

Morris, Marshall, Faulkner and Company, Fine Art Workmen in Painting, Carving, Furniture and the Metals

The growth of Decorative Art in this country owing to the effort of English Architects has now reached a point at which it seems desirable that Artists of reputation should devote their time to it. Although no doubt particular instances of success may be cited, still it must be generally felt that attempts of this kind hitherto have been crude and fragmentary. Up to this time want of artistic supervision, which can alone bring about harmony between the various parts of a successful work, has been increased by the necessarily excessive outlay consequent on taking one individual artist from his pictorial labour.

The Artists whose names appear above hope by association to do away with this difficulty. Having among their numbers men of varied qualifications, they will be able to undertake any species of decoration, mural or otherwise, from pictures, properly so called, down to the consideration of the smallest work susceptible of art beauty. It is anticipated that by such co-operation, the largest amount of what is essentially the artist's work, along with his constant supervision, will be secured at the smallest possible expense, while the work must necessarily be of a much more complete order, than if any single artist were incidentally employed in the usual manner.

These artists having been for many years deeply attached to the study of the Decorative Arts of all time and countries, have felt more than most people the want of some one place, where they could either obtain or get produced work of a genuine and beautiful character. They have therefore now established themselves as a firm, for the production, by themselves and under their supervision of –

i   Mural Decoration, either in Pictures or in Pattern work, or merely in the arrangement of colours, as applied to dwelling houses, churches, or public buildings.
ii   Carving generally, as applied to Architecture.
iii   Stained Glass, especially with reference to its harmony with Mural Decoration.
iv   Metal Work in all its branches, including Jewellery.
v   Furniture, either depending for its beauty on its own design, on the application of materials hitherto overlooked, or on its conjunction with Figure and Pattern Painting. Under this head is included Embroidery of all kinds, Stamped Leather, and ornamental work in other such materials, besides every article necessary for domestic use.

It is only requisite to state further, that work of all the above classes will be estimated for and executed in a business-like manner: and it is believed that good decoration, involving rather the luxury of taste than the luxury of costliness, will be found to be much less expensive than is generally supposed.

B.   RATIONALISM, ECLECTICISM, AND REALISM IN FRANCE

Introduction

The same spirit of contention and debate that characterized British theory in the middle decades of the century can also be found in France. And while many of the issues are similar, many are also unique. The Gothic Revival, which we have seen emanating from the efforts of Eugène-Emmanuel Viollet-le-Duc and Jean-Baptiste-Antoine Lassus, hits its stride in the 1840s, but it is already meeting resistance. A strong impulse toward a Renaissance-inspired yet modern style was given by Henri Labrouste and his design for the Bibliothèque Sainte-Geneviève, built during the 1840s. Historical studies, meanwhile, were revealing for the first time the architectural history between the late Roman Empire and Gothic times. To all of these influences one might add the great strides French engineers were making in the design of iron structures. Politically, things were also uneasy. The unhappiness with the outcome of the revolution of 1830 had never been placated, and France underwent another bloody revolution 18 years later. After much jockeying, Louis Bonaparte (nephew of Napoleon) proclaimed a "Second Empire" in 1852, and set about reforming – unsuccessfully – such institutions as the Ecole des Beaux-Arts. Bonaparte and Georges-Eugène Haussmann, nevertheless, were quite successful in transforming the city of Paris into a modern metropolis, a process whose cost in the end essentially brought the country to the brink of bankruptcy. This regime ended with a foolish declaration of war against Prussia in 1870, which resulted in a humiliating and catastrophic defeat for France, and yet another revolution.

203   ALBERT LENOIR AND LÉON VAUDOYER
from "Studies of Architecture in France" (1844)

We saw earlier Viollet-le-Duc set down one clear avenue of historical thought with his nine-part essay on Gothic architecture in the *Annales Archéologiques*, which ran between 1844 and 1847. His hymn to the structural rationalism of this style was, however, not unopposed. Another view of French architectural history was championed in a lengthy series of articles published in *Le Magasin pittoresque*, beginning in 1844. They were co-authored by Albert Lenoir and Léon Vaudoyer.

Vaudoyer, of course, was one of the dissenting students at the French Academy in Rome in the late 1820s and early 1830s. When he returned to Paris he heeded Hugo's call to study Gothic architecture and during this decade, together with Hippolyte Fortoul, he devoted much time to exploring the origins of Gothic and Romanesque architecture in France and Germany. Lenoir was meanwhile taking a different route to the same end. The son of a famed antiquarian, he first befriended Vaudoyer in Rome in 1830 and traveled extensively with him throughout the Italian countryside surveying Italian medieval architecture. He was also more closely connected with Saint-Simonian circles, and in 1836 he traveled to the Middle East to explore his contention that European medieval architecture had evolved from a synthesis of architectural schools emanating out of Byzantium in the East and northern Italy in the West. Back in Paris, he wrote extensively for the governmental historical commission that was in the process of classifying and recording French monuments. In 1839 he and Vaudoyer were hired by the Saint-Simonian journal *Magasin pittoresque* to prepare a series of historical articles entitled "Studies of Architecture in France," a task that once again would run in serial form until 1847.

All of this would seem to make Lenoir and Vaudoyer natural allies with Viollet-le-Duc, but in fact their conclusions regarding the relevance of medieval architecture were vastly different. The following excerpt is, in fact, a stinging rebuttal to Viollet-le-Duc's first article in the *Annales Archéologiques*, and to the suggestion that contemporary architecture should somehow return to the path defined by the Gothic style. For Lenoir and Vaudoyer, the Gothic style, while beautiful and powerful as an artistic development, was nevertheless an overextension of the preceding Romanesque period of development, and in fact had collapsed from its own lack of evolving principles well before the introduction of the Renaissance style into France. Again the Saint-Simonian notion of "continual progress"

Albert Lenoir and Léon Vaudoyer, from "Etudes d'architecture en France" in *Le Magasin pittoresque*, 12 (1844), pp. 261–2, trans. Harry Francis Mallgrave.

precluded any simple return to the past, although both Lenoir and Vaudoyer in fact looked to the Renaissance as a period for artistic inspiration.

These considerations in themselves provide a new proof of what we have already demonstrated – namely, it was not the Renaissance that had dethroned the Gothic; the latter had already declined before it had to fear the influence of the new doctrines, and the causes of its decline or lack of longevity were inherent in its founding principle.

While admiring these marvelous cathedrals of the thirteenth century and while being strongly impressed by their powerful architectural effects, we cannot consider the Ogival style as the most beautiful development of Christian art, because this style is for us really a corruption of the Romanesque style from which it directly evolved. Romanesque architecture is the architecture of dogma and of faith; it is always sacerdotal. Ogival architecture is an art emancipated and liberated from ecclesiastical authority. By analogy, can we not recognize the same difference between a Romanesque church and a Gothic church as that which existed between a Greek and Roman temple: an overdone abstraction of all of the perfection that Greek art had achieved, which had never been given to Christian art to attain? Among the Gothic churches, which are generally conceded to be closest to perfection? Are they not precisely those that approach the most primitive style of Romanesque churches? If at Notre-Dame de Paris and Notre-Dame de Chartres we substitute some full arches for the ogival ones, we will find a true Romanesque church. At Reims and Amiens, on the contrary, we see the luxury of ornaments increasing in a proportion that one is unable to ignore as a beginning of decline; this decline becomes even more apparent in the churches of the fifteenth century, and is found complete at the beginning of the sixteenth century, even though the Renaissance, which had been naturalized and introduced into civil construction, was not accepted for use in religious edifices. Now if the grand reforms that had taken place in sixteenth-century architecture had not come, what would have happened to Gothic? Would it have become reinvigorated, performed on itself its own Renaissance within the circle of principles after which it had marched, and without returning to the teachings of pagan antiquity? It is rather doubtful when we see how quickly Christian art collapsed after the Romanesque style, which had ruled for six centuries, after it was abandoned and replaced by the Ogival style, whose principle was in not having any, if it was not that of liberty without limits.

We know there are some people who lament the results of the Renaissance, and who do not hesitate to contest the benefits of this grand social revolution, who are rather biased or rather wrongfully passionate in asserting that the Renaissance was harmful in destroying the originality of our national art, and that without the Renaissance the art of the Middle Ages would still today be the expression of our religious sentiments. Others, going even farther, demand nothing less than to return to Gothic Architecture, and to the negation of everything that has happened since. But is it possible to concede such beliefs and not also – logically – soon lament the habits, usages, and the language of our ancestors? Are we able to protest the course of things and insist on stopping the march of humanity, which is often uncertain to be sure, sometimes askew or stationary, but never retrograde.

Therefore we neither share these regrets nor have such wishes, persuaded that we are that the Middle Ages, within its limitations, having filled the measure of what was possible in art, and having arrived at the last period of its decadence, had been powerless to regenerate its own fount. The moment had come where the Middle Ages gave way to the Renaissance, and was absorbed in this ardent and fecund movement, in which antiquity enthusiastically came to dissipate the gloom of ten centuries.

What! Will Gothic be our national art! And must we repudiate all the advances that have been made since! What! Was French genius so limited that since the fifteenth century our art has lost all its originality or character! We cannot believe it. Art in general, and architecture in particular, are subject to the impulse of ideas that propels the epoch in which they are created. Architecture, we have already had the occasion to note, is the most faithful interpretation of the principles, habits, and spirit of a civilized nation; it is with architecture as with language, and if this comparison has already often been made, it is because there is nothing more exact and more striking. If the Renaissance was accomplished in French architecture, it was because it was at the same time accomplished in our habits, in our institutions, and in our literature. Children of the Roman civilization, we have all borrowed from antiquity; therefore, who is to say that we have not retained a proper originality? Is the French language not formed of Greek, Latin, and Italian elements, and is it therefore not appropriate to the French spirit? But let us not be deceived. If the art of the Middle Ages itself brought some fame to our country, it is because it had remained for such a long time under the influence of the traditions and models of antiquity. One should not suppose that we are unable to recognize the range, grandeur, and originality of these marvelous productions of Christian art; while professing a deep sympathy for the efforts and the goal of the Renaissance. We are ready to concede that it had a false and shabby side and that, directed by a spirit of imitation a little too pronounced, it did not realize all that it was possible to achieve. But what we will never understand is how one is able to reject its spirit and contest its happy effects.

204   EUGÈNE-EMMANUEL VIOLLET-LE-DUC
from "On the Construction of Religious Buildings in France" (1845)

Notwithstanding the criticisms of Lenoir and Vaudoyer, Viollet-le-Duc in his nine articles from the *Annales Archéologiques* both set out his rationalist conception of medieval architecture and at the same time placed it within a dialectical system of structural reasoning unseen in earlier historical analyses. History for many later Saint-Simonians had become a process of linear evolution, always pointing forward; for Viollet-le-Duc, however, it remained hieratic and defined by key organic or vital moments, such as the Greek and the Gothic periods. Viollet-le-Duc's journey through his historical analyses is thus one of revelation: the successive unfolding of rational decisions and innovations, all of which raised Gothic architecture to sublime heights. Above all the style was and remains French, that is, particularly adapted to the French climate, French materials, and the genius of the French

Eugène-Emmanuel Viollet-le-Duc, from "De la construction des édifices religieux en France" [On the construction of religious buildings in France] from *Annales Archéologiques*, Vol. II (1845), pp. 136–8, trans. Harry Francis Mallgrave.

people. The following excerpt, from near the end of his second chapter, speaks to the moment when Romanesque architecture, such as seen in the church at Vézelay, makes its crucial transition to the Gothic style with its more complex system of vaulting supported by flying buttresses.

The consequences of this new system were such that in less than 40 years Gothic architecture achieved its development, arrived at its greatest perfection, and came to be regarded as an "art" subject to fixed "rules," to an "order," taking this word in its true sense. Thus we scarcely need to repeat that the beautiful period of Gothic architecture must be studied with all the care, all the respect, and all the attention that we have put and are putting into the study of antique monuments. The great problem that the architects of the twelfth century had to struggle with in order to raise vaults on tall walls, the efforts that they made, and the admirable results that they obtained – these issues must be for us a subject of conscientious research. There are many things to understand about this time, many things to observe; there is a science and an art unknown until then and lost today; even though we believe we know everything, we have so many things to rediscover.

The discovery and use of the flying buttress completed a revolution that transpired over a century. We see the Romanesque tradition rapidly giving way. Materials, their use, the manner of cutting them, construction, ornaments, profiles – all were changed, subjected to new laws and to new proportions. The caprice that we meet so frequently in the monuments of the tenth and eleventh centuries gave way to strict rules that appear to have come out of a "school." Toward the end of the twelfth century and the beginning of the thirteenth century, nothing was left to chance, to the whim of the artist or worker: each profile had its place, its function. Ornaments, distributed with a certain parsimony, are found only in some parts of the edifice, such as in the capitals, under the dripstones of the cornices, in the groves of the archivolts of the doorways, on the crowns of the buttresses, along the gable, under the spring of the vaults. The statuary itself was subject to an order; it only occupies certain hallowed places where it cannot be distracted. It is limited in dimensions that scarcely exceed human dimensions. Finally, we find during this period an "art," if not also as much beauty (this is a matter of taste that we do not intend to discuss) as Greek art of the good period; it is not less limited, or less reasoned, or less knowing, or less correct or wise. We know there are, still today, many for whom this assertion may appear as a paradox, if not a grave error. We understand the objections that will be made, and we shall try to respond here.

First of all we pose this question: Is it the form or the spirit of antique architecture that must be studied? It is both, some will say, but not form to the detriment of the spirit. Unfortunately this is a mistake too often made. The first sentiment that we experience when we see and study the best Greek monuments of antiquity is a profound admiration for their "good sense," for the pure and simple reason, "devoid of poetry," that presides in these structures. But to what end has this reason and "good sense" led these Greek architects? To using the materials at their disposal according to their strength, their nature, and their quality; to fulfill the given program; to submit their buildings to the uses and customs of their citizens, to limit the dimensions required by these uses; to make only the necessary expenditure, to put equal care in the execution of all the parts of the edifices, to take a thousand precautions in order to avoid all the causes of ruin. Here is the "spirit" of Greek architecture. Here is what this architecture teaches us first and above all else: before the art of profiling a capital or an entablature, or decorating a frieze or a pediment. Therefore if we follow the "spirit" and not the form, if we use our materials and take into account their qualities, if we satisfy the program of "where we live," if we limit ourselves to our uses and our customs, if we moderate our expenses, then on the day that someone asks us for a church, will we design a Greek temple? Certainly not. And what monuments satisfy all these conditions better than our edifices of the twelfth and thirteenth centuries!

By virtue of good sense, reason, understanding of materials, their proper use, antique monuments differed essentially by their form. Is that not a quality? Needs, uses, climate, different materials, a new religion – are they nothing? Must not everything modify the form of architecture? Certainly nothing is more logical. Reason and good sense will always and everywhere be the same; it is the "spirit" that must always govern every human work, and especially with an art as positive as architecture. But with customs, religions, and different climates the "form" is infinite. Thus let the men of the thirteenth century have their art here, like the Greeks had theirs under Pericles. To prefer the Greek form to the Gothic form is the matter of taste. But do not deny our fathers their wisdom, reason, good sense, knowledge, and experience, because they possessed these qualities to a high degree, and perhaps they even had more of the spirit of antiquity than all of those who have imitated them since the Renaissance.

205 CÉSAR DALY
from "On Liberty in Art" (1847)

A new forum for debate was opened in France in 1840 with the creation of the *Revue générale de l'architecture et des travaux publics.* Its founding editor and publisher, César Daly, was born in Verdun, the son of a French noblewoman and Irish sea captain. He was first schooled in England but in the early 1830s he was back in France and studying under Félix Duban in Paris. During this period Daly also pledged his efforts to realizing the ideas of Charles Fourier, who, like Saint-Simon before him, placed great emphasis on a new and organic architectural style arising from the radical reformation of existing patterns of social existence and from constant evolutionary development. In his architectural thinking, Daly was close to the circle of Duban, Labrouste, and Vaudoyer, although he differed from them in some of his strong futurist views.

In the 1840s Daly's position was, however, still evolving. He was never an ideologue or partisan of a particular style and he was not entirely inimical to the Gothic circle of Viollet-le-Duc – who wrote several articles for the *Revue générale*, beginning in 1851. But in this article of 1847, Daly announces his firm rejection of the Gothic Revival in France. His opponent in this instance is Ludovic Vitet, a historian and friend of Viollet-le-Duc, and the first *Inspecteur des monuments historiques.* If Vitet's position regarding the Gothic is somewhat more complex than Daly makes it out to be, this passage nevertheless launches Daly's campaign that would eventually be directed at both Gothic enthusiasts and the declining classical school, represented by the Ecole des Beaux-Arts.

César Daly (1811–94), from "De la liberté dans l'art [On liberty in art]: A Monsieur Ludovic Vitet" in *Revue générale de l'architecture et des travaux publics*, Vol. VII (1847), pp. 393–4, trans. Harry Francis Mallgrave.

In my youth I had an old professor who was very fond of recounting short historical anecdotes; and as his erudition exhausted itself faster than my curiosity, he was often forced to repeat his stories.

This circumstance gave me the advantage of hearing him recite several times the story of a famous Saxon king who, in walking along the seashore, was tired of seeing the incoming tides too quickly bringing his excursions to an end. "Your power is without limits," said a courtesan to the king, "command the sea, set down some limits, and it will obey you." The king commanded but the sea approached with a rumble and soon the courtesans and his majesty were obliged to flee the indocile ocean. The moral of this story, interpolated my worthy mentor, is easy to deduce; there are some movements entirely outside of our control, there are some forces against which we can have only limited action.

Such a shame, is it not true, monsieur? Such a shame that this old professor was not part of the architectural section of the institute, which has for so long endeavored to restrain art, this other ocean that always breaks into foam along a remote shore of history! With a little more discretion, the institute would have escaped in '89 what menaces it.

Oppression calls for revolt, and the reaction is always equal to the action. The official institute had decreed that everyone should be passionately smitten with antiquity, and only for the antique. There is now born an official institute that wants to impose the exclusive cult of the Gothic. The ideal of the first institute lies in horizontal lines; the second admires only vertical lines. Both, however, want to force art to worship its relics, to give life to or galvanize its mummies; they are one and the same. For the first, as for the second, art is only a fetishism.

And the public? The artists?

Artists are tyrannized by these extreme parties, who both have tender feelings for a decayed art, who both wish to oppose their century, and who differ only by age: one being old and the other older.

The public, as the artists understand them, are treated as sick, even as idiots; by the authority of the dead they are not allowed liberty, neither in taste, nor in feelings, nor in reason.

"You will only drink something hot, very hot, even on a scorching day," says someone on the left.

"It is a regime of icy drinks that you will follow, even on the most severe cold days," cries him on the right.

Here it is Armagnac, there burgundy; but monsieur, the liberty of the artist, the truth and the dignity of art – who in France troubles himself with them?

In the midst of this conflict, what is the situation of the artist who conscientiously searches for truth?

206 LÉONCE REYNAUD
from *Treatise on Architecture* (1850)

We saw Reynaud earlier with two excerpts from his article for the *Encyclopédie nouvelle* (chapters 139 and 154 above) of 1834. He next went into architectural practice, and in 1837 he was appointed a professor at the École Polytechnique. In 1842 he moved to the Ecole des Ponts et Chaussées and eventually became the school's director. His two-volume *Traité d'architecture* is in many ways the most comprehensive explication of the advanced Saint-Simonian view of history: an outline of architecture's progressive and synthetic development, which in his day was incorporating the new material of iron into its formal vocabulary. Reynaud admired in particular Henri Labrouste's Bibliothèque Sainte-Geneviève (1838–50) as an example of this new type of iron construction.

But iron, even more so than wood, lends itself to every form. It permits lighter and bolder construction, greater spacing of the points of support, and it reduces bulk considerably. It is resistant to fire and it is easy to ensure it a long life. Also, each day iron's applications are extended and its benefits multiplied. Now in our palaces and in most public buildings, the decking and the roofing are executed in iron. Our private habitations even begin to follow this example. Iron has already been used in some remarkable buildings, to the exclusion of every other material. It allows us to erect bridges, for the openings of which no combination of carpentry would suffice. Finally, iron offers advantages in replacing wood in the building of those immense vessels that testify so highly to the power of mankind. We should add, however, that iron's conductibility of heat does not permit it to replace stone and wood everywhere, and that in many circumstances iron construction is not the most economical in those cases that require the outlay of initial prototypes.

From another point of view iron recommends itself to the serious study of architects. For a long time architecture has been accused of not renewing the forms that it employs in a building. We pretend that we have no system of architecture because we reproduce elements already known. Without doubt these complaints are somewhat unjustified; they bear witness in their exaggeration to a somewhat unclear appreciation of the conditions and merits of the art. They seem to say that the forms on which architecture has been called upon to operate are things of caprice and of pure convention, and they ignore one of the most precious qualities of the fine arts – their universality. Nevertheless, if we note that they apply neither to painting nor to statuary (to speak only of the arts of design), and even less to architecture, which remains faithful to the same type, we will also come to recognize that it has something in it well founded, and that if the expression is false and the demands are excessive, the sentiment is true. The public – without resorting to a full account of the different conditions imposed on architecture – feels rightly that this art cannot remain foreign to the progress of science and industry; and when the public sees us so far beyond our predecessors in these two branches of human activity, it must be astonished at finding, almost exclusively, the forms and elementary proportions of Greece or Rome in our edifices.

Léonce Reynaud, from *Traité d'architecture*, Vol. I (second edition, 1860). Paris: Dalmont et Dunod, 1860, pp. 530–2., trans. Harry Francis Mallgrave.

The variations that it is able to ascertain appear insufficient, because the public does not completely appreciate the merits of the forms of our stone buildings.

But this new material that comes before us will require new forms and new proportions, because it differs essentially from all those materials that have been employed in buildings up to now. What is suited to stone will in no way be suited to iron. In the industrial world, therefore, there is not the principle of a complete renovation of the art, but of new elements, of a new branch that is no doubt destined to considerable development and progress, to which it seems impossible to assign any limits. Science will equally be called upon here to exercise a direct influence on architecture, and it will not allow iron to undergo the long period of trial and error that it had to go through before it found the forms and the proportions most convenient for stone construction. It will immediately give what – deprived of its assistance – we might otherwise have to put off until after long and expensive efforts. Science will not dictate absolute laws; it will not fix the harmonious proportions that are outside of its province. It will not dominate art, but it will elaborate the bases on which feeling supports its creations, it will set the limits between which architectural taste will freely act.

207 EUGÈNE-EMMANUEL VIOLLET-LE-DUC
from ''Architecture'' in *Reasoned Dictionary* (1854)

By the early 1850s Viollet-le-Duc was already beginning to revise his earlier position. He was no longer committed to the Gothic revival in the sense of advocating the imitation of Gothic forms, but he still believed that a renewal of contemporary practice could be brought about by employing the rational constructional analysis that had been a feature of Gothic architecture. This phase of his theory appears in the first volume of the ten-volume *Dictionnaire raisonné de l'architecture français du XIe au XVIe siècle* (1854–68) – one of the great scholarly efforts of the nineteenth century. His objective in this dictionary is not to provide models for contemporary use, but to dissect France's medieval legacy for its ''imperious laws of logic'' and ''native originality and independence that derives from our national genius.'' As the following excerpt from his article ''Architecture'' demonstrates, Gothic architecture is to be admired in particular for what it discloses of the French mind and French spirit, a rationalist legacy therefore unique to France.

We must take into account the particular character of an important part of France if we are ever going to understand the great movement in the arts that burst out around the end of the twelfth century. We can only make reference to it generally here, since we will deal with it in connection with our analysis of each specific topic and of the forms adopted by each type of architecture. It is necessary to point out, though, that this great movement in the arts

Eugène-Emmanuel Viollet-le-Duc, from ''Architecture,'' in *Dictionnaire raisonné de l'architecture français du XIe au XVIe siècle* (1854), trans. Kenneth D. Whitehead, in *The Foundations of Architecture: Selections from the Dictionnaire raisonné*. New York: George Braziller, 1990, pp. 72–4. © 1990 by George Braziller, Inc. Reprinted with permission of George Braziller, Inc.

remained confined within specific limits so long as architecture, in both theory and practice, remained in the hands of the religious establishments. In that situation, everything contributed to keeping it within bounds: compulsory traditions that had to be followed; the rigor of life in the cloister; the reforms attempted and carried out among the clergy during the eleventh and part of the twelfth centuries. Once architecture had passed out of the hands of the clergy into the hands of the laity, however, the national genius was not slow in quickly making itself dominant. Eager to free itself from the Romanesque envelope in which it found so little comfort, the national genius ended up stretching the boundaries of that envelope until they burst. One of the earliest efforts in that direction involved the construction of vaults. What was needed was to try to take advantage of the rather confused results that had been obtained up to that point; this goal had to be pursued with the same rigorous logic that characterized all intellectual efforts in that era. The basic principle, which we have already developed in the entry "Flying Buttress," was that vaults exert oblique thrusts; thus it was necessary, in order to maintain them in place, to construct a counter oblique resistance. By the middle of the twelfth century, builders had already recognized that the round, or semicircular, arch had too great a thrust to allow it to be raised to great heights on thin walls or separate pillars, especially over large open spaces, without enormous piers or abutments. So they replaced the round arch with the pointed arch. They continued to use the round arch only for windows or narrow spans. They abandoned the barrel vault entirely, since its thrust could be supported only by a continuous abutment. Reducing the points of resistance of their structures to the piers, they ingeniously arranged it so that all the weight and thrust of their vaults were conducted to these piers, which they then supported by independent flying buttresses, which transferred to the outside all the weight of these large edifices. To provide a firmer foundation for their piers or separate buttresses, they charged them with supplementary weight, out of which they then fashioned some of their richest decorative motifs. As they thus progressively reduced the mass of their structures, they recognized the tremendous resistance strength that the pointed arch possessed while, at the same time, it had only a slight separating action. Accordingly, they began to use the pointed arch everywhere, totally abandoning the round arch, even in civil architecture.

From the beginning of the thirteenth century on, then, architecture developed in accordance with a wholly new method – a method in which all the related parts could be rigorously deduced, one from the other. Now, it is by means of such changes of method as this that revolutions in the sciences and in the arts begin. Construction dictates form: piers destined to carry several arches will have as many separate columns as there are arches; these columns will have a greater or a lesser diameter depending upon the weight they must carry, and they will be raised up to the vaults that they are designed to support; their capitals, too, will assume an importance proportionate to the load they carry. Arches will be wide or slender, or will rest upon one or several rows of springers, depending upon their function. Walls, having become superfluous, will disappear completely in the most magnificent constructions, to be replaced by gratings decorated with stained glass. Everything that is necessary to the construction will become just another motif for decoration: roofs, waterspouts, the introduction of daylight, the means of access and circulation on different stories of the building, even its ironwork, supporting structures, sealing, leading, heating, and ventilation. All these things will not be concealed, as has been a regular construction practice since the sixteenth century; they will, moreover, be kept right out in the open, and, through various ingenious methods, they will contribute to the total richness of the architecture – always taking for granted, of course, the level of good taste that will invariably govern how they are decorated. There will, in short, never be any mere ornament that could really have been dispensed with in one of these exquisite structures of the beginning of the thirteenth century. Each and every ornament will also represent the fulfillment of some specific need. If we move outside France and look at some of the imitations of these French buildings, though, we will encounter some rather strange things; for these imitations are often found to have copied the mere forms without any inner understanding of why an architectural member has taken the form that it has. Consideration of this fact may serve to explain how it is that, in accordance with our national habit of always trying to seek our good at a distance somewhere (as if distance somehow enhanced value), the loftiest criticisms of the type of architecture commonly styled "Gothic" almost always have in view the cathedrals of Milan, Siena, Florence, or certain German churches. It never seems to occur to such critics of the "Gothic" to take a trip of a few short miles, where they could seriously study the actual structure and features of the cathedrals of Amiens, Chartres, or Reims. French architecture of the Middle Ages should surely not be studied in those places where it was nothing but an import; it should be studied on the soil that gave it birth, and among the various moral and material elements that nourished it. Furthermore, this architecture is so intimately tied to our national history, to the achievements of the French mind, as well as to our national character (whose major traits, tendencies, and directions are vividly reflected in this same architecture) that it is only barely understandable why all this is not better known and appreciated, or why the study of it is not required in our schools every bit as much as is the teaching of our national history.

208 GUSTAVE COURBET
from "Statement on Realism" (1855)

Reynaud's remarks on iron, published in the first volume of his *Traité d'architecture* (1850), actually precede the sudden popularity of this material in the 1850s. Paxton's impressive design for the Great Exhibition of 1851 would have an enormous impact on the use of iron in both Europe and the United States. In France iron construction was similarly given a boost when Napoleon III ordered the work on the Halles Centrales halted in 1853, so that its architect Victor Baltard (1805–74) might redesign the city's central market as a series of cast-iron structures. Paris also followed London by hosting its own international exhibition in 1855 – the *Exposition universelle des produits de l'industrie*. Here the engineer Alexis Barrault designed the main exhibition hall as a tripartite nave of three barrel vaults (cast-iron trusses) with a span of 48 meters in the center.

The Paris Exposition of 1855 is also notable in one other important respect. After the painter Gustave Courbet had two of his paintings – *The Painter's Studio* and *Burial at Ornians* – rejected by the official exposition committee

Gustave Courbet (1819–77), from "Statement on Realism" which appeared as a preface to Courbet's catalogue of 1855, "Realism – Gustave Courbet." The English translation is taken from *Gustave Courbet: 1819–1877*. London, 1977, p. 77.

because of their prosaic subject matter, he displayed these works off-site at his unofficial but widely visited *Pavilion de Realism*. Hence the phenomenon first pejoratively coined "realism" rather quickly translated itself into a powerful artistic and literary movement – one with a significant architectural impact. In its most general meaning, realism can be defined as the attempt to represent the real world in a truthful and objective manner, that is, to disregard many of the artistic pretensions of the past. Artists must therefore deal with the present and its problems with a sense of independence and individuality. The following statement appeared as a preface to Courbet's catalogue of 1855, "Realism – Gustave Courbet," and is sometimes attributed to Courbet's friend and accomplice in popularizing the movement, the writer Champfleury.

The title 'realist' has been imposed on me in the same way as the title 'romantic' was imposed on the men of 1830. Titles have never given the right idea of things; if they did, works would be unnecessary.

Without going into the question as to the rightness or wrongness of a label which, let us hope, no one is expected to understand fully, I would only offer a few words of explanation which may avert misconception.

I have studied the art of the ancients and moderns without any dogmatic or preconceived ideas. I have not tried to imitate the former or to copy the latter, nor have I addressed myself to the pointless objective of 'art for art's sake'. No – all I have tried to do is to derive, from a complete knowledge of tradition, a reasoned sense of my own independence and individuality.

To achieve skill through knowledge – that has been my purpose. To record the manners, ideas and aspect of the age as I myself saw them – to be a man as well as a painter, in short to create living art – that is my aim.

209 CHARLES BAUDELAIRE
from "The Painter of Modern Life" (1859)

Central to the realist movement was the notion of "modernity," a term that captures the lure and celebration of the present while at the same time expressing a sense of impatience or disdain for the traditions of the past. The poet and critic Charles Baudelaire popularized this notion with his literary homage to the artist Constantin Guys (1805–92), here simply identified as "Monsieur G." The "transitory, fugitive element" underlying modernity for Baudelaire was in part represented by the *flâneur*, the urban stroller or idler who takes in the sensations and active imagery of the streaming metropolis with both a sense of thrill and dread over the accelerating pace of life. Being "modern" now takes on a certain polemical edge, and its translation into architectural terms is

Charles Baudelaire (1821–67), from "The Painter of Modern Life" (1859, published 1863) in *The Painter of Modern Life and Other Essays*, trans. and ed. by Jonathan Mayne. New York: Da Capo Paperback, 1986, pp. 12–14. © 1965 by Phaidon Press Limited. Reprinted by permission of Phaidon Press Limited.

equally evident in the transformation and expansion of the city of Paris (through the creation of several new boulevards) by Baron Georges-Eugène Haussmann.

Modernity

And so away he goes, hurrying, searching. But searching for what? Be very sure that this man, such as I have depicted him – this solitary, gifted with an active imagination, ceaselessly journeying across the great human desert – has an aim loftier than that of a mere *flâneur*, an aim more general, something other than the fugitive pleasure of circumstance. He is looking for that quality which you must allow me to call 'modernity'; for I know of no better word to express the idea I have in mind. He makes it his business to extract from fashion whatever element it may contain of poetry within history, to distil the eternal from the transitory. Casting an eye over our exhibitions of modern pictures, we are struck by a general tendency among artists to dress all their subjects in the garments of the past. Almost all of them make use of the costumes and furnishings of the Renaissance, just as David employed the costumes and furnishings of Rome. There is however this difference, that David, by choosing subjects which were specifically Greek or Roman, had no alternative but to dress them in antique garb, whereas the painters of today, though choosing subjects of a general nature and applicable to all ages, nevertheless persist in rigging them out in the costumes of the Middle Ages, the Renaissance or the Orient. This is clearly symptomatic of a great degree of laziness; for it is much easier to decide outright that everything about the garb of an age is absolutely ugly than to devote oneself to the task of distilling from it the mysterious element of beauty that it may contain, however slight or minimal that element may be. By 'modernity' I mean the ephemeral, the fugitive, the contingent, the half of art whose other half is the eternal and the immutable. Every old master has had his own modernity; the great majority of fine portraits that have come down to us from former generations are clothed in the costume of their own period. They are perfectly harmonious, because everything – from costume and coiffure down to gesture, glance and smile (for each age has a deportment, a glance and a smile of its own) – everything, I say, combines to form a completely viable whole. This transitory, fugitive element, whose metamorphoses are so rapid, must on no account be despised or dispensed with. By neglecting it, you cannot fail to tumble into the abyss of an abstract and indeterminate beauty, like that of the first woman before the fall of man. If for the necessary and inevitable costume of the age you substitute another, you will be guilty of a mistranslation only to be excused in the case of a masquerade prescribed by fashion. (Thus, the goddesses, nymphs and sultanas of the eighteenth century are still convincing portraits, *morally* speaking.)

It is doubtless an excellent thing to study the old masters in order to learn how to paint; but it can be no more than a waste of labour if your aim is to understand the special nature of present-day beauty. The draperies of Rubens or Veronese will in no way teach you how to depict *moire antique, satin à la reine* or any other fabric of modern manufacture, which we see supported and hung over crinoline or starched muslin petticoat. In texture and weave these are quite different from the fabrics of ancient Venice or those worn at the court of Catherine. Furthermore the cut of skirt and bodice is by no means similar; the pleats are arranged according to a new system. Finally the gesture and the bearing of the woman of today give to her dress a life and a special character which are not those of the woman of the past. In short, for any 'modernity' to be worthy of one day taking its place as 'antiquity', it is necessary for the mysterious beauty which human life accidentally puts into it to be distilled from it. And it is to this task that Monsieur G. particularly addresses himself.

210   EUGÈNE-EMMANUEL VIOLLET-LE-DUC
from *Lectures on Architecture,*
Lecture VI (1859)

In the late 1850s and 1860s Viollet-le-Duc's theory began to evolve once again in light of the intense architectural debate taking place in France. In 1856 Henri Labrouste closed his popular design studio, which he had opened in 1830 in defiance of the Ecole des Beaux-Arts. Fifteen students, led by Anatole de Baudot (1834–1915), approached Viollet-le-Duc and asked him to open a studio. The latter responded with a full architectural program of study, the cornerstone of which would be a series of lectures that he immediately set out to compose. Even though the studio failed and his students left him, Viollet-le-Duc continued with his task and completed his first series of ten lectures by 1863. Of these, the sixth lecture stands apart in its general tenor. Whereas the first five lectures are largely didactic and historical, Viollet-le-Duc in his sixth lecture speaks directly to contemporary issues and with both a sense of urgency at contemporary prospects and a mature system of historical development. Greece and the Middle Ages are both periods of great accomplishment and style, but they now have little to offer the present except the logic and discipline of an overriding principle. The inspiration of the artists must be conjoined to them and the functional steam locomotive now becomes a symbol of the new industrial age.

I admit that in what appertains to Architectural Art we are far from rightly appreciating our own times, – what they demand, and what they reject. We are just at the same point with regard to Architecture that the Western World at large was at the time of Galileo in regard to the sciences. The conservators of *the fixed principles of beauty* would, if they had the power, willingly confine, as a dangerous maniac, him who should attempt to prove that there exist principles independent of form; – that, while principles do not vary, their expression cannot be permanently riveted to one invariable form. For nearly four centuries we have been disputing about the relative value of ancient and modern Art; and during these four hundred years our disputes have turned not upon principles, but upon ambiguous terms and figures of speech. We architects, shut up in our art – an art which is half science, half sentiment, – present only hieroglyphics to the public, which does not understand us, and which leaves us to dispute in our isolation. Shall we never have *our* Molière to treat us as he did the doctors of his time? May we not hope some day (while still admiring them) to part company with Hippocrates and Galen? [. . .]

Eugène-Emmanuel Viollet-le-Duc, from Lecture VI, *Entretiens sur l'architecture* (1859), trans. Benjamin Bucknall, and published in 1877 in Viollet-le-Duc, *Lectures on Architecture.* New York: Dover, 1987 (facsimile edition), pp. 172, 176–7, 183–4.

There are times when man needs some of the barbarian element, just as the soil needs manure; for production requires a process of mental fermentation, resulting from contrasts, from dissimilarities, from a disparity between the real and the ideal world. The periods most fruitful in intellectual products have been periods of the greatest agitation (it must be understood that I include the arts among intellectual products – with no offence to those who produce "works of art" as a velvet weaver makes yards of velvet), – periods in which the student of history finds the greatest contrasts. If a society attains to an advanced degree of civilisation, in which everything is balanced, provided for, and adjusted, there ensues a general equality of well-being, – of the good and the proper, – which may render man materially happy, but which is not calculated to arouse his intellect. Movement, struggle, even opposition, is necessary to the arts; stagnation in the mental order, as in the physical, soon induces decay. Thus Roman society placed in the centre of the West, and absolute mistress of the known world, became enfeebled and corrupted, because discussions and contrasts were wanting. Morals and Art decline, simply because everything in this world which does not renew itself by movement and the infusion of foreign elements, becomes subject to decay. Ideas are like families: they must be crossed if we would not see their vitality enfeebled.

What themes shall the poet find amid a perfectly well-ordered, well-governed, well-behaved society, where all have the same number of ideas, and of the same kind, on every subject? Extremes and contrasts are necessary to the poet. When a man of strong feelings sees his country invaded; when he is the witness of shameful abuses; when his sense of right is outraged; when he suffers or hopes, – if this man is a poet, he is inevitably inspired; he will write and arouse emotions in others: but if he lives in the midst of a polished, tolerant, easy-going community, by whom extremes alone are regarded as want of taste – what will he find to say? He will perhaps describe the flowers, the brooks, the verdant meadows, or, stimulating his imagination to a fictitious warmth, he will plunge into the domain of the unreal, the unnatural, the impossible; or, on the other hand, he will give expression to an undefined longing, a groundless disgust of life, and sufferings for which no adequate cause can be alleged. No! – the true poet, sounding to its depths this social condition, apparently so calm and unvaried, will seek in human hearts feelings which never die, wherever man is to be found: beneath the uniform garb in which all the members of this community are dressed, he will find various passions, noble or base; he will compel us to recognise again those contrasts whose manifestations we seek to suppress: thus and thus only will he make himself heard and read. The more civilised and regular society becomes, the more is the artist compelled to analyse and dissect passions, manners, and tastes, – to revert to first principles – to lay hold of and display them in naked simplicity before the world, – if he would leave a deep impression upon this externally uniform and colourless society. Hence it is more difficult to be an artist in times like our own, than among rude, unrefined, people, who openly display their good or evil passions. In primitive epochs, *style* imposed itself on the artist; now, the artist has to acquire style.

But what is style? I am not speaking now of style as applied to the classification of the arts by periods, but of style as inherent in the arts of all times; and to make myself better understood, I remark that independently of the style of the writer in each language, there is a style which belongs to all languages, because it belongs to humanity. This style is inspiration; but it is inspiration subjected to the laws of reason, – inspiration invested with a distinction peculiar to every work produced by a genuine feeling rigorously analysed by reason before being expressed; it is the close accord of the imaginative and reasoning faculties; it is the effort of the *active* imagination regulated by reason. [...]

We may say as much of the ideas, systems, and principles which regulate art. When ideas, systems, and principles are modified, the forms corresponding should be modified also. We admire a hundred-gun ship of war, rigged as a sailing vessel; we perceive that there is in this work of man – the principle being admitted – not only a wonderful product of intelligence, but also forms so perfectly adapted to their purpose, that they appear beautiful, and in fact are so; but however beautiful these forms may be, as soon as steam-power has supervened, they must be changed, for they are not applicable to the novel motive force; hence they are no longer *good*; and on the principle just now cited they will no longer be beautiful for us. Since in our days, when we are subjected to an imperative necessity, we subordinate our works to that necessity, we are so far capacitated for acquiring style in art, which is nothing more than the rigorous application of a principle. We erect public buildings which are devoid of style because we insist on allying forms derived from traditions with requirements which are not in harmony with those traditions. Naval engineers in building a steam-ship, and machinists in making a locomotive, do not endeavour to reproduce the forms of a sailing vessel of the time of Louis xiv., or of a stage-coach: they simply conform to the novel principles with which they have to deal, and thus produce works which have a character, a style of their own, as indicating to every eye a definite purpose. The locomotive, for example, has a special physiognomy which all can appreciate, and which renders it a distinct creation. Nothing can better express force under control than these ponderous rolling machines; their motions are gentle or terrible; they advance with terrific impetuosity, or seem to pant impatiently under the restraining hand of the diminutive creature who starts or stops them at will. The locomotive is almost a living being, and its external form is the simple expression of its strength. A locomotive therefore has style. Some will call it an ugly machine. But why ugly? Does it not exhibit the true expression of the brute energy which it embodies? Is it not appreciable by all as a thing complete, organised, possessing a special character, as does a piece of artillery or a gun? There is no style but that which is appropriate to the object. A sailing-vessel has style; but a steamer made to conceal its motive power and looking like a sailing-vessel will have none; a gun has style, but a gun made to resemble a crossbow will have none. Now we architects have for a long time been making guns while endeavouring to give them as much as possible the appearance of crossbows, or at any rate that of arquebuses; and there are persons of intelligence who maintain that if we abandon the form of the arquebuse we are barbarians, – that Art is lost, – that nothing is left for us but to hide our heads in shame.

211   CÉSAR DALY
from *Revue générale*, Vol. 21 (1863)

I
n his introductory editorial of the *Revue générale* for 1863, César Daly reflected back on the previous 23 years of his publication: both the great promise that the journal held out for a new style of architecture and the failure of his generation to find a unifying architectural principle. He still staunchly defends freedom and taste in art, but this belief over the years had led him to regard the eclecticism of his day – of which so many of his contemporaries were complaining – as a necessary and useful transitional stage to prepare the way for the "new world" of art and society. Once again he opposes all forms of intellectual and moral exclusivity in architectural design, such as what the advocates of the classical and Gothic camps demanded. At the same time these two passages contain a hint of the resignation that was descending over the architectural profession in general. The lively architectural debates of the past half century seemed to have accomplished very little in altering the course of development, although the changes of outlook in retrospect appear nothing less than profound.

Every system of signs, symbols, and representations that express feelings or convey intelligent human communication is a language. Architecture, from this point of view, is also a language, but a language that supports as many revolutions and radical transformations as history presents in distinct styles.

The architect who has studied only one style of architecture is like the Frenchman who knows only his maternal language; he is enslaved to the style, which *thrusts itself* upon him each time he attempts an artistic composition.

And this tyranny is so complete that he, possessed by a form of art whose yoke it is impossible for him to shake off, is only able to master his preferred form of art with an incomplete understanding. He is thus master of himself but he is not a master. In effect, he is similar to the Frenchman who is totally ignorant of Latin, who is only imperfectly the master of his national language. He is the same as the architect who is concerned only with a single architectural style, who can only understand it very incompletely because he is ignorant of its origin, its primitive *raison d'être*, and the successive transformations of a series of artistic forms that his preferred style has received by a tradition of preceding styles.

Does the knowledge of the rules of grammar or the general philosophy of languages not provide an understanding, a more perfect appreciation of the special grammar of each language?

Similarly we can ask – *à fortiori* – if it is possible to master fully a particular style of architecture when we remain absolutely ignorant of all the other historical styles of this art? [...]

* * *

The contemporary architect is not able to contemplate the promised land of the future art and know exactly in which direction to set out today [...] Master of every style, initiated at least in the feelings that they express, in the moral and physical causes that have defined

César Daly, from "Introduction" to the *Revue générale*, Vol. 21 (1863), pp. 5–6, 8–9, trans. Harry Francis Mallgrave.

them, the architect – if he is only intelligent and *erudite*, a *man of taste* whom the ardent flame of poetry has not touched – *will reproduce* the past, but he will reproduce it at least with independence in his selection. He will introduce there the transformations dictated to him by the tact and the discernment that allows an in-depth understanding of both ancient things and contemporary demands. Powerless to create, he will follow the path of *eclecticism* – that wisdom of societies in the midst of change. He will hold prudently to this isthmus destined to facilitate for our weakness the passage from the collapsing old world to the new world that is emerging slowly from the depths of the unknown. But if he has some *genius*, he *will create* with the independence of his genius. New Columbus, he will boldly rush to the discovery of this brilliant world, to this *terra incognita* whose existence is universally presented, even though it is not shown on the geographic maps of art. In any case, prudence or boldness, erudite or inspired, the architect familiar with history will at least march openly and in full possession of his liberty; because *liberty* is the daughter of *science*, just as *slavery* is born of *ignorance*.

Thus to obtain liberty by science, to recognize the *direction of architectural progress in the future* by the revelations of the tradition of what *architectural progress accomplished in the past*, and to facilitate our practical progress along "the good path" – for these reasons this *Revue* studies without exception the *entire past* of our art.

The past forms the detritus that redoubles the active fecundity of the present and prepares the rich harvests of the future. The past, furthermore, contains the germ of what must be, as the acorn contains the oak, and like the child at the bosom of his mother contains the strong man enjoying the plenitude of his faculties. But it is all the past that contains this germ and only a fragment of some kind – either a single race, or a single country, or a single epoch, or a single historical style.

212   CÉSAR DALY
from *Revue générale*, Vol. 23 (1866)

Three years later, in a similar introductory editorial of 1866, Daly's position had evolved still further. He is now less tolerant of eclecticism, although he does not entirely reject it. He remains firmly opposed to both the classical and Gothic schools. But he also here has a new villain that must be confronted: the so-called rationalist school. This editorial again underscores the great complexity of events. The overt object of Daly's attack is the creation of a new architectural school in 1865, the Ecole Centrale d'Architecture (later the Ecole Spéciale d'Architecture), whose first director was Emile Trelat. It had been founded in response to failed reform efforts at the Ecole des Beaux-Arts, and in the desire to direct architectural education closer to the new or emerging technologies. Viollet-le-Duc was initially supportive of the pedagogical program of the new school, and thus this editorial is also an attack on his (still evolving) rationalist theories. But the Fourierist Daly, at the same time, is not in principle opposed to the inroads of the new materials and technologies; he is rather concerned that such purely rationalist thinking will deprive architecture of its artistic side and result in a cold world unresponsive to human poetry, sentiment, or

César Daly, from "Introduction" to the *Revue générale*, Vol. 23 (1866), p. 8., trans. Harry Francis Mallgrave.

feeling. Also very evident here is the widespread anxiety of this time that architecture as a profession will be overtaken by engineering, in his words transforming the "architectural art into an industrial architecture."

What have we done?

The *classical school* turned toward antiquity in order to demand an aesthetic from it. However our feelings are not identical with those of antiquity.

The *Gothic school* addressed itself to the Middle Ages in order to demand a doctrine of art from it. But the genius of our civilization completely opposes the feudal and fanatical genius that characterizes the Middle Ages.

And finally the *rationalist school* comes to proclaim that reason – which has never created a work of art since the beginning of time – must constitute the sole judge, *"the first and the last judge"* of architectural works, apparently without suspecting that in stripping architecture of all poetry, it will leave only an industry of building and therefore suppress (as a simple stand-in for civil engineers) the entire body of architecture. Perhaps it will leave them the resources to become, for a time, modest designers for their knowledgeable victors.

Civil engineers, who ignore what effectively constitutes architecture, dream of such revolutions; there is nothing astonishing or nothing reprehensible in that! But that some architects lend them a hand proves simply that these architects have never understood *art*.

And while the founders of the Ecole Centrale d'Architecture are amazed when eminent architects have refused to participate in a course of teaching that leads to the ruin of the *architectural art*, and that only profits the building art, we can only admire our naivety and pay homage to the lucid inspirations and the artistic instinct of others.

The historical schools – classical and neogothic – in drawing near to antiquity and the Middle Ages have only succeeded and are only able to succeed by creating an indifference toward architecture in the hearts of the masses.

And the rationalist school, in denying in large part architecture's aesthetic and poetic feeling, in regulating everything in the name of logic, radically kills the *art* in architecture.

For us, the classical, neogothic, and rationalist schools are only different facets of the eclectic unity. And to summarize clearly and succinctly our ideas, let us formulate here the three great theses that we have set out previously to discuss: either to produce serious instruction in contemporary aesthetics (and consequently regulate the practice of architecture and mark the direction of its progress) or to make or simply to appreciate the critique of architectural works today.

These theses are the following:

1. *What does eclecticism, envisaged in its relation with society, philosophy, and art, have to do with the architectural art?*

2. *Is architecture destined to disappear before civil engineering? Will the engineer some day absorb the architect?*

3. *What resources does eclecticism offer to contemporary architecture for raising it from its apparent humiliation and preparing for the organic future of art?*

To treat these three questions thoroughly would be to write a philosophical history of modern architecture; at the same time it would lay the foundation of architectural aesthetics of the nineteenth century. [. . .]

As we go along, the *Revue* will make progress in the exposition of its doctrines of historical philosophy and aesthetics; the terrain of its critique will be found more and more consolidated and enlarged.

But the events of our day rush forward rapidly, and the obvious symptoms indicate from what side the critique is already being applied with success. Evidently the struggle tends to concentrate itself between those who want to constitute *reason* as the sole judge of architecture, and those who want, on the contrary, to appeal to the tribunal of *sentiment clarified by reason*. We thus well intend, here and now, to work our doctrinal expositions in parallel with the critique of works executed around us.

The doctrine without an applied critique is abstract science; it is the absence of life. The critique without doctrine is an individual and momentary fantasy substituted for the law of eternity and humanity.

We want truth and life, science and action, theory and practice.

213 BOURGEOIS DE LAGNY
from "Salon of 1866" (1866)

D aly's critique of the rationalist school took on another pejorative coloration in the same year when the architect Bourgeois de Lagny, in writing for the newly founded journal *Moniteur des Architectes*, effectively linked the same rationalist school and its philosophy to the movement of French realism. The immediate object of de Lagny's attack was the young architect Joseph-Eugène-Anatole de Baudot, a devoted pupil of Viollet-le-Duc and later an important innovator in the use of concrete construction. But for de Lagny, also falling into the category of realist architects was Louis-Auguste Boileau, the architect of the cast-iron, Gothic church St.-Eugène (1854–5), and later of the famed Parisian department store, Magasins du Bon Marché (1869–79).

Architecture, unlike its sister arts of painting and sculpture, has not been engaged in those endless discussions of our day between idealism and realism, classicism and romanticism. These two artistic forms, which have their *raison d'être* in the other arts, are in architecture almost absorbed into a single line of thought. Architectural realism (or construction with the absence of art) has played only a very secondary role in the development of monumental art; and this latter art, when it is worthy of this name, is composed of *ideals* with regard to the state of civilization of each period and nation. It is not subject to the forms of realism or construction; that is, only to the extent that these forms correspond to the manifestation of feelings, ideas, and sensations that the architect wants to prevail through the use of marble, stone, iron, and other materials that usage and progress of the building-art put at his disposition. Monumental art even rejects these materials as improper to all serious and noble construction. Iron and cast iron, so widely used today, fall into this category. The architect employs them only in a secondary way in public edifices designed for a long

Bourgeois de Lagny, from "Salon de 1866," in *Le Moniteur des Architectes* (June 1, 1866), pp. 81–3, trans. Harry Francis Mallgrave.

duration, in those works destined to transmit to future generations the glorious mementos of an epoch – monuments of popular belief, religion, race, or national significance.

Between the realism of construction and the idealism of architecture there are opposing goals that lead to very different means of execution. What the builder most forcefully reveals in his work – a good aesthetic – leads the architect to modify it. Beauty in architecture (in literature it is Chateaubriand who says it), beauty consists in choosing and hiding: choosing what manifests the grace of contours, the harmony of proportions, the elegance of forms, the originality of dispositions and effects; and hiding, on the contrary, everything that smacks of pain and effort, that takes away from majesty by constraining it, everything that shows a struggle with the material, a resistance of force and its weight. When architecture assumes this character, it belongs to those rude and barbaric periods of civilization, in which the human struggle with nature had not yet ceased, as seen in the Egyptian period of antiquity and the Romanesque period in more recent times. At the most one is permitted to use the architectural forms of those periods in our buildings where *utility* overweighs *beauty*, where the economics of public or private funds compel the architect not to give into the impulses of the imagination, and to treat an element of the disposition of the construction itself as an object of decoration.

214   EUGÈNE-EMMANUEL VIOLLET-LE-DUC
from "Style" in *Reasoned Dictionary* (1866)

Viollet-le-Duc did not wait long to pick up the gauntlet in what became the final stage of this debate. He responds to the attacks of Daly and others with two philosophical essays in 1866. In one – his entry on "Style" in the eighth volume of his *Dictionnaire raisonné* – he now defines the term in very abstract terms simply as "the manifestation of an ideal based on a principle." In his logical, almost mathematical precision, he has clearly moved beyond his earlier support of Gothic Revivalism and is attempting to define architecture in universal terms. Iron construction is not to be belittled; near the end of this essay, he announces that a new style must arise out of a new structural principle, "out of adherence to a law that is unimpeded by exceptions."

We will speak here of *style* only as it belongs to art understood as a conception of the human mind. Just as there is only *Art* in this sense, so there is only one *Style*. What, then, is style in this sense? It is, in a work of art, the manifestation of an ideal based on a principle. [...]

Thus, even while we recognize that a work of art may exist in an embryonic state in the imagination, we must also recognize that it will not develop into a true and viable work of

Eugène-Emmanuel Viollet-le-Duc, from "Style," in *Dictionnaire raisonné* (1866), trans. Kenneth D. Whitehead, in *The Foundations of Architecture: Selections from the* Dictionnaire raisonné. New York: George Braziller, 1990, pp. 231–2, 240–2. © 1990 by George Braziller, Inc. Reprinted with permission of George Braziller, Inc.

art without the intervention of reason. It is reason that will provide the embryonic work with the necessary organs to survive, with the proper relationships between its various parts, and also with what in architecture we call its proper proportions. Style is the visible sign of the unity and harmony of all the parts that make up the whole work of art. Style originates, therefore, in an intervention of reason.

The architecture of the Egyptians, like that of the Greeks, possessed style because both architectures were derived by means of an inflexible logical progression from the principle of stability on which both were based. One cannot say the same of all the constructions of the Romans during the Roman Empire. As for the architecture of the Middle Ages, it, too, possessed style once it had abandoned the debased traditions of antiquity – that is, in the period from the twelfth to the fifteenth centuries. It possessed style because it proceeded according to the same kind of logical order that we have observed at work in nature. Thus, just as in viewing a single leaf it is possible to reconstruct the entire plant, and in viewing an animal bone, the animal itself, it is also possible to deduce the members of an architecture from the view of an architectural profile. (See the entry "Trait.") Similarly, the nature of the finished construction can be derived from an architectural member.

215 EUGÈNE-EMMANUEL VIOLLET-LE-DUC
from *Lectures on Architecture*, Lecture XII (1866)

T he second response of Viollet-le-Duc, probably written sometime later in 1866 or shortly thereafter, is the twelfth lecture of his *Entretiens sur l'architecture*. The lecture is astonishing if only for the designs of large iron-and-masonry structures that Viollet-le-Duc provides to the reader. This short excerpt does not do full justice to the nuances of his theory, but it represents his final resting point – his willingness to move beyond the historical past and embrace iron in the much-desired creation of a new style.

Hitherto cast or rolled iron has been employed in large buildings only as an accessory. Where edifices have been erected in which metal plays the principal part, as in the *Halles Centrales* of Paris, – in these buildings masonry ceases to take any but an exceptional part, serving no other purpose than that of partition walls. What has nowhere been attempted with intelligence is the simultaneous employment of metal and masonry. Nevertheless it is this which in many cases architects should endeavour to accomplish. We cannot always erect either railway stations, markets, or other immense buildings entirely of masonry, such buildings being very heavy in appearance, very costly, and not presenting sufficiently ample interior accommodation. A structure in masonry, regarded as an envelope protecting from cold or heat, offers advantages which nothing could replace. The problem to be solved

Eugène-Emmanuel Viollet-le-Duc, from Lecture XII, *Entretiens sur l'architecture* (1866), trans. Benjamin Bucknall and published, originally in 1881, as *Lectures on Architecture*, New York: Dover, 1987 (facsimile edition), pp. 58–9.

for providing great edifices destined to accommodate large assemblages would therefore be this: – To obtain a shell entirely of masonry, walls and vaulting, while diminishing the quantity of material and avoiding obstructive supports by the use of iron; to improve on the system of equilibrium adopted by the mediæval architects, by means of iron, but with due regard to the qualities of that material, and avoiding the too close connection of the masonry with the metal; as the latter becomes not only a cause of destruction to the stone, but perishes itself very quickly when not left free. Some few attempts have been made in this direction, but timidly, – for instance by merely substituting columns of cast iron for stone pillars. Iron, however, is destined to play a more important part in our buildings; it should certainly furnish very strong and slender supports, but it should also enable us to adopt vaulting at once novel in plan, light, strong and elastic, and bold constructions forbidden to the mason, such as overhanging projections, corbellings, oblique supports, etc. Is it not evident, for example, that while retaining the system of vaulting employed during the Middle Ages, the thrust of that vaulting might be resisted by the means represented in figure 3? The use of rigid shafts or cast-iron columns as oblique supports, is a means of which our builders have not yet thought, I hardly know why, for this system is fruitful in deductions. It somewhat contravenes the principles of Greek and even Roman architecture; but if we would invent that *architecture of our own times* which is so loudly called for, we must certainly seek it no longer by mingling all the styles of the past, but by relying on novel principles of structure. An architecture is *created* only by a rigorously inflexible compliance with modern requirements, while the knowledge already acquired is made use of, or at least not disregarded.

216 ÉMILE ZOLA
from *The Covered Market of Paris* (1872)

Although this short passage from a novel of the writer Émile Zola falls outside of our chronological time-frame, it is nevertheless a fitting postscript to four decades of continuous discussion. As we have already seen (chapter 137 above), Victor Hugo in the second edition of *Notre-Dame de Paris* added his chapter "Ceci tuera cela" ("This will kill that"), in which he spoke of the death of (medieval) architecture at the hands of the printing press. The realist Zola reiterates this theme, only now it is the death of earlier conceptions of architecture through modern works erected in accordance with the realist spirit of the time. The Parisian church of Saint-Eustache – a quasi-Renaissance, late-Gothic church – was completed in 1532. Les Halles centrales were the famous iron structures that Victor Baltard erected between 1853 and 1870 to serve as the central marketplace for the city. The scene of this passage is a dialogue between two protagonists, taking place on a carriage ride through Paris. In the following text the ellipses are original.

Émile Zola (1840–1902), from *Le ventre de Paris* [The covered market of Paris] (1872), trans. Harry Francis Mallgrave (with ellipses in original). Paris: Le Livre de Poche, 1978, pp. 337–9.

In passing in front of the rue de Roule, he observed the side portal of Saint-Eustache, which can be seen from afar, above the giant shed of a covered street of les Halles. He came back to it again and again, wanting to find a symbol there.

"It is a curious juxtaposition," he said, "this fragment of the church framed by this avenue of cast iron . . . *Ceci tuera cela*, iron will kill stone and the time is near . . . Do you believe it is a coincidence, you, Florent? I think that the necessity of the alignment did not alone put the rose window of Saint-Eustache in the very middle of les Halles centrales. See, everything there is obvious: it is modern art, realism, naturalism, whatever you wish to call it, which has grown up in the face of ancient art . . . Isn't this your view of the matter?"

Florent remained silent, as he continued:

"This church, moreover, is of a bastard architecture; the Middle Ages agonized there, and the Renaissance stammered there . . . have you noticed some of the churches that we have built today? They resemble anything that one wants . . . libraries, observatories, pigeon houses, casernes; but surely people are not convinced that the Almighty lives inside them. The masons of Almighty God are dead, simple prudence will no longer build these ugly carcasses of stone in which we have no one living. . . . Since the beginning of the century, we have built only one original monument, a monument that did not copy any part, which shot up naturally in the sun of the epoch; and this is les Halles centrales, are you listening, Florent, a bold work, go on, and which is only again a timid revelation of the twentieth century. . . . This is why Saint-Eustache is done for, but of course! Saint-Eustache is over there with its rose window, devoid of its pious people, while les Halles stretching itself out next to it is bustling with life. . . . That is what I see, my man!"

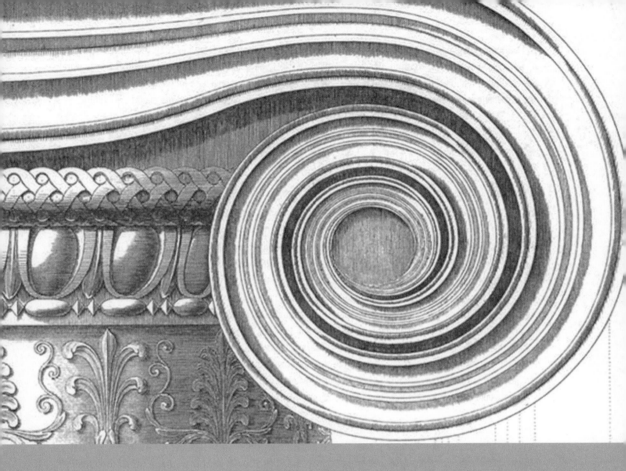

C.   TECTONICS AND STYLE IN GERMANY

Introduction

What France was losing in architectural influence in the second half of the nineteenth century, Germany was in large part gaining. But here too the process was not an easy one. In the 1840s Germany was still a country divided, and the efforts of 1848–9 to unify the country under a national constitution had disastrous social consequences when the titular national crown was rejected by the Prussian monarch, leading to political insurrection. With the defeat of the republican forces, many of Germany's leading intellectuals and artists either went into exile (escaping arrest) or willingly emigrated to such other countries as the United States and Canada. The competing camps of the *Rundbogen* architects, the Gothic movement, and the classicists were joined in the 1840s by a Renaissance movement, paralleling the situation in both France and Britain. In the 1860s Prussia began to exert its growing economic and political might: first by destroying the Habsburg armies and their pan-Germanic intentions in the summer of 1866, and second by marching into France in 1870. The formal unification of Germany was declared from an occupied Versailles in 1871, an event announcing the arrival of a new world power. What is not to be overlooked during these years is that a very substantial base for modern architectural theory was also being laid in Germany, a theoretical basis that would begin to blossom toward the end of the century.

217   KARL VON SCHNAASE
from *Dutch Letters* (1834)

These few lines, drawn from a larger study, have an especial importance to German thought. They define the first — and quite precocious — attempt to analyze architecture through its spatial (hence perceptual) relationships. Hegel in his lectures, as we saw earlier (see chapter 160 above), made an allusion to the spatiality of Gothic architecture. Schnaase, quite independently, approaches the matter from a slightly different but crucial perspective. He sees medieval architecture as the continuous development of the spatial interior, which he deems to be its creative answer to the exterior conception (building as object) of antique architecture. In reflecting here on the spatial play of the side aisles of the Antwerp Cathedral with its central nave, he not only sees a spatial understanding as the most important factor in the structural evolution of medieval architecture but also becomes the first historian to consider architecture as a spatial art. This passage is thus the base on which numerous psychologies of space would be built in German theory in the second half of the century.

Only through this [the cross-vault] does what was suggested in the relationship of piers become fully realized. Here it is clearly seen that the space between the piers includes particular surfaces; that spiritual movement that we found in the perception of surfaces is here represented corporeally. For the shafts that spring from the piers and meet in the keystone of the vaults also define the sightlines of the whole as well as of the individual surfaces that are concentrated between them. And as this movement contained in the floor plan is represented in the vaulting, both visibly unite with each other; the whole itself is recognized in the bounded bodies. But because the individual corresponding surfaces of the floor plan and of the vaults are joined and the whole is only formed through them, we do not perceive them in a quiet state of completion; they are only seen in a constant process of forming individual and independent parts and making their transition into the whole. In fact we are thereby transposed into the interior, where not only the more complete form but the forming force itself, in its living creativity, becomes visible. The soul of this life, however, is the cross-vault. For while its shafts always cut themselves off from the side walls in striving toward the middle, and are joined there in the peak of a triangle, they unite the two sides in the middle lines indicated by the keystones. And as the points of these lines arising individually and forming the peaks of the triangle also allude to the sections of the side walls (as their basic lines), they seem, so to speak, to spring forth from the side lines and to dissolve themselves in them. Thus from the interior arises a continual state of [spatial]

Karl von Schnaase (1798–1875), from *Niederländische Briefe* [Dutch letters]. Stuttgart: J. G. Cotta, 1834, pp. 199–201, trans. Harry Francis Mallgrave.

transition, from ideals to real boundaries, and a return from this to that – a pulsating organic life.

The living principle therefore resides not in the relations of the whole, but in the individual spaces that, in repeating themselves, are produced there. From this there follows another remarkable distinction between the antique and Christian architecture. In the former the relations of breadth and depth of the whole are more or less fixed, and they determine the character of the building. But the Gothic church, while also displaying these relations to a certain extent, has no such inner necessity; it is, in essence, only a consequence of the natural limits of human imagination and therefore retains a raw indeterminacy. In many cases we can enlarge the depth by adding a cross-vault without altering the character of the building. The latter is rather determined by the individual parts, and the relationships that take place through them. Therefore that between the width of the piers and the interval between them is, so to speak, the mother of all other relations. This relation is therefore also rather fixed and usually does not change, except in individual buildings in unusual cases where the building's function demands something uncommon. On a larger scale, however, it varies with whole nations according to their spiritual distinctiveness.

218   KARL BÖTTICHER
from *Greek Tectonics* (1843)

The address of 1846 from which we cited passages earlier (chapter 169 above) was written within the context of the German style debate of the 1840s. But Bötticher had earlier begun to devise a theoretical model that would have great significance for German architectural theory in the second half of the century. It was apparently during the late 1830s that Bötticher – on the advice of Schinkel – began to explore the ornamental forms of Greek architecture with regard to their symbolic meaning, specifically the development of the Greek tectonic language. His thesis was that every detail of a Greek temple (including the curvature of its profiles and moldings) not only had a specific working function to satisfy but also a higher symbolic function – its *art-form* – to idealize. The curvature of the echinus of a Doric capital, for instance, might be inclined more vertically or horizontally to reflect the architect's wish to accentuate or mitigate the structural load to be transmitted into the column. Ornamental forms painted on the echinus might also have arisen out of similar sensibilities relating to weight. His distinction between a "core-form" (also work-form; abstractly, the actual structural work to be performed) and the "art-form" (its symbolic or artistic representation) became a cornerstone of German tectonic theory, and gave rise to an abundance of theorizing on the application of these concepts to new materials and technologies.

The principle of Greek tectonics is demonstrably fully identical with the principle of creative nature: the *concept* of each creation corresponds to its form. From this single principle arises a *law* of form, which far transcends the individual *arbitrariness* of the working individual. It

Karl Bötticher, from Preface to *Die Tektonik der Hellenen* [Greek Tectonics] (1843), trans. Harry Francis Mallgrave from 1852 edition published in Potsdam by Ferdinand Riegel, pp. xiv–xvi.

encompasses within its totality the only true and highest freedom and is an inexhaustible source for invention. We take this principle to be true in large religious *monuments*, yet it also extends itself to the smallest implement or the least significant utensil that serves a domestic chore. Therefore even in the *latter* sphere, in which is preserved an inexhaustible richness of the most charming ideas of noble customs and refined living needs, we must necessarily include the sacred practices and real uses for the completion of the range of ideas.

The Greek building in its design and construction shows itself in every respect to be an *ideal* organism *articulated* for the production of the *spatial need* in an *artistic* way. This space-serving organism, from the whole to the smallest of its members (*membra*), is an imagined creation; it is an invention of the human mind and has no model in nature from which it could have been designed. Every *one* of its members proceeds only from the *whole*; for this reason, each part is an *imperative* and *necessary* part, an *integrating* element of the whole, which conveys and transfers its *special* function and place to the *whole*. From such a conception, the working hand of the architect [*Tektonen*] fashions each member into a bodily *scheme*, which for the cultivation of spatiality *most perfectly* fulfills each member's *unique* function and its structural *interaction* with all *other* members. As one endows a form with an appropriate material, and indeed the form of an *architectural* member, as one arranges all of these members into a self-sufficient mechanism, the material's inherent life, which in a *formless* condition is *resting* and *latent*, is resolved into a dynamic expression. It is compelled into a *structural function*. It now gains a higher existence and is bestowed with an *ideal* being, because it functions as a member of an *ideal* organism.

The realization of the concept of each member can be considered through two elements: through the *core-form* [*Kernform*] and through the *art-form* [*Kunstform*]. The core-form of each member is the *mechanical* and *necessary* component, the *structurally* functioning scheme. The art-form, by contrast, is only the functionally *clarifying characteristic*. Yet this characteristic represents not only the *unique* nature of each member but also its relationship to *adjacent* members. It also encompasses the *juncture* of the parts working with it. And just as mechanically all members are joined into a static unity, so also are the *juncturing symbols* of all members *figuratively* bound into a uniquely inseparable organism. Thus this clarifying characteristic is, so to speak, only an outer covering (*Hülle*) of the member, its symbolic attribution – *decoratio*, χόσμοσ. It arises simultaneously with it or at the movement that the member's mechanical structure is conceived. They both have the *same* idea and both are born together. Only with *its* appearance does the concept of each member become *evident*; its dead material contains the remnants of an organic *animation*, a structural *working-together* in a condition of the most permanent rest and unchangeableness. In fact, every material gains meaning only when it appears through an impression of an image-form, as something *marked with a spirit*, something *animated by ideas*. In truth we must confess that the representation of this invisible, inner-working activity is *polyhymnic* mimicry; mute and rigid, it betrays its idea and concept only through a characteristic sign.

For in the end it is sculpturally possible to reveal these symbols – even the grandest of symbolic concepts – in a corporeal scale. The function of each individual member stands up to the structural interplay and organic relation of all *reciprocal* and *measurable* forces personified to the eye; the architectural concept has become proportionally measurable.

219 EDUARD VAN DER NÜLL

from "Suggestions on the Skillful Relation of Ornament to Untreated Form" (1845)

One of the characteristics of Germanic theory throughout the nineteenth century — again harking back to its philosophical foundation — is the emphasis it places on construction and materials, what is generally referred to today as tectonics. This essay by the Viennese architect Eduard van der Nüll is an instructive case in point. He was trained at both the Vienna Polytechnical Institute and the Academy of Fine Arts. Winning the gold medal jointly with August Siccard von Siccardsburg, van de Nüll traveled with his later partner to Italy, France, England, and Germany before returning home in 1844. There he was appointed a professor of ornament at the Academy of Fine Arts, the leading architectural school of the Habsburg Empire. This essay and its title was thus intended as a synopsis of his teaching principles, which makes his emphasis on construction all the more startling for one teaching the nuances of ornamentation. This essay — by more than a half-century — presages the constructional emphasis of van der Nüll's later student, Otto Wagner. Van der Nüll and Siccardsburg would go on to win the competition for the famed Vienna Opera, but the former committed suicide in the spring of 1868 after the nearly completed work was subject to some unfavorable reviews.

We have underscored three demands in this essay, upon which is based the artistic completion of a work of architecture:

1) the logical treatment of the material with which we have to create;

2) the professional education that allows rational construction;

3) the gift to denote precisely the still untreated form called forth by reason, and to ennoble it with a sense of beauty.

These three conditions, internally keen in themselves, create the whole that becomes perfected according to its possibility.

If a work of architecture is to point to the future as a monument of our time, reason in the choice of the material will be the best way of fulfilling this purpose, and feeling will be called upon to achieve the expression of solidity in the form. This more precise determination of the purpose of a building (not this or that style of an earlier epoch) conditions the choice of construction. We will strive to make purposeful construction as visible as possible, to avoid the fine and the lean, to favor the worthy and the commanding, and to strive to show already in the untreated form the effective reasons for the constructional parts. The additional ennoblement of form can only further intensify the pleasure of the viewer, which is why we suggest that the purpose be very precisely denoted by the ornamental treatment.

Eduard van der Nüll (1812–68), from "Andeutungen über die kunstgemässe Beziehung des Ornamentes zur rohen Form" [Suggestions on the skillful relation of ornament to untreated form], Österreichische Blätter für Literatur und Kunst (1845), trans. Harry Francis Mallgrave from Gustav Peichl (ed.), Die Kunst des Otto Wagner, Vienna: Akademie der bildenden Künste, 1984, pp 33–4.

The material and the purpose of the building – both condition and distinguish its characteristics. We noted earlier that a complete break from antiquity will only lead us down the path of errors. We should master profiling, the divisioning of the ornamental order, and many other things, but new methods of construction will also always produce new characters. Only in this way, we believe, can the totality of younger talents band together more closely and unify, until in the end, after many centuries, the characteristics of new ways of construction will be ennobled by art. It will inspire later generations to advance along this path, and thus we will achieve a truly original and national architectural style.

220 HEINRICH LEIBNITZ
from *The Structural Element in Architecture* (1849)

Bötticher's effort to probe systematically the structural and decorative system of the Greek temple found many followers in the nineteenth century. What Bötticher had supplied was essentially an analytical paradigm (work-form/art-form) that could be applied to other styles or periods. In this little-known book of 1849, the historian Heinrich Leibnitz accepts Bötticher's model and attempts to advance it with his consideration of the history of structural development. What Leibnitz is striving for is a way out of historicism. After defining architecture through the work-form/art-form model (see below), he embarks on a survey of the principal innovations in structural development – beginning with caves and dolmens – and concludes with the thesis that iron can never be a formative material in architecture because it "contradicts static feeling and destroys the mass." In essence he, like so many others of his generation, was working on the assumption that architectural repose necessarily relies on mass and its (art-form) ornament, and that any structural system that contradicts or negates its artistic presentation would never find acceptance. What cannot be overlooked here, however, is the *abstract* nature of Leibniz's scheme. Building upon such a model, it would fall to the next generation of architects and theorists to imagine alternative psychologies of form that would have less concern for the traditional historical styles.

It has long been recognized that *architecture* forms a moment in the cultural history of a people that is particularly suited to portray all exterior as well as spiritual relations of a people, and provide a sure insight into a people's inner nature and ethical viewpoint.

Within the areas of artistic investigation, the study of architecture's historical monuments therefore forms a richly cultivated field, and exhaustive scholarship as well as refined artistic sensitivity has here unearthed treasures of which our present architecture has not failed to make use. Two great epochs, ushered in and linked by intermediate periods, present us

Heinrich Leibnitz, from *Die struktive Element in der Architektur und sein Verhältniss zur Kunstform* [The structural element in architecture and its relation to the art-form]. Tübingen: Ludwig Friedrich Fues, 1849, pp. 3–4, 5–7, trans. Harry Francis Mallgrave.

today with a series of styles that have poured forth the wealth of their overpowering forms. Their partisans stand opposed to one another in isolated camps and – based on the principle of their viewpoint – seek to demonstrate the superiority of one or another art-form as well as its application to present architecture. But until now the results have not been positive. This condition of vacillation is very evident in today's architecture. Whereas here we encounter the massively articulated and squat building forms of Greek antiquity, and over there soar the colossal masses of the Gothic period with their myriad divisions and ornamental richness, we also find a large number of other buildings decked out with the manifold forms of those intermediate periods, unfortunately often in an unharmonious and false way. We are reminded of the bawdy wife who adorns her plump body with the noble relics of stolen jewelry.

Yet what is the cause of this incessant, urgent movement, this unbridled striving after new forms from the past? [. . .]

★ ★ ★

The aim of this treatise is thus to review the principal architectural moments through the course of their historical development and in this way compare that higher moral meaning of a building, while keeping in view the *structural* element as the *core-form*. But in order to denote the viewpoint to which we will unswervingly adhere in this study, let us propose the following general principle:

We understand *architecture* to be that building activity capable of imprinting the stamp of spiritual-moral (ethical) meaning on mechanically assembled works arising from naked need, therefore raising the materially necessary form into an *art-form*.

Architecture, in its tasks, certainly first proceeds from mechanical necessities. It will assemble its forms according to the nature of the material and indeed following the laws of rational combination for a spatial mechanism. For unlike sculpture and painting, it is not an imitative art; it finds in nature no immediate model. It is rather an *abstraction*.

As it thus employs raw material for a three-dimensional creation and gives each individual part in a building a specific function and activity in relation to all others, it also forces them to express the life latent and concealed in the formless material and in the mechanical development of forces and structural activity. Thus it forms a whole that proceeds from spiritual or physical needs, and accordingly is conceived and assembled, and makes evident also its *mechanical* nature in the whole as well as in the individual parts.

Still, this form will not yet be an *art-form*.

Form is indeed a mechanical abstraction conditioned by structural laws, similar to how the parts of a machine perfectly fulfill the function for which they are created. But form will always be rigidly constrained as long as it lacks an exterior character habitus – the characteristic – that can now elevate this *mechanism* into a living and significant *organism* denoting its inner essence. This moment will only take place when this mechanical *core-form* is endowed with a plastic *art-form* – similar to a transparent veil. While such a veil will certainly approach the perceived objects of nature and the exterior world (for instance, plants), its form and essence are analogous to the concept of the relevant building member, and thus it is capable of representing spiritually the mechanical function, which it also performs on a physical level.

This characterizing element will be the creation of form or *ornament* in architecture. Its purpose does not reside in the structural functioning of a building, but rather in articulating symbolically the function of the core-form, in precisely displaying all its relations, and thus in endowing the work with that independent life and that ethical sanction through which it can alone be raised into a work of art.

221 GOTTFRIED SEMPER
from *The Four Elements of Architecture* (1851)

The earlier selections from the Semper essay on polychromy (see chapters 134 and 138 above) represented the architect at the very beginning of his career. By 1851 Semper's situation had transformed itself in every which way. In 1834, in part due to his essay on polychromy, he was appointed a professor of architecture at the Dresden Academy of Fine Art. Shortly thereafter he launched a very successful architectural career, beginning with his much-applauded design for the Dresden Royal Theater (1835–41). His happy situation, however, changed dramatically with the political events of 1848–9, as the various Germanic states struggled with the issue of unification and a constitutional form of government. In May 1849 Semper, who supported national unity, was caught up in the so-called Dresden Uprising, which resulted in his political exile from Germany.

Of necessity he turned to theory. In 1851 he published the first synopsis of his ideas, which he entitled *The Four Elements of Architecture*. Much of the text deals with his earlier ideas on polychromy and constitutes his response to the earlier criticisms of the art historian Franz Kugler. But in the fifth chapter of the book Semper lays out two parts of his later theory, which views the history of architecture as a process of symbolic and formal development. The first is the notion that architecture derives its essential forms from four primordial or original motives found in the technical arts of ceramics, roofing (carpentry), mounding (terracing and masonry), and weaving (walling). The second notion is his so-called *Bekleidung* or "dressing" thesis. This archaeological and spatial theme suggests that the textile motive for the wall underwent an intricate process of formal development, as the conceptual rudiments of weaving evolved into textile wall hangings and later into solid wall dressings (paneling and paint) that emulated in style their original textile origin. This line of reasoning would become the start of a very elaborate theory that Semper would ultimately devise and publish in his two volumes entitled *Style*.

The first sign of human settlement and rest after the hunt, the battle, and wandering in the desert is today, as when the first men lost paradise, the setting up of the fireplace and the lighting of the reviving, warming, and food-preparing flame. Around the hearth the first groups assembled; around it the first alliances formed; around it the first rude religious concepts were put into the customs of a cult. Throughout all phases of society the hearth formed that sacred focus around which the whole took order and shape.

Gottfried Semper, from *Die Vier Elemente der Baukunst* (1851), trans. Wolfgang Herrmann and Harry Francis Mallgrave, in *Gottfried Semper: The Four Elements of Architecture and Other Writings*. Cambridge: Cambridge University Press, 1989, pp. 102–6. © 1989 by Cambridge University Press. Reprinted with permission of Cambridge University Press.

It is the first and most important, the *moral* element of architecture. Around it were grouped the three other elements: the *roof*, the *enclosure*, and the *mound*,[1] the protecting negations or defenders of the hearth's flame against the three hostile elements of nature.

According to how different human societies developed under the varied influences of climate, natural surroundings, social relations, and different racial dispositions, the combinations in which the four elements of architecture were arranged also had to change, with some elements becoming more developed while others receded into the background. At the same time the different technical skills of man became organized according to these elements: *ceramics* and afterwards metal works around the *hearth, water* and *masonry works* around the *mound, carpentry* around the *roof* and its accessories.

But what primitive technique evolved from the *enclosure?* None other than the art of the *wall fitter* (*Wandbereiter*), that is, the weaver of mats and carpets. This statement may appear strange and requires an explanation.

It was mentioned previously that there are writers who devote much time to searching for the origin of art and who believe they can deduce from it all the different ways of building. The nomadic tent plays a rather important role in their arguments. Yet while with great acumen they detect in the catenary curve of the tent the norm of the Tartar–Chinese way of building (although the same shapes occur in the caps and shoes of these people), they overlook the more general and less dubious influence that the carpet in its capacity as a *wall*, as a vertical means of protection, had on the evolution of certain architectural forms. Thus I seem to stand without the support of a single authority when I assert that the carpet wall plays a most important role in the general history of art.

It is well known that even now tribes in an early stage of their development apply their budding artistic instinct to the braiding and weaving of mats and covers (even when they still go around completely naked). The wildest tribes are familiar with the hedge-fence – the crudest wickerwork and the most primitive pen or spatial enclosure made from tree branches. Only the potter's art can with some justification *perhaps* claim to be as ancient as the craft of carpet weaving.

The weaving of branches led easily to weaving bast into mats and covers and then to weaving with plant fiber and so forth. The oldest ornaments either derived from entwining or knotting materials or were easily produced on the potter's wheel with the finger on the soft clay. The use of wickerwork for setting apart one's property, the use of mats and carpets for floor coverings and protection against heat and cold and for subdividing the spaces within a dwelling in most cases preceded by far the masonry wall, and particularly in areas favored by climate. The masonry wall was an intrusion into the domain of the wall fitter by the mason's art, which had evolved from building terraces according to very different conditions of style.

Wickerwork, the original space divider, retained the full importance of its earlier meaning, actually or ideally, when later the light mat walls were transformed into clay tile, brick, or stone walls. Wickerwork was the *essence of the wall.*[2]

Hanging carpets remained the true walls, the visible boundaries of space. The often solid walls behind them were necessary for reasons that had nothing to do with the creation of space; they were needed for security, for supporting a load, for their permanence, and so on. Wherever the need for these secondary functions did not arise, the carpets remained the original means of separating space. Even where building solid walls became necessary, the latter were only the inner, invisible structure hidden behind the true and legitimate representatives of the wall, the colorful woven carpets.

The wall retained this meaning when materials other than the original were used, either for reason of greater durability, better preservation of the inner wall, economy, the display of greater magnificence, or for any other reason. The inventive mind of man produced many such substitutes, and all branches of the technical arts were successively enlisted.

The most widely used and perhaps the oldest substitute was offered by the mason's art, the stucco covering or bitumen plaster in other countries. The woodworkers made panels (πίναχες) with which to fit the walls, especially the lower parts. Workers handling fire supplied glazed terra cotta[3] and metal plates. As the last substitute perhaps can be counted the panels of standstone, granite, alabaster, and marble that we find in widespread use in Assyria, Persia, Egypt, and even in Greece.

For a long time the character of the copy followed that of the prototype. The artists who created the painted and sculptured decorations on wood, stucco, fired clay, metal, or stone traditionally though not consciously imitated the colorful embroideries and trellis works of the age-old carpet walls.

The whole system of Oriental polychromy – closely connected and to a certain extent one with the ancient arts of paneling and dressing – and therefore also the art of painting and bas-relief arose from the looms and vats of the industrious Assyrians,[4] or from the inventions of prehistoric people who preceded them. In any case, the Assyrians should be considered the most faithful guardians of this primordial motive.

In the oldest annals of mankind Assyrian carpets were famed for their splendid colors and the skill with which fantastic pictures were woven into them. Written descriptions of mystical animals, dragons, lions, tigers, and so forth agree fully with the images we see today on the walls of Nineveh. If such a comparison were still possible, we would recognize a perfect accord not only in the objects depicted but also in the manner of treatment.

Assyrian sculpture clearly kept within limits imposed by its origin, even though the new material permitted a new means of raising the figures from the background. A struggle toward naturalism is evident, whose limits were set not by hierarchical power, but (apart from the despotic rules of a ceremonial court) by the accidental features of a technique foreign to sculpture yet still responsive to the echoes from the past. The postures of the figures are stiff but not so rigid as to have become mere characters; they only look as though they were chained. Within a composition they are already, or rather, are *still* pictorial adaptations of a celebrated historical act or a court ceremony, not like the Egyptian images, which are simply a means to record a fact and are really a painted chronicle. Even in their arrangement, for instance, in their adherence to equal head heights, the Assyrian figures are more distinguished than Egyptian images. Sharp, threadlike contours, the hard shapes of the muscles, a predilection for ornamental accessories and embroidery are indicative of their origin; there is exaggeration, but not a lifeless style. The faces do not show the slightest trace of an artistic effort to render the inner state of the soul; they are, even with their constant smiles, without any individual expression. In this respect they are less advanced than Egyptian sculpture and resemble more the early works of the Greeks.

In actual wall murals the same technique is evident. According to Layard, the wall paintings at Nimrud are surrounded and interwoven with strong black contours; the ground is blue or yellow. The friezelike borders of the pictures that contain inscriptions also indicate their technical affinity with carpets. The character of the cuneiform corresponds fully with this technique. Would it be possible to invent for needlework a more convenient way of writing?

Alongside these substitutes for the earlier carpets, the latter were still widely used as door curtains, window curtains, and so forth, as can be seen by the richly decorated rings with which they were secured. The simple inlaying of the wooden floors is a sign that they, too, were covered with carpets. Carpets were also the models for the art of mosaic, which remained for the longest time true to its origin.

The interior walls above the gypsum panels were lined with a lightly burned, glazed, or, as one might say, lacquered brick. They were glazed only on one side and covered with painted ornaments that were totally inconsistent with the shape of the stone, but that crossed over it in every direction. Other evidence shows that the stones were in a horizontal position when they were glazed. They were, therefore, first arranged horizontally, then ornamented and glazed, and finally attached to the sun-dried brick wall in proper order as a dressing (*Bekleidung*). This also proves that the glaze was a general covering and its idea was independent of the material to which it was applied. A late-Roman or Medieval use of colored stones for patterning a wall had not been conceived in these earliest periods of art.

NOTES

1   At first glance the mound or the terrace appears as secondary and as necessary only in the lowlands, where solid dwellings had already been erected; yet the mound joined at once with the hearth and was soon needed to raise it off the ground. Allied with the building of a pit, it may have also served as support for the earliest roofs. Moreover, it is probable that man, not as an individual but certainly as a social being, arose from the plains as the last mud-creation, so to speak. The legends from times immemorial of all nations, which often conceal an idea of natural philosophy, agree on this point.

2   The German word *Wand* [wall], *paries*, acknowledges its origin. The terms *Wand* and *Gewand* [dress] derive from a single root. They indicate the woven material that formed the wall.

3   It is highly probable that the wish to give tiles a colored glazing first led to the discovery of burnt bricks. The glazed tiles from Nineveh that I had the opportunity to examine closely in Paris are in an almost unburnt state. Their glaze must have been extraordinarily fusible. Terra cotta dressings are the forerunners to brick walls, and stone plaques the forerunners to ashlar.

4   It is remarkable that most of the colors on the Assyrian alabaster panels of Khorsabad and Nimrud have disappeared, while it is evident that they must have existed to complete the remnants still surviving. In contrast to Egyptian and Greek paintings, the surviving traces are not thickly applied but appear as if stained into the surface; it is probable that the colors were composed mainly of vegetable matter.

222 GOTTFRIED SEMPER
from *Science, Industry, and Art* (1852)

I n December 1850, while living in exile in London, Semper was introduced to Henry Cole. The meeting was significant because Cole, as we have seen, was in the process of planning the Great London Exhibition of 1851. Cole became aware of Semper's status as a political refugee and his desperate financial plight, and he put the architect's name on a list of designers who might assist the foreign nations in displaying their wares at the exhibition. In the spring of 1851 Semper thus prepared the displays of Turkey, Canada, Sweden, and Denmark, and in the process had ample opportunity to examine the enormous range of goods shown at the exhibition. The result was this critique of the event, which he wrote in the fall of 1851, around the time of the exhibition's closing. While many critics of the exhibition were quick to point out the artistic failings of the event, Semper's essay differs from most others in that he attributes these failings not so much to poor taste or to the problem of historicism, but rather to the changed technical conditions – new materials and techniques – of the industrial age. These conditions, in his view, had fundamentally altered the ground of art and were in fact in the process of destroying art in the traditional sense. This process of disintegration was not necessarily a good or bad thing; it was simply an inevitability that would eventually create a new, nonhistorical art. Semper here also presents a new definition of style – not a historical language of forms but a qualitative standard of design.

How long did the inventor of oil painting toil with an old process that no longer satisfied certain purposes before he discovered his new process? Bernard Palissy searched half his life for an opaque enamel for his faience before he finally found what he sought. These men knew how to use the invention because they needed it, and because they needed it they searched and found it. In this way, gradual progress in science went hand in hand with the mastery and the awareness of how and to what end the invention could be applied.

Necessity was the mother of science. Developing empirically and with youthful spontaneity, science soon drew confident deductions on the unknown from the narrow field of acquired knowledge, doubting nothing and creating its world from hypotheses. Later it felt confined by its dependence on application and became an object in itself. It entered the field of doubt and analysis. A craze for classification and nomenclature superceded the ingenious or fanciful systems.

In the end genius reconquered the vast amount of material collected by research and purely objective investigation was forced to submit to hypothetical inference and to become the latter's servant in the procurement of further factual evidence derived from analogies.

Philosophy, history, politics, and a few higher branches of the natural sciences were raised to this comparative viewpoint by the great men of the past two centuries, while in the other sciences, because of the abundance and complexity of their material, inferences

Gottfried Semper, from *Wissenschaft, Industrie und Kunst: Vorschläge zur Anregung nationalen Kunstgefühles* [Science, industry, and art: proposals for the development of national taste in art] (1852), pp. 133–6, 142–4. © 1989 by Cambridge University Press. Reprinted with permission of Cambridge University Press.

only timidly begin to join with research. Searching every day more judiciously, research makes astonishing discoveries. Chemistry, in joining with physics and calculus, dares to defend the boldest hypotheses of the Greeks and the long-pitied broodings of the alchemists. Science at the same time inclines decidedly toward the practical and at present stands exalted as its guardian. Every day it enriches our life with newly discovered materials and miraculous natural forces, with new methods of technology, with new tools and machines.

It is already evident that inventions are no longer, as before, a means for averting privation and for enjoyment. On the contrary, privation and enjoyment create the market for the inventions. The order of things has been reversed.

What is the inevitable result of this? The present has no time to become familiar with the half-imposed benefits and to master them. The situation resembles that of the Chinese, who should eat with a knife and fork. Speculation interposes itself there and lays out the benefits attractively before us; where there is none, speculation creates a thousand small and large advantages. Old, outdated comforts are called back into use when speculation cannot think of anything new. It effortlessly accomplishes the most difficult and troublesome things with means borrowed from science. The hardest porphyry and granite are cut like chalk and polished like wax. Ivory is softened and pressed into forms. Rubber and gutta-percha are vulcanized and utilized in a thousand imitations of wood, metal, and stone carvings, exceeding by far the natural limitations of the material they purport to represent. Metal is no longer cast or wrought, but treated with the newest unknown forces of nature in a galvano-plastic way. The talbotype succeeds the daguerreotype and makes the latter already a thing forgotten. Machines sew, knit, embroider, paint, carve, and encroach deeply into the field of human art, putting to shame every human skill.

Are these not great and glorious achievements? By no means do I deplore the general conditions of which these are only the less important symptoms. On the contrary, I am confident that sooner or later everything will develop favorably for the well-being and honor of society. For now I refrain from proceeding to those larger and more difficult questions suggested by them. In the following pages I only wish to point out the confusion they now cause in those fields in which the talents of man take an active part in the recognition and presentation of beauty.

II

If single incidents carried the force of conviction, then the recognized triumphs at the Exhibition of the half-barbaric nations, especially the Indians with their magnificent industries of art, would be sufficient to show us that we with our science have until now accomplished very little in these areas.

The same, shameful truth confronts us when we compare our products with those of our ancestors. Notwithstanding our many technical advances, we remain far behind them in formal beauty, and even in a feeling for the suitable and the appropriate. Our best things are more or less faithful reminiscences. Others show a praiseworthy effort to borrow forms directly from nature, yet how seldom we have been successful in this! Most of our attempts are a confused muddle of forms or childish triflings. At best, objects whose seriousness of purpose does not permit the superfluous, such as wagons, weapons, musical instruments, and similar things, we sometimes make appear healthier by the refined presentation of their strictly prescribed forms.

Although facts, as we said, are no argument and can even be disputed, it is easy to prove that present conditions are dangerous for the industrial arts, decidedly fatal for the traditional higher arts.

The *abundance of means* is the first great danger with which art has to struggle. This expression is illogical, I admit (there is no abundance of means but only an inability to master them); however, it is justified in that it correctly describes the inverted state of our conditions.

Practice wearies itself in vain in trying to master its material, especially intellectually. It receives it from science ready to process as it chooses, but before its style could have evolved through many centuries of popular usage. The founders of a flourishing art once had their material kneaded beforehand, as it were, by the beelike instinct of the people; they invested the indigenous motive with a higher meaning and treated it artistically, stamping their creations with a rigorous necessity and spiritual freedom. These works became universally understood expressions of a true idea that will survive historically as long as any trace or knowledge of them remains.

What a glorious discovery is the gaslight! How its brilliance enhances our festivities, not to mention its enormous importance to everyday life! Yet in imitating candles or oil lamps in our salons, we hide the apertures of the gas pipes; in illumination, on the other hand, we pierce the pipes with innumerable small openings, so that all sorts of stars, firewheels, pyramids, escutcheons, inscriptions, and so on seem to float before the walls of our houses, as if supported by invisible hands.

This floating stillness of the most lively of all elements is effective to be sure (the sun, moon, and stars provide the most dazzling examples of it), but who can deny that this innovation has detracted from the popular custom of *illuminating* houses as a sign the occupants participate in the public joy? Formerly, oil lamps were placed on the cornice ledges and window sills, thereby lending a radiant prominence to the familiar masses and individual parts of the houses. Now our eyes are blinded by the blaze of those apparitions of fire and the facades behind are rendered invisible.

Whoever has witnessed the illuminations in London and remembers similar festivities in the old style in Rome will admit that the art of lighting has suffered a rude setback by these improvements.

This example demonstrates the two main dangers, the Scylla and Charybdis, between which we must steer to gain innovations for art.

The invention was excellent but it was sacrificed in the first case to traditional form, and in the second case its basic motive was completely obscured by its false application. Yet every means was available to make it more lustrous and to enrich it at the same time with a new idea (that of a fixed display of fireworks).

A clever helmsman, therefore, must be he who avoids these dangers, and his course is even more difficult because he finds himself in unknown waters without a chart or compass. For among the multitude of artistic and technical writings, there is sorely needed a practical guide to invention that maps out the cliffs and sandbars to be avoided and points out the right course to be taken. Were the theory of taste (aesthetics) a complete science, were its incompleteness not compounded by vague and often erroneous ideas in need of a clearer formulation especially in its application to architecture and tectonics in general, then it would fill just this void. Yet in its present state it is with justification scarcely considered by gifted professionals. Its tottering precepts and basic principles find approval only with so-called experts of art, who measure the value of a work thereby because they have no inner, subjective standards for art. They believe they have grasped beauty's secret with a dozen precepts, while the infinite variation in the world of form assumes characteristic meaning and individual beauty just by the denial of any scheme.

Among the notions that the theory of taste has taken pains to formulate, one of the most important is the idea of style in art. This term, as everyone knows, is one for which many interpretations have been offered, so many that skeptics have wanted to deny it any clear conceptual basis. Yet every artist and true connoisseur feels its whole meaning, however difficult it may be to express in words. Perhaps we can say:

> Style means giving emphasis and artistic significance to the basic idea and to all intrinsic and extrinsic coefficients that modify the embodiment of the theme in a work of art.

According to this definition, absence of style signifies the shortcomings of a work caused by the artist's disregard of the underlying theme, and his ineptitude in exploiting aesthetically the means available for perfecting the work.

Just as nature in her variety is yet simple and sparse in her motives, renewing continually the same forms by modifying them a thousandfold according to the graduated scale of development and the different conditions of existence, developing parts in different ways, shortening some and lengthening others – in the same way the technical arts are also based on certain prototypical forms (*Urformen*) conditioned by a primordial idea, which always reappear and yet allow infinite variations conditioned by more closely determining circumstances. [...]

* * *

III

I hear two objections being raised:

"That what has been said of the influence of science and speculation on the practice of art pertains only to a few countries, and the conditions that prevail with the originally hut-dwelling, backwoods Anglo-Saxons are not relevant to old Europe with her still living traditions of art. And supposing those conditions were to become widespread here, then true art would appear even more pure and sublime on *monumental buildings*, as with the Greeks who had almost no civil architecture."

Let us not delude ourselves! Those conditions most certainly are going to have a general validity for us, because they correspond to circumstances that prevail in all countries; and second, we are becoming aware only too painfully that high art especially is being fatally hit.

High art, too, has for some time being going into the marketplace, not to speak there with the people, but to be offered for sale.

Who was not seized with grief and sadness in strolling though the Lombard–Austrian market, which was crammed with lovely naked and veiled slave figures in marble? Did we not clearly see that they felt ashamed of the traits of their once high lineage? And they glanced around so seductively in their humiliation in search of a buyer! There were indeed no fewer than eight or ten chained male and female slaves in the Exhibition.

In contrast, in the great central gallery stout bodies put on a display of gymnastic, bending, equestrian, and all other possible exercises! Among them were some better reminiscences and lyric outpourings. A few were truly new in their self-contained motives, yet for most we ask: What was their actual relevance?

A work of art destined for the marketplace cannot have this relevance, far less than an industrial object can, for the latter's artistic relevance is supported at least by the use for which it is expected to have. The former, however, exists for itself alone, and is always distasteful when it betrays the purpose of pleasing or seducing a buyer.

Busts and portrait statues seem to be the soundest area of our plastic art, but whoever becomes better acquainted with the field also knows how perverted and foul is the situation here. To oblige idling artists we populate public squares with famous men. The arts must be protected! Yet a hero cult similar to the Greek exists neither with those who commission the works nor with the public. The people do not look at them any more as soon as a habit of noticing a place empty is replaced by another habit of seeing a pedestal there. If I am not mistaken, among the numerous statues of famous men of the past, present – and future that decorated the exhibition building, there were many that were made for sheer speculation. Nevertheless, the portrait statue remains perhaps the most important starting point for the improvement of art.

Painting was excluded from the Exhibition, or else the market would have appeared even more mottled. That what was said about sculpture also applies to painting needs no lengthy line of reasoning. Have not the art associations and art-exhibitor groups already set up and arranged for a fixed and permanent cycle of yearly fairs to market their paintings!

"Yet," I hear it said, "our monuments with their frescoes, painted glass, statues, pedimental fields, and friezes will always remain the hoard of true art!"

Yes, that would be true, if they were not borrowed or stolen! They do not belong to us. From the undigested elements out of which they are assembled nothing new has taken shape, nothing we can call our own. They have not become part of our own flesh and blood. Although they are presently being collected with great care, they have not yet been disintegrated sufficiently.

This process of disintegrating existing art types must be completed by industry, by speculation, and by applied science before something good and new can result.

223 JACOB BURCKHARDT
from *The Civilization of the Renaissance in Italy* (1860)

Throughout the first half of the nineteenth century, the battle of the styles across Europe had largely been a campaign between classicists and gothicists – with a third camp also forming in Germany around the *Rundbogen*. Beginning around mid-century a new stylistic force came into view: the culture of the Renaissance. It is true that a few architects (such as Henri Labrouste and Gottfried Semper) had pointed the way in the late 1830s with their use of Renaissance forms, but nevertheless this period was still held in little esteem by both critics and historians. Classicists decried the period as a second-coming of classicism, and therefore as something less original than antique culture. Gothicists disdained its secularization on the one hand, and the abuses of the papacy on the other. The person who would transform this image of the Renaissance in the German-speaking lands was the Swiss historian Jacob Burckhardt, who in 1860 published one of the great historical books of all time.

The Civilization of the Renaissance holds a seminal place within Western historiography as the first comprehensive cultural study of an era. Burckhardt's thesis is that the Renaissance was not simply a period of classical renewal, but was rather a time of profound social and personal transformation, in which "humanist" ideas for the first time gain their ascendancy in Western culture. Everything from the popularity of Roman ruins to witchcraft now fall under the historian's magnifying glass, as Burckhardt literally resurrects the nuances and mindset of an entire culture. This short excerpt speaks to the Renaissance "personality."

In the Middle Ages both sides of human consciousness – that which was turned within as that which was turned without – lay dreaming or half awake beneath a common veil. The veil was woven of faith, illusion, and childish prepossession, through which the world and history were seen clad in strange hues. Man was conscious of himself only as a member of a race, people, party, family, or corporation – only through some general category. In Italy this veil first melted into air; an *objective* treatment and consideration of the State and of all the things of this world became possible. The *subjective* side at the same time asserted itself with corresponding emphasis; man became a spiritual *individual*, and recognized himself as such. In the same way the Greek had once distinguished himself from the barbarian, and the Arab had felt himself an individual at a time when other Asiatics knew themselves only as members of a race. It will not be difficult to show that this result was due above all to the political circumstances of Italy.

In far earlier times we can here and there detect a development of free personality which in Northern Europe either did not occur at all, or could not display itself in the same manner. The band of audacious wrongdoers in the tenth century described to us by Liudprand, some of the contemporaries of Gregory VII (for example, Benzo of Alba), and a few of the opponents of the first Hohenstaufen, show us characters of this kind. But at the close of the thirteenth century Italy began to swarm with individuality; the ban laid upon human personality was dissolved; and a thousand figures meet us each in its own special

Jacob Burckhardt (1818–97), from *Die Kultur der Renaissance in Italien* [The civilization of the Renaissance in Italy] (1860), trans. 1878, first published in 1945 by Ludwig Goldscheider. Oxford: Phaidon Press, 1981 (facsimile edition), pp. 81–2.

shape and dress. Dante's great poem would have been impossible in any other country of Europe, if only for the reason that they all still lay under the spell of race. For Italy the august poet, through the wealth of individuality which he set forth, was the most national herald of his time. But this unfolding of the treasures of human nature in literature and art – this many-sided representation and criticism – will be discussed in separate chapters; here we have to deal only with the psychological fact itself. This fact appears in the most decisive and unmistakable form. The Italians of the fourteenth century knew little of false modesty or of hypocrisy in any shape; not one of them was afraid of singularity, of being and seeming[1] unlike his neighbours.

NOTE

1   By the year 1390 there was no longer any prevailing fashion of dress for men at Florence, each preferring to clothe himself in his own way.

224   JACOB BURCKHARDT
from *The History of the Italian Renaissance* (1867)

After completing his grand cultural study in 1860, Burckhardt resumed his earlier focus on the arts and contemplated writing a companion volume on Renaissance painting, sculpture, and architecture. Only the last project was completed and published. Not a survey – it is a different kind of work in that it dissects Renaissance architecture through its theory, building type, plan, spatial development, compositional elements and detailing, and decoration. This short excerpt on Poliphilus and the "spatial style" is important in two respects. First, it advances Schnaase's spatial analysis of architecture and expands the traditional notion of style as a formal language. Second, its distinction of the "spatial style" from the "organic styles" underscores the importance of new uses and complexity of plan in furthering architectural development. Learning the spatial lessons of Renaissance spatial design would, by implication, assist the nineteenth-century architect in designing for the new and more complex building types.

Meanwhile, neither theorists nor poets talk as clearly as we should like about the great transition which was taking place before their eyes and was partly brought about by them. Sometimes they are unaware of the state of events, sometimes these seem self-evident to them. Only later could the Renaissance be identified, in contrast to all earlier styles, as one of spatial and surface relationships.

Jacob Burckhardt, from *Die Geschichte der Renaissance in Italien* [The history of the Italian Renaissance] (1867), trans. James Palmes, *The Architecture of the Italian Renaissance*, ed. Peter Murray. Chicago: University of Chicago Press, 1985, p. 32.

The spatial style which the new era brought to architecture is in complete contrast to the organic styles; which does not prevent it from exploiting in its own way the forms produced by the latter.

The organic styles have always only one principal type: the Greek one the rectangular peripteral temple, the Gothic the many-aisled cathedral with Western towers. As soon as they are diverted to a different use, particularly one involving complex ground-plans, they are ready to be transformed into spatial styles. The Imperial Roman style is already close to this transition, developing a notable spatial beauty, which survives in differing degrees in the Byzantine, Romanesque, and Italian Gothic styles, but reaches its zenith in the Renaissance.

225 GOTTFRIED SEMPER
from *Style in the Technical and Tectonic Arts* (1860)

I n the years 1860–3, while now residing and teaching in Switzerland, Semper published the first two volumes of his work entitled *Style*. The lengthy study (the third volume of which was never completed) might be likened to Charles Darwin's near-contemporary book *The Origin of Species* (1859), in that Semper too – although entirely apart from the theoretical model of Darwin – attempted to write a history of architectural development based on a few elementary "motives." The book is also different in its underlying idealism. Semper vehemently rejected the idea that architectural design could be subject to certain laws (historical or evolutionary) and comes down decidedly on the side of the architect and his freedom in inventing new paths of development. The four motives are grouped into the classes of textiles, ceramics, tectonics (carpentry), and stereotomics (masonry).

Excerpts from three parts of the first volume (devoted solely to textiles) reveal three different aspects of his thought. The first passage forms the opening pages of his Prolegomena or philosophical prologue and discloses his broader intention to write an "empirical theory of art," in opposition to the abstract, speculative slant of German aesthetics.

The second passage, in which he overtly opposes the ideas of Bötticher, shows his method of analysis. His point is that the Greeks, in employing their painted surfaces, not only moved beyond the Asiatic principle of decorative incrustation but also idealized their forms in a way that denied their very materiality.

The third passage – containing his famous footnote on the "masking of reality" – carries his "dressing" thesis to its logical conclusion. The motive for monumental architecture is here traced back to the improvised scaffold or stage of the early Greek drama, and monumental motives for architecture, Semper believed, should still reside in this "haze of carnival candles." The "masking of reality" for Semper, at its highest level, is a double masking of the architectural work: a (symbolic) masking of the material and of its thematic content. It is an almost violent response to what he termed the materialists of his day, or to those who were striving to invent a new style solely from architecture's structural and material premises. Semper is essentially taking a last stand in defense of traditional

Gottfried Semper, from *Der Stil in den technischen und tektonischen Künsten* (1860), trans. Michael Robinson and Harry Francis Mallgrave in *Style in the Technical and Tectonic Arts, or Practical Aesthetics*. Los Angeles: Getty Publications Program, 2003, pp. 71–2, 378–9, 249–50. © 2003 by Getty Publications. Reprinted with permission of Getty Publications.

values in design, but his ideas nevertheless would still have a major impact. Like Viollet-le-Duc, his writings form one end of a bridge that, when complete, touches down in the early twentieth century.

The nocturnal sky shows glimmering nebulae among the splendid miracle of stars – either old extinct systems scattered throughout the universe, cosmic dust taking shape around a nucleus, or a condition in between destruction and regeneration.

They are a suitable analogy for similar events on the horizon of art history. They signify a world of art passing into the formless, while suggesting at the same time a new formation in the making.

These phenomena of artistic decline and the mysterious phoenixlike birth of new artistic life arising from the process of its destruction are all the more significant for us, because we are probably in the midst of a similar crisis – as far as we who are living through it (and therefore lacking a clear overview) are able to surmise and judge.

At the least, this view has many adherents, and in truth there is no lack of supporting evidence. The only thing that remains uncertain is whether these signs indicate a general decline arising from more profound social causes, or whether they suggest conditions that are otherwise healthy but that have temporarily caused confusion in those fields and human faculties concerned with discerning and representing beauty. Perhaps sooner or later they will lead to happier things in this sphere as well and work to the general good and honor of humanity.

The first hypothesis is bleak and unproductive because it denies artists who subscribe to it any support for their efforts. If the world of art were collapsing, Atlas himself would be too weak to hold it up; those who find pleasure in building do not want to restrict themselves to tearing down something rotten.

The second hypothesis, by contrast, is practical and productive – whether it is right or wrong.

As long as whoever embraces it guards against the presumption of seeing himself as the founder and savior of a future art, he will view his work more modestly as something in the process of becoming, or rather, as the *becoming of art* in general, and set for himself the following task: *to explore within individual cases the regularity and order that become apparent in artistic phenomena during the creative process of becoming and to deduce from that the general principles, the fundamentals of an empirical theory of art.*

Such an approach will provide no handbook for artistic practice, for it will not show *how to create* a particular art-form but rather how it *comes into being.* The work of art will be seen as a result of *all* the factors involved in its creation. Technique will therefore be a very important issue to consider, but only insofar as it affects the principle of art's creation. Nor will this approach merely produce a history of art. In passing through the field of history, it will not apprehend and explain the works of art of different periods and countries as facts but rather it will *expand upon them*, as it were, by identifying in each the necessarily different values of a function composed of many variables. It will do this primarily with the intention of revealing the inner law governing the world of the art-form, just as it governs the world of nature. For nature in its infinite abundance is nevertheless very sparing with its motifs; it constantly repeats its basic forms, modifying them a thousand times according to the formative stage reached by living beings and the various conditions of their existence. It shortens some elements and lengthens others, develops some elements fully, then merely alludes to them elsewhere. Nature has its own evolutionary history, within which old motifs are discernible in every new form. In just the same way, art is based on a few standard forms and types that derive from the most ancient traditions; they reappear constantly yet offer infinite variety, and like nature's types they have their own history. Nothing is arbitrary; everything is conditioned by circumstances and relations.

★ ★ ★

The Hellenic temple was *built* in accordance with the Egyptian principle but in a more developed way: as perfect isodomic masonry *outfitted* (ἀσκητόν) according to the Asiatic principle of incrustation, understood in the higher *structural-symbolic* sense. Through this combination the incrustation was freed of material service; it appeared only as a carrier of the formal idea, while at the same time emancipating the latter from the building material by hiding the joints in the stone. Thus form is explained only in terms of itself and by the organic idea contained within it, as happens with a living creature. We do not ask what material the creature is made of, even though the quality and quantity of materials are crucial conditions of existence and profoundly affect it.

Therefore the Greek architectural style did not draw a distinction between the "core schema" and "art schema," a distinction that unmistakably contains a slavish tendency to Egyptianization. Professor Bötticher – and let this be said with all regard for his learning, taste, and acumen – was inspired by Hermes Trismegistus, who was also the guiding spirit of Pythagoras when he wrote his exegesis on Hellenic temples.

The figure column (caryatid) was for Greece what the pier statue was for Egypt – namely, the expressive limit of the architectural principle of each country. The difference between them cannot be defined more succinctly or more comprehensibly than by comparing these two opposites!

The Hellenic principle obviously had to be based on formal traditions that favored masking the material construction. It could never have arisen without these traditions – for instance, on pure speculation – and these traditions were Asiatic!

It was merely a matter of transforming the forms of the Asiatic construction of the dressing that were based on mechanical necessity into dynamic, even organic, forms, a matter of endowing them with a soul. Anything that had no morphological purpose, anything that was foreign or opposed to the purely formal idea, had to be excluded or removed to a neutral ground. In reviewing what existed previously – and in animating it – the act of creation did not reside in inventing new types, which would have remained incomprehensible to the masses or had a chilling effect.

This new style had to avoid all *unnecessary* references to weight and inertia of masses, and so it banished the arch from the store of art-forms. It used the attributes of mass only to emphasize precisely the activity and life of the organic members. In short, it emancipated form from the material and from naked need.

As part of this trend the Hellenic architectural principle had to vindicate and nurture *color* as the subtlest and most incorporeal dressing. This was the most perfect means to dispose of reality, for while it dressed the material it was itself immaterial. It also corresponded in other regards to the freer tendencies of Hellenic art.

Polychromy replaced the barbarian dressing with precious metals, and incrustations with the precious stones, paneling, and other ornamental accessories with which Asiatic work was so extravagantly outfitted.

This is already clear from the contrast between barbarian and Hellenic art outlined above. It is fully confirmed by things we can still see on the remains of monuments, and not least by the reports of the ancients themselves.

★ ★ ★

For now I will merely point out that the outward reason for monumental undertakings has always been, and still is, the wish to commemorate and immortalize some religious or solemn act, an event in world history, or an act of state. There is nothing to keep us from assuming, from casting aside all doubt, that the first beginnings of a monumental art, which everywhere requires an existing, relatively high culture and even luxury, was in an analogous way suggested to its founders by similar *festive celebrations*. The festival apparatus – the improvised scaffold with all its splendor and frills that specifically marks the occasion for celebrating, enhances, decorates, and adorns the glorification of the feast, and is hung with tapestries, dressed with festoons and garlands, and decorated with fluttering bands and trophies – is the *motive* for the *permanent* monument, which is intended to proclaim to future generations the solemn act or event celebrated. [. . .]

I cite these examples mainly to draw attention to the principle of the *exterior decoration and dressing* of the structural framework – a principle that is necessary for improvised festive buildings and always and everywhere carries within itself the nature of the thing. From this I conclude that the same principle of veiling structural parts, combined with the monumental treatment of the tent covers and carpets that were stretched between the structural parts of the scaffold that is the source of the motif, must appear equally natural when seen in early architectural monuments.[1]

NOTE

1 I think that the *dressing* and the *mask* are as old as human civilization and that the joy in both is identical to the joy in those things that led men to be sculptors, painters, architects, poets, musicians, dramatists – in short, artists. Every artistic creation, every artistic pleasure, presumes a certain carnival spirit, or to express it in a modern way, the haze of carnival candles is the true atmosphere of art. The destruction of reality, of the material, is necessary if form is to emerge as a meaningful symbol, as an autonomous human creation. Let us forget the means that must be used to achieve a desired artistic effect, and not blurt them out and thus woefully forget ourselves. The unspoiled feeling led primitive man in this direction in all early artistic endeavors. The truly great masters of art in every field returned to it, except that in times of high artistic achievement these individuals also *masked the material of the mask*. This instinct led Phidias to his conception of the subject matter for the two tympana of the Parthenon. Evidently he considered his task, the representation of the double myth and its actors (the deities), *as the material to be treated* (just like the stone in which he formed them), which he veiled as much as possible, thus freeing it of all material and outward expression of its nonpictorial and religious-symbolic nature. Therefore his gods confront and inspire us, individually and collectively, first and foremost as expressions of true human beauty and grandeur. What was Hecuba to him?

For similar reasons drama could have meaning only in the beginning and at the height of the progressive education of a people. The oldest vase paintings give us an idea of the early material masks of the Hellenes. In a spiritual way, like those stone dramas by Phidias, the ancient mask is taken up again by Aeschylus, Sophocles, and Euripides and at the same time by Aristophanes and the other comic dramatists. Thus the proscenium frames an image of a noble piece of human history that did not simply occur somewhere once but happens everywhere as long as human hearts beat. What was Hecuba to them? The spirit of the mask breathes in Shakespeare's dramas. We meet the humor of masks and the haze of candles, the carnival spirit (which, in truth, is not always joyous), in Mozart's *Don Giovanni*. For even music needs a means to destroy reality. Hecuba means nothing to the musician, either, or should mean nothing.

But masking does not help when the thing *behind* the mask is not right or when the mask is no good. If the material, the indispensable, is to be completely destroyed in the artistic creation in the sense meant here, then the material must first be completely mastered. Only complete technical perfection, only the judicious and proper treatment of the material according to its properties, and above all only the consideration of these properties in the act of shaping form can cause the material to be forgotten, can liberate the artistic creation from it, can elevate even a simple landscape painting to become a high work of art. [. . .]

226   GOTTFRIED SEMPER
from *Style in the Technical and Tectonic Arts* (1860)

In the second volume of *Style* – containing the sections on ceramics, tectonics (timber construction), and stereotomy (stone construction) – Semper's text often reads like a catalogue of technical concerns, but scattered throughout are passages that would much influence German architectural debates throughout the remainder of the century. His remarks on the architectural exploitation of "space" and "iron" are instructive cases in point. The idea of architectural space for Semper had earlier resided in the walling or textile motive, but in his discussion of stone construction he develops this theme for vaulting techniques, and, in the process of considering Roman innovations, emphasizes the importance of this "mighty spatial art" for architecture.

In Semper's several remarks on the use of iron, he sets up the logical dilemma for all those coming after him, in their attempts to treat iron. On the one hand iron (in this case cast iron) is by nature "infertile soil for art" because of its slight dimensions and tendency toward invisibility. On the other hand, when those thin members might be enhanced by tubular construction, or when trusses are designed more artistically, "it might be possible to pin our hopes for the future of art on it." Over the next 40 years, every major German architect would read these words and struggle with the solution.

Gottfried Semper, from *Der Stil in den technischen und tektonischen Künsten* (1860), trans. Michael Robinson and Harry Francis Mallgrave in *Style in the Technical and Tectonic Arts, or Practical Aesthetics*. Los Angeles: Getty Publications Program, 2003, pp. 753–4, 756–7, 658–60. © 2003 by Getty Publications. Reprinted with permission of Getty Publications.

The Two Main Factors in the History of Stone Construction

All events throughout architectural history can be divided into two major groups defined by the manner and extent to which stone construction embodied an architectural-spatial idea.

The first group is stone architecture that merely *employs* the cutting of stone. Following the oldest tradition shared by all peoples of ancient heritage, the role assigned to stereotomy (and, in the final analysis, stone cutting) was only *subservient* – sometimes for the monumental production of the wall dressing, sometimes for producing a monumental (tectonic) framework in stone. In cultural-historical terms, this represents the earliest starting point for monumental art – even if it was its most perfect conclusion as well. In this sense, it came closest to the idea of perfection, which is the starting point and goal of all art.

The second group consists of architectural works in which the spatial idea is directly expressed through stone construction – works in which the spatial idea is conditioned a priori by the influence of stone, from which the architect's mental conception of space essentially emanated.

This happened when joint cutting, the arch, and especially the vaulted ceiling were added to the store of architectural art-forms. This occurred only after a protracted period during which these things failed to be taken into consideration for the expression of the spatial idea or, rather, were excluded from it in principle.

The new architectural principle this step created was to a certain extent in conflict with tradition and with the older types shared by monumental architecture and the other arts – although these types had so powerful an inner truth and were so deeply rooted in general architectural consciousness that they could never quite lose their validity. As these older types entered into new combinations thanks to the new principle, their continuity suffered somewhat and their original meaning became obscured. In compensation for this and the loss of ancient *melodic clarity* and *plasticity*, however, it was only by means of these combinations that architecture obtained the true means for developing that most magnificent *symphony* of mass and space toward which it had probably been striving since the earliest times (consider, for example, the Egyptians and probably also the Assyrians). Architecture had been denied this achievement because the material limits of stone tectonics were too confining before the adoption of the vault. [...]

The Romans

In contrast to the revolutionary Hellenes, the Romans were in customs, religion, and art the conservative supporters and preservers of everything originally *Greco-Italic*. They were late in borrowing the system of full ashlar construction, and so the magnificent development of the singularly Roman way of building proceeded undisturbed. Isodomon had been the hieratic privilege of the Hellenized temple, but Roman work proper, the idea of world domination expressed in stone, found a more suitable concrete form (indeed the only permissible one) in a kind of hollow construction – the poured wall with an ashlar crust and related masonry processes. It was necessary *to transfer the concameration – the vaulted cell system that had been known since ancient times but had been used only for substructures – to aboveground construction.* This was a new use for hollow construction and represented a solution to the problem of how to create from the surrounding rooms themselves the supports and abutments necessary to vault even massive central halls while expending a minimum on material and in labor and obtaining the largest possible space.

The Romans were in no way the *inventors* of this mighty spatial art, which would have related to Greek architecture as a symphony concert does to a hymn accompanied on the lyre, had it been developed to the same level of perfection as was Greek architecture. It had been in preparation for a long time and had its own priests and prophets before the Alexandrian period, among them Hippodamos and other founders of Asian cities, active as early as Athens's golden age. One can discern its dark seeds in tholoi, crypts, nuraghi, and other mysterious works of those early mystic inhabitants of the Mediterranean lands who worshiped the cult of the earth spirit. One can only speculate about the way in which Chaldean-Assyrian architecture related to Alexandrian-Roman buildings in this regard – that is, to what extent earlier tectonics was displaced from its old areas of application by the vault and dome. Any such speculations call to mind the semimythical accounts left by later writers, as well as the authentic representations of extensive domed structures that appear on Assyrian and Lycian relief panels, and above all Parthian and Sassanian ruins, calculated entirely according to the Roman vaulting principle and also closely related in plan to ancient Assyrian layouts. [. . .]

★ ★ ★

Metal Bar Construction (Iron)

In principle, there is no difference in construction between solid wooden planks and bars of iron or any other metal. The only difference lies in the proportions and dimensions of the constructional parts, corresponding to the well-known physical differences between the two materials. It should also be noted that metal does not share all of wood's deficiencies as a tectonic material, or at least does so to a lesser extent. It is not hygroscopic; it does not warp, shrink irregularly, or stretch.

Yet metal bars, unlike wood, have the disadvantage of excessive flexibility and elasticity, and cast iron is very brittle.

This comparison shows that metal-bar construction is infinitely more distant from monumental art than wood construction is. Here, much more strongly than with wood, the proportions appropriate to absolute stability contradict the proportions appropriate to the mechanical activities of the parts.

At the same time, all the formal motives that arise from the deficiencies of wood disappear.

Certainly the use of certain motives unique to metal-bar construction for formal ends can be defended, such as the motives of fitting things together and the ligatures found in the joints. But on the whole this is infertile ground for art. It is not possible to speak of a monumental metal-bar style or cast-iron style; their ideal is *invisible architecture!* For the thinner the metal tissue, the more perfect it is.

Things are different when metal is used either for tubular construction (a form with which we are familiar from the first volume) or for lattice construction (which in principle is close to the former). Both are equally important to our theory of style (see "Metallurgy").

If metal bars are less suitable as an architectural material, this makes them all the more suited to the tectonic tasks that we have recognized as contrary to the monumental – namely, the most delicate and light utensils and domestic furnishings, where they find their own niche. [...]

Hollow Lattice Construction (Wood and Metal)

A tubular, or rather a hollow-body tectonics predominated in domestic furnishings as well as in architecture from the earliest times. It held its own, at least, alongside actual bar tectonics, from which it differs on one point of great importance to our aesthetic-stylistic consider-ations. Because of the rigidity of the elements from which it is constructed, and in accordance with basic structural laws and material efficiency, a hollow-metal vertical support no longer needs (and in fact must reject) those diagonal braces and reinforcements without which solid construction (if consistently developed according to its own principles) cannot even exist – in neither real nor aesthetic-formal terms (that is, for the eye). In recent times the principle of hollow construction has been taken up in bridge building and even in civil architecture. Thus far it has been taken up only in a technical sense and spirit, but it might be possible to pin our hopes for the future of art on it. Our building style will once again meet the standards of monumental forms; the latter will no longer be mere lies, and the old Indo-Germanic traditions in art will once again be understood.

Yet this will hardly affect our tubular and truss railway bridges in the near future, although much could be done if all their elements were used correctly to develop the form. So far all they offer are naked constructional schemes that draw rigid, none-too-fortuitous lines across the landscape. The netted walls, which in themselves have great aesthetic potential, lack articulation and alternation. The piers that support them are nothing but raw, unfinished masses. They need to be imbued with life as organisms following the antique idea once again, made to function eurythmically, and their profiles should be regulated to the load (see "Metallurgy").

227 RUDOLF HERMANN LOTZE
from *History of German Aesthetics* (1868)

A slightly different interpretation to the problem of iron posed by Semper was given by the physician and philosopher Rudolf Hermann Lotze, who received a doctorate in medicine and philosophy at the tender age of 21 and subsequently pursued many paths: focusing his multitude of published writings on pathology, psychology, philosophy, logic, and aesthetics. Lotze, like many of his generation, opposed the idealist schemes of Schelling and Hegel, while at the same time he did not fully accept the psychological realism of his predecessor Johann Friedrich Herbart, whose professorial chair at Göttingen University Lotze himself assumed in 1844. In the chapter on architecture in his *History of German Aesthetics*, he begins by recounting the Germanic debate of recent years, and especially the ideas of Hübsch, Semper, and Bötticher. What he now injects into the debate regarding iron is a psychologist's point of view, that is, the psychological habits of the spectator are just habits and therefore not incompatible with the new forms and proportions of the evolving technologies.

In most vivid contrast to this still continuing religious tendency of our time stands *technical-industrial* development. It poses for architecture sufficient new tasks, yet without having formed a style fully corresponding to it; but what it has nurtured tends to be subject to the hypercriticism of those caught up in old theories. Whoever remembers the early days of the railroad will perhaps recall that many of the provisional terminals built in light wood construction in fact made a harmonious impression with the totality of railroad activity. The characteristic of industrial mechanics consists in achieving the large through the simplest and smallest possible structure. Corresponding to this bold spirit was the airiness of earlier structures, which was greater than in those colossal piles of stone, mostly in a Romanesque style, which have now replaced them. The locomotive with its fantastic construction and mobility – a small vulcanian monster of gigantic power – appears very foreign when placed within these broad masses, the same masses whose forms also stand in opposition to railroad lines and light-spanned bridges, as well as with the noisy bustle of traveling life.

Paxton's glass-and-iron building has invented a new principle for the construction of bright exhibition spaces. Its failing has been exposed with greater acuity than one has devoted to the further development of the valuable seed. People criticize it because the slenderness of the iron columns does not impart the aesthetic impression of strength that a certain visible width of supported mass demands. Only nature has not established a proportion between thickness and height that in itself ensures this impression; in this regard our aesthetic feeling is dependent on experience. A timber support may appear perfectly secure to us, whereas a stone support of the same dimension may be very threatening; it is just our habituation to the wooden column that initially makes us suspicious of the more slender metal one. Furthermore, while it may be true that the ornamentation of the iron

Rudolf Hermann Lotze (1817–81), from *Geschichte der Aesthetik in Deutschland* [History of German aesthetics] (1868), trans. Harry Francis Mallgrave.

structure is lacking and without a sense of style, we should expect from new constructional methods – which are not merely a display of heavy masses but rather a complex and cohesive tension and riveting of the individual parts – the gradual development of a completely new kind of decoration, and not simply an imitation of the old. To take for granted or reapply the old presumption in the new overlooks the surprising results that this way of building has up to now successfully produced.

Most serious are the objections as to the durability of metal, and we might hold little hope that further experience will refute them in a satisfactory way. But it is also questionable if monumental duration is imperative in *any* architecture. Eternal duration is generally not essential for beauty: "Yet I made, said God, only the ephemeral beautiful." In our lively and active time perhaps what matters is to express the transitory needs that we feel, to express beautiful reality in a fleeting way, and to create works for themselves, for the living, instead of what the future may set for them. What survives will be a style that is the *art* of building, not the individual *work*, and there will be no misfortune in this approach.

228   GOTTFRIED SEMPER
from *On Architectural Style* (1869)

Semper's final theoretical deliberation took the form of a public lecture he gave in Zurich in March 1869. He was at the time contemplating starting the long-anticipated third volume of *Style*, in which he promised to address the issue of contemporary architecture. His plans never went forward, and thus this lecture represents his last word on several important themes. Three excerpts are presented. In the first the 66-year-old architect briefly touches on the contemporary scene, and concludes with his denunciation of present efforts to apply Darwin's theory of natural selection to the (evolutionary) invention of a new style. In the second he reiterates his earlier comments in *Style* on Roman architecture, but now identifies the "mighty art of space creation" with the future of architecture in general. In the third – his closing comments of the lecture – Semper effectively resigns on the matter of a new style and now passes the problem on to the younger generation.

In recent times more was done here in style making and more eagerly than anywhere else, partly on royal command, partly on the whim of architects presumed to be men of genius. In Munich the celebrated Maximilian style was created at his majesty the king's most gracious command, founded on the following profound idea: Our culture is a mixture made up of elements from all earlier cultures; consequently, our modern architectural style should also be a mixture of every conceivable style of architecture from every time and nation. The entire history of culture should thus be mirrored in it! The upshot of such reasoning is evidenced by the latest developments in that city of the muses on the Isar.

In addition to this there is, as we said, the chorus of private style inventors, who shine their cheap inventive spirit on every large and small residence, railway station, and every-

Gottfried Semper, from *Über Baustyle* [On architectural styles] (1869), trans. Wolfgang Herrmann and Harry Francis Mallgrave, in *Gottfried Semper: The Four Elements of Architecture and Other Writings*. Cambridge: Cambridge University Press, 1989, pp. 267–8, 281, 284. © 1989 by Cambridge University Press. Reprinted with permission of Cambridge University Press.

where. In most cases they start from the erroneous assumption that the question of style is chiefly a constructive question and do not acknowledge the inherited traditions of artistic symbolism. What they have achieved by this reasoning is nothing other than the dubious distinction of having done their bit for the prevailing Babylonian confusion.

Another sort of stylist is found in the so-called tourist architects, who bring home every autumn one new style from their excursions into distant lands and know how to find a buyer for it.

Finally, we should mention those who seek in a return to the medieval or so-called Gothic style the future of the national architecture and their own future – and they are hardly ever mistaken regarding the latter.

To these practical solutions to the question of style there is an opposing school of opinion, according to which architectural styles cannot be invented at all, but evolve in different ways in conformance with the laws of natural selection, heredity, and adaptation from a few primitive types (*Urtypen*), rather similar to the way the species are presumed to evolve in the realm of organic creation. Herman Grimm, the biographer of Michelangelo, says: "It can be safely assumed that where sudden transitions appear in architectural styles, these may be ascribed either to the influence of more remote models, or to the loss of transitional links." Very similar views on this subject are also expressed by other authorities in art history.

This application of the famous axiom, "nature makes no leaps" and of Darwin's theory on the origin of species to the special world of the small re-creator – man – seems somewhat questionable to us, in view of what the study of monuments shows. Very often they present the monumental symbols of national cultures continuing alongside or following behind one another in a consciously retained opposition.

We can quite rightly describe the old monuments as the fossilized receptacles of extinct social organizations, but these did not grow on the backs of society like shells on the backs of snails, nor did they spring forth from blind natural processes, like coral reefs. They are the free creations of man, on which he employed his understanding, observation of nature, genius, will, knowledge, and power.

★ ★ ★

A few centuries after Alexander, the Romans assumed his legacy with their idea of world sovereignty and borrowed from him that mighty art of space creation, which would have related to Greek architecture as a symphonic concert does to a hymn accompanied by a lyre – were it as perfect as the symphony and had it (emancipated from abject servitude to need, the state, and religion) moved, like the symphony, toward a free, self-sufficient idealism. Herein lies its future and the future of architecture in general.

★ ★ ★

Permit me still one other practical application of the fable! People reproach us architects for a lack of inventiveness – too harshly, since nowhere has a new idea of universal historical importance, pursued with force and consciousness, become evident. We are convinced that wherever such an idea would really take the lead, one or the other of our young colleagues will prove himself capable of endowing it with a suitable architectural dress.

Until that time comes, however, we must reconcile ourselves to make do as best we can with the old.

229　RICHARD LUCAE
from "On the Meaning and Power of Space in Architecture" (1869)

In 1869 Semper was not the only one contemplating the significance of space as a new architectural medium. Within weeks of his lecture, the Berlin architect Richard Lucae, a great admirer of his and later the director of the Berlin Bauakademie, coincidentally delivered a lecture on the same theme. Lucae was obviously impressed with the new spatial experiences of railway stations, the Sydenham Crystal Palace, and Alpine tunnels. His remarks — phenomenological in their twentieth-century character — make him one of the first modern architects to discuss the psychological experience of perceiving large spaces: their form, lighting, character, and our movement through them. It might be compared with earlier British discussions on the sublime. This lecture helps to lay an important cornerstone of what would later be seen as twentieth-century modernism. It also stands at the beginning of writings on the meaning of iron and space that dominate German theory in the last quarter of the century.

Let us take an example from modern life. Let us take the hall of a recently built train station in a large city. We receive a very different impression depending on whether we are embarking on or returning from a trip. If we are embarking we walk along the broad avenue among the thousands of people who also want to depart; we crowd along here and there and we see the building only where we are carried into an opening. We are oblivious to the impression of the tension of the broad glass roof when we arrive; here the hall with its protective roof becomes the friend who pleasantly and hospitably greets us. The lasting impression that the space has on us, however, is that of the security with which the colossal roof is supported on two side walls, how it floats freely above our astonished eyes, and the bold and overpowering effect of the breadth of space without supports. It is the same feeling that we experience when we stand before the tunnel that has been bored through the Alps, namely, that the same ingenious spirit who has created this has created that. Unfortunately almost scale alone exerts its power here, for we have mostly relegated the space to a prosaic purpose and thereby had thought we could do without art. Surely other spatial factors, such as light and form, could be artistically used to raise this space to a higher aesthetic level. If a meaningful idea of beauty were at the same time added to the great structural ideas of these roof forms, our eyes might find rest and pleasure in the confusing iron bars and iron chords crisscrossing each other in every direction. Then we would not notice, figuratively speaking, the individual instances of this mathematical calculation translated into iron and simply organize it into a clear sum, into a system appearing as a beautiful form. For the purely mathematical structure is not a finished achievement of art, but only a skeleton, like the human body [. . .]

★ ★ ★

Richard Lucae (1829–77), from "Über die Bedeutung und Macht des Raumes in der Baukunst" [On the meaning and power of space in architecture] (1869), trans. Harry Francis Mallgrave.

If we are in the Pantheon in Rome, we find ourselves in a space in which the architecture was originally not created for the purpose that it serves today, and yet probably no one has experienced it who has not had a powerful impression.

In the Pantheon we are fully isolated from the exterior world. Nothing connects us with it other than a windowless opening at the top of the powerful half-globe, which majestically but heavily sits on the giant rotunda. We become forced into a kind of self-communion, although the uniformity of the space has a somewhat soothing effect on our feelings. It is a magical circle in which we seek the way out. Here a force overcomes us, of which we know not what it wants with us. We are in the sway of a mysticism against which our free sensation might resist; although we are magically drawn in, we yearn to be beyond it and back among people. Even if the space of the Pantheon is more solemn than any other, in its seriousness it is almost demonic and at the same time scarcely allows us any edification.

The feeling that we find lacking in the Pantheon's uniformity of form and perfect unity of the light and that gives our thoughts no decisive goal – this feeling of edification overwhelms us in Saint Peter's in Rome.

We stroll down the central nave like down an enormous street – involuntarily to the point at which the idea of the whole building resides. We do not stand simultaneously at the beginning and the end of the space, as in the Pantheon. The powerful barrel vaults lead our eyes there, where the half-light around us suddenly withdraws into a supernatural force of light. Surely an inhabitant of the primeval forest, someone who had not heard of Saint Peter or Christianity, would not pause before he arrives under the dome of Michelangelo. Here is a space that seals us off from the profane world of commerce. Here the source of light leads us into a region that shields our eyes from the banality of life.

And yet our sensations here are different from those of the Pantheon. In the latter, between the fully enclosing walls, we had the feeling of being in an impressive underground grotto, in which the light flows down to us along the fine lines of the ceiling; in Saint Peter's, its spiritual rays have been compressed under the gigantic vault and lift it high, taking us with it into its supernatural habitat. Freely the glance wanders through the wide arches of the church nave, bringing itself to a point of blissful consciousness as we experience always anew the wonder of the space that opens itself here.

If we accept the tenet that "the sublime is only that toward which we experience the small and the large at the same time," we must also accept the fact that unfortunately modern art has lost sight of the concept of the sublime. Nevertheless, architecture could have preserved it, for surely the gigantic dome of Saint Peter's exerts this power. Here we stand under the impression of a work of the human hand that in its appearance approaches the sublimity of creation.

We cannot conclude our survey without touching on a space unique in its kind – the Crystal Palace in Sydenham, near London.

Whereas in the powerful train hall we had the feeling that it, taken in the strict sense of art, was not a complete space, the magic of Sydenham for us resides in the fact that we are in an artificially created environment that has already ceased to be a space. We are separated from nature but yet we are scarcely conscious of it; the barrier that separates us from the landscape is scarcely perceptible. If we reflect on it, it is as if one has poured air, as it were, like a liquid; thus here we have the sensation that the free air has kept its solid shape after the form in which it had been poured was again taken away. We find ourselves, so to speak, in a piece of sculpted atmosphere. The sun's rays come to us not through individual openings. They fill the space with a completely beautiful naturalness. And as the sun of this space does not give or allow the light to be anything special or particular, so we must also be content with the fact that its colors borrow their limits from the objects outside. In this way it is like a magical, poetic form of light, which always works most beautifully in surroundings such as these, where it crowns a gentle hill in open landscape.

ADDITIONAL RECOMMENDED READINGS

Part I, section A

Coldstream, Nicola, *Medieval Architecture* (Oxford: Oxford University Press, 2002).

Favro, Diane, *The Urban Image of Augustan Rome* (New York: Cambridge University Press, 1996).

Frankl, Paul (revised by Paul Crossley), *Gothic Architecture* (New Haven: Yale University Press, 2001).

Hersey, George L., *The Lost Meaning of Classical Architecture* (Cambridge, MA: MIT Press, 1988).

Krautheimer, Richard, *Early Christian and Byzantine Architecture* (Harmondsworth: Penguin, 1979).

Kruft, Hanno-Walter, *A History of Architectural Theory from Vitruvius to the Present* (London: Zwemmer, 1994).

McEwen, Indra Kagis, *Vitruvius: Writing the Body of Architecture* (Cambridge, MA: MIT Press, 2003).

Onians, John, *Bearers of Meaning: The Classical Orders in Antiquity, the Middle Ages, and the Renaissance* (Princeton: Princeton University Press, 1990).

Panovsky, Erwin, *Gothic Architecture and Scholasticism* (New York: Meridian, 1976).

Payne, Alina, et al. (eds.), *Antiquity and its Interpreters* (New York: Cambridge University Press, 2000).

Rowland, Ingrid D., et al., Introduction to *Vitruvius: Ten Books on Architecture* (New York: Cambridge University Press, 1999).

Rykwert, Joseph, *The Dancing Column: On Order in Architecture* (Cambridge, MA: MIT Press, 1996).

Scott, Robert A., *The Gothic Enterprise: A Guide to Understanding the Medieval Cathedral* (Berkeley: University of California Press, 2003).

Stalley, R. A., *Early Medieval Architecture* (Oxford: Oxford University Press, 1999).

Part I, section B

Benevolo, Leonardo, *The Architecture of the Renaissance* (Boulder, CO: Westview Press, 1978).

Blunt, Anthony, *Baroque and Rococo* (New York: Harper and Row, 1982).

Hersey, George L., *Architecture and Geometry in the Age of the Baroque* (Chicago: Chicago University Press, 2002).

Lotz, Wolfgang, *Studies in Italian Renaissance Architecture* (Cambridge, MA: MIT Press, 1981).

Millon, Henry A., *The Triumph of the Baroque: Architecture in Europe, 1600–1750* (New York: Rizzoli, 2000).

Murray, Peter, *The Architecture of the Italian Renaissance* (New York: Schocken Books, 1963).

Panofsky, Erwin, *Renaissance and Renascences in Western Art* (New York: Harper & Row, 1969).

Payne, Alina A., *The Architectural Treatise in the Italian Renaissance: Architectural Invention, Ornament and Literary Culture* (New York: Cambridge University Press, 1999).

Smyth, Craig Hugh, *Mannerism and Maniera* (Vienna: IRSA, 1992).

Wittkower, Rudolf, *Architectural Principles in the Age of Humanism* (London: Academy Editions, 1973).

Wittkower, Rudolf, *Art and Architecture in Italy 1600–1750* (Harmondsworth: Penguin, 1973).

Part II, section A

Berger, Robert W., *The Palace of the Sun: The Louvre of Louis XIV* (University Park, PA: Pennsylvania State University Press, 1993).

Blunt, Anthony, *Art and Architecture in France 1500–1700* (Harmondsworth: Penguin, 1977).

Herrmann, Wolfgang, *The Theory of Claude Perrault* (London: Zwemmer, 1973).

Middleton, Robin D., "The Abbé de Cordemoy and the Graeco-Gothic Ideal: A Prelude to Romantic Classicism," *Journal of the Warburg and Courtauld Institutes*, XXV (1962).

Pérez-Gómez, Alberto, Introduction to *Claude Perrault: Ordonnance for the Five Kinds of Columns after the Method of the Ancients* (Santa Monica: Getty Publications Program, 1993).

Rykwert, Joseph, *The First Moderns: The Architects of the Eighteenth Century* (Cambridge, MA: MIT Press, 1980).

Part II, section B

Harris, John, *The Palladian Revival: Lord Burlington, His Villa and Garden at Chiswick* (New Haven: Yale University Press, 1994).

Jourdain, Margaret, *The Work of William Kent: Artist, Painter, Designer and Landscape Gardener* (London: Country Life Limited, 1948).

Kaufmann, Emil, *Architecture in the Age of Reason: Baroque and Post-Baroque in England, Italy, and France* (Cambridge, MA: Harvard University, 1955).

Rykwert, Joseph, *The First Moderns: The Architects of the Eighteenth Century* (Cambridge, MA: MIT Press, 1980).

Summerson, John, *Architecture in Britain 1530–1830* (Harmondsworth: Penguin, 1977).

Summerson, John, *Inigo Jones* (New York: Yale University Press, 2000).

Tinniswood, Adrian, *His Invention So Fertile: A Life of Christopher Wren* (London: Jonathan Cape, 2001).

Wilson, Michael, *William Kent: Architect, Designer, Painter, Gardener, 1685–1748* (London: Routledge & Kegan Paul, 1984).

Wittkower, Rudolf, *Palladio and English Palladianism* (London: Thames and Hudson, 1974).

Part III, section A

Braham, Allan, *The Architecture of the French Enlightenment* (Berkeley: University of California Press, 1989).

Harris, John, *Sir William Chambers, Knight of the Polar Star* (London: Zwemmer, 1970).

Herrmann, Wolfgang, *Laugier and Eighteenth Century French Theory* (London: Zwemmer, 1985).

Kalnein, Wend Graf and Levey, Michael, *Art and Architecture of the Eighteenth Century in France* (Harmondsworth: Penguin, 1972).

Kaufmann, Emil, *Architecture in the Age of Reason: Baroque and Post-Baroque in England, Italy, and France* (Cambridge, MA: Harvard University Press, 1955).

Middleton, Robin and Watkin, David, *Neoclassical and 19th Century Architecture* (New York: Electa, 1987).

Praz, Mario, *On Neoclassicism* (Evanston, IL: Northwestern University Press, 1969).

Rykwert, Joseph, *The First Moderns: The Architects of the Eighteenth Century* (Cambridge, MA: MIT Press, 1980).

Part III, section B

Kaufmann, Edgar, Jr., "Memmo's Lodoli," *The Art Bulletin*, vol. 46 (March 1964), 159–72.

Middleton, Robin, Introduction to *Julien-David Le Roy: The Ruins of the Most Beautiful Monuments of Greece* (Los Angeles: Getty Publications Program, 2004).

Potts, Alex, Introduction to *The History of the Art of Antiquity* (Los Angeles: Getty Publications Program, 2005).

Searing, Helen, "Lodoli Architetto," in *In Search of Modern Architecture: A Tribute to Henry-Russell Hitchcock* (New York: The Architectural History Foundation, 31–7).

Smart, Alastair, *Allan Ramsay: Painter Essayist and Man of the Enlightenment* (New Haven: Yale University Press, 1992).

Tsigakou, Fani-Maria, *The Rediscovery of Greece: Travellers and Painters of the Romantic Era* (New Rochelle: Caratzas Brothers, 1981).

Wiebenson, Dora, *Sources of Greek Revival Architecture* (University Park, PA: Pennsylvania State University Press, 1969).

Wilton-Ely, John, *The Mind and Art of Giovanni Battista Piranesi* (London: Thames and Hudson, 1978).

Wilton-Ely, John, *G. B. Piranesi: Observations on the Letter of Monsieur Mariette* (Los Angeles: Getty Publications Program, 2002).

Part III, section C

Etlin, Richard A., *Symbolic Space: French Enlightenment Architecture and Its Legacy* (Chicago: University of Chicago Press, 1994).

Kaufmann, Emil, *Three Revolutionary Architects: Boullée, Ledoux, and Lequeu* (Philadelphia: American Philosophical Society, 1952).

Middleton, Robin, "Jacques François Blondel and the *Cours d'Architecture*," *Journal of the Society of Architectural Historians*, vol. 18 (1959), 140–8.

Middleton, Robin, Introduction to *Nicolas Le Camus de Mézières: The Genius of Architecture; or the Analogy of that Art with our Sensations* (Santa Monica, CA: Getty Publications Program, 1992).

Pérouse de Montclos, Jean-Marie, *Etienne-Louis Boullée, 1728–1799, Theoretician of Revolutionary Architecture* (London: Thames & Hudson, 1974).

Rosenau, Helen, *Boullée & Visionary Architecture, Including Boullée's 'Architecture, Essay on Art'* (New York: Harmony Books, 1976).

Vidler, Anthony, *Claude-Nicolas Ledoux: Architecture and Social Reform at the End of the Ancien Régime* (Cambridge, MA: MIT Press, 1990).

Part IV, section A

Ashfield, Andrew and de Bolla, Peter (eds.), *The Sublime: A Reader in British Eighteenth-Century Aesthetic Theory* (New York: Cambridge University Press, 1996).

Beard, Geoffrey, *The Work of John Vanbrugh* (London: B. T. Batsford, 1986).

Downes, Kerry, *Vanbrugh* (London: Zwemmer, 1977).

Harris, John and Snokin, Michael (eds.), *Sir William Chambers: Architect to George III* (New Haven: Yale University Press, 1996).

Hart, Vaughan, *Nikolaus Hawksmoor: Rebuilding Ancient Wonders* (New Haven: Yale University Press, 2002).

Hipple, Walter John, *The Beautiful, The Sublime, & The Picturesque in Eighteenth-Century British Aesthetic Theory* (Carbondale, IL: Southern Illinois University Press, 1957).

Leatherbarrow, David, "Architecture and Situation: A Study of the Architectural Writings of Robert Morris," *Journal of the Society of Architectural Historians*, vol. 44, no. 1 (March 1985), 48–59.

Watkin, David, *The English Vision: The Picturesque in Architecture, Landscape and Garden Design* (London: John Murray, 1982).

Part IV, section B

Ashfield, Andrew and de Bolla, Peter (eds.), *The Sublime: A Reader in British Eighteenth-Century Aesthetic Theory* (New York: Cambridge University Press, 1996).

Burke, Edmund, *A Philosophical Enquiry into the Origin of our Ideas of the Sublime and the Beautiful*, ed. J. T. Boulton (London: Routledge & Kegan Paul, 1958).

Fleming, John, *Robert Adam and His Circle in Edinburgh & Rome* (London: John Murray, 1962).

Harris, Eileen, *The Genius of Robert Adam: His Interiors* (New Haven: Yale University Press, 2001).

Hipple, Walter John, *The Beautiful, The Sublime, & The Picturesque in Eighteenth-Century British Aesthetic Theory* (Carbondale, IL: Southern Illinois University Press, 1957).

Part IV, section C

Ashfield, Andrew and de Bolla, Peter (eds.), *The Sublime: A Reader in British Eighteenth-Century Aesthetic Theory* (New York: Cambridge University Press, 1996).

Ballantyne, Andrew, *Architecture, Landscape and Liberty: Richard Payne Knight and the Picturesque* (New York: Cambridge University Press, 1997).

Daniels, Steven, *Humphry Repton: Landscape Gardening and the Geography of Georgian England* (New Haven: Yale University Press, 1999).

Darley, Gillian, *John Soane: An Accidental Romantic* (New Haven: Yale University Press, 1999).

Watkin, David, *Sir John Soane: Enlightenment Thought and the Royal Academy Lectures* (New York: Cambridge University Press, 1996).

Part V, section A

Bergdoll, Barry, *Léon Vaudoyer: Historicism in the Age of Industry* (New York: Architectural History Foundation, 1994).

Bergdoll, Barry, *European Architecture 1750–1890* (Oxford: Oxford University Press, 2000).

Lavin, Sylvia, *Quatremère de Quincy and the Invention of a Modern Language of Architecture* (Cambridge, MA: MIT Press, 1992).

Levine, Neil, "The Book and the Building: Hugo's Theory of Architecture and Labrouste's Bibliothèque Ste-Geneviève," in *The Beaux-Arts and Nineteenth-Century French Architecture*, ed. Robin Middleton (Cambridge, MA: MIT Press, 1982), 139–73.

Middleton, Robin, "Hittorff's Polychrome Campaign," in *The Beaux-Arts and Nineteenth-Century French Architecture* (Cambridge, MA: MIT Press, 1982).

Middleton, Robin, "The Rationalist Interpretations of Classicism of Léonce Reynaud and Viollet-le-Duc," *AA files*, vol. 2 (Spring 1986), 29–48.

Pérez-Gómez, Alberto, *Architecture and the Crisis of Modern Science* (Cambridge, MA: MIT Press, 1983).

Picon, Antoine, Introduction to *Durand: Précis of the Lectures on Architecture, with Graphic Portion of the Lectures on Architecture*, trans. by David Britt (Los Angeles: Getty Publications Program, 2000).

Van Zanten, David, *The Architectural Polychromy of the 1830s* (New York: Garland, 1977).

Van Zanten, David, *Designing Paris: The Architecture of Duban, Labrouste, Duc, and Vaudoyer* (Cambridge, MA: MIT Press, 1987).

Younés, Samir, *The True, the Fictive, and the Real: The Historical Dictionary of Architecture of Quatremère de Quincy* (London: Papadakis, 1999).

Part V, section B

Atterbury, Paul and Wainwright, Clive (eds.), *Pugin: A Gothic Passion* (New Haven: Yale University Press, 1994).

Bergdoll, Barry, *Léon Vaudoyer: Historicism in the Age of Industry* (New York: Architectural History Foundation, 1994).

Lewis, Michael J., *The Politics of the German Gothic Revival: August Reichensperger* (New York: Architectural History Foundation, 1993).

Lewis, Michael J., *The Gothic Revival* (London: Thames & Hudson, 2002).

Middleton, Robin, "The Rationalist Interpretations of Classicism of Léonce Reynaud and Viollet-le-Duc," *AA files*, vol. 2 (Spring 1986), 29–48.

Pevsner, Nikolaus, *Some Architectural Writers of the Nineteenth Century* (Oxford: Clarendon Press, 1972).

Stanton, Phoebe, *Pugin* (New York: Viking Press, 1971).

Part V, section C

Bergdoll, Barry, "Archaeology vs. History: Heinrich Hübsch's Critique of Neoclassicism and the Beginnings of Historicism in German Architectural Theory," *The Oxford Art Journal*, vol. 5, no. 2, (1983), 3–12.

Bergdoll, Barry, *Karl Friedrich Schinkel: An Architecture for Prussia* (New York: Rizzoli, 1994).

Herrmann, Wolfgang, Introduction to *In What Style Should We Build? The German Debate on Architectural Style* (Santa Monica, CA: Getty Publications Program, 1992).

Neumeyer, Fritz, Introduction to *Friedrich Gilly: Essays on Architecture, 1796–1799* (Santa Monica, CA: Getty Publications Program, 1994).

Schwarzer, Mitchell, *German Architectural Theory and the Search for Modern Identity* (New York: Cambridge University Press, 1995).

Snodin, Michael (ed.), *Karl Friedrich Schinkel: A Universal Man* (New Haven: Yale University Press, 1991).

Watkin, David and Mellinghoff, Tilman, *German Architecture and the Classical Ideal* (Cambridge, MA: MIT Press, 1987).

Zukowsky, John (ed.), *Karl Friedrich Schinkel 1781–1841: The Drama of Architecture* (Chicago: Art Institute of Chicago, 1994).

Part V, section D

Boller, Paul F., Jr., *American Transcendentalism, 1830–1860: An Intellectual Inquiry* (New York: G. P. Putnam, 1974).

Brawne, Michael, *The University of Virginia, the Lawn: Thomas Jefferson* (London: Phaidon, 1994).

Cohen, Jeffrey A. and Brownell, Charles E., *The Architectural Drawings of Benjamin Henry Latrobe*, 2 vols. (New Haven: Yale University Press, 1994).

Curran, Kathleen, *The Romanesque Revival: Religion, Politics, and Transnational Exchange* (University Park: Pennsylvania State University Press, 2003).

Curran, Kathleen, "The German Rundbogenstil and Reflections on the American Round-Arched Style," *Journal of the Society of Architectural Historians*, vol. 47 (Dec. 1988), 351–73.

Donoghue, John, *Alexander Jackson Davis: Romantic Architect, 1803–1892* (New York: Arno Press, 1977).

Ennis, Robert B., *Thomas U. Walter, Architect, 1804–1887* (Philadelphia: Athenaeum, 1982).

Gilchrist, Anges Addison, *William Strickland, Architect and Engineer: 1788–1854* (New York: Da Capo Press, 1969).

Hamlin, Talbot, *Greek Revival Architecture in America* (New York: Dover, 1964; orig. 1944).

Hamlin, Talbot, *Benjamin Henry Latrobe* (New York: Oxford University Press, 1955).

McLaughlin, Jack, *Jefferson and Monticello: The Biography of a Builder* (New York: Henry Holt, 1988).

Metzger, Charles R., *Emerson and Greenough: Transcendental Pioneers of an American Esthetic* (Westport, CT: Greenwood Press, 1954; reprint 1974).

Newton, Roger Hale, *Town & Davis, Architects: Pioneers in American Revivalist Architecture, 1812–1870* (New York: Columbia University Press, 1942).

Nichols, Frederick Doveton, *Thomas Jefferson's Architectural Drawings* (Charlottesville, VA: Thomas Jefferson Memorial Foundation, 1961).

Pierson, William H., *American Buildings and their Architects: Technology and the Picturesque, the Corporate and the Early Gothic Styles* (New York: Anchor Books, 1980).

Schuyler, David, *Apostle of Taste: Andrew Jackson Downing 1815–1852* (Baltimore: Johns Hopkins, 1996).

Scully, Vincent J., *The Shingle Style and the Stick Style: Architectural Theory and Design from Downing to the Origins of Wright* (New Haven: Yale University Press, 1971).

Shackelford, George Green, *Thomas Jefferson's Travels in Europe, 1784–1789* (Baltimore: John Hopkins Press, 1995).

Stanton, Phoebe, *The Gothic Revival and American Church Architecture* (Baltimore: John Hopkins Press, 1968).

Vickery, Robert, *The Meaning of the Lawn: Thomas Jefferson's Design for the University of Virginia* (Weimar: VDG, 1998).

Wright, Nathalia, *Horatio Greenough: The First American Sculptor* (Philadelphia: University of Pennsylvania Press, 1963).

Part VI, section A

Beaver, Patrick, *The Crystal Palace: 1851–1936, A Portrait of Victorian Enterprise* (London: Hugh Evelyn, 1970).

Bell, Quentin, *The Schools of Design* (London: Routledge & Kegan Paul, 1963).

Bell, Quentin, *Ruskin* (New York: George Braziller, 1978).

Bonython, Elizabeth, *King Cole: A Picture Portrait of Sir Henry Cole, KCB, 1808–1882* (London: Victoria and Albert Museum, n.d.).

Collins, Peter, *Changing Ideals in Modern Architecture 1750–1950* (London: Faber & Faber, 1965).

Hilton, Tim, *John Ruskin* (New Haven: Yale University Press, 2000).

Kemp, Wolfgang, *The Desire of My Eyes: The Life and Work of John Ruskin* (New York: The Noonday Press, 1990).

Kohane, Peter, "Architecture, Labor and the Human Body: Fergusson, Cockerell and Ruskin," Ph.D. diss., University of Pennsylvania, 1993.

Pevsner, Nikolaus, *Some Architectural Writers of the Nineteenth Century* (Oxford: Clarendon Press, 1972).

Salmon, Frank, *Building on Ruins: The Rediscovery of Rome and English Architecture* (Aldershot: Ashgate, 2000).

White, James F., *The Cambridge Movement* (Cambridge: Cambridge University Press, 1962).

Part VI, section B

Bercé, Françoise, *Viollet-le-Duc: Architect, Artist, Master of Historic Preservation* (Washington, DC: The Trust for Museum Exhibitions, 1987).

Bergdoll, Barry, Introduction to Kenneth D. Whitehead, *The Foundations of Architecture: Selections from the Dictionnaire Raisonné* (New York: George Braziller, 1990).

Bergdoll, Barry, *Léon Vaudoyer: Historicism in the Age of Industry* (New York: Architectural History Foundation, 1994).

Hearn, M. F., *The Architectural Theory of Viollet-le-Duc: Readings and Commentary* (Cambridge, MA: MIT Press, 1990).

Lipstadt, Hélène, "César Daly and the *Revue générale de l'architecture*," Ph.D. diss., Harvard University, 1981.

Lipstadt, Hélène, "The Building and the Book in César Daly's *Revue Générale de l'Architecture*," in *Architecturereproduction*, ed. Beatriz Colomina (New York: Princeton Architectural Press, 1988), 25–55.

Murphy, Kevin D., *Memory and Modernity: Viollet-le-Duc at Vézelay* (University Park, PA: Pennsylvania State University Press, 2000).

Van Zanten, Ann Lorenz, "Form and Society: César Daly and the Revue Générale de l'Architecture," *Oppositions* 8 (Spring 1977), 137–45.

Van Zanten, David, *Building Paris: Architectural Institutions and the Transformation of the French Capital, 1830–1870* (New York: Cambridge University Press, 1994).

Part VI, section C

Herrmann, Wolfgang, *Gottfried Semper: In Search of Style* (Cambridge, MA: MIT Press, 1984).

Mallgrave, Harry Francis, *Gottfried Semper: Architect of the Nineteenth Century* (New Haven: Yale University Press, 1996).

Mallgrave, Harry Francis, Introduction to *Gottfried Semper: Style in the Technical or Tectonic Arts of Practical Aesthetics* (Los Angeles: Getty Publications Program, 2004).

Schwarzer, Mitchell, *German Architectural Theory and the Search for Modern Identity* (New York: Cambridge University Press, 1995).

ACKNOWLEDGMENTS

I have benefited greatly from several excellent reviewers at both the planning stage and final stages of this process. Although several of these readers remain anonymous, I am indebted to those who have encouraged me in the project, made suggestions, and/or provided material – among them Andrew Morrogh, Barry Bergdoll, Peter Kohane, Mario Carpo, Martin Bressani, Marco Frascari, Michael J. Lewis, and María Ocón Fernández. I owe a particular debt of gratitude to Christina Contandriopoulos, who not only provided an abundance of support during my stay at the Canadian Centre for Architecture but also afterwards. I thank the very capable library staff of the Canadian Centre for Architecture in Montreal, and also Peg Wilson, who handled various interlibrary loan requests for me locally.

Text Acknowledgments

I and the publisher gratefully acknowledge the permission granted to reproduce the copyright material in this book:

1. Marcus Vitruvius Pollio (c.90–c.20 BC), from Book 1 of *De architectura* [On architecture] (c.25 BC), trans. Morris Hicky Morgan, in *Vitruvius: The Ten Books on Architecture*. New York: Dover, 1960 (orig. 1914), pp. 5, 13–17.
2. Marcus Vitruvius Pollio, from Book 2, Chapter 1 of *De architectura* [On architecture] (c.25 BC), trans. Morris Hicky Morgan, in *Vitruvius: The Ten Books on Architecture*. New York: Dover, 1960 (orig. 1914), pp. 38–41.
3. Marcus Vitruvius Pollio, from Book 3, Chapter 1 of *De architectura* [On architecture] (c.25 BC), trans. Morris Hicky Morgan, in *Vitruvius: The Ten Books on Architecture*. New York: Dover, 1960 (orig. 1914), pp. 72–3.
4. Marcus Vitruvius Pollio, from Book 4, Chapter 1 of *De architectura* [On architecture] (c.25 BC), trans. Morris Hicky Morgan, in *Vitruvius: The Ten Books on Architecture*. New York: Dover, 1960 (orig. 1914), pp. 102–7.
5. Old Testament, from *I Kings*, chapters 6 and 7 in the King James version of the *Holy Bible*.
6. Old Testament, from *The Book of Ezekiel* (c.586 BC), chapter 41, "The Measuring of the Temple," in the King James version of the *Holy Bible*.
7. New Testament, from *The Revelation of Jesus Christ to Saint John* (c.95 AD), chapter 21, in the King James version of the *Holy Bible*.

8. Abbot Suger (c.1081–1151), from *The Book of Suger, Abbot of Saint-Denis* (c.1144), trans. Christina Contandriopoulos from the French translation of the Latin text, ed. and trans. Françoise Gasparri, in *Les Classiques de l'histoire de France*, Vol. 1. Paris: Belles Lettres, 1996, pp. 25–39. Reproduced by permission.

9. William Durandus (c.1237–96), from *Rationale divinorum officiorum* (1286), translated in 1843 as *The Symbolism of Churches and Church Ornaments*. The passage used here is from the third edition (London: Gibbings & Co., 1906), pp. 20–2.

10. Antonio di Tuccio Manetti (1423–97), from *The Life of Brunelleschi* (1480s), in the *The Life of Brunelleschi by Antonio di Tuccio Manetti*, ed. Howard Saalman, trans. Catherine Enggass. University Park: Pennsylvania State University Press, 1971, pp. 50, 52, 54. © 1971 by Pennsylvania State University Press. Reprinted with permission of Pennsylvania State University Press.

11. Leon Battista Alberti, from Prologue and Book 1 of *De re aedificatoria* [On the art of building] (1443–52) in *On the Art of Building in Ten Books*, trans. Joseph Rykwert, Neil Leach, and Robert Tavernor. Cambridge, MA: MIT Press, 1988, pp. 3, 5–6, 7. © 1988 by The MIT Press. Reprinted with permission of the MIT Press.

12. Leon Battista Alberti, from Book 6 of *De re aedificatoria* [On the art of building] (1443–52) in *On the Art of Building in Ten Books*, trans. Joseph Rykwert, Neil Leach, and Robert Tavernor. Cambridge, MA: MIT Press, 1988, pp. 155–7. © 1988 by The MIT Press. Reprinted with permission of the MIT Press.

13. Leon Battista Alberti, from Book 9 of *De re aedificatoria* [On the art of building] (1443–52) in *On the Art of Building in Ten Books*, trans. Joseph Rykwert, Neil Leach, and Robert Tavernor. Cambridge, MA: MIT Press, 1988, pp. 301–3. © 1988 by The MIT Press. Reprinted with permission of the MIT Press.

14. Il Filarete (Antonio di Piero Averlino) (c.1400–70), from his untitled treatise on architecture (1461–3) in *Filarete's Treatise on Architecture*, 2 vols, ed. and trans. John R. Spencer. New Haven: Yale University Press, 1965, pp. 4–8 (Book I, 1v–2r; 2v–3v). © 1965 by Yale University Press. Reprinted with permission of Yale University Press.

15. Il Filarete (Antonio di Piero Averlino), from his untitled treatise on architecture (1461–3) in *Filarete's Treatise on Architecture*, 2 vols., ed. and trans. John R. Spencer. New Haven: Yale University Press, 1965, pp. 101–3 (Book VIII, 59r–60r). © 1965 by Yale University Press. Reprinted with permission of Yale University Press.

16. Sebastiano Serlio (1475–1554), from Book 3 (69v) of *Tutte l'opere d'architettura et prospettiva* [The complete works on architecture and perspective] (1540) in *Sebastiano Serlio on Architecture*, Vol. 1., ed. and trans. Vaughan Hart and Peter Hicks. New Haven: Yale University Press, 1996, p. 136. © 1996 by Yale University Press. Reprinted with permission of Yale University Press.

17. Giacomo Barozzi da Vignola (1507–73), from Preface to *Regola delli cinque ordini d'architettura* [Rules of the five orders of architecture] (1562), trans. Richard J. Tuttle in his essay "On Vignola's *Rule of the Five Orders of Architecture,*" from *Paper Palaces: The Rise of the Renaissance Architectural Treatise*, ed. Vaughan Hart and Peter Hicks. New Haven: Yale University Press, 1998, pp. 361–2. © 1998 by Yale University Press. Reprinted with permission of Yale University Press.

18. Andrea Palladio (1508–80), from *I quattro libri dell'architettura* [The four books of architecture] (1570), trans. Isaac Ware (1738), in *Andrea Palladio: The Four Books of Architecture*, ed. Adolf K. Placzek. New York: Dover Publications, 1965 (reissue), pp. 1, 79–80.

19. Juan Bautista Villalpando (1552–1608), from *In: Ezekielem Explanationes* [Ezekiel commentaries] (1604), trans. Daniel Pfeiffer, from the Spanish edition, *El tratado de la arquitectura perfecta en la última visión del profeta Ezequiel*, Madrid: Colegio Oficial de Arquitectos, Patrimonio Nacional, 1990, p. 129.

20. Georgio Vasari (1511–74), from Preface to *Le vite de piu eccellenti architetti, pittori, et scultori italiani* [Lives of the most eminent Italian architects, painters, and sculptors] (1550, 1568), trans. Mrs. Jonathan Foster, in *Lives of the Most Eminent Painters, Sculptors, and Architects*, Vol. 1. London: George Bell and Sons, 1888, pp. 300–3.

21. Georgio Vasari, from "Life of Michelangelo" in *Le vite de piu eccellenti architetti, pittori, et scultori italiani* [Lives of the most eminent Italian architects, painters, and sculptors] (1550, 1568), trans. Mrs. Jonathan Foster, in *Lives of the Most Eminent Painters, Sculptors, and Architects*, Vol. 5. London: George Bell and Sons, 1888, pp. 270–2.

22. Peter Paul Rubens (1577–1640), from Preface to *Palazzi di Genova* [Palaces of Genoa] (1622), trans. Harry Francis Mallgrave.

23. René Descartes (1596–1650), from *Regulae ad Directionen Ingenii* [Rules for the direction of the mind] (1628), trans. John Cottingham, Robert Stoothoff, and Dugald Murdoch in *The Philosophical Writings of Descartes*, Vol. I. Cambridge: Cambridge University Press, 1985, p. 13.

24. Roland Fréart de Chambray (1606–76), from Preface to *Parallele de l'architecture antique et de la moderne* [A parallel of ancient architecture with the modern] (1650), trans. John Evelyn in *A Parallel of the Antient Architecture with the Modern*, printed in London by The Roycroft for John Place's shop in Holborn, 1664, pp. 1–3.

25. Paul Fréart de Chantelou (1609–94), from *Diary of the Cavaliere Bernini's Visit to France* (1665) in Fréart's *Diary of the Cavaliere Bernini's Visit to France*, ed. Anthony Blunt, trans. Margery Corbett. Princeton: Princeton University Press, 1985, pp. 7–9, 260–2. © 1985 by Princeton University Press. Reprinted by permission of Princeton University Press.

26. François Blondel (1618–86), from "Discours prononcé par Mr Blondel a l'ouverture de l'Academie d'Architecture" [Inaugural lecture to the Academy of Architecture] (1671), published at the beginning of the first volume of his *Cours d'architecture* (Paris, 1675), trans. Harry Francis Mallgrave.

27. François Blondel, from *Cours d'architecture: enseigné dans l'Academie Royale d'Architecture* [Architecture course: instruction at the Royal Academy of Architecture] (Paris: The Author, 1675), trans. Harry Francis Mallgrave.

28. René Ouvrard (1624–94), from *Architecture harmonique, ou application de la doctrine des proportions de la musique à l'architecture* [Harmonic architecture, or the application of the doctrine of musical proportions to architecture] (1677), trans. Christina Contandriopoulos and Harry Francis Mallgrave, from facsimile edition of *La theorie architecturale à l'age classique*, ed. Françoise Fichet, Paris: Pierre Mardaga, 1979, pp. 176–8.

29. Claude Perrault (1613–88), annotations to French translation of *Les dix livres d'architecture de Vitruve* [Ten books of architecture of Vitruvius]. Paris: Coignard, 1673, trans. Harry Francis Mallgrave and Christina Contandriopoulos.

30. François Blondel, from *Cours d'architecture*, Vol. II (1683), trans. Harry Francis Mallgrave from 1698 Paris edition, part III, p. 235.

31. Claude Perrault, from *Les dix livres d'architecture de Vitruve* [Ten books of architecture of Vitruvius], second edition (Paris, 1684), pp. 79–80, trans. Harry Francis Mallgrave.

32. Claude Perrault, from *Ordonnance des cinq espèces de colonnes selon la méthode des Anciens* (1683), trans. Indra Kagin McEwen, in *Ordonnance for the Five Kinds of Columns after the Method of the Ancients*. Santa Monica: Getty Publications Program, 1993, pp. 47–8, 49, 50–1. © 1993 by Getty Publications. Reprinted with permission of Getty Publications.

33. Jean-François Félibien (1658–1733), from Preface to *Recueil historique de la vie et des ouvrages des plus celebres architectes* [Historical survey of the life and works of the most celebrated architects] (1687). Paris: Sebastien Mabre-Cramoisy, trans. Harry Francis Mallgrave.

34. Charles Perrault (1628–1703), from Preface to *Parallèle des anciens et des modernes en ce qui regarde les arts et les sciences* [Parallel of the ancients and the moderns with regard to the arts and sciences] (1688), trans. Christopher Miller from *Parallèle des anciens et des modernes*, Vol. 1 (Paris: Jean-Baptiste Coignard, 1688) and published in *Art in Theory 1648–1815: An Anthology of Changing Ideas*, ed. Charles Harrison, Paul Wood, and Jason Gaiger. Oxford: Blackwell, 2000. Translation © 2000 by Christopher Miller. Reprinted with permission of Christopher Miller.

35. Charles Perrault, from the memorandum "Dessin d'un portail pour l'Église de Sainte-Geneviève à Paris" [Design of a portal for the church of Sainte-Geneviève in Paris] (1697), trans. Harry Francis Mallgrave from *Bulletin monumental*, 115:2 (1957), pp. 94–6.

36. Michel de Frémin (c.1631–1713), from *Mémoires critiques d'architecture* [Critical memoirs on architecture] (1702), trans. Christina Contandriopoulos and Harry Francis Mallgrave from a facsimile edition published by Gregg Press, Farnborough, 1967, pp. 26–8, 30–1, 33–4, 37.

37. Jean-Louis de Cordemoy, from *Nouveau traité de toute l'architecture ou l'art de bastir* [New treatise of all architecture or the art of building] 1706, second edition 1714), trans. Harry Francis Mallgrave from a facsimile edition of the 1714 edition published by Gregg Press, Farnborough, 1966, pp. 108–9, 139–40.

38. Henry Wotton (1568–1639), from the Preface and Part I of *The Elements of Architecture*. London: John Bill, 1624.

39. Christopher Wren (1632–1723), from "Tracts" on architecture (mid-1670s), in *Wren's "Tracts" on Architecture and Other Writings*, ed. Lydia M. Soo. New York: Cambridge University Press, 1998, pp. 153–5 (Tract I).

40. Christopher Wren, from "Tracts" on architecture (mid-1670s), in *Wren's "Tracts" on Architecture and Other Writings*, ed. Lydia M. Soo. New York: Cambridge University Press, 1998, pp. 157–8 (Tract II), 188 (Tract IV).

41. Anthony Ashley Cooper, Third Earl of Shaftesbury (1671–1713), from *Characteristics of Men, Manners, Opinions, Times* (1711) in *Characteristics*, ed. John M. Robertson. London: Grant Richards, 1900, I: pp. 225–9, II: pp. 136–7, II: pp. 267–72.

42. Anthony Ashley Cooper, Third Earl of Shaftesbury, "A Letter Concerning Design" (1712) in *Second Characters or the Language of Forms*, ed. Benjamin Rand. London: Thoemmes Press, 1995 (a reprint of the 1914 edition), pp. 19–24.

43. Colin Campbell (1676–1729), Introduction to Vol. I of *Vitruvius Britannicus, or the British Architect* (3 vols., 1715–25). New York: Benjamin Blom, 1967 (facsimile edition).

44. Nicholas Du Bois, Translator's Preface to Giocomo Leoni's edition of *The Architecture of A. Palladio; in Four Books, containing A short Treatise of the Five Orders, and the most necessary Observations concerning all Sorts of Buildings*. London, John Watts, 1715.

45. William Kent (1685–1748), "Advertisement" to *The Designs of Inigo Jones, Consisting of Plans and Elevations for Publick and Private Buildings*, Vol. I (1727).

46. James Gibbs (1682–1754), Introduction to *A Book of Architecture, Containing Designs of Buildings and Ornaments* (1728), pp. i–iii.

47. Robert Morris (1701–54), from *An Essay in Defence of Ancient Architecture; or, a Parallel of the Ancient Buildings with the Modern: Shewing the Beauty and Harmony of the Former and the Irregularity of the Latter* (1728). Farnborough: Gregg International Publishers, 1971 (facsimile edition), pp. 19–25.

48. Alexander Pope (1688–1744), last two verses from *Of False Taste: An Epistle to the Right Honourable Richard Earl of Burlington*, third edition, pp. 13–14. London: L. Gilliver, 1731.

49. Isaac Ware (d. 1766), "Advertisement" to *Andrea Palladio: The Four Books of Architecture* (1737). New York: Dover Publications, 1965 (facsimile edition).

50. Robert Morris, from "An Essay upon Harmony as it Relates Chiefly to Situation and Building." London: T. Cooper, 1739 and Farnborough: Gregg International Publishers, 1971 (facsimile edition), pp. 7–14, 31–2.

51. Johann Bernhard Fischer von Erlach (1656–1723), from Preface to *Entwurf einer historischen Architektur* [Outline for a historical architecture] (1721), pp. 4–5., trans. Harry Francis Mallgrave.

52. Voltaire (François-Marie Arouet, 1694–1778), from *Lettres philosophiques sur les anglais* [Philosophic letters on the English] (1733), trans. William F. Fleming, in *The Works of Voltaire: A Contemporary Version*, Vol. XIX, pp. 5–6. New York: Dingwall-Rock, 1927.

53. Jacques-Gabriel Soufflot (1713–80), from "Mémoire sur les proportions de l'architecture" [Memoir on architectural proportions] (1739), trans. Harry Francis Mallgrave from Michael Petzet (ed.), *Soufflots Sainte-Geneviève und der französische Kirchenbau des 18. Jahrhunderts*. Berlin: Walter de Gruyter, 1961, pp. 131–2.

54. Jacques-Gabriel Soufflot, from "Mémoire sur l'architecture gothique" (1741), trans. Harry Francis Mallgrave from Michael Petzet (ed.), *Soufflots Sainte-Geneviève und der französische Kirchenbau des 18. Jahrhunderts*. Berlin, Walter de Gruyter, 1961, p. 142.

55. Carlo Lodoli (1690–1761), from Notes for a projected treatise on architecture (c. 1740s), trans. Edgar Kaufmann Jr., from Memmo's *Elementi d'architecturra lodoliana* (Zara, 1834) and first published in *The Art Bulletin* 46:1 (March 1964), pp. 162–4.

56. Baron de Montesquieu (Charles Louis de Secondat, 1689–1755), from Preface to *L'Esprit des Lois* (1748), trans. Thomas Nugent, in *The Spirit of the Laws*. New York: Hafner Press, 1949, pp. lxvii–lxix. © 1949 by Hafner Publishing Company. Reprinted with permission of The Free Press, a division of Simon & Schuster Adult Publishing Group.

57. Jean-Jacques Rousseau (1712–88), from *Discours sur les sciences et les arts* (1750), trans. Roger D. Master and Judith R. Master, in *Jean-Jacques Rousseau: The First and Second Discourses*. New York: St. Martin's Press, 1964, pp. 36–9. © 1969 by Bedford/St. Martin's. Reprinted with permission of Bedford/St. Martin's.

58. Jean Le Rond d'Alembert (1717–83), from "Discours préliminaire des editeurs" [Preliminary discourse of the editors] (1751), trans. Richard N. Schwab, in *Preliminary Discourse to the Encyclopedia of Diderot*. Indianapolis: Bobbs-Merrill, 1963, pp. 3–6.

59. Jacques-François Blondel (1705–74), from the entry "Architecture," trans. Harry Francis Mallgrave from facsimile edition of Diderot's *Encyclopédie, ou Dictionnaire raisonné des sciences, des arts et des métiers*, Vol. 1 (1751). New York: Readex Microprint Corporation, 1969, pp. 616–18.

60. Charles-Étienne Briseux (1660–1754), from Preface to *Traité du beau essentiel dans les arts* [Treatise on essential beauty in the arts] (1752), trans. Harry Francis Mallgrave from original edition. Paris, 1752, pp. 1–2.

61. Marc-Antoine Laugier (1713–69), from *Essai sur l'architecture* (1753), trans. Wolfgang and Anni Herrmann, in *An Essay on Architecture*. Los Angeles: Hennessey + Ingalls, 1977, pp. 11–13, 14–15. © 1977 by Hennessey + Ingalls. Reprinted with permission of Hennessey + Ingalls.

62. Marc-Antoine Laugier, from *Essai sur l'architecture* (1753), trans. Wolfgang and Anni Herrmann, in *An Essay on Architecture*. Los Angeles: Hennessey + Ingalls, 1977, pp. 100–2, 103–4. © 1977 by Hennessey + Ingalls. Reprinted with permission of Hennessey + Ingalls.

63. Isaac Ware (d. 1766), from *A Complete Body of Architecture, Adorned with Plans and Elevations, from Original Designs*, printed in London for T. Osborne and J. Shipton, 1756, p. 131 (Chapter II).

64. Isaac Ware, from *A Complete Body of Architecture, Adorned with Plans and Elevations, from Original Designs*, printed in London for T. Osborne and J. Shipton, 1756, pp. 694–5 (Chapter IX).

65. William Chambers (1723–96), from *A Treatise on Civil Architecture, in which The Principles of that Art are Laid Down, and Illustrated by a Great Number of Plates*, published in London for the author by John Haberkorn, 1759, pp. 17–18, 64.

66. William Chambers, from *A Treatise on the Decorative Part of Civil Architecture*, third edition. London: Joseph Smeeton, 1791 and New York: Benjamin Blom, 1968 (reissue), p. 107.

67. James Stuart (1713–88) and Nicholas Revett (1720–1804), from "Proposals for publishing an accurate description of the Antiquities of Athens" (1748) in a footnote to *The Antiquities of Athens*, Vol. I. London: John Haberkorn, 1762, Preface, v.n.

68. Robert Wood (1716–71) and James Dawkins (1717–c.1771), from *The Ruins of Palmyra, otherwise Tedmor, in the Desart*. London, 1753, pp. 15–16.

69. Johann Joachim Winckelmann (1717–68), from *Gedanken über die Nachahmung der griechischen Werke in der Mahlerey und Bildhauer-Kunst* (1755), trans. Elfriede Heyer and Roger C. Norton, in *Reflections on the Imitation of Greek Works in Painting and Sculpture*. La Salle: Open Court, 1987. © 1987 by Open Court Publishing Company. Reprinted by permission of Open Court Publishing Company, a division of Carus Publishing Company, Peru, IL.

70. Allan Ramsay (1713–84), from "A Dialogue on Taste" (1755) in the journal *The Investigator* (London, 1762), pp. 37–8.

71. Julien-David Le Roy (1724–1803), from *Les Ruines des plus beaux monuments de la Grece* [The ruins of the most beautiful monuments of Greece]. Paris: H. L. Guerin and L. F. Delatour, 1758, trans. Harry Francis Mallgrave.

72. Julien-David Le Roy, from *Les Ruines des plus beaux monuments de la Grece* [The ruins of the most beautiful monuments of Greece]. Paris: H. L. Guerin and L. F. Delatour, 1758, pp. 9–10, trans. Harry Francis Mallgrave.

73. James Stuart and Nicholas Revett, from Preface to *The Antiquities of Athens*. London: John Haberkorn, 1762, pp. i–v.

74. Johann Joachim Winckelmann, from *Geschichte der Kunst des Alterthums* [History of the art of antiquity] (1764), trans. Harry Francis Mallgrave.

75. Johann Joachim Winckelmann, from *Geschichte der Kunst des Alterthums* [History of the art of antiquity] (1764), trans. Harry Francis Mallgrave.

76. Johann Joachim Winckelmann, from *Geschichte der Kunst des Alterthums* [History of the art of antiquity] (1764), trans. Harry Francis Mallgrave.

77. Giovanni Battista Piranesi (1720–80), from *Osservazioni di Gio. Battista Piranesi sopra la Lettre de Monsieur Mariette aux Auteurs de la Gazette Littéraire de l'Europe* (1765), trans. Caroline Beamish and David Britt, in *Giovanni Battista Piranesi: Observations on the Letter of Monsieur Mariette*. Los Angeles: Getty Publications Program, 2002, pp. 87–9, 95–6. © 2002 by Getty Publications. Reprinted with permission of Getty Publications.

78. Giovanni Battista Piranesi, from *Parere su l'Architettura* [Opinions on architecture] (1765), trans. Caroline Beamish and David Britt, in *Giovanni Battista Piranesi: Observations on the Letter of Monsieur Mariette*. Los Angeles: Getty Publications Program, 2002, pp. 105–6, 107–8. © 2002 by Getty Publications. Reprinted with permission of Getty Publications.

79. Giovanni Battista Piranesi, from "An Apologetical Essay in Defence of the Egyptian and Tuscan Architecture" (1769) in *Divers Manners of Ornamenting Chimneys*. Rome: Generoso Salomoni, 1769, pp. 2–3, 32–3.

80. Germain Boffrand (1667–1754), from *Livre d'architecture* (1745), trans. David Britt in *Book of Architecture Containing the General Principles of the Art*, ed. and introduced by Caroline van Eck. Aldershot: Ashgate Publishing, 2003, pp. 21–2, 28–9, 35, 36, 39, © 2003 by Ashgate Publishing Ltd. Reprinted with permission of Ashgate Publishing Ltd.

81. Étienne Bonnot de Condillac (1714–80), from *Essai sur l'origine des connaissances humaines* (1746), trans. Hans Aarsleff in *Essay on the Origin of Human Knowledge*. Cambridge: Cambridge University Press, 2001, pp. 11–12, 56.

82. Julien-David Le Roy, from *Histoire de la disposition et des formes differentes que les chréstiens ont données à leur temples, depuis le Règne de Constantin le Grand, jusqu'à nous* [History of the arrangement and different forms that the Christians have given to their churches from the reign of Constantine the Great until today] (1764), trans. David Britt, in *The Ruins of the Most Beautiful Monuments of Greece*. Los Angeles: Getty Publications Program, 2003, pp. 368, 372–3 (excerpts). © 2003 by Getty Publications. Reprinted with permission of Getty Publications.

83. Jacques-François Blondel, from *Cours d'architecture, ou traité de la decoration, distribution & construction des bâtiments* [Course of architecture, or treatise on the decoration, distribution and construction of buildings]. Paris: Chez Desaint, 1771, pp. 373–4, 411–12, 419–20, trans. Harry Francis Mallgrave.

84. Nicolas Le Camus de Mézières (1721–89), from *Le génie de l'architecture; ou, l'analogie de cet art avec nos sensations* [The genius of architecture; or, the analogy of that art with our sensations] (1780), trans. David Britt, in *The Genius of Architecture*. Santa Monica: Getty Publications Program, 1992, pp. 69–70, 73–4. © 1992 by Getty Publications. Reprinted with permission of Getty Publications.

85. Nicolas Le Camus de Mézières (1721–89), from *Le génie de l'architecture; ou, l'analogie de cet art avec nos sensations* [The genius of architecture; or, the analogy of that art with our sensations] (1780), trans. David Britt, in *The Genius of Architecture*. Santa Monica: Getty Publications Program, 1992, pp. 93–5. © 1992 by Getty Publications. Reprinted with permission of Getty Publications.

86. Jean-Louis Viel de Saint-Maux, from *Letters sur l'architecture des anciens et celles des modernes* [Letters on the architecture of the ancients and the moderns] (1787), trans. Harry Francis Mallgrave from facsimile edition. Geneva: Minkoff Reprint, 1974, pp. 7–8, 10–13, 16–18.

87. A. C. Quatremère de Quincy (1755–1849), from *Encyclopédie méthodique: architecture*. Paris: Panckouke, 1788, pp. 478–9, 500, trans. Harry Francis Mallgrave.

88. Étienne-Louis Boullée (1728–99), from *Architecture, essai sur l'art* [Architecture, essay on art] (c.1794), edited and annotated at the Bibliothèque Nationale in Paris by Helen Rosenau, trans. Sheila de Vallée, published in *Boullée & Visionary Architecture*, New York: Harmony Books, 1976, pp. 86, 87, 89.

89. Étienne-Louis Boullée, from *Architecture, essai sur l'art* [Architecture, essay on art] (c.1794), edited and annotated at the Bibliothèque Nationale in Paris by Helen Rosenau, trans. Sheila de Vallée, published in *Boullée & Visionary Architecture*, New York: Harmony Books, 1976, pp. 107, 115.

90. Claude Nicolas Ledoux (1736–1806), from *L'architecture considérée sous le rapport de l'art, des moeurs et de la legislation* [Architecture considered in relation to art, morals, and legislation]. Paris: C. F. Patris, 1802, pp. 9–12, trans. Harry Francis Mallgrave.

91. John Soane (1753–1837), from Royal Academy Lectures on Architecture (V and XI; 1812–15) in *Sir John Soane: Enlightenment Thought and the Royal Academy Lectures*, ed. David Watkin. London: Cambridge University Press, 1996, pp. 563, 648.

92. John Locke (1632–1704), from *An Essay Concerning Human Understanding* (1690), ed. Alexander Campbell Fraser. New York: Dover, 1959, Vol I: pp. 37–8, 121–4.

93. William Temple (1628–99), from "Upon the Gardens of Epicurus; or, of Gardening in the Year 1685" (1692), in *Five Miscellaneous Essays by Sir William Temple*, ed. Samuel Holt Monk. Ann Arbor: University of Michigan Press, 1963, pp. 29–30.

94. John Vanbrugh (1664–1726), Letter to the Duchess of Marlborough (June 11, 1709) in *The Complete Works of Sir John Vanbrugh*, Vol. 4, ed. Geoffrey Webb. London: The Nonesuch Press, 1928, pp. 29–30.

95. Anthony Ashley Cooper, Third Earl of Shaftesbury, from "The Moralists" (1709) in *Characteristics of Men, Manners, Opinions, Times, etc.*, (orig. 1711), ed. John M. Robertson. New York: E. P. Dutton & Co., 1900, Vol. II: pp. 124–5.

96. Joseph Addison (1672–1719), from *The Spectator* (1712), reprinted in *The Spectator*. London: George Routledge & Sons, 1868, pp. 593–5 and 597–8.

97. Robert Castell (d. 1729), from *The Villas of the Ancients Illustrated*, printed by the author, 1728, pp. 116–18.

98. Batty Langley (1696–1751), from *New Principles of Gardening* (1728). Farnborough: Gregg International Publishers, 1971 (facsimile edition), pp. 193–5.

99. Robert Morris, from *Lectures on Architecture* (1734–6). Farnborough: Gregg International Publishers, 1971 (facsimile edition), pp. 63–70.

100. William Chambers, from *Designs of Chinese Buildings, Furniture, Dresses, Machines, and Utensils*, published by the author, 1757. New York: Benjamin Bloom, 1968 (reissue), pp. 14–18.

101. John Locke, from *An Essay Concerning Human Understanding* (fourth edition, 1700), ed. Alexander Campbell Fraser. New York: Dover, 1959, Vol. I, ch. XXXIII, pp. 529–33.

102. Joseph Addison, from *The Spectator* (26 June 1712), reprinted in *The Spectator*. London: George Routledge & Sons, 1868, pp. 598–600.

103. Jean-Baptiste du Bos (1670–1742), from *Critical Reflections on Poetry, Painting, and Music* (orig. 1719), trans. Thomas Nugent from the fifth edition of du Bos's work. London: John Nourse, 1748, pp. 21–8.

104. Francis Hutcheson (1694–1746), from *An Inquiry into the Original of Our Ideas of Beauty and Virtue in Two Treatises*, fourth edition (1738, orig. 1725). London: D. Midwinter et al., 1738, pp. 1–2, 4–6, and 8–10.

105. George Berkeley (1685–1753), from the "Third Dialogue" of *Alciphron, or the Minute Philosopher in Seven Dialogues* (1732), in *Alciphron, or the Minute Philosopher in Focus*, ed. David Berman. London: Routledge, 1993, pp. 65–71.

106. David Hume, from *A Treatise of Human Nature* (1739–40). Amherst, NY: Prometheus Books, 1992, pp. 298–9.

107. Allan Ramsey, from "A Dialogue on Taste" (1755) in the journal *The Investigator* (London, 1762), pp. 32–5.

108. Alexander Gerard (1728–95), from *An Essay on Taste* (1756, published 1759), facsimile edition published by Walter J. Hipple for the Scholars' Facsimiles & Reprints, Gainesville, 1963, pp. 11–14 and 33–5.

109. David Hume, from "Of the Standard of Taste" (1757) in facsimile edition of *Four Dissertations*, ed. John Immerwahr. Bristol: Thoemmes Press, 1995, pp. 213–17.

110. Edmund Burke (1729–97), from *A Philosophical Enquiry into the Origin of our Ideas of the Sublime and Beautiful* (1757) in *The Works of Edmund Burke*, Vol. I, London: G. Bell & Sons, 1913, pp. 118–22.

111. Edmund Burke, from *A Philosophical Enquiry into the Origin of our Ideas of the Sublime and Beautiful* (1757) in *The Works of Edmund Burke*, Vol. I, London: G. Bell & Sons, 1913, pp. 74–5, 100–8.

112. Lord Kames (Henry Home, 1696–1782), from *Elements of Criticism* (1762). London: Vernor and Hood, 1805 (eighth edition), pp. 370–4.

113. Robert Adam (1728–92) and James Adam (1732–94), from Preface to *The Works in Architecture of Robert and James Adam, Esquires* (1773–8), ed. Robert Oresko. London: Academy Editions, 1975 (facsimile edition), pp. 45–7.

114. Thomas Whately (d. 1772), from *Observations on Modern Gardening* (1770). New York and London: Garland Publishing, Inc., 1982 (facsimile edition), pp. 127–32, 146–50.

115. Horace Walpole (1717–97), from "The History of the Modern Taste in Gardening" (1771) in *Horace Walpole: Gardenist*, ed. Isabel Wakelin Urban Chase. Princeton: Princeton University Press, 1943, pp. 25–9.

116. William Chambers, from *A Dissertation on Oriental Gardening*. W. Griffin, 1772, pp. 11–17.

117. William Gilpin (1724–1804), from *Observations on the River Wye*. London: R. Blamire, 1782, pp. 15–22.

118. Joshua Reynolds (1723–92), from *Discourses on Art* (1786), ed. Robert R. Wark. New Haven: Yale University Press, 1959, pp. 240–4.

119. John Soane, from *Plans, Elevations, and Sections of Buildings Erected in the Counties of Norfolk, etc.* (1788). Farnborough: Gregg International Publishers, 1971 (facsimile edition), pp. 8–11.

120. Uvedale Price (1747–1829), from *Essays on the Picturesque, as Compared with the Sublime and the Beautiful*, Vol. I (1794). J. Mawman, 1810, pp. 43–53, 87–92.

121. Richard Payne Knight (1751–1824), from "Postscript" to the second edition of *The Landscape, a Didactic Poem in Three Books* (second edition, 1795). London: W. Bulmer, 1795 and Farnborough: Gregg International Publishers, 1972 (facsimile edition), pp. 98–104.

122. Humphry Repton (1752–1818), from *Sketches and Hints on Landscape Gardening* (1795), from the 1890 edition of *Sketches and Hints*, entitled *The Landscape Gardening and Landscape Architecture of the Late Humphry Repton*. Farnborough: Gregg International Publishers, 1969 (facsimile edition), pp. 111–14.

123. Uvedale Price, from "An Essay on Architecture and Buildings as connected with Scenery" (1798) from *Essays on the Picturesque*, Vol II. J. Mawman, 1810, pp. 211–14, 258–60, 265–9.

124. Richard Payne Knight, from *An Analytical Inquiry into the Principles of Taste* (second edition). London: Luke Hansard, 1805, pp. 220–5.

125. John Soane, from Royal Academy Lectures on Architecture (V, VIII, XI; 1812–15) in *Sir John Soane: Enlightenment Thought and the Royal Academy Lectures*, ed. David Watkin. London: Cambridge University Press, 1996, pp. 563, 600, 645–6.

126. Jean-Nicolas-Louis Durand (1760–1834), from *Précis des leçons d'architecture données à l'École Royale Polytechnique* (1802–5), trans. David Britt, in *Précis of the Lectures on Architecture*. Los Angeles: Getty Publications Program, 2000, pp. 83–5. © 2000 by Getty Publications. Reprinted with permission of Getty Publications.

127. A. C. Quatremère de Quincy, from *De l'architecture égyptienne considérée dans son origine, ses principes et son gout, et compare sous le meme rapports à l'architectur greque* [On Egyptian architecture considered in its origin, its principles, and its taste, and compared on the same points with Greek architecture]. Paris: Barrois l'Aîné et Fils, 1803. pp. 239–42, trans. Harry Francis Mallgrave.

128. Christian Ludwig Stieglitz (1756–1836), from *Archaologie der Baukunst der Griechen und Römer* [Archaeology of the Architecture of the Greeks and Romans] (1801), pp. 258–61, trans. Harry Francis Mallgrave.

129. A. C. Quatremère de Quincy, from *Le Jupiter olympien, ou l'art de la sculpture antique considérée sous un nouveau point de vue* [The Olympian Jupiter, or the art of antique sculpture considered from a new point of view]. Paris: Firmin Didot, 1814, pp. viii, 36, trans. Harry Francis Mallgrave.

130. Charles Robert Cockerell (1788–1863), from "On the Aegina Marbles" from *Journal of Science, Literature, and Art* VI (1819), pp. 340–1.

131. William Kinnard, annotations to Stuart and Revett's *The Antiquities of Athens*, second edition (1825).

132. Otto Magnus von Stackelberg (1787–1837), from *Der Apollotempel zu Bassae in Arcadien und die daselbst ausgegrabenen Bildwerke* [The temple of Apollo at Bassae in Arcadia and the carvings excavated there] (1826), pp. 33–4, trans. Harry Francis Mallgrave.

133. Jacques Ignace Hittorff (1792–1867), from the lecture "De l'architecture polychrôme chez les Grecs, ou restitution complete du temple d'Empédoclés, dans l'acropolis de Sélinute" [Polychrome architecture among the Greeks, or complete restitution of the temple of Empedocles on the acropolis of Selinus] (April 3, 1830), trans. Harry Francis Mallgrave from *Annals de L'Institut de Correspondence Archéologique*, Vol. 2. Paris, 1830, pp. 263–4.

134. Gottfried Semper (1803–79), from *Vorläufige Bemerkungen über bemalte Architectur und Plastik bei den Alten* [Preliminary remarks on polychrome architecture and sculpture in antiquity] (1834), trans. Harry Francis Mallgrave and Wolfgang Herrmann, in *Gottfried Semper: The Four Elements of Architecture and Other Writings*. New York: Cambridge University Press, 1989, 58–60, 65–6. © 1989 by Cambridge University Press. Reprinted with permission of Cambridge University Press.

135. Léon Vaudoyer (1803–72), excerpts from three letters of 1829, 1830, and 1831 in *Léon Vaudoyer: Historicism in the Age of Industry*, ed. Barry Bergdoll. Cambridge, MA: MIT Press, 1994, pp. 293n.47, 296n.92, 294–5n.61.

136. Émile Barrault (1799–1869), from *Aux Artistes: du passé et de l'avenir des beaux-arts* [To artists: of the past and future fine arts]. Paris: Alexandre Mesnier Libraire, 1830, pp. 9–10, 12–18, trans. Harry Francis Mallgrave.

137. Victor Hugo (1802–85), from *Notre-Dame de Paris* (1832), trans. Walter J. Cobb, in *The Hunchback of Notre-Dame*. Signet, 1964, pp. 184–5. © 1965 by Walter J. Cobb. Used by permission of Dutton Signet, a division of Penguin Group (USA) Inc.

138. Gottfried Semper, from *Vorläufige Bemerkungen über bemalte Architectur und Plastik bei den Alten* [Preliminary remarks on polychrome architecture and sculpture in antiquity] (1834), trans. Harry Francis Mallgrave and Wolfgang Herrmann, in *Gottfried Semper: The Four Elements of Architecture and Other Writings*. New York: Cambridge University Press, 1989, pp. 46–7. © 1989 by Cambridge University Press. Reprinted with permission of Cambridge University Press.

139. Léonce Reynaud, from the entry "Architecture" in *Encyclopédie nouvelle* (1834), trans. Harry Francis Mallgrave from facsimile edition. Geneva: Slatkine Reprints, 1991, pp. 771–2.

140. Horace Walpole, from Letter to H. Zouch (March 15, 1759), in *The Yale Edition of Horace Walpole's Letters*, Vol. XVI, ed. W. S. Lewis. New Haven: Yale University Press, 1952, p. 27.

141. Horace Walpole, from *A Description of the Villa of Horace Walpole at Strawberry Hill* (1774) in *The Works of Horatio Walpole, Earl of Orford*, Vol II. London: G. O. and J. Ribonson, 1798, pp. 395–8.

142. Johann Wolfgang von Goethe (1749–1832), from "Von deutscher Baukunst" [On German architecture] (1772), trans. John Gage, in *Goethe on Art*. London: Scolar Press, 1980, pp. 106–8. © 1980 by John Gage. Reprinted with permission of John Gage.

143. François René Chateaubriand, from *Le génie du christianisme* (1802), trans. Charles I. White, in *The Genius of Christianity; or the Spirit and Beauty of the Christian Religion*. Baltimore: John Murphy, 1856, pp. 384–7.

144. Friedrich von Schlegel (1772–1829), from *Briefen auf einer Reise durch die Niederlande, Rheingegenden, die Schweiz und einen Teil von Frankreich* [Notes on a trip through the Netherlands, the Rhine country, Switzerland, and a part of France] (1806), trans. E. J. Millington, in *The Aesthetic and Miscellaneous Works of Frederick von Schlegel*. London: H. G. Bohn, 1849, pp. 154–8.

145. Joseph Görres (1776–1848), from "Der Dom in Köln" [The Cathedral at Cologne] (1814), trans. Harry Francis Mallgrave from the *Rheinischer Merker*, 151 (November 20, 1814), pp. 125–7.

146. Georg Moller (1784–1852), from *Denkmähler der deutschen Baukunst* [Monuments of German architecture] (1815–21), trans. W. H. Leeds, in *Moller's Memorials of German-Gothic Architecture*. London: John Weale, 1836, pp. 5–7.

147. Thomas Rickman (1776–1841) from *An Attempt to Discriminate the Styles of English Architecture from the Conquest to the Reformation*. London: Longman, Hurst, Rees, Orme, and Brown, 1817, pp. 37–9.

148. William Whewell (1794–1866), from *Architectural Notes on German Churches; with Notes Written during an Architectural Tour in Picardy and Normandy* (1830). Cambridge: J. and J. J. Deighton and London: John W. Parker, 1842 (third edition), pp. 47–52.

149. Robert Willis (1792–1874), from *Remarks on the Architecture of the Middle Ages, Especially of Italy* (1835). Cambridge: Pitt Press, 1835, pp. 18–21.

150. Augustus Welby Northmore Pugin (1812–52), from *Contrasts: or, A Parallel between the Noble Edifices of the Middle Ages, and Corresponding Buildings of the Present Day; Shewing the Present Decay of Taste* (1836). Leicester: Leicester University Press, 1973 (facsimile edition), pp. 1–3.

151. Augustus Welby Northmore Pugin, from *The True Principles of Pointed or Christian Architecture* (1841). London: Academy Edition, 1973 (facsimile edition), pp. 1–2.

152. John Mason Neale and Benjamin Webb, from *The Ecclesiologist* (first issue), published in 1841, and later bound in Cambridge by Stevenson, 1842, pp. 1–4.

153. Victor Hugo, from *Notre-Dame de Paris* (1832), trans. Walter J. Cobb as *The Hunchback of Notre-Dame*. Signet, 1964, pp. 106–7 (excerpt). © 1965 by Walter J. Cobb. Used by permission of Dutton Signet, a division of Penguin Group (USA) Inc.

154. Léonce Reynaud, from entry on "Architecture," in *Encyclopédie nouvelle* (1834), trans. Harry Francis Mallgrave from facsimile edition. Geneva: Slatkine Reprints, 1991, pp. 776–7.

155. Eugène-Emmanuel Viollet-le-Duc (1814–79), from "De la construction des édifices religieux en France" [On the construction of religious buildings in France], trans. Harry Francis Mallgrave from *Annales Archéologiques* (1844), pp. 179–81.

156. Immanuel Kant (1724–1804), from *Kritik der Urtheilskraft* [Critique of Judgment] (1790), trans. J. H. Bernand as *Critique of Judgment*. New York: Hafner Press, 1951, pp. 65–7, 73. © 1951 by Hafner Press. Reprinted with permission of The Free Press, a division of Simon & Schuster Adult Publishing Group.

157. August Schlegel (1767–1845), from *Vorlesungen über schöne Litteratur und Kunst* [Lectures on literature and the fine arts] (1801–2) in *A.W. Schlegels Vorlesungen iber schöne Litteratur und Kunst*. Heilbronn, 1884 and Kraus, 1968 (facsimile edition), pp. 160–2, 178–9, trans. Harry Francis Mallgrave.

158. Friedrich Gilly (1772–1800), from "Einige Gedanken über die Notwendigkeit, die verschiedenen Theile der Baukunst … zu vereinen" [Some thoughts on the necessity of endeavoring to unify the various departments of architecture in both theory and practice] (1799), trans. David Britt, in *Friedrich Gilly: Essays on Architecture 1796–1799*. Santa Monica: Getty Publication Programs, 1994, pp. 169–71. Reprinted with permission of Getty Publications.

159. Karl Friedrich Schinkel (1781–1841), literary fragments (c. 1805), trans. Harry Francis Mallgrave from Schinkel's papers as assembled by Goerd Peschken, *Das architecktonische Lehrbuch*. Berlin: Deutscher Kunstverlag, 1979, pp. 21–2.

160. Georg Wilhelm Friedrich Hegel (1770–1831), from *The Philosophy of Fine Art* (1820s), trans. F. P. B. Osmaston, in *The Philosophy of Fine Art*, Vol. III. London: G. Bell and Sons, 1920, pp. 89–91.

161. Friedrich von Gärtner (1792–1837), from Letter to Johann Martin von Wagner (January 13, 1828) in Kathleen Curran, *The Romanesque Revival: Religion, Politics, and Transnational Exchange*. University Park: Pennsylvania State University Press, 2003, p. 51. © 2003 by Pennsylvania State University Press.

162. Heinrich Hübsch (1795–1863), from *Im welchem Style sollen wir bauen?* (1828), in *In What Style Should We Build? The German Debate on Architectural Style*, ed. and trans. Wolfgang Herrmann. Santa Monica: Getty Publication Programs, 1992, pp. 67–9, 99. © 1992 by Getty Publications. Reprinted with permission of Getty Publications.

163. Rudolf Wiegmann (1804–65), from "Bemerkungen über die Schrift [Remarks on the book]: *Im welchem Style sollen wir bauen?*" (1829) in *In What Style Should We Build? The German Debate on Architectural Style*, ed. and trans. Wolfgang Herrmann. Santa Monica: Getty Publication Programs, 1992, pp. 105–6, 111. © 1992 by Getty Publications. Reprinted with permission of Getty Publications.

164. Karl Friedrich Schinkel, from Notes for a textbook on architecture (c. 1830), trans. Harry Francis Mallgrave from *Das architekonische Lehrbuch*, ed. Goerd Peschken. Berlin: Deutscher Kunstverlag, 1979, pp. 114–15.

165. Karl Friedrich Schinkel, from Notes for a textbook on architecture (c. 1835), trans. Harry Francis Mallgrave from *Das architekonische Lehrbuch*, ed. Goerd Peschken. Berlin: Deutscher Kunstverlag, 1979, pp. 149–50.

166. Rudolf Wiegmann, from "Gedanken über Entwickelung eines zeitgemässen nazionalen Baustyls" [Thoughts on the development of a national architectural style for the present], trans. Harry Francis Mallgrave from *Allgemeine Bauzeitung*, Vol. 6 (1841), pp. 208, 213.

167. Johann Heinrich Wolff (1792–1869), from "Einige Worte über die von Herrn Professor Stier bei der Architektenversammlung zu Bamberg zur Sprache gebrachten … architektonischen Fragen" [Remarks on the architectural questions broached by Professor Stier at the meeting of architects at Bamberg, 1845] (1845), trans. Wolfgang Herrmann, in *In What Style Should We Build? The German Debate on Architectural Style*. Santa Monica: Getty Publication Programs, 1992, pp. 143–5. © 1992 by Getty Publications. Reprinted with permission of Getty Publications.

168. Eduard Metzger, from "Beitrag zur Zeitfrage: In welchem Stil man bauen soll!" [Contribution to the contemporary question: in what style should one build!], trans. Harry Francis Mallgrave from *Allgemeine Bauzeitung*, Vol. 10 (1845), pp. 177–8.

169. Carl Gottlieb Wilhelm Bötticher (1806–99), from "Das Prinzip der hellenischen und germa-nischen Bauweise hinsichtlich der Übertragung in de Bauweise unserer Tage" [The principles of the Hellenic and Germanic ways of building with regard to their application to our present way of building] (1846), trans. Wolfgang Herrmann, in *In What Style Should We Build? The German Debate on Architectural Style*. Santa Monica: Getty Publication Programs, 1992, pp. 156–9. © 1992 by Getty Publications. Reprinted with permission of Getty Publications.

170. Thomas Jefferson (1743–1826), from Letter to Madame de Tessé, March 20, 1787; Letter to Major L'Enfant, March 10, 1791; Letter to Littleton Waller Tazewell, January 5, 1805; Letter to Messrs. Hugh L. White and Others, May 6, 1810, in *Thomas Jefferson: Writings*. New York: The Library of America, 1984, pp. 891–2, 975–6, 1149–50, 1222–3.

171. Benjamin Latrobe (1764–1820), Letter to Thomas Jefferson, May 21, 1807, from *Thomas Jefferson and the National Capital*, ed. Saul K. Padover. Washington: United States Government Printing Office, 1946, pp. 389–92.

172. George Tucker, from "Thoughts of a Hermit – For the Port Folio: On Architecture" in the journal *Port Folio*, IV (1814), pp. 559, 566–9.

173. William Strickland (1788–1854), from introductory lecture on architecture, delivered at the Franklin Institute, November 13, 1824. The manuscript is part of the "Wyck Papers" at the American Philosophical Society in Philadelphia.

174. Thomas U. Walter (1804–87), from "Of Modern Architecture," a lecture delivered at the Franklin Institute, December 9, 1841. The manuscript is part of the "Walter Papers" held by the Athenaeum of Philadelphia.

175. Arthur Delavan Gilman (1821–82), from "Architecture in the United States," a book review published in the *North American Review*, April 1843, pp. 436–9.

176. Thomas Alexander Tefft (1826–59), from the lecture "The Cultivation of True Taste" (1851), pp. 13–16. The manuscript is part of papers held by the Rhode Island Historical Society.

177. Ralph Waldo Emerson (1803–82), from the essay "Self-Reliance" (1841), in the Library of America edition of *Ralph Waldo Emerson: Essays & Lectures*, New York, 1983, pp. 259–60, 277–9.

178. Ralph Waldo Emerson, from "Thoughts on Art" (1841) in *The Works of Ralph Waldo Emerson*. New York: Tudor Publishing, 1900, Vol. IV, pp. 66–71.

179. Horatio Greenough (1805–52), from Letter to Washington Allston (October 1831) in *Letters of Horatio Greenough: American Sculptor*, ed. Nathalia Wright. Madison: University of Wisconsin Press, 1972, pp. 88–91.

180. Horatio Greenough, from "American Architecture" (1843) in Horatio Greenough, *Form and Function: Remarks on Art, Design, and Architecture*, ed. Harold A. Small, Berkeley: University of California Press, 1947, pp. 53–5, 57–9, 60–2.

181. Horatio Greenough, from "Structure and Organization" (1852) in Horatio Greenough, *Form and Function: Remarks on Art, Design, and Architecture*, ed. Harold A. Small, Berkeley: University of California Press, 1947, pp. 116–18, 120–2, 127–8.

182. Henry David Thoreau (1817–62), comments from his journal (January 11, 1852) from *The Writings of Henry David Thoreau*, Vol. III: Journal, ed. by Bradford Torrey, Boston: Houghton Mifflin Co., 1906, pp. 181–3.

183. Andrew Jackson Downing (1815–52), from *A Treatise on the Theory and Practice of Landscape Gardening, Adapted to North America; with a View to the Improvement of Country Residences*. New York: Wiley and Putnam, 1841, pp. 296–300.

184. Andrew Jackson Downing, from *Cottage Residences* (1842), reprinted in *Victorian Cottage Residences*. New York: Dover, 1981, pp. vi–x.

185. Andrew Jackson Downing, from *Hints to Persons about Building in the Country*. New York: Wiley and Putnam, 1847, pp. xiv–xvii.

186. Andrew Jackson Downing, from *The Architecture of Country Houses* (1850). New York: Dover Publications, 1969 (facsimile edition), pp. xix–xx.

187. Calvert Vaux (1825–95), from *Villas and Cottages: A Series of Designs Prepared for Execution in the United States* (1857). New York: Harper and Brothers, 1864 (second edition) and New York: Dover, 1970 (facsimile edition), pp. 28–32.

188. James Jackson Jarves, (1818–88), from *The Art-Idea* (1864). Cambridge, MA: The Belknap Press of Harvard University Press, 1960 (facsimile edition), pp. 286–90.

189. Thomas Hope (1769–1831), from the pamphlet *Observations on the Plans and Elevations Designed by James Wyatt, Architect, for Downing College, Cambridge,* printed by D. N. Shury, London, 1804, pp. 15–17.

190. Thomas Hope, from *An Historical Essay on Architecture* (1835). London: John Murray, 1840 (third edition), pp. 489–92.

191. Thomas Leverton Donaldson (1795–1885), from "Preliminary Discourse Pronounced before the University College of London, upon the Commencement of a Series of Lectures on Architecture" (1842).

192. John Ruskin (1819–1900), from *The Seven Lamps of Architecture.* London: Smith, Elder, and Co., 1849, pp. 31–2, 136–7, 190–2.

193. James Fergusson (1808–86), Augustus Welby Pugin, Edward Lacy Garbett (d. 1898), and Robert Kerr (1823–1904), from the debate in *The Builder* (1850), pp. 122, 134–5, 209, 219, 541–3.

194. Edward Lacy Garbett, from *Rudimentary Treatise on the Principles of Design in Architecture, as Deducible from Nature and Exemplified in the Works of the Greek and Gothic Architects.* London: J. Weale, 1850, pp. 260–4.

195. John Ruskin, from "The Nature of Gothic," in *The Stones of Venice,* Vol. 2 (1851–3). The text is taken from an undated, nineteenth-century American edition of the book, published in New York by John W. Lovell, pp. 159–62.

196. Matthew Digby Wyatt (1820–77), from *The Industrial Arts of the Nineteenth Century: A Series of Illustrations.* London: Day and Son, 1851, pp. vii–viii.

197. Richard Redgrave (1804–88), from "Supplementary Report on Design" in *Reports by the Juries.* London: William Clowes & Sons, 1852, pp. 708, 712–13.

198. Owen Jones (1807–88), from *The Grammar of Ornament* (1856). New York: Van Nostrand Reinhold Company, 1982 (facsimile edition), pp. 154–6.

199. John Ruskin, from "The Deteriorative Power of Conventional Art over Nations," in *The Two Paths: Being Lectures on Art, and Its Application to Decoration and Manufacture, Delivered in 1858–9.* London: Smith, Elder and Co., 1859, pp. 34–5.

200. Robert Kerr, "The Battle of the Styles," from the summary in *The Builder,* May 12, 1860, p. 294.

201. James Fergusson, from *History of the Modern Styles of Architecture: Being a Sequel to the Handbook of Architecture.* London: John Murray, 1862, pp. 328–9.

202. William Morris (1834–96), Prospectus for Morris, Marshall, Faulkner and Company (1861) from Ray Watkinson, *William Morris as Designer.* New York: Reinhold Publishing Corporation, 1990, pp. 16–17.

203. Albert Lenoir and Léon Vaudoyer, from "Etudes d'architecture en France" in *Le Magasin pittoresque,* 12 (1844), pp. 261–2, trans. Harry Francis Mallgrave.

204. Eugène-Emmanuel Viollet-le-Duc, from "De la construction des édifices religieux en France" [On the construction of religious buildings in France] from *Annales Archéologiques,* Vol. II (1845), pp. 136–8, trans. Harry Francis Mallgrave.

205. César Daly (1811–94), from "De la liberté dans l'art" [On liberty in art]: A Monsieur Ludovic Vitet" in *Revue générale de l'architecture et des travaux publics,* Vol. VII (1847), pp. 393–4, trans. Harry Francis Mallgrave.

206. Léonce Reynaud, from *Traité d'architecture*, Vol. I (second edition, 1860). Paris: Dalmont et Dunod, 1860, pp. 530–2., trans. Harry Francis Mallgrave.

207. Eugène-Emmanuel Viollet-le-Duc, from "Architecture," in *Dictionnaire raisonné de l'architecture français du XIe au XVIe siècle* (1854), trans. Kenneth D. Whitehead, in *The Foundations of Architecture: Selections from the* Dictionnaire raisonné. *New York: George Braziller, 1990, pp. 72–4.* © 1990 by George Braziller, Inc. Reprinted with permission of George Braziller, Inc.

208. Gustave Courbet (1819–77), from "Statement on Realism" which appeared as a preface to Courbet's catalogue of 1855, "Realism – Gustave Courbet." This text is sometimes attributed to Courbet's friend and accomplice in popularizing Realism, the writer Champfleury. The English translation is taken from *Gustave Courbet: 1819–1877.* London, 1977, p. 77.

209. Charles Baudelaire (1821–67), from "The Painter of Modern Life" (1859, published 1863) in *The Painter of Modern Life and Other Essays*, trans. and ed. by Jonathan Mayne. New York: Da Capo Paperback, 1986, pp. 12–14. © 1965 by Phaidon Press Limited. Reprinted by permission of Phaidon Press Limited.

210. Eugène-Emmanuel Viollet-le-Duc, from Lecture VI, *Entretiens sur l'architecture* (1859), trans. Benjamin Bucknall, and published in 1877 in Viollet-le-Duc, *Lectures on Architecture*. New York: Dover, 1987 (facsimile edition), pp. 172, 176–7, 183–4.

211. César Daly, from "Introduction" to the *Revue générale*, Vol. 21 (1863), pp. 5–6, 8–9, trans. Harry Francis Mallgrave.

212. César Daly, from "Introduction" to the *Revue générale*, Vol. 23 (1866), p. 8., trans. Harry Francis Mallgrave.

213. Bourgeois de Lagny, from "Salon de 1866," in *Le Moniteur des Architectes* (June 1, 1866), pp. 81–3, trans. Harry Francis Mallgrave.

214. Eugène-Emmanuel Viollet-le-Duc, from "Style," in *Dictionnaire raisonné* (1866), trans. Kenneth D. Whitehead, in *The Foundations of Architecture: Selections from the* Dictionnaire raisonné. New York: George Braziller, 1990, pp. 231–2, 240–2. © 1990 by George Braziller, Inc. Reprinted with permission of George Braziller, Inc.

215. Eugène-Emmanuel Viollet-le-Duc, from Lecture XII, *Entretiens sur l'architecture* (1866), trans. Benjamin Bucknall and published, originally in 1881, as *Lectures on Architecture*, New York: Dover, 1987 (facsimile edition), pp. 58–9.

216. Émile Zola (1840–1902), from *Le ventre de Paris* [The covered market of Paris] (1872), trans. Harry Francis Mallgrave (with ellipses in original). Paris: Le Livre de Poche, 1978, pp. 337–9.

217. Karl von Schnaase (1798–1875), from *Niederländische Briefe* [Dutch letters]. Stuttgart: J. G. Cotta, 1834, pp. 199–201, trans. Harry Francis Mallgrave.

218. Karl Bötticher, from Preface to *Die Tektonik der Hellenen* [Greek Tectonics] (1843), trans. Harry Francis Mallgrave from 1852 edition published in Potsdam by Ferdinand Riegel, pp. xiv–xvi.

219. Eduard van der Nüll (1812–68), from "Andeutungen über die kunstgemässe Beziehung des Ornamentes zur rohen Form" [Suggestions on the skillful relation of ornament to untreated form], *Österreichische Blätter für Literatur und Kunst* (1845), trans. Harry Francis Mallgrave from Gustav Peichl (ed.), *Die Kunst des Otto Wagner*, Vienna: Akademie der bildenden Künste, 1984, pp. 33–4.

220. Heinrich Leibnitz, from *Die struktive Element in der Architektur und sein Verhältniss zur Kunstform* [The structural element in architecture and its relation to the art-form]. Tübingen: Ludwig Friedrich Fues, 1849, pp. 3–4, 5–7, trans. Harry Francis Mallgrave.

221. Gottfried Semper, from *Die Vier Elemente der Baukunst* (1851), trans. Wolfgang Herrmann and Harry Francis Mallgrave, in *Gottfried Semper: The Four Elements of Architecture and Other Writings*. Cambridge: Cambridge University Press, 1989, pp. 102–6. © 1989 by Cambridge University Press. Reprinted with permission of Cambridge University Press.

222. Gottfried Semper, from *Wissenschaft, Industrie und Kunst: Vorschläge zur Anregung nationalen Kunstgefühles* [Science, industry, and art: proposals for the development of national taste in art] (1852), pp. 133–6, 142–4. © 1989 by Cambridge University Press. Reprinted with permission of Cambridge University Press.

223. Jacob Burckhardt (1818–97), from *Die Kultur der Renaissance in Italien* [The civilization of the Renaissance in Italy] (1860), trans. 1878, first published in 1945 by Ludwig Goldscheider. Oxford: Phaidon Press, 1981 (facsimile edition), pp. 81–2.

224. Jacob Burckhardt, from *Die Geschichte der Renaissance in Italien* [The history of the Italian Renaissance] (1867), trans. James Palmes, *The Architecture of the Italian Renaissance*, ed. Peter Murray. Chicago: University of Chicago Press, 1985, p. 32.

225. Gottfried Semper, from *Der Stil in den technischen und tektonischen Künsten* (1860), trans. Michael Robinson and Harry Francis Mallgrave in *Style in the Technical and Tectonic Arts, or Practical Aesthetics*. Los Angeles: Getty Publications Program, 2003, pp. 71–2, 378–9, 249–50. © 2003 by Getty Publications. Reprinted with permission of Getty Publications.

226. Gottfried Semper, from *Der Stil in den technischen und tektonischen Künsten* (1860), trans. Michael Robinson and Harry Francis Mallgrave in *Style in the Technical and Tectonic Arts, or Practical Aesthetics*. Los Angeles: Getty Publications Program, 2003, pp. 753–4, 756–7, 658–60. © 2003 by Getty Publications. Reprinted with permission of Getty Publications.

227. Rudolf Hermann Lotze (1817–81), from *Geschichte der Aesthetik in Deutschland* [History of German aesthetics] (1868), trans. Harry Francis Mallgrave.

228. Gottfried Semper, from *Über Baustyle* [On architectural styles] (1869), trans. Wolfgang Herrmann and Harry Francis Mallgrave, in *Gottfried Semper: The Four Elements of Architecture and Other Writings*. Cambridge: Cambridge University Press, 1989, pp. 267–8, 281, 284. © 1989 by Cambridge University Press. Reprinted with permission of Cambridge University Press.

229. Richard Lucae (1829–77), from "Über die Bedeutung und Macht des Raumes in der Baukunst" [On the meaning and power of space in architecture] (1869), trans. Harry Francis Mallgrave.

Every effort has been made to trace copyright holders and to obtain their permission for the use of copyright material. The publisher apologizes for any errors or omissions in the above list and would be grateful if notified of any corrections that should be incorporated in future reprints or editions of this book.

INDEX